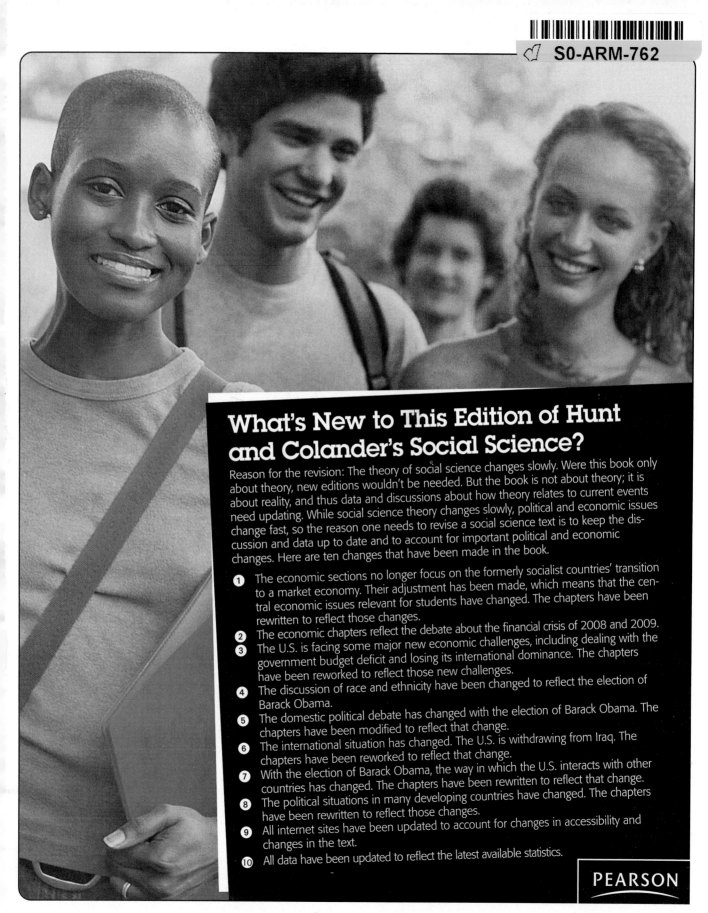

What's New to This Edition of Hunt and Colander's Social Science?

Reason for the revision: The theory of social science changes slowly. Were this book only about theory, new editions wouldn't be needed. But the book is not about theory; it is about reality, and thus data and discussions about how theory relates to current events need updating. While social science theory changes slowly, political and economic issues change fast, so the reason one needs to revise a social science text is to keep the discussion and data up to date and to account for important political and economic changes. Here are ten changes that have been made in the book.

1. The economic sections no longer focus on the formerly socialist countries' transition to a market economy. Their adjustment has been made, which means that the central economic issues relevant for students have changed. The chapters have been rewritten to reflect those changes.

2. The economic chapters reflect the debate about the financial crisis of 2008 and 2009.

3. The U.S. is facing some major new economic challenges, including dealing with the government budget deficit and losing its international dominance. The chapters have been reworked to reflect those new challenges.

4. The discussion of race and ethnicity have been changed to reflect the election of Barack Obama.

5. The domestic political debate has changed with the election of Barack Obama. The chapters have been modified to reflect that change.

6. The international situation has changed. The U.S. is withdrawing from Iraq. The chapters have been reworked to reflect that change.

7. With the election of Barack Obama, the way in which the U.S. interacts with other countries has changed. The chapters have been rewritten to reflect that change.

8. The political situations in many developing countries have changed. The chapters have been rewritten to reflect those changes.

9. All internet sites have been updated to account for changes in accessibility and changes in the text.

10. All data have been updated to reflect the latest available statistics.

PEARSON

Social Science

An Introduction to the Study of Society

FOURTEENTH EDITION

Elgin F. Hunt
Late Chairman of Social Science Department
Wilson Junior College

David C. Colander
Department of Economics
Middlebury College

Allyn & Bacon

Boston   Columbus   Indianapolis   New York   San Francisco   Upper Saddle River
Amsterdam   Cape Town   Dubai   London   Madrid   Milan   Munich   Paris   Montreal   Toronto
Delhi   Mexico City   Sao Paulo   Sydney   Hong Kong   Seoul   Singapore   Taipei   Tokyo

Executive Editor: Jeff Lasser
Project Manager: Lauren Macey
Editorial Assistant: Elaine Almquist
Executive Marketing Manager: Kelly May
Sr. Production Project Manager: Roberta Sherman
Manufacturing Buyer: Debbie Rossi
Cover Administrator: Kristina Mose-Libon
Editorial Production and Composition Service: Elm Street
Photo Researcher: Martha Shethar

Library of Congress Cataloging-in-Publication Data

Hunt, Elgin F.
  Social science : an introduction to the study of society / Elgin F. Hunt, David C. Colander.—14th ed.
       p.   cm.
  Includes bibliographical references and index.
  ISBN-13: 978-0-205-70271-8
  ISBN-10: 0-205-70271-6
 1. Social sciences.   I. Colander, David C. II. Title.
  H85.H86   2020
  300—dc22

                              2009054359

10 9 8 7 6 5 4 3 2 HAM 14 13 12 11 10

Allyn & Bacon
is an imprint of

www.pearsonhighered.com

ISBN 10:   0-205-70271-6
ISBN 13: 978-0-205-70271-8

To the sales reps – the unsung heroes
of textbook publishing

Contents

*C*hapter 7   Psychology, Society, and Culture   123

Part III   Institutions and Society

*C*hapter 8   The Family   146

Chapter 9   Religion   168

Chapter 10   Education   187

Chapter 21 International Institutions and the Search for Peace   418

Preface

Social science is taught in diverse ways. Some courses take a global perspective, some an anthropological perspective, some a psychological perspective, some a sociological perspective, and some a historical perspective—to name just a few. In my view, although each individual social science perspective has something to offer, what distinguishes the social science course is that it looks at problems from as many different perspectives as possible, relying on the scholar's common sense to choose the perspective that is most useful for a particular problem. The commonsense perspective is the social science perspective.

Social science is an important course. All too often our educational system rushes students into specializations before the students have an overall picture—before they know where they want to go. Once they have an overall picture, specialization is necessary, but to specialize before having an overall picture is unfair to students. Students who specialize too early don't develop a commonsense perspective; they aren't sensitive to the interrelationships and resonances among disciplines. At worst, they become slaves of their discipline's approach. At best, they have the wisdom to recognize that there are many approaches to a problem, but their lack of training forces them to recreate the wheel. Knowledge of the other disciplines would have saved them the trouble and been far more efficient.

That's why I am a strong advocate of the social science course. It is one of the most important courses students take in college, and in my view it is a necessary prerequisite to taking courses in specific disciplines. It puts those other courses in perspective.

The changes in this edition have been made to strengthen the presentation and to keep the book current. I have reworked sections that reviewers thought needed work and updated all chapters. The major changes are in the political, economic and international sections. The economic chapters in the previous edition reflected the formerly socialist countries' transition to a market economy. Their adjustment is now more complete and I have rewritten the chapters to reflect that. All major economies of the world are now pragmatic market economies. The interesting policy questions in economics now center less around socialism vs. the market, but what type of market economy we want to have. With the financial crisis of 2008 and 2009, such issues will be much in the news and I have rewritten the economic chapters to reflect that. This meant a major change to Chapter 16, and almost total rewriting of Chapter 17, which now has the name, "The Economy, Government, and the Economic Challenges Facing the United States."

The political chapters have been rewritten to bring them up to date with the constantly changing political winds. For the U.S. this means a substantial change. With the election of Barack Obama as president, and his attempt to deal with the financial crisis, politics in the U.S. are quite different in 2010 than they were in 2007. It is not only internal politics that have changed. President Obama has changed the tone of U.S. foreign policy, and the international chapters have been modified to capture that change in tone.

There were also smaller changes made to many of the other chapters both to reflect the newest developments in social science thinking and to keep the book current. For example, in Chapter 1 I added a discussion of how social science thinking underlies both the law and international relations to help tie in those sections with the broader social science theme.

In Chapter 2, I added a discussion of Ben Stein's documentary *Expelled: No Intelligence Allowed* to spice up the discussion about intelligent design. Other chapters have similar small changes, all made with the goal for keeping this book totally up to date. Finally, I updated all the internet questions and connections to keep the questions current and to see that the sites are still accessible. I will post links on my website http://community .middlebury.edu/~colander/links.html) so that you can assign the students the questions and they will only have to click on the link.

Despite all these changes the book remains what it was in the previous edition—a relatively neutral (at least as neutral as I am able to be) commonsense overview and introduction to the social sciences and social science thinking about the major issues of our day.

Acknowledgments

As always, the book benefits from the suggestions of reviewers, colleagues, and students who have e-mailed me. I'd like to thank them all. For this edition, I'd specifically like to thank some great reviewers: Ali Al-Taie, Shaw University; William Plants, University of Rio Grande; and David S. Schjott, Northwest Florida State College.

Over the last few editions the reviewers have included: Emmanuel Agbolosoo, Navajo Community College; Ali Al-Taie, Shaw University; Verl Beebe, Daytona Beach Community College; John Beineke, Kennesaw State College; Thomas J. Bellows, The University of Texas at San Antonio; Dallas A. Blanchard, University of West Florida; Ducarmel Bocage, Howard University; William K. Callam, Daytona Beach Community College; Pam Crabtree, New York University; Bruce Donlan, Brevard Community College; Anthony Douglas, Lornan, Mississippi; Dr. William M. Downs, Georgia State University; Phil A. Drimmel, Daytona Beach Community College; J. Ross Eshleman, Wayne State University; Dana Fenton, City University of New York, Borough of Manhattan Community College; Cyril Francis, Miami–Dade North Community College; Richard Frye, Neuro-Diagnostic Lab, Winchester Memorial Hospital, Winchester, Virginia; Judy Gentry, Columbus State Community College; Paul George, Miami–Dade Community College; Don Griffin, University of Oklahoma; Charles F. Gruber, Marshall University; Ghulam M. Haniff, St. Cloud State University (Minnesota); Roberto Hernandez, Miami–Dade New World Center; Charles E. Hurst, The College of Wooster; Sharon B. Johnson, Miami–Dade Community College; Kenneth C. W. Kammeyer, University of Maryland; Rona J. Karasik, St. Cloud State University; Lynnel Kiely, Truman College; H. D. Kirkland, Lake City Community College; Patricia E. Kixmiller, Miami–Dade Community College; D. R. Klee, Kansas City, Missouri; Casimir Kotowski, Harry S. Truman City College; Errol Magidson, Richard J. Daley Community College; James T. Markley, Lord Fairfax Community College; Stephen McDougal, University of Wisconsin–La Crosse; David J. Meyer, Cedarville University; Karen Mitchell, University of Missouri; Catherine Montsinger, Johnson C. Smith University; Lynn Mulkey, Hofstra University; Roy Mumme, University of South Florida; Eleanor J. Myatt, Palm Beach Junior College; Quentin Newhouse Jr., Howard University; Annette Palmer, Howard University; Robin Perrin, Pepperdine University; Joseph Pilkington-Duddle, Highland Beach, Florida; William Primus, Miami–Dade North Community College; Roger Rolison, Palm Beach Community College; William H. Rosberg, Kirkwood Community College; Dan Selakovich, Oklahoma State University; Henry A. Shockley, Boston University; Ruth Smith, Miami–Dade Community College; Scharlene Snowden, City University of New York, Medgar Evers College; Larry R. Stucki, Reading Area Community College; Barry Thompson, University of Rio Grande; Judy Thompson, University of Rio Grande; Elizabeth Trentanelli, Miami–Dade College; Edward Uliassi, Northeastern University; David Wells, Glendale Community College; Ted Williams, City College of Chicago; William Plant of the University of Rio Grande W. M. Wright, Lake City

Community College; Norman R. Yetman, The University of Kansas; and George Zgourides. Primus, Miami–Dade North Community College.

At the end of an earlier edition, I included a sheet for students to grade the book and to send me suggestions for improvement. A number of students did this, and their suggestions have played an important role in shaping the book. Most, I'm happy to say, were highly positive, but a few attacked the book and the course. One particularly memorable student flunked me on just about every chapter and wrote the following:

> Until you and this so called science become legitimized I'd rather spend time gorging myself and then vomiting. Guesses, hypotheses, maybes, might be's don't belong in college; they belong in elementary school.

That student obviously read the book, because he is correct: The book doesn't tell the student what is right or wrong, and it does report guesses, hypotheses, and maybes. But that student is wrong about what does and what doesn't belong in college. Guesses, hypotheses, and maybes are precisely what belong in college, because by the time students are in college they can be expected to have the maturity to understand that knowledge is nothing but good guesses, reasonable hypotheses, and logical maybes.

Social science doesn't tell you what's right. It presents the observations and the theories as fairly as it can and lets you decide.

This edition I made good use of research assistants who I had do background research, fact checking, proofreading, and providing me with council about what worked and what didn't. These students include Kent Diep, Steven Jones, Jing Zhong, Zach Colander, Andrew Chong, Sam Parnell and Erik Elderbrock. I thank them all.

I would also like to acknowledge the contributions of Executive Editor Jeff Lasser and Editorial Assistant Lauren Macey who played valuable roles in helping me prepare this Fourteenth edition. I also thank Helen Reiff, Erik Elderbrock, and Aaron Brush who worked on the index. Lauren Traut helped smooth out the process and the team at Elm Street Publishing Services oversaw the production of this book; I thank them for all their hard work. I want to thank my family for helping me find the time to work on the book.

Finally, I want to mention the unsung heroes—the sales reps who came to me with names of reviewers and suggestions for changes and to whom this book is dedicated. These sales reps are the backbone of any college publishing company, and I thank them. One rep in particular deserves special recognition. After the death of Elgin Hunt, who was the initial author of this book, she recruited me for *Social Science;* she convinced me and Macmillan to do the book, and she continued to provide unending support and encouragement. This book was always known at Macmillan as "Wendy's book," and it remains Wendy's book, even though it is now published by Allyn and Bacon.

D. C. C.

Social Science and Its Methods

After reading this chapter, you should be able to:

- Define social science and explain why it is important
- List the various social sciences
- State the nine steps that make up the scientific method
- Discuss some reasonable approaches to problems in social science
- Differentiate the historical method from the case method and the comparative method
- Distinguish educated common sense from common sense
- Explain why a good scientist is always open to new ways of looking at issues

Theories should be as simple as possible, but not more so.

—Albert Einstein

On September 11, 2001, eighteen men boarded airplanes with the intent of crashing them into the World Trade Center, the Pentagon, and the White House or Capitol. They succeeded with three of the planes, causing enormous destruction. The fourth plane crashed, but thanks to passengers who discovered the highjackers' plans and attacked the highjackers, the destruction of the White House or Capitol was prevented. What forces drove the highjackers to undertake such action? What forces led the passengers to organize together to thwart them? What might have prevented the highjackings? Such questions fall under the purview of **social science**—the scientific study of social, cultural, psychological, economic, and political forces that guide individuals in their actions.

Formal social science is relatively new. Nevertheless, a vast amount of information has been accumulated concerning the social life of human beings. This information has been used in building a system of knowledge about the nature, growth, and functioning of human societies. Social science is the name given to that system of knowledge.

All knowledge is (1) knowledge of human beings, including their culture and products, and (2) knowledge of natural environment. Human culture has been changing, and knowledge about it has been gradually accumulating ever since the far distant time when humans first assumed their distinctively human character. But until rather recent times, this knowledge was not scientific in the modern sense. **Scientific knowledge** is knowledge that has been systematically gathered, classified, related, and interpreted. It is concerned with learning the concepts and applying those concepts to particulars, rather than just learning a vast amount of information.

Primitive peoples acquired much of their knowledge unconsciously, just as we today still begin the use of our native language and acquire many of the basic elements in our culture unconsciously. For the most part, they accepted the world as they found it, and if any

Social Science versus the Soaps

Faced with the events that affect our lives, we have two options: We can lose ourselves in a parody of reality, such as becoming experts on the soaps (is Laura really sleeping with John's wife's brother?), or we can try to understand those events—what actually happens. Some educators, following the philosophy of Plato, try to argue the moral superiority of the latter: Better to be an unhappy learned person than a happy fool. Others find that unconvincing. Following Jeremy Bentham, the social philosopher, they prefer happiness. The problem they have with the soaps is that soaps don't make you happy; soaps quickly become boring. You soon play out the options in your head and, often, create far better scenarios than the television writer. It's a bit like tic tac toe: one move (if you know what you are doing), and the game is done. Pinochle is somewhat more interesting, and the good TV shows approach the complexity of pinochle. But here again, after seven or eight cards have been played, the possibilities soon become evident. Chess is a step above this, with its infinite number of possibilities. But still, after twenty or so moves (and often fewer), good chess players can anticipate the outcome and choose to call a draw, resign, or declare victory.

Quite frankly, soaps, tic tac toe, pinochle, and chess are not for this author. I prefer a far more complicated game—one in which I'm both a player and a pawn. That game could be called the game of life, or it could be called the game of society. It is played by some 7.8 billion people, each having a wide variety of possible moves that range from shooting up a playground full of schoolchildren to trying to travel farther into outer space, construct faster computers, or improve humans by modifying their genes. The players in the game of society are divided into two types: male and female. These two types have certain drives, and desires, and certain rules that are passed on to them, either through their genes or through society's mores.

The ultimate goal of the game is often unclear, although its day-to-day objects can be said to consist of continuing to play the game and to keep the game itself alive. What winning or losing the game might be is clouded. Probably, if we commit suicide, we are losers. If we make a million dollars, are admired by our acquaintances for it, and are happy, we are probably winners. Many people even question whether we are playing the game of our own free will or whether we are merely the pawns of a god who has predetermined all our actions.

This game is far more diverse and interesting than other games. The possibilities are endless and the challenge immediate. It has elements of danger, like Russian roulette (if we really *do* goof, we *will* blow ourselves up). And it has its peaceful moments. But what makes it the most interesting game of all is that we are both the players and the played, at times moving ourselves as we make stupid or foolish choices and contrive sophisticated or imaginative solutions, and at other times watching other players as they make their choices and contrive their solutions. *Trying to understand this game is what social science is all about.* And the reason I am a social scientist instead of a TV fan is that I watch society and try to understand what makes society work. It's a whole lot more challenging and fun than watching the soaps. Moreover, unlike the soaps, watching society has a purpose—if we can understand society, we might be able to make it better.

Social science has fascinated enormous numbers of people, and a whole set of ponderings about the game has already developed. These ponderings concern the nature, growth, and functioning of human societies. This book introduces you to the past ponderings of social scientists.

explanations seemed called for, they invented supernatural ones. Some primitive peoples believed that every stream, tree, and rock contained a spirit that controlled its behavior.

In modern times, our emphasis is on the search for scientific knowledge. We have divided human knowledge into a number of areas and fields, and every science represents the systematic collection and study of data in one of these areas, which can be grouped roughly into two major fields—social science and natural science. Each of these fields is subdivided into a number of specialized sciences or disciplines to facilitate more intensive study and deeper understanding. Social science is the field of human knowledge that deals with all aspects of the group life of human beings. **Natural science** is concerned with the natural environment in which human beings exist. It includes such sciences as physics and chemistry, which deal with the laws of matter, motion, space, mass, and energy; it also includes the **biological sciences,** which deal with living things. The third field of study is the **humanities,** which deals with literature, music, art, and philosophy. The humanities are closely related to social science in that both deal with humans and their culture. Social science, however, is most concerned with those basic elements of culture that determine the general patterns of human behavior. The humanities deal with special aspects of human culture and are primarily concerned with our attempts to express spiritual and esthetic values and to discover the meaning of life. Whereas the social sciences study issues in a systematic, scientific way, the focus of the humanities is more on the emotions and feelings themselves than on the system employed to sharpen that focus.

The importance of social science goes far beyond the specific social sciences. It is social science thinking that underlies much of the law as well as our understanding of international relations and government. All these fields are the natural byproducts of social science inquiry. Thus, a knowledge of social science is necessary for anyone trying to understand current world events.

Social Science

No field of study is more important to human beings than the social sciences. To understand society is to learn not only the conditions that limit our lives but also the opportunities open to us for improving the human condition. Increasing our knowledge of human society is as important as learning more about mathematics, physics, chemistry, or engineering, for unless we can develop societies in which human beings can live happy, meaningful, and satisfying lives, we cannot reap the benefits from learning how to make better automobiles and skyscrapers, traveling in space, or constructing faster computers. Albert Einstein summed it up: "Politics is more difficult than physics and the world is more likely to die from bad politics than from bad physics."

Because all expressions of human culture are related and interdependent, to gain a real understanding of human society we must have some knowledge of all its major aspects. If we concentrate on some phases and neglect others, we will have a distorted picture. But social science today is such a vast complex that no one student can hope to master all of it. Thus, social science itself has been broken up into anthropology, sociology, history, geography, economics, political science, and psychology. (The boxes in this chapter provide a brief introduction to each of these disciplines.)

This list of social science disciplines is both too broad and too narrow. It is too broad because parts of the fields of history, geography, and psychology should not be included as social sciences. For instance, parts of history and geography belong in the humanities, and parts of psychology belong in the natural sciences. The list is too narrow because new social sciences are emerging, such as cognitive science and sociobiology, that incorporate new findings and new ways of looking at reality. (See box on The Evolving Social Sciences.)

Because all knowledge is interrelated, there are inevitable problems in defining and cataloging the social sciences. Often, it is difficult to know where one social science ends and another begins. Not only are the individual social sciences interrelated, but the social sciences as a whole body are also related to the natural sciences and the humanities. The strains of the old song, "The hip bone's connected to the thigh bone,..." are appropriate to the social sciences. To understand history, it is helpful, even necessary, to understand geography; to understand economics, it is necessary to understand psychology. Similar arguments can be made for all of the social sciences.

One of the difficulties in presenting definitions and descriptions of the various social sciences is that social scientists themselves don't agree on what it is they do, or should be doing. In preparing this chapter, we met with groups of social scientists specializing in specific fields and asked them to explain what it was that distinguished their field from others.

The Evolving Social Sciences

The themes of this book are evolution and change. Thus, it would be surprising if the divisions among the social sciences that currently exist still remain ten years from now. Indeed, with the development of new technology and technological advances in the physical sciences, the distinction among the various sciences is blurring and new sciences are developing. As these fields develop, the boundaries of the various social sciences change.

Interaction among the various social sciences is creating new fields, such as economic psychology, psychological economics, and sociopolitical anthropology. In economics and political science, too, a group of economists is calling for the reintegration of these two fields into political economy, and some schools do have departments of political economy.

Change is also occurring in the natural sciences, and there is interaction between the natural and social sciences. New developments in genetic theory, which will be discussed in Chapter 2, have caused many to believe it is time for a new social science, called cognitive science, which combines psychology, linguistics, philosophy, social anthropology, and molecular biology. Although it is still in the process of formation, a tentative definition of **cognitive science** is the study of how the mind identifies problems and how it solves those problems. For instance, there are more ways to write the letter *s* than there are people who know how to write that letter (all people who write plus the printing press and computer software and innumerable typefaces designed for them). Let us identify the problem as how to recognize the letter *s* when we see it. We know the result of the exercise: Everyone who knows how to read can instantly recognize most renditions of the letter *s* (the handwriting of a few college students and some physicians excepted). But we do not currently know *how* we do it. Or, how do you know the face of your roommate from the face of your mother, from the face of the letter carrier, from the face of Brad Pitt? There has been speculation about how the mind works for almost as long as there have been minds, theories, and even experiments, but few specific riddles have been conclusively solved.

Whether these upstart disciplines take hold remains to be seen, but that some change will take place is certain.

There was little agreement among specialists in a particular social science, let alone among all social scientists. A cynic once said, "Economics is what economists do." If we replaced "economics" and "economists" with any of the other social sciences and its practitioners, we would have as good a definition as possible. Unfortunately, it would not be very helpful to those who do not know what social scientists do.

One important difference among the individual social scientists did come out of these discussions: Even when two social scientists are considering the same issue, because their training is different they focus on different aspects of that problem. Geographers fixate on spaces and spatial relativities, economists on market incentives, and political scientists on group decision making. Thus, although we might not be able to define, unambiguously, the domains of the various social sciences, you will get a sense of the various approaches as we consider issues from various perspectives throughout the book.

The study of social science is more than the study of the individual social sciences. Although it is true that to be a good social scientist you must know each of those components, you must also know how they interrelate. By specializing too early, many social scientists can lose sight of the interrelationships that are so essential to understanding modern problems. That's why it's necessary to have a course covering all the social sciences. In fact, it wouldn't surprise me if one day a news story such as the one in the box on the next page appeared.

To understand how and when social science broke up, you must study the past. Imagine for a moment that you're a student in 1062, in the Italian city of Bologna, site of one of the first major universities in the Western world. The university has no buildings; it consists merely of a few professors and students. There is no tuition fee. At the end of a professor's lecture, if you like it, you pay. And if you don't like it, the professor finds himself without students and without money. If we go back still earlier, say to Greece in the

Unified Social Systems Theory Derived

Dateline 2050. Researchers today announced the development of a unified theory of the social sciences. The new theory, which had its early foundations in the work of Ludwig von Bertalanffy, is the equivalent in social science of the unified field theory in physics, which tied together the various forces of nature into a general theory. The formulation of the unified field theory in 2020 solved the problem that stymied earlier physicists such as Albert Einstein. It intensified the efforts of social scientists to develop their own unified theory. The theory, which is also called a unified social systems theory, ties together the various social sciences that in the nineteenth and twentieth centuries diverged into anthropology, sociology, history, geography, economics, political science, and psychology. The theory combines the work on complex systems begun by John von Neumann in the late 1940s and early 1950s with game theory, also begun by von Neumann, to form a coherent whole, and captures many of the interrelationships that were previously lost in the fragmentation or divisions of social science. That work was extended in the complexity revolution in science that came into its own in the early 2000s. By combining these theories with recent advances in the separate social sciences, the resulting new unified social science theory provides new insights into how society works.

When asked what set her on this path, the social scientist who developed the theory said it was the experience in her first social science class, in which she used the classic Hunt and Colander text, *Social Science*. In that class, with the aid of the insights her teacher provided, the scientist grasped the first inklings of how these various theories might be put together, setting the stage for her later achievement.

sixth century B.C., we can see the philosopher Socrates walking around the streets of Athens, arguing with his companions. He asks them questions, and then other questions, leading these people to reason the way he wants them to reason (this became known as the *Socratic method*).

Times have changed since then; universities sprang up throughout the world and created colleges within the universities. Oxford, one of the first universities, now has thirty colleges associated with it, and the development and formalization of educational institutions has changed the roles of both students and faculty. As knowledge accumulated, it became more and more difficult for one person to learn, let alone retain, it all. In the sixteenth century, one could still aspire to know all there was to know, and the definition of the Renaissance man (people were even more sexist then than they are now) was one who was expected to know about everything.

Unfortunately, at least for someone who wants to know everything, the amount of information continues to grow exponentially while the size of the brain has grown only slightly. The way to deal with the problem is not to try to know everything about everything. Today we must specialize. That is why social science separated from the natural sciences and why social science, in turn, has been broken down into various subfields, such as anthropology and sociology.

There are advantages and disadvantages to specialization, and many social problems today are dealt with by teams of various social scientists. Each brings his or her specialty to the table. For example, one of the authors is an economist but works on projects with geographers, sociologists, anthropologists, political scientists, and psychologists. More and more interdisciplinary majors are being created; one of the authors of this book teaches in both the economics department and the international politics and economics department at his school. Interdisciplinary graduate schools of public policy have grown enormously. In these programs, students study all the social sciences while specializing in one. Figure 1.1 provides a graphic overview of the evolution of knowledge and the present social sciences. (The appendix at the end of this chapter expands on the ideas in this diagram.)

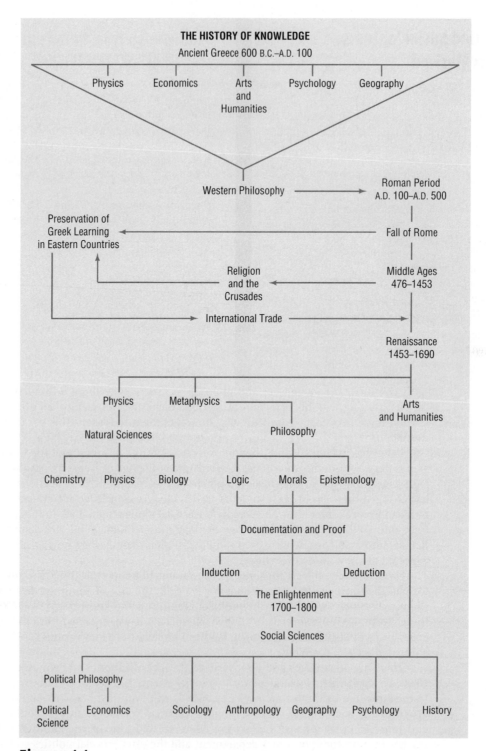

Figure 1.1

Knowledge at a glance. The development of knowledge in messy, but assuming that a picture is worth a thousand words, we offer this sketch of the development of knowledge. Maybe it's worth five hundred words.

Anthropology

Anthropology is the study of the relationship between biological traits and socially acquired characteristics. Sometimes called the study of humans, it consists of two broad fields:

1. Physical anthropology
2. Cultural anthropology

Some of the concerns of physical anthropology are:

■ Influence of evolution of natural environment on the physical characteristics of humans

■ Human evolution: how modern *homo sapiens* evolved from earlier species

Some of the concerns of cultural anthropology are:

■ Archaeology, or the remains of extinct civilizations that left no written records

■ Organization of preliterate societies

■ Characteristics of subgroups or subcultures within contemporary society

Among the topics that interest anthropologists are excavation of formerly inhabited sites, fossils, the gene pool, technology and artifacts, linguistics, values, and kinship.

Social Science as a System of Rules

Today the amount of knowledge is increasing faster than ever. How, then, can a unified social science theory ever be formulated? The answer is found in abstraction and the ability to discover rules or relationships (rather than simply facts) and rules relating rules to other rules.

To understand the importance of knowing rules, think back to grade school when you learned addition. You didn't memorize the sum of 127 and 1,448. Instead you learned an algorithm (a fancy name for a rule) about adding (7 + 8 = 15; write down the 5 and carry the 1...). Then you had to memorize only a few relationships. By changing the number system from a base ten system to a binary system (0 and 1 are the only numbers), you cut substantially the amount of memorization (all you need to know is 0 + 0 = 0; 0 + 1 = 1; and 1 + 1 = 10) and you could apply the same rule again and again, adding all possible numbers (an insight that played an important role in the development of the computer). Knowing the rules saved you from enormous amounts of memorization, but nonetheless gave you access to a large amount of information.

Another way to look at the problem is to think of the library. If you have a small library, you can know nearly everything in it, but once your library gets larger, you will quickly find that having more books makes it harder to know what's in there. However, if you put in place a filing system, such as the Dewey decimal system or the Library of Congress system, you can access the books through a filing system. The rules of the filing system give you the key to great amounts of information, just as the rules of addition, subtraction, or algebra do. General rules, once learned, can be applied to large numbers of particulars. The higher you go (rules about rules about rules), the more you can know with less memorization.[1]

All this is relevant to social science and the 2050 dateline because social science, too, is held together by rules or relationships. If there is to be a unified social science theory, it will be because some student started thinking about rules and how the rules of the various social sciences can fit together. If you understand the general concepts, you can apply them in a variety of circumstances. Thus the future "unified social scientists" will not necessarily know all the facts of a particular social science. Each of the specialties will retain its identity and will likely become even more specialized. But as that specialization occurs, it creates the need for a new specialization that concentrates on tying together the various component parts of social science. The new unified social scientists will know the general rules of the individual social sciences and the rules of how one social science interacts with another, but they will not know all the specific facts of any one of them.

The preceding argument is a heavy one to throw at you in the first pages of a textbook because it asks you not only to know the lessons of the individual social sciences, but also to

---

[1]It was an architect, Ludwig Mies van der Rohe, who compressed such exposition into a famous statement, "Less is more."

Sociology

Sociology is the systematic study of relationships among people. Sociologists assume that behavior is influenced by people's social, political, occupational, and intellectual groupings and by the particular settings in which they find themselves at one time or another. Sociologists differ in their approach. Their three major choices are:

1. Functionalism
2. Conflict
3. Interactionism

Sociology's vast subject matter can be identified as a study of people:

- Where they collect
- How they socialize and organize
- Whom they include in and exclude from their groups
- What they do to their environment
- When they confront formulas for control, such as politics, law, finance, religion, education, and social pressures
- Why they change

Geography

Geography is the study of the natural environment and how it influences social and cultural development. Some of the concerns of geography are:

- Ecology
- Climate
- Resources
- Accessibility
- Demography

Geography has practical applications manifest in:

- Maps
- Trade patterns
- Industrial and agricultural decisions
- Settlement of population
- Aggression and acquisition

go beyond and strive for an understanding of their synthesis. Going beyond is ultimately what learning is all about and what makes it so challenging. We would like to be able to say that we can guide you to a unified social science theory, but the truth is that all we can do is give you a boost and encouragement. After surveying the social sciences, you can decide in which one, if any, you want to specialize; whether you should work toward tying them all together; or whether you should bag the whole approach and go into a premed program.

The Scientific Method and Its Application

The **scientific method** is a set of rules about how to establish rules. The use of the scientific method is perhaps the most important tool you can have in studying social science because it enables you not only to learn the lessons of the individual social sciences, but also to go beyond and strive for an understanding of their synthesis.

Conditions Favorable to Scientific Inquiry. Scientific inquiry is possible only in a society in which certain attitudes are developed or tolerated. Successful scientific investigation requires from the investigator not only intelligence but certain mental attitudes as well. One of these is curiosity, which makes people ask two questions: Why? and How? Another is skepticism, which makes people reexamine past explanations and reevaluate past evidence. To reexamine and reevaluate, investigators need objectivity, which enables them to seek impartially for the truth, to make every effort not to allow personal preconceptions, prejudices, or desires to color the observed facts or influence the interpretation of those facts. When these three attitudes—curiosity, skepticism, and objectivity—come together, scientific inquiry can flourish.

In preliterate tribal societies, the obstacles to the development of scientific methods of inquiry are very great. Such societies are much more bound by custom and tradition than are modern societies. The traditional way of doing things is regarded as the only right way. Moreover, any serious deviation from established procedures is likely to be regarded as a danger to the group.

We cannot classify Europe in the Middle Ages as either preliterate or tribal. Nevertheless, respect for tradition, for ancient authorities, and for religious

History

History is the study of past events. It is a social science in the sense that it is a systematic attempt to learn about and verify past events and to relate them to one another and to the present. Every event has a historical context within which we commonly say the event must be studied. The subject matter of history is everything that has already happened. The study of history involves:

- Identifying
- Classifying
- Arranging
- Patterning

The fruits of the study of history are:

- Imposition of order
- Appreciation of variety
- Possibilities of prediction
- Realization of limitation

dictates was so strong then that the growth of a scientific spirit was stunted. The free development of modern science had to wait until such events as the Crusades, the Renaissance, the great voyages of discovery, and the Reformation had loosened the hold of tradition.

Nature of the Scientific Method. Modern science is based on the assumption that this is an orderly universe, ruled by the law of cause and effect. Any given set of circumstances always produces the same result. If seemingly identical situations have different results, they were not really alike; some significant difference existed and was overlooked. Further investigation should disclose what this difference was.

Science offers no final explanations of the universe and its phenomena. Time, space, matter, energy—existence itself—are mysteries the ultimate nature of which are probably forever beyond the grasp of the human search. But an accepted scientific theory may be regarded as an explanation, up to a certain point, of a scientific law.

Scientific investigation is seldom simple. Each field of knowledge has its special problems, and investigators must always adjust their methods to the peculiarities of the situation they are dealing with. A method of investigation that is of great importance in some fields is the setting up and carrying out of controlled experiments.

The Experimental Method and Its Limitations. The **experimental method** is a method of separating out causal factors. It consists of running an experiment many times with only one variant. If the results of the experiments are different, that one variant is most likely the cause.[2] In chemistry, physics, and biology, such controlled experiments play an important role in discovering facts and testing hypotheses. In these sciences, an investigator can create a situation in which all the significant factors that bear on a problem can be controlled.

But there are limits to the use of the experimental method when a scientist cannot control the situations that are significant for the solution of problems. In the social sciences, very little use can be made of the method of controlled experiment except in dealing with certain relationships that involve rather small groups, because the investigator cannot control the situations. For example, one way to prove or disprove the proposition that high tariffs bring prosperity would be to apply very heavy duties to all goods entering the United States for a considerable period of time, while holding constant all other factors affecting business activity. If a sustained increase in prosperity followed, we would then have substantial evidence to support the thesis that high tariffs are a cause of prosperity. No investigator, let us say an economist, can control the country's tariff policy; and even if she could, while the high tariff was in effect many other social changes would be taking place, such as strikes, the establishment of new industries, and perhaps even wars. Some of these other changes would doubtless have much more influence on the state of national prosperity than

---

[2]But it is always possible that some other factor was not "held constant." If you remember chemistry experiments in high school, you know how hard it is to keep all other things constant.

The Saga of Hans, the Thinking Horse

The scientific method can be seen in the saga of Hans, the Thinking Horse. Around 1900, according to reports published in a Berlin, Germany, newspaper, there was a horse that was good at math, and when his owner asked him math questions, the horse could answer by tapping out the correct number with one of his front hooves. People who witnessed the horse's ability were puzzled, and they called in a number of social scientists to investigate the phenomenon. To their amazement, they found that not only could Clever Hans, as he was known, add and subtract when his owner asked him—he could also calculate square roots. The social scientists were convinced that, against all odds, they had indeed been shown a thinking horse.

Another social scientist, though, a skeptical young psychologist by the name of Oskar Pfungst, had a different idea. He retested Hans, asking a set of questions to which Pfungst himself did not know the answers. He discovered that although Hans succeeded on nearly every question if the questioner knew the answer, the horse failed nearly every question when the questioner did not know the answer. A social scientist's skepticism had shown that Hans could not really reason, even though it seemed as if he could. This true story demonstrates the important trait of skepticism. The scientific community declared that Hans was just a horse.

But a quality those scientists did not show was imagination. Even though Hans could not think and reason, he had an amazing ability: He could almost read minds. When it came to people who knew the answers to the questions they were asking, he could monitor changes in his questioners' posture, their breathing, their facial expressions, and their inflections and speech patterns. He could interpret the signals they were sending and then provide the responses they wanted. This is an ability that some humans have—although generally to a lesser degree than Hans—and it is an ability that can supplement thinking. Yet it was only at the end of the twentieth century that comparative psychologists showed the imagination to start analyzing this kind of ability in detail.

The lack of imagination exhibited by some scientists in the past limited the scope of the scientific programs they followed. A good scientist must have both skepticism and imagination.

would the high tariff and would make it impossible to separate out the effects of the high tariff from the effects of all these other events.

Most problems of interest to social scientists involve very large groups of people, often society as a whole. Controlled experiments cannot be used to solve such problems. When, however, social scientists can solve a problem by working with small groups, they may be able to make a limited use of the experimental method if the people involved will cooperate. Also, they can study **natural experiments,** which occur when two similar areas or entities choose different policies, and the effects of the different policies can be systematically studied. With natural experiments, researchers do not get perfect control, but they get some.

In the future, with further advances in computer technology, social scientists will study policy issues using virtual social systems in which a computer model of numerous interacting individuals creates a virtual system that can analogue what occurs in the real world. Because of the complexity of social systems, such virtual systems remain a hope for the future, not a reality.

Social experiments are sometimes called experiments, but, unless they have a "control" that followed a different path and hence can be studied as a natural experiment, they are not what we mean by experiment. A social experiment is simply the introduction and "trying out" of new social policies. For example, Oregon's change in the financing of health insurance or Florida's experiments with vouchers for financing education might be called social experiments. The distinction involves the ability to have a control and to be able to replicate the experiment. The less the control, and the less the ability to repeat the experiment, the less sure we are of the results.

Methodology and the Social Sciences

Because it is so difficult to experiment in social science, some people have insisted that it is not science. Except for the prestige carried by the word, whether we call the study of society

Economics

Economics is the study of the ways in which men and women make a living, the most pressing problem most human beings face. It considers the social organization through which people satisfy their wants for scarce goods and services. Its subject matter is often summarized as:

- Production
- Distribution
- Consumption

Some of the topics it includes are:

- Supply and demand
- Monetary and fiscal policy
- Costs
- Inflation
- Unemployment

Economics seeks to explain, guide, and predict social arrangements by which we satisfy economic wants.

Political Science

Political science is the study of social arrangements to maintain peace and order within a given society. It deals with government, and its interests are:

- Politics
- Laws
- Administration
- Theory of the nature and functions of the state
- International relations

It has both a philosophical and a practical base. It examines the theory of systems of government, but it also studies actual practices by which government:

- Taxes
- Prohibits
- Regulates
- Protects
- Provides services

a science is not important. It is merely a question of definition. If we mean by *science* the natural sciences only, then social science is not true science. If we mean by science only the so-called exact sciences, then again social science is not included. If, however, we use the term *science* broadly, to include all systematic attempts to expand knowledge by applying the scientific method, then social science must definitely be included in the scientific family. What is really important is that social scientists have discovered many significant relationships that are sufficiently dependable to add greatly to our understanding of social behavior and to serve as useful guides in dealing with some social problems.

There has been much debate about the correct methodology to be used in social science. Thomas Kuhn, a famous philosopher of science, defined a **paradigm** as a scientific theory and the core of beliefs that surround it. He argued that scientific progression occurs by paradigm shifts in which, for a long time, scientists will resist change and hold on to an old theory even as evidence mounts up against it, and even when another theory better fits the data. Eventually, however, the evidence in favor of the new theory is so great that suddenly scientists shift their thinking. The process can be likened to the way a drop of water forms on a faucet. It grows larger and larger until it falls. A good example in the sciences is Einstein's relativity theory in physics, which was initially scoffed at but was later adopted because it was consistent with a wider range of physical phenomena than was the earlier gravitational theory of Sir Isaac Newton.

Social scientists have discussed at great length whether Kuhn's theory of paradigm shift is appropriate for the social sciences. If it is, it gives legitimacy to competing theories. If it is not, then the generally accepted theory can be considered the best. The issue has never been resolved, but our understanding of the relevance of theories has advanced.

Imre Lakatos, another famous philosopher of science, has extended Kuhn's arguments by saying that in social science there are generally many competing theories, each being extended through competing **research programs,** or groups of scientists working on a particular problem. For example, in psychology there are the behaviorists and the Freudians. In sociology there are functionalists, conflict theorists, and interactionists. We could cite different theories within each social science. Advocates of each of the paradigms compete for researchers. The group of researchers most successful in competing for followers is the one most likely to grow.

Psychology

Psychology deals with the mind and personality of the individual. It is a social science because humans are social creatures. It focuses on the individual and physical processes, such as:

- Biological structure
- Development and maturation

Of the various branches of psychology, the most relevant to social science is social psychology. Social psychology is the study of the individual's behavior as it influences and is influenced by the behavior of others. Some specific topics that interest psychologists and social psychologists are:

- Socialization
- Environment and heredity
- Adjustment and maladjustment

These social scientists deal with natural phenomena such as emotion, memory, perception, and intelligence.

Other philosophers of science go further. Some, like Paul Feurabend, argue that all methodology is limiting and that the correct methodology is no methodology. Still others argue that sociological issues, such as what is likely to advance a scientist's career, rather than the truth of a theory determine what the scientist believes.

In this book, we emphasize the competition among various theories. By doing so, we hope to show how, in social science, controversy plays an important role in the development of our knowledge.

Probably the best way to understand the scientific method is to consider a couple of examples that do *not* follow the scientific method. For instance, consider astrology or numerology. These pseudostudies hold that by analyzing the alignment of the stars or the position of certain numbers, individuals can discover or predict events that will affect them. However, the accuracy of the discoveries or the reliability of the predictions has never been satisfactorily demonstrated to most social scientists. Even though we might turn to our horoscopes and say, "Aha! That seems to fit my character or my experience," if we critically consider these predictions, often we see that the statements are so broad that they can be applied more or less appropriately to a wide range of happenings or possibilities. This is not to say that the social sciences always avoid that. Economics, for instance, often comes up with predictions from large, highly sophisticated mathematical models (called *econometric models*), and some of these predictions are no better for steering a course than back-of-the-envelope estimates.

A good social scientist generally takes an agnostic (not believing but also not disbelieving) position about claims until they can be tested and retested. Consider, for example, parapsychology, which argues that people can transmit certain information independently of all conventional forms of communication. Shirley MacLaine's best-selling book *Out on a Limb* convinced many people that the claim of parapsychology is true. Most social scientists remain unconvinced. They hold that, to date, the theories have not been sufficiently demonstrated. In stating that these theories have not been tested, a good social scientist is not dogmatic. It is possible that we social scientists become so tied to our way of looking at the world that we are unable to consider the possibilities of other ways. Who is to say that the tests we accept as conclusive are the "right" tests? Or that our training hasn't biased the tests?

Ultimately, however, we must make a working judgment about what is and what isn't an acceptable test, and social scientists' methodology is an expression of that working judgment. It should, however, be presented as a working judgment, not as a set of definitive criteria of what is true and what is false. That's why, generally, good social scientists remain agnostic over a wide range of issues that they just don't have time to investigate. Thus, in many ways, what you will get out of a study of social science and an understanding of its methods is a healthy understanding of the limitations of your powers to know.

The Methods of Social Science

The basic procedures of the scientific method are as important in social science as in physical science. Social scientists must observe carefully, classify and analyze their facts, make generalizations, and attempt to develop and test hypotheses to explain their generalizations. Their problem, however, is often more difficult than that of physical scientists. The facts gathered by the social scientist—for example, those concerning the cultures of different peoples—have similarities, but each fact may also be unique in significant respects. Facts of this kind are difficult to classify and interpret. Further, as we have already noted, the generalizations or laws that the social scientist can make are likely to be less definite and certain than those of the physical scientist.

The difficulty of discovering relatively exact laws that govern social life results from several circumstances. First, the things of greatest importance in our social life—satisfactions, social progress, democracy—are not really measurable. Second, society is extremely complex. It is difficult and usually impossible to find and evaluate all the many causes of a given situation, though often we can discover the factors that were most important in bringing it about. Third, in every social situation there is the human element. Frequently, the course of social events depends on the reaction of a few individuals who are leaders, and, except in routine situations, we can seldom predict individual behavior with complete certainty.

If the social scientist finally does succeed in finding uniformities or "laws" of social behavior and in setting up hypotheses to explain them, there is still another difficulty—namely, that investigators can seldom employ controlled experiments to test their hypotheses. To a considerable extent, the social scientist must substitute careful observation and the mental process of abstraction for experiments. The investigator abstracts from a given situation some one factor in order to consider what effect it would have if acting alone. To do this, the investigator imagines that any other factors present remain constant or inert and asks, for example, a question such as: If other factors affecting economic life remained constant, what would be the economic effect of raising tariff rates on imports?

A social scientist with a thorough knowledge of a situation may correctly calculate the effect of a given causal factor by assuming that all other things remain equal. However, to reach correct conclusions by this method, the investigator must be both competent and painstaking. Even then, the dangers of error are great. If anything, there is more need for competence in the social scientist than in the physical scientist. The theories of a physical scientist often can be proved right or wrong by experiments, but this is seldom true of those of the social scientist. An unfortunate result is that it is easier in social science than in physical science to be needlessly vague, to perpetuate errors, and to cover up incompetence.

Social scientists also have more difficulty than physical scientists in being objective. Because they deal

"I'm a social scientist, Michael. That means I can't explain electricity or anything like that, but if you ever want to know about people. I'm your man."

with human beings and are human themselves, social scientists find it hard to put aside their own likes and dislikes, their sympathies, prejudices, and frustrations. As a result, they sometimes fall into the trap of trying to justify their own hopes, beliefs, or biases instead of seeking to discover the truth. We should always be on guard against those who pose as social scientists but who, in fact, substitute propaganda and charisma for objectivity and competence.

This does not mean that social science is any less scientific than the natural sciences, or that it is less objective. It simply means that social scientists must be continually on guard against such traps and must be as clear and objective as possible.

The differences between physical science and social science lead to slightly different structures of research. Although there is no ideal structure, a reasonable approach to a problem in social science is the following:

1. Observe.
2. Define the problem.
3. Review the literature. (Become familiar with what others have observed.)
4. Observe some more.
5. Develop a theoretical framework and formulate a hypothesis.
6. Choose the research design.
7. Collect the necessary data.
8. Analyze the results.
9. Draw conclusions.

Using this outline as a rough guide, and recognizing that the specific project and each specific social science determine the exact nature of the methodology to be used, you have a reasonably good method of attack.

Observing. Notice that social science begins with observation. Social science is about the real world, and the best way to know about the real world is to observe it.

Defining the problem. Of the various research steps listed, this one is probably the most important. If you've carefully defined your terms, you can save an enormous amount of energy. Put simply, if you don't know what you're doing, no matter how well you do it, you're not going to end up with much. The topic might be chosen for a variety of reasons, perhaps because it raises issues of fundamental social science importance, perhaps because it has suddenly become a focus of controversy, or perhaps because research funds have become available to investigate it.

Reviewing the literature. Knowledge of the relevant literature is essential because it provides background, suggests approaches, indicates what has already been covered and what hasn't, and saves you from redoing what has already been done. It is a way of using other people's observations.

Observing some more. After you have defined your problem and reviewed the literature, your observation will be sharper. You will know more precisely what you are looking for and how to look for it.

Developing a theoretical framework and formulating a hypothesis. Make a statement predicting your results and then clarify what each of the terms in the statement means within the framework of your research. Suppose your hypothesis is: "High price increases sales of fashionable magazines." You should specify how high is high, and compared to what specific price is the price stated to be high; how much of an increase is significant over the circulation the magazine enjoyed at the lower price; what sales are included (newsstand, subscription, or both); and what is "fashionable." Different researchers may define the same term differently, which is one of the reasons why the same research subject can produce different results.

Choosing a research design.   Pick a means of gathering data—a survey, an experiment, an observational study, use of existing sources, or a combination. Weigh this choice carefully because your plan is the crux of the research process.

Collecting the necessary data.   Data are what one collects from careful observation. Your conclusions will be only as good as your data, so take great care in collecting and, especially, in recording your data. If you can't document what you've done, you might as well not have done it.

Analyzing the results.   When all the data are in, classify facts, identify trends, recognize relationships, and tabulate the information so that it can be accurately analyzed and interpreted. A given set of facts may be interpreted two different ways by two different analysts, so give your analysis careful, objective attention. After this step has been taken, your hypothesis can then be confirmed, rejected, or modified.

Drawing conclusions.   Now you can prepare a report, summarizing the steps you've followed and discussing what you've found. A good report will relate your conclusions to the existing body of research, suggest where current assumptions may be modified because of new evidence, and possibly identify unanswered questions for further study.

These steps differ slightly from those used by a natural scientist, but only slightly—the primary difference comes in testing a hypothesis. In some natural sciences, it is possible to conduct controlled experiments in which the same experiment can be repeated again and again under highly regulated conditions. In the social sciences, such controlled experiments are more difficult to construct.

The line between social science and natural science is not fixed. In some natural sciences, perfectly controlled experiments are impossible. In cosmological physics, for example, one can't create the universe again and again. Thus, one must speculate about a hypothesis, draw conclusions from that hypothesis, and see whether the conclusions match what one observes in the universe. Alternatively, in the social science of psychology, certain controlled experiments are possible—for example, individuals can be given specific stimuli under specific conditions again and again. Thus, the difference between the way one deals with the natural sciences and the way one deals with the social sciences can be blurry.

Let's take an example of the use of the social science method—Joseph Holz's study of the implications of teen pregnancy. First, he studied all the writing on teen pregnancy. Then he set up the following hypothesis: Teen motherhood causes the mothers to be economically and socially worse off than they otherwise would have been. To test this hypothesis, he used data that had been collected over many years tracking the lives of teenage women. From that he extracted two groups—a set of teenagers who had become pregnant and borne the child and a set of teenagers who had become pregnant but had miscarried. He then compared their economic and social positions when they were in their mid-thirties. If teen motherhood caused the mother to be worse off, then the teens who had borne their babies should have been in a worse position than those who miscarried. They weren't. He found no significant difference between the two groups: Both were low income, significantly dependent on welfare benefits, and had completed the same number of years of school. The initial hypothesis was false. Teen pregnancy did not make mothers worse off; it was simply a symptom of a larger set of problems. This larger set of problems was so severe that whether mothers had borne a child in their teens made little difference to their economic and social positions.

Holz's findings were published as the government was conducting a costly campaign against teen motherhood, and his conclusions were unpopular with both liberals and conservatives. Liberals did not like them because his study suggested that much of the family planning advice and sex education developed by liberals was of little help in improving these women's lives. Conservatives didn't like them because his study implied that more substantive changes than simply eliminating teen motherhood were needed to improve these women's lives and break the cycle of poverty. But good social science methodology is not about pleasing anybody—it is about understanding social issues and social problems.

Although Holz's experiment was not fully controlled, it was as close as one could come to a controlled experiment in the social sciences. It selected similar groups to compare in such a way that no obvious reason existed as to why these two groups should differ.

Social Science Approaches to Problems

As you review the literature about various social science studies, you will see that social scientists can use many different approaches and methods as they study problems. We first consider alternative approaches; then we consider alternative methods.

Alternative Approaches.   The approach one takes when analyzing a problem reflects one's worldview—the lens through which one sees the world. Four approaches that social scientists use are the functionalist theory approach, the exchange theory approach, the conflict theory approach, and the symbolic interaction theory approach.

The functionalist theory approach.   This approach emphasizes the interconnectedness of social life and the difficulty of affecting only one part of society with a policy. Followers of the **functionalist theory approach** are hesitant to make social judgments because all aspects of society have certain functions.

The exchange theory approach.   Closely related to the functionalist approach, the **exchange theory approach** emphasizes the voluntary exchanges of individuals as reflecting individuals' choices. Thus, the structure of society reflects individuals' desires. The exchange theory approach lens is one of relative harmony in society, sometimes upset by dysfunctional elements.

The conflict theory approach.   The **conflict theory approach** sees far less harmony than the exchange theory approach. Followers of this approach see social behavior in terms of conflict and tension among competing groups or classes. Whereas the exchange theory approach sees individuals' voluntary choices, the conflict theory approach sees force and power directing individual actions.

The symbolic interaction theory approach.   The **symbolic interaction theory approach** sees individuals as deriving meaning from the symbols they learn from. Followers of this approach see reality as reflecting less what people do and more what they think and feel. Their motives and perceptions, rather than actions, are emphasized.

These approaches are not necessarily independent of one another. Some social scientists use a combination of approaches to study problems, while some use one at one time and another at another time.

Alternative Methods.   In addition to using different approaches, social scientists also use different methods. These include the historical method, the case method, and the comparative and cross-cultural methods.

The historical method.   Because most social developments—such as the government of the United States—have unique characteristics, in order to understand them as fully as possible the social scientist must rely heavily on a study of their historical background. We can never understand completely how any historical situation came to exist, because there are limits to our historical knowledge and causes become increasingly complex and uncertain as we trace them further into the past. We can, however, make both historical events and present social situations much more intelligibly by using the **historical method**—tracing the principal past developments that seem to have been directly significant in bringing about a social situation. To trace these past developments, a historian will use many of the same methods as other social scientists such as collecting birth and marriage certificates and classifying those data.

It has been noted that history never really repeats itself. Nevertheless, present and past situations often have such striking similarities that a knowledge of the past can give us insights into present situations and sometimes into future trends.

The case method.   Writers on the methodology of social research have devoted a great deal of attention to the case method—its characteristics, its variations, the uses it can serve, its advantages, and its limitations. Here we only describe its basic nature. The **case method** involves making a detailed examination and analysis of a particular issue or problem situation. This can involve a case study of a single person such as that by a psychologist of his client, a single area or town such as a sociologist's study of why a town changes, or even a study of whole countries such as an economist's when comparing various countries.

A case study can be intended to discover how to bring about desirable changes in a particular problem situation: for example, to find the most effective ways of upgrading or rehabilitating a slum area. More often, the chief purpose of a case study is to throw light on many similar situations that exist in a society. The hope is that an understanding of one or a few cases will illuminate the others and thus aid in solving the social problems they present. The case or cases selected should be typical of the group they purport to represent.

The preceding requirement can be a limiting factor in the usefulness of the case method. Suppose we wanted to make a study of the class structure of U.S. society as a whole. Obviously, it would be easier to select as cases for study several relatively small and isolated cities in various sections of the country. But it is questionable whether these would give us a true picture of the country as a whole, because today a great proportion of our people live in large metropolitan areas where the class structure is likely to be much more complex than in smaller and more isolated communities. However, to study and describe in detail the class structure of such an area may be prohibitively difficult and expensive, and therefore impractical.

The comparative and cross-cultural methods.   The **comparative method** was formerly often employed in the hope of discovering evolutionary sequences in the development of human institutions—that is, patterns of social development or progress that would be universal. For example, it was sometimes assumed that definite stages existed in the development of governmental institutions, and it was thought that these stages could be discovered by comparing a society at one level of development with some other society at a different level. Today, this attempt to find patterns of social evolution that can be applied to all societies has been largely abandoned.

However, comparison of different societies still plays an important role in anthropological studies through what is called the **cross-cultural method.** This method consists of making detailed studies of the culture patterns of a number of societies for the purpose of comparing the different ways in which their people meet similar needs. These studies sometimes show surprising similarities in the cultural traits of widely separated peoples who appear to have had no direct or indirect contacts with one another.

Comparison of the characteristics of different societies involves problems. At times, it is difficult to decide whether two or more societies are independent or should be treated as one. Or consider definitions: If we are comparing the family institution in different societies, we must define *family* broadly enough to cover cultural variations yet specifically enough to make comparisons meaningful. Sociologists do not always agree on just what a family is. Again, if we are comparing unemployment in urban-industrial societies, we must agree on what we mean by *unemployment*. For example, in the early 1980s, the unemployment rate in Mexico, computed by U.S. standards, was approximately 30 percent. Mexican economists, however, argued that this figure was meaningless because Mexican work habits and culture were different from those in the United States. Much of what was measured as unemployment, they said, was actually individuals working at home and not earning money in the marketplace. Thus, although they had nonmarket jobs, they had been counted as unemployed.

Common Sense in the Social Sciences

Probably the most important lesson to remember when conducting any research is that you should use what might be called an educated common sense. You can understand the analytic argument for common sense by considering the mind as a supercomputer storing enormous amounts of information, not all of which may lie at the surface of recall. This holds true even with the vast increase in computer power. Processing speeds of computers double every eighteen months, according to Moore's Law. That increase has made it possible to do enormous things even with home computers. However, compared with the capabilities of the human mind, even the most powerful computer counts by using its fingers and toes. The mind processes trillions of pieces of information in millinanoseconds (we don't know what they are either, but we do know they are very small). When the results of the models and the minds diverge, it seems reasonable to rely on the more powerful computer—the mind. It makes sense to do so, however, only if the best information has been input into the mind. Common sense is not sufficient; we must use educated common sense.

To see the difference between common sense and *educated* common sense, consider the problem: Does the earth circle the sun or does the sun circle the earth? Uneducated common sense tells us that the sun circles the earth, and that commonsense conclusion became built into society and society's view of itself throughout the Middle Ages. To believe otherwise was heresy. In 1540, Copernicus tried to fit that commonsense view with observations that classical Greeks had made of the heavens. As he went about this task, he discovered that he could get a good fit of the data with the theory only if he assumed the earth moved around the sun. His was an **educated common sense**—rational thought based on observation and the best information available. It was that kind of educated common sense that ultimately led to the scientific method. As specialization makes us focus on narrower and narrower issues, it is important to keep in the back of our minds that scientific analysis has made us look at only part of the problem and that we must also use our educated common sense to interpret the results reasonably.

The Use of Statistics

Whenever possible, social scientists rely on quantitative data—data that can be reduced to numbers—but often quantitative data are not available, so social scientists must rely on qualitative data such as interviews or heuristic summaries of information in the literature. When using qualitative data, it is much more difficult to draw specific inferences from the data, because the "facts" one finds depend on how one interprets the qualitative data. One way to partially overcome such "interpretive problems" is the "Delphic method" in which another specialist in the field reviews your interpretation and then you modify your interpretation in response if you see fit, explaining your reasons for accepting or rejecting the suggested modifications. Another way is to translate the qualitative data into quantitative data, creating "proxies" (stand-ins) for any missing quantitative data, although that often simply hides the interpretative issues rather than eliminating them.

If quantitative data are available, social scientists rely on **statistical analysis**—information in numerical form that has been assembled and classified—to provide the social scientist with the information needed to understand social relationships and processes. Statistics do not enable us to measure directly such basic social values as good citizenship, happiness, or welfare, but they are useful in measuring other factors that underlie social life, such as the size of the population of a country, or the number of families whose incomes fall below some level that we set as the minimum for decent and healthful living. Statistical relationships also give us insights into social problems. If we find that the proportion of males in juvenile detention centers who come from broken homes is substantially greater than the proportion of males in the population at large who come from such homes, this suggests that broken homes may be an important factor contributing to juvenile delinquency. But statistics must always be interpreted with care, for it can be easy to read into them conclusions they do not justify. Also, it is sometimes possible to manipulate them so that they appear to show what we want them to show.

Although statistics measure the results of social activity and highlight trends, they have other useful functions: testing theories and discovering relationships. For example, *correlation* is the relationship between two sets of data. A high correlation between sets of data means that if an element in one set rises, its corresponding element in the other set is also likely to rise. Other statistics determine how sure we are of a relationship. We do not discuss these statistics because an introductory social science course is not the place to learn them, but it *is* the place to learn that such techniques of testing relationships exist, and they may be worth your while to study at some point in the future.

If we are going to use statistics, we must have data. Data are the raw numbers describing an event, occurrence, or situation. Social scientists' data come from measuring and counting all occurrences of a particular happening. For example, we might find, "In 2007, there were *x* number of murders and *y* number of suicides." One way to get data is to conduct a **survey,** a method whereby data are collected from individuals or institutions by means of questionnaires or interviews. For instance, we might conduct a survey in which selected people are questioned or polled on such matters as their incomes, their beliefs on certain issues, or the political candidate for whom they intend to vote. Figure 1.2 gives an example of such a survey. Statistics can tell us how large a portion of a group must be surveyed before we can be reasonably sure that the results will reflect the views of the entire group. Such techniques are used extensively in surveys such as the Gallup or Harris public opinion polls.

The use of statistics has been greatly facilitated, and therefore greatly expanded, by the computer. The computer has made it possible to record, arrange, and rearrange voluminous information quickly and analytically. Today, enormous amounts of data and other resources are available to anyone with a computer or other access to the Internet.

With the expansion of social data and the enormous increase in computing power, it is increasingly possible for social scientists to look for relationships in the data alone, rather than to be guided in that search by theories. Using highly sophisticated statistical techniques, social scientists analyze data, looking for patterns. After they find a pattern, they fit that pattern to a theory. For example, social scientists Stephen Levitt and John Donohue searched the data and found a relationship between the passage of the abortion rights law in the United States and a decrease in crime in later periods. Based on this evidence, they argued that because abortion reduced the number of unwanted children, those children who were born had more guidance, and that it was the law making abortion legal, not any change in law enforcement or increase in the number of inmates

1. Do you worry very much about the AIDS problem?

    <u>*50.4*</u> No

    <u>*49.6*</u> Yes ──────┐

    > If yes, what are your specific worries?
    >
    > <u>*1.8 Past-oriented (did past partners tell truth)*</u>
    >
    > <u>*26.6 Present-oriented (e.g., general fear, casual*</u>
    > <u>*relationships uncertain, others apathetic)*</u>
    >
    > <u>*20.5 Future-oriented (e.g., rapid spread, new*</u>
    > <u>*means of spreading may be found)*</u>

Directions: For the following items, indicate the degree of your agreement or disagreement by placing an "X" in the appropriate column.

	Strongly Agree	Agree	Disagree	Strongly Disagree
2. Fraternities are the center of social life on campus.	*32.5%*	*47.9%*	*18.8%*	*0.9%*
3. Fraternities encourage too much illegal drinking.	*9.4%*	*28.2%*	*53.0%*	*9.4%*
4. Fraternities encourage too much vandalism.	*6.9%*	*15.5%*	*59.5%*	*18.1%*
5. The fraternity system encourages the development of positive female–male relationships.	*3.5%*	*33.9%*	*47.8%*	*14.8%*
6. I worry about contracting AIDS.	*4.3%*	*41.9%*	*39.3%*	*14.5%*
7. There is too much fear of AIDS today.	*5.2%*	*19.0%*	*50.0%*	*25.9%*
8. There should be much more mandatory testing for AIDS.	*13.8%*	*46.6%*	*33.6%*	*6.0%*
9. Regarding AIDS, the best statement to describe my concern is "It won't happen to me."	*1.7%*	*25.6%*	*45.3%*	*27.4%*

Figure 1.2

One of the best ways by which social scientists collect information is through a survey. This is one page of a fourteen-page survey conducted by college students for their sociology class. Because of time pressures in that particular survey, they were unable to perform an extensive analysis of their data. For this reason, they urged caution in the use and interpretation of the information.

jailed, that was mostly responsible for the decrease in crime rates that the United States experienced in the 1990s.

Whenever making such claims, social scientists should be very careful not to confuse **correlation**—the simultaneous movement of two variables—with **causation**—in which change in one variable brings about change in the other variable. The difference can be seen in the following example. When it is expected to rain, more people carry umbrellas, so umbrella usage and rain are correlated. But the fact that people carry umbrellas does not cause it to rain, or so most of us believe.

The Interdisciplinary Approach

Modern industrial societies and their problems are becoming increasingly complex, and because no one person today can master all the social sciences, growing emphasis is placed on the interdisciplinary approach to many social problems. The **interdisciplinary approach** means that a group of social scientists with different specialties will work together on a certain problem, not all of whose aspects any one of the group fully understands. For some problems, such as those surrounding pollution, it may be necessary to call in, say, a physical scientist, a geologist, and an engineer. But in facing all of these problems, the need for educated people who have a broad sense of problems and interrelationships—who understand the need for a unified social science—is also becoming more and more evident.

Though few social relationships can be reduced to exact and invariable laws, human beings in large groups everywhere show great likenesses of behavior when conditions are really similar. Thus, there is reason to believe that we can, through systematic study and research, greatly increase our understanding of the nature and development of human societies, and to hope that the attitudes fostered by the interdisciplinary approach itself and the knowledge to which it leads us can ultimately result in greater tolerance and cooperation among diverse groups and among nations.

Social Science and Society

Some people believe that the social sciences are lagging behind the natural sciences. They maintain that not only does social science have no exact laws, but that it has also failed to eliminate great social evils such as racial discrimination, crime, poverty, and war. They imply that social scientists have failed to accomplish what might reasonably have been expected of them. However, such critics are usually unaware of the real nature of social science and of its special problems and basic limitations. For example, they forget that the solution to a social problem requires not only knowledge but also the ability to influence people. Even if social scientists discover the procedures that should be followed to achieve social improvement, they are seldom in a position to control social action. For that matter, even dictators find that there are limits to their power to change society.

Agreeing on Policy

One of the great problems in a democracy is getting the majority of people to reach substantial agreement on the major policies that should be followed to create a better society. Social scientists can aid in bringing about this agreement by helping people to understand the issues, the difficulties involved, and the possible steps to a solution. If we express social objectives in sufficiently general terms, agreement is not so hard to obtain. Most people would like to have a heaven on earth characterized by peace and goodwill, with freedom, justice, security, health, and happiness for all. But when it comes to drawing up a blueprint for reaching these objectives, disagreements and obstacles become apparent. Social scientists themselves are not always in complete agreement on what our specific social goals should be or on how we can best work toward them.

In any case, the function of social science and of those who practice it is not primarily to determine social objectives. Its major function is to discover how our objectives can be achieved. The determination of the goals themselves—our social values—is not a scientific problem but one having to do with our likes and dislikes, our esthetic concepts, our moral standards, and our philosophical and religious beliefs. (We will have more to say about social values in the following chapter.)

Values, Terminology, and Rhetoric

This chapter began with a quotation from Albert Einstein who said that "theories should be as simple as possible, but not more so." The same thing could be said about ideas and the expression of those ideas. Unfortunately, specialists have an incentive to develop a terminology that is anything but simple and that often obscures rather than clarifies. One of the many social science teachers who has written us about this book (and in doing so, these teachers have played an important role in its development) described a history conference she attended where "we were treated to such goodies" as

> The sociopolitical internecine amortizations of agronomous proletarization, if solely counterproductive of Jurassic multi-dimensional interstitial extrapolated Augustinian and Aristotelian epistemological diagrammetric middle-sector dichotomies, as measured in the context of paradigmatic vestigiae (though challenged none too effectively, if I am not remiss in saying so, by Freylinghausen's hypothesis delivered at the University of Bordeaux in April 1896) are existentially and polaristically categorized by Nordlinger's Metternichian thermodynamics as tangentially interrelated with studies promulgated by Darffenstangenovich on a scale of one to twenty factored to the 24th power.

Although she may have used a bit of literary license in transcribing the conference proceedings, her point is well taken. She was attending a conference on her specialty, yet she didn't understand what was being said. It happens all the time, not only to students, but to teachers as well. Although there may be valuable ideas in what many specialists have to say, we can't profit from them if we can't understand them, or if we must spend hours translating them.

In his wonderful book, *The Sociological Imagination,* C. W. Mills made precisely this point. He argued that in many social sciences, "high theory" is top-heavy with jargon. As an example, he interpreted sociologist Talcott Parsons's terminology: He reduced it by 80 to 90 percent and at the same time made it more intelligible. Mills wasn't making the point that Parsons's insights weren't good ones; to the contrary, Mills believed that Parsons was a brilliant sociologist. But Parsons's language obscured his brilliant ideas.

Another characteristic of language is that it embodies value judgments and preserves ways of looking at problems. A good social scientist recognizes this and is always open to dealing with reality by alternative modes of expression and new ways of looking at issues.

Conclusion

If this chapter has succeeded in its intended purpose, it should have given you a sense of what it means to be a social scientist. As you saw, the social sciences are evolving: They interact and they move among the humanities, the natural sciences, and the individual social sciences depending on who is working with them. They are fluid, not static, and that fluidity will present problems to anyone who attempts too fixed a definition of any of them.

The ability to handle the fluid definitions, to recognize the shadows as well as the objects without flinching, is an important characteristic that good social scientists exhibit—one which, if learned, will serve you well as you study this book and play the game of life.

Key Points

- Social science is the name given to our knowledge about the nature, growth, and functioning of human society.
- The scientific method is a set of rules about how to establish rules.
- A good social scientist generally takes a wait-and-see position about claims until they are tested and retested.
- A reasonable approach to a problem in social science is to observe, define the problem, review the literature, observe some more, develop a theoretical framework and formulate a hypothesis, choose the research design, collect the necessary data, analyze the results, and draw conclusions.
- Three typical methods in social science are the historical method, the case method, and the comparative method.
- It is important to use educated common sense in the social sciences.
- A good social scientist is always open to new ways of looking at issues.

Some Important Terms

anthropology (1)
biological science (2)
case method (17)
causation (21)
cognitive science (4)
comparative method (17)
conflict theory approach (16)
correlation (21)
cross-cultural method (17)
economics (1)
educated common sense (18)
exchange theory approach (16)

experimental method (9)
functionalist theory
    approach (16)
geography (1)
historical method (17)
history (1)
humanities (2)
interdisciplinary approach (21)
natural experiments (10)
natural science (2)
paradigm (11)
political science (1)

psychology (1)
research program (11)
scientific knowledge (1)
scientific method (8)
social science (1)
sociology (1)
statistical analysis (19)
survey (19)
symbolic interaction theory
    approach (16)

Questions for Review and Discussion

1. What is scientific knowledge? How does it differ from knowledge acquired "unconsciously"?
2. Distinguish among the three major fields of human knowledge. What is the emphasis of each?
3. Name the principal social sciences and define the field with which each deals.
4. Why would it have been difficult to carry on scientific investigation in primitive societies or even in the Middle Ages?
5. What is the scientific method?
6. What basic assumption underlies the use of the scientific method?
7. What is the experimental method?
8. Why is it difficult to formulate precise laws in the field of social science?
9. Are there any advantages to having competing research programs?
10. In what sense is social science scientific?
11. Why is it often impossible to study social problems by means of the experimental method?

12. Explain the ways in which the problems of social science differ from those of the exact natural sciences.
13. What are the advantages of the interdisciplinary approach to the study of many social problems?
14. Social science has been broken down into specialties. Why is it a problem to put them back together through a unified theory?
15. What new social science fields do you think will be important ten years from now? Why do you think so?

Internet Questions

1. Using an Internet search engine directory (for example, http://dir.google.com or http://dir.yahoo.com), look at the lists of topics included under Social Science or Society. How many fields are listed? What fields would you add (or delete) in a list of your own?
2. The website www.buildfreedom.com/content/scientific_method.shtml uses an abbreviated version of the scientific method to solve the social problem of dating. Use this process to "solve" another everyday problem.
3. Go to www.wikipedia.org and choose one of the branches listed under Social Sciences. What are the subdisciplines or branches listed under your choice?
4. Take the survey about alcohol use at www.alcoholscreening.org. After taking the survey, look at the feedback you are given based on your answers. What can the results for this survey be used for?
5. Go to www.ncpa.org/pi/crime/pd08599g.html and read the discussion about Donohue and Levitt's study of abortion and crime rates mentioned in the text. What are some of the alternative arguments that critics use to explain why the crime rate has decreased?

For Further Study

Greene, Brian, *The Fabric of the Cosmos*, New York: Knopf, 2004.

Hecht, Jennifer Michael, *Doubt: A History: The Great Doubters and Their Legacy of Innovation*, San Francisco: Harper, 2004.

Mills, C. Wright, *The Sociological Imagination,* New York: Oxford University Press, 1959.

Repcheck, Jack, *Copernicus' Secret: How the Scientific Revolution Began*, New York: Simon & Schuster, 2009.

Slater, Lauren, *Opening Skinner's Box: Great Psychological Experiments of the Twentieth Century*, New York: Norton, 2004.

Tilly, Charles, *Why*, Princeton, NJ: Princeton University Press, 2006.

Wilson, Edward O., *Consilience: The Unity of Knowledge*, New York: Knopf, 1998.

WWW Anthropology Resources on the Internet www.anthropologie.net

WWW Economic History Services http://eh.net/

WWW Encyclopedia of Psychology www.psychology.org (accessed June 16, 2009)

WWW Political Resources on the Net www.politicalresources.net

WWW Social Science Research Council www.ssrc.org

WWW Sociological Resources on the Internet www.socioweb.com

WWW Virtual Library in Economics www.helsinki.fi/WebEc

WWW Virtual Library in Sociology http://socserv.mcmaster.ca/w3virtsoclib

Historical Roots of Social Science

Natural scientists tell us that the world has been around for some 6 billion years and that living things have been around for at least 3 billion. We will go back, however, only about 2,600 years, when Western philosophy began on the fringes of ancient Greece (some theorists hold that the Greeks responded to ideas from Eastern civilizations, but there are limits to even our broad sweep). The Greeks came to realize that their ancient account of how the world was created and administered—by an enormous collection of gods, or pantheon—was not the only possible explanation. They are credited with being the first to establish rational theory, independent of theological creed; to grasp rational concepts and use them as a way of looking at reality and seeing logical connections; and to be empirical and antimystical. Two great Greek thinkers of the third and fourth centuries B.C., Plato and Aristotle, are responsible for establishing a basis for knowledge as we know it and deal with it today.

The philosophical debates of the Greek period were in many ways the same ones that go on today, explaining how, when all things change, things must also be simultaneously unchanging; otherwise, something would have to be created out of nothing—a logical impossibility. These ideas would later develop into modern physics, including the laws of thermodynamics and the proposition that matter can neither be created nor destroyed—merely transformed. The Greeks also considered many of the issues that later became the social sciences; for example, they considered the role of the state (political science), the way minds interact with society (psychology), and individuals' interaction within the market (economics). Thus, the history of the social sciences begins with the Greeks. The history, however, is not continuous.

Much of the Greek contribution to knowledge would have been lost (who knows what other contributions actually have been lost?) were it not for its preservation by Eastern civilizations. On their forays into the East during the Crusades (the religious wars from 1095 to 1272 in which Christians in Europe attempted to capture Christianity's traditional territory in the Middle East), Europeans became reacquainted with the learning of the ancient Greeks, and they brought back the body of ancient Greek learning to Europe, where it was generally available by the twelfth century. These ideas spread slowly throughout Europe over the next three hundred years, and by the middle of the fifteenth century, rediscovery of Greek civilization in Europe was widespread. Because the period from about 1453 (the fall of Constantinople) to the end of the seventeenth century was characterized by the rebirth and proliferation of ancient knowledge, it became known as the **Renaissance** (a French word meaning "rebirth").

The Renaissance must have been a wonderful time for scholars. The totality of knowledge was still comprehensible by the human mind. An ideal in the Renaissance was that an educated person could know everything and exercise all skills and social graces. A true Renaissance man was willing to take on all comers on any issue.

As the store of knowledge grew, it became harder and harder to know everything, and so people began to specialize. A natural division opened, one between the humanities (the study of literature, music, and art) and physics. The physics part of this division was not refined enough, and soon physics was broken up into empirical studies (which developed into the various natural sciences) and metaphysics (nonempirical studies that developed into philosophy).

The Renaissance was preceded by the **Middle Ages** (a period from roughly A.D. 476, and the end of the Roman Empire, to A.D. 1453, the defeat of Christian religious armies in Constantinople by the Islamic Turks). In the Middle Ages, religion was so central to life that the study of religion was taken for granted, and it tied together all the other fields of study. For example, painters painted religious pictures, musicians wrote religious music, and the study of literature was the study of the Bible and its commentators. Questions that today seem the obvious ones, such as, Why are people divided into classes? and Why are the poor poor? were simply not asked. Things were the way they were because that was God's will. Once one knew God's will, the issue was how to carry it out. For example, medieval scholars believed in a "just" price and that collecting interest on savings was immoral. They taught those principles and condemned those who did not follow their teachings.

As the Renaissance dawned and continued, that religious tie provoked tension as scholars in the various fields of study came to conclusions different from the church's doctrines, beginning a long conflict between religious learning and beliefs and so-called rationalist learning and beliefs.

The tension between religious explanations and rationalist explanations was (and still is) inevitable. The rationalist approach places human reason above faith. In a rationalist approach, one looks for logical connections and is continually asking the question, Can you prove it? This meant that somehow the rationalists had to figure out what it meant to prove something. A religious approach places faith above reason. A religious explanation had no need to prove anything: Explanations were accepted on faith.

Throughout the Renaissance, rationalism more and more replaced religion as the organizing principle of knowledge, and as it did, the various fields of knowledge became divided along rationalist lines. The humanities still reflected religious issues; the rationalist revolution came much later to the humanities. To the degree that they were considered, most of the issues we now classify under social science were studied as part of history. History was part of literature and the humanities. It was simply a documentation of what had happened—it never asked *why* something happened. To ask why meant failure to accept God's will. Thus, it was primarily from philosophy, not history, that most of the social sciences emerged.

The natural sciences and philosophy divided along modes of inquiry and answers to the question, Can you prove it? The study of philosophy itself evolved into a variety of fields, such as logic, morals, and epistemology (the study of knowledge).

The Enlightenment

The **Enlightenment** is the period in which rationalism definitely replaced religion as the organizing principle of knowledge. The Enlightenment began between A.D. 1650 and A.D. 1700 and continued for about one hundred years. It is in this period that the development of the social sciences took hold and flourished.

By the time of the Enlightenment, it had become evident that to know everything—to be a Renaissance scholar—was impossible. Not only was it impossible to know everything, but it was also impossible to know everything about just one subject—say, all of physics or all of philosophy. Individuals began to specialize their study. For instance, chemistry and astronomy were separated from physics.

As philosophers delved into their subject, they further divided philosophy into parts. One part was metaphilosophy, the study of issues that most scholars agreed were not empirically testable. One such issue was: Because God is all-powerful, can he create a rock so heavy he cannot move it? The other division of philosophy dealt with issues that could, in principle at least, be empirically tested. For instance: What type of political organization of society is preferable? It is from the second division that the social sciences evolved. (They were called sciences because they were in principle meant to be empirically testable.)

The Enlightenment spawned social science because the Enlightenment rejected the assumption that the classical world of the Greeks and the Romans was perfect. In the Enlightenment (roughly the whole of the eighteenth century), there was a general belief that civilization had improved and so too should the thinking about civilization. Moreover, in the seventeenth century, just preceding the Enlightenment, there was continual turmoil—a long drawn-out war between France and England and a religious conflict between Catholics and Protestants about how to interpret God's will. That fight broke down the religious explanations and made people very much aware of social problems. Which of the two explanations, Catholic or Protestant, was right? Why were they fighting? What could be done about it? The social sciences developed as individuals attempted to explain those social problems and suggest what could be done to solve them.

Although the existence of social problems that require solutions may seem obvious to you, it was not always so obvious. This view is the product of the Enlightenment, which established the "three humiliations" of human beings. These are:

1. The earth is not the center of the universe.
2. Humans are creatures of nature like other animals.
3. Our reasoning ability is subject to passions and subconscious desires.

Frontispiece from Diderot's Encyclopédie, *written during the Enlightenment.*

Before we experienced these humiliations, thinkers could rely on an order they believed was established by God. Social problems were set up by God and were to be accepted or endured. Only after the beginning of the Enlightenment did people begin to believe that society and culture are themselves products of history and the evolution of culture—that they had changed and would continue to change.

As is often the case, the change in viewpoint had a paradoxical counterpoint, and human beings' "humiliation" was accompanied by a belief in human beings' power. If society could change, then the change could be, at least to some extent, guided and directed by human beings.

Since its conception, social science has entwined these two aspects. Sometimes it is simply trying to understand, and it accepts our limited powers and our place in the cosmos, and at other times it is trying to change society.

From Philosophy to Social Science

The evolution of philosophy into the social sciences can be seen in France, where philosophers joined to produce an encyclopedia, edited by Denis Diderot and Jean d'Alembert, which appeared over a span of several years in the mid-1700s. The full title of this encyclopedia proclaimed it to be a rational dictionary of science, art, and industry. Unlike earlier compilations, it contained systematic articles on man, society, and method, and a number of the first definitions of the social sciences can be traced to this mammoth work.

There are many ways to look at social problems, and as scholars began considering human beings in reference to their social environment, the diversity soon became apparent. The history of each of the social sciences becomes hopelessly tangled with that of each of the others at this point. In the Enlightenment, scholars were debating one another and ideas were quickly evolving. To capture even a flavor of the interaction and debate leads to a formidable morass, hardly conducive to a social science course. So we will stop our consideration here.

Some Important Terms

Enlightenment (26)
Middle Ages (25)
Renaissance (25)

Human Origins

After reading this chapter, you should be able to:

- Summarize Darwin's theory of evolution
- Explain the role of mutation in the theory of evolution
- Relate DNA to genes and genetic engineering
- Distinguish between the theory of punctuated equilibrium and the theory of continuous equilibrium
- Summarize briefly the evolution of human beings over the last 30 million years

If a single cell, under appropriate conditions, becomes a man in the space of a few years, there can surely be no difficulty in understanding how, under appropriate conditions, a cell may, in the course of untold millions of years, give origin to the human race.

—Herbert Spencer

Our ancestors in the not-so-distant past believed that the globe we live on was the major focus of the universe and that all the heavenly bodies revolved around it. Today, we know that it is only an infinitesimal part of the cosmic universe of space and matter. To human beings, however, this tiny part is more important than all the rest, for the greatest concerns of human beings are themselves, the planet on which they live, their origin, their destiny, and their relationships with each other. Even if they hope for a future life in some far-off heaven, they still long to make their earthly life meaningful and satisfying.

Human beings are first of all social creatures. They normally spend their entire lives in association with other human beings and as members of various organized social groups. The quality of association and membership varies according to the nature of the social group. For members of a family, association normally is constant and close, but as residents of a town or city, human beings' association with the majority of the other residents is only occasional and often impersonal. Modern technology, especially the Internet, is both increasing and developing that association. As people spend more time on-line, they spend less time with their families and geographic neighbors, but they often establish associations with people all over the world.

Physical geography is still important and most people still define themselves as members of a larger society, all bound together to some degree by a common language, common interests, geographic areas, ways of living, common loyalties, and reliance on a common national government for their defense and for much of their general welfare. To a great extent, the ability of people to live happy and satisfying lives depends on the nature of the society they live in.

The Origin of the Human Species

Where and when the human species originated is not known with absolute certainty, but the conventional view is that it was in Africa some 5 to 7 million years ago. Modern scientists believe that millions of years ago, the process of evolution produced our first human ancestors when a humanlike creature branched off from the apes. They believe that then a long series of changes created a group of hominids who displayed over time more and more of the basic physical characteristics that distinguish modern human beings from all other forms of life. Fossils of humanlike species have been found that date back about 5 million years, and research in this field is progressing so rapidly that it is possible that by the time you read this even older evidence will have been found. After splitting off from apes, humanlike species are believed to have continued to gradually change to other types of humanlike species in the evolutionary process.

Darwin and the Theory of Evolution

Evolution in its broadest sense refers to any process of progressive change. Thus, one may speak of the evolution of the novel, of art, or of religion. But when used without qualification, **evolution** ordinarily means organic evolution, or the theory that all the complex life forms of today have descended from earlier ones that existed long ago. The theory of evolution was popularized by the English biologist Charles Darwin, who devoted his life to systematically finding evidence to support the concept of evolution and to explaining natural selection, which he believed was the mechanism by which evolution was accomplished.

Darwin, in the capacity of a naturalist, made a five-year voyage with a British surveying expedition on the ship *Beagle* (1831–1836). During this time, he had unusual opportunities to study a great variety of plant and animal life. He was puzzled by the similarities and differences he found and by the progressive steps that often seemed evident in going from the simpler to the more complex forms of life. Ultimately, he developed his theory of natural selection to explain these relationships. The first major work in which he presented his conclusions was *The Origin of Species* (1859). Later, in another famous book, *The Descent of Man,* he dealt specifically with the evolution of the human race.

Though Darwin was largely responsible for the widespread acceptance by scientists of the concept of evolution, he was neither the first to suggest the idea nor the first to be impressed by the remarkable physical similarity of human beings to certain animals. As far back as the fourth century B.C., Aristotle believed in the gradual development of complex organisms from simpler ones, and a generation before Darwin, the French zoologist J. B. Lamarck had published a theory of evolution. Although flawed, it had many insights. Also, a hundred years before Darwin, the great Swedish naturalist Carolus Linnaeus organized the various species by similarity of their physical attributes. In doing so, he invented the term **primates,** a group of animals including human beings, apes, and monkeys whose outstanding characteristics are their larger, complex brains; high intelligence; and hands and feet adapted for grasping. In his studies, Linnaeus could not overlook the resemblances among these three kinds of creatures.

Natural Selection.   Darwin's concept of evolution was based in part on **natural selection,** the proposition that individual members of the various species that have characteristics more favorable for meeting the conditions of life are more likely to survive and pass on their characteristics to future generations. Darwin believed that every species is characterized by the appearance of such individuals; thus, the direction that evolution takes is largely determined by "the survival of the fittest."

Genetics studies how the hereditary characteristics of species and individuals are transmitted biologically to their offspring. The precise process of how evolution occurs is still unsettled, but it generally is believed that genetics plays an important role.

The foundation work in genetics was done by Gregor Mendel in the late nineteenth century.[1] He discovered that plants and animals have what he called inheritance factors, now known as **genes,** which he defined as discrete units within cells that retain their original character for generation after generation. Because of this retention, these genes determine the characteristics of future generations. Thus, the study of evolution is closely connected to the study of genetics.

Mutation.   Genetics explains the way we are, but it does not explain why and how we change. That occurs through a process called **mutation:** random genetic changes that lead to new characteristics. In mutation, an offspring may have quite different characteristics from those of its parents.

Although we do not completely understand why these mutations occur, we do know that if the resulting offspring survive, their new characteristics can be passed on to future generations. Mutations are random. They seem to be accidents, partial failures of the process by which a species is able to reproduce its kind. We also know that the incidence of mutations is increased by exposure to certain chemicals or types of radiation. Most mutations are neutral, but some are fatal and some are beneficial to the offspring. Beneficial mutations make evolution possible. Over long periods of time, evolution can bring about great changes in the character of a plant or animal species, and in the process the structure and biological functioning of the species often become much more complex.

Examples of changes in a species that seem to be the result of gene mutations and the operation of natural selection (survival of the fittest) are not difficult to find. The peppered moth in Great Britain is a case that has been studied in detail. This moth spends much of its time clinging to trees and is a favorite food of some birds. Until the middle of the nineteenth century, all peppered moths found by naturalists who collected specimens seem to have been light in color. Because the bark of the trees was usually light and often lichen-covered, this served as protection by making it difficult for the birds to see them. But after the Industrial Revolution had been under way for some time, so much soot fell in some areas of central Britain that the tree trunks and branches became darker. This made dark moths harder to see than light ones, and therefore the dark moths lived longer on average and produced more progeny. Because moths go through a great many generations in a relatively short period of time, in some of the more highly industrialized areas of Britain natural selection almost completely replaced the light peppered moths with the dark ones.

Genes contain two **alleles,** one from each parent, that affect particular characteristics. In sexually reproducing organisms, the alleles transmit characteristics from the parents to the offspring. A **dominant allele** controls the characteristic that is transmitted to offspring. A **recessive allele** will not transmit its characteristics unless both alleles in the pair are recessive. However, if two recessive alleles are paired, they will determine the characteristic affected. The peppered moth presents a relatively simple example of the operation of natural selection. The color of these moths is known to result from a dominant allele, a pair of dominant alleles for dark color, or a pair of recessive alleles for light color.

Human characteristics result from this same combination of dominant and recessive alleles. In the case of eye color, brown eyes are dominant and blue eyes are recessive. A person must have two recessive alleles to have the recessive characteristics; otherwise, the dominant characteristics prevail.

---

[1]As is the case with many major scientific breakthroughs, the significance of Mendel's work was not immediately understood. Although he published his results in 1866, their importance was not recognized until 1900.

Theories, Proofs, and the Darwinian Story

The peppered moth example has been cited in this text and in most other textbooks about evolution for at least the last twenty years. Why do textbook authors choose this example? We do so in large part because it fits the Darwinian story of evolution so well. Recently, social scientist Michael Majerus pointed out that the moth photos, on which much of the story was based, were staged and that there were serious design flaws with the original peppered moth experiments.

Despite the problems he found in the experiment, Dr. Majerus, and most moth experts, believe that the basic story about the peppered moths holds up and that the story they tell is "qualitatively right." But the recent discussion of the problems with the original experiment provides good insight into the scientific method. The scientific method directs scientists to question everything because there is always a chance that a "proof" will slip through the cracks, leading to false beliefs, especially when a theory comes to be strongly believed by most scientists. The problem is that when reports of observations fit the way we already think, we tend to be less questioning than we otherwise would be. After reviewing the broader evidence, almost all scientists continue to believe that some version of the Darwinian story of evolution holds, but they are continually testing it in order to refine and improve it so that it better fits the empirical data.

However, many people in our society—especially those with a strong Christian affiliation—interpret the Bible literally and are hesitant to accept accounts of evolution inconsistent with the Bible. The debate between these two groups is unlikely to be resolved. Science relies on empirical evidence to settle such disputes and almost all empirical scientists believe that the preponderance of empirical evidence on evolution supports some version of the theory of evolution. True, the evidence is incomplete, and science has no explanation for the ultimate beginning of everything, and there is always the possibility that scientists are collectively fooling themselves—they have done so before. Scientists admit to this possibility because good science requires them always to be skeptical even about issues they think they know; but what will convince them is contradictory empirical evidence, not arguments about the limitations of human knowledge.

Whereas good scientists are always on the lookout for contradictory evidence, good religious people are not. Almost all religions, and certainly the Christian religion, require people to accept things on faith. Religious beliefs are supposed to be held regardless of the empirical evidence—the more the empirical evidence contradicts the foundation of faith, the stronger the faith must be. This means that the two sides do not have a common method of resolving the debate.

Whether scientists should have a more open mind to additional hypotheses that complement or are in addition to evolution, but do not contradict it—such as the hypothesis that there is an intelligent design underlying the evolutionary process—is an open question. The problem with these hypotheses is that it is difficult, and perhaps impossible, to find empirical evidence that would lead us to choose one hypothesis over another. Other than the fact that we exist, and that our existence must have some cause, there seems to be no test of the intelligent design hypothesis. Thus, most scientists tend to find the arguments made by Ben Stein in his documentary, "Expelled: No Intelligence Allowed" (www.expelledthemovie.com), as primarily propaganda for a particular faith rather than an argument for a serious scientific addition or alternative to the theory of evolution. That said, the close-mindedness and unwillingness of some scientists to even address the issue, or to allow people to put their ideas forward, goes against the openness that is essential to scientific inquiry. Lastly, science has no explanation for existence; evolution is a theory of change, not a theory of existence.

The first human beings, or their humanlike precursors, probably evolved in tropical regions where survival was possible without clothing. It is likely that they had very dark skin because light skin would have given little protection against the burning rays of the sun. There is debate about whether these people spread into other parts of the world or, instead, whether people developed independently in various parts of the world. Whichever the case, it is believed that in time they became capable of spreading out from Africa, eventually to most of the world. This was probably because their physical characteristics changed. For instance, early hominids probably did not walk upright, but when they developed that ability, they could travel more efficiently. More important, perhaps, was their development of tool making. With tools, they could hunt or scavenge other animals, so they could consume more protein and fat than their low-energy vegetarian diet would have provided. Not only their bodies but also their brains would have been charged with more energy. The brain needs lots of energy to grow. As their diet expanded, hominids could physically and intellectually expand their territory.

All early hominids were probably dark-skinned. As they moved, that changed. In the most northern of the territories into which they expanded, the sun was very weak, especially in the long winters, and was often hidden by clouds or fog. Dark skin, which had been an advantage in warm, sunny climates, became a disadvantage because the sun's rays, by penetrating human skin, help produce vitamin D, which is an essential element in nutrition. Populations that remained in these colder regions for very long periods of time—perhaps 100,000 years or more—seem gradually, through gene mutations and the process of natural selection, to have developed much lighter shades of skin.

Limitations of Natural Selection. Natural selection does not completely account for all evolutionary changes. In small groups, some such changes may result from gene mutations that are harmless but do not create characteristics that contribute to survival. But other characteristics developed by such groups may increase their chances of survival, and so they grow in number and spread over wider areas. Natural selection may explain the dark skins of black Africans and the lighter skins of northern Europeans, but it is not an obvious explanation of some other racial characteristics, such as the different construction of the eyes in Asian and Occidental people, nor does it account for as much similarity as exists. Therefore, work in this area will likely continue.

Recent Developments in Genetics

In recent years, scientists have significantly extended our knowledge of genetics. Whereas once it was thought that genes were the building blocks of life, today scientists have unraveled the gene and discovered a small building block, **DNA,** or deoxyribonucleic acid, the basic chemical building block of genes. Scientists had known for a long time that DNA existed, but it was only in 1953 that James Watson and Francis Crick unraveled its double helix structure, discovering that DNA resembled a spiral staircase. They found that each of the steps serves as a code word and determines how amino acids are linked into the proteins of which all living things are made. It was like discovering the blueprint for life (but not how life was originally created or what force had drawn the blueprint).

In the 1970s, a further advance was made. Professor Paul Berg altered, or spliced, a gene. Rather than merely reading the blueprint, he had changed it. This opened up a whole new field. If scientists could change a gene, they could exercise some control over living organisms by cloning—that is, duplicating—existing forms and possibly building new ones. This process is called **genetic engineering,** rearranging genetic material to create new, man-made life forms or change existing ones. In response—demonstrating one of the interconnections between science and other fields that we see throughout this text—the price of genetic engineering stocks on Wall Street went wild as everyone tried to get in on the action.

In 1973, an international project, the Human Genome Project, was begun. Its purpose was to map, or identify, all the human genes. By 2001, the project was completed, with the mapping of a human being's entire set of genes. It's like having a set of directions to what makes us biologically what we are. This achievement was reached through the competitive efforts of government—the National Human Genome Research Institute directed by James Watson and his successor, Francis S. Collins—and a private enterprise, Celera Genomics, headed by J. Craig Ventner. They found that humans had only about 25,000 genes, about 6,000 more than a worm, and that humans share many genes with a wide variety of animals.

This genetic map has given us a much better understanding of the biological causes of differences among people and what can cause changes in people. Scientific research using this enormous amount of raw information has taken off in many directions and will likely have to be complemented by a study of the many proteins that are the building blocks of

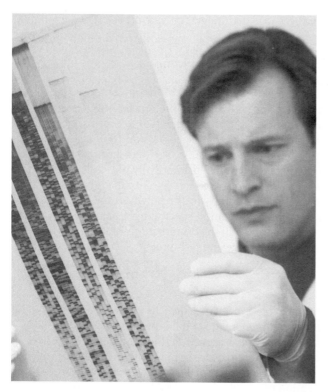

Analyzing DNA.

cells. Thus, a new applied science—proteomics—is building on the genome project. This study is still in its early stages, although some scientists believe that soon they will be able to combine the nonliving chemicals that make up DNA, and by combining them in the right proportions, be able to turn those chemicals into something living. The major breakthroughs from genetic engineering for medicine are, however, probably decades away.

Having our genetic codes presents many social and ethical dilemmas. Can we extend life spans by one hundred years? If we can, should we? Can we create new life forms? If so, what rights would they have?

Back in 1988, cloning got a lot of publicity when white mice that had been genetically altered were patented by the U.S. Patent Office so that the laboratory that had developed these mice could sell them to other laboratories for various scientific procedures. Before that, there had already been genetic engineering of plants to improve basic grains such as rice, leading to India's "green revolution" and more food at less cost for its people. In 1997, Scottish scientists succeeded in cloning sheep. Since that time, many more species of animals have been cloned. Some people even believe that it may be possible to clone extinct species, a fantasy explored in the book and movie *Jurassic Park.*

Further research on cloning has shown its limitations. Only a small percentage of eggs that start out as clones end up as live animals, and many of those live animals have defects. Scientists have traced the problem to faulty DNA methylamines, which essentially means that the DNA of clones gets slightly mixed up, and hence gives faulty instructions to the growth process. Because of the problems with cloning, most scientists agree that although we may be able to clone a human, we should not do so. However, it is always possible that some rogue scientist might attempt to do so; and such an attempt would force society to face the difficult ethical issues raised by cloning. One such issue involves embryonic stem cell research. (Stem cells are all-purpose cells that can develop into alternative types of cells). The American Medical Association has endorsed limited human embryo cloning for medical purposes, but there are major debates about whether it is appropriate.

Some Implications of Recent Developments

Changes in technology present society with extraordinarily difficult questions. If, for instance, parents could choose characteristics for their children, what characteristics would they choose, and how would their decisions affect the overall population? Will a line be drawn forbidding cloning of human beings but permitting genetic alteration and possibly control of existing human beings? Who would draw such a line and how would its boundaries be enforced? The information gathered by researchers may be used in unforeseen and possibly undesirable ways. For instance, a government might collect knowledge about its citizens and use it to manipulate them. Or pension systems might use it to identify potentially long-lived people and charge them more for pensions. Or insurance companies might use the information to deny medical coverage to individuals predisposed to certain diseases. We can expect significant social repercussions from this scientific enterprise throughout the twenty-first century.

Moral, political, religious, scientific, and governmental forces will undoubtedly mobilize on an international scale for debates on these issues. Thinking about them gives you a sense of how new discoveries can have profound effects on the social system in which we live. In short, our future social evolution will likely be substantially influenced by the information we have about our human evolution. What we know will change what we are.

Should the Species Be Regrouped?   As our knowledge of biology has progressed and we have developed far more information about the genetic makeup of life-forms, our abilities to differentiate species and to place them in orders of progression have changed enormously. The divisions of the species that we currently use were created by Carolus Linnaeus (1707–1778). His divisions were determined primarily by physical traits. As our knowledge of genetic makeup has improved, we have come to realize that physical similarities do not necessarily imply genetic similarity, and vice versa. Given the importance of genetic makeup, it would seem logical to organize species by genetic components. However, division by physical characteristics is still the dominant division used. This is an example of the inertia in any system of knowledge and terminology. They evolve slowly.

Sociobiology

The study of genetics is not the only evolution-related field to experience progress; the study of evolution itself has progressed, and on one front it has been extended.

A group of scientists called *sociobiologists* has argued that human behavior evolves in the same direction that anatomy and body chemistry do: to increase the chances of survival of the species. Behavior that does not increase chances of survival will eventually lead to destruction. **Sociobiology** is a combination of sociological and biological reflections that theorize a genetic basis for human behavior.

A leader in sociobiology, Harvard entomologist (one who studies insects) Edward O. Wilson has provided an example that may help clarify the reasoning sociobiologists use. People are born with an inherent fear of strangers. This fear is a necessary genetic trait; it is a form of "prepared learning" that can be seen in infants less than a year old. If infants did not have this fear, they would be more susceptible to attack and thus less likely to survive. Over generations, more individuals who exhibit this trait generally will survive than individuals who do not, and eventually the genetic trait will become inherent in the species.

The argument may seem simple and of little consequence, but if we replace "strangers" with "persons of another race" the argument becomes more problematic and conflicts with our society's views on equity. People can justify or at least rationalize any behavior as being "in their genes." Therefore, sociobiology has provoked strong attacks that it "justifies racism." In response, sociobiologists point out that their argument is not that

"It'll never work out. She's patented, he isn't."

genes directly control behavior, but rather that genes play a role. Wilson states, "We're suggesting that there is a mechanism which one sees during evolution continuously around the circuit: genetic change, cultural change, genetic change, and so on." The issues raised are highly controversial and are reminiscent of the free will–determinism issue early Christian philosophers debated. Do we do what we do because we are programmed to do it, or do we do it by choice? We suspect the debate will continue for some time.

The concerns about the almost singular focus of sociobiology on genetic natural selection has led to the development of a new field of psychology—evolutionary social psychology. This field accepts that biological and genetic factors play a role in explaining behavior but argues that other factors are also important.

Punctuated Equilibrium versus Gradual Change

Evolution theory is also challenged on another front. Darwin saw evolution as a gradual process of natural selection and survival of the fittest as the most likely phenomenon. Now evolutionists such as paleoanthropologist Niles Eldredge and polymath Stephen Jay Gould[2] argue that evolution is characterized by long periods of relative stability that are punctuated by sudden changes, followed by more stability, followed by more changes, and so on. One hypothesis why this occurs is that changes in environment cause species to diversify and specialize into several new niches, creating new lineages. In Gould's theory, a species will be unchanged for thousands or hundreds of thousands of years and then suddenly something will happen that will change it (perhaps gene splicing?) or even wipe it out. The authors think of Gould's theory as macroevolution—periodic sudden large changes—and of the concept of gradual evolution as microevolution, a continuous, almost unnoticeable succession of small changes.

The debate centers on fossil evidence from millions of years ago that paleoanthropologists find in their digs. In the study of evolution, archaeologists have found fossils that demonstrate the changes various species such as humans have undergone. However, large gaps that scientists expected to fill eventually somehow remain. It is here that Gould's theory enters. Gould's **punctuated equilibrium** theory holds that evolution is a stop/go process of sudden change, with long intervening periods of no change.

The difference between punctuated equilibrium and gradual evolution can be seen in Figure 2.1. The straight upward-sloping line represents the traditional view, and the new view, punctuated equilibrium, is depicted by the horizontal lines with sudden upward jumps or stages every million or so years. An example of sudden jumps has been found in snail fossils at Lake Turkana in Kenya by Harvard archaeologist Peter Williamson. He discovered that, over a 2-million-year period, there were two sudden changes in which major evolutionary changes occurred, and in between almost no change occurred. Thus, in Gould's view, evolution is merely a series of revolutions interspersed with long periods of calm. The punctuated equilibrium theory of evolution has attracted interest because it explains parts of the phenomenon that the old theory could not. For example, his theory could explain the sudden disappearance of dinosaurs millions of years ago. If evolution were a continual process, they would have died off slowly.

Gould's punctuated equilibrium theory was challenged in 1988 in the work of Peter Sheldon. Researchers before Gould had noted a significant gap in a set of crab-related

---

[2]A *polymath* is a person of encyclopedic learning, and the term has been applied to Gould because he was a biologist, geologist, and historian; he was also a leading theorist on large-scale patterns in evolution and an informative writer.

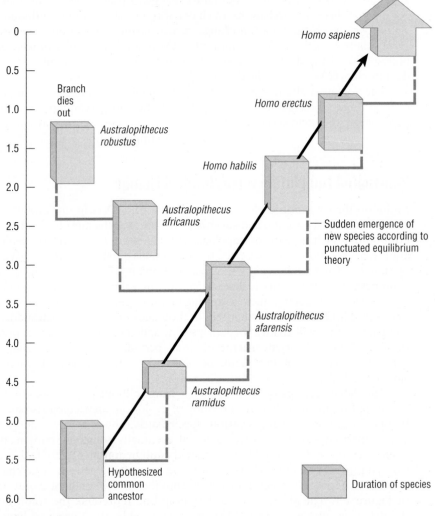

Figure 2.1

A possible theory of evolution. In the traditional view, evolution is represented by the straight, upward-sloping line. In an alternative view that has been advanced in recent years, equilibrium is represented by the horizontal lines with sudden upward jumps at intervals of thousands or hundreds of thousands of years. Note that the lengths of the time periods on the vertical axis are the estimates of some authorities. Other authorities give other lengths of time, but all authorities agree that the time periods are very, very long. In the interest of simplicity, the graph does not show all the species that are now extinct but are thought to have existed at various periods along the way to Homo sapiens.

creatures called trilobites (see Figure 2.2). In the evolution of these trilobites, it appeared that there was a sudden stop, and then the set picked up again but with some different characteristics, especially in the number of ribs they had. The absence of trilobites that would have filled the gap with a steadily changing number of ribs had been cited as supporting Gould's theory. However, through painstaking work, Sheldon found specimens that filled in the gaps, showing that the average number of ribs the trilobites contained changed slowly over time. Sheldon's findings generated much debate, and the general feeling was that both sides were in some way correct and that some changes may be punctuated and others may be gradual. But these views are evolving as more evidence is likely to be found in years to come.

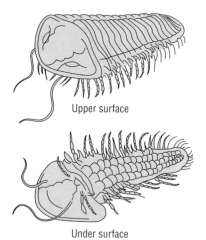

Upper surface

Under surface

Figure 2.2

Trilobites resembled modern wood lice. The discovery of their fossils challenged Gould's theory of punctuated equilibrium.

The Evolution of Human Beings

Much of what happens in abstract scientific theory does not make news, except for articles in such periodicals as *National Geographic* or *Scientific American.* However, because it has seemed to some people to go against the Bible's version of creation, evolution has stirred popular press controversy from Darwin's time to ours, especially on the part of fundamentalists who believe in literal interpretations of the Bible.

Science, Faith, and Controversy

Just how much controversy it has caused can be seen in some famous court trials that have dealt with the issue. In 1925, for example, a Tennessee high school biology teacher, John Scopes, was prosecuted for and found guilty of breaking a state law forbidding the teaching of evolution in the public schools. The law and others like it in several neighboring states were not repealed until the late 1960s. In recent years, evolution has again made headlines, this time over attacks by a group called scientific creationists. **Scientific creationism** is not a science, but rather the belief that all present life-forms were spontaneously created at one point in time. Proponents have helped pass statutes in a number of states requiring the teaching of what are actually religious objections to evolution wherever the latter is presented in public school classes and textbooks. In response, publishers have suggested to their authors that they tone down the discussion of evolution in textbooks so that it is acceptable to the scientific creationists. The result has been that some textbooks have devoted only minimal discussion to evolution. Many educators have complained, and in 1985 California did something about those complaints. It informed publishers that unless their books dealt with the issue head on, their books would be dropped from public school purchases in California.

To put the matter bluntly, no organization of U.S. professional scientists has given any scientific support to creationism. In fact, almost all recognized scientific authorities strongly reject such assaults on academic freedom, the traditional scientific method, and the American principle of separation of church and state. A 1982 federal court decision endorsed the scientists' view by throwing out an Arkansas law mandating the study of scientific creationism in the state's public schools on grounds that creationism is not a science but religion, as it rests on a spiritual, not objective, premise and thus violates the separation of church and state principle that is part of the U.S. approach to government.

At the close of the twentieth century, the Kansas State Board of Education decided that individual school boards could choose whether to teach evolution. This step evoked spirited discussion throughout the country and does not represent a major trend in U.S. education. One of the objections to the provision was that its implementation would place graduates of Kansas school systems outside the mainstream of U.S. scientific theory and thus at a disadvantage in many future careers. Few Kansas school boards chose to discontinue the teaching of evolution, and in the state elections of 2000, several proponents of discontinuance who were running for reelection to the state board were defeated. The controversy has continued and in the early 2000s, local school boards of various states have had occasional clashes over textbook choices because of the evolution issue.

These debates are relevant here because scientific creationists have used Gould's new evolutionary theory of sudden rather than gradual evolutionary changes as scientific evidence to support their position. They say that the physical evidence of earth's multibillion-year existence can be explained by a series of creations, each one replacing the one before it. But as Gould explained in the court case, his theory is not antievolutionary; it merely challenges the *process* whereby evolution occurs.

The actual issues of what should be taught in classrooms are too complex to be addressed here. However, it must be stressed that although there have been sound professional scientific criticisms from time to time of the specifics of evolution, responsible scientists have not denied its basic point. The phrase *scientific creationism* is in many ways a contradiction in terms. Creationism begins and ends with a belief that life sprang from a sudden act of divine power and has not appreciably changed. This is an essentially religious version of natural origins. Science studies cause and effect and thus looks for continuity. This is not to say that religious faith cannot coexist with science. Ultimately, "existence" or "being" must be explained, and no scientific theory can yet explain how something was created out of nothing.[3]

In the mid-1990s, a more acceptable but still controversial method of integrating religion into science developed. It was called **intelligent design** and it was the center of a fight about a textbook entitled *Of Pandas and People*. The central thesis of intelligent design is that the world is too complex to have developed on its own and that it can only be explained with some concept of initial intelligence. This is different from scientific creationism in that it does not challenge evolutionary evidence. It simply adds to it a theory of what is behind evolution. Critics see it as a sneaky way to introduce creationism into schools, while supporters see it as an acceptable hypothesis because it discusses issues that science and empirical evidence do not contradict.

Predecessors of Modern Humans

Some of the most interesting finds have concerned the evolution of humans. Though humans are closely related to the other primates, we are not certain how they evolved. However, with allowance for oversimplification, a basic outline can be drawn up.

The origin of life is thought to have occurred billions of years ago as one-celled organisms arose from the primordial ooze. Over the millennia, the organisms evolved into a wide variety of life-forms. Primates, from which humans developed, evolved some 65 to 70 million years ago, and a monkey–apelike creature from which the human species evolved is thought to have appeared somewhere between 22 and 38 million years ago. This apelike species is considered the common ancestor of modern apes and humans. Figure 2.3 gives you a general sense of that evolution. Each box in it represents a different species.

First let us explain that a **species** is a broad category of individuals who look alike and can mate with each other to produce fertile offspring. Today's humans are the only members of the species *Homo sapiens* (reasoning man).[4] They are also the only surviving human species. At least two other human species, *Homo habilis* (man with tool-making ability) and *Homo erectus* (man who stands up straight), have long since become extinct. All three of these types of humans belong to the same umbrella category, or genus.

---

[3]Most religions solve this problem by postulating a god who created all, but as many Sunday school students have pondered, that still leaves open the question of who created God. At some point, faith must still play a role, and when an explanation relies on faith rather than reason, it becomes a religious explanation. Even the "big bang" cosmological theory has no explanation of what "banged."

[4]To distinguish early modern humans from contemporary modern humans, some authorities use the term *homo sapiens sapiens* for the latest humans. In simplifying, we have not made this distinction, but it is useful to know that the term exists and what it means.

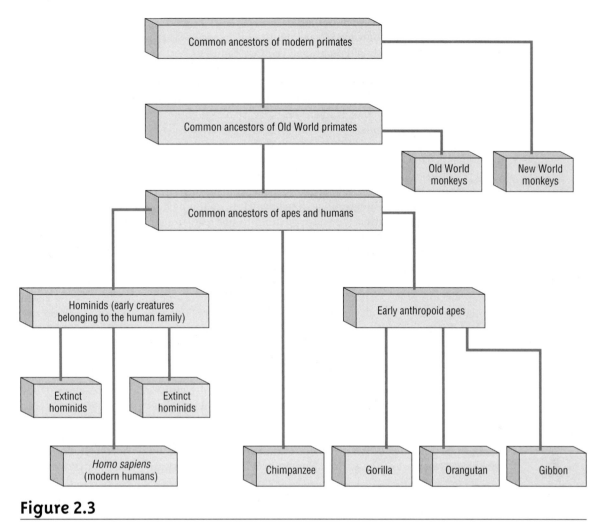

Figure 2.3

Possible lines of descent of humans and other higher primates from their common ancestral type.

A human type more distantly related to us than any of the species just mentioned belongs to a separate genus, *Australopithecus,* creatures who have been extinct for millions of years. Humans and *Australopithecines* belong to the family *Hominidae,* along with several kinds of apes, both living and extinct. And the whole family belongs to the larger group of primates.

From Apelike Creature to Hominid.   The date when these apelike creatures began to change to **hominids,** humanlike creatures who stood on two feet, is unclear, but it is believed to have been somewhere between 6 and 10 million years ago in Africa, and several million years later in Europe and Asia. The fossil record for these timespans is poor or nonexistent, so the estimate is based on genetic differences between living humans and living primates combined with estimates of how long it has taken for the differences among these creatures to occur.

Much debate exists about the lines of descent of humans and other primates. In trying to resolve this debate, researchers are turning more and more to the realm of molecular biology and chemical analysis of DNA done in the laboratory. According to fossil evidence, the evolutionary split between human beings and apes might have occurred as early as 25 million years ago and continued for a long time. This view was strengthened by a fossil said to be of a 15-million-year-old prehuman jawbone found in 1991 in southern Africa. This evidence, however, is contradicted by comparison of blood substances from human beings with those from chimpanzees, indicating the divergence was far more recent—perhaps only 7 million years ago. The DNA analysis has tended to support the later dating and, in fact, recent work by David Reich of Harvard has suggested that chimps and humanoids interbred for hundreds of thousands, or even millions, of years. Even today, chimps' genetic structure differs from humans' by only 1.2 percent. While his hypotheses are still debated, the general belief that genetic analysis will provide important clues about human evolution is shared by most scientists.

Although there is a dispute as to when the transition from ape to hominid occurred, anthropologists generally agree that all the primates, including hominids, once lived in trees and that during this period they developed limbs of great strength, with prehensile fingers and toes for grasping branches. Most primates, including the gibbon and the orangutan, still live in trees, but gorillas, like humans, live on the ground. Chimpanzees sleep in tree nests but spend much of the daytime on the ground. Apparently, one reason for this descent to the ground was their increase in size. Gorillas typically weigh from 400 to 600 pounds and are far too heavy for life in the trees. Even chimpanzees are too heavy to swing about through the branches unless they choose them with care. The great apes can walk on two legs but they have not achieved the human's erect posture and normally walk on all fours.

Perhaps the most important physical difference between human beings and apes is in the size and complexity of the brain. Between various animal species, there seems as a rule to be some relationship between intelligence and the weight of the brain, especially its weight in relation to the body. But the most important factor is the organization of the brain. The chief advantage of large size seems to be that it provides space for additional cells and for more complex mechanisms. On the average, chimpanzees are smaller than humans, but some weigh as much as 120 or 130 pounds. The brain of a small human typically weighs about three times that of a chimpanzee of the same body weight, and a normal human cerebral cortex, the part of the brain most concerned with memory and thought, may have ten

The Search for Eve

The development of genetic research has introduced a new battleground in the debate about our past. The work of molecular biologists has challenged many evolutionists' conviction about the timing of the human family tree and where it first took root. Until the early 1990s, some molecular biologists argued that the evolution from prehistoric to modern *Homo sapiens* occurred in one place and that humans descended from one woman who lived approximately 200,000 years ago.

These molecular biologists examined the genetic differences between chimpanzees and humans and found that the differences were surprisingly small—so small, in fact, that they believe chimpanzees parted company from humans only about 5 to 7 million years ago. The microbiologists went on to examine mitochondrial DNA, which is inherited only through the mother, from the placentas of 147 pregnant women, choosing women from all over the world. They found that the differences in DNA among people all over the world were amazingly small, which suggests that the differences among peoples of the world are also small. Hypothesizing that about 2 to 4 percent of the DNA components will mutate over the course of a million years, they came to the conclusion that, around 200,000 years ago, a woman must have existed from whom all now-living human beings are descended. Their research caused much debate. In 1992, however, they discovered an error in their calculations and admitted that their results were far less conclusive than they had previously believed, but they still believed it had elements of truth.

This research has continued. Bryan Sykes, an Oxford geneticist, argues that he has found "the seven daughters of Eve," that these women lived 45,000 years ago, and that all existing humans descended from them.

This eighteenth-century drawing from Diderot's Encyclopédie shows what some people at that time imagined early humanlike creatures to have looked like.

times as many cells as the cerebral cortex of a typical ape. Today, there seems little doubt that this complex brain is an essential basis of the human power to acquire a vast store of memories, to use word symbols, and to carry on abstract thought.

With respect to behavior, there are both striking similarities and striking differences between apes and human beings. Like humans, apes have family life and care for their young. They have emotional responses, can express gratitude and shame, and often are sociable and cooperative. On occasion, they compete with one another, and sometimes they engage in play. Certain chimpanzees have responded well to training in various types of behavior such as smoking, riding a bicycle, eating with a knife and fork, and drinking from a bottle. They have also shown ability to solve problems requiring reasoned judgment. But to all these accomplishments, there are limits that argue unmistakably for the superior intellectual qualities of human beings.

The problem for physical anthropologists is to fill in the gaps of precisely how humans evolved, or if the evolutionary theory of punctuated equilibrium discussed earlier is true, to explain why the changes occurred when they did. In the last century, and especially since the 1930s, anthropologists have made tremendous strides in solving the puzzle. Archaeological finds date our ancestors back about 6 million years and a wide variety of early hominid fossils have been given forbidding names such as *Africanus ramidus, Zinjanthropus,* and *Orrorin Tugenessis.*

A key element in determining when to date the start of modern human history is when these early hominids began using tools. Discoveries of tools with skeletons have been dated from 2.5 to 1.6 million years ago. This group of hominids is called *Homo habilis* because *habilis* means "maker."

Remaining Gaps. Despite advances in fossil discoveries, significant gaps remain in our knowledge of our ancestors, even among experts with their detailed and technical grasp of the subject. For instance, what happened during the intervening years? Were these apelike beings the predecessors of modern humans or only of apes? Did humans start out in a number of places or in only one, from which they dispersed throughout the world? These questions still are unanswered and probably always will be. However, genetic studies are leading to more specific answers. The latest genetic data suggest that all humans descended from Africa and spread throughout the world along the lines shown in Figure 2.4.

From Hominids to Homo Sapiens. The earliest known species of *Homo* (human), **Homo habilis,** emerged from these early ancestors. *Homo habilis* had a larger brain but smaller teeth than these early ancestors and probably produced stone tools and other stone objects.

As we move closer to our own century, our information increases somewhat, but despite substantial progress, it is still sketchy and incomplete. An important find occurred in 1891 in Java when a Dutch surgeon, Dr. Eugene Dubois, unearthed another piece of the puzzle: **Homo erectus.** *Homo erectus* lived from about 1.8 million years ago to possibly as recently as 250,000 years ago and was a hunter who knew how to use fire.

It is believed that about 1.8 million years ago in Africa, *Homo erectus* developed from *Homo habilis* and then dispersed to Europe and Asia about a million years ago. *Homo erectus*'s brain was even larger and the teeth even smaller than *Homo habilis*'s. The lessening of tooth size indicates that dependence on hard food such as nuts and seeds, which requires powerful teeth and jaws, was decreasing as human diet veered toward softer foods such as fruit and, increasingly, meat. *Homo erectus* seems to have been very strong—which would have facilitated hunting.

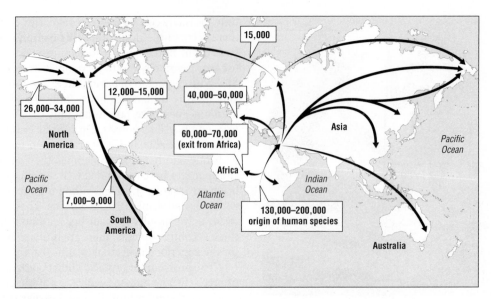

Figure 2.4

Early human migration.

Among *Homo erectus*'s nonbiodegradable waste are found more sophisticated objects than *Homo habilis* made, such as axes, and there is evidence, from ashes and charred material, that toward the end of *Homo erectus*'s existence, *Homo erectus* learned to use fire.

In 1997 two Spanish paleontologists, José Bermudez de Castro and Juan Arsuaga, announced that their study of 800,000-year-old fossils found in Spain leads them to believe that **Homo antecessor** (man who goes before) is a separate species who is a possible common ancestor of Neanderthals and *Homo sapiens* (discussed next). They speculated that the fossils they found in northern Spain represent emigrants from Africa.

Homo erectus seems to have become extinct nearly 500,000 years ago. The reasons are not at all clear. Artifacts of *Homo erectus,* although more sophisticated than those of their predecessors, do not show much change over more than a million years. Thus, one theory holds that *Homo erectus* may have been too conservative and inflexible to adapt to changing conditions.

Another theory is that *Homo erectus* did change, separating into two branches. One branch was the Neanderthals and the other was the modern human, *Homo sapiens.* **Homo sapiens** is a group of hominids who began to differ from their predecessors by their larger brains and by the better quality tools they made. European and African sites have yielded some fossils of these human ancestors ranging roughly from 200,000 to 300,000 years old, but according to genetic evidence they may have existed as long ago as 800,000 years—earlier than the fossil record. We call ourselves today members of *Homo sapiens.* A 2003 fossil find of modern man in Ethiopia fits with recent genetic studies of the time and place of the emergence of humankind. These support the replacement theory—"Out of Africa"—that a late migration of humans eventually supplanted all other humanlike species around the world at the time, such as Neanderthals.

Homo sapiens (reasoning man) was a species composed of people more highly developed than *Homo erectus.* They first appeared in Africa and Europe about the same time that *Homo erectus* was disappearing. Once again, we see the new people displaying larger brains than the people they were replacing, and they differed so much from *Homo erectus* that they were assigned to a new species. It is the species to which all modern human beings belong today. However, early *Homo sapiens* shared many characteristics with *Homo erectus.* They seem to have been unable, for instance, to adapt to harsh climates, or to find food more easily than did *Homo erectus*.

Neanderthals.   Remains from periods longer than 100,000 years ago are few. We do know, however, that the evolutionary network produced the **Neanderthals,** who bore a close resemblance to modern human beings, about 100,000 years ago. Despite this close resemblance, the recent fossil evidence and genetic studies strongly suggest that the Neanderthals were not our ancestors. Instead, they probably shared a common ancestor with modern man. If modern features already existed in Africa 160,000 years ago, we could not have descended from a species like the Neanderthals.

Neanderthals get their name from the Neander Valley in Germany, where in 1856 the first evidence of their existence was found. They lived in Europe and spread to Asia, although a few researchers believe they developed independently in Asia. Physically, they differ from all other people, modern or extinct, in the shape of their heads and, strangely, in the length of their thumbs, which were about as long as their other fingers.

It used to be thought that Neanderthals were dim-witted, slouching cavemen completely covered with hair. But this reputation is based on just one fossil, which modern scholarship has proved happens to be that of an old, diseased, and injured man. He was approximately forty or forty-five years old when he died—very old for people at that time. Healthy Neanderthals probably walked erect. Objects found at Neanderthal sites show that Neanderthals could make complex tools, and characteristics of their skulls, and what can be deduced from skulls about their brains, mean that they probably could speak, although perhaps not with the full range of sounds that modern humans make. Sites also show that they did not necessarily live in caves, but if they did they altered the caves to make them more livable. Sometimes they built shelters rather than settled in caves. In 1996, scientists digging at a Neanderthal site in Slovenia announced they had found what appeared to be a musical instrument, a flute made from a bear bone.

As we will discuss in later chapters, the development of language capability was a major evolutionary step. (See the box on the uniqueness of the human species.) It allowed the species much greater interaction and hence social development than could occur in non-speaking species. In doing so, it made the passing on of learned knowledge about the environment much more efficient. It also allowed the species to develop concepts of time, space, and quantity, thereby creating the potential for symbolic interaction.

The Neanderthals were powerfully built but somewhat shorter—about five feet four inches—than present-day males. They had sloping foreheads, heavy ridges over the eyes, large wide noses, and protruding jaws, and the Neanderthal brain was larger than that of the average modern person. A tribute to their humanity is the fact that among the buried remains are people who were handicapped or aged, which means that Neanderthals cared enough and were organized enough to provide for these economically unproductive members of their communities.

To date, few Neanderthal sites have been found from the period 35,000–60,000 years ago. Because this is also the period in which they seem to have disappeared, there is little or no evidence of why they disappeared. Theories of what happened include the following: (1) they interbred with another group, Cro-Magnons (discussed below), and eventually Neanderthal characteristics were completely absorbed into Cro-Magnons; (2) they battled with Cro-Magnons in a struggle and were annihilated; and (3) they wandered away into regions that were too environmentally inhospitable for survival. Recent genetic testing seems to confirm, at least in Europe, that Neanderthals were replaced by rather than absorbed into the Cro-Magnon gene pool.

Cro-Magnons.   There is another group of people whose origins are uncertain but who may have been the immediate precursors of *Homo sapiens*. **Cro-Magnons** were anatomically modern, tall, well-built people with skull capacity comparable to that of present-day humans. They are called Cro-Magnons from the name of the French village near which the

*I*s the Human Species Unique?

There is an ongoing debate among social scientists about whether the human species is unique. The argument that human beings are unique emphasizes that (1) only humans can think and reason, (2) only humans can communicate with others by means of language, and (3) only humans can use tools. Each of these points is debatable. Social scientists who argue that human beings are not unique point out that animals have solved enormously complex problems, some better than humans have.

Certain social scientists argue that language is not limited to humans and have shown that chimpanzees can communicate by sign language and by touching geometric symbols. One chimp has learned over 150 different signs, and a psychologist has taught a gorilla, Koko, more than 500 words. Moreover, Koko can express emotion: When her pet cat was killed in a traffic accident, she mourned its death. After a time, she "asked" to be given another cat to care for and love. Moreover, the gorilla specifically asked that it be replaced with a Manx cat (a highly unusual breed remarkable for having no tail).

The ability to use tools, disputants hold, is another characteristic not unique to human beings. Yes, humans have a greater ability to devise and use tools, and that ability has given them power over other creatures, but power is not necessarily differentiation, and animals use a variety of tools and social structures. For example, the cattle-tending ant gets honeydew by cultivating aphids and other insects who secrete it, and it even constructs shelters, such as underground galleries, in which to herd its aphids.

To counter these arguments, supporters of human uniqueness assert that the power of the human mind to solve complex problems goes far beyond that of animals and that although animals can learn words, they cannot learn syntax, an important aspect of language. As the linguist Noam Chomsky put it, to say that animals can communicate with each other by language is like saying that because people can rise into the air by jumping they can fly like birds, only not as well.

What difference does it make whether human beings are unique? A lot. Consider the following questions: Is it morally wrong to use animals in experiments? Should we eat meat? If you believe that human beings are unique, it is relatively easy to argue that animals can and should be used by human beings. If human beings are not unique, then it is much harder (but not impossible) to argue in favor of using animals in ways that we would not use human beings.

In the space between these two views on the morality of killing living creatures, we find a number of places where we can draw a line. It may, for example, be okay to kill a cockroach, but not a dog, a cow, or a pig. Precisely where to draw that line is the problem, however, and some radical thinkers have even argued that not only is there nothing distinctive about human beings, but that it is moral for society to eliminate individuals whose life is no longer worth living—for instance, people with brain damage or individuals who have lived out their "useful" lives and are no longer able to care for themselves.

Don't expect any of these debates to be settled any time soon; rather, we ask you to acknowledge here, and throughout this book, that recognizing the arguments of many sides, considering them thoroughly and objectively, and coming to a conclusion that does not stubbornly exclude every other theory are the essential qualities of a good social scientist.

Teaching KoKo to read.

first specimens were found in 1868. Cro-Magnons and other early anatomically modern sapiens existed before Neanderthals disappeared. In western Europe, no Cro-Magnon skeletons have been found older than 30,000 years, but 40,000-year-old tools that archaeologists believe must have been made by modern people have been found at a number of western European locations. Cro-Magnons appear to have flourished only beginning about 35,000 years ago. Their remains have been found at various European sites and, in smaller numbers, in the Near East, China, Indonesia, Australia, and Africa.

The remains indicate that they were not as strong as Neanderthals, probably because they didn't need to be. Less strength, for instance, means less food is necessary, so the same total amount of food could support a larger population.

Conclusion

Modern people are distinguished from their ancestors by more than physical characteristics. By about 35,000 years ago, they were exhibiting cultural sophistication, for example in the cave paintings that can still be seen, especially in southern France and northern Spain. The closer we come to our own times, the more evidence we find of such strategies as coping with cold climates by the construction and use of clothing and the building of shelters. There is also evidence of increasingly complex social organization and even some limited trade with groups as much as ninety miles apart.

There is, as is true of much anthropological theory, debate about these findings. For instance, one method of dating was a controversial technique that relates the age of the human remains to the detection of when the artifacts discovered with the human remains were last heated. There are innumerable unanswered questions about the development of human beings. For example, what in the theory of natural selection explains the various emergences of human behavior? And did most sophisticated behavior appear at roughly the same time, or were there successive advances? Because work continues in this fascinating field, it is likely that the answers to at least some of these questions, and to some of the other questions you can think of, will one day be discovered, or at least deduced.

The Cro-Magnons, like the Neanderthals, were hunters and gatherers; they roamed from place to place in search of food and survivable weather. As we see in the next chapter, about 11,000 years ago that changed. The change was due to a technological development.

At this point, we stop our consideration of the origins of human beings, leaving the development in what anthropologists call the Stone Age, a period beginning more than 600,000 years ago and lasting to about 10,000 B.C. We make this break not because Stone Age humans were physically different from modern human beings, but because of the technological developments of the Stone Age, which significantly modified the way individuals interrelate.

Key Points

- Darwin's theory of evolution centers on the survival of the fittest or natural selection; beneficial mutation makes evolution possible.
- Genes contain DNA, the building block of living organisms. DNA contains the codes that determine an organism's development.
- Sociobiologists argue that behavior that decreases chances of survival will eventually be eliminated from human behavior.

- Whether evolution is punctuated or continuous is still much in debate.
- The evolutionary split between human beings and apes occurred more than 25 million years ago.
- The search for human origins has led to many fossil finds but not to a definitive statement: "This is where human beings began."
- Cro-Magnons may have been the immediate precursors of *Homo sapiens*.

Some Important Terms

alleles (30)
Cro-Magnons (43)
DNA (32)
dominant allele (30)
evolution (29)
genes (30)
genetic engineering (32)
genetics (30)

hominids (39)
Homo antecessor (28)
Homo erectus (28)
Homo habilis (28)
Homo sapiens (28)
intelligent design (38)
mutation (30)
natural selection (29)

Neanderthals (43)
primates (29)
punctuated equilibrium (35)
recessive allele (30)
scientific creationism (37)
sociobiology (34)
species (38)

Questions for Review and Discussion

1. Why do we say the human being is a social creature?
2. Why are humans, apes, and monkeys all placed in the biological order of primates?
3. Explain Darwin's theory of evolution.
4. How have modern geneticists modified Darwin's theory?
5. Can scientists create life? What possibilities can you see in genetic engineering?
6. How does sociobiology explain the development of human behavior?
7. What is the theory of punctuated equilibrium, and why is it important?
8. Should scientific creationism be taught in schools? Why or why not?
9. How long ago do you think humanlike creatures appeared on earth? Why is it so hard to determine the date, and why do you think we keep trying?
10. Who are some of the earliest precursors of human beings? What makes them like us? What makes them unlike us?
11. What three abilities gave humans advantages over all other creatures? Are humans unique?

Internet Questions

1. Read the short essay at www.sfgate.com/cgi-bin/article.cgi?f=/c/a/2002/05/27/MN226754.DTL. What are some of the examples given as evidence for punctuated equilibrium? Is one mechanism of evolution singled out for these cases?
2. Pick one of the articles about a recent discovery in paleoanthropology listed on www.talkorigins.org/faqs/homs/recent.html. What was found? Where was it found?
3. Go to www.youtube.com/watch?v=4LThjf-Qbi4 and watch the video. What are homologous structures? What are vestigial organs?
4. According to the information at http://discovermagazine.com/2006/apr/chimp-genome (accessed June 25, 2009), even though humans and chimps share 98.7 percent of their genes, what makes them so different?
5. Go to www.expelledthemovie.com and watch the trailer to Ben Stein's documentary, "Expelled: No Intelligence Allowed" on Darwinism and what he considers the suppression of intelligent design. Is it an alternative to the theory of evolution, and how does the scientific community explain their dislike of this theory?

For Further Study

Arusaga, Juan Luis, *The Neanderthal's Necklace: In Search of the First Thinkers*, translated by Andy Klatt, New York: Four Walls Eight Windows, 2004.

Darwin, Charles, *The Origin of Species*, Irvin, Charlotte, and William Irving, eds., New York: Ungar, 1959 (first published in 1859).

Dawkins, Richard, *Climbing Mount Improbable*, New York: Norton, 1996.

Dennett, Daniel C., *Darwin's Dangerous Idea: Evolution and the Meaning of Life*, New York: Simon & Schuster, 1995.

Hess, Elizabeth, *Nim Chimpsky: The Chimp Who Would Be Human*, New York: Bantam, 2008.

Jolly, Alison, *Lucy's Legacy: Sex and Intelligence in Human Evolution,* Cambridge, MA: Harvard University Press, 1999.

Maddox, John, *What Remains to Be Discovered: Mapping the Secrets of the Universe, the Origins of Life, and the Future of the Human Race,* New York: Free Press, 1999.

Marks, Jonathan, *What It Means to Be 98% Chimpanzee: Apes, People, and Their Genes,* Berkeley: University of California Press, 2002.

Olson, Steve, *Mapping Human History: Discovering the Past through Our Genes,* Boston: Houghton Mifflin, 2002.

Oppenheimer, Stephen, *Out of Eden: The Peopling of the World,* London, UK: Constable and Robinson, 2003.

Singh, Simon, *Big Bang: The Most Important Scientific Discovery of All Time and Why You Need to Know About It*, New York: Fourth Estate (Division of HarperCollins), 2005.

Slifkin, Nosson, *The Science of the Torah*, Brooklyn, NY: Yashar Books, 2005.

Zimmer, Carl, *At the Water's Edge: Macroevolution and the Transformation of Life,* New York: Free Press, 1998.

WWW   Action Bioscience www.actionbioscience.org

WWW   Creation/Evolution Newsgroup Archive www.talkorigins.org

WWW   Genetic Engineering News www.genengnews.com

WWW   Human Genome Project http://genomics.energy.gov

WWW   Thailand National Center for Genetic Engineering and Biotechnology www.biotec.or.th

WWW   A Science Odyssey: Human Evolution, Interactive www.pbs.org/wgbh/aso/tryit/evolution/shockwave.html

WWW   Sociobiology http://webspace.ship.edu/cgboer/sociobiology.html (accessed June 25, 2009)

Origins of Western Society

After reading this chapter, you should be able to:

- Explain why the domestication of animals and control of land were central developments that created society as we know it today
- Trace the development of modern civilization from Mesopotamia and Egypt to today
- Explain the Greek and Roman origins of modern civilization
- Distinguish three periods of the Middle Ages
- Explain the importance of the Renaissance to modern civilization
- Define the Age of Revolutions

Time is a river of passing events, and its current is strong. No sooner is a thing brought to sight than it is swept by and another takes its place—and this too will be swept away.

—Marcus Aurelius

Throughout most of the remainder of this book, we look at and contrast the origins, development, and operation of societies' cultures so that we can better understand modern problems. However, at this point, it seems advantageous to take a whirlwind tour of history and the development of Western culture. On this tour, we see some of the influences that have led to the formation of the types of societies we have, and although what we can cover in a chapter is severely limited, we can at least introduce you to some of the terminology we use when we describe historical periods. The chief purpose of our tour, though, is to gain some historical perspective and use it to find continuity and similarities among periods and developments that, if we glance at them casually and individually, seem different from one another.

In the next section, we take you on that whirlwind tour, covering millennia in half pages. In doing so, we consider the origins of Western culture as embodied in the social, political, and economic institutions that shape our modern society.

From the Stone Age to the Agricultural Age

We ended the last chapter with a cliffhanger, saying some technological development significantly changed the nature of humankind and society. If you guessed that this development was the bow and arrow, you were right in guessing that Stone Age humans developed these, but wrong in thinking that was what caused the change. The bow and arrow improved Stone Age humans' ability to hunt but did not change the basics of their daily lives. Another technological development *did* fundamentally change society. Central developments that created society as we know it today occurred when human beings learned that they could exercise control over the land (through cultivation by hoe) and animals (through domestication for carrying, riding, pulling, and the systematic practice of egg gathering and milking). These developments moved human beings from the Stone Age to what we call the **Age of Agriculture,** a period beginning about 11,000 years ago and characterized at first by the storing of wild crops and then by the cultivation of land, domestication of animals, and creation of permanent communities. The Age of Agriculture changed the habits of most human beings from those of roving hunters to those of people living in a more or less fixed community.

The importance of these developments for society cannot be overemphasized. People could live in one place; they could accumulate more physical items and pass those on to their children. Moreover, once they could be assured of food, they could devote time to other aspects of life. During the Age of Agriculture, pottery was invented, making it easier to store surplus liquids; it was discovered how to make cloth from both flax (linen) and wool. Moreover, because agriculture and domesticated animals required constant care, people built permanent buildings, usually in clusters. Thus began villages.

The agricultural revolution produced significant population growth in what is now the Middle East and Europe, although village living fostered disease because there was little or no understanding of the need for sanitation. Moreover, the same technological developments that made farming possible also made warfare more effective. Horses provided better transportation, and bows and arrows provided better attack mechanisms. Archaeological excavation has revealed various weapons from this period. Although many could be used in hunting, they are also suitable for attacking and for holding off attackers. Conflict and the lack of sanitation kept the level of population from exploding.

Early Civilizations

Slowly over this period people addressed two issues that are crucial to the preservation and extension of the human life span: They learned about the need for sanitation, and they began to try to solve the problem of constant fighting. These developments were most pronounced in the Middle East. Approximately 4000 B.C., large numbers of people began moving into the lowlands of Mesopotamia (modern-day Iraq) and Egypt. During this time, writing developed (about 3000 B.C.) and with it began what we call recorded history. Because of that development we have a much better knowledge of this period than of pre-recorded history.

The Cradle of Modern Civilization: Mesopotamia and Egypt

Although we do not know the reason for the development of cities in the Middle East, we can deduce that it was made possible by improved methods of cultivation, which created a surplus of food and improved sanitation conditions. Once in existence, cities took on the purposes of administration, commerce, and entertainment. It seems likely that in order to protect themselves from constant warfare, individuals submitted to a powerful leader, and for that protection they had to pay a certain percentage of their farm output. Thus began our basic political institution, which is the gathering of people into a spatially and ethnically defined unit organized and run by a small group. This group's efforts provide the stability within which individuals in the unit can work, play, buy, sell, and plan because they have been willing to recognize and pay administrators who will enforce accommodation among the members of the unit and defend the peace against outsiders.

Agricultural surpluses also created questions about the division of the surplus and the opportunity for other groups to take it away. Because of constant disputes among various localities, it probably became obvious to people that some method of stopping the fighting

*M*ilestones of Civilization

Stone Age	2,500,000–10,000 B.C.[*]
Humans appear in China	25,000 B.C.
Age of Agriculture	11,000 B.C.
Copper Age	6500 B.C.
Egyptian civilization	5000 B.C.
Near Eastern (Mesopotamian) civilization	4000 B.C.
Bronze Age	3800 B.C.
Indian civilization	3000 B.C.
Chinese civilization	1800 B.C.
Iron Age	1000 B.C.
Greek civilization (at its height)	700 B.C.–500 B.C.
Roman civilization	753 B.C.–A.D. 476
Japanese civilization	A.D. 57
Middle Ages	A.D. 476–A.D. 1453
Crusades	A.D. 1095–A.D. 1291
Renaissance	A.D. 1400–A.D. 1600
Reformation	A.D. 1517–A.D. 1690
Voyages of discovery	A.D. 1450–A.D. 1600
Age of Revolutions	A.D. 1750–A.D. 1850
Victorian era	A.D. 1837–A.D. 1901
Edwardian era	A.D. 1901–A.D. 1914
World War I	A.D. 1914–A.D. 1918
World War II	A.D. 1939–A.D. 1945
Postwar nuclear era	A.D. 1945[†]

[*]Many of these dates are estimates or are subject to debate, or both.

[†]Many wars have occurred since 1945 and are still occurring, but the end of World War II began an era conventionally called "postwar."

would make everyone better off, either because one group had won over all others or because they could come to an agreement. To further these ends, small localities coalesced into more or less unified kingdoms.

As the size of a kingdom increased, the leader of the kingdom likely became more and more removed from the ordinary inhabitants. As this happened, the leader became closely identified with divinity, either as a god or as a delegate of a god, and a feature of these early Middle Eastern countries was the king-god. The king-gods, in turn, appointed priests, and thus began pagan religious institutions.

As the kings gained power, they also gained control of the ownership of land, which was in the process of being transferred from individuals who farmed the land to the nobility who protected the land. We see in this process the organization of society into a military aristocracy, a priesthood, and, finally, a laboring class of landless peasants. Wars created the lowest class; the captured losers in a war became slaves. By about 3000 B.C., this organization had become stable and within it people, freed from the basic struggle merely to live another day, could begin to trust, create, and provide for the future. If we name the result *civilization,* we may say that by about 3800 B.C., a group called the Sumerians had civilized the Mesopotamian area, which is in modern-day Iraq.

To have an organization requires codifying its rules. To do that, one must recognize that what has been going on has in fact been going on and that a certain order exists in those activities. For example, when a child was murdered, the parents probably became angry and attempted some type of revenge, which brought on revenge for revenge in a cycle of individual retribution. If rules that incorporated the revenge could somehow be established, impulsive

Early writing: hieroglyphics.

The stele of Hammurabi. The ancient legislator is shown on the left. He is discussing his laws (carved below) with the Sun God.

killing could be avoided. To do that, someone had to record those rules so that they could be known and followed, by both the leaders and the subjects.

The **Code of Hammurabi** is an early collection of rules, or laws, set up by King Hammurabi of Mesopotamia about 4,000 years ago. The code set up an "eye for an eye" system of retribution, combined with humanitarian rules such as prohibitions against defrauding the helpless.

The Mesopotamian political organization did not last; another group of individuals, less civilized and more warlike, soon overran the Sumerians. This group was the Semites. Even though the Semites won their war, they did not win the cultural competition, and their culture was soon absorbed into the Sumerian culture.

As the Semites were absorbed into the Mesopotamian culture, another culture, similar to the Mesopotamian, was flourishing in Egypt. Like Mesopotamian society, Egyptian society was ruled by a king-god. Because of the geography of the area, Egypt was free of hostile invasions (the sea and the desert made it difficult for attackers to menace Egypt). Combined with the warm, predictable climate and the fertile farmland of the Nile, this led to an extremely productive society that generated significant agricultural surpluses. The pyramids, great funerary temples, and rock-cut tombs in which the kings and queens of Egypt were laid to an uneasy rest are evidence both of the power of the king-gods and of the enormous surpluses generated by that culture.[1]

---

[1]Almost every known burial site has been shorn of its contents, whether by ancient marauders or modern archaeologists.

Development of the Greek Civilization

Throughout southern Europe, parallel developments like those in Mesopotamia were taking place, although they did not reach into most of those regions until much later. In Crete, part of ancient Greece, pictographic writing was known as early as 3000 B.C., but what we have defined as the civilizing process did not flourish until later—its heyday there was from about 2000 B.C. to about 1200 B.C., when physical Cretan civilization was suddenly destroyed, probably by an earthquake, tidal wave, volcanic eruption, some combination of these disasters, or even an invasion by the Doric tribes of the north. What exactly happened cannot be determined, simply because of the sheer finality of whatever it was that destroyed human constructs.

From about 700 B.C. to 500 B.C., a new Greek civilization emerged, and many of the roots of Western civilization and institutions are to be found here. For example, Western political organizations have their foundations in the Greek **polis,** or political community. The Greek polis was originally an agricultural village. These villages or cities were also independent political units. The two most famous are Sparta and Athens (today Sparta is a town of about 16,000 inhabitants, whereas Athens bustles with close to 5 million people and is the capital of modern Greece). The citizens of such a unit were seen as relatives of each other, theoretically descended from a common ancestor. The Greek philosopher Aristotle argued that the polis was a natural outgrowth of the human being's nature. He felt that without law and justice the human being was the worst of animals; with law and justice, the best.

The concept of the polis and its increasingly skillful and sophisticated implementation resulted in the growth of such cities and in the growth of their contacts with each other and with other civilizations. With the development of trade, industry, and colonization, a new class of people, the merchants, became wealthy and important. This change caused trouble for the polis: division within the ruling aristocracy and the establishment of tyranny, or rule by a tyrant, a monarch or leader who had gained power in an unregulated but not necessarily wicked way and who governed through one-man rule. This is one example among many in the history of economic changes and shifts in the distribution of wealth leading to changes in both politics and the social relations among people. Although the concept of "tyrant" was antithetical to the polis, and the custom of rule by tyrant lasted only about a hundred years, tyrants played a role in reducing civil wars among the polis and in encouraging economic and social change necessary for the development of technology, the arts, and literature; reducing the grip of the aristocracy; and, paradoxically, giving more people the potential for roles in government.

The Persian Empire

In the fifth century B.C., the Persian Empire arose in lower Mesopotamia, and in the fourth century B.C. the Macedonians conquered the various city-states that made up the world of Greece. The Macedonians had no polis and were ruled loosely by a king. A council of aristocracy served as a check on the king's power, and by 338 B.C. one of these kings, King Philip II, had conquered Athens and other Greek city-states, a plan that he conceived and carried out over a period of thirty years. Philip was assassinated in 336 B.C., and his rule was assumed by his son, Alexander the Great, who was not yet twenty years old. By the time Alexander died, overcome by a sudden and unidentified disease when he was only thirty-three years old, he had solidified his father's conquest of Greece and then gone on to conquer Egypt, almost all of what we now call the Middle East, and the greater part of India. To Alexander is attributed the demand, "Bring me more worlds to conquer."

Greek Civilization in the Persian Empire. Notice that in contrast to the previous sections, we titled the last section "The Persian Empire," not "The Development of the Persian Civilization." The reason is that the Persian legacy was not cultural; its legacy was primarily the creation of an empire. Alexander's empire did not end the cultures and civilizations that

The Eastern Connection

In this chapter and throughout this book, we have concentrated on Western culture, institutions, and history. We have done so because we have to stop somewhere; to include the East we would have to make the book twice as long. However, it would be inappropriate not to mention some of the multitudinous ideas in Western culture that first developed in the East.

In terms of beginnings of civilizations, the East developed slightly later than the West, but once developed, it quickly surpassed the West in political and economic organization, in technology, and in sophisticated philosophy.

Language—India, five or six thousand years ago. The language is Indo-European, and today half the world's population speaks languages derived from it. These include Hindi, Lithuanian, Russian, Greek, Gaelic, Latin, German, all the Scandinavian languages, English, Italian, French, Spanish, Portuguese, Romanian.

History—India dates the beginning of the modern era at 3102 B.C.

Bronze casting—China, 1600 B.C.

Monotheism (only one god, not multiple gods)—Iran, sixth century B.C.

Sanskrit grammar, with 3,873 rules—India, 500 B.C.

Kite—China, 400 B.C.

Great Wall of China—begun in 209 B.C.

Cable suspension bridge—China, 100 B.C.

Sophisticated eye surgery, including cataract removal—India, before A.D. 33

Trade—by the second century A.D., China was trading with Rome

Wheelbarrow—China, A.D. 231

A centralized nation-state—as early as the sixth century A.D., Japan had a system of centralized government (borrowed from China)

Paper money—China, A.D. 811 (it was called flying cash because it could be transported so much more easily than silver or copper coins)

Arabic numerals (0, 1, 2, 3, 4, etc.)—India, ninth century A.D.

Movable type (made of clay)—China, A.D. 1045

Movable type (made of metal)—Korea, A.D. 1302

made up the Persian Empire and, although conquered militarily, Greek culture won out over the Persian culture. Even the Persian Empire did not last long. After Alexander's sudden death in 323 B.C., the empire quickly collapsed. It is the Greek, not the Persian, cultural legacy that most strongly influenced modern society.

Many Greek ideas and institutions were revived almost 1,800 years later in what became known as the Renaissance. (*Renaissance* can be translated "rebirth," and Greek ideas were some of the concepts that were reborn.) Because of their predominance in the

The Persian Empire (shown in the shaded area) at its height.

How the Greeks Tried Laughing All the Way to the Peace Talks

In 413 B.C., Athens suffered a terrifying defeat: Its navy was destroyed. The opposing army, the Spartans, was nearby and well equipped. Allies not only deserted Athens but also joined the enemy. Aristophanes, a famous comic writer, chose to face this despair by writing a play.

Lysistrata is about a unique way to enforce peace. The plot is simple: The heroine, Lysistrata, organizes the women of both sides to refuse sex with their husbands and lovers until the men agree to end the war.

Initially, most of the women are unwilling to give up sex. Lysistrata convinces them by rational arguments that her plan will work. She persuades the older women to join, giving them a vital task—guarding the public treasury so that no money can be disbursed for the war. She holds them together when they waver after suffering without men for a long period (well, five days—but it's clear Aristophanes thought that was a long time). She knows, and she makes them realize, that if they stick together, and if they can endure longer than the men can endure, they will win. When the men debate with her, she wins every point.

The men give in first. And their reward is even more than they hoped, because the women remind them that both sides worship the same gods, both sides have in the past done noble deeds in aid of the other, and in this quarrel surely they can compromise. After a little bickering, the opposing armies do come to an agreement, after which both sides join in a satisfying feast of all domestic joys (including, but not limited to, eating and drinking).

As you can see, the play is far more complex than it may have seemed at first. It is about sex, money, reason, greed, graft, war, politics, organization, cunning, religion, prejudice, psychology, folly, resolve, accommodation, denial, and triumph. It is even about love. In short, it is about the issues of social science.

P.S. *Lysistrata* is a play. In real life, the Spartans did not attack Athens immediately, and while they hesitated, the Athenians were able to build a whole new navy, defend their city, and win an honorable peace. What part the women of Athens played in the real peace must be left to your imagination.

Renaissance, the ideas of Greek society played a central role in the subsequent history of Western civilization.

Roman Civilization

As we mentioned earlier, individuals were organizing into social groups throughout southern and middle Europe in a period beginning about 4000 B.C. If we had thousands of pages to explain and you had hundreds of years to study, we could recount the history and interaction of these groups. We are forced to be selective, however, and the next civilization that we have time and room for is the Roman civilization, which developed in what is now Italy. It developed later than many of the others, and as late as 1000 B.C. it remained a collection of unorganized tribes.

About 1000 B.C., Italy was invaded by its warlike neighbors who imposed their language and social organization on almost all of Italy. In the eighth century B.C., small villages were amalgamated into the city-state of Rome, and by the sixth century B.C., it had overthrown its foreign conquerors and become the center of Italy and Italian culture. Rome's dominance constituted what we call the Roman Empire, and it was to last almost a thousand years.

The Roman state was one in which the king, or caesar, was elected, although the office appears to have tended to remain in the same family. The ruler had extraordinary powers and could make arrests and even order capital punishment, but what was called the senate had veto power, and it was ultimately from the senate that the ruler derived his authority.

Individuals in Rome fell into two categories: patricians and plebeians. The patricians had all the power and privilege; the plebeians could hold no public or religious office. However, the need for the plebeians to fight in the constant wars that Rome undertook gave them power, and by 450 B.C. they were strong enough to enforce their demand for a major codification of Roman law. As the patrician–plebeian distinction broke down, another class distinction—based on wealth, contacts, and birth—developed, and most of the Roman leaders came only from the few families in this new aristocracy.

Ruins of the Roman Forum.

Roman civilization endured until the fifth century A.D., but it did not remain static. The Roman republic was transformed into the Roman Empire, and pagan religion gave way to Christianity; by the fourth century A.D., Christianity was the state religion.

The Romans exercised their power for centuries, and their influence pervades Western civilization today. They overran Greek civilization and incorporated it into their own, so that when Roman influence is transmitted to us, Greek influence is transmitted to us. Here are some of the things that make us live as Romans today:

- The dominance of the family
- The custom of women to rule in household matters and to have certain legal property rights
- Political patronage
- The "network" system of contacts for social and professional advancement
- Ingenuity in solving technical problems
- Reliance on and practice of all manner of engineering and inventive art
- The concept of empire
- Existence of a military-industrial complex
- Second homes and resorts
- Large agricultural holdings
- The lure of city life
- A flexible legal system that is constantly changing to suit circumstances, relying on a body of precedents to interpret and modify statutes
- The names of all of our months and the organization of our calendar

From the four phenomena that are the most striking in Roman history—military undertakings, engineering, law, and political administration—we pick out the last as basic to all the rest. Roman political administration was efficient, reasonable, flexible, realistic, and humane. Because the government was so well organized, Rome was able to devote its ample excess energies to building, manufacture, agriculture, literature, trade, moral philosophy, and world conquest. Rome also had the leisure and Latin language to develop, refine, and express its thoughts, principles, discoveries, speculations, and decrees. Today, Latin forms the basis of hundreds of thousands of words in the English language, although semantically English is a Germanic language. However, Rome's success also had its negative side: Along with the benefits came complacency, ambition, greed, arrogance, and tyranny. Because these traits are more dramatic than the steady march of its well-ordered society, today we often think of ancient Rome in terms of the religious conflict, savage combat, extravagant public carnivals, graft, brutal suppression of opposition, and dissolution that eventually weakened control over enormous territory[2] and caused popular uprisings, financial collapse, and military defeat—in short, the fall of the **Roman Empire,** the enormous territory encompassing Great Britain, most of Europe, northern Africa, and the Middle East administered by the Romans.

Rome was attacked by other groups from both the north and the south, and by about 500 A.D. the population of the empire had declined from an estimated 1.5 million to about 300,000, and Rome, as a civilization, ended. Why did it end? It is hard to say, and maybe that is not even the right question. Edward Gibbon argues in *The Decline and Fall of the Roman Empire* that perhaps the question should not be, Why did Rome fall? but, Why did it last so long?

The Middle Ages (A.D. 476-1453)

With the fall of Rome came the advent of a period we now call the **Middle Ages,** from about A.D. 476 to A.D. 1453, between Roman civilization and modern civilization.

The Middle Ages began in 476 with the defeat of the Roman Empire by wandering tribes that roamed over much of what is now northern and central Europe.[3] Even though the northern tribes had conquered Rome, Roman culture at least partially conquered the northern tribal culture. The tribes began to adopt some of the technological, social, religious, and political structures that the Roman Empire had developed.

As Roman culture spread north, Muslim culture spread across North Africa and into all of Spain and Portugal. Muslim armies, formed of warriors known as Moors, attacked Europe, spread into Spain, and then moved into France. In 732, they lost a major battle against the Frank tribe, but their influence remained strong in Spain and Portugal.

Because Muslims controlled the Mediterranean Sea and Europe's contacts with the Orient were curtailed, Europe was forced into a kind of isolation. The coastal cities became less prosperous, and workers were displaced from seagoing occupations to agriculture. Wandering decreased, agricultural activity increased, and life became centered on a manor, or **feudal estate**—an area ruled by a lord. The land on the feudal estate was worked by **serfs,** peasants who were bound to a particular manor (feudal estate) and subject to their feudal lord's will. Christianity, which had been flourishing in the Roman Empire, retained and strengthened its influence partly because it had modeled its administrative structure on the efficient civil Roman organization.

The church consolidated its political and military power by asserting its independence from civilian rulers and by fending off attempts by the Muslims to encroach further on Europe. It also had the time and energy to fight bitter quarrels within its own ranks on matters of religious doctrine. Meanwhile the holders of large manors quarreled, reconciled, and rearranged their allegiances among themselves and the various kings and civil administrators. The local lords, the kings, and the church constantly jockeyed for power, wealth, and land as they all struggled to control these available resources and seize them from one another.

---

[2]The empire was constantly conquering, annexing, and losing pieces of territory, but at its largest, about A.D. 200, it included what we call today the Middle East, North Africa, Spain, Great Britain, and most of present-day Europe.

[3]The Eastern Empire, which had been officially divided from the western Roman Empire in 395 A.D., survived until 1453, when the Turks conquered its capital, Constantinople. Today, Constantinople is the Turkish city of Istanbul.

O rigins of Pakistani Society

Although there isn't space here to discuss the origins of Eastern society, it is so important that you have some sense of Eastern culture that we offer brief insights into other countries' social, cultural, political, and economic institutions throughout the book. Here, Pakistan will be our example.

As a nation-state, Pakistan has been around for about sixty years, but it has origins that predate the birth of Islam (622 A.D.), the religion today of the majority of its inhabitants. By 5000 B.C., a civilization was already flourishing in the Indus Valley, then still a part of India. Excavations of its two greatest cities, Mohenjo Daro and Harappa, show that it had an extensive system of civic administration as well as sewage, drainage, and irrigation systems.

About 1500 B.C., this civilization was supplanted by a group of Indo-European tribes from central Asia who established their own rule over India and instituted a caste system to maintain a permanent hold over the conquered people, from whom, however, they assimilated many things. In the fourth century B.C., when Alexander the Great advanced up the Indus River, a group called Mauryas was already laying the foundations of the first Indian Empire, which saw the growth of economics, learning, and Sanskrit (Sanskrit is one of the earliest languages, the mother of dozens of the world's modern languages). The Mauryas's religion was Buddhism, different from the Hinduism of the conquered people. Then in the eighth century A.D., the Arabs invaded north India and fostered the religion of Islam there.

The Indian Empire was united by a Turkish dynasty, the Mughals, the greatest of whom was Akbar (1542–1605). He gave administrative unity to the country; advanced the notion of secular as opposed to religious rule; promoted the concept of Indian indivisibility; encouraged tolerance among all races and religions; raised splendid monuments and cities; married Hindu princesses to solidify alliances; and patronized poets, painters, and scholars. Akbar was a Muslim and under his rule much of India converted to Islam.

In 1757, India was conquered by the British, who originally came as traders but who exploited internal dissensions to take over the country. In 1947 British rule ended. At that time, Pakistan was created, but the new country was physically divided by a portion of north India that lay between Pakistan's eastern and western sections. This situation proved unworkable, and in 1971 the eastern section broke away to become the independent state of Bangladesh.

Today, Pakistan is an independent, unitary country located on the northwest border of India. Its other bordering neighbors are Afghanistan, Iran, and China.

Manor life in the early Middle Ages was relatively straightforward: You were born; you lived a life similar to that of your parents in the same place that they lived, and you died, leaving your children to continue the process. The manor estate was owned by the feudal lord, although ownership was not defined in the way we define it today. Land was not thought of as something that could be bought and sold, but rather as something that belonged to the lord because it belonged to the lord. The peasants, or serfs, did the work on the farm and in return received protection from the lord and enough food to live. The lord provided some security from attack.

What is simple has a tendency to become complex. As the lords became accustomed to managing the land, they began to feel like real owners and to act like owners. Toward the end of the tenth century, the concept of land ownership gained acceptance. This was logically followed by preoccupation with acquiring more and more land while concern for preserving the old feudal way of life faded.

At the end of the tenth century, a series of strong rulers in what are now the countries of France and Germany succeeded in imposing centralized government on parts of Europe. Administrative systems developed in which the interests of the various classes—the lords, the church, the peasants, and the townspeople—were represented. The decline of the feudal manor meant that many of the workers who had been attached to those manors went back into the towns looking for other kinds of jobs. Because of technological improvements having to do with methods of plowing and rotating crops, it took fewer agricultural workers to provide more food. As the towns grew, their economies grew, too. People bought and sold within the town, towns traded with each other, regions had an interest in keeping the peace in order to protect trade, and Europe became strong enough even to venture into the Mediterranean Sea.

Two motives interacted to begin the end of Europe's isolation: religion and commerce. In the Middle Ages, religion played a central role in all individuals' lives. In fact, the Catholic Church was the primary institution for people outside of the manor. It controlled education and knowledge, and it told people how they should live their lives. Moreover, the church owned enormous amounts of land and had significant economic and political power. That power was demonstrated by the **Crusades,** a series of religious wars between the eleventh and thirteenth centuries that, the church said, were necessary to recover Jerusalem (modern-day Israel) from the infidels.

The contacts the Crusaders made with Arab culture introduced new products to Europe, taught the Europeans what Arabs had learned about science and mathematics, and revived interest in Greek culture. The Crusades stimulated trade and made the merchants of Venice, Pisa, and Genoa rich. This new merchant class changed the internal structure of the society of the Middle Ages because most merchants had been formerly landless adventurers. Its growth and the growth of the cities in which trade prospered changed the nature of the social system.

Whereas life on the manor was structured and individuals' roles were well defined, in the cities there was ambiguity about roles, and individuals had the freedom to choose what they could be. Although by modern standards the cities were merely small towns, they offered the opportunity for wealth and the amusements and intellectual variety that we associate with cities. The freedom of the cities had attracted many serfs and peasants, especially those whom new agricultural technology had dispossessed from manor lands. When this occurred, the landed nobility lost power and in their weakened state were taken advantage of by the merchants, who sided with the kings. The loose associations that had previously existed were solidified into modern **nation-states,** separate countries with defined borders and populations with the same language and more or less the same interests, administered by rulers who sought to foster the particular nation-state's economic, political, social, and cultural growth.

As Europe grew richer, the nation-states and the church had more to fight about. All were rich and wished to be richer, were powerful and wished to be more powerful. The worst fight was between the English and the French and was called the Hundred Years' War. It raged from 1337 until 1453, more than a hundred years, but there were periods of peace, or at least periods of exhaustion when both sides rested. What was it about? It was about whether the French should rule in England or the English should rule in France. It was about prestige, about who was smarter and stronger, about boundaries and national identity. It was about what all wars are about.

Worse even than the Hundred Years' War was the **Black Death,** or bubonic plague, a disease transmitted by rats. In the 1290s, bubonic plague arrived in Sicily, carried there by sick rats from ships in the Middle East trade. The plague was carried from country to country by commercial routes, attacking all of Europe as far as Norway, where it died out about 1350. It had probably just run out of victims. There are all kinds of estimates of how many people died, but a generally accepted figure is 40 percent of Europe. Population levels did not recover for 200 years.

This population change had enormous social and economic consequences. For example, so many people were killed by the plague that the surviving workers were able to command much higher wages. Cities grew wealthier. Even the Catholic Church profited because it received so many inheritances and religious fees. Landholders, on the other hand, suffered because their workers died off, the demand for food dropped (fewer people to eat it), and they had to pay higher prices for the things they bought.

Struggles within the church went on all during this period. One of the questions was, Shall it be the pope or shall it be the individual churches who set policy? The papacy was weakened by these quarrels, and monarchs moved into the power vacuum. Religious life

Is a Modern Plague Possible?

It was trade that made the West rich, but it was also trade that brought the bubonic plague to Europe. Can such a calamity happen again? The answer is yes. One indication that it can happen again was seen in 2003 when SARS, which killed approximately 10 percent of its victims, spread from China around the world. SARS had no cure, and it spread like the common cold.

With the increased interconnections among countries that occur with globalization, it is becoming increasingly difficult to keep an illness geographically constrained. In 2003, it looked as if SARS was being contained, but new concerns were raised about a possible bird flu pandemic spreading throughout the world. In 2009, the rapid spread of the H1N1 virus—commonly known as swine flu—from Mexico to more than seventy countries led the World Health Organization (WHO) to declare a global pandemic, demonstrating how easily a deadly disease can circle the world. So, in answer to the question: Is a modern day worldwide plague possible?—the answer is yes.

An engraving depicting victims of the plague.

became subject to civil control. Although the papacy still had a stronghold in Rome, its power base shrank and it lost much of its unquestioned authority over the rest of Europe. Religious debates had fostered new ways of looking at the world, and intellectual Europe was ready for new ideas.

New ideas were about to arrive. In 1453, Constantinople, which was under Christian control, fell to the Turks, who were Muslims. Among the refugees who escaped to Europe were Greek scholars, who brought with them learning and traditions that fueled the Renaissance.

The Renaissance

The Middle Ages ended sometime in the fifteenth century, when scholars of the time decided that they were embarking on a "new beginning." They called the new beginning the Renaissance. **Renaissance** means "rebirth," and it occurred after the Middle Ages when the knowledge of the ancient Greeks and Romans was reestablished and reason, critical thinking, and the arts flourished. Architecture, sculpture, painting, and even engineering and critical investigation were created by artists such as Leonardo da Vinci, Raphael, Michelangelo, and Donatello. The Renaissance encouraged critical thinking, and people no longer necessarily accepted the dictates of the church elders on all topics under the sun.

In 1517, such critical thinking put in motion a set of events that came to be known as the Protestant Reformation, when a German Augustinian friar by the name of Martin Luther posted ninety-five theses against indulgences on the door of the castle church of Wittenberg. Indulgences are reductions in, or even elimination of, the time a sinner would

Marco Polo's Travels

One of the ways in which the West learned about the culture of the East was through the tales of explorers. One of the most famous was Marco Polo, who traveled throughout the East. The map traces Marco Polo's travels. His description of where he went isn't always easy to identify on modern maps, but he followed this plan more or less. He was one of the earliest travelers from West to East. He reached Beijing on a trading mission in 1275 and remained in China for seventeen years. As late as the nineteenth century, the book he wrote about his travels continued to be almost the only source of information the West had about the remote areas of central Asia. Some of the things the West learned about from Marco Polo were tattooing, coal, condensed milk, paper money, and fuel oil.

otherwise have to spend being punished in the next world. They are granted by the Catholic Church to sinners in return for actions such as saying certain prayers or visiting certain holy shrines. In Luther's day, the practice had been corrupted because the church sold indulgences for profit. Luther was outraged by this practice. He believed that human beings must be saved not by indulgences but by faith alone. Luther's posting of the theses was a direct challenge to the pope's absolute authority. With this challenge, Luther and other Protestant theologians began a forced retrenchment of church power and created a complex of hostilities between groups that can still be seen today, for example, in the antagonisms between Protestants and Catholics in Northern Ireland.

The importance of free thinking and rationality to the events that shaped our world can be seen in the popular saying to the effect that the philosopher Erasmus (1466–1536), who was one of the strongest advocates of rationality, "laid the egg that Luther hatched."

Throughout the Renaissance, the influence of religion remained strong. The Protestant Reformation challenged only those aspects of the Renaissance that paid obeisance to traditional religion. The Reformation replaced it with a religion that gave a stronger role to the individual. Other Renaissance values, such as the importance of education, religion, and obedience to God, were maintained.

As we discussed earlier, until the latter part of the Middle Ages the individual feudal lords had strong powers, and although they were tied together into loose confederations with a king or monarch, often the individual lords had more power than the monarch. The expansion of trade, the development of cities, and the creation of a new merchant class led to a new set of alliances that made possible the development of the modern state. The Renaissance solidified that development. The states continued to develop throughout the 1700s, and by the end of that century, most of the states of Europe that we are now familiar with had been formed as monarchies.

Artist's impression of fifteenth-century Florence.

Throughout this period, the middle class, consisting of merchants and wealthier peasants, continued to grow, but the focus on traditional life remained. Change was considered bad, and tradition remained the important focal point, governing the direction of society.

The Development of Modern Economic and Political Institutions

Throughout the Middle Ages and the feudal system, markets existed, but they were not the chief ways by which individuals acquired the goods they needed for existence. Markets and trade did, however, provide luxuries and a variety of goods, and throughout the Middle Ages a set of fairs developed during which individuals bartered these goods. Merchants acquired more and more income from the trade at these fairs and gradually became strong enough to join with the king in reducing the rights of the lords. These changes occurred simultaneously with the Renaissance. In the Middle Ages, people looked at the economy quite differently than we do today. Economic activity was not seen as necessarily good in itself; tradition, rather than the profit motive, guided people's actions. Everyone knew one's place and roles were well defined. There were a few free individuals, such as the merchants, and as a byproduct of their traveling from place to place, a variety of cities or marketplaces sprang up where individuals from the manors could go to trade with the merchants. But all of these events would not have brought much change were it not for the Crusades, which sped up and significantly increased the breakdown of the manorial system.

From Serfdom to Mercantilism

During this time, there was a gradual transition from the system of **serfdom,** feudal obligations owed by vassals to their lords based on a percentage of their agricultural output or days of labor, into payments of money due for rent owed. Thus, the central economy shifted from a system of traditional obligations to a system based on the exchange of products and services for money. The lords were in favor of this movement because the expanding trade required them to have money in order to deal with the merchants. The expanded wants generated by this trade left many lords impoverished, and the

If You Hated Inquisition I, Wait until You See Inquisition II

The phenomenon known as the Inquisition was not exclusively medieval and did not occur just once.

Inquisition I: The Medieval Inquisition

The medieval Inquisition began in 1233 when the Roman Catholic pope replaced local bishops with his own appointees. Their duty was to inquire into heresy (theories of religion that differed from the official Roman Catholic version). The inquisitors would give notice that they were coming to a locality and why. People would have a month to come forward voluntarily and swear they were not heretics. Usually the inquisitors believed them and that was that. But some people did not come forward.

In every age and country there are a bunch of nosy neighbors, and nosy neighbors would denounce this or that person to the inquisitors. Then the inquisitors would hold a trial. The accused could have legal counsel and could appeal to the pope if the decision was adverse. However, the accused could not find out who had accused him or her (on the other hand, the accused could give the inquisitors a list of his or her enemies, and if an enemy's name was the same as an accuser's name, the accusation of that enemy was thrown out). The pope's appointees were generally willing to believe heretics who swore that they would give up their heresy and be good. But if people were found guilty, they were turned over to the local ruler for punishment. The most common punishment was imprisonment, although once in a while one of these unfortunate people was burned alive at the stake. It was not until the 1800s that the custom was abolished. Until then it was a fact of life in France, Italy, and Germany.

Inquisition II: The Spanish Inquisition

This is properly known as the "Spanish Inquisition," and it was much worse than Inquisition I. It was established by the Spanish rulers Ferdinand and Isabella, the same folks who brought you Christopher Columbus, the New World, and America. (No one is all bad; but no one is all good, either.) Inquisition II was harsher and tried many more people than the medieval Inquisition. It is the so-called Spanish Inquisition that is famous for torturing both the accused and the unlucky witnesses, for handing out guilty verdicts right and left, and for using the preferred punishment of burning at the stake. Because Inquisition II was run by the Spanish kings and queens, the Roman Catholic pope did not really approve of it, but papal authority did not succeed in abolishing it until 1820.

P.S. People were usually heavily drugged before they were burned at the stake. Sometimes, though, the authorities were mean and nasty, and if they thought the accused was especially wicked, the drugs were omitted.

merchants had incomes significantly exceeding those of the richest lords. At that point, the landed aristocracy began to view their ancestral manors not just as something that belonged to them but as possible sources of cash, and when sheep became profitable they began to enclose the land that had been previously held in common, so that the sheep could graze on it. This made it more and more difficult for the tenants to support themselves. Enclosure dispossessed many tenants and created a new type of labor force—individuals without land who moved into the cities and led a marginal existence or wandered from place to place.

Although serfdom was not formally abolished in France until 1789, and in Germany not until the 1850s, by the 1700s the market economy was definitely emerging, although it had yet to receive full legal and political status. The new economic order was **mercantilism,** an early phase of capitalism in which private ownership and profits were important, but in which there was significant state control. In a mercantilist system, the king granted rights for individuals to conduct a variety of trades, the state was intricately involved in all aspects of commerce and business, and countries all tried to export more goods than they imported and to build up their gold reserves. Technological developments continued throughout this time, but in the 1700s technological changes themselves fundamentally altered the methods of, and needs for, labor.

𝒜 Ripple from the Third Crusade

When returning to England from the Third Crusade at the end of the twelfth century, King Richard the Lion-Hearted was taken captive by Henry VI of France, and the English were forced to pay a large ransom for him. In order to pay that ransom, Richard's younger brother, John, who was ruling England in Richard's absence, had to establish high taxes, which did not decline after Richard's release. The high taxes, together with John's military and administrative failures, caused a revolt against the English monarchy. The English nobles, backed by the church and by solid citizens of the towns, forced John, who had come to the throne after Richard's death, to accept the Magna Carta. The **Magna Carta,** "the great charter," forced the king to agree that free men had rights and liberties that could not be trampled on. We quote from the Magna Carta to show how bad the conditions must have been that forced the revolt, and to show you why the Magna Carta is said to be the basis of some of the rights we ourselves take for granted today.

No constable . . . shall take anyone's . . . chattels without . . . paying for them in money.

No sheriff . . . shall take horses or wagons . . . except on permission.

We . . . will not take the wood of another man . . . except by permission of him to whom the wood belongs.

No free man shall be taken, or imprisoned, or dispossessed, or outlawed, or banished . . . except by the legal judgment of his peers, or by the law of the land.

To no one will we sell, to no one will we deny or delay, right or justice.

The Emergence of Nation-States

As the individual states grew and trade picked up, the monarchs attempted to consolidate and broaden their power by supporting the merchants in voyages to Africa (in search of gold) and India (in search of spices). Such voyages avoided the Arab land routes by which gold had been making its way to Europe and the long, arduous overland route between western Europe and India through which pepper, cloves, and other spices came. Thus we have a variety of voyages of discovery such as Columbus's that tremendously broadened possibilities for society. It was through these voyages in search of still better routes to India that what became the United States enters the picture of Western development.

Various coins. The shell could have been spent in Africa as recently as a hundred years ago. The next two are ancient Chinese, and then we progress through time and space: North India, the Middle East, Rome, and Arabia—until we reach our own penny and quarter.

Drawing of early Industrial Revolution factory, from Diderot's Encyclopédie.

The emergence of nation-states led to numerous wars both within and among nations. These included the French Wars of Religion (1562–1598), the Thirty Years' War (1618–1648), the Glorious Revolution in England (1688), the Great Northern War between Sweden and Russia (1700), the War of the Spanish Succession (1702–1714), and many others. Such wars continue through much of history; and both conflict and the threat of conflict are the most important problems still facing the modern world.

The Industrial and Political Revolutions of the 1750s to the 1850s

The period of time from 1750 to 1850 is often called the **Age of Revolutions** because of the enormous economic and political changes that occurred during that time.

In the 1750s, once again technological changes had enormous influence on all parts of society. These technological changes were so important that the next significant period is called the **Industrial Revolution,** a period from 1750 to about 1900 characterized by the invention of machines that had the effect of greatly increasing total output and reorganizing work patterns and social relationships. Although the Industrial Revolution began in England, its influence soon spread throughout the world. The revolution was spurred by technological developments such as John Kay's flying shuttle[4] (1733), James Hargreaves's spinning jenny (1765), James Watt's steam engine (1769), and Richard Arkwright's power loom (1769). These inventions made it possible to produce much more output than had hitherto been possible, and in doing so created the need to reorganize the types of work that individuals did.

In order to produce these machines and use the technology, individuals were needed in cities to work in factories. Thus people leaving the rural manors had an alternative. Because pay was often initially higher in factories than on the farm, a migration began into the cities where people hoped to get jobs. The Industrial Revolution further strengthened the power of the merchants, who had allied themselves with the monarchy.

---

[4]This was a technological advance but not, like the U.S. shuttle, a space vehicle. The invention of the flying shuttle frustrated the textile industry because it enabled workers to weave so much cloth that the spinners of thread from which it was woven could not keep up; it was a challenge to the textile industry that was met by offering a prize to anyone who could invent something to increase the threadspinners' productivity. The prize was won when the spinning jenny was invented.

On the political front, this period witnessed both the American and French Revolutions. In 1776, the American Revolution began, weakening the English empire and establishing the rights of individuals relative to the state and ruler. The pressures that had erupted in the American Revolution were founded in the same conditions as those that later caused the French Revolution. Because of the wars that had marked much of the 1700s, governments had significant debts on which they continually had to pay high interest. On the eve of the French Revolution (1789), the interest paid on the French debt was more than half of France's total budget. As the merchants grew tired of paying this debt, the middle class aligned itself with some members of the aristocracy, leading to a revolution in the way societies were organized. The power of the king was eliminated, and there was a declaration of the rights of man and citizenship. The French Revolution, embodying the ideas of the emerging social sciences, changed the political and economic organization of society.

The Industrial Revolution took hold in the 1800s. The middle class grew enormously and, with its newfound political power, pursued an increasingly important role in running the economy. During this time, significant social experimentation took place as the state and the organization of society went through the process of reform and of throwing off tradition. Throughout this period, societies and individual countries became more clearly defined, and by 1850 in western Europe the concept of a nation-state with parliamentary government ruled the day.

But these nation-states had to learn to live together, and their failure to do so and to discover a way to negotiate settlements of disputes among them led to continued warfare and significantly changed the boundaries separating nation-states. As a result of wars, many new nation-states have sprung into being, whereas from time to time old ones have died out. During the nineteenth century, Turkish authority was expelled from most of Europe, and new states took its place on the Balkan Peninsula: Greece, Bulgaria, Serbia, Romania, Albania, and Montenegro. Approximately twenty new states were formed from the old holdings of Spain and Portugal in the New World. About the middle of the nineteenth century, China and Japan opened their doors to Western trade. They, too, entered the community of nation-states, in 1842 and 1854, respectively.

World War I was a war between Germany, Austria-Hungary, and Turkey on one side and Britain, France, Belgium, Italy, Luxembourg, Bulgaria, parts of Yugoslavia, Russia, Japan, and the United States on the other side that lasted from 1914 to late in 1918. It tore down the old multinational states of Austria-Hungary and Estonia, and redrew other parts of the European map. Lasting from 1939 to 1945, **World War II** was a much more international war and was fought between Germany, Japan, and Italy on one side, and the United States, Canada, the British Empire, most of Europe, much of Asia including China, many of the Western Pacific countries, and the Union of Soviet Socialist Republics (USSR) on the other side. It led directly to the establishment of Israel, and the divisions of Korea and Germany. After World War II, a surge of nationalism took place in the colonial areas of Africa and Asia, and in the 1960s a number of African and Asian states emerged from the British and French empires.

Beginning in the late 1980s, additional dramatic changes took place. The USSR broke up, and political subdivisions within the USSR, such as Russia, Georgia, Uzbekistan, and the Ukraine, all became independent countries. The wall between East and West Germany was torn down, and those two countries reunited to become one Germany. Poland, Czechoslovakia, Hungary, Romania, and other communist-dominated countries of eastern Europe changed their political systems, orienting themselves more toward the West than to the former USSR.

In the late 1990s, these changes made the United States the world's sole superpower, giving it the power to exert its will throughout the world. Whether it used that power wisely is much in debate. In any case, it is unlikely to continue as the sole superpower. Both the European Union (EU) and China are growing in economic and military power, and the future will likely have power within the world more divided than it was in the past.

Conclusion

That's it: the history of Western civilization in a chapter—not the most thorough or complete history, but one that will give you some sense of the origins of our society and the institutions we consider throughout much of the rest of the book.

Key Points

- The development of agriculture and the domestication of animals played key roles in the establishment of fixed communities, which were essential to modern civilization.
- Egypt and Mesopotamia formed the cradle of modern civilization.
- The Greek civilization that significantly influenced our own emerged from about 700 to 500 B.C.
- In the fifth century B.C., Roman civilization emerged and remained dominant until the fifth century A.D.

- In the Middle Ages, the church dominated life.
- The Renaissance was a period when the arts flourished and people were encouraged to question some church dictates.
- The Age of Revolutions, from about 1750 to 1850, led to the emergence of our modern economic and governmental systems.

Some Important Terms

Age of Agriculture (49)
Age of Revolutions (64)
Black Death (58)
Code of Hammurabi (51)
Crusades (58)
feudal estate (56)

Industrial Revolution (64)
Magna Carta (63)
mercantilism (62)
Middle Ages (56)
nation-states (58)
polis (52)

Renaissance (59)
Roman Empire (56)
serfdom (61)
serfs (56)
World War I (65)
World War II (65)

Questions for Review and Discussion

1. What are some of the developments that changed human beings from roving hunters to people living in fixed communities? What responsibilities and functions did the towns grow to provide?
2. What are some of the legal systems that have existed in Western society? Do you think any of their provisions have relevance today?
3. What conditions enabled certain classes of society to grow wealthy? Do you think concentrations of wealth were a positive or a negative factor for the nature of society?
4. Name some human characteristics that persist over time in the development of Western society.
5. In thinking about your life today, can you identify any ideas that may have come from the Greeks? From the Romans? From the Middle Ages? If so, what are they? (If you prefer, choose some of the other periods discussed, such as the Reformation and the Industrial Revolution.)

6. How did the Arab world influence the development of Western society in the Middle Ages? Do you see any parallels with the situation in the Middle East today?
7. What did the peasant get from the feudal lord, and what did the feudal lord get in return? Do you think it was a fair exchange?
8. How did the church affect life in the Middle Ages? Did its influence change in the Renaissance?
9. How did trade and commerce develop? What do you think your life would be like today if the only things you could buy were those that were grown or manufactured within ten miles of your house?
10. What was revolutionized by the Industrial Revolution?
11. Name some of the wars that altered the course of Western society. Why do you think they led to change?

12. Identify some of the institutions that have grown up in Western society. How are they changing society today?
13. What is the most important problem facing Western society today? What solutions can you think of?

14. Throughout the chapter, the influence of the Muslim world has been brought into the discussion. How do you think this influence will play out over the next fifty years?

*I*nternet Questions

1. Using thinkquest (http://library.thinkquest.org/C006522/life/), read about the lives of women and children during the Renaissance. Now go to www.youtube.com/watch?v=wL5CviNAhnk and watch the video. Compare aspects of everyday life in the Middle Ages to that in the Renaissance. What stereotypes exist concerning women in the Middle Ages, and where did these stereotypes originate?
2. Go to http://industrialrevolution.sea.ca/impact.html and read about the industrial revolution. How did the social structure change during the industrial revolution?

3. Read about the Black Plague at www.eyewitnesstohistory.com/plague.htm. What were the symptoms? How did people try to avoid the disease?
4. What are the five major groupings in the Age of Revolutions (1763–1848)? Pick one and list the important events. You can use www.thenagain.info/webchron/WestEurope/agerevs.chron.html.
5. Go to www.mnsu.edu/emuseum/prehistory/aegean. Read about the ancient Greek civilization of the Mycenea. How did this civilization fall?

*F*or Further Study

Diamond, Jared, *Collapse: How Societies Choose to Fail or Succeed*, New York: Viking, 2006.

Diop, Cheikh Anta, *The African Origin of Civilization: Myth or Reality?*, Chicago: Lawrence Hill Books, 1994.

Fletcher, Joann, *Chronicle of a Pharaoh*, New York: Oxford University Press, 2000.

Guetzmann, William N., and K. Geert Rouwenhorst, eds., *The Origins of Value*, Oxford, UK: Oxford Press, 2005.

Harris, Lee, *Civilization and Its Enemies: The Next Stage of History*, New York: Free Press, 2004.

Heilbroner, R., *The Worldly Philosophers*, rev. ed., New York: Simon & Schuster, 1980.

In Arab Lands, Bonfils Collection, University of Pennsylvania Museum, intro. by Douglas M. Haller, Cairo, Egypt: University of Cairo Press, 2000.

Johnson, Steven, *The Invention of Air: A Study of Science, Faith, Revolution, and the Birth of America*, New York, NY: Riverhead, 2008.

Kelly, John, *The Great Mortality: An Intimate History of the Black Death, the Most Devastating Plague of All Time*, New York: HarperCollins, 2005.

Larner, John, *Marco Polo and the Discovery of the World*, New Haven, CT: Yale University Press, 2000.

Lobo, Tatiana, *Assault on Paradise*, trans. Asa Zatz, Willimantic, CT: Curbstone Press, 1999.

Margolis, Howard, *Copernicus: How Turning the World Inside Out Led to the Scientific Revolution*, New York: McGraw-Hill, 2002.

Maurice, Charles S., and Charles W. Smithson, *The Doomsday Myth: 10,000 Years of Economic Crises,* Stanford, CA: Hoover Institution Press, 1984.

Newman, Paul B., *Daily Life in the Middle Ages,* Jefferson, NC: McFarland, 2001.

Schiavone, Aldo, *The End of the Past: Ancient Rome and the Modern West,* trans. Margery J. Schneider, Cambridge, MA: Harvard University Press, 2000.

Staloff, Darren, et al., *Great Minds of the Western Intellectual Tradition,* audio/videotapes, Springfield, VA: The Teaching Company, 2000.

Tritle, Lawrence, *From Melos to My Lai: War and Survival (Down the Centuries),* Cambridge, MA: Harvard University Press, 2000.

WWW   Ancient World Database http://eawc.evansville.edu/eawcindex.htm

WWW   The Fertile Crescent Interactive www.mnsu.edu/emuseum/prehistory/middle_east/index.shtml

WWW   Internet Modern History Sourcebook www.fordham.edu/halsall/pgc.asp?page=mod/modsbook.html

WWW   Medieval Crusades www.medievalcrusades.com

WWW   Timeline of Ancient Greece www.ancient-greece.org/resources/timeline.html

WWW   Timeline of Ancient Rome www.exovedate.com/ancient_timeline_one.html

Society, Culture, and Cultural Change

After reading this chapter, you should be able to:

- Explain why culture is necessary to hold society together
- List some important elements of culture
- Summarize briefly three popular theories of cultural change
- List five factors that cause culture to change
- List three factors stabilizing culture
- Discuss the cultural lag theory and its limitations
- Explain the doctrine of cultural relativism

Culture is the sum of all the forms of art, of love, and of thought, which, in the course of centuries, have enabled man to be less enslaved.

—André Malraux

Human beings are social beings. We cannot understand their nature independently of their social environment. That is why we call our discipline *social science.*

To understand human beings' role as social beings, we must understand culture. To understand culture and its key role in social science, it is helpful to consider an analogy to physics. When we studied physics in high school, we were taught that there are electrons, protons, and neutrons. Together, these made up atoms, atoms made up elements, and elements made up matter. Since that time, learning physics has become much more difficult. Physicists have discovered even smaller particles, which they tell us are the building blocks of all matter. These building blocks include quarks, leptons, and ghostly particles called gluons, whose existence is assumed by physicists because something has to hold matter together. Quarks and leptons make up matter; gluons hold matter together.

Why are quarks, leptons, and gluons relevant to social science? Because just as physicists need to assume the existence of gluons to hold matter together, social scientists must assume a force that holds society together. Without gluons, quarks and leptons would fall apart and the world as we know it would not exist. Society has a similar force holding it together. Why don't you just haul off and clobber your neighbor when he or she does something wrong? Why don't countries always enter into war to get what they want? What sensibility makes it possible for society to continue to exist and to coordinate the individual wills of some 6.8 billion individuals? The answer is culture, and the social science equivalent to the gluon is culture, embodied in social institutions, mores, conventions, and laws.

Culture and Multiculturalism

Culture is the total pattern of human behavior and its products, embodied in thought, speech, action, and artifacts. It is the way of thinking and doing that is passed on from adults to children in their upbringing and can be thought of as the shared language, norms, and values of a society. Culture is dependent on the capacity for learning through the use of tools, language, and systems of abstract thought. It includes not only patterns of behavior as such but also the attitudes and beliefs that motivate behavior. Culture creates human beings and human societies. Reciprocally, by slow accumulation over many generations, culture is the product of human societies and of the individuals who compose them.

Cultures as we know them have evolved through a long process of change. **Cultural evolution** is the name given to this gradual, accumulative process. Any modern culture is largely the product of the originality and initiative of great numbers of individuals in times past, though in most cases the contribution of any one person has been so small that it cannot even be identified.

Because culture is learned by association with other human beings, the character and personality of all human beings are in large part reflections of the society in which they live. Individuals acquire their knowledge, skills, customs, ideals, religion, and morals from their social environment. This is made possible through socialization. **Socialization** is the process that shapes the personality of individuals so that they can adjust to and become members of society. In the United States, most of us feel, think, and act like U.S. citizens because we have spent all our lives in a mainstream U.S. social environment. If, from earliest childhood, we had associated only with a group of Inuits who never had any contacts with the mainstream U.S. culture, we probably would neither understand nor feel comfortable with that culture.

This does not mean that all people in a culture are alike in their personalities. Significant differences in our family backgrounds and in many other aspects of our personal social environment. To develop human nature, we must be human beings and inherit human potentialities; no two people will ever react to the same environment in exactly the same way. Biologically inherited differences affect the intelligence and temperament of every person and therefore affect thinking and behavior. In any given individual, social inheritance and biological inheritance are so closely bound together that we can never be sure of the relative influence of each. However, for nearly all of us the general pattern of life is largely determined by our social environment. Almost everything we believe or know or do we learn from observing other people, from listening to other people, or from reading and thinking about what other people have written.

Multiculturalism

The United States does not have a single culture, but instead has a blend of overlapping cultures. For example, urban black culture is different from Hispanic culture, which is different from Jewish culture, which is different from rural Midwestern culture, and so on. The blending of these various cultures is not always smooth, and at times is disruptive. Hip-hop, classical, and country music do not a symphony make. Nonetheless, the similarities of the various U.S. subcultures hold together, and allow us to speak of a single U.S. culture, which actually is a composite of various subcultures.

Political debates about culture often focus on whether the government should support monoculturalism or multiculturalism. Technically, monoculturalism emphasizes the shared aspects of subcultures, whereas **multiculturalism** emphasizes the differences among subcultures. However, the term *multiculturalism* has developed a somewhat different meaning. Specifically, the term was used in the 1980s as a way to emphasize that most university curricula reflected a Eurocentric bias at the expense of other U.S. subcultures. Thus, to support multiculturalism was to be against the Eurocentric bias in university curriculums. As often happens when terms become part of a political debate, monoculturalism and multiculturalism were seen as opposites. We don't see it that way. We see both as supportable. Specifically, if the U.S. monoculture were committed to **pluralism**—the value that cultural diversity is good—there would be no contradiction between the two. The debate is simply about getting the right mix. The advantage of monoculturalism is that shared culture tends to hold society together; the advantage of multiculturalism is that it incorporates diversity and lets subgroups revere their own history and view that history as a strong building block of the larger culture.

The Shared Beliefs in Culture

Culture is an enormously vague concept that is difficult to grasp. Perhaps the easiest way to understand culture is to answer a few questions:

1. Should children, age eleven to fifteen, sleep in the same beds as their parents?
2. Should women be allowed to drive?
3. Should females be circumcised?
4. Should people wear swimming suits on public beaches?

Most of you from the United States, I suspect, answered the questions (1) no, (2) yes, (3) no, and (4) yes. Why do I suspect that? Because you come from a shared culture. But if you were from another country, or a part of the United States that is not affected by mainstream U.S. culture, your answers would likely be different. For example, according to Richard Shweder in his book, *Why Do Men Barbecue? Recipes for Cultural Diversity,* in Mali and Somalia women are repulsed by the idea of not circumcising women. Similarly, in Saudi Arabia some women (although it is a decreasing number) see it as simply inappropriate for a woman to drive. Many more examples could be provided, but these should be sufficient to give you a sense of how culture is the shared beliefs of a society.

Culture and the Nature of Society

Even though the personality of each individual is in large measure molded by society, it is clear that society can have no existence apart from the people who constitute it. **Society** is a group of individuals living as members of a community. The characteristics of every society are gradually shaped and changed over succeeding generations by innovations introduced by the people who belong to it. The influence of any one individual may be small, but the contributions of many individuals over long periods of time can be great.

It is important to pay close attention to our definition of society. A group of people does not necessarily constitute a society. A number of people who come together temporarily, and perhaps accidentally, are merely a crowd, or an unorganized aggregate. To constitute a society, a group must be bound together by established relationships. It must, in other words, be organized.

Though the basis of any society is a group of individuals, equally important to its establishment is the continued existence of the group over a period of time. A crowd brought together for a football game is an aggregate, but it is not a society. Its members are physically close together, and for the moment are united by a common interest. However, any sense of unity they may have is superficial and temporary. When the game is over, they disperse. They are not together long enough to organize into a society. But if the same people were marooned for a year on an uninhabited island, they would be forced to organize themselves into a society.[1] They would develop common ideas, interests, and techniques for living and working together. It is the sense of living together as a community that makes up a society.

Culture and Its Role in Human Societies

There is a problem in precisely defining culture because it has a variety of aspects. But our earlier definition of it is probably the best. Culture is the way of life that the people of a society follow. It includes all knowledge, beliefs, art, morals, law, customs, and any other capabilities acquired by a human being as a member of society.

In short, culture is the total pattern of human behavior and its products embodied in thought, speech, action, and artifacts. Culture is also dependent on the capacity for learning through the use of tools, language, and systems of abstract thought.

As you can see, the culture of a society includes everything of human origin in the lives of its members—that is, everything they learn through their direct or indirect contacts with other people. It includes the customary ways of behaving in everyday life, religious beliefs, moral standards, the way family life is organized, the methods used to provide food and shelter, language, government, and forms of artistic expression.

The Elements of Culture

Culture develops only through the association of human beings and thus presupposes society; at the same time, culture is what makes a human society possible. Only when people develop in some degree a common culture can they function as an organized group, for only then do they know what to expect of one another and how to behave to meet the requirements of the group. A society can exist because human beings have the capacity for creating culture and, what is equally important, for sharing it with their contemporaries and transmitting it to succeeding generations. Culture creates societies and societies depend on culture. In short, culture embodies social norms (its conventions, mores, and laws) and institutions together with a society's technology, its material products, and its values. Figure 4.1 presents the elements of culture upon which society rests. Let us consider briefly some of the elements of culture.

Social Norms: Conventions, Mores, and Laws. Conventions are the simple, everyday customs of a group that represent the usual ways of behaving. Conventions change slowly, and many of them are very persistent. In our society, it is customary or conventional to sleep on a bed; to eat at a table; to handle our food with knives, forks, and spoons; and to greet an acquaintance on the street. All these are conventions. Conventions are established customs to which we attach little moral significance. We may think that people whose conventions are different from ours are themselves different, but we try to understand those differences, not ostracize people because of their differences. For example, we will probably wonder about a woman who shaves her head, but our social practice will be to try to act as if we notice nothing unusual.

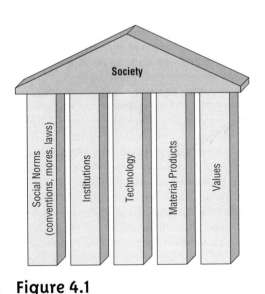

Figure 4.1

The elements of culture.

---

[1]The television program *Survivor* assembled a small group of people on an uninhabited island. The basic purpose was to allow viewers to watch the difficulties this group would have in making decisions. Had there truly been no hope of rescue, and no need to "eliminate" individuals periodically, the group would probably have organized and cooperated in a much more socially beneficial manner.

Punk dressers challenge social norms in Great Britain.

Mores (pronounced mor-rays) are conventions that would have serious consequences if they were violated. They include those customs that must generally be observed by all members of a society for the culture to survive. People who disregard mores are usually seen as more than slightly odd or eccentric—their character definitions are beyond weird. Although a violation of a society's mores would not necessarily land a person in jail, it would incur social punishment in the form of peer disapproval. For example, a claims adjuster who showed up at the insurance office and completely disrobed would have violated one of society's mores and, even if not arrested for indecent exposure, would nevertheless face informal punishment. On the other hand, a person who wears informal clothing to a wedding reception is merely violating a convention.

In contrast to mores and conventions, which are merely customs taken as understood in governing the conduct of the group, laws are more exact, and are generally recorded, codified, and enforced as a means of securing public obedience. **Laws** are the principles and regulations established in a community by some authority and applicable to its people, whether in the form of legislation or of policies recognized and enforced by judicial decision. Violations of laws may carry severe punishments and/or ramifications for the offender. Being caught speeding results in a small fine, whereas premeditated murder may be punishable, at least in some states, by death. What is against the law and the punishment for violation of laws vary in different societies. For example, in some Islamic societies it may be against the law for a woman to appear in public with her face uncovered, and stealing may be punished by the loss of one's hand. In the United States, there are no laws about covering one's face, and stealing results in a jail sentence, at most.

Social Institutions. A **social institution** is an established complex pattern of behavior in which a number of persons participate in order to further important group interests. Institutions are usually organized around some central interest or need. Government, for example, provides the necessary order and coordination among individuals. The school provides for formal education of the young while the family, one of the most basic of all social institutions, helps meet many of the needs of daily life, such as those for shelter, food, close companionship, and affection. The church, temple, mosque, and synagogue are the institutions that enable people to express their religious beliefs by joining others in worshipping a deity or deities in established rituals. Social institutions not only provide order and coordination, they also provide for social change. For example, religious groups played a significant role in the civil rights movement in the United States, a movement that forced U.S. society to treat African Americans more equitably and to remove some of its blatantly discriminatory laws.

Material Products. Strictly speaking, culture is never material. It is in the minds and personalities of people. It is what they have learned from their social environment—attitudes, beliefs, knowledge, and ways of behaving. However, important in every culture is knowledge of how to produce and use a variety of material products, including food, clothing, houses, tools, machines, and works of art. **Cultural objects (artifacts)** are products of human skill and effort that are essential to the functioning of a society. Cultural objects are more than mere expressions of the culture that produces them; they become essential to its functioning because without them people could not carry on the necessary activities of daily life. This is strikingly true in a modern industrial society. Such a society would be paralyzed if it could not use computers, airplanes, cars and trucks, telephones, power plants, factories and their machines, supermarkets, and fast-food outlets, to name a few.

Language. **Language** is a body of words and the system for their use common to a people of the same community or nation, the same geographical area, or the same cultural tradition.

Language is intrinsic in the societies and cultures of humans. Benjamin Lee Whorf argued that each particular language embodies and propagates a worldview. Groups of people speaking the same language, therefore, communicate in the same cultural tone. Cultural assumptions and observations are locked into a society's language. For instance, communication between multilingual people transmits cultural differences between societies.

Language plays a central role in the development and transmission of culture. It allows communication, which is essential for the coordination of activities. It allows cultures to save and transmit a knowledge of their history. Writing allows many further uses of language, widening its ability to store and accumulate knowledge. Writing allows cultures to be preserved and passed on in expanded ways. But language also creates limitations. The structure of the language influences the way individuals look at issues and can therefore incorporate many hidden biases.

Social Values. Social values are the motivating power that makes institutions function effectively. They are the things that a given society considers desirable because they are believed to contribute to the good life and the general welfare. In our cultural environment, honesty, courage, justice, and respect for law and for the rights of others are highly regarded social values. So also, on a somewhat different level, are financial success, health, and education.

Individuals' desires tend to reflect the values stressed in the societies to which they belong. U.S. society is often said to be materialistic. This may not be a wholly correct characterization, yet it contains an element of truth. In our modern United States, we have great respect for success in business, entertainment, and sports, and we place great emphasis on the importance of raising standards of living and abolishing poverty. Because we put such a high value on material welfare, many of our people have come to regard the earning of more and more money as their major life objective. Others, of course, look on money merely as a means to achieve more important objectives. These more important objectives may involve such "higher" social values as the education of one's children; charity; the appreciation and encouragement of art, science, and religion; and the rendering of public service.

Social values make institutions function effectively. The church, temple, mosque, or synagogue, for instance, will be a dynamic force in society only as long as a large portion of their members firmly believe in a supreme being or spiritual guide and have faith that their reli-

---

ℱWIW :-)

Text messaging by email, phone, and instant messenger programs is becoming more and more common—so much so that a new language is developing, both with abbreviations and acronyms, and with symbols that add emotion. Below is a sampling of some of the abbreviations and emotions. Younger students will likely know them all, and more. Older students and professors can find many more by searching the Internet.

143	I love you	:-)	smiley face/happy
2G2BT	Too good to be true	;-)	wink
A3	Anytime, anywhere, anyplace	:-(	frown/sad
YSYD	Yeah sure you do	:-@	scream
SUITM	See you in the morning	:-I	indifference
TTYL	Talk to you later	:-/	perplexed
FWIW	For what it's worth	;-}	leer
LOL	Laughing out loud	:-e	disappointment
		:->	devilish grin
		:-D	shock or surprise
		:-P	wry smile
		:-!	foot in mouth
		:-&	tongue tied
		:-	male
		>-	female

Fast-food restaurants have been integrated into U.S. culture. They are as American as Old Glory.

gious organization is an essential instrument for the growth of the soul and the creation of a good society. Where religion has a strong hold on a society, it is usually a conservative force tending to preserve established moral values.

Social values are relative rather than absolute. They often vary widely from one culture to another, and each individual acquires from his or her own culture ideas of what is desirable or undesirable, good or bad, right or wrong. In some societies, sexual relations before marriage are regarded as a cardinal sin; in others, they are permitted or even expected. In some societies, women must be very plump to be regarded as beautiful; in others, they must be rather slim. In most if not in all modern societies, the killing of infants is regarded with horror, but some nonliterate tribal societies see it as commendable under certain circumstances—for instance, if the infants have physical disabilities.

Cultural Integration

Cultures or societies contain certain aspects that are similar among all cultures. These aspects or traits are called universals. A **cultural universal** is an aspect of culture that is found in all cultures. Religion, for example, is a cultural universal, as is the existence of some form of government, family life, and national ideals. **Cultural alternatives** are those cultural characteristics not necessarily shared by other cultures. For example, some cultures might place the elderly in a subordinate role, whereas others might place them in an exalted role. Therefore, exalting old age is a cultural alternative; not all societies do it.

Traits differ not only among cultures; they also differ within cultures. **Cultural integration** is the degree to which a culture is internally consistent and homogeneous. In large, complex modern cultures such as the United States, there tends to be more diversity. In small, preliterate cultures such as the Amazon Indian culture of the Yahma tribe today there tends to be less diversity. Thus, these cultures are more unified.

In U.S. culture, which greatly values freedom of choice with respect to both ideas and things, life is more complex and stressful. Many social problems such as crime, teenage rebellion, alcohol and drug abuse, and emotional disorders result from our greater ability to choose options. For example, if culture determined what job you would have when you graduate, your life would probably be less stressful. Even cultures that place a high value on freedom must achieve some measure of balance between shared cultural traits and the potentially disintegrative forces of nonshared traits. Since about 1960, we have seen in the United States a decline in the social behavioral consensus that was more typical of the earlier years of the twentieth century. Some social scientists believe that this flexible value system could cause serious trouble for our society. Whether they are right, and whether our society will move toward more shared cultural traits, remains to be seen.

As you can see, culture is the glue that holds society together, but like glue it can also cause difficulties for society. The reason is that societies are in constant transition, and to be successful a society must adjust to new technologies and relations with other societies. The glue that really held society together in one time period may be the sticky mess that in another time period entraps some members of society. Therefore, to understand the role of culture in society, we must consider the process of social change, the factors that contribute to that change, and the effect that change has on culture.

Culture, Society, and Social Change

The culture of a society is constantly evolving to fit new situations. For instance, wars can create almost instantaneous change and can focus a society's interest, money, and energy on a single goal—winning. Total emphasis is placed on war-related activities rather than on more diverse activities. Whether a country wins or loses, the postwar society will substantively differ from the prewar society. Some of these changes will be the result of an opponent's war effort, and others will be the result of interaction with members of other societies.

The rate of social change has gradually gained momentum through the course of human social development. In early times, it started slowly. Many thousands of years ago, all human beings belonged to small, preliterate groups. Though the groups varied greatly in the nature and complexity of their cultures, as a rule the customs and traditions of each were so firmly established that its members tended to follow much the same way of life over a great many generations. Then the rate of social change increased. In effect, social change has behaved much like a snowball rolling down a hill. First, it starts out small and moves slowly; then, as it picks up more snow and gets larger, it gains momentum.

Certain factors have been especially important in contributing to an increased rate of change. Outstanding among these is the development of agriculture. The growing of crops forced people to live in permanent dwellings. Increasing the food supply through storage brought about an increase in population and, gradually, the growth of towns and cities. Another important factor is the invention of writing, which made it possible to record human knowledge and to transmit it to future generations more adequately than ever before. As the sum total of human knowledge increased, the rate of its accumulation accelerated.

Later developments that did much to speed up the rate of social change include the invention of printing, the rise of modern science, and the Industrial Revolution, which began in England in the mid-1700s. The Industrial Revolution represented a shift in the methods of production; it entailed the replacement of hand tools by machines and power tools, and initiated the movement away from small-scale agriculture to the development of large-scale industry. This necessitated enormous numbers of workers for the factories, fewer workers in the fields, and therefore enhanced urbanization, the movement of people from rural to urban areas. A more recent factor of great importance in accelerating change has been the annihilation of distance through the development of rapid transportation and communication. Today, we can use satellite transmission to simulcast events and ideas all around the world while they are actually happening or being formulated.

Not only is the rate of technological change increasing, but so is the interaction among cultures. This is especially true in developing countries. Western science and technology are now spreading throughout the world at an accelerating pace, and further westernization is a likely prospect for many developing countries. The **Internet**—an interconnected set of computers through which people can communicate and transfer information—has transformed communication among individuals and is in the process of making our world one enormous community. With social interaction Internet sites such as MySpace and FaceBook proliferating, young people are interacting with others in ways that were previously impossible, changing what determines and constitutes a community. (Older people often have a much harder time adapting to the avenues of social interaction that the new technology allows.)

One result of increasingly close contacts with distant lands is that the peoples of the world are becoming more and more alike in their customs, the products they use, and the ways they earn a living. Wide cultural differences among peoples can still be found and may never completely disappear. Today, bitter enmities seem ineradicable within countries such as Bosnia and between countries such as India and Pakistan. However, cultural differences are, on the whole, diminishing, and at a more rapid rate than ever before.

We would be wrong, however, to see the diffusion of cultural traits as a one-way street. Styles of dress, food specialties, art forms, and modes of thought in other continents and societies are bringing changes to our own culture. Change in itself is not necessarily good or bad. It only means that old situations are replaced with new ones. Evolution has more definite implications than change. Evolution implies a gradual development from simpler forms of life, art, technology, or social organization to more complex forms. **Social evolution** is the long and complex process of change and interaction by which cultures gradually develop. Whether this change is desirable is debatable. From a Western, ethnocentric perspective, we often think of change as progress, but from a broader perspective, change is not necessarily progress—it may be regressive change. Change cannot be seen as progress unless we know what the life goals are and how those changes help us meet those goals. Views of what life goals should be differ; hence, views of whether social evolution is progressive differ.

Popular Theories of Social Change

Human beings have a tendency to glorify the past. Some become firmly convinced that the good old days of their youth and childhood were far superior to the present. One of the earliest theories of social change was held by certain Greek philosophers who believed that humankind once lived in an ideal golden age. From this, we gradually descended to a silver, then a bronze, and finally an iron age.

A quite opposite theory of social change has been popular in Europe and the United States in the last century or two. This is the doctrine of inevitable progress, the belief that the world is getting better and better. Not even two world wars and a multitude of smaller wars have been able to shake the faith of those who firmly hold this doctrine.

Another theory of social change, popularized by Oswald Spengler and Arnold Toynbee, is that such change runs in cycles. According to their theory, institutions, societies, and civilizations pass through cycles of growth, climax, and decline. Modern civilization is no exception and is bound ultimately to disintegrate. This cycle theory of social change is based on the idea that history repeats itself. Some cycle theorists maintain that modern civilization is now on the verge of a decline, and to support this contention they point to the fate of certain past civilizations, including ancient Greece and the Roman Empire. Cycle theories vary considerably, but they all tend to support the thesis that civilizations first advance, ultimately reach a peak, and finally decline.

Other attempts to explain social change have relied on the supernatural, racial characteristics, economic conditions, cultural diffusion, or invention. Any given culture, however, is the result of too many factors to be explained adequately by any simple formula. Yet one thing is sure: Change is inevitable. Humans' relationship to their environment is dynamic, no matter where they live, and this dynamic relationship produces change.

Factors Causing Cultural Change

We now look at some of the most important social forces that cause cultural change, together with the problems that change has brought about. We begin with a discussion of technological development; then we examine the role of religion, ideologies, cultural diffusion, wars, planned group action, geography, and climate.

Technological Development. Technological development begins with discovery and invention. A **discovery** is learning something about the physical or social environment that was not known before. In the past, explorers have discovered new islands and continents,

Robot replacing workers. This 1882 cartoon was called "Demon destroying the People."

Alphabets of different cultures, from Diderot's Encyclopédie.

astronomers have discovered laws that regulate the motions of the heavenly bodies, and anthropologists have discovered many interesting differences between the cultures of preliterate peoples. Discoveries about the natural world often furnish the basis for inventions. For example, the discoveries about electricity from some of the great scientists made it possible for Thomas Edison to invent the incandescent electric lightbulb and other useful devices.

An **invention** is a new way of doing something or a new object or mechanical device developed to serve some specific purpose. It is a cultural innovation devised by one or several individual members of a social group. Inventions may be either material or nonmaterial. Familiar machines such as the lawn tractor and the airplane are material inventions. Old-age insurance and crop rotation are examples of nonmaterial inventions. One of the greatest of all nonmaterial inventions was the alphabet, which made possible our present system of writing and printing.

An invention is really a special kind of discovery, and hence no sharp line can be drawn between the two. We can call the making of fire by striking together flint stones either a discovery or an invention. All mechanical inventions involve the discovery that materials combined and used in certain ways will produce certain desired results. Inventions bring about changes in technology, and in modern societies technological change has been a powerful force behind social change.

A good example is the computer, which is changing our lifestyle and culture in many ways. Computerized robots are replacing workers in many jobs, tiny robots are being developed for medical uses, and the Internet is changing the way we shop and communicate with others. Similarly, developments in biotechnology are changing our lives and soon may make it possible for us to choose characteristics for our children and to influence medical treatment.

Technological change has become so important to understanding society that we devote an entire chapter, Chapter 6, to a deeper consideration of the issues.

Cultural Diffusion. Once a new cultural element is well established in one society, it may spread to others. **Cultural diffusion** is the name given to the spread of cultural traits from one social group to another. In other words, not all the elements found in the culture of a given group were invented or developed within that group. In most cases, the greater part of the content of any culture has been borrowed from other cultures. In most societies, cultural diffusion is an extremely important factor in social change. Societies isolated from outside contacts tend to be static, whereas those that can readily communicate with other groups constantly acquire new cultural elements. However, contact does not always lead to cultural diffusion. For example, the Amish society in the United States has significant contact with mainstream U.S. culture. Despite this contact, Amish society has maintained its separate cultural identity through careful nurturing and has shunned many modern technological developments.

Cultural diffusion, more than any other factor, has been responsible for the development of Western civilization. Western civilization was nurtured in Europe, and its center is still there. Yet most of the basic elements of this civilization did not originate in Europe but were borrowed from other peoples in other parts of the world. Our modern number system, so much more flexible than that of the Romans, was borrowed from the Arabs, who in turn borrowed it from the Hindus in India. Without this number system or a good substitute, it would be almost impossible for us to carry on the mathematical calculations now required by both business and science. Again, our alphabet, which with modifications is used for writing and printing all European languages, was borrowed originally from the Phoenicians of Africa. It seems probable that they, or a neighboring people speaking a similar Semitic language, were the original inventors.[2]

Ideas and Ideologies.   Social change may also be initiated by new ideas. Relatively simple, practical ideas may result in inventions that soon are accepted and become a recognized part of the cultural pattern—a new type of dance, a new kind of business corporation, or a new mechanical gadget. However, not all new ideas are of this type. Some represent important changes in social attitudes and basic social values. Such ideas may in time gain a powerful hold on minds, as did the concepts of "liberty, equality, and fraternity" of the French Revolution, or the civil rights movement in the United States in the 1960s. Often they come to represent hopes and aspirations that, though they can never be fully realized, can be approached in a variety of ways. Once ideas of this kind become well established in any society, they become a powerful force for continuing social change in directions that are thought to lead toward their realization. Religions, which embody people's conception of what is good and what is bad, often are vital forces for social change. For example, as we stated earlier, religious groups played an important role in the civil rights movement, and in the early 2000s Christian churches were exerting pressure on government on issues as diverse as abortion and foreign policy.

Even in the modern world, it usually takes considerable time for major new ideas to gain a firm foothold. Various writers have maintained that social change is always motivated by the discoveries or theories of great thinkers of a past generation. Karl Marx, for example, had little effect on society during his lifetime; British economist John Maynard Keynes's economic ideas of the 1930s did not have any great impact on the public and on government policies until the 1960s.

An **ideology** is an organized system of ideas for remodeling society to bring it "nearer to the heart's desire." We may regard it as a composite of ideas, values, and emotions. Those who believe in an ideology often support it with religious fervor. Fascism, communism, socialism, and democracy are all ideologies. Each has its system of values, and each would organize society—supposedly to further the common good—according to a somewhat different pattern. No ideology ever achieves the ideal society that its adherents envision. We regard our U.S. society as democratic, but we often are keenly aware that we fall short of the democratic ideal in many ways.

Collective Action.   Most social changes take place gradually and are not planned and carried out by a central agency. At times, however, social changes of importance are brought about more or less rapidly by planned group action. Group action by an entire society, such as a modern nation, usually means government action, because the government is the only agency that can make and enforce rules that in theory apply to the whole social group. Japan is a nation that has experienced a great social transformation within the past 150 years. It has changed from a feudal society to a modern, highly industrialized democracy. Much of this change has been brought about by government policies that were specifically designed to bring Japan into the modern world.

The outstanding twentieth-century examples of drastic and far-reaching social changes carried out by governments on a vast scale are found in the former Soviet Union and in China. There, in two of the largest and most populous countries of the world, when the communist leaders came into power they completely changed in a relatively short time

---

[2]The Phoenician alphabet contained only consonants. The Greeks, who were the first Europeans to appropriate this alphabet, added vowels.

many basic aspects of the political, social, and economic structure. In an attempt to create societies based on the communist ideology of Karl Marx, the state seized vast amounts of property from the middle- and upper-class owners, uprooted millions of peasants from their holdings and put them to work on collective farms or communes, and took over the operation and expansion of practically all productive enterprises. But the achievement of such broad and rapid changes was possible only through the establishment of powerful dictatorships that had small regard for the rights and freedoms of individuals.

In the 1990s, many of these communist dictatorships ended. Eastern Europe went through dramatic upheavals: Several communist systems were overthrown; the Soviet Union broke up into various countries; and all of these countries experienced enormous political, social, and economic change. What the end result will be won't be known for many years. It may be an adoption of a Western-style market economy, or it may be the establishment of some new system.

Important social changes can also be brought about in democratic countries through planned government action, but only if the action has popular support. However, such changes are implemented more slowly and are much less drastic than those that can be made by a communist society or a dictatorship. In democracies, social changes planned by government are usually embodied in legislation that is designed to meet certain social problems. For example, in the United States, acts of Congress and of state legislatures have almost eliminated the employment of child labor; at the same time, they have helped increase school attendance, both by providing free public schools and by making school attendance compulsory. Legislation under the New Deal, from about 1932 to 1937, established in their original forms our farm income–support program and our Social Security system. It also stimulated the growth of labor unions by strengthening their legal position and their bargaining power. Now, in the 2000s, those structures are being questioned.

Legislation, however, has its limitations. To be effective in promoting social change in a democracy, it must either reflect the established beliefs of the people or it must change those beliefs relatively quickly. If legislation violates what the majority of citizens believe to be their just rights and privileges, it has little chance of success. For instance, the Prohibition amendment to the U.S. Constitution, legally in force from 1919 to 1932, failed and was finally repealed because the majority of Americans felt that outlawing the sale of liquor was an unreasonable violation of their personal liberties.

Geography and Climate.   When people live in a given region over a long period of time, they become adjusted to local conditions of geography and climate. A society, for example, set on the edge of an ocean would be more prone to utilize marine resources—fish for food, shells as jewelry, and perhaps greater trade owing to the oceanic access—than would a landlocked society. Changes in the natural environment can and do occur. In extreme cases, droughts, earthquakes, the exhaustion of important natural resources, changes in climate, and the like may require radical cultural adjustments.

Geography and climate are also important factors in social change when people migrate from one region to another. The European settlers who emigrated to the Americas, Africa, Australia, and New Zealand found many differences of climate, topography, and natural changes, especially in food, clothing, houses, and ways of earning a living. We consider these issues in more detail in Chapter 5.

Language and Cultural Change

Social change takes place over long periods of time and often is difficult to discern. Because our perceptions of the past are imperfect, our knowledge of the past is also limited and imperfect. We don't know what was; we only know what is. One way to get an idea of the change that takes place is to consider the evolution of languages. Some social scientists believe that all modern languages sprang from a single root—a tiny population that probably lived in Africa or Asia about twenty thousand years ago. A sense of this evolution is shown in Figure 4.2. According to this theory, all differences in modern-day languages are the result of independent evolution of varying branches of this root language.

How much a language can evolve can be seen by comparing the Old English phrase for "How are you?" in a book like *Beowulf* (eighth century A.D.): "Hal! Geard weallas!" (it reads like a foreign language) to that same phrase in Shakespeare (sixteenth–seventeenth century A.D.): "How art thou?" to a modern variant: "How ya doin'?" Given how much languages can change without our noticing, we should not be surprised by how much cultures can change and how different cultures can be from one another.

Figure 4.2

According to some linguists, all of our languages sprang from a single root of a mother language. The diagram shows the hypothesized language tree.

Factors Stabilizing Culture

The various factors of social change lead to a dynamic, continually altering society. Change and culture will often conflict, with culture providing strong resistance to social change. In the present-day United States, underlying the many changes constantly taking place in our culture is a great body of stabilizing elements that give continuity to our way of life.

Stability of Social Norms.   In spite of the high value that some industrial societies place on so-called progress, human beings appear basically conservative. The human mind and personality are so constituted that once people acquire certain beliefs, attitudes, and patterns of behavior, they have difficulty changing them. This is especially true of the basic elements in our culture that we acquire unconsciously in the impressionable years of early childhood. Our beliefs and attitudes may include some approval of change—for example, changes in fashions—but only within limits. The mores, the principal institutions of our society, and even many of its conventions are so firmly impressed on us that they become an essential part of our own personalities. For example, the tradition that women need to be protected from the harsh realities of commercial competition, the rough and tumble of military life, and the demands of heavy physical labor played a role in the failure of the passage of the Equal Rights Amendment to the U.S. Constitution.

Habit.   A chief reason for the persistence of conventions, mores, and social institutions is that they become largely habitual for all members of the social group. **Habits** are ways of behaving that have been learned so well that they can be carried on without conscious attention. Once acquired, however, they are difficult to change because they become a part of the individual's personality.

Value Attachment.   Another reason for the persistence of conventions, mores, and institutions is that we and our group attach values to them. In the case of conventions, these values may be small, but in the case of mores and certain basic institutions they are great. When we believe that established patterns of behavior have high moral value and when, in addition, they arouse in us strong emotions, these patterns become resistant to change.

Social changes of any importance, even though favored by the majority, are likely to meet opposition from many individuals and groups who have vested interests. A **vested interest** is a privilege or advantage that an individual enjoys because of the status quo, which is the existing state of affairs. A skilled plasterer has a vested interest in the plastering trade, and is not likely to favor substituting wallboard for plaster. Various unions in the building industry, in order to protect the jobs of their members, have fought against prefabricated housing and have insisted on retention of slower, more expensive, on-the-spot building methods.

Industry and labor are not alone in opposing, for selfish reasons, the introduction of new elements into our culture. Many people stand to lose by changes in the status quo, not only materially but in power or prestige. Theologians, philosophers, and scientists have again and again opposed new ideas and new knowledge for fear that their own established beliefs and theories would be discredited.

Social Change versus Social Stability

Many of the things we value in our modern society—for example, our relatively high standards of living—could not have been brought about without a receptive attitude toward social change, because all change produces new situations. However, if change occurs very rapidly it may create new problems for which we are unprepared. Instead of introducing a better world, it can bring on periodic crises and give people a constant sense of uncertainty and insecurity. Every social group feels the need for some degree of stability. If this stability is to be maintained, change in our basic institutions must be gradual. It must take place by evolution rather than by revolution.

For any large modern society to meet the needs of its people requires a remarkably complex organization; the organization can be challenged, it can be adapted, it can be changed, but any belief that it can be destroyed and quickly replaced with something better is unrealistic. Social revolutions are never complete, and they bring few of the results that were envisioned. The communist revolution in Russia, after years of struggle and confusion, produced Stalin; and the National Socialist revolution in Germany produced Hitler.

Social Change and Social Problems

Although not all social scientists would agree on the exact nature of a social problem, for our purposes the following definition suffices. For a social problem to exist, two conditions must be fulfilled. First, there must be wide recognition of some condition that adversely affects the welfare of a significant number of people. Second, there must be a belief that this condition can and should be changed. In other words, a **social problem** is a situation that has been recognized as adversely affecting the welfare of large numbers of people and for which it is believed a solution exists. To admit the existence of a social problem clearly implies the possibility of change, for no matter how undesirable a situation may be, it is not a problem unless we believe there is a way to change it. In primitive societies, drought, famine, and pestilence may not have been regarded as problems because nothing could be done about them. They were simply accepted. However, they became problems if it was believed there were ways to avert them—for instance, by making adequate sacrifices to the gods.

In a sense, social problems are always individual problems, for it is individuals who experience their adverse effects. We call them social problems for two reasons: first, because they affect such a significant proportion of people as to constitute a threat to the welfare or safety of the whole group; and second, because they cannot be adequately met by individuals. If they are to be solved at all, it must be by some kind of group action. This becomes clear when we consider such major social problems as widespread poverty, disease, recurrent periods of mass unemployment, crime, family disorganization, and war.

As would be expected, a large modern society is much more likely to possess complex social problems than a smaller society. Larger societies often contain important subgroups with differing cultural patterns, and these subgroups are likely to be subject to inconsistencies, strains, and conflicts that speed up social change and often are intensified by it.

When we attempt to define and study any particular social problem, we encounter certain difficulties. For one thing, every social problem is closely related to a number of other social problems and is therefore highly complex. To fully understand one problem, we must know something about the others. Thus, to understand fully the problem of family disorganization and divorce, we may, for example, need to know something about poor housing, unemployment, and social classes.

There is seldom any simple or complete solution for a major social problem. The causes are always complex, and practical remedies are difficult to find or implement. Moreover, the action necessary to solve or mitigate a social problem may be effectively blocked by public indifference and ignorance and by the opposition of vested interests. This does not mean that all attempts at social improvement are useless. It does mean, however, that a number of our major social problems are likely to remain with us in some form or degree for the indefinite future.

Cultural Lag and Social Problems

Though some elements in culture may change while others remain relatively constant, the various aspects of a given culture are by no means entirely independent of one another. To illustrate, religion may have a substantial influence on technological change. On the one hand, it may encourage technological change by teaching that material progress is in accord with the divine will; on the other hand, it may discourage such change by teaching that mechanical innovations are works of the devil.

The late eminent sociologist William F. Ogburn assigned great importance to what he called *cultural lag* as a source of social disorganization. According to his theory, the culture of any society constitutes a pattern of interrelated elements. Once integration and stability have been achieved, a change in any one part of the pattern may create strains and disturbances in the closely related parts. Eventually, adjustments will be made to restore harmony, but meanwhile there may be a considerable time lag during which tension persists. In modern industrial societies, it is technological change that sets the pace. According to Ogburn's theory, technological progress produces rapid changes in the material aspects of our culture, but the nonmaterial aspects fail to adjust, or they do so only after an excessive time lag. As a result, many troublesome social problems are created.

Cultural lag is the slowness in the rate of change on one part of a culture in relation to another, resulting in a maladjustment within society. A frequently cited cultural lag is the failure of political organizations to adjust to advances in transportation. To illustrate, the present system of counties and county governments in the United States was established when the only way to travel to the county seat was by horse and buggy. Because twenty miles or so was the practical limit of a day's travel, larger units of local government would have been difficult to administer. Today there is no such restriction on travel,

*A*re You PC?

Social change affects our everyday life. A recent example of this is the PC phenomenon, which has been much in debate on college campuses and elsewhere since the early 1990s. PC stands for "politically correct." To be PC is to be attuned to some unstated but nonetheless strong and reasonably well-defined set of social norms that emphasizes minority rights, women's rights, social justice, and environmentalism. It is a derogatory term that was created in response to the social pressure on individuals to meet those norms.

In the early 1980s, the pressures on many college campuses for individuals to be PC were rather strong, but the phrase did not exist. New courses, course requirements, and departments were instituted at many schools in women's studies, ethnic studies, and the environment.

The underlying philosophy of some of these pressures went against the grain of some individuals, as did the sometimes strong-arm tactics (such as sit-ins and taking over buildings) supporters used to implement and demand change. Supporters justified these strong-arm tactics on the grounds that ours is a repressive

society and given that repression, the ends justify the means. This justification went against the grain of another Western social norm—toleration and respect for others' rights—leading a number of people, including some who support the social norms that the strong-arm tactics were meant to achieve, to repudiate the movement. It also led to the creation of the term *PC*. This term that had been used by Nazis to describe individuals who held the belief that the white Aryan race was superior to all others. The Nazi association of the term brought out the dissonance between the strong-arm tactics used by some PC supporters and the norms of toleration and respect for individual rights.

The debate between PC supporters and opponents concerns conflicting social norms—toleration versus social justice. PC supporters argue that one should not be tolerant of injustice, and that if our society were truly tolerant and maintained respect for all others, the movement wouldn't be needed. But because our society isn't, it is necessary to be intolerant of injustice and intolerance. Social science doesn't tell us whether the PC movement is right or wrong, but it does help us put it in perspective and have a better appreciation for the inevitable tensions that social change brings about.

for by automobile we can travel more than 100 miles in two hours or less. Business can be conducted by fax or through the Internet instantaneously. For example, I worked on this book while teaching university professors in Bulgaria and communicating with my U.S. publisher by phone and email. Students of government now maintain that most of our rural counties are far too small to be efficient units of local government. However, our governmental institutions are so resistant to change that any substantial modification of existing county lines is almost impossible.

Limitations of the Cultural Lag Theory

The cultural lag theory is useful, provided we clearly understand its meaning and its limitations. In the first place, we must not assume that changes in the material aspects of culture always precede changes in the nonmaterial aspects. There is a constant interaction between the two, and in the long run technological progress itself is largely dependent on certain nonmaterial factors such as social attitudes and forms of social organization. Most, if not all, of the material products of culture originate in the human mind, and new material devices will not be invented and put to use unless the nonmaterial cultural atmosphere is favorable. The rapid material progress characteristic of present-day society is itself the result of earlier changes in our nonmaterial culture, changes that made possible the development of modern machine technology. We have already called attention to some of these earlier developments. One was the increased receptivity to change that was brought about by historical movements such as the Renaissance, the Reformation, and the great voyages of discovery. Another closely related factor was the development of mental attitudes that made it possible to apply the scientific method to the search for truth.

In the second place, when changes occur in the material culture we may sometimes have difficulty in agreeing on the kinds of adjustments needed in the nonmaterial culture. Consider, for example, the invention of the automobile and its widespread adoption as a means of transportation. The automobile brought about many social changes, including changes in the customs of courtship and dating. One of its effects was to enable dating couples to escape, to some degree, the close supervision of their elders. Did this represent an unsatisfactory adjustment of our nonmaterial culture to the automobile? Some observers maintained that it did. They considered it an example of cultural lag and argued that new ways of supervising dating couples had to be devised to maintain moral standards. Others, however, regarded greater freedom in the relations between the sexes not as a problem but as a development that represented social progress.

But even if there is general agreement that the nonmaterial culture has not satisfactorily adjusted to changes in the material culture, making the desired adjustments may be difficult or, conceivably, impossible. The word *lag* implies optimistically that the satisfactory solution of social problems resulting from technological change is merely a matter of time, but in some cases this time may never come. Our society's increased medical knowledge of fetal abortive processes has only added to the social conflict surrounding that issue, for instance.

Contrasts among Cultures

The interaction between culture and social change leads not only to social problems within a society but also to problems among various societies. The reason is that different cultures often evolve along quite different paths. For example, in our culture women and men are considered equal. In certain other cultures, a woman's role is fundamentally different from a man's role. (For example, in some Islamic societies a woman is not allowed to drive a car.)

Archaic tribal societies often differ from one another greatly, but unless they are brought into contact with powerful outside influences, they tend to be relatively stable.

Industrial societies are much more subject to change. In them people's wants tend to multiply rapidly, as do the products with which to satisfy them. From one culture to another, family relations, economic activities, government, religion, and art take on an endless variety of forms.

The Interaction of Humans and Society

Though we are all, in part, products of our cultural environment, no two persons will have exactly the same personal experiences. Furthermore, they will not inherit biologically the same physical and nervous constitutions, and these inherited differences will cause them to react differently to many of the elements in their cultural environment.

Thus, the study of humankind is a complicated one that moves from unique traits of individuals to general aspects of society and back again to unique aspects of individuals. Therefore, such a study must encompass a wide range of issues.

Cultural Relativism

The doctrine of **cultural relativism** asserts that all cultures are for the most part equally valid. That is, cultures develop in a way that best suits the population's needs, and the cultural traits within a culture have a specific purpose.

Today, few students of society would question the proposition that any culture that has enabled a group to meet its basic needs, and to survive over a long period of time, is worthy of respect, as are the individuals who practice its customs and follow its moral precepts. Cultures are not as a whole good, bad, right, or wrong; they simply exist and must be judged relative to their own value system. Therefore, to understand other cultures, we must try to look at them through the eyes of those who have been brought up under their influence rather than through our own eyes. If we do this, we may find that these cultures meet needs we have failed to recognize. For example, nineteenth-century missionaries to certain South Sea islands were shocked to find that the native women wore no clothing above the waist. Part of their mission was to convert the women to wearing Mother Hubbards, shapeless dresses that kept their bodies well covered. To the missionaries, this seemed a great gain. But from a health standpoint, it may have been unfortunate. In the tropical rainy climate of the

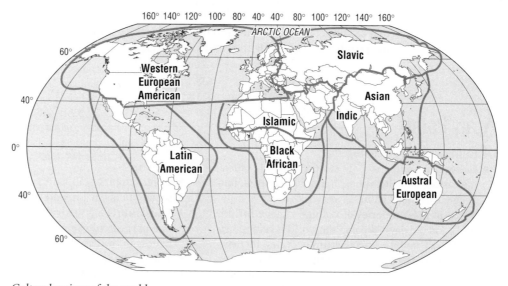

Cultural regions of the world.

islands, the Mother Hubbards were wet much of the time, and they may have contributed to poor health.

Ethnocentrism is the tendency to judge other cultures by a person's own culture and its standards, the belief of a group that its people and its way of life are superior to all others. An extreme example in the twentieth century was the Nazi doctrine that the Germans were a superrace. In modern societies, feelings of ethnocentrism and chauvinism increase during times of insecurity or economic depression. Pre-Nazi Germany was in a severe depression, which many believe enabled Adolf Hitler to rise to power. In the late twentieth century, we saw, or were forced to recognize, the power of religion as a divisive force. In countries such as Northern Ireland, India, Pakistan, and the former Yugoslavia, opposing religious groups have fought bitterly with each other within their own borders, and their internal differences can affect their relations with foreign countries as they sometimes attempt to influence beliefs in other nations. Frequently, these religious convictions are mixed with political problems, making the cultural issues complex and recalcitrant.

At one time, ethnocentrism may have had a survival value for some nonliterate tribal societies by giving them confidence in the superiority of their own people and own way of life. But nowadays, although ethnocentrism still contributes to the cohesion of a society, survival is likely to depend on achieving understanding and cooperation among races, peoples, and nations. Although some ethnocentrism is necessary to hold a society together, the conscious cultivation of ethnocentrism generally results in misunderstanding, prejudice, ill feeling, and conflict.

Approach to the Study of Society

In this book we are primarily concerned with the nature of modern U.S. society. Most of the discussion is therefore centered on our own culture and its basic values and on the problems that arise in connection with efforts to achieve these values. However, we can understand our own society better if we see it in perspective. Hence, throughout the book we call attention to other societies and cultures, to the characteristics common to all cultures, and to the differences that distinguish them.

Because it is not the function of science to determine social values, we simply assume for the most part the validity of the basic ideals of our own democratic society, and occasionally we attempt to clarify these ideals. But our principal efforts are concerned with giving a picture of the general character of U.S. society. We explain its values and its social institutions. We also discuss its failures to achieve its goals and the frustration and conflict that are sometimes the result, and we consider the nature of its major problems and explore the possibilities of solving them through social action.

$\mathcal{K}$ey Points

- Culture holds society together.
- Important elements of culture include social norms, social institutions, material products, language, and social values.
- Three popular theories of cultural change include the "good old days" theory, "the world is getting better" theory, and the "change runs in cycles" theory.
- Five factors that cause culture to change are technology, cultural diffusion, ideas and ideologies, collective action, and geography and climate.
- Three factors stabilizing culture are stability of social norms, habit, and value attachment.
- The cultural lag theory states that a change in any one part of culture may create strains and disturbances in the closely related parts.
- The doctrine of cultural relativism states that all cultures are for the most part equally valid.

Some Important Terms

conventions (71)
cultural alternatives (74)
cultural diffusion (77)
cultural evolution (69)
cultural integration (74)
cultural lag (83)
cultural objects (artifacts) (72)
cultural relativism (85)
cultural universal (74)
culture (69)

discovery (76)
ethnocentrism (86)
habits (81)
ideology (78)
Internet (75)
invention (77)
language (72)
laws (72)
mores (72)
multiculturalism (69)

pluralism (70)
social evolution (76)
social institution (72)
socialization (69)
social problem (82)
social values (73)
society (70)
vested interest (81)

Questions for Review and Discussion

1. What is the definition of culture given in the text?
2. What is cultural evolution?
3. Do the authors see monoculturalism and multiculturalism as opposites? Why or why not?
4. What are some examples of conventions, mores, and laws found in U.S. society?
5. What are social institutions?
6. What are social values? Give some examples. Do you think Americans could ever accept infanticide as a positive social value? Why or why not?
7. Why are the cultures of primitive societies more integrated than the cultures of modern industrial societies?
8. Explain the relationship between culture and society.
9. What developments of the last five or six centuries do you think have been of greatest importance in speeding up the rate of social change? Explain why in each case.
10. Distinguish between the concepts of social evolution and social change.
11. Explain the relation to social change of the following: discovery and invention, cultural diffusion, ideas and ideologies.
12. Why does social change usually encounter strong resistance? Is this fortunate or unfortunate? Explain.
13. What is a social problem? Why is a particular social problem often difficult to define or isolate?
14. State the theory of cultural lag and discuss its limitations.
15. What is cultural relativism? How does this concept relate to ethnocentrism?
16. Of today's major social problems, which three seem to you most critical? Defend your choices.
17. Sometimes we are dissatisfied with aspects of our social system. Should we therefore dismantle it completely and start over? Why or why not?

Internet Questions

1. The site www.toolpack.com/culture.html discusses cultural change at the organizational (business) level. What is organizational culture? Name the four companies used as examples of successful cultures.
2. Look through the website for the United States Golf Association, www.usga.org. Is the USGA a social institution? Do golfers comprise a society?
3. Go to www.youtube.com/watch?v=Wy9wXCxVxhw and watch part one of the video about the Navajo. What resulted from the interaction of Anglo-American and Navajo cultures? What term from this chapter best illustrates the views of Civil War general William Sherman and the actions of the U.S. government concerning the education of Navajo children?
4. Go to www.youtube.com/watch?v=_HJNVPKRtzY &feature=related and watch the second part of the video about the Navajo. Why were the Navajo codes never broken by the Japanese?
5. According to www.bmezine.com/culture/A60524/cltamode.html, what is the underlying reason that businesses often reject applicants with body piercings or tattoos?

For Further Study

Eberstadt, M., *Home-Alone America: The Hidden Toll of Day Care, Wonder Drugs, and Other Parent Substitutes*, New York: Sentinel, 2004.

Friedman, Thomas L., *The World Is Flat: A Brief History of the Twenty-First Century*, Penguin/Allen Lane, 2006.

Henig, Robin Marantz, *Pandora's Baby: How the First Test-Tube Baby Sparked the Reproductive Revolution*, New York: Houghton Mifflin, 2004.

Mead, Margaret, *Continuities in Cultural Evolution*, New Haven, CT: Yale University Press, 1964.

O'Keefe, Kevin, *The Average American: The Extraordinary Search for the Nation's Most Ordinary Citizen*, New York: Public Affairs, 2005.

Schlosser, Erik, *Fast Food Nation*, New York: Perennial/HarperCollins, 2004.

Shweder, Richard, *Why Do Men Barbecue? Recipes for Cultural Diversity*, Cambridge, MA: Harvard University Press, 2003.

Suskind, Ron, *The One Percent Doctrine: Deep Inside America's Pursuit of Its Enemies Since 9/11*, New York: Simon & Schuster, 2006.

Varmus, Harold, *The Art and Politics of Science*, New York, NY: W. W. Norton, 2008.

Weiner, Mark S., *Black Trials: Citizenship from the Beginnings of Slavery to the End of Caste*, New York: Knopf, 2004.

Zeigler, Alexis, *Conscious Cultural Evolution: Understanding Our Past, Choosing Our Future*, Charlottesville, VA: Ecodem Press, 2000.

WWW   Adherents of Cultural Relativism www.quantonics.com/Famous_CRites.html

WWW   Business Culture Guide www.executiveplanet.com

WWW   Center for Applied Linguistics www.cal.org

WWW   Cultural Studies Central www.culturalstudies.net

WWW   Folklore and Mythology Electronic Texts www.pitt.edu/~dash/folktexts.html

WWW   Internet Society www.isoc.org

WWW   Social Change Links gsociology.icaap.org

Geography, Demography, Ecology, and Society

After reading this chapter, you should be able to:

- Identify the major countries on a map of the world
- Explain why many people believe population growth is a problem
- State the Malthusian theory and explain how technology can affect its predictions
- Explain how culture and environment interact
- Explain how geography, population, culture, and the natural environment interact—and affect the ecological balance

Ecology is rather like sex—every new generation likes to think they were the first to discover it.

—Michael Allaby

In the last chapter, we discussed culture, the glue that holds society together. In this chapter, we look at society from three slightly different perspectives—geographic, demographic, and ecological—discussing each in terms of its interrelationships with culture. Each of these perspectives highlights certain problems that societies face and provides a foundation for a better understanding of those problems.

Geography

In 1988, the National Geographic Society commissioned a study called "Geography: An International Gallup Survey." It tested 10,820 people in nine countries on their ability to identify sixteen spots on a map of the world. U.S. citizens could identify about half the places, but citizens aged eighteen to twenty-four could identify fewer than seven. People in Sweden did the best. In the early 2000s, the situation hadn't changed; as a follow-up, National Geographic-Roper conducted a survey on geographic literacy among young adults and found that only 37 percent could find Iraq on a map, and less than half of the U.S. citizens could identify France or Japan; just one-half could find the state of New York. The survey also looked at the world's cultural, economic, and natural resources. U.S. citizens were least likely to know that the Taliban was based in Afghanistan, and over one-third estimated the population of the United States to be ten times the actual number. (You can take an on-line version of the Roper test yourself by visiting www.nationalgeographic.com/roper2006/html.)

On the next page, you'll find a map of the world. To keep our quiz easy, we are asking you to identify only thirteen countries (leaving out the other three spots the National

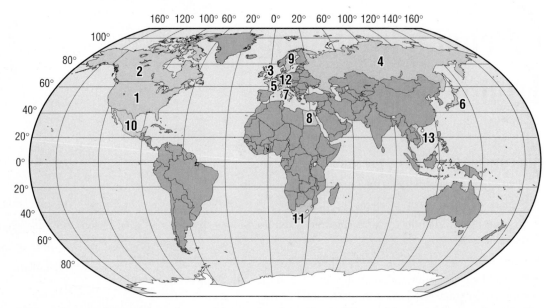

A geography quiz. Can you name the countries numbered on this map? Be careful—countries sometimes change their names suddenly. Within the past twenty years, Burma renamed itself Myanmar, Kampuchea changed its name back to Cambodia, and Zaire changed its name to Democratic Republic of the Congo (its name before it was called "Zaire" was "The Congo"). The answers to our quiz follow (they're printed upside down).

1. United States 2. Canada 3. United Kingdom 4. Russia 5. France 6. Japan 7. Italy 8. Egypt 9. Sweden 10. Mexico 11. South Africa 12. Germany 13. Vietnam

Geographic asked about). The countries we ask you to name are numbered. Let's hope you're as smart as the Swedes (who scored about 75 percent).

Even if you scored 100 percent, you do not necessarily know geography.[1] Geography is far more than the knowledge of where places are. **Geography** is a social science that focuses on the spatial interaction of human beings with each other and with their physical environment. Geography considers questions such as why cities are located where they are, how the environment shapes society's culture, and why some areas develop while others don't. For example, one explanation why central Africa was little touched by Western culture before twentieth-century technological advances in transportation is that most of its rivers are too difficult to navigate—it was just too expensive and difficult to get a boat up the rivers into the interior of the continent.

Where does such knowledge fit into the social sciences? As we emphasized in Chapter 1, enormous overlap exists among the social sciences. Therefore, it is not only geographers who have considered the location of cities, the effect of environment on culture, and why some areas develop rather than others. Sociologists have considered these points, too. In fact, sociologists and some social scientists other than geographers were the first to raise many of the issues we discuss in this chapter. When geographers are asked about this, they say that sociologists actually are geographers. That claim seems to be a bit of social science equivocation, but it is less important to know which social science has had a particular idea than it is to know the idea itself.

---

[1]If you think you did well on our little quiz, remember that the places we chose were some of the most obvious. If we had asked you for cities, rivers, and oceans, the quiz would have been more difficult.

Do You Understand Space?

Geographical facts are concerned with space. Where is New York City, and how far is it from Wichita, Kansas? If you had the time and money, could you drive from Singapore to Paris?

Here is a short quiz on such geographical facts. The answers are below, but they are printed upside down (a manipulation of space).

1. What is the capital of California?
2. In what country is the mouth of the river Nile?
3. What is the largest city in the United States?
4. What is the difference between the Arctic and the Antarctic?
5. Japan is an archipelago. What is an archipelago?
6. If you superimposed Indonesia on a map of the United States, it would be as wide as the continental United States. Where is Indonesia?
7. Popocateptl is a volcano that had not erupted since 1802, but in late 2000 it began to spew flames and ashes considered so dangerous the government evacuated more than 40,000 people from their homes along the base of the mountain.

Where is Popocateptl? Vesuvius is another famous volcano. It erupted in a.d. 79, burying an entire city in cinders and ashes. Where is Vesuvius?

8. What is the largest city in Canada?
9. What country or countries border the Black Sea?
10. Venice is famous because so many of its "streets" are really canals. Can you name another city that is laced with waterways that serve as streets?

Answers: 1. Sacramento. 2. Egypt. 3. New York City. 4. There are a lot of differences, but the most dramatic is that the Arctic is at the northern top of the world and the Antarctic is at the southern bottom of the world. Others: The Arctic is water; the Antarctic is land. The Arctic has people and polar bears; the Antarctic has penguins but not native people. 5. A string of islands. 6. Northwest of Australia. 7. Popocateptl is in Mexico and Vesuvius is in Italy. Both are still active. 8. Toronto. 9. Russia, Georgia, Ukraine, Turkey, Bulgaria, and Romania. 10. There are many. Stockholm, Amsterdam, Bangkok, Jakarta, and Vancouver are some. Where are those cities, by the way? (Sweden, Netherlands, Thailand, Indonesia, Canada.) You probably can think of some others.

Demography

Societies are made up of people. Whereas geography approaches the study of society by means of a spatial dimension, demography approaches it through a people dimension.

Demography is the study of the number and characteristics of a population. It is concerned not only with the number of people in an area but also with the factors that may be causing their number to increase or decrease. These include matters such as the state of health care and sanitation, the extent to which birth control is practiced, and the availability of food and other resources. Further, demography concerns the distribution of people among countries and regions and the different kinds of people who make up any given population and their physical, mental, and cultural characteristics. In this connection, demographers classify and count people on the basis of characteristics such as age, gender, marital status, occupation, income, nationality, and race.

Population Estimates

When we add up the population statistics for all countries, we conclude that there were slightly less than 7 billion people in 2010. Population is divided up unevenly among countries and regions (see Figure 5.1). China has the largest population of any country, with about 1.3 billion people; and Asia, with about 4 billion people, has the largest population of any region.

A global inventory of human settlements (taken by satellite). The lighted areas show dense settlements that have income necessary to pay for lighting.

(a) The twenty most populous countries
in 2009 (in millions) (estimated)

China	1,339
India	1,166
European Union	492
United States	307
Indonesia	240
Brazil	199
Pakistan	176
Bangladesh	156
Nigeria	149
Russia	140
Japan	127
Mexico	111
Philippines	98
Vietnam	87
Ethiopia	85
Egypt	83
Germany	82
Turkey	77
Dem. Rep. of the Congo	69
Iran	66

(b) Growth in world population: 1950 to 2050

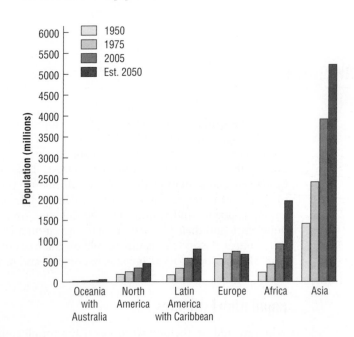

Figure 5.1

The populations of the twenty largest countries are listed in (a). In (b), distribution of the world's population by regions is given for 1950, 1975, 2005, and estimates for 2050. (Some of the changes are due to changes as to which region countries are included.) Note that Oceania includes Australia. (Sources: CIA World Factbook; Population Division of the Department of Economic and Social Affairs of the United Nations Secretariat.)

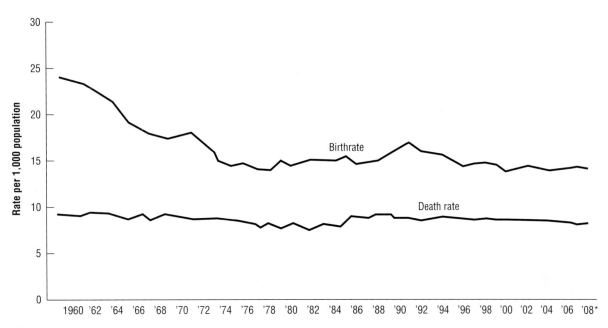

Figure 5.2

U.S. birthrates and death rates, 1960 to 2008. (Sources: U.S. Bureau of the Census; U.S. Department of Health and Human Services, National Vital Statistics Report.)

*2008 estimate.

Determinants of Population Growth

Because two key determinants of the population of any country are its death rate and its birthrate, these deserve special consideration. Figure 5.2 shows the U.S. birthrates and death rates since 1960.

The current world death rate is considerably lower than in the distant past. How much further the death rate will drop in coming years will depend both on changes in the age composition of the world population and on the rate of advance in medical science. Although some further reduction in the death rate can be predicted, unless we make great advances in controlling degenerative diseases and the aging process itself, the future of population growth will depend largely on the trend of the birthrate. As death rates decline, the world population will increase unless birthrates also fall. Developing countries have already seen their populations increase because of their declining death rates, despite the efforts of some of them to decrease their birthrates.

In Europe and the United States, the birthrate has been declining since the nineteenth century, although upswings have occurred periodically in one country or another. In the United States, for example, although the birthrate rose slightly in the beginning of the 1990s, most demographers believed this was a temporary phenomenon, and the long-run decline of the birthrate will likely continue due to social and economic forces that make people less willing to accept the trouble, expense, and responsibility involved in raising large families.

Birth control has been so effective in the United States, Japan, and western Europe that their population growth has slowed to a crawl or even begun to decline. In less developed countries where children play an important economic as well as social role in the family, the population growth has continued at a high rate despite governmental attempts to slow it down. In India, a program to force sterilization was a factor in the fall of the government of Indira Gandhi in 1977. She was later reelected and the program was significantly modified.

In China, strong social and economic pressures to have only one child are applied to families. These include peer pressure (families deciding to have more than one child often are socially ostracized), economic pressure (families deciding to have more than one child are deprived of certain rights to housing, whereas those agreeing to have only one child are financially rewarded), and counseling (the party leaders visit and explain the reasons and need for birth control). The one-child program has not halted the rise in the birthrate because, despite official pressures and even fines of as much as $1,000 for families having more than one child, many couples are choosing to have more children.

Probably the most original approach to reducing the birthrate exists in Thailand, where the head of the family planning services uses a condom as his calling card. There, rather than university names or slogans on T-shirts, many wear T-shirts with the message, "A Condom a Day Keeps the Doctor Away." Contraceptive information is printed on things such as bottle caps, towels, and ice cream sticks.

The Growth of Population over Time

The past history of population has been one of significant but not continual growth. Instead, it has been marked by periods of expansion and contraction. Since 1800, however, the world population has grown rapidly.

Why Population Has Grown Rapidly since the 1800s. The great increase in world population since 1800 has resulted directly from a continuing decline of the death rate. Two factors are responsible for this: first, great advances in sanitation and health care, and second, a relatively rapid increase in the per capita output of both food and manufactured goods, so that for large numbers of people standards of living rose substantially above subsistence level. In part, the increase in per capita output was made possible by the opening up for trade and settlement of some of the undeveloped areas of the world. Principally, however, the increase was a result of the Industrial Revolution. The great advances of science and technology in the nineteenth and twentieth centuries made it possible for the world to support a rapidly rising population. Furthermore, in Western industrial countries, not only has it been feasible to support larger populations, but it has been possible to support them at higher standards of living than were known in the past.

Unequal Population Growth since the Late 1800s. In the latter part of the nineteenth century, some of the less developed parts of the world began to experience some of the benefits of modern science, industry, and transportation. Sanitation and improved health care began to reduce the death rate and to increase the rate of population growth. Some of the less developed regions of the world, such as Asia and Latin America, made substantially greater gains in population than Europe, the United States, and Canada.

However, increases in population in the developing areas of the world often occurred at the expense of standards of living. Birthrates remained high and production expanded slowly. If an increase in the food supply temporarily put off famine or relieved malnutrition, it was soon matched by a further increase in population. Since 1900, the population of Asia has increased fivefold; today, nearly 60 percent of the people of the world are found there.

Population Growth in the Future. As you can see in Figure 5.3, demographers believe that world population will grow more and more slowly. They see the net gains in population decreasing at the beginning of the twenty-first century and almost ending by the beginning

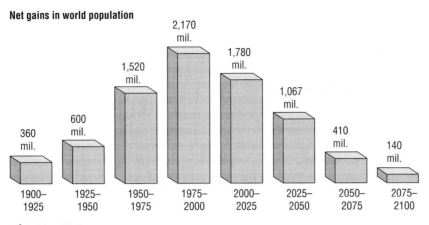

Net gains in world population

Period	Net gain
1900–1925	360 mil.
1925–1950	600 mil.
1950–1975	1,520 mil.
1975–2000	2,170 mil.
2000–2025	1,780 mil.
2025–2050	1,067 mil.
2050–2075	410 mil.
2075–2100	140 mil.

Figure 5.3

Population growth's peak period. Current trends suggest that additions to world population will come more slowly in the future. (Source: Population Division of the United Nations.)

of the twenty-second century. That decrease will not help equalize the population among areas; the rate of population growth is, and will probably continue to be, much higher in some areas than in others.

The Problem of Counting

The population figures given in this chapter are *estimates*; some are not very good estimates. In fact, we have practically no population figures based on an actual census except for those of relatively recent years. A **census** is an official, systematic count of the number of people who live in a given area. Usually, when people are counted, other kinds of information about them, such as age and gender, are also gathered. Lacking any census figures, we can make only rough guesses about populations and population changes that occurred before the latter part of the eighteenth century.

The first reliable census of a European country was taken by Sweden in 1749. In the United States, the first census was taken in 1790. About that time, several other European countries began to take censuses, and by 1850 reasonably accurate figures were available for western Europe, the United States, and some countries in other parts of the world. Today, we have fairly dependable population statistics for most countries, yet even the simplest numbers, such as how many people there are in a country, often are subject to debate. Although U.S. census figures are about the best in the world, after all the counting of our full 1990 census was done, there were still disputes about how many people were missed. The Census Bureau accepted that it actually missed about 12 million people in its count and that it double counted about 7 million people, making its count about 5 million (12 million minus 7 million) too low. Final compilation of the U.S. census of 2000 shows the total U.S. population at 281,421,906. This means that 33 million people were added to the total population from 1990 to 2000, representing the largest increase ever in population from census to census. The U.S. Census Bureau believes that this may be because this time there was better counting of undocumented immigrants.

Why are the statistics not better? Ask yourself how you would work out a system to count more than 300 million people constantly on the move, including homeless people and illegal aliens, and you'll quickly see why. There is a significant debate about whether sampling techniques should be used to "fill in" for the numbers of people who are missed when they are not individually counted. The issue was politically charged because allocation of federal grants is often dependent on formal census counts. The moral of this story is that social scientists use census data, but they use them carefully. They use their own estimates of the future even more carefully.

The Malthusian Theory

For more than a century, most discussions of the population problem have started from the theory of Thomas Robert Malthus concerning the relationship of population to the means of human subsistence. Malthus was a Church of England clergyman and an early English economist. In 1798, he published a short treatise called "An Essay on the Principle of Population as It Affects the Future Improvement of Society." During the next thirty years or more, he revised this treatise six times. The seventh and final edition was not published until 1834, after the author's death. Throughout all these editions, the basic argument remained the same, but in the second and later editions Malthus brought together a considerable amount of data to support his population doctrines.

Population and Means of Subsistence

Reduced to its simplest terms, the **Malthusian theory** is the belief that a population tends to outrun the means of subsistence. This was not a new idea, but Malthus developed it with such clarity and force that his treatise attracted wide attention. He contended that people are impelled to increase their numbers by a powerful natural urge, the attraction between male and female. As a result, if there are no obstacles population will increase rapidly and without limit. Furthermore, it will increase in geometric ratio—that is, by multiplication. By this Malthus meant that if a population could double in, say, twenty-five years, it would double again in the next twenty-five years, and so on indefinitely. He believed, however, that the means of subsistence could be increased only in arithmetic ratio—in other words, slowly and

Crowded street in New Delhi.

to a limited extent. Consequently, population would always tend to press against the food supply. When the food supply became inadequate to support more people, any further increase in population would be prevented by the "positive" checks of malnutrition, famine, disease, and war.

Malthus's belief that population growth would necessarily tend to outrun means of subsistence was based on the law of diminishing returns. In terms of the relationships between land, labor, and food output, the **law of diminishing returns** means that if more and more people are employed on a given area of land, even though total output may continue to expand, beyond a certain point average output per worker will shrink.

The amount of good farmland in the world is limited. Once all the undeveloped regions of the earth have been settled and cultivated more or less intensively, further attempts to increase food production will become less and less effective because they will bring into operation the law of diminishing returns. It will still be possible to increase output by employing more workers on the land already cultivated or by cultivating land that is less fertile. However, assuming no advances in agricultural technology, this will bring about a decrease in the average output per worker, a decrease that will become greater and greater as attempts are made to raise production to higher and higher levels. It is possible that advances in agricultural technology might, for a long time, more than offset this tendency toward diminishing returns, but they could not do so indefinitely if population continued to grow. Sooner or later, the amount of land per person would become impossibly small.

Malthus recognized that certain preventive checks might conceivably slow population growth by reducing the birthrate. These preventive checks he summarized under the general heading of "moral restraint." By this term he apparently referred to premarital chastity and late marriage. However, he did not believe that these preventive checks were likely to be practiced sufficiently to have much effect in keeping down births. Malthus apparently opposed both postmarital abstinence and contraception. He thought that marriage and its sexual satisfaction should carry with them the risks of bringing children into the world along with the responsibility to support them. Otherwise, people would get something for nothing and be deprived of their main incentive for economic improvement.

Because Malthus had little hope that the preventive checks would be effective in keeping population from exerting pressure on the means of subsistence, he was pessimistic about the chances of greatly improving the economic condition of most people. However, in the final edition of his essay, he recognized that conditions in Europe were slowly improving in spite of the growth of population, and he expressed the hope that some way might yet be found to make possible the "gradual and progressive improvement" of human society.

The Concept of Optimal Population

Given the level of technological development, in any country growth of population beyond a certain point would mean lower standards of living. Relative shortages of farmlands, fuels, timber, metals, and other resources would develop. On the other hand, a very small population would also have disadvantages. In very thinly populated areas, it is often difficult to maintain law and order, to provide medical and hospital services, or to provide schools. Also, there are not enough people to build adequate roads or to make it worthwhile to operate public transportation services. The **optimal population** is the population that would maximize welfare for its members. What, then, is the optimum, or best, size of population from the standpoint of maximizing welfare?

Actually, there is no way of determining with even approximate accuracy what the optimal population of a country would be at any given stage in its development. Yet for any country, there is likely a point beyond which an increase in population would strain its resources and reduce average output per worker, and hence reduce standards of living.

This view, however, is disputed by Julian Simon, author of *The Ultimate Resource,* who argued that people are the ultimate resource and that there can be no such thing as too many people. People create ideas, and as they do they create the technology by which the world can support an ever-larger population.

Most demographers do not share Simon's optimism. They believe that India, Pakistan, and China have already exceeded their optimal quantity and that the United States and western Europe are approaching theirs. But such views are primarily held by demographers from the United States and western Europe who have a Western cultural bias, and any statements about optimal population are inevitably culturally determined.

Poor have-not nations, for example, lay the blame for shortages of resources and other goods on the excessively wasteful policies of developed countries, with their emphasis on consumption rather than conservation. Some critics claim that Western nations are using the population issue and the need for reduced birthrates in countries with high birthrates as another form of imperialist control over these areas, which were so recently freed from colonialism.

The Question of Population Quality

In the past, some students of human society have been concerned about the possibility that social forces would bring about a serious deterioration of the biological quality of human populations. They feared that the danger would be greatest in the countries that have made the most social and economic progress. This deterioration, they felt, might take two forms: (1) a decline of the physical quality and stamina of individuals, with an increasing incidence of physical defects, and (2) a decline of native intelligence—that is, the capacity for mental development.

Their arguments as to why this might happen were varied. One was that the advances we have made in medicine and science have meant, among other results, that it is easier for children who are weak or have physical disabilites to survive, grow to maturity, and have children of their own. Modern medicine makes the principle of the survival of the fittest inoperative, or greatly weakened. In short, they argue that, in a worst-case scenario, humanitarianism and science, instead of saving the human race, will ultimately destroy it.

A second argument being made today is a socioeconomic one. It goes as follows: With the development of the two-income family, intelligent individuals will choose careers over marriage and family and will have few children, leaving the less advantaged and less educated to bear the majority of the children. To support this view, they usually point to the difference in the birthrate between the upper and middle classes on the one hand and the less advantaged classes on the other.

No one can be certain to what extent economic and social success result from inborn qualities that the upper classes possess in greater measure than the other classes. We know that individual success depends on both social environment and biological inheritance. There is always an interplay between the two. But to move from this obvious fact to a belief that we can determine whether society will be better or worse off when one socioeconomic group has children while another does not is a difficult step that few are willing to take. Moreover, most people are unwilling even to consider the social measures required to ensure that only certain groups have reproductive rights.

Given modern developments in genetic engineering, these issues are likely to become more and more important. For example, it is now possible with amniocentesis to check a fetus for gender and for some birth defects long before it is born. Eggs from one woman can be transplanted into another, and sperm can be frozen to be used for artificial insemination. Some time in this century, it may be possible to change the genetic characteristics of sperm and eggs so that children's characteristics can be controlled. In principle, couples might go to a genetic engineering company and order the type of child they want ("girl who will grow up to be 5 feet 7 inches tall and weigh 128 pounds, with an IQ of 217," and so forth). The questions society faces are: Should such technological advances be allowed to continue? And if they are, who should do the specifying?

Some societies have taken an active role in trying to control the genetic qualities of their population. For instance, Singapore, whose government has successfully administered severe laws against drug dealing, pornography, and littering, attempted in the 1980s to institute a program whereby extra privileges were promised to women university graduates who married and had children. At the same time, it was proposed that bonuses of $5,000 be awarded to less educated mothers who submitted to sterilization. The government's stated reasons for these proposals were that uneducated women were having twice the number of children as college graduates were, and the prime minister claimed that this would "deplete the talent pool" and that the "level of competence would decline." However, women and others perceived the program as unfair; scientists questioned the assumptions on which it was based; less educated women did not want to be sterilized, even for $5,000; women did not want to be treated as breeding stock; and the experiment was withdrawn after about a year and a half.

"Frankly, I think we'll regret introducing these organisms into the environment."

*E*cology: The Interaction of Geography, Demography, and Environment

Geography and demography come together in a consideration of environmental issues and ecology. The **environment** is the sum of all the external influences that impinge on the human organism. These influences exert their effects through physical stimuli that produce sights, sounds, tastes, smells, and other bodily sensations. These sensations make us aware of our environment, and through them we are able to interpret this environment and react to it.

The **social environment** is composed of the elements in our surroundings that are human or of human origin. The **natural environment** is composed of the nonhuman elements in our surroundings. The general character of our social environment depends chiefly on the culture of the group to which we belong. The character of our natural environment depends primarily on the climate, water resources, soil, topography, plant and animal life, and mineral resources of the part of the world we live in. However, once human beings have lived in an area for a long time, they are certain to have made changes, for better or worse, in their environment. It then becomes difficult to draw a sharp line between the constructed physical environment and some aspects of the natural environment.

The Ecological Balance

Ecology is the science concerned with the interactions between living things and their environment. The environment of each species of organism includes not only the inanimate world but also all other living species that affect it directly or indirectly. It includes the population density of its own members and the character of their behavior.

Human ecology is the part of ecology that deals with the way in which human societies adjust to their environments. It considers the processes by which populations adapt to their surroundings, taking into account the technology and the types of social organization by which adjustment is achieved. Human ecology applies some of the findings of the biological sciences to problems dealt with by the social sciences.

In the world of nature, there is normally a movement toward ecological balance. **Ecological balance** is the term applied to the state achieved when each plant or animal species, with its own characteristics and needs, has adjusted to its environment and survived, and when other species, which have likewise adjusted to the environment, prevent it from expanding indefinitely and from crowding them out. Most species depend on other species for food or for meeting other needs. Though the natural ecological balance is not absolutely static, normally it changes slowly over long periods of time. New species that can make superior adjustments evolve and may destroy or crowd out old species and render the latter extinct, or changes in climate may occur such that some species cannot survive.

Modern times have brought rapid changes in the ecological balance in many parts of the world. Sometimes, the results have been good from the human point of view, but sometimes they have been almost disastrous. When rabbits were introduced into Australia where they had no natural enemies and multiplied by the millions, they became a national problem. By building the St. Lawrence Seaway, engineers allowed lampreys to enter the Great Lakes, where they almost completely destroyed the whitefish. People

A forest of skyscrapers and signs in New York City.

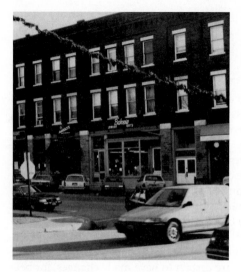

Hometown, USA.

have caused the introduction of insect pests from one part of the world to another, often with disastrous results. After World War II, the nearly worldwide use of an insecticide called DDT did indeed control or eliminate undesirable insects, but it also destroyed or damaged other forms of animal life and even human health.

Examples of threats to the ecological balance are many: global warming, industrial pollution, smokestack emissions, acid rain, depletion of water tables, and paving over of fertile soil and plant and animal habitats. These by no means exhaust the list, and we have not even attempted to describe ecological catastrophes on whole continents, such as Africa. Since the 1970s, the United States has had to face the fact that many industrial, military, and agricultural chemicals are not only lethally affecting animal life but also exercising long-term effects on human health, and that the cost of eliminating these chemicals and repairing their ravages (where possible) is astronomical. The costs are incalculable of policing hazardous waste disposal, discovering and salvaging previously used sites, finding alternative chemicals to those that have caused trouble, and devising safe methods for disposal of wastes from indispensable activities such as radioactive medical technology. Today, given snowballing technological growth, the possibility of irreversible change is enormous. For example, the explosion in worldwide commerce and travel has already meant that plants, animals, and insects have traveled outside their natural habitats and are crowding out or eliminating plants and animals in the localities to which they emigrate. Some scientists predict that, in that same way, the migration of viruses will spread nearly untreatable disease far from the sites to which such viruses were formerly confined.

Pollution

A major concern of ecologists is **pollution**—the destruction of our natural resource base by the productive process. Over the past fifty years, there has been extensive pollution of rivers, lakes, and forests by sewage and industrial wastes. As early as the 1950s, even in such a large body of water as Lake Erie, pollution reached a level that destroyed commercial fishing and made most beaches unusable. Pure air also has become scarce in many of our urban centers, where the inhabitants often must breathe a mixture of air combined with auto fumes, dust, and various waste products from trash fires, incinerators, and the smokestacks and flares of industrial plants. Improperly disposed toxic chemicals and various noxious waste products have invaded the soil in some areas, and sometimes whole communities must be moved while their former homesites are cleaned up. In other communities, people suspect that various illnesses are caused by this kind of problem, but no cleanup seems immediately practical. In the United States, a federal law enacted near the end of the twentieth century mandated that by 2000 nuclear waste must be safely disposed of in sites where no leakage will occur for "thousands of years." This mandate has proved impossible to implement, partly because it is seemingly beyond current technology, but principally because people do not want such a site anywhere near where they live, and we are seeing much vigorous disagreement as localities all strive to avoid being chosen. NIMBY (Not In My Back Yard) has become a watchword of modern times.

Some pollution is an inevitable consequence of production, presenting society with a trade-off: Do we want more material things, or do we want a more pristine environment? In making that decision, both the costs and benefits must be considered.

Although people can agree on the need for conservation and strong antipollution efforts when costs are not considered, when costs are considered there is significantly less agreement. Let's consider some of these costs. They involve restrictions on individual actions, relocation of industry and jobs, new bureaucracy, and the development of expensive new technology. In assessing the issue of pollution, the costs as well as the benefits must be considered. Therefore, it is unlikely that we will decide to institute a "no pollution" policy; that would be impossible to implement. And even approaching a standard of "little" pollution would be too expensive. Instead we are likely to choose an "optimal level" of pollution.

Since the 1960s, the United States has made considerable gains in fighting pollution, but it has not been easy. The central problem is what is called the "tragedy of the commons." Because the environment belongs to society and not to specific individuals, no individual has the incentive to care for it. A number of governmental antipollution agencies have been established. The **Environmental Protection Agency (EPA)** is the most important government antipollution agency; it directs antipollution efforts and monitors environmental problems. Some of its gains have been impressive. In the early 1950s, Lake Erie was so polluted by untreated sewage from surrounding areas that many forms of animal life could not inhabit it. Today, it is well on the way to recovery. Sewage treatment plants were mandated, and firms were prevented from dumping industrial waste into the lake.

Laws also were passed dealing with oil spills so that companies responsible for the spillage are responsible for cleaning them up. Similar laws have been passed concerning other types of pollution.

Many environmental issues have international dimensions. An example is our recent effort to control global warming. The large majority of scientists believe that the emission of industrial waste gases is causing global warming and that this global warming could have dire consequences in the future. In 1997, delegates from 160 countries attended a ten-day conference on this subject in Kyoto, Japan. This conference resulted in the issuance of a document called the **Kyoto Protocol,** which provided that industrialized countries must cut emissions of these gases, especially carbon dioxide.

Some in the United States were upset that only industrial countries would be required to reduce emissions and that developing countries such as China and India would not have to comply. The exception of developing countries was justified by the argument that they began emitting later than industrial countries, and they need to "catch up" economically. The Kyoto Protocol set 2000 as the date for its accomplishment. Unfortunately, no industrial nation met that deadline, and by 2000, U.S. emissions were about 13 percent above 1990 levels.

The problems of the protocol, which has no enforcement mechanism, were dealt with by setting the deadline further and further ahead. Ultimately, the U.S. announced that it would not support the protocol because it believed it would be bad for the U.S. economy and, moreover, would not work even if attempted.

A toxic waste disposal site.

Instead, President Bush declared the protocol fatally flawed: he set forth what he called the Clear Skies Initiative, which was a plan to combat global warming through voluntary measures, with a cap-and-trade approach that rewards industries that reduce pollution. In a cap-and-trade approach, a total amount of pollution is determined (the cap) and new sources of pollution must buy the rights to pollute from existing polluters who agree to lower their pollution by an offsetting amount so that total pollution does not increase. With the election of President Barack Obama, the U.S. policies on climate change changed. Obama introduced a cap and trade system for the U.S., and demonstrated a willingness to work with other countries in the world to attempt to arrive at a world climate policy that would show global warming. The U.S. played an active role in the Copenhagen Climate Conference in 2009. Nonetheless, the political problems of achieving a meaningful climate change policy acceptable to all countries was immense, and there were enormous fights in Copenhagen between developed and developing countries about who should pay the enormous costs to combat global warming. So, even with a U.S. seemingly committed to the goal of fighting global warming, it is unclear whether the actual policies seen as politically feasible will be sufficient to do the job or just "feel good window dressing" policies. Obama's decision in 2009 to allocate hundreds of billions of dollars of pollution permits free to firms was not an encouraging sign.

Conservation and the High Price of Gasoline

With the extremely fast growth of the Chinese economy, and the overall growth of the world economy, demand for energy and raw materials has increased substantially over the past decade. This increase in demand has set in motion an increase in the price of many raw materials, the most noticeable of which has been oil. It has also led to many calls for U.S. citizens to conserve energy and other natural resources.

Many of those who favor conservation lament the high price of gas and oil, but economists point out that it is the way in which the market coordinates available supply with demand. Specifically, the higher price leads to more exploration and research into alternative technologies, such as hydrogen-based fuel cells, or cars designed to run on ethanol. That leads to an increase in the supply of energy. Simultaneously, the increase in price cuts back on the quantity of the gas demanded.

If $3.00 a gallon gas does not end the U.S. consumer's desire for SUVs, $10.00 a gallon gas probably will; and if China's economy continues to grow at its current rate, no new major technological development occurs, and no new oil supplies are found, then such prices are possible, as the market does its job. In a market economy, if society resists adjusting its use of resources to the available supply through conservation, a rise in the price of the resources will force society to conserve.

Conclusion

This chapter has reviewed geographic, demographic, and ecological problems that society faces and has shown some of the ways society meets them. Of the three types, the geographic problems are the most constant, but with new technologies even these can change. The Internet, for example, has made it possible for more individuals to work in more rural areas and has increased the range of areas where businesses can operate.

Demographic problems are constantly changing: As societies become richer, their population growth generally decreases on its own. Nonetheless, population problems play central roles in many countries' social problems. Whereas demographic problems generally decline as a country gets richer, ecological problems often become more severe. But the wealth of society also gives it the means to deal with those ecological problems. Whether it actually does deal with them is a political issue; often, even though the means are there, the political will is not.

Social scientists study such problems and work on alternative solutions that circumvent the political problems. Finding an acceptable alternative is seldom easy, but that work generally leads to a better understanding of the problem and of alternative solutions.

Key Points

- Knowing the geography of the world is an important skill.
- The world population has fluctuated over time, but since the 1800s it has grown substantially.
- The Malthusian theory is the belief that population tends to outrun the means of subsistence.

- The law of diminishing marginal returns: If more and more people are employed on a given area of land, beyond a certain point—even though the total output may continue to expand—average output per worker will shrink.

- The birthrate and the death rate interact to determine population growth.
- The ecology of our world is affected by human action, the life and death of species, climate changes, productive changes that result in pollution, and conservation measures.
- There is often a trade-off between economic production goals and environmental goals.

Some Important Terms

census (95)
demography (91)
ecological balance (99)
ecology (99)
environment (99)
Environmental Protection Agency (EPA) (101)

geography (90)
human ecology (99)
Kyoto Protocol (101)
law of diminishing returns (96)
Malthusian theory (96)
natural environment (99)

optimal population (97)
pollution (100)
social environment (99)

Questions for Review and Discussion

1. What are some of the questions that geography is concerned with?
2. How does geography interact with sociology?
3. How many people are there in the world?
4. What is the world's most populous country? Explain some of the problems that a country faces in trying to limit its population growth, including the problems it will have if it is successful.
5. What is the Malthusian doctrine? Have the predictions of Thomas Malthus come true?
6. Identify some of the reasons why the world population has grown in the past 200 years.
7. What are some possible ways to limit population? Mention natural causes as well as those encouraged by government or other policies.
8. In practice, are all policies for limitation of population growth acceptable? If not, which ones would you argue against?
9. What are some of the costs of pollution? What are some of the gains from pollution? It is very expensive to clean up areas that have been polluted. What are some ways you can think of to pay for such cleanups?
10. You are a government planner in the country of Growthlandia. You would like to know where to build new schools, where to close schools, and whether it makes sense to embark on an ambitious program to expand the number of job opportunities. What would you like to know about the composition of Growthlandia's population now and how that population is likely to change in the next fifteen years?
11. How would your life be different if gas cost $10 per gallon?

Internet Questions

1. Go to an atlas site (for example, www.atlapedia. com) and look at a country or region. Look at its physical and political map. What borders it? Which borders are natural?
2. Go to www.maxshores.com/kudzu and read about kudzu. What is it? What are its benefits to the southeastern United States?
3. What does the U.N. see as one of the most powerful constraints on realizing women's rights and achieving the Millennium Development goals in its Progress of the World's Women Report for at http://www.unifem.org/progress/2008?
4. Go to www.geohive.com/earth. Looking at the latest figures for populations of countries by sex, what two countries have the highest percentage of females? Of males?
5. What is the ozone layer according to the EPA, www.epa.gov/docs/ozone/science/q_a.html#q1? What is today's UV index value for your zip code (www.epa.gov/sunwise/uvindex.html)?

For Further Study

Bargmann, Julie, *Toxic Beauty: A Field Guide to Derelict Terrain*, Harrisburg, PA: Phaidon Press, 2005.

Bureau of the Census, *Current Population Reports*, Washington, DC: Population estimates for the United States issued monthly; special reports from time to time.

Colbert, Elizabeth, *Field Notes from a Catastrophe: Man, Nature, and Climate Change*, New York: Bloomsbury, 2006.

Friedman, Thomas L., *The World Is Flat: A Brief History of the Twenty-First Century*, New York: Farrar, Straus and Giroux, 2005.

Friedman, Thomas L., *Hot, Flat, and Crowded*, New York, NY: Farrar, Straus & Giroux, 2008.

Goodell, Jeff, *Big Coal: The Dirty Secret Behind America's Energy Future*, Boston: Houghton Mifflin, 2006.

Malthus, Thomas, *An Essay on the Principle of Population, or, A View of its Past and Present Effects on Human Happiness,* New York: Cambridge University Press, 1992 (first published in 1798).

Mead, Margaret, ed., *Cultural Patterns and Technical Change*, New York: New American Library/Mentor, 1956.

Newbold, K. Bruce, *Six Billion Plus: Population Issues in the Twenty-First Century,* Lanham, UK: Rowman & Littlefield, 2002.

Riggs, Stan, and Dorothea V. Ames, *Drowning the North Carolina Coast*, College Park, MD: North Carolina Sea Grant, 2003.

Simon, Julian, *The Ultimate Resource*, Princeton, NJ: Princeton University Press, 1981.

Smith, Norris, *Changing U.S. Demographics,* New York: H.W. Wilson, 2002.

Speth, James Gustave, *Red Sky at Morning*, New Haven, CT: Yale University Press, 2006.

Statistical Abstract of the United States, Washington, DC: U.S. Bureau of the Census, issued annually.

WWW Ecology Global Network http://ecology.com/index.php

WWW The Environmental Protection Agency www.epa.gov

WWW Foundation for Clean Air Progress www.cleanairprogress.org

WWW GeoHive—Global Statistics www.geohive.com/default1.aspx

WWW Test your Geographic Knowledge www.mccollam.com/fun/geoquiz

WWW National Geographic Maps http://maps.nationalgeographic. com/maps (accessed June 22, 2009)

WWW www.nationalgeographic.com/roper2006/pdf/FINALReport2006GeogLitsurvey.pdf

WWW The United Nations www.un.org

WWW The U.S. Bureau of the Census www.census.gov

Technology and Society

After reading this chapter, you should be able to:

- Define technology and explain its importance
- Explain how the Industrial Revolution significantly changed all aspects of society
- Discuss the role that technology plays in social change
- Present both sides of the limits-to-growth debate
- List some of the important technological developments of the past
- Speculate on likely important technological developments in the future

Political activity is shadow-play . . . ; technology is the underlying reality. Engineers, not poets, are the secret legislators of the world.

—David Warsh

Technology is the universe of tools, means, and methods through which we interact with our environment. We devote a separate chapter to technology because it is an integral cog in social and cultural change. It both causes social change and is itself influenced by culture. In our brief overview of history, we saw the importance of technology—in the initial establishment of cities, made possible by crop cultivation; in the spread of population to overcome environmental limitation, through the use of fire; and in the evolution of our thinking about society, by means of printing. That evolution is continuing. Computers, robots, gene splicing, nuclear research, interactive information systems—all are currently in the process of changing our society, presenting us with new problems and new horizons. Exactly how that technology will affect society is hard to predict, but it is certain to change.

We begin our consideration of technology with a short quiz (p. 106). In the left column, we list six technological advances that have helped shape our society. In the middle column is a set of dates and in the right column a list of names. These are only some of the best-known discoveries; the list could go on and on. Moreover, each of these technological developments has a compelling story accompanying its introduction, and even more interesting effects that it has caused. For example, the process of canning food was developed in 1810 by an enterprising Frenchman, Nicholas Appert. The stimulus for this invention came from Napoleon Bonaparte. As early as 1800, Emperor Napoleon recognized the importance of preserving food after nearly losing the Battle of Marengo because of a lack of provisions. The emperor realized that a reliable method of food preservation would enhance his chances of military success. Therefore Napoleon offered a set of prizes for technological improvements, including food preservation, believing that France lagged behind its rival, Great Britain, in technology.

Can You Match the Date and Name with the Invention?

1. First motorcar	(a) 1876	(aa) Alexander Graham Bell
2. Telephone	(b) 1896	(bb) Thomas Edison
3. Incandescent lightbulb	(c) 1854	(cc) Guglielmo Marconi
4. Radio	(d) 1835	(dd) Elisha Otis
5. Elevators	(e) 1876	(ee) William Henry Fox Talbot
6. Photography	(f) 1885	(ff) Karl Benz

1—f, ff; 2—a or e, aa; 3—a or e, bb; 4—b, cc; 5—c, dd; 6—d, ee.

When Appert, a cook who had worked in a wine cellar as a champagne bottler, heard about the prizes, he began work on a method to preserve food. It was many years before he perfected his process. Drawing on his experience as a cook and a bottler, Appert had an idea that he might be able to preserve food in champagne bottles by filling them with food, sealing them, and boiling the bottles. Although he did not know why the food in the bottles did not spoil (we now know it was because he had sterilized the contents of the bottles), still he was successful, and soon bottled food (and later, canned food) allowed individuals to eat vegetables in winter and to preserve meat over long periods. The desired result—better provisioning of armies—was accomplished, along with the far more widespread benefits that preserved food meant for public health.

Canned food was important in the early 1800s because mechanical refrigerators did not exist. At that time, the only way to refrigerate food was by storing ice, which was cut from ponds in the winter and kept till the next winter, insulated by hay in windowless structures known as icehouses. In the United States, some southern states imported ice all year from these icehouses. (As you can imagine, much of it melted, and one year in Apalachicola, Florida, the price rose to $1.25 a pound—about $50 in today's dollars.)

John Gorrie, a doctor trying to solve the problem of malaria, which was rampant in Florida at the time, discovered that the disease occurred more frequently in hot, humid weather. He felt he could reduce its incidence if he could lower the temperature of his hospital wards. At first he did this by blowing fans over blocks of ice, but when an ice shortage pushed the price to high levels, he decided there must be a better way. He was aware of some recent discoveries in chemistry—specifically, that compressed gases, when expanding rapidly, will absorb heat from their surroundings. He constructed a steam engine that would compress air (a gas) in a cylinder. As the piston withdrew, it would allow the air to escape and expand into another cylinder. Gorrie put a brine solution around this cylinder and found that it would get cold because the air inside the cylinder was cold. By pumping this cold air into his hospital wards, he invented the first air conditioner.

Gorrie also discovered that by placing water around the brine solution, he could draw heat from the water to such an extent that the water turned to ice. Gorrie realized the enormous possibilities of the ice-making machine and tried to market it, but could not find any financial backing; he died a poor and broken man. For the next twenty years, people tried to perfect the invention, but with only moderate success. By the early 1900s, however, the process was sufficiently developed, and refrigerators became a commercial reality.

The social effects of refrigerators were enormous. People could buy larger quantities of food at lower prices. They no longer had to make as many trips to the store, which meant that neighborhoods provided fewer social and commercial contacts. Eventually, refrigerators played an important role in destroying the basis for neighborhood stores and replacing them with the modern supermarket and modern advertising, both of which created profound changes in urban, suburban, and rural society.

Changes in refrigeration technology are ongoing. Thermal acoustic methods of cooling, in which sound waves are used to do the cooling, and magnetic field cooling are being explored as more efficient and less harmful methods of achieving refrigeration.

We recount these stories of the development of the food canning process and of refrigerators not because these inventions are unique—we could have chosen numerous other examples—but because seeing a particular instance gives us a better sense of the tremendous and far-reaching influence that technological progress can have on society.

The Industrial Revolution

The technological developments chosen for the quiz at the beginning of this chapter date from the 1800s. In part, that is because the discoverers of many earlier inventions are unknown. (Actually, historians often debate the origin of many technological discoveries, including modern ones.) But it is also because in the nineteenth century there was simply an enormous number of technological improvements. We limited the quiz to a few items you are likely to be able to identify. Many eighteenth-century inventions have become so outdated that many people today have never seen them, such as the steam locomotive that used to pull railroad cars. After a lull, technological improvement began to expand enormously about 1760. The period after that date is called the Industrial Revolution.

The **Industrial Revolution** is the name given to the sum of all the changes in economic and social organization characterized by the replacement of hand tools with power-driven machines and by the concentration of industry in large establishments. It had its beginnings in England around 1760. There, for the first time people began to employ power machines for industrial production and to build factories to house them. By 1800, this movement had made substantial progress.

The English Industrial Revolution was brought about by a cumulation of inventions. A new invention in one industry was followed by improvements and inventions in related industries. This is well illustrated by the textile inventions of the eighteenth century. These inventions were first employed in the cotton goods industry, which was relatively small and new, and the machinery was operated by water power. When James Watt devised a greatly improved steam engine, the revolution really took off. Machinery for producing cotton textiles was modified and applied to the production of woolen cloth, the output of which expanded by leaps and bounds. Costs and prices were so reduced that a great new demand developed for both wool and cotton products.

The developments just described gave England an advantage over its competitors. Because England was able to mechanize its industries so much sooner than other countries, it was for many years the workshop of the world. Its production, trade, and wealth rose to what were then regarded as high levels. But in time industrialism began to spread to other nations.

The Development of Industrialism in the United States

In the early nineteenth century, the machine industry and factory system began to develop in the United States. The Napoleonic Wars (1803–1815) and the War of 1812 gave U.S. industrialization a strong push because they made it difficult for the United States to import English textiles.[1] To make up for the resulting shortage, many new textile factories were established in this country. Employers had to pay higher wages than their counterparts in the

---

[1]Two of the adversaries in the Napoleonic Wars were France and England; two of the adversaries in the War of 1812 were the United States and England. Both wars disrupted U.S. trade with England.

The interior of a nineteenth-century cotton factory.

English factories, but as long as English textiles were not available, they could operate profitably. When peace came to Europe and normal trade was reestablished, many of these new factories were forced to close down. Others, however, survived, and from that time on the United States gradually became more and more industrialized.

In some respects, conditions in the United States favored industrialization. First, our domestic market was rapidly growing. Second, raw materials were plentiful. Third, labor was relatively scarce and wages were higher than in Europe, partly because workers kept leaving their jobs to settle on free or cheap land along the frontier. Although this raised costs of production, it also put a premium on the introduction of labor-saving machines. To reduce costs, as many operations as possible were shifted to power machines. As a result, production increased much faster than the number of workers, standards of living gradually rose, and wealth began to accumulate.

Standardization, Interchangeability, and Mass Production

Early machines were crude by our standards. Because their parts did not fit together perfectly, they ran with a great deal of noise and clatter and frequently broke down. Often their products were imperfect, so that further work had to be done on them by hand to make them acceptable. One of the greater advances in industrial technology was the gradual development of precision machines that would run smoothly and that could also turn out standardized, accurately made, and hence interchangeable parts for more or less complex finished products such as watches, guns, washing machines, and automobiles. This development made it physically possible for a machine to produce thousands of units of a given part, all so nearly alike that they could be freely substituted for one another. **Standardization**—the production of uniform, substitutable parts—was made possible by a humble but far-reaching development, the improvement of measurement devices. Similar small improvements have played large roles in shaping our society, so it is worth describing this one in detail to give you a sense of the mundane aspect of technological development.

To understand the problem of standardization, think of a car. If you blow a piston, you go out and buy a new one. Getting the new piston is not cheap, but it is a lot cheaper than if you had to have a machinist make a new piston to fit your individual engine. It would probably cost twenty or thirty times as much. Extending this analogy to other areas, much of the machinery—for example, dishwashers, tractors, and photocopiers—we use today relies on **interchangeability,** the ability to substitute one part for another. Without it, there would be far fewer goods than we now have, and those that we do have would be more expensive.

So interchangeability is important; that's obvious. But if it is obvious that interchangeability has so many advantages, why weren't early machines built with interchangeable parts? The reason is a technical one: To achieve interchangeability in machines, tolerances (variations in size and shape) must be less than one-thousandth of an inch. With the tools available in the 1700s and early 1800s, even the best, most skilled machinist could not approach such tolerances, so interchangeability was only a dream until some method of achieving those tolerances could be found.

As has happened with many inventions, the strongest impetus for standardization came from the armed forces. Before and during the Civil War (1861–1865), each rifle had to be produced separately. If one broke, a skilled machinist or gunsmith was needed to repair it. These craftsmen, using a variety of tools, would fashion a musket or even a rifle. Each musket had to be built precisely; that is, all the parts, such as the stock, barrel, and lock, had to fit together and work as a coordinated whole (hence the phrase, "lock, stock, and barrel"). But precision did not mean interchangeability. A gunsmith would work the individual components until they fitted together, but as he modified each part to fit the others, he made it specific to that weapon; the part worked in no other. To repair rifles, armies had to have their own musket makers who would fix individual muskets that had broken in the field. Armies would also keep armories where they made individual weapons, and armories were an important part of the defense capacity of any country.[2]

In about 1820, one of the skilled musket makers, John Hall, argued that this procedure was inefficient and that armies would have a tremendous advantage if their muskets had interchangeable parts. An army would only have to carry spare parts, which could easily be used to repair a broken weapon. It would not only be cheaper, but it would also be far more efficient. As we stated earlier, technological requirements for interchangeable parts were enormous because if all parts were to be interchangeable, each musket had to fit together precisely and be identical to every other in a way that two individuals each producing an entire musket could not accomplish.

To meet the problem, Hall developed a method of precision machine production. The movement to precision machine production required a number of small but extremely important technological breakthroughs, which included measuring from a standard pattern rather than from each piece and the development of dies by which individual parts were compared and tested. With these developments, machines could reach a level of precision and consistency necessary for interchangeability, a level much higher than even the most skilled worker could achieve.

Rather than a machinist measuring each part, a machinist could make an initial part, or die, and then a machine employing a micrometer could produce a duplicate, using a process similar to the one hardware stores use today to duplicate keys. The machine traces the original and fashions the new part to conform. By means of this process, each part is sufficiently identical so that interchangeability is possible. There are, of course, some minute variations, but by making each part and measuring it relative to the original with a micrometer, a skilled machinist can keep the variations between the individual pieces at an acceptable level for interchangeability.

Social and Economic Effects of Interchangeability. Once interchangeability was introduced, the production process quickly changed and the pace of the Industrial Revolution quickened. In the early 1900s, Henry Ford carried through this development with the introduction of the

---

[2]Later we discuss the modern military-industrial complex (the interconnection between the military and business) and its implications for society. It is important to remember that the military-industrial complex is not a new phenomenon but has existed for as long as societies themselves have existed.

A mass-produced robotic doll.

assembly line, a production technique in which each worker in a factory performs a single operation on an item as it is passed along. Because of this innovation, the price of a car was lowered in the 1920s from about $1,600 to $300.

With standardization and machine production, while one machine was making one part other machines could be making other parts, and by using an assembly line great quantities of the finished product could be turned out by merely assembling the proper parts. Thus standardization led to **mass production,** the use of standardized parts to construct great quantities of a product on an assembly line.

Naturally, it does not pay to make large amounts of a product if they cannot be sold. But when the market is large enough, the use of standard interchangeable parts makes mass production possible and substantially reduces costs. To construct an expensive machine to make a standardized part would not pay if the machine could be used to produce only a few units of output, because the sale of these few units would have to cover the entire cost of the machine. But if mass production is possible and a machine can be employed to produce thousands or hundreds of thousands of units, the portion of the cost that must be charged to each unit becomes small or even negligible. It then pays to use a machine in place of human labor whenever one can be devised to perform a necessary operation. When standardized parts made by machines are combined into a finished product on a modern assembly line, as in the automobile industry, mass production reaches a high level of efficiency.

The effects on society of interchangeability and mass production were enormous. Individual skilled workers were no longer held in high esteem; their pay fell, their social position fell, and the skill level necessary to produce goods fell. In response, they led movements against the use of new machines. As the status of skilled workers fell, the status of the owners of machines rose. Fortunes were built by industrialists, and high society had to make room for these newly rich. Business provided a way to move up the social ladder, and as businesspeople moved up, they brought their own values and worldview. Armies and arms became less costly; war and killing increased.

As the interchangeable-parts approach to production spread, these effects were multiplied. With the development of low-priced cars, the limitations geography placed on society changed and the nature of cities changed. Low-priced tractors increased productivity in farming, lowering food prices and forcing more and more people off the farms. None of these changes would have occurred as early as they did if Hall had not figured out a way to machine-tool more exactly.

We could continue describing the myriad effects that flowed from the improved measuring systems, but the previous discussion should be sufficient to start you thinking about these and other technological developments. As you ponder these issues, remember that technological developments are still occurring. The development of gene-splicing techniques, robots, computers, and the Internet has already changed our society and working habits significantly.

For example, in early societies strength and physical ability were important characteristics necessary for the existing level of technology. Because women bore children, were uniquely able to feed them, and on average were physically weaker than men, they generally stayed home caring for the children while males hunted. The Industrial Revolution lessened that division but did not eliminate it. The developments in technology, however, have diminished the importance of an individual's physical strength, making the male–female roles based on them irrelevant, if they ever were relevant. (Some authorities claim that men's physical advantages over women are minimal.) Thus, many of the cultural aspects of society, such as the patriarchal family, have come into question.

New technological developments can be expected to further this change, but they will also lead to new ways to deal with it. The technology of the Industrial Revolution, for example, required individuals to work in a factory with everyone on hand at the same time. This technology eventually led to an eight-to-five workday with weekends off. With the development of computers, fax machines, email, and the Internet, the need for a workplace separate from one's home has decreased, and more people are working at home or with flexible hours. Such changes have made work and family life easier for two-income families, and the movement toward flexible work schedules can be expected to continue.

Technology and Globalization

The development of technology is generally associated with specialization and increased trade because trade allows individuals and companies experiencing a technological change to become better at what they do (this is called learning by doing). As they become better at it, they can produce products at lower cost. Additionally, trade allows companies to take advantage of economies of scale—the bigger a firm's production facilities, the lower its per unit costs of the good. For example, making one car is extremely expensive; making many cars has a much lower per-car cost.

If a company can produce something more cheaply, it can out-compete other firms and hence make enormous profits. With those profits, it can spend more on research and development and gain even more of the market, as long as other firms cannot duplicate that technology quickly. When this happens internationally, it falls under the heading **globalization**—*the integration of world economies.* Globalization has been occurring at a fast rate in recent years, and traditional societies are often shaken by change, as less expensive goods come in from more technologically advanced countries.

Technology also affects traditional societies in another way. Firms are always looking for cheaper ways to produce goods. If they can hire workers in a traditional society at a lower rate than they can in their own society and are allowed to do so, they will often transfer production facilities. Another aspect of globalization involves the movement of production facilities and technology from one economy to another. In recent years, enormous amounts of manufacturing activity in the United States have been transferred to countries such as India and China, with profound effects on their economies and culture. It has made them better off materially, but has also introduced large income inequalities and westernization of their culture, which many people consider a loss.

The Internet is speeding the process of globalization, making it possible for firms to easily compare prices of goods throughout the world and to communicate cheaply over long distances. U.S. service sector jobs, such as claim agents, suppliers of help-line support, X-ray technicians, and tutors, which previously had not experienced international competition, are now being **outsourced**—many U.S. high-wage workers have been replaced by low-wage foreign workers. With continuing technological advances subjecting more and more jobs to outsourcing, and the large differential between U.S. wages and those in many foreign countries, the effects of globalization will likely be enormous over the coming decade.

Modern Technology and the Need for Skilled Workers

A belief once widely held is that machines reduce the need for human skills. It was said that before the machine age the individual worker was an artisan who performed by hand all the operations on the product. The worker was a weaver, a shoemaker, a candlemaker, or a tailor. Standards of technique were high, and because one worker made the entire product, a high level of skills was demanded. After the advent of machines, individual skills became almost useless. Machines performed the principal operations required to make a product, and the worker became an automaton whose function was to operate or feed the machine, perhaps doing nothing but moving a lever up and down or placing a piece of metal in a machine, removing it when the machine had operated, and repeating this task all day long. Such work required no skill, and so the typical worker became a common laborer instead of an artisan.

The reasoning presented here is plausible but highly misleading. Before the age of the machine, skilled craftspeople represented a tiny portion of the working population in most countries. The great majority of the people lived and worked on the land. The work was heavy, the hours long, and the returns small. It is true that the introduction of machines put certain skilled artisans out of work or forced them to work in factories as unskilled labor. For example, after the introduction of the power loom in England in the eighteenth century, the price of cloth dropped so sharply that skilled handweavers could no longer make a living at their trade. This does not mean, however, that the introduction of machinery reduced the total demand for workers with special skill or training. Quite the contrary. The skills required became different, but in the long run the machine industry made it necessary for a much larger portion of the population than ever before to acquire specialized skills, training, or knowledge. Furthermore, in modern factories purely routine and mechanical jobs such as feeding materials into a machine are continually disappearing because machines can be devised to perform these operations automatically. An outstanding characteristic of modern automation is the constant shifting of routine activities from people to machines.

To compensate for this loss of routine jobs, modern machine technology has created great numbers of jobs that require specialized skills or knowledge: engineers, construction workers, plumbers, electricians, machinists, and mechanics. There are people trained in the organization and administration of industrial enterprises, in advertising and selling, and in various phases of transportation. In addition, there are accountants and a great many skilled clerical workers.

The development of robots has reduced the number of routine jobs even more but has increased the need for skilled technicians who assemble and repair them, the systems engineers who devise plans for using them to solve business problems, and the programmers who put these plans into operation.

Machines and Unemployment

In addition to the belief that machines reduce the demand for skilled workers, there is an even more persistent notion that has little foundation in past experience—the idea that advances in machine technology, by replacing labor, progressively decrease total job opportunities and total employment. This belief had a strong appeal in the 1930s when millions were out of work. At that time, many writers argued that our economy had become "mature" and that in order to provide enough jobs in the future, it would be necessary either to spread the work around by progressively shortening the work week or else to have the government keep creating more jobs through an expanding program of public works. In addition to shortening the work week, it was often proposed that young people should be kept in school longer and that older workers should be retired at earlier ages.

No one questions that machines displace individual workers from certain jobs and that in the short run this often creates difficult problems. For example, the use of diesel engines and electric power by railroads has made obsolete the position of "fireman"—the employee who shoveled coal into the locomotive boiler that produced the steam for the train's steam engine—but because of union support, railroads had to fill this position for many years after steam power ceased being used by trains. However, such problems are temporary. Ultimately, advances in machine technology tend to reduce costs and prices (assuming a constant value of the dollar) or to hold them down, and by enabling people to buy more goods, they create new employment opportunities. If some industries employ fewer workers, others employ more. At the same time, new products are introduced and new industries are established.

Technology and Social Change

As you can see from our discussion of the Industrial Revolution, technology plays an important role in determining a society's culture. The patterns of a society's daily activities are greatly influenced by its technology—that is, by the kinds of goods, including services, that it knows how to produce and by the methods it employs to produce them. In primitive societies, for example, production is carried on with the aid of simple hand tools, and people spend most of their time hunting, fishing, tilling the soil, preparing food, making clothing, and constructing crude shelters. On the other hand, in modern industrial societies such as ours, millions of men and women spend most of each week in offices, factories, or laboratories, and often they travel long distances by automobile, bus, or train to reach their places of work. Therefore, to understand cultural and social change, we must understand its interaction with technology.

That technology has played a dominant role in shaping our modern world is beyond question. Culture, to be sure, is much more than technology. But modern civilization as we know it could not have developed without its technological base. Technology largely determines the way in which people use their habitat and the extent to which they can benefit from the potential resources it may contain. When Columbus came to America, the territory that is now the United States could probably support, by the methods of production known to the Native Americans, fewer than half a million people. Today the same territory supports more than 500 times as many and provides them with a much more plentiful and dependable supply of material goods. This difference cannot be explained in terms of the natural environment. It is explained mainly by the fact that our modern industrial technology is vastly superior in productive efficiency to the technology the Native Americans had.

Problems Created by Technology

Although technological progress has conferred great benefits on the human population, it also has created many problems. Work in the first factories took people away from their homes all day and disrupted the established pattern of domestic life. It also forced large numbers of people to live close to their new places of work, which in turn resulted in crowded industrial towns and cities. On the other hand, there is evidence that even the early factories gave the masses more opportunities to earn and a better chance of survival. One indication of this is the fall in the death rate and the increase in the rate of population growth that has occurred over time.

The effects of technology on society are so pervasive that some social scientists claim that technology is the primary determinant of social and cultural relations. Some social scientists argue that mass production and the assembly line, where each individual does one task repeatedly, developed not because they were more technically efficient, inasmuch as you can get more output from a certain amount of work, but because they established and fortified social divisions. For example, suppose two kinds of a machine can produce widgets. One requires each individual to work on a part with no one supervising; the other requires a supervisor directing individuals to perform specific tasks. Even if the first kind of machine provides a cheaper way to produce a widget, if the decision were left to the supervisor, he or she would be unlikely to choose the one that eliminated the supervisor's job.

Social scientists who use this line of reasoning argue that the social class structure of capitalism is inevitable with the capitalist means of production. They argue that even communist countries, which in theory attempted to avoid class divisions, nevertheless maintained the class divisions of capitalist society as long as they used capitalist technology and capitalist modes of production. When a technology is designed for a boss and a worker, unless these divisions are maintained the technology cannot be effective. Communism self-destructed

Qwerty

When considering the interrelationships between technology and social institutions, it is instructive to think about the keyboard.

You will note that the first six letters on the top of the keyboard spell QWERTY. When you learned keyboarding, you learned to memorize the positions of these keys, and you got to where you could type anywhere from 5 to 150 words per minute. You might wonder how the letters were given those positions, instead of being arranged some other way. They were put there on purpose by an inventor, Christopher L. Sholes. Initially, typewriters were built with letters in serial fashion, but it was found that people could type too fast on such a keyboard, and often the keys would lock together when pressed in succession too quickly.

Sholes developed the QWERTY keyboard to minimize the occurrence of such stickiness. Of course, the problem of keys sticking was relevant only for the earliest typewriters. The "golf ball" typewriters developed in the 1960s and the electronic typewriters that followed had no such problem at all, and neither do computer keyboards. Yet QWERTY, the innovation devised for a specific purpose at an earlier time, remains standard for all of these keyboards. Redesigning the keyboard would mean that teachers must retrain and experienced typists must relearn how to move their fingers, so it seems unlikely that such a change will take place.

Precisely the same set of issues is relevant to a variety of existing technologies and social institutions. Although they may have had a purpose at one time, they might be limiting now. The mere fact that they are limiting does not mean they will be changed.

because it did not develop its own technology. Only by developing an alternative technology, one not designed to hold workers down, can any society divest itself of class structure.

This argument is subject to much criticism, but the fact remains that capitalist technologies have inevitably developed a class system. (But so too have precapitalist and noncapitalist countries.) Concern about this effect of technology kept China from encouraging Western technology. Through much of Mao Zedong's Cultural Revolution of the 1960s and well into the 1970s, China attempted to purge many of those Western technologies. However, under a new leader in the late 1970s and early 1980s, China reversed its position and began the conscious introduction of Western technology into its system, with the intention of pushing economic development. The debate, however, continues, especially because the recent upheavals in formerly socialist societies have been marked by increasing inequality.

Similar debates can be heard in discussions of the future of the class structure in the United States. For example, the economic theorist Michael Piori has argued that technology is pushing society in the opposite direction, and that with the use of computers and robots the very nature of capitalist societies will change. He argues that with the new developing technologies, robots will do the work of blue-collar workers and thus class distinction will no longer be embodied in technology. He believes that in the future there will be far less class distinction in the United States than there now is.

Piori's views that technological development will reduce class distinctions are not shared by all. In fact, some economists have argued that recent technological developments are responsible for increasing inequality and class divisions. Specifically, they argue that technological developments in telecommunications, which have made for cheap global communication and transport (such as containerized super ships) have created downward pressure on many developed countries' workers' wages, forcing those workers into low-paying service jobs. The result is the creation of an upper class that lives a cloistered existence in gated communities, quite separate from the middle and lowerclasses that make up the majority of the U.S. population.

Technology and Crime

It isn't only class structure that is affected by technology; so is crime. Previously, many people's image of crime had been of someone using a gun to rob a bank or store. Technology has changed that. Today, we have cyber crimes, such as identity theft, illegal transfers of moneys out of someone's bank account, and cyber stalking by Internet predators. Just as in the legal economy, the most successful criminals today are highly educated.

As crime technology changes, so too does crime fighting. Today, technology plays a central role in fighting crime. While the popular TV series *CSI* and *Numb3rs* portray exaggerated depictions of crime detection technology, the role of technology in law enforcement has indeed made a college education an important step for anyone thinking of advancing in that career.

Natural Resources, Economics, and Technology

One of the debates that often surfaces among social scientists concerns whether there are sufficient resources for society to continue to grow and whether we will some day reach a limit to growth. It is relevant to our discussion here because technology provides a necessary link between resources and the economy. To see this link, we need to consider the nature of economic activities, natural resources, and technology.

Economic activities are those activities concerned with making a living, and they necessarily play a major role in every culture. Their character is largely determined by three factors. First, all human beings have wants for many kinds of scarce goods. **Scarce goods** are goods that exist in limited quantities and that we can obtain only if we produce them or if we offer something valuable in exchange for them. The desire to satisfy specific wants is the motive behind all economic activity.

The second factor that guides economic activity is available resources. Economic goods such as food, clothing, housing, and weapons cannot be created out of nothing. If people are to have goods, they must find the materials in nature—natural resources—from which the goods can be produced. Unless people can find such materials, their wants will remain unsatisfied no matter how great their efforts. With ingenuity, however, they may discover that they can turn to their advantage materials that at first seemed quite useless. The third factor controlling economic activity is technology, meaning knowledge of how to use resources to produce desirable goods, including services.

Both the technology of a society and the economic activities in which its people engage are greatly influenced, though by no means wholly determined, by the extent to which various natural resources are available. For example, power is an essential in a modern industrial economy, but even a modern economy cannot make extensive use of power unless substantial amounts of power-producing resources are available. Furthermore, the methods used to generate power tend to depend on the relative availability and cost of water power, coal, natural gas, petroleum, sun, wind, and fissionable materials such as uranium. In the future, the methods employed are also likely to be greatly influenced by the success with which we can eliminate the contributions most of them make to polluting or otherwise damaging our environment.

The key element in the process is that natural resources have meaning only in reference to technology. Because technology transforms natural resources into products that can satisfy economic wants, the supply of natural resources depends on the type of technology we have. If a technology develops that can turn sand into a steel-like substance cheaply, then there will be an almost unlimited amount of building material. If we can develop a technology that can turn sunlight into energy cheaply, energy will be almost unlimited. Thus, technology holds the key to growth and the solution to shortages.

Natural Resources and the Limits of Economic Growth

With regard to natural resources, the United States is in a relatively fortunate position, for it is probably better supplied with them than any other similar area in the world. This endowment of natural resources has provided the material basis for our phenomenal economic development and our present political and military strength. We have great areas of fertile farmlands and forests. We are relatively well provided with sources of power such as petroleum, natural gas, coal, and sites for hydroelectric plants. We also have large reserves of iron ore and other important minerals. True, we lack certain metals, such as nickel, chromium, and tin, but ordinarily we have no difficulty in importing these.

Although our position is still strong with respect to most basic resources, the outlook for the future is not clear. Concern about future availability of resources reached a high point in the 1970s as ecologists argued that we were headed for doom. Their argument was twofold: Either we were going to run out of natural resources, or the pollution resulting from production was going to destroy us.

Most economists believe that much of the ecological concern at that time was overdone. We still have vast reserves of low-grade iron ore; similarly, we have vast reserves of shale oil and sand oil. The problem is one of costs and developing the technology that makes extraction of these natural resources economically feasible. The remaining reserves involve a high cost of extraction and therefore cannot be utilized unless the price to the consumer is raised. At 50 cents per gallon for gas, there would likely be a gasoline shortage; at $10 per gallon, there will likely be enough for many years to come. In fact, this is how the market system is designed to work. As a good becomes scarcer, its price rises. Because of that price increase, we use less of it and individuals devote more resources to designing new technologies to achieve the same result without using that resource. For example, plastics were developed during World War II because of the shortage of natural rubber. Similarly, in response to higher prices for gasoline in the 1970s, the average size of automobiles decreased significantly. Then, as gasoline prices fell in the 1980s and 1990s, larger and more powerful cars once again came into vogue. In the early 2000s, high demand for oil by China and the war in Iraq raised the price of gasoline to an average $3 per gallon. That increase and concern about the supply of gasoline has sparked an interest in hybrid cars that derive at least part of their power from electricity.

Goods can become scarce by other means than by being used up. In the United States, the federal government is pushing to have automobile manufacturers develop vehicles to run on energy that is less polluting than gasoline. Therefore, in the early twenty-first century, we will see more vehicles designed to run on electricity and natural gas because government policy has made gasoline "scarce" through limiting its use; it has also made gasoline expensive, because people who won't give up gasoline engines will pay more to obtain that scarce good.

Over the long run, changes in the relative availability of natural resources have an even greater effect on our culture. For example, cities developed as an efficient means of bringing people together before the existence of automobiles and low-cost transportation. When gasoline was introduced, it stimulated the development and spread of automobiles, which in turn reduced the relative advantages of cities. In the 1950s, we saw the result: a movement back to the country to the areas around cities that became known as suburbia. In the 1970s, as the price of gasoline rose, the relative advantages of city life increased and many city areas were revitalized.

Despite these benefits, we still should be concerned about natural resource shortages. High prices can cause hardships, and the cultural change that accompanies relative price changes often is difficult. To be aware of the need for change and to be careful with resources can lessen the impact of that change or at least reduce the problems associated with it.

Global Warming

One of the ecological effects of modern society is **global warming,** the gradual warming of the earth's temperature due to the burning of fossil fuels. Most scientists are convinced that global warming is taking place, and we know that the average surface temperature of the earth is already higher than it was a hundred years ago. The Intergovernmental Panel on Climate Change, established by the United Nations, includes 2,000 scientists, and their consensus is that global warming is a significant potential problem. These conclusions were reinforced in later studies. In 2007, the Panel predicted that if nothing is done about global warming in the year 2100, the average surface temperature of the earth will be more than 10 degrees Fahrenheit warmer than it was in 1900. Contrast this projected increase over only 100 years with the estimate that in the thousands of years from prehistoric times until now the earth has warmed, at most, only 9 percent. Not all scientists agree. A few scientists argue that such temperature changes are part of a natural fluctuation over thousands of years and may not be related to emissions of gases caused by fossil fuel burning but the large majority see global warning as a man made phenomenon.[3]

Nevertheless, the question remains: What should we do about global warming? At the 1992 Earth Summit in Brazil, most of the countries of the world signed treaties to cope with global warming and other environmental problems. Those treaties provided for worldwide reduction of polluting gases followed by periodic assessments of the economic consequences. Despite the 1992 Summit agreement, by 2000 U.S. emissions of waste industrial gases rose significantly. Another attempt to limit polluting gases was the Kyoto Protocol, which was adopted in 1997 and initiated in 2005. This Kyoto Protocol required industrial countries agreeing to it to reduce greenhouse gas emissions. To encourage that to happen it established several "flexible mechanisms" such as a emissions trading market that created incentives to reduce emissions. Most observers consider the Protocol a step in the right direction, but too small a step to make a real difference in global warming. For one thing, it exempted developing countries such as China and India, which led the United States, the largest industrial country in the world, to refuse to sign it, in part because it exempted developing countries. In December 2009, the U.N. organized a climate summit in Copenhagen to attempt to arrive at a new international treaty to attempt to slow down global warming. They did not arrive at a treaty, but some countries agreed to a non-binding agreement that they hoped would provide a framework for future efforts at a global climate treaty.

Global warming remains a contentious issue, with political, economic, environmental, cultural, and health implications that mean the problem will be near the forefront of global concern for many years to come.

Technology of the Past

At the beginning of this chapter, we gave you an easy quiz on technological developments. To put you in the right frame of mind to consider the technology of the future, for which we need to take a wider view of technological development, we now look further into the past and consider technology over a broader horizon. Remember that humans have become humans only through the developments of technology, some of which occurred within human beings through biological evolution.

---

[3]Carbon dioxide is the principal polluting gas, but environmentalists have also targeted five others: methane, nitrous oxide, hydrofluorocarbons, perfluorocarbons, and sulphur hexachloride.

Looking to that past and taking a broad view of technology, we can see that some major "technological" developments occurred thousands of years ago. Some are presented here.

Teeth. The ability to use teeth to crack hard foods such as nuts, seeds, and rind gave *Ramapithecines* access to more foods than other early creatures had. *Ramapithecines* appeared about 15 million years ago and some authorities class them as hominids; others call them common ancestors to hominids and apes. Neanderthal teeth (100,000 to 36,000 years ago) show that they were used to hold objects.

Hands. The ability to use their hands to throw and shake things gave an advantage to primates who stood on two feet. Anthropologists believe that primates began to stand on two feet at least 4 million years ago.

Brains. About 2 million years ago, primate brains began to grow larger. Primates began to use their brains and hands not only to use objects as tools but also to make tools. Some of the earliest made tools were for chopping and digging.

Fire. Cave evidence that may be as old as 700,000 years shows by the charred remains of cooked animals that hominids had learned to make and use fire. It seems that among the animals they cooked were other hominids.

Wooden shelters. As early as 400,000 years ago, hominids had begun to use trees to build shelters.

Spears. Cro-Magnons had spears by at least 35,000 years ago. They could hunt and eat large animals, if the large animals did not eat the Cro-Magnons first.

Bows and arrows. By about 20,000 years ago, humans knew how to use bows and arrows to kill small, fleet animals from a distance. Hunters were safer and at the same time had a wider choice of protein.

As you can see from the list, technology (the means by which humans interact with their environment) progressed slowly at first, as humans learned to use their physical attributes in new ways. Then, as the human brain developed further, a new method of technological change occurred—change brought about through thought and reasoning. This change sped up the process of technological change, and by 7,000 years ago it had led to the development of cities, to writing, and to recorded history.

We stopped our list at 20,000 years ago because we compiled it not in any attempt to be comprehensive, but to make you think about what technology is and what it can be used for. What results can you think of that came from controlling fire and the energy it produces? How do combinations of one technology with others extend the range of human habitats? What do hunting and building imply about cooperation and planning? Do you draw any conclusions from the preponderance in the list of actions such as biting, throwing, chopping, burning, and impaling? If you were to continue the list, what lifestyles would you see developing?

Technology of the Future

We considered past developments simply to set you thinking about technologies of the future and the effects that the development of those technologies might have on society. What we meant you to learn from our consideration of the past is that society fifty years from now is likely to be quite different from society today, and the technologies we develop will play an important role in shaping that future.

But what technologies will develop? Some seem obvious. Computers will progress and become more and more integrated with household appliances. Refrigerators will keep track of what you need to order from the on-line grocery store and place your order for you. On-demand television on the Internet will free people from having to watch a particular show at a particular time. Interaction with these new devices will be via voice recognition,

Modern technology: (left) The International Space Station. (right) A virtual reality demonstration.

not keyboards. Likewise, discoveries in biotechnology will change entirely the way we interact with our bodies; cures for cancer and other diseases will be found, our bones and tissues will be programmed to repair themselves, and we will have the ability to choose characteristics of our offspring.

In considering the effects of technology on the future, you will quickly see that predicting the future is one of the most difficult but enjoyable activities of social science; it allows the imagination to roam. Will spaceships like the *Enterprise* develop out of our current space shuttle efforts? Will we find new technologies that totally change our lives, such as instant transportation or intelligence transfers? The possibilities are endless and not always pleasant for specific individuals. For example, if a machine were developed to implant knowledge in students without the use of teachers, many educators would likely be out of a job, and rather than students going to school for sixteen years, they would merely attend school for information updates once a year.

Timeline: The Future

2015 Breakthrough in medicine; method delays aging process and extends average life expectancy by ten years (world population increases; causes Social Security programs to fail).

2017 Developments with Buckeyballs redefine matter; diamonds and metals no longer scarce.

2018 Fusion reactor created that makes energy "too cheap to meter"; oil companies go broke; gas stations are eliminated.

2020 Genetic engineering means fabricated human replacement organs roll off assembly line. Amputated limbs can be regrown.

2025 Human cloning perfected; all parts of body can now regenerate themselves.

2050 Computer chips developed to place in the human head; eliminates the need for teaching.

2110 Temperature rise on earth means snow and ice at the poles melt and oceans flood all low-lying areas. Miami is no more.

2160 Various complicated life-forms reproduced from organic chemicals create significant debate about morality and meaning.

2190 Major viral outbreak from genetic engineering experiment; half the world population dies.

2210 Instant transportation created; old-fashioned means of transportation—cars, legs, and so forth—no longer needed.

2240 Human body shapes modified to eliminate useless appendages.

2270 Life-forms discovered in different galaxies now reachable with instant transportation.

2280 The starship *Enterprise* returns safely to home base.

Such fanciful ideas are probably a long way off, but clearly life in 2050 will be significantly different from life in 2010. Early in this century, robot factories may be commonplace and you may have a robot helping you with both your housework and job. Gene-splicing and genetic engineering could bring about even more changes. Numerous created life-forms could be kept in special areas and released for special purposes. For example, if there is an oil spill, oil-eating bacteria would be released. If we need more gasoline, new organisms that improve the process of making gas would be sold to oil firms. Or if you need a new type of plant to decorate a room, you would design it and put in your order.

The technology of the future will probably involve changes that are much more imaginative than those we have just speculated on. Some imaginative technological changes and their potential effects are listed in the box on the previous page. Each of these ideas is fanciful, but each has been advanced by futurists at one time or another. They are placed here not because we expect them to materialize, but to make us reflect and think about their implications for society and culture. Each would change society in ways that are difficult to fathom. Each would have social, economic, and cultural consequences that in turn would affect society's ability to use that technology to its advantage and not to its detriment. Seeing that society uses technology for good rather than evil is what social science is all about.

The Social Basis for Technological Progress

Because of the extensive social changes these new technological developments involve, they may never come about. Technological progress occurs only as long as social conditions encourage and make it possible; quite likely, someday conditions could change in such a way as to stop it. There have been times and places in the history of the world when people have lost ground instead of making progress.

Many factors might in the long run greatly retard our technological progress. The costs of the research and equipment necessary for meeting certain problems of pollution are likely to be resisted by many corporations and also, where government is directly involved, by many taxpayers. Technological progress also tends to be slowed by organized pressure groups that have an interest in limiting the output of certain products and in opposing the introduction of new methods or products in order to maintain the demand and the prices for the things they sell. For example, labor unions often oppose the introduction of methods or materials that might reduce the jobs available to their members, and producers of building materials sometimes seek to discourage the introduction of substitutes for their products, even though these may be better and cheaper and may use materials that are more plentiful. Again, many farmers demand that the government take measures to reduce farm output in order to raise farm prices and incomes.

A more subtle influence that might slow up technological progress would be the growth among our people of a less receptive attitude toward change. This might result not only from a lack of interest in consuming more goods but also from a feeling of indifference toward improving both the quality of goods and the quality of the environment; or it might result from a gradual dilution of the spirit of adventure and from an increasing emphasis on security. Change and progress often seem dangerous and disturbing. They put some people out of jobs and force them to seek types of employment not to their liking. They cause some business enterprises to fail, even though others may be expanding rapidly. A society that puts its whole emphasis on stability and security is not likely to look with favor on radical technological innovations.

Future Shock?

A pioneer in the field of futurology, Alvin Toffler, warned in his 1971 book *Future Shock* of the "shattering stress and disorientation that we induce in individuals by subjecting them to too much change in too short a time." According to Toffler, the accelerating rate of change, particularly in technology, in the last part of the twentieth century had occurred so fast that it overwhelmed the adaptive powers of ordinary persons. He argues that we must learn to understand and control the rate of change at this "turning point in history at which people either vanquish the processes of change or vanish, at which point, from being the unconscious puppets of evolution they become either its victims or its masters." Thus, Toffler became a leading advocate of controlled technological change. On the other side are the advocates of stronger reliance on the new technology. For them, the new technology is seen as a way of escaping economic problems such as high rates of unemployment and slow growth.

Which of the two forces—the forces for change or the forces for preventing change—will win out is unclear. Regardless of the outcome, their interaction will make the world of the future an exciting one to live in and an exciting one for social scientists to study.

Key Points

- Technology comprises the tools, means, and methods through which we interact with our environment.
- The Industrial Revolution significantly changed all aspects of society through its introduction of interchangeability and mass production of material products.
- Technology influences culture, and culture influences technology.

- The limits-to-growth debate has two sides, and we will find out which side is correct only when it is too late to do anything about it.
- The development of teeth, hands, brains, fire, wooden shelters, spears, and bows and arrows are some of the important technological developments of the past.
- Potential technological developments in the future are limited only by the imagination.

Some Important Terms

assembly line (110)
economic activities (115)
globalization (111)
global warming (117)

Industrial Revolution (107)
interchangeability (109)
mass production (110)
outsource (111)

scarce goods (115)
standardization (108)
technology (105)

Questions for Review and Discussion

1. Give an example of a technological advance that has greatly influenced your own life and explain what its effect on you has been.
2. Name some technological change that took place in the past and explain how you think it has changed conditions ever since.

3. What was the Industrial Revolution? What are some of the reasons it was successful in the United States?
4. Why are standardization and interchangeability so important to mass production?
5. When it became possible for machines to make products formerly made by hand, what effects did

this have on the number of people employed? On the level of wages? On the profit of employers? On the quality of the products?

6. Explain how the technology of the assembly line led to other technological and cultural changes.

7. If the use of robots in factories becomes widespread, will this mean a loss of jobs and a rise in unemployment? Why or why not?

8. The jobs of some individuals are replaced by particular technological changes. What are some ways to deal with this problem?

9. Technology can be very expensive in terms of its effect on the quality of the air, water, soil, and general environment. How can this expense be dealt with?

10. Technology can be very expensive in terms of the amount of money it costs. Where do you think this money comes from?

11. Do you think the advantages of technology are worth the disadvantages? Why or why not?

12. Are there any technological changes you think should not be made? What are they? If you oppose a particular technological change, what alternative solution do you have for the problem that change was meant to address?

13. Try your hand at predicting a technological change that may occur in the future. What effects on society might that change produce?

Internet Questions

1. Using the website www.inventionfactory.com/history/main.html, find out what the Brooklyn Bridge is suspended from. How thick are the cables?

2. Go to www.usbr.gov/projects and look up the Hoover Dam. How large is the structure? Where is it located and when was it built?

3. Go to www.npr.org/templates/story/story.php?storyId=19174580 and either read the article or listen to it. Who makes Blu-ray discs? What new technology may make Blu-ray discs obsolete? What earlier formatting war is mentioned in the article, and which brand came out on top then?

4. Go to www.livescience.com/php/trivia/?quiz=inventions and take the quiz. How do you score?

5. Go to www.sierraclub.org/energy/overview. What country is the largest emitter of carbon dioxide (CO_2)? Name one possible outcome of a 2°C rise in temperature.

For Further Study

Ackerman, Frank, and Lisa Heinzerling, *Priceless: On Knowing the Price of Everything and the Value of Nothing*, New York: New Press, 2004.

Brown, David E., ed., *Inventing Modern America: From the Microwave to the Mouse*, Cambridge, MA: MIT Press, 2002.

Essinger, James, *Jacquard's Webb: How a Hand Loom Led to the Birth of the Information Age*, Oxford: Oxford University Press, 2004.

Mead, Margaret, ed., *Cultural Patterns and Technical Change*, New York: New American Library/Mentor, 1956.

Menzel, Peter, and Faith D'Aluisio, *Robo Sapiens: Evolution of a New Species*, Cambridge, MA: MIT Press, 2000.

Othmer, James P., *The Futurist*, New York: Doubleday, 2006.

Shreeve, James, *The Genome War: How Craig Ventner Tried to Capture the Code of Life and Save the World*, New York: Knopf, 2004.

Toffler, Alvin, *Future Shock*, New York: Bantam, 1971.

Warshcauer, Mark, *Technology and Social Inclusion: Rethinking the Digital Divide*, Cambridge, MA: MIT Press, 2003.

Wilmut, Ian, and Roger Highfield, *After Dolly: The Uses and Misuses of Human Cloning*, New York: Norton, 2006.

WWW   Arts and Science Collaborations, Inc. www.asci.org

WWW   The Center for Democracy and Technology www.cdt.org

WWW   EPA, Climate Change www.epa.gov/climatechange (accessed June 22, 2009)

WWW   National Institute of Standards and Technology www.nist.gov/ (accessed June 22, 2009)

WWW   Science and Technology www.avs.org

WWW   Sierra Club www.sierraclub.org (accessed June 22, 2009)

WWW   Time 100, Builders and Titans www.time.com/time/time100/builder/index.html

WWW   Wired www.wired.com (accessed June 22, 2009)

WWW   World Peace Through Technology http://peacetour.org/

Psychology, Society, and Culture

After reading this chapter, you should be able to:

- Explain how culture and personality are related
- Summarize the nature/nurture debate
- State the importance of positive and negative reinforcement
- Discuss Maslow's hierarchy
- Differentiate the id, ego, and superego
- Explain how IQ is calculated and the problems with its use
- Define *deviance* and name five sociological theories about deviance

If I am not for myself,
who will be?
And if I am only for myself,
who am I?
And if not now, when?
—**Rabbi Hillel**

Culture is created by the individuals within that culture, but individuals' personalities are shaped and molded by culture. In this chapter, we take a social psychology perspective and consider the relationship between the individual and society. Much of our discussion will center on personality. **Personality** is the total organization of the inherited and acquired characteristics of an individual as evidenced by the individual's behavior. Culture's role in shaping individual personality is major, whereas each individual's influence on culture is usually slight. As individuals, people must accept their culture much as they find it, and if they hope to lead satisfactory lives as human beings, they must adjust to it.

This dependence of the individual on culture sometimes makes culture appear to be an independent entity, something that has an existence and continuity regardless of the people who are its carriers. This impression is strengthened when we view culture historically and note that many of its basic elements persist generation after generation. Two hundred years ago, the English language in its essential characteristics was not very different from what it is today. Yet, of all those who spoke English then, not a single person is now alive.

For some purposes, it is convenient to think of culture as if it had an independent, objective existence. In the final analysis, however, this is untrue. All cultures have been created by people. When we analyze culture closely, we find only a series of patterned reactions characteristic of the individuals who belong to a given group. It is people who hold beliefs, have attitudes, practice customs, and behave in conformity with patterns accepted by the group. Cultures are built up so slowly and gradually that it is seldom possible to isolate the contributions made by particular individuals. In a large society, the individual is only one among millions. Furthermore, most individuals accept the social situation in which they find themselves and make little attempt to change it.

The fact that people as individuals are shaped by their culture does not mean that they are deprived of all freedom to control their behavior, to choose their mode of life, and even to affect the conditions that surround them. Any general cultural pattern is flexible to a degree and permits some variations from the norms. In simple primitive societies, the permissible variations may be rather limited, but in modern complex societies they are great. However, in any society the average individual is seldom aware of the extent to which culture restricts freedom. Culture becomes so internalized—so much a basic part of personality—that most of the time people do not wish to behave in ways other than those culturally approved. Only in special situations do they become keenly aware of conflicts between their own desires and the kind of conduct that is socially permissible.

Socialization of the Individual

Socialization plays a major role in the development of human personality. This does not mean that a child's personality may not be greatly influenced by its biological inheritance and by contacts with the physical environment. For the most part, however, a child learns from people the patterns of behavior and the attitudes, beliefs, and expectations that motivate behavior. All of these are largely cultural in origin, and therefore, as a child grows and develops, his or her behavior reflects to an ever-greater degree the culture of the society into which he or she was born.

Significance of the Early Years of Childhood

The experiences of the young child within the family group seem to have the greatest influence on the development of human personality. Very early a normal baby begins to recognize familiar faces, sense approval and disapproval, seek attention, and in other ways react to the social environment.

Our personalities develop in this early childhood. Although tremendous gaps exist in our knowledge, we have discovered some of the ways in which children learn. One of the leaders in this discovery was noted psychologist Jean Piaget who developed several widely accepted theories on the development of children. His first point is obvious: Very young children think differently from adults. For example, many children think their shadow is a living entity that follows them wherever they go. Similarly, imaginary friends fly around the room at night, and inanimate objects, from marbles to vacuum cleaners, have very human characteristics. Reality for them blends in with imagination. As we grow older, most of us learn to separate reality from imagination. If, however, an individual lacks the right environment, he or she will not be able to do so and may go through an entire lifetime living in a semifantasy world.

Piaget finds it useful to divide a child's life into four stages (shown in Figure 7.1). From birth to two years, a child is primarily concerned with learning about physical objects. From two to six or seven years, the youngster learns about symbols in language, dreams, and fantasy. Next, he or she begins to learn about abstract concepts such as numbers and the relationships between them. Finally, from ages twelve to fifteen, the child masters purely logical thought and learns to understand double messages, such as irony and double entendres.

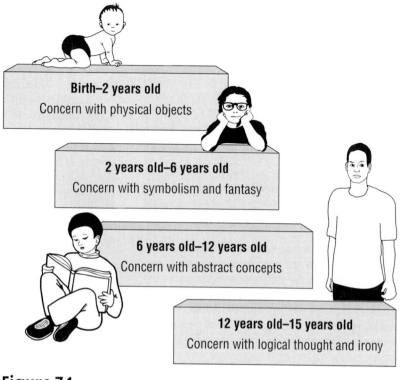

Figure 7.1

Piaget's four stages.

In order to develop normally both emotionally and mentally, a child must be accepted and receive affection, but overprotection and overaffection are not desirable, for they tend to lead to dependency and immaturity. At the other extreme, parental rejection and lack of affection create feelings of insecurity and inferiority and often bring on compensatory reactions such as aggressive, rebellious, or domineering behavior.

As young children grow, they come into contact not only with parents, brothers and sisters, and other members of the household, but also with outsiders such as neighbors and playmates. They acquire greater physical competence and greater skill in the use of language and continually make adjustments to new people and new situations. These early experiences leave nearly indelible impressions and influence the "set" of each one's personality.

Significance of Differences in Individual Environment

It is questionable whether any two individuals have precisely the same hereditary characteristics, though in the case of identical twins there is a close approximation to this situation. Certainly, no two individuals have exactly the same social environment. Some of the differences in individual environments are obvious to the most casual observer, but other differences are not so easy to see.

We are all aware that in a country such as the United States people often grow up in social environments that differ widely. To begin with, there are noticeable differences in the language, attitudes, and customs of the people in different regions. Also, even in the same region there are differences between rural life and city life; and in a city of even moderate size there can be found a great variety of more or less distinct social groups. Among the more important of these groups are those set off from one another by differences in income and social prestige, religion, nationality, or race. But differences in individual social environment go further than this. In any given social group, families are likely to differ significantly from one another in their modes of life, so that a child brought up in one family may have a quite different environment from that of a child reared in another.

All these differences are fairly obvious. It is not quite so obvious, but nonetheless true, that two children brought up in the same family at the same time may have quite dissimilar environments. This is because social environment depends not only on people, but also on the nature of personal relations with them. One child in a family may be loved by the parents, given every advantage, perhaps be overindulged, whereas another child may be disliked, neglected, even mistreated. Clearly, such children do not have at all the same environment, and the differences are sure to have deep and lasting effects on their mental and emotional development, on their personalities, and on their relations with other people in later years.

Effects of Extreme Isolation on Children

The study of children who have been largely isolated from social contacts demonstrates the importance of socialization by showing what happens in its absence. It also considers the possibility of compensating in later years for development that failed to take place earlier at the normal time.

It is impossible to find children who have been completely isolated from other human beings from the time of birth. The reason is simple. The human infant is so helpless that it cannot possibly survive without receiving some care from older people who understand its needs. However, cases have been reported of children who, in early life, have been partially or completely isolated from human contact over considerable periods. These reports are of two types: (1) cases of **feral children**—children who have lived in a wild or untamed state with animals—and (2) cases of children kept isolated in a room, basement, or attic and given little attention except for being provided with food and drink. (Less extreme examples of isolation occur with children who are merely neglected, or who are cared for, more or less impersonally, in institutions.)

Stories of feral children appeal to the imagination. They have been told in all ages about children believed to have been cared for when very young by boars, wolves, bears, or other animals. These stories have nearly always been spread by hearsay, and it is doubtful whether any of them are based on fact. Perhaps the oldest of such tales is about the legendary founders of Rome, the twins Romulus and Remus, who are said to have been abandoned as infants and suckled by a wolf. As you might have noticed, our history of the world skipped these legendary twins.

The one report that has some credibility is of two children found in a wolf den in India. They could not talk, and they are reported to have run on all fours and in other respects to have exhibited animal-like behavior. Under human care, they responded very little to the attempts made to socialize and educate them, and both died at an early age. Most psychologists believe that they most likely suffered from **infantile autism,** a condition in which a child is unable to respond emotionally to others. Most psychologists believe these children, not very long before they were found, had been abandoned because they were autistic.

Though stories of feral children should be regarded with skepticism, there appear to be well-authenticated cases of children who for considerable periods of time have been locked in basements, attics, or upstairs rooms and isolated from almost all normal human contacts. One case involved a girl named Isabelle who, because she was illegitimate, was

According to legend, the founders of Rome were human twins, Romulus and Remus, who were nurtured by a wolf.

kept secluded in a dark room with her deaf-mute mother until she was six and a half years old. In another case, a girl named Anna was kept in a room alone until she was about six.

In each of these cases, when the girl was discovered her behavior in many respects resembled that of an infant or a wild animal. But Isabelle, when placed in a normal social environment and given special training, caught up rapidly. In a few years, she was making good progress in school and gave the impression of a bright, cheerful, energetic little girl. However, when Anna was placed in a normal environment, she made much less progress, and she was still considered mentally disabled when she died at the age of ten and a half.

We have no way of knowing why Anna failed to develop as much as Isabelle. Perhaps Isabelle's close contact with her deaf-mute mother gave her a sense of being loved and secure, and thus she enjoyed a great advantage over Anna in her emotional development, or it may be that she received more expert attention after she was removed from isolation. It is also possible that Isabelle's biological inheritance was superior to Anna's.

In 1970, a thirteen-year-old girl, who was given the name Genie, was found. She had been tied up and kept in a room without human contact by her elderly parents, who were psychologically disturbed. She had been fed only milk and baby food and was never spoken to. She was incontinent, could not speak, and weighed only fifty-seven pounds. After she was brought to a hospital, she learned to communicate, but, although her mother said that she had been normal at birth, Genie's IQ was only 74 and her language ability never fully developed.

Personality and Its Development

To have a full understanding of the relationship between individuals and society, it is helpful to have a clear concept of the meaning of personality. It has been said that every human being is in some respects like all others, in some respects like some others, and in some respects like no others.

As we mentioned earlier, personality may be defined as the total organization of the inherited and acquired characteristics of an individual as evidenced by the individual's behavior.

It is the product of the interaction between an individual's original biological nature and his or her social and natural environment. Therefore, it bears the imprint of four things:

1. The inherited potentialities of the individual
2. Natural environment
3. The culture of the individual's society
4. Unique personal experiences

However, once personality has begun to form it becomes an independent force that may play a dominant part in its own future development and in the adjustment of the individual to the total environment.

The Nature/Nurture Debate

The human baby is a helpless creature at birth. It cannot walk; it cannot talk; it cannot even sit up, turn itself over, or grasp an object it is offered. It is not equipped, as are most animals, with a large number of hereditary **instincts**—inherited complex patterns of behavior that do not have to be learned. Instincts enable animals to satisfy needs that arise at various stages of their development. A good example is the nest-building instinct of birds.

Human babies at birth have instincts, but they also have an innate capacity for growth and development. Gradually, a baby learns to adjust to its environment, and in the process it slowly becomes conscious of itself as a person, separate from its environment. As it develops physically, its power to learn keeps increasing, but all the patterns of behavior that will later characterize it as a normal human being must be learned, and the learning process is not always easy.

The drives that a baby inherits are urges to satisfy basic needs such as those for sleep or food. When these are not satisfied, they are felt as tension or discomfort. These drives provide the stimulus for learning. One of the most powerful of human drives is hunger. To satisfy hunger, a baby depends on its mother's breast or a bottle. But when it becomes hungry, nourishment is not always present, and as its discomfort increases, the baby cries. This may bring the breast or the bottle and with it the pleasure that is felt as hunger is satisfied. Before long, the baby associates crying with the appearance of the nourishment, and so it cries as soon as hunger begins in order to bring the satisfaction. This illustrates the beginning of the learning process and perhaps also the beginning of the development of personality.

B. F. Skinner, a psychologist who did extensive research in this area, strongly emphasized the influence of society on the individual. He saw individuals' personalities shaped in large part by conditioning. He believed that individuals' behaviors could be changed by **operant conditioning**—altering individuals' habits by behaviors (operants) that themselves have an observable effect on the environment affecting an individual. Operant conditioning often is discussed in terms of **positive reinforcement, negative reinforcement,** and **punishment.** Procedures that strengthen behavior are called reinforcement; those that suppress behavior are called punishment. There are two types of reinforcement and two types of punishment, as outlined in Table 7.1.

It is important to note that punishment is not the same as negative reinforcement. If you speed and get a speeding ticket, you experience a positive punishment. If, however, the judge offers you the choice of attending a driver education class or losing your license, that's an example of negative reinforcement. You attend the class to avoid a worse alternative—losing your license. To summarize, positive and negative reinforcement are both procedures that strengthen behavior. Positive and negative punishment are both procedures that weaken behavior.

The effects of reinforcement and punishment on personality leave individuals with some hard choices. For example, should parents console or ignore a crying child? Consoling can reinforce negative crying behavior; on the other hand, ignoring might make the child feel unloved and have a negative influence on the child's development.

Table 7.1

Types of Punishments and Reinforcements

PROCEDURE	STIMULUS EVENT	EFFECTS	EXAMPLES
Positive reinforcement	Applying a desirable stimulus	Strengthens responses that precede occurrence of stimulus	Praise
Negative reinforcement	Applying an undesirable stimulus	Strengthens responses that allow escape from stimulus	Harsh criticism
Positive punishment	Applying an undesirable stimulus	Weakens responses that precede occurrence of stimulus	Speeding ticket
Negative punishment	Loss of a desirable stimulus	Weakens responses that lead to loss of stimulus	"Time-out"

Skinner did extensive work with laboratory animals such as rats and rabbits to test his theories. He and his adherents have shown that animals can be taught to do things such as push on a bar to receive food or water. Such laboratory work is, on the whole, noncontroversial (except when the experiments directly harm animals). But when Skinner's theories are extended to humans and to the way humans learn, they can be controversial.

Some researchers have emphasized the influence of punishment and reinforcement so strongly that little room remains in their theories for any other determinants of personality. Moreover, they have derived from these theories a number of proposals for education and controversial rehabilitation programs. For example, Skinnerians developed programmed texts that provide fast positive reinforcement for students. Also, some sex criminals may submit themselves to a rehabilitation program in which whenever they are shown sexually arousing pictures, they experience an electric shock (negative reinforcement) designed to modify their behavior.

Skinner's emphasis on the environment's role in shaping personality is disputed by many psychologists who emphasize instead the role of **heredity,** the genetic transmission of characteristics from parent to offspring. The debate between the two sides has often been called the nature/nurture debate. The **nature/nurture debate** focuses on whether heredity or environment is more important in determining the personality and the success in life of an individual. It is like asking, Which is more important in making an automobile run—the gasoline or the engine? Quite obviously, if the car is to run at all, both gasoline and an engine must be provided. Likewise, if a baby is to develop normally, it must have both a reasonably adequate biological inheritance and a reasonably adequate social environment.

If we could somehow take two identical individuals and place them in different environments, we could answer the question. However, no two people are physiologically identical (even identical twins have some slight differences), and no two people have the same environmental background. Instead, researchers must concentrate on groups of people to determine whether heredity or environment is more important. For example, are people's sexual desires determined by nature or nurture? This is an open question, but in 1991 a respected researcher found distinct differences in the brains of homosexuals and the brains of heterosexuals, which suggests a stronger role for nature. He emphasized, however, that his study was tentative. Another study, by Anthony Bogaert of Brock University, found that boys with older brothers had a higher probability of being gay than those without, and that the more brothers one had, the higher the probability of being gay. That wasn't the case for stepbrothers, however, so the reason is more likely nature than nurture. He hypothesized that it had something to do with antibodies developed by the mother of boys that affects the sexual orientation of future children. Despite these many provocative studies, we still have no definitive answer, but there is a leaning toward nature setting the scene for nurture. Surely, we will hear more about this debate in the future.

Recently, a test of the nature/nurture question was conducted with respect to obesity. The population studied consisted of adopted children, and the question posed was, Would the children resemble their biological (nature) or their adoptive (nurture) parents? In this study, it was found that children of obese biological parents tended to be obese. The obesity of the adopted parents had little effect. In this case, nature seems more important than nurture.

Recent discussions of the nature/nurture debate have tended to emphasize the complex interaction between the two. For example, measures of the inheritability of intelligence rise with age, from 40 percent in childhood to 60 percent in adulthood. James Flynn, a psychologist in New Zealand, suggests the reason is that a slight difference in intelligence at birth leads caregivers to treat children differently, with the seemingly brighter child being more strongly reinforced in learning, while the seemingly less bright child receives negative reinforcement.

Explanations of Behavior

The nature/nurture debate is part of a larger debate in psychology about how best to understand behavior. We distinguish four general approaches:

1. The **cognitive approach** focuses on nature; it sees thought as the initiator and determinant of behavior. In this approach, human actions represent reactions to physical processes in the brain. It looks to **cognitive science**—the scientific study of the mind—for explanations of behavior.

2. The **psychoanalytic approach** also focuses on nature, but it does not look to cognitive science. Rather, it takes a more mystical approach, focusing on certain innate tendencies of people. The most well-known of the psychoanalytic approaches is Freud's, which we discuss later in this chapter. Freud's approach focuses on the unconscious and its relation to conscious thoughts and actions. The psychoanalytic approach has produced a variety of therapeutic approaches besides that of Freud, one of which is Albert Ellis's "rational emotive therapy," also discussed later.

3. The **behavioralist approach** focuses on actions, not thoughts. B. F. Skinner was an advocate of this approach. The behavioralist approach has a recent addition—what might be called the biopsychological approach. Flowing from biology as much as it does from psychology, this approach views behavior simply as responses to chemical stimuli in the body (although its basis often is not put so bluntly). In this approach, one's genetic structure is believed to determine the ranges of behavior one will display; the chemical messengers determine specific behaviors within that general range. The mind is seen as just another part of the physical world.

4. The **humanist approach** emphasizes the entire person and his or her interrelationship with culture. Abraham Maslow's work, discussed later, is an example of this humanist approach.

These approaches are not mutually inconsistent, and recently a group of therapists emphasizing a combination approach—a cognitive behavioralist approach—have been gaining ground. The cognitive behavioralist approach emphasizes that thoughts can be "operants of the mind." Thus cognitive approaches focusing on thought are opened up to behavioralist analyses focusing on behavior.

Before we move on to discuss how these different approaches lead to different treatments of maladjustment, let us briefly consider Abraham Maslow's theory of the well-adjusted

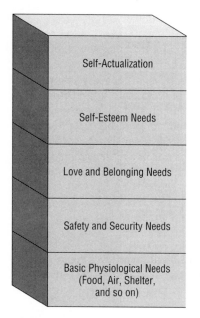

Figure 7.2

Abraham Maslow's hierarchy.

individual and Freud's conception of the personality to give you a little better idea of the differences that varying approaches can lead to.

The Well-Adjusted Individual

Probably the most famous theory of the development of a healthy personality is that of Abraham Maslow, known as Maslow's hierarchy. **Maslow's hierarchy** states that there are five levels of human achievement, each of which must be satisfied before the next is attempted. They are shown in Figure 7.2.

Self-actualization, the level of human achievement in which one is well adjusted to one's reality, is the highest level, according to Maslow. A person need not be famous, or the best in the field, in order to be self-actualized. Rather, we are self-actualized when content with life and capable of handling the problems that all of us must face. Because each level of the hierarchy must be satisfied before the next can be attempted, few of us reach self-actualization; even for those few who attain that highest level, it is a constant effort to stay there and not slide back down.

What do we mean by good social adjustment? There are dangers in setting up social adjustment as an ideal to be sought. If an individual were perfectly adjusted to the environment in the sense of having no problems or tensions and not wishing that anything were different, that person would stagnate. On the other hand, if we mean by a well-adjusted person, someone who loves life and finds it interesting and stimulating, that person must have dissatisfactions, problems to be dealt with, and goals to be achieved. Good adjustment must be a dynamic concept, and there is no simple formula for it that will apply equally well to everyone.

The truly well-adjusted person has developed a strong and balanced personality that can suffer misfortunes and recover from them. It should be emphasized that disappointment, pain, and grief are common experiences of life that come to all of us from time to time. The well-adjusted person can deal with these without being crushed.

Much research has gone into studying the genetic component of adjustment. In one study, psychologists David Lykken and Auke Tellegen surveyed 732 pairs of identical twins and found that their level of happiness was the same regardless of their surroundings. Another study reinforced this finding and discovered that the actual circumstances a person experiences have little to do with the satisfaction that person experiences. For example, people in China were happier in measures of subjective well-being than people in Japan, even though people in Japan were ten times richer.

In a book that attempted to pull all these ideas together, University of Pennsylvania psychologist Martin Seligman tried to explain what these findings meant for people searching for the "good life." One of his suggestions gives a sense of the ideas he raises. Specifically, he suggests: Keep your illusions. For example, he argues that happy couples—the couples who stay together happily—are ones who do not see their partner objectively, but instead see him or her through rose-colored glasses and think that the partner is better than he or she actually is. Other research, however, leads to different views. For example, research comparing people who have pessimistic personalities with people who have optimistic personalities found that those with pessimistic personalities are more attuned to reality and less stressed than people with optimistic personalities. We leave a consideration of these ideas to you as an optional research project, but we're sure you will do it (even though deep down we have our doubts) because, although we have underlying pessimistic personalities, we are trying to be optimists, which is another of Seligman's suggestions of how to have the good life.

Adjustment and Normality

Good adjustment and normality do not have precisely the same meaning when applied to personality, but their relationship is close. Conversely, a normal person in any society is necessarily a reasonably well-adjusted person. In cultural terms, a **normal person** is one who has acquired the basic attitudes and behavior patterns of the culture sufficiently well to be accepted and approved by the group. In any society, a well-adjusted person is likely to be recognized as a normal person. This normal person may not in all respects represent the typical person in the group, or the statistical average, but the normal person's behavior must not deviate too far from what is acceptable. Cultural norms are determined by the group. Types of behavior that in one culture would be quite normal might in another culture be regarded as wholly abnormal.

The Freudian Concept of Personality

Probably the best-known name in psychology is Sigmund Freud, who lived from 1856 to 1939 and spent most of his life in Vienna, Austria. He was trained as a physician but specialized in neurology, and in those days this meant that most of his patients were people with emotional problems.

Freud became famous as the originator of the system of psychotherapy known as **psychoanalysis,** a method of analysis based on the exploration of unconscious mental processes as manifested in dreams and disturbed relationships with others. Essentially, the method of psychoanalysis is that of free association. A patient is induced to express anything that comes to mind in the hope of uncovering memories or ideas of which the patient is unaware but that may be causing mental and emotional conflicts. For example, perhaps a terrifying experience in early childhood has been repressed below the level of consciousness. The psychoanalyst believes that if the patient can be helped to recall such an experience, the patient will be able to deal with it realistically, so that the mental disturbances it has been causing will disappear. But to bring unconscious mental processes to the level of consciousness takes time and persistence on the part of both the psychoanalyst and the patient.

In time, Freud became recognized as one of the great original thinkers in the field of psychology, and today most psychologists believe he made important contributions to our understanding of the human personality. But his theories have been the center of much controversy.

The Id, Ego, and Superego.   To Freud, personality consisted of three major systems or "structures," which he called the id, the ego, and the superego. In the normal person, these three personality systems cooperate to enable the individual to satisfy basic needs and desires within the environmental setting, but when they are in serious conflict with one another, various mental disorders will result.

According to Freud, the **id** is the part of our personality controlled by the pleasure principle. It is driven by the goals to seek pleasure and avoid pain. It is the immature, selfish side of our personalities. Its counterpart, the **superego,** is our primitive conscience, which develops as we grow older and is guided solely by our morals. The third major structure of the personality is the **ego**—the personality component that most immediately controls behavior and is most in touch with external reality—which plays referee between the other two systems, sometimes allowing us to seek pleasure, at other times allowing the superego to guide us to more restrictive behavior. The id, ego, and superego are, of course, not independent entities. Rather, they are convenient terms to designate different groups of forces that interact within the human personality.

Defense Mechanisms. Among the many elements of Freud's psychology are **defense mechanisms**—behaviors that individuals use to avoid facing issues. These include:

- Displacement, in which one redirects one's anger away from the real target and toward an innocent target. For example, a frustrated worker kicks his dog.

- Reaction formation, in which an individual connects an anxiety-causing impulse with an overemphasized opposite. For example, people who are unconsciously attracted to the same sex may develop an intense hatred of gays.

- Projection, in which unacceptable urges in oneself are attributed to others. For example, a spouse tempted to have an affair becomes unduly suspicious of his or her partner.

- Rationalization, in which one gives excuses for one's shortcomings. For example, after you fail an exam and flunk out of school, you say it was all boring anyhow, and you prefer doing active, not mental, work.

- Fantasy, in which one avoids one's real worries by living in a fantasy world. For example, you don't study but rather spend all day dreaming of the great job you will never get because you didn't study.

- Sublimation, in which one transforms an unacceptable need into an acceptable ambition. You study hard because you hate the textbook author's stupid jokes.

Defense mechanisms include other behaviors that we all follow to varying degrees, but this list should give you a good idea of what is meant by defense mechanisms.

The Oedipus Complex. Probably the best-known aspect of Freud's work is the **Oedipus complex**—a child's sexual attraction to the parent of the opposite sex—so called because of its analogy to the Greek myth about Oedipus, the man who unknowingly killed his father and married his mother. Freud's formulation of the Oedipus complex grew out of the fact that rather early in his career he believed he had uncovered, in the unconscious mental processes of his neurotic patients, fantasies of sexual relations with the parent of the opposite sex, combined with jealous anger against the parent of the same sex. Later he came

*P*erfection Blueprint

If the perfect child will make the perfect adult, the early 1980s produced a recipe to satisfy society's appetite for good adjustment. Judith Martin wrote two no-nonsense books that explained how to perfect the child. Briefly stated, her rules are for parents to nag, to start early, to set a good example, and to keep at it. She based her system on the belief that if the child acts perfect, the child is perfect.

She has no patience with uncertainties such as, "Who is to decide what is right and wrong, what is proper and improper?" and "What difference does it make which spoon you choose for the soup?" If you teach your child to sit up straight and your child learns to do that, then, Martin believes, your child will look nice, will seem to be paying attention in school, will be paying attention in school, will be learning lessons, and will be on the road to success and perfection.

She advocates advancing by increments, or steps. Say please and thank you to the baby; withhold the candy until the toddler says please; give the child a place at the dinner table when she no longer spits spinach around the kitchen; let the kid eat in a restaurant when he has learned not to interrupt adults' conversation; send the eighth-grader off to buy her own clothes when she has learned to polish her own shoes and press her shirt before starting out for school.

There are old-fashioned sayings that summarize these ideas, such as "Manners maketh man" and "Handsome is as handsome does" and even "Go along to get along." Social scientists call this process socializing. Or it could be called civilizing. Whatever you may think of her methods, Martin has hold of a basic principle. If individuals can be molded to a standard set by the society in which chance has deposited those individuals, the standards will be preserved, the people will get along with each other, everyone will know what to expect, there will be no surprises, and the world will run smoothly.

Motivational speakers such as Tony Robbins abound. They will tell you that you can do anything you want, if only you try their simple methods.

to believe that a strong sexual attraction to the parent of the opposite sex, along with jealousy of the other parent, is a universal experience of childhood in the years before the age of five. After this period, the Oedipus complex is repressed and disappears from the conscious mind because of recognition of the impossibility of fulfilling the sexual wishes; also, in the case of a boy, because of fear of retaliation from the father. At this stage, the child begins to identify with the parent of the same sex. Freud believed that the Oedipus complex was an essential factor in the development of every child's personality and hence in determining the nature of all human societies.

The Oedipus complex received much publicity and aroused widespread opposition. Many people found it difficult to accept in the form in which Freud presented it. He made it clear that the Oedipus complex referred to a definite desire of the child for sexual relations with the parent of the opposite sex, and to jealousy of the other parent because of the sexual relationship, but in our society it seems doubtful that most very young children have even a vague concept of the existence or nature of sexual relations. Certainly many do not, and in that case it is hard to see how they can desire them or be jealous on account of them. Even among psychoanalysts who subscribe to most of Freud's theories are those who question or reject the theory of the Oedipus complex.

Pop Psychologies

Modern scientific psychology is supplemented by what might be called pop psychology, in which the more scientific theories are translated and digested, making them available for popular consumption. One such translation is transactional analysis, or TA, which in some respects is similar to Freud's theories. It was made famous by Thomas A. Harris's bestselling book *I'm O.K., You're O.K.*, and it breaks down the human personality into three "parts"—parent, adult, and child—which roughly coincide with the superego, ego, and id of Freud. According to TA, when two people interact they must be using the same mode of personality (preferably the adult voice). When one's parent mode attempts to address another person's child mode but the receiver is thinking in the adult voice, confusion of the message and frustration result. Other pop theories include ESP (extrasensory perception), scream theory, and channeling. Most recent pop psychologies of the early 2000s have a common theme—the quick fix. These theories include psychohypnosis, neuro-linguist programming (NLP), timeline therapy, and emotional freedom techniques (EFT), and although we do not discuss these here, they make interesting research topics.

*I*ntelligence, Personal Adjustment, and Normality

Before we move on to discuss some of the approaches various psychological theories lead to, let us consider the issue of intelligence and its role in determining personal adjustment and normality. Although this subject is not directly related to personal adjustment, it is an important topic that often causes confusion.

In every human society, individuals have varied **intelligence,** which is the ability of a person to understand the situations that confront him or her and to make satisfactory adjustments to them insofar as such adjustments depend on learning and thinking. Low intelligence has prevented some people from making an adequate adjustment to their environment. But only in recent decades have systematic efforts been made to define and measure intelligence or other mental qualities.

Mental Tests

Mental tests are intended to discover or to measure the mental characteristics of an individual. One of the earliest mental tests is described in Greek mythology. During the Trojan War, according to the story, a Greek named Ulysses paid no attention to the government's call to arms. The authorities visited him and found him plowing up the beach and sowing salt. Determined to see whether he was pretending to be insane, they placed Ulysses's only son in the plow's path. Ulysses quickly turned aside, and the test was deemed conclusive proof that he was sane.

Modern mental tests are based on the assumption that we can predict the reactions of an individual in various situations by giving specially designed tests in which similar conditions are involved. Furthermore, we assume that by presenting an individual with a large variety of sample situations, we can estimate how that person's abilities compare with those of other people.

Psychologists employ various types of tests to determine the characteristics of an individual. One type attempts to measure general intellectual ability; this is known as an intelligence test. Another type explores the individual's basic interests by presenting various hypothetical choices and asking the subject to express preferences. A third type is intended to measure aptitudes for certain kinds of work. A fourth is known as a test of achievement and is essentially a test of how well certain skills have been learned or certain kinds of knowledge have been assimilated. A fifth is intended to discover special abilities or disabilities and is generally given to children or adults with disabilities. Finally, a sixth type of test used by psychologists tries to determine the individual's personality structure and basic emotional needs. This type of test is known as a personality, or emotional adjustment, test.

All these tests are used by clinical psychologists to diagnose the power and potentialities of the individual as they exist at any given stage of development. On the basis of such tests, psychologists are able to learn something about the mental difficulties of an individual and judge the possibilities of helping the individual to overcome them.

Mental Age and the IQ.   The best-known psychological test is the IQ, or general intelligence test, which attempts to reduce the many dimensions of intelligence to a single number that estimates a person's mental age. To do this, researchers devised a wide variety of test items, from the simple to the complex, and arranged them in order of difficulty. They then tried these items out on a large number of children at various grade levels. On the basis of this experience, they assigned a mental-age value to each item. Their procedure in assigning questions or problems to various ages was as follows: If a certain item was responded to correctly by as many as 65 to 75 percent of the children whose age was, say, eight years, but by a smaller percentage of children below that age, it was considered a test of eight-year-old intelligence. They then grouped several items of appropriate difficulty, usually five, to test children of each age. If a child could answer the questions for all levels up through those for eight-year-olds, but none of those for the years above that, mental age was considered to be eight regardless of actual or chronological age. But the child received proportionate credit for any questions actually answered.

For example, if the child could answer all the questions for eight-year-olds, and three out of five of those for nine-year-olds, mental age was considered 8.6. If the child could also answer two out of five of the questions for age ten, a mental age of nine was assigned. Later, other psychologists refined the technique so that each mental year consisted of twelve mental months. For example, each test item might represent two mental months, in which case six items would represent a mental year. Each person tested would then receive two months' credit toward a mental age for each item answered correctly.

Once the concept of mental age was developed, it was only a step to the notion of expressing a ratio between the mental age and the chronological age of an individual. This ratio was called the **IQ, or intelligence quotient**—an index of an individual's tested mental ability as compared to the rest of the population. IQ is calculated by dividing mental age by actual age and multiplying the resulting fraction by 100. Multiplying by 100 expresses the ratio or fraction as a percentage, but it is not customary to write "percent" after the number expressing IQ. The formula for finding IQ may be written as follows:

$$IQ = \text{Mental Age/Chronological Age} \times 100.$$

Let us see how this formula works in practice. A child eight years old having a mental age of eight is an average child. IQ would be $8/8 \times 100 = 100$. It is apparent, therefore, that an IQ of 100 represents average intelligence. If a child eight years old had a mental age of twelve, as indicated by an intelligence test, that eight-year-old would obviously be very bright. This would be indicated by IQ, which would be $12/8 \times 100 = 150$.

Today it is often the practice to assign an individual a percentile rank rather than an IQ. **Percentile rank** is a ranking of an individual with reference to other individuals in a certain group when all individuals in the group are ranked in order from the most capable to the least capable. The hundredth percentile consists of the 1 percent of the group who have made the highest scores. The first percentile consists of the 1 percent who have made the lowest scores. Similarly, the 50th and 51st percentiles consist of those who have made average scores. Figure 7.3 shows the IQ rankings for society.

Mental tests indicate that great differences exist in intelligence in our population. This fact has long been known, but tests have made our knowledge more definite. Though these and other psychological tests are used more widely than ever before in schools, in government, and

IQ Score	Category		Percentage
20		PROFOUND	
30			
40	Retarded	SEVERE	0.4%
50			
60		MODERATE	
70	Mildly Retarded		2%
80	Borderline		7%
90	Dull Normal		17%
100	Normal		25%
110			25%
120	Bright Normal		17%
130	Superior		7%
140			2%
150			
160			
170	Very Superior		0.4%
180			
185			
200			

Figure 7.3

Percentage of children at different IQ groupings.

in business, they are also subjected to increasing criticism because of cultural biases in the tests. Nevertheless, mental tests are probably the best means we have for comparing the mental powers of large numbers of individuals.

Limitations of IQ and Other Tests.   Many of the early experimenters believed they had devised tests that did not depend on acquired knowledge but were essentially a measure of innate or inherited mental ability. Hence, they thought the scores of individuals on such tests could not be affected by any ordinary differences in environment. However, various studies and experiments have demonstrated beyond a reasonable doubt that factors such as differences in family environment and schooling may have a substantial effect on the scores individuals make on standard intelligence tests. For example, when identical twins are separated early and reared in different types of homes, the twin reared by parents of superior social, economic, and educational status almost invariably does better on an intelligence test than the other member of the pair, and sometimes the difference is fairly substantial.

Another example is that people who take the same test thirty years after entering high school will score in direct relation to how much education they have received in that span of time. Yet another chink in the armor of IQ test infallibility comes from Robert Rosenthal of Harvard University and Lenore Jacobsen, an elementary school principal in San Francisco, who successfully convinced a group of teachers that certain students were gifted. According to *Pygmalion in the Classroom,* in which the study is published, the students, who actually were chosen at random, surpassed their classmates and became high-level achievers. These "brighter" students scored an average of 12.22 points higher on achievement tests administered at the beginning and end of the year, compared with only an 8.42 point improvement from their classmates. The only difference between the two groups was in how the teachers responded to their learning needs.

Another indication of the limitation of the IQ test is the fact that scores on the same test have been increasing over time. Because it is almost impossible that intelligence is rising that fast, this suggests that there are sociological aspects to the test and that the test reflects those sociological aspects.

In recent years, some social scientists have argued that standardized intelligence tests are racially biased as well. Again, this relates to the environment in which the child is raised. A black child raised in a low-income area may not know what the capital of Greece is, but the lack of that one bit of information does not indicate less learning ability than a child from a high-income background enjoys. Others disagree, arguing that it is not "white information" that is tested.

The conclusion we can draw from such studies is that the scores people make on intelligence tests are a result of their previous experiences as well as of their inherited mental aptitudes. Where conditions of environment have been similar, differences in scores may be a rough indication of differences of innate mental aptitude. However, we must be cautious in assuming that any two given individuals have really had the same, or nearly the same, environment.

Some educators say that these intelligence tests are knowledge tests, not necessarily tests of intelligence. Currently there is a trend to use different kinds of tests, such as assessing a portfolio of a student's work or testing on a computer where the computer selects the next question based on how the test-taker has answered the preceding questions. However, it is expensive to develop new tests, to persuade schools to adopt them, and to train educators to administer and grade them. The standard IQ tests currently employed will probably continue to be widely used for many years.

Intelligence Is Far More Than Mental Manipulation.   All tests are useful only if we recognize their limitations. IQ tests tell us something about the probable intelligence of an individual at the time a test is taken, but they do not and cannot measure innate or inherited mental potentialities. A possibly more serious limitation grows out of the difficulty of defining intelligence in such a way that all the elements that enter into it can be

*Y*our IQ Is 132? So What?

Is the intelligence level of people in the United States falling? If it is, why?

Charles Murray, an author who treats various social and political issues, thinks the intelligence level in the United States is falling and that he has found out why. He explained his theories in a book called *The Bell Curve* (written with coauthor Bruce Herrnstein).

In that book, he concludes that the average level of U.S. intelligence is falling because some large groups of nonwhite Americans and some large groups of nonwhite immigrants to the United States have lower IQs than large groups of whites (but East Asians, he says, have higher IQs than whites). He reaches this conclusion because of the results of his research on IQs (the average IQ of some groups is lower than that of others) and because he takes the further step of treating IQ as the measure of intelligence.

Many social scientists consider Murray's arguments wrong and prejudiced. Murray insists they are not. He points out that although large groups may exhibit a particular average test score level, individuals in any of the groups may vary widely in intelligence, and no assumptions should be made about any individual's intelligence based on the overall scores for a particular group. Murray explains that his position is that one group is not inferior to another, just different.

Whether Murray's research is prejudiced against or toward any particular group or individual, he is open to criticism just because he equates IQ with intelligence. The book claims that IQ measures intelligence and that IQ/intelligence depends primarily on what you're born with, rather than what you get from living. But although IQ scores are definitely measurable, and one group or another does on average score higher or lower than others, there is a lot of doubt among social scientists as to what an IQ score means. So Murray's work is widely criticized. Still, Murray's controversial books on social policy topics are useful to consider; they make for spirited and challenging discussion, whatever their effect on the real world of politics and social interaction may be.

correctly rated by a test. It is doubtful whether the concept can be defined with much precision and whether the relative intelligence of different individuals, especially at the higher levels, can be determined with much accuracy. Defining intelligence is problematic, but our earlier definition—that intelligence is the ability of a person to understand the situations that confront him or her and to make satisfactory adjustments to them insofar as such adjustments depend on learning and thinking—is probably the best we can do.

The more intelligent a person is, the better able he or she is to do the following:

- Perceive a situation as a whole rather than partially or incompletely
- Learn quickly
- Concentrate thought and learning in a desired direction
- Find satisfactory solutions, either with or without help from others

High intelligence probably requires considerable imagination and originality, for to solve a difficult problem we may need to think of and to evaluate a number of novel approaches.

When we assume that a so-called mental test measures intelligence, we are assuming that the mental abilities required for correct answers to its questions are the same as those needed for solving the sometimes complex problems encountered in real life. This is not always true, for mental tests have many limitations. For example, they must be completed within a limited period of time on the theory that this makes the scores of individuals more comparable. But some of the world's greatest achievements have been made by people who have acquired the habit of thinking through difficult problems slowly, checking at every step to avoid missing some important consideration. Furthermore, to allow one's mind and imagination to wander with a purpose, to take time to search for the unusual or unlikely aspects of a situation, is one kind of intelligent behavior. It is also an important ingredient in originality or creativity. IQ tests don't measure such abilities. Much research has been done on multiple intelligence models, which assume that there are several different dimensions of intelligence, and that these dimensions cannot be reduced to a single meaningful number such as is attempted with IQ. Researchers have yet, however, to come up with an acceptable alternative.

𝒲ho Stands Stress Better: Men or Women?

It used to be thought that women were more emotionally and psychiatrically disabled and had more symptoms of stress than men. However, in 1984 the National Institute of Mental Health (NIMH) completed a six-year study of psychiatric ailments and concluded that although women tend to suffer more than men from phobias and depression, men suffer more than women from alcohol abuse, dependence on drugs, and long-term antisocial behavior. Taking all psychiatric disorders into account, the NIMH study found that both men and women are about equally likely to be affected.

Even so, women have often continued to be perceived as more subject to psychiatric problems because the study also showed that women seek professional help twice as often as men do. In fact, though, it could be argued that women have a healthier attitude than men because they do seek help, whereas, according to the study, men tend to mask their depression with alcohol.

You can probably see the tendencies in your own life. Women talk with other women; they discuss their problems and they expose and examine their weaknesses. Men generally hide them and are far less likely to have close male friends with whom they discuss personal problems. Instead, male friends do things together. It is the "macho" thing to do.

Intelligence and Personal Adjustment

Intelligence, especially if we mean intelligence measured by IQ tests, has little relation to one's ability to adjust except at the highest IQ levels (above 150) and lowest IQ levels (below 60). Both of these extreme groups often have a harder time adjusting to society than do people in the middle ranges.

The reason that IQ generally is not important is that personal adjustment has more to do with emotional stability and coming to terms with what one is as a person than it does with one's ability to score high on a test.

Even if IQ tests did measure intelligence accurately, it should be pointed out that intelligence and success are not synonymous. Many high-IQ individuals have difficulty coping with life; they might be able to solve a complicated mathematical problem, but they haven't the faintest idea how to interrelate with other people. Business leaders generally fall in the average (normal and bright normal) IQ category, not the superior or very superior categories. They have qualities such as internal fortitude, drive, ambition, ability to work with others, and imagination, which are necessary and probably more important than superior intelligence for business success. We can speak from experience; being at a university we're around people with high IQs all the time and, quite frankly, many of them can be real pains.

𝒟eviance

One of society's tasks is to coordinate the actions of millions of individuals so that they fit together. Society's way of doing this is to develop **norms**—expectations about what constitutes appropriate or acceptable behavior. By definition, most people follow those norms. Individuals' actions are called **deviant** when those actions conflict with society's norms.

A number of things should be noted about the concept of deviance. The first is that it is a relative concept. An act can only be considered deviant relative to some norms, and there is enormous arbitrariness in setting those norms. Thus picking one's nose in public and wiping the result on one's hair would be considered somewhat deviant in the United States. In the Yanomamö tribe in South America, that is the norm; not following that norm is the deviant behavior. To make this relativity clear, some sociologists have emphasized that it is society's reaction to the act, not the act itself, that makes something deviant.

Some societal norms are codified into law. A **crime** is a deviant behavior that violates legal norms. All crime is deviant behavior, but not all deviant behavior is crime. In this chapter, we concentrate on deviance.

There has been extensive theorizing about deviance. Most of that theorizing quickly gets too complicated for a general social science course, but in the remainder of this chapter we briefly introduce you to some of the broadest of these perspectives on deviance, surveying some psychological, biological, sociological, and economic explanations for deviance.

Major Theories on Deviance

All of us exhibit some deviant behavior. Every so often any well-adjusted person says, "Phooey on the norms!" and lets go, blowing off steam to release tension. Such limited deviant behavior is often condoned and even admired by society. It gives the person an identity, a personality. However, there is a line and if one crosses it, one's individuality becomes too much for society. Society wants you to be different, but not too different.

There are a variety of perspectives on deviance and explanations of why people step over the line. Psychologists tend to look within individuals—into their upbringing or into their genetic makeup. Sociologists, by contrast, tend to look for factors outside individuals—such as social conditions within society.

As soon as these explanations are explored more carefully, one quickly gets caught up in competing perspectives, each of which has its own terminology and theoretical nuances. We'll leave those issues for a sociology or psychology course and try here to introduce you briefly to some of the major perspectives and theories.

Psychological and Biological Explanations of Deviance

We do what we do because certain chemicals are released to the brain. These chemicals tell us what actions to perform. The chemicals that are released are themselves determined by a combination of what we eat, our genetic makeup, and the way we are brought up. Psychological and biological explanations of deviance focus on such biological or physiological explanations of criminal behavior.

Some of the psychological explanations of deviance focus on **personality disorders,** abnormalities in individual personalities caused by hereditary factors or by upbringing. These disorders might result, for example, from emotional deprivation—lack of love—in childhood or from being brainwashed by television programs in which crime is glorified. Or, alternatively, these explanations focus more on neurological and biological issues resulting from heredity or psychological causes. Let's consider one of those subissues: the issue of genetic and biological predisposition to deviance and crime. Genetic and Biological Predisposition to Deviance.

The idea that there is a criminal type has long been a popular belief among laypeople and among some criminologists. For example, in the late nineteenth century, noted Italian criminologist Cesare Lombroso claimed that criminals are less sensitive to pain and more subject to epilepsy than normal individuals. He found criminals to have heads higher at the rear than at the forehead, longer lower jaws, flattened noses, scanty beards, long ears, and other physical peculiarities. He explained these peculiarities as atavistic reversions to the characteristics of early savage ancestors. Later studies have totally discredited Lombroso's theory.

Modern approaches have not concentrated on body type but rather on genetic structure. Some studies have argued that a causal link exists between the presence in some males of an extra Y or "male-producing" chromosome (designated the XYY syndrome) and criminal behavior. Much of this work has been discredited, and in 1971 Richard Fox labeled it a modern myth.

The advent of sociobiology has brought another resurgence of biological explanations of criminal behavior. Sophisticated studies, such as one by Sarnoff Mednick and Karl Christiansen in 1977, have suggested some biological predisposition to criminal activity.

They found that boys adopted at birth whose biological parents were criminals were more likely to be criminals than those with noncriminal parents, even though neither group knew about their parents.

Yet another attempt to establish a biological basis for crime took place in 1985, when James Q. Wilson of Harvard and Richard Herrnstein of the University of California published *Crime and Human Nature,* in which they argue that crime is a matter of relating costs (getting caught and punished) with the benefits of crime. The authors hold that for certain types of individuals, such as those with athletic builds and slightly lower than average IQ (92), the costs are outweighed by the immediate benefits; that is, punishment for crime occurs with a lag, whereas the benefits of crime are immediate. They hold that this means individuals' time preference (how much they value the present relative to the future) plays an important role in determining whether a person is predisposed to crime. As with most theories that focus on a biological basis for crime, these theories are much in debate.

Sociological Explanations of Deviance

The group that has had the most to say about deviance and crime is composed of sociologists. To introduce you to the sociologists' perspective, we will briefly discuss differential association theory, control theory, labeling theory, strain theory, and illegitimate opportunity theory. These theories are part of two broad sociological perspectives: (1) a symbolic **interactionist perspective,** which sees individuals interpreting social life through symbols that we learn from the groups to which we belong, and (2) a **functionalist perspective,** which sees all activities in society as having a function. Differential association theory, control theory, and labeling theory fall within the symbolic interactionist perspective. Strain theory and illegitimate opportunity theory fall within the functionalist perspective.

Differential Association Theory. **Differential association theory** argues that deviant behavior often is simply behavior that is conforming to norms. The difference is that they are deviant norms. For example, some groups develop a different set of values or norms—such as toughness and the ability to take chances—considered deviant from the dominant norms.

This theory, put forward by sociologist Edwin Sutherland, argues that whether people deviate or conform is most influenced by the groups with whom they associate. Because different groups have different forms of deviant behavior, people who associate with different groups experience an "excess of definition" and in some groups seem deviant. For example, street gangs can require individuals to "stand up" to an insult, and if one is insulted one is expected to respond by defending one's honor with physical violence.

Differential association theory comes more into play when significantly different cultures interact. In the Hmong culture of Southeast Asia, one of the ways one finds a wife is to "capture" her and forcibly have sex with her. In the United States, that is called kidnapping and rape, both of which are serious crimes.

Most people will agree that differential association theory explains some deviant behavior, but most also argue that it should not be used to condone it. Society must have norms, and individuals must learn to conform to those norms and abide by those that have been codified into law.

Labeling Theory. **Labeling theory** focuses on the significance of labels given to people (such as names and reputational labels). These labels assigned by society to groups can tend to make the actions of certain groups criminal and the actions of certain other groups noncriminal. A classic study of the effects of labeling was done by sociologist William Chamblis. He studied two groups of adolescent lawbreakers in a high school. He labeled one group "the Saints" and the other group "the Roughnecks." Both groups were wild, into drinking, truancy, vandalism, and theft, but the Saints were seen by their teachers as headed for success whereas the Roughnecks were seen as headed for trouble. The cause of this distinction was family background and social class. The Saints came from respectable, middle-class families. The Roughnecks came from working-class families. This led to a number of differences: The Saints had cars so their debauchery was spread over the entire town and was less conspicuous; the Roughnecks did not have cars and their actions, taking place in the same area day after day, made them conspicuous and drew the attention of the police. They also had different "styles of interaction" when caught by police. The Saints were seemingly apologetic and penitent; they showed a seeming respect for the police and generally were let go with warnings. The Roughnecks showed contempt for the police and consistently had the book thrown at them. The results were predictable: The Saints became doctors and lawyers while the Roughnecks became criminals.

The issues here are obviously more complicated than can be captured by this brief discussion of Chamblis's study, but the idea should be clear: Labels make a difference in how people are treated and in many cases can become self-fulfilling.

Control Theory. **Control theory** argues that the desire to rebel is more akin to our natural desires but that certain forces prevent us from doing so. Control theory argues that the question is not, Why do people deviate from society's norms? Rather, the question is, Why don't we deviate more than we do? To prevent such deviation, society has developed norms and institutions that subtly control us and our actions. Much of the subtle control is instilled by parents during our childhood, and thus the type of family we come from and the type of friends we have in early childhood play major roles in determining how much deviance we will exhibit.

Strain Theory. **Strain theory** falls within the functionalist sociological perspective. Functionalists argue that deviance is a necessary part of a society; it clarifies moral boundaries and affirms norms; it promotes social unity and brings about necessary social change.

Successful industrialized societies must arouse discontent in people to instill within them the desire to advance and better themselves. Strain theory was developed by sociologist Robert Merton and other functionalists. **Strain theory** argues that when the social structure does not provide equal access for economic success, but instills in all people a functional striving for economic success, the result is a social strain. This social strain can result in a variety of reactions, one of which is crime. Notice the difference between strain theory and the psychological theories. Strain theory sees deviance as a product of society, not of individuals. Society creates crime and criminals.

Illegitimate Opportunity Theory. A slightly different take on the functionalist perspective on crime is the illegitimate opportunity theory, put forward by sociologists Richard Clower and Lloyd Ohlin. This theory argues that crime is all around us but that different social classes have distinct styles of crime. All individuals are imbued with the desire to achieve material success, but the lower social classes have significant barriers to achieving that success legally. They are, however, presented with **illegitimate opportunity structures**—opportunities to make larger amounts of money through "hustles" such as drug dealing, pimping, and gambling. Society sees all these as crimes. The more privileged class does not face the barriers and its crimes are "white-collar crimes" such as tax evasion and false advertising, which are not prosecuted as much and are not so widely seen as bad.

Economic Explanations of Deviance

Economists tend to see all issues through a prism of costs and benefits. Thus, their explanation for crime and deviance is that the costs of crime exceed the benefits and that the way to decrease crime and deviance is to increase its costs. For example, the death penalty increases the cost of a crime to an individual, and economists argue that having the death penalty helps prevent killings. Critics argue that killing generally is an irrational act—a crime of passion in which the penalty plays only a very small role; thus, having the death penalty will not significantly reduce killings. (Both sides are still debating the empirical evidence.)

Similarly, economists argue that lower-income individuals are more likely to commit an "equal payoff" crime than are high-income individuals because the cost to the higher-income individuals of going to jail is higher. Similarly, a rich person is less likely to be deterred by a fine than a poorer person because the same fine has less meaning to the rich person. Finland has an interesting application of this view. It makes all traffic fines income sensitive, so that a rich person pays a much higher fine than a poor person. Thus, a rich person might have to pay $200,000 if caught speeding.

Even economists admit that much is left out of their cost–benefit approach to crime (and to many issues). But they argue that its simplicity and clear statement often shed some light on an issue that is missed by other approaches, especially when the economic approach is combined with a good understanding of the strengths and weaknesses of other social science approaches.

Summary of Various Perspectives on Deviance

Our discussion has only touched on the various theories of deviance. Many, I am sure, led to reactions from you such as "But how about…." To really get into those issues, you'll have to take a psychology or sociology course on deviance. Before we move on, however, let us point out that the theories are not mutually exclusive, and our brief overview of them has not done them justice. Deviance is not a simple issue, and truly understanding that issue requires study beyond that which can be presented in an overview course such as this.

Conclusion

As you can see from the discussion in this chapter, and as you probably know from your own life, adjusting personality to fit society and adjusting society to fit personality are not easy. These adjustments involve a continual effort extending from birth to death. For many of us, it will seem an almost insurmountable effort in which the cards are stacked against us. It is precisely this feeling that leads so many into pop psychology.

This chapter presents a variety of theories and therapies, and almost all of them have some value. Perhaps the most useful lesson here is not so much what the theories are (although this knowledge is necessary) as it is that psychological problems are prevalent among most members of society. It is all too easy to see ourselves as out of step and others as well adjusted (or vice versa).

In terms of the course, the important lesson is to understand the processes by which individuals and societies interrelate. Society is composed of individuals, but society as a whole is much more than the sum of those individuals. Thus individual development and societal development make up a two-way street.

An evolving society will always have its adjustment problems, and each one of us who is a part of society plays a small role in that adjustment. As we adjust, so too does society.

Key Points

- Culture is created by the individuals within that culture, and individuals' personalities are in turn shaped and molded by culture.
- Both nature and nurture affect personality and individual development.
- Positive and negative reinforcement help shape an individual's personality.

- Self-actualization is the highest level of Maslow's hierarchy of needs.
- Freud saw personality as consisting of three major systems: the id, the ego, and the superego.
- Defense mechanisms are behaviors that individuals use to avoid facing issues.

- IQ tests can be useful, but only if their limitations are kept in perspective.
- Deviant behavior is not a crime unless there is a law against that behavior.

- Five sociological explanations of crime are differential association theory, control theory, labeling theory, strain theory, and illegitimate opportunity theory.

Some Important Terms

behavioralist approach (130)
cognitive approach (130)
cognitive science (130)
control theory (142)
crime (139)
defense mechanism (133)
deviant (139)
differential association theory (141)
ego (132)
feral children (126)
functionalist perspective (141)
heredity (129)
humanist approach (130)

id (132)
illegitimate opportunity
   structures (142)
infantile autism (126)
instincts (128)
intelligence (134)
interactionist perspective (141)
IQ (intelligence quotient) (135)
labeling theory (141)
Maslow's hierarchy (131)
nature/nurture debate (129)
negative reinforcement (128)
normal person (132)

norms (139)
Oedipus complex (133)
operant conditioning (128)
percentile rank (136)
personality (123)
personality disorders (140)
positive reinforcement (128)
psychoanalysis (132)
psychoanalytic approach (130)
punishment (128)
self-actualization (131)
strain theory (142)
superego (132)

Questions for Review and Discussion

1. Does culture control people or do people control culture? Explain the relationship between the two.
2. Some outstanding individuals have made significant contributions to our culture. Name someone who you think has done this, and discuss that person's contribution.
3. Discuss some of the factors in childhood that influence an individual's personality.
4. Explain how, according to Skinner, operant conditioning shapes personality.
5. Which is more important in the development of personality, environment or heredity? Explain the relationship between the two.
6. Contrast the four approaches to the determination of behavior: cognitive, psychoanalytic, behavioralist, and humanist.
7. According to Maslow, what are the five levels of human achievement?
8. What are some of the characteristics of a well-adjusted individual?
9. Explain some of the contributions that Sigmund Freud made to the understanding of human personality.
10. Explain the IQ test and what it tries to measure.
11. Why may an act be a crime in one society but not in another?
12. Explain how criminal behavior could be behavior conforming to a group norm.
13. According to the strain theory, is crime necessary for a successful industrial society?
14. In what way is the labeling theory similar to the illegitimate opportunity theory of criminal behavior?

Internet Questions

1. Jung was a psychologist and a peer of Freud. The site www.terrapsych.com/jungdefs.html has a glossary of Jungian terms. What is an Electra complex?

2. The site www.indiana.edu/∼reading/ieo/digests/d94.html is about home schooling/socialization debates. Go to Stough, 1992. According to Stough's research, does home schooling limit socialization?

3. Go to www.psych.umn.edu/psylabs/mtfs/special.htm to answer the question: As twins grow older, do they become less similar to one another?

4. Take a free IQ test, such as that found at www.intelligencetest.com. What aspect of intelligence do you believe the test is designed to evaluate? What other aspects of knowledge are there?

5. Pick a child from the list on www.feralchildren.com/en/index.php. What or who was the caregiver? Do you believe the story? For all the children listed, what was the most common caregiver? Where would she or he most likely be from?

*F*or Further Study

Alford, Henry, *How To Live: A Search for Wisdom from Old People (While They Are Still on This Earth)*, New York, NY: Twelve Publishers, 2009.

Burroughs, Augusten, *Running with Scissors*, New York: Picador Press, 2004.

Dyer, Wayne W., *The Power of Intention: Learning to Co-Create Your World Your Way*, Aldershot, UK: Hay House, 2005.

Haidt, Jonathan, *The Happiness Hypothesis*, New York: Basic Books, 2006.

Johnson, Steven, *Mind Wide Open: Your Brain and the Neuroscience of Everyday Life*, New York: Scribner, 2004.

Mahon, Darrin M., *Happiness: A History*, New York: Atlantic Monthly Press, 2006.

Martin, Judith, *Miss Manners' Guide to Rearing Perfect Children*, New York: Atheneum, 1984.

Maslow, A. H., *Psychology of Science: A Reconnaissance*, Chicago: Regnery-Gateway, 1969.

Nationwide In-Person Surveys of Adults, Chicago: National Research Center and U.S. Bureau of the Census, 2005.

Pinker, Steven, *How the Mind Works*, New York: Norton, 1997.

Sen, Amartya, *Identity and Violence: The Illusion of Destiny*, London: Penguin UK, 2006.

Slater, Lauren, *Opening Skinner's Box: Great Psychological Experiments of the Twentieth Century*, New York: Norton, 2004.

Small, Meredith F., *Kids: How Biology and Culture Shape the Way We Raise Our Children*, New York: Doubleday, 2001.

Thurman, Robert, *Infinite Life: Seven Virtues for Living Well*, Oxford: Oxford University Press, 2005.

WWW   B. F. Skinner Foundation www.bfskinner.org

WWW   The Jean Piaget Society www.piaget.org

WWW   Library of Congress, Freud: Conflict and Culture www.loc.gov/exhibits/freud

WWW   Maslow's Hierarchy of Needs http://chiron.valdosta.edu/whuitt/col/regsys/maslow.html

WWW   Mental Help.net Personality Disorders www.mentalhelp.net/poc/center_index.php?id=8&cn=8 (accessed June 22, 2009)

WWW   Personality Tests www.2h.com/personality-tests.html

WWW   Social Psychology Network www.socialpsychology.org

The Family

After reading this chapter, you should be able to:

- List four variations in family patterns and discuss where such variations can be found
- List three functions of the family and explain how variations in family patterns serve those functions
- Discuss the state and problems of the U.S. family today
- Discuss the effects of technology on the family and what effect future changes in technology are likely to have on the family

It is characteristic of man that he alone has any sense of good and evil, or just and unjust, and the like, and the association of living things who have this sense makes a family and a state.

—Aristotle

Of all the institutions that shape our personalities and help us adjust to changing environments, the **family**—a group of persons closely related by marriage, blood, or some other bond who deal as a unit with the outside world—is the most important. It is within the family that we are initially socialized. If our family unit isn't working, we are likely to have personal and social problems. In the United States, families are recognized by civil and religious authorities. Families typically are formed by **marriage**—a social institution marking a commitment between individuals to live as a family, which is recognized by civil and/or religious authorities.

In the United States, many still tend to think of the family in terms of a mother, father, and one or more dependent children, often with the father working and the mother staying at home. This vision of the family is still strong, but that kind of family is now in the minority in the United States; in fact, fewer than 10 percent of our households meet this description. Moreover, the concept is by no means accepted in all parts of the world.

Similarly, many of our other ideas about marriage and the family are not universally held. For example, in the United States we have come to assume that everyone should have a free choice in selecting a mate, but this is definitely not a worldwide custom. Some societies have quite different ideas of marriage and family. One stable point can be claimed, however: Throughout history, among all peoples in the world, the family has been the continuing and basic primary group.

With the recent political push by some in the United States to legalize same-sex marriage, the history of marriage as an institution becomes important. Looking at that history, we see that it has both a religious and a secular component. Marriage's civil history goes back furthest; and, from early on, governments have adopted changing rules about what constitutes marriage (for example, whether polygamy is allowed) and the rights that individuals have in marriage. These rules become built into society's legal code (for example, until recently, in Western society, when women married, they had to transfer all their property to their husband) and those legal codes form the civil or secular foundation of marriage.

Marriage's religious rules differ among different religions. In the west, the history of marriage goes back to the Middle Ages when the Catholic church sanctioned marriage as a sacrament between a man, a woman, and God. Other religions took different views, and some religions saw marriage as simply a government issue.

The dual civil–religious aspect of marriage complicates debates about marriage and leads to the possibility of individuals being married in the eyes of a religion, but not in the eyes of the law, and vice versa. Polygamy and same-sex marriage in the United States are examples of marriages accepted by some religions but not by most state laws.

Variations in the Family Pattern

In addition to the **two-parent family**—mother, father, and one or more children—there are also the **single-parent family,** consisting of either a mother or father, but not both, with one or more children; the **extended family,** consisting not only of parents and children, but also of other relatives such as grandparents, aunts, and uncles; and the **gay family,** consisting of two men or two women and their children.

Number of Mates

In the Western world, monogamy is the traditional, and in most places the only, legal form of matrimonial relationship. **Monogamy** is a form of marriage in which there is one husband and one wife. This is by far the most widespread form of marriage all over the world, even where other forms are allowed or encouraged. Given the increasing frequency of divorce in the United States, some researchers have suggested that we should develop a new name—**serial monogamy**—to describe our standard formal relationship, which is marriage between one husband and one wife followed by a dissolution of that marriage and a subsequent marriage between that same husband or wife and another opposite-sex partner.

Polygamy is the term used for plural marriage, but this is divided into two types: **polygyny,** meaning one husband and two or more wives, and **polyandry,** meaning one wife and two or more husbands. A polygamous family may be thought of as two or more nuclear families bound together because all the children have one parent in common. Some writers also recognize a form of plural marriage called group marriage, or cenogamy. **Cenogamy** is a form of union in which several men are married to several women, but such relationships are uncommon. **Same-sex marriage** is a union between adults of the same gender. Around 1970, at least in the United States, this last term began to be used as such relationships were formed more and more openly. These relationships and the question of their legal status create new social, legal, and political problems with which our society is still struggling.

Where polygyny is sanctioned, it is generally practiced both for its prestige value and for its economic advantages. Among the Tupis of South America, for instance, as well as in sections of Africa, wealth and distinction are measured in terms of how many wives a man has. Often the wives not only perform domestic services but also work in the fields, and thus contribute to the support of the entire family group. Sometimes, as in the Trobriand Islands of Micronesia, the income of a chief depends on the annual endowments received from the families of his wives. The first wife usually has the responsibility of administering the affairs of the household, but she is not necessarily the favorite wife. In many cases, each wife keeps a separate household, and the husband rotates his attention among them.

Polyandry is comparatively rare. It is found mainly in some parts of Tibet and among some aboriginal tribes of India, where a woman may marry two or more brothers. There

An arranged Indian wedding.

are also cases of polyandry among a certain few indigenous people of Canada, in the Marquesas Islands, and among the Bahima in Africa, but it is the least common of the main forms of marriage.

Selection of Mates

The rules governing the choice of mates are as diverse as the societies in which they have developed. The rules differ not only from one society to another but also among subgroups, such as social classes, within a society. They usually include various limitations on the persons of the other sex who are eligible to marry any given individual.

Let us first consider some of the rules governing eligibility. For instance, in India a person of one caste finds it difficult to marry an individual from another, and until recently, in a country such as South Africa a person of one race was not permitted to marry someone from another race. In some societies, one may never marry a blood relative, no matter how distant, and in others one may marry only within the kinship group.[1] The governing factors on the one hand are the fear of incest, or sexual activity among people who are close kin, and the desire for alliances. At the other extreme is the fear of marrying anyone too unlike the social group to which one belongs (in the case of certain small groups, this necessarily means marrying a relative). In the majority of modern societies, both forces operate, and therefore most people find their search for acceptable marriage mates limited to persons not closely related but within the same general social group.

Rules govern the actual choice of a marriage partner. Some societies have **arranged marriages,** marriages that are arranged by one or more persons other than the marriage partners because it is believed that a marriage is as much the concern of the families as of the individuals involved. The arguments in favor of such marriages include alliances of wealth, property, or political power, or the belief that young people are too immature, inexperienced, and impulsive to consider properly all the factors necessary for an enduring and successful marriage.

Many Asian families in the United States still arrange marriages for their children, many of whom are highly educated. In some societies, wives are obtained by kidnapping or

---

[1]Marriage within the kinship or other social group is known as *endogamy. Exogamy* refers to marriage outside the group.

by capture, perhaps in a raid on a neighboring tribe. Sometimes the kidnapping is genuine, and sometimes it is a ritual that carries out a previous understanding.

The other principal type of selection we call personal-choice mating. **Personal-choice mating** implies the custom of personal freedom in mating, with relatively little interference from others. This is the type of marriage we are familiar with in mainstream society. However, this freedom of choice is not restricted to our own country, nor indeed to our own time, although we again emphasize that mating activities are almost always be carried on within the framework of the prevailing local laws and mores.

The techniques involved in personal-choice mating differ from one society to another, as do the moral and legal sanctions governing them. For example, among the polar Eskimos in earlier days there was not only complete freedom of choice by mutual agreement in the making of a permanent marriage, but before marriage there was also a sanctioned period of group living, during which experimental mating took place among the youth of the community. Children resulting from this arrangement were not considered illegitimate but belonged to the mother and the man who eventually became her husband. One of the criteria often used by the man in choosing a wife was her demonstrated ability to bear children, just as one of the criteria for the woman in choosing her husband was his demonstrated ability to provide for her and her children.

Family Control

No one type of family control has ever been universal, but three main patterns have prevailed: patriarchy, matriarchy, and the egalitarian family. A **patriarchy** is a form of social organization in which the father is the supreme authority. A **matriarchy** is a form of social organization in which the mother is the supreme authority. An **egalitarian family** is one with shared control, with neither the father nor the mother as superior.

In a patriarchal culture, the father is not only the head of the family, but society also considers that the children belong to him and that he has authority over their lives, even, in some cases, the right to give or sell them in marriage. The patriarchal family was found among the early civilizations around the Mediterranean and has been carried down through Christian civilizations to modern times. Our colonial fathers maintained the patriarchal system, and there are still many families in the United States, as well as in other parts of the world, in which the father is the recognized authority in the family, although with some modifications.

Societies in which family control actually rests with the mother are exceptional. In most so-called matriarchal cultures, as among the Zuni Indians in the southwestern part of the United States, the mother usually does not have direct control, as one might suppose. More often, the mother's brother wields authority and controls the children. But the family takes the mother's name and usually lives with the mother's parents or other relatives. The husband may move in with them, but he is apt to spend more time with his own mother or his sisters' families, helping to control their children. Because he has no control status with his own children, he is more of a playmate and friend to them.

Family control in the United States has gradually shifted toward the partnership, or egalitarian, form. As women have increasingly gained equal educational, economic, and political rights and privileges, the control of the family has more and more come to be shared by both marriage partners.

Reckoning of Descent

In the Western world, we use the **bilateral method** of reckoning descent, counting our ancestors on both our father's and our mother's side because our biological inheritance comes from both. However, this is not the universal practice. Some societies use the **unilateral method,** in

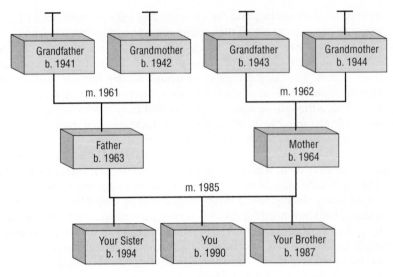

Figure 8.1

How to draw a family tree.

which an individual is deemed to belong to either the father's or the mother's family and ancestors are reckoned only in the male line of descent or in the female line. A **patrilinear system** determines descent through the male line; a **matrilinear system** determines descent through the female line. This may not seem logical to us, but it does simplify matters for those who use it. Imagine being asked to name your ancestors for twenty generations back. The African chief who reckons his ancestry by patrilineal descent would know the twenty names required. In our society, we would have to remember 1,048,576 names. Few carry their family tree back that far, but many families keep a family tree like the one in Figure 8.1.

Names and naming systems are important symbols. In the United States, although we generally acknowledge our descent bilaterally, the name we carry usually is that of our father or husband, emphasizing the patrilineal line of ancestry; however, in recent times, more married women have been keeping their birth names.

The preceding examples illustrate the many diverse customs that prevail in families throughout the world. Despite such diversity, are there basic points regarding marriage and the family on which all societies agree? There must be some underlying reasons for the survival of this institution through all the changes that have taken place over centuries. Perhaps the answers can be found in the functions of the family, for although ways of carrying out these functions differ in every society, they remain the force motivating the family as an institution.

Functions of the Family in Society

The family has many functions:

It must reproduce the species; otherwise the species will end.

It must see to it that the young are reasonably well adjusted, so that they don't cause trouble for society and that they grow up to be productive in the biological and physical sense.

It must provide sufficient satisfaction for parents to keep them well adjusted so they don't make trouble for society.

Society relies on families to fulfill these functions, and when they don't succeed, other social institutions must adapt. Let's consider an example: the biological function of families, or the need to reproduce.

Until recently, few married couples were voluntarily childless, but in the last twenty years the number of families having no children has been increasing. During this time, many women, both married and unmarried, delayed childbearing and pursued professional education, gaining a foothold in their careers. Often they married other professionals. The incomes of these professional couples tended to be high but so were their expenses and their ambitions. They chose to put off having children, which they were able to do because, among other reasons, of advances in contraceptive techniques and increasing sanction of these techniques.

A number of those couples who put off having children are experiencing what might be called the thirty-seven-year-old syndrome, in which couples approaching the end of the woman's childbearing years are opting to have at least one child before the woman reaches an age at which pregnancy is unwise or impossible. This countervailing trend became apparent in the 1980s and has continued through the early 2000s. A phenomenon surfacing at about the same time was that of unmarried women not only welcoming but actively seeking pregnancy, sometimes with partners selected only for this occasion or through any of a number of other fertilization methods.

Reasons for desiring more or fewer children vary in different societies. In agricultural societies, especially if land is plentiful, people are likely to desire large families because children tend to be an economic asset. In industrial societies, where children are more costly, families tend to have fewer of them. If the trend toward childless couples continues, society will have to find some other way to reproduce itself. For the United States, this may well mean an increase in immigration.

Matching Family Patterns with Family Functions

What family structure best meets these functions? That's hard to say because it depends on individuals' psychological development and the technology and exigencies of the society. Let's consider the variations of family groups in reference to modern Western society.

Number of Mates

As we stated above, our society is primarily a monogamous one in which a family group includes a male and a female. Why?

One of the reasons is that this family grouping works well for reproduction. Given current technology, that's the way society reproduces itself. If reproductive technology required three (or only one) for reproduction, there would be pressure for a different number of mates.

Another reason is that children take enormous amounts of time. A one-parent family has a difficult time meeting either the child's or the parent's psychological needs. As a matter of fact, a two-parent family has a difficult time meeting the child's and the parents' psychological needs, especially if both parents are working. This places two types of pressure on social institutions. One pressure is for an extension of the family, either by including a third mate or by extending the family and including grandparents, aunts, or uncles as part of the primary family unit. The second pressure is for society to develop institutions such as day care to remove part of the childrearing burden from the family.

A third important reason the family group consists of a monogamous male and female is for the psychological adjustment of the individuals. According to some social scientists, "three's a crowd" is more than just a pat phrase. Individuals have psychological needs to be accepted and loved, making mates of some type necessary, and the need for security argues for a single mate. Some individuals might prefer more than one mate for themselves, but

The little darlings (sometimes).

few would prefer that their mate have more than one mate. The development of strong friendships outside of marriage often results in strong feelings of jealousy. Those feelings are in part genetic; most species have developed instincts that encourage the propagation of the individual's genes, and humankind is no exception.

Recent work in evolutionary psychology emphasizes this psychological aspect. Some experts claim that those traits leading to procreation will be fostered in individuals and that there is a relationship between physiology and human characteristics. Thus, while there is a strong tendency toward one-to-one mating, there is also a strong tendency in both the male and the female to stray and have other mates.

Finally, a fourth reason is that from society's point of view the monogamous relationship provides a mate for most people because males and females are born in nearly equal numbers.

As we stated above, although the majority of relationships are monogamous, there is a frequency of turnover of mates—called serial monogamy—and a certain amount of infidelity within some marriages. Thus, while our system is monogamous, it is not so in a strict sense.

Selection of Mates

Western societies generally allow individuals to select their own mates. Such a selection process is by no means universal; families in Eastern societies generally choose mates for the children. The problem with family selection is the possible incompatibility of mates and a failure to fulfill the psychological function of marriage, although as some of our Eastern friends point out, given the number of divorces and unhappy marriages in the West, self-selection doesn't seem to do such a good job of meeting the psychological functions.

The advantage of family selection is that it is more likely to fulfill economic and social stability goals. When hormones play an important role in mate selection, economic and social considerations often are forgotten.

Of course, as we saw in Chapter 4, social stability is not necessarily a goal of society. Cultural diffusion is also necessary, and one of the reasons Western societies have adapted better than Eastern societies to the changing technologies may be that self-selection of mates creates social instability that allows and generates change.

Family Control and Reckoning of Descent

Western societies generally are patriarchal and use a bilateral method of reckoning descent. These customs do not seem to fulfill significantly any of the functions of the family other than the need for the psychological adjustment of the male. Society does need to fulfill the child-rearing function, and it is true that women bear and nurse children and have evolved both genetically and

A traditional family.

Living and Loving

A key role of the family is procreation. A society needs children, but not too many. Maintaining the proper balance of numbers of children is a difficult social problem. Take Singapore, for example, a small, rich country in Asia. Singapore's population control incentives were very successful and reduced the birthrate from a 4.7 percent annual increase in 1965 to a 1.5 percent annual increase in the late 1980s. Then the government began worrying that the country would have too few young people to support the elderly, so it switched tactics and strongly encouraged marriage.

The government established a number of programs to encourage the 30 percent of college-educated women who were unmarried to get married. The programs included dating services, "love classes," and advice to men about how to act on a date. One of the program booklets lists "some nutty ideas" for dates, such as "playing Scrabble on the beach armed with a dictionary and a thesaurus."*I leave it to you to decide whether this advice is transferable to the United States. Perhaps we could modify it some: Why not ask your date if he or she wants to go to the beach and discuss the questions at the end of this chapter? How about....

The measures didn't work so well in Singapore either. After they were introduced, the birthrate continued to fall. In the early 2000s, Singapore established financial incentives for having children. A second child earns couples about $3,000, and a third child is worth about $6,000.

Even countries that don't provide direct financial incentives for having children offer implicit subsidies. In the United States, taxpayers get a child tax credit, and in other countries parents get paid leaves and free child care, policies that are designed to make children less costly.

*A thesaurus is a reference book set up like a dictionary, except it provides a list of synonyms.

socially so that, on average, a woman is better able to deal with children than a man is, at least until the child reaches the age of about three. Maternal instincts exist. But this patriarchal reality only suggests that the male will most likely maintain the uninterrupted income-earning activities, not that the male will have control of the family.

What maintains the patriarchal system is, in large part, social and genetic inertia. Male dominance is built into the social and genetic structure of society. The fact that it is built in does not mean that it cannot, or will not, be changed. It simply means that it will only be changed through conscious effort and moral commitment to equality.

Other Western Family Characteristics and Functions of the Family

We could go on listing Western family characteristics and discussing their function, but there isn't space, and besides, it is an activity best left to you. Think of other characteristics, such as the age at marriage. Estimate what the average age is (later in the chapter we give you the information), and then try to explain what functions are served by getting married at that age. Why not earlier, say at age thirteen or so, as soon as people are sufficiently developed sexually to have children?

Is an Arranged Marriage in Your or Your Child's Future?

Dating is a pain, love is nonexistent, and romance is for the birds. According to Ramdas Menon, a sociologist at Texas A&M University, more and more Americans, especially those with Asian, African, and Middle Eastern backgrounds, are taking this view and leaving the problem of whom to marry up to their parents. They want their parents to arrange marriages for them, often to people they never meet until the parents of the prospective bride and prospective groom have settled things among themselves. Does this make sense? Maybe it does. It takes pressure off the mates. The custom also preserves culture, brings individuals from similar backgrounds together, often unites and strengthens economic ties, and keeps premarital expectations low.

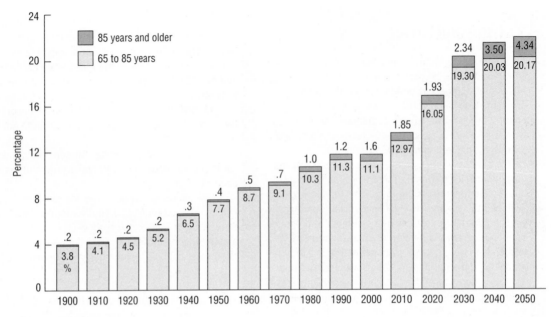

Figure 8.2

The aging of the United States. By the year 2050, over 20 percent of Americans will be over the age of 65 and almost one-fifth of these will be over 85. (Source: U.S. Bureau of the Census.)

Another interesting question in relation to the functions of the family is what is likely to happen to the family as the age structure of society changes. Consider Figure 8.2, which shows the increase in the elderly as a percentage of the total population. What is likely to happen to the family as this occurs? How will the family unit deal with the changes incurred by such a population shift?

In the next section, we look at the U.S. family today. As you read, consider the functions of the family and how well the characteristics fulfill those functions.

The Family in the United States Today

One of the causes of the revolutionary changes in twentieth-century life in the United States was our massive transition from an agricultural, rural nation to one that is mainly commercial-industrial and urban. With the mass movement of people to cities throughout the late nineteenth and early twentieth centuries, housing costs increased and both family and home size shrank. People no longer worked mainly at home, although initially most women stayed home to care for the family. However, technological advances in labor-saving household appliances and family planning freed women for leisure and market-oriented activities. Children's help around the house was no longer required as much as it was on the farm; the number of children per family declined, and the city's recreational offerings often drew parents and children in different directions.

Modern transport—the car in particular, which came into widespread use in the 1920s—served to make us an on-the-go nation; home became a place to sleep or to get away from. The car itself and the two-car family helped in large measure to build the post–World War II commuter suburb. Postwar affluence, fed by commercial wealth, advertising, and the credit economy, helped lure us away from the waste not, want not Puritan ethic of the nineteenth century, when debt meant disgrace. Smaller families and the dramatic increase in the

As more and more women have entered the labor force, fathers have had to become nurture providers, not always with the most finesse.

number of families in which both parents work—often earning two high incomes—have led to a return from the suburbs to city life, as many seek the distractions and satisfactions of the fast track.

With women playing more vital roles away from home, their dependence on males for survival has lessened. Moreover, many other forces have driven women toward more self-sufficiency and a search for satisfaction both in marriage and outside of it. Today, both males and females demand more of marriage and of each other, which adds to the stresses of modern life. The fully liberated man (of whom there are still only a few) shares major decisions, roles, and work with his wife, but many women find that they continue to be allotted the major share of the domestic duties, even while working full time. In other households, the patriarchal male finds great difficulty in accepting the wife's autonomy, but a great many do, nevertheless, make the adjustment.

Even with shared responsibilities, the two-earner family cannot provide full-time care for children. This situation has placed more responsibility on the schools, many of which provide not only lunches but breakfasts and may stay open beyond the normal school day to provide some place for the child to remain until the parents' workday is over. Fortunate families have found good day-care centers, but these are not equitably distributed and tend to be expensive. Moreover, most good centers have waiting lists. Many children come home after school to empty houses or apartments and fend for themselves, sometimes even supervising younger brothers or sisters, until a parent arrives. These children have become known as **latchkey children**—children who have their own house key and immediately lock themselves in once inside their homes.

The sexual revolution of the 1960s and the enhanced sense of independence experienced by both men and women loosened many moral restraints. The mobility and easy anonymity of modern cities have made it possible for husbands and wives to widen their circle of friends. Often this freedom has caused them to become less content with one life-long mate. A phenomenon described as serial marriage has resulted, in which people have several husbands or wives over the course of their lives, although not more than one at a time. Because each partner may bring to the new marriage one or more children and may be sharing the custody of those children with other former mates, family relationships can become complicated and challenging to emotional and material resources.

How to Be a Good Wife

One way to get an idea of the change that has occurred in the nature of the family is to look at old textbooks. For example, a 1960 home economics textbook included a section entitled "How to Be a Good Wife." It included suggestions such as the following:

- Have dinner ready for him when he comes home from work; let him know you have been thinking about him and his needs.
- Touch up your makeup and be refreshed when he arrives.
- Prepare the children; wash their hands and faces. They are little treasures and he would like to see them play the part.
- Clean up the house before he arrives. Make him feel that he has reached a haven of rest and order.
- At the time of his arrival, eliminate all noise. Greet him with a warm smile.
- Let him be the first to talk.
- Never complain. Try to understand his world of strain and pressure and his need to be home and relax.

When I showed the list to my wife, she smiled and reminded me to have dinner ready for her and the kids when she got home from work.

Despite these changing roles, the family remains an important element of life in the United States. In many ways, the family has merely adapted to the changing cultural climate in the United States, and, we suspect, most of you see marriage and a family somewhere in your future. Many people who had moved away from family relationships are returning.

Table 8.1 gives you an overview of some U.S. family characteristics. Notice that only about half of all U.S. households consist of married couples, and that there are more un-married female-headed households than there are male-headed households. The greater number of female-headed households is in large part due to the fact that women live longer than men. For a better sense of the changes that are occurring, in the next part of the chapter we consider the issue of dating in the United States. Because much of the material presented about dating is familiar to you, we approach it in a slightly different way—as if it were written by an anthropologist about people from another culture. This allows you to take a more objective look at issues in which you are active.

Table 8.1
U.S. Family Household Characteristics

CHARACTERISTIC	TOTAL HOUSEHOLDS (In Thousands) NUMBER
All	116,783
HOUSEHOLD TYPE	
Family household	77,873
Nonfamily household	38,910
HOUSEHOLD TYPE	
Family household	
HOUSEHOLD MEMBERS	
Family members only	73,989
Family and nonfamily members	3,884
FAMILY TYPE	
Married Couple	58,370
Male Householder	5,100
Female Householder	14,404
Nonfamily household	
HOUSEHOLD MEMBERS	
Nonfamily members only	38,910
FAMILY TYPE	
Male Householder	17,872
Female Householder	21,038

(in thousands)

TYPE OF FAMILY	NUMBER IN MILLIONS	PERCENTAGE OF TOTAL
Married couple	58,370	50
Male head of household	22,972	19.7
Female head of household	35,442	30.3

Source: US Bureau of the Census, *Current Population Survey,* 2009.

Dating in the 1940s.

Dating

Because U.S. custom allows self-selection of mates, people who eventually marry must first meet. Some of the ways people meet are through school, work, religious institutions, sports, walking the dog, amateur dramatic societies, networks of friends, and the Internet where sites such as MySpace and Facebook allow people to meet others outside their immediate geographic area.

After two people meet, they get to know each other better through formal or informal dating. Dating allows people to get acquainted with each other on an intimate and, hopefully, a mature plane. It also gives them an opportunity to evaluate themselves in an interpersonal situation outside the family and serves as a form of recreation. In the 1950s, dating was often formal, with the boy picking up the girl and escorting her to a social event. Although the boy was no longer required to ask her parents' permission to take the girl out (as he would have been in the 1800s), he was obliged to see the parents and exchange some conversation when he came to the girl's house to pick her up. At these—often awkward—meetings, the parents would "size up the lad" and inform him that they expected their daughter home by a certain hour (say midnight if it were a weekend evening). In the 2000s, arranging a date is more informal. Often one person, male or female, will phone or speak to the other and suggest they get together and possibly do something, such as go to a movie or ride in a sports car. The ritualistic meeting of the parents can come later, or not at all, whatever seems to occur naturally.

Sometimes this relationship moves to formal dating, but often it does not, although both individuals have a sense (often different) of how much freedom the relationship allows them in terms of seeing, talking to, and being with other individuals. A vocabulary often develops to describe how individuals feel about relationships. For example, at my college some students who want a one-to-one relationship are described as "velcro."

Most relationships are not necessarily expected to end in marriage. Usually an individual has relationships with a variety of people before finding one that seems right. In fact, there are likely to be several right ones, or no right one. An eighth-grade girl explains: "Next year we'll be in high school, and then I'll ditch him to date a sophomore. No freshman girl ever dates a freshman!" Older individuals are likely to be less concerned about age or year in school and more concerned with emotional, economic, and social compatibility. The difficulty in finding a satisfactory mate is so great that singles ads in newspapers, in magazines, and on the Internet are booming. Here's one such ad:

> IS THERE A CARING considerate, attractive, ambitious woman out there who seeks companionship, fun, possible marriage? Considerate, attractive, ambitious M.D., 37, 5 ft. 8 in., tired of the singles race, divorced, two children, income in the $150 thousand range, looking for psychologically aware, vibrant, professional, bikiniable woman to share opera, skiing, sailing, art galleries. She's blond, in her 20s, doesn't smoke, and wants me. Send photo/phone.

Some make better reading than the preceding, and many are more interesting than the soaps.

Sex and Singles

There are enormous differences in sexual codes, even within the same town; the sexual revolution that started in the 1970s spread in a complicated pattern. The sexual revolution also brought with it an increase in sexually transmitted diseases. Depending on the individual's upbringing, sexual relations can begin at any stage of the relationship. Prohibitions against sexual relations are decreasing among college students, and "hooking up" in which one has sex with someone else supposedly without any emotional commitment, has increased. Today, students often talk about "friends with benefits" rather than about their "girlfriend" or "boyfriend."

In large cities and in suburban communities, sexual relations often begin as early as age twelve, which as we stated earlier is an argument for starting marriage much earlier. In families in which religion or other organized moral standards prevail, however, the slogan "good girls don't" still carries some weight, and in such families, girls wait until the serious stage of a relationship, or later, before having intercourse. It should be noted that a dual standard still exists; there is a less strict guideline than "good boys don't."

Over one-third of U.S. births are now to unmarried women, and for black women the proportion is even higher. Almost 70 percent of all black children are born to unmarried mothers. In the black community as a whole, over 50 percent of all one-parent families are headed by mothers who have never been married.

Through the 1980s, the issue of teenage pregnancy was seen as a predominantly black issue, but beginning in the 1990s, with an increasing proportion of white teenage pregnancies, the issue now extends beyond racial lines. In the early 2000s, teenage birthrates have declined across all race and ethnic lines, although rates for African American and Hispanic teens continue to be higher than those for other groups, with about 20 percent of African American births being to teenage mothers compared to 10 percent for whites. The birthrate is about 42 per 1,000 teenage women, and although this is a 33 percent decrease over the last ten-year period, it is still the highest rate of all industrialized nations. (Both increased use of contraception and increased abstinence are credited for the decline.)

Another issue that confronts singles—indeed, anyone, married or single, who is not in a monogamous relationship—is sexually transmitted disease. In addition to centuries-old venereal diseases such as gonorrhea and syphilis, there are now herpes, chlamydia, genital warts, and HIV, which can lead to acquired immunodeficiency syndrome (AIDS), a breakdown in the immune system.

Even intense relationships often do not lead to marriage. Individuals often have a number of serious relationships before they finally marry. It is also common for couples to live together for periods of anywhere from a month to many years before making a decision to marry, and some decide never to marry. A Gallup poll taken in the 1980s found that about 50 percent of the responding college students thought it was helpful to live together before marriage; many thought it didn't matter one way or the other, and only about 27 percent thought it was harmful. However, all but 2 percent thought it was extremely important to remain faithful to one's mate after marriage.

In deciding whether (and whom) to marry, romantic love plays a role, but increasingly individuals are considering, in addition to love, other issues, especially in relationships in which both members are planning a career. Whose career will come first? What happens if they are assigned jobs in different locations? If one supports the other in order to further his or her education, what obligations are incurred? To meet these complex issues a number of couples are entering into formal marriage contracts (prenuptial agreements) that spell out the obligations and expectations of both so that the love relationship is not shattered.

After a period of decision, most individuals marry. Marriage is a more or less permanent contract between a man and a woman under which they are expected to live together and to provide a home for their children. The contract has legal, and in many cases religious, sanctions.

Entering into this contract creates many new responsibilities involving not only the couple but also the families from which they came and various other social groups. The partners immediately assume new statuses: the husband/wife status, the in-law status, and the family status. Even if the parties have previously lived together, marriage involves a major change.

Such an important shift of roles, even though desirable and pleasurable, involves a good deal of adjustment. This has not been made easier by the swift pace of social change in the United States. In a static society, the role expected of each spouse is well understood, but in a dynamic society such as ours it is easy to be uncertain about just what is expected. This confusion may be increased in cross-marriages between faiths, nationalities, or races. Even if hazards are eliminated, our common heritage of diversity is constantly changing the social pattern for everyone. Hence, adaptability has become an important personality characteristic in marital adjustment.

Children

As we stated earlier, for an increasing number of families marriage and having children are not necessarily linked. This has contributed to creating what is sometimes called an underclass that has little chance of escaping the poverty it grew up with. This underclass has to deal with a different set of pressures than the middle class.

People in the underclass often get a poor education and little encouragement to take advantage of the educational opportunities open to them. They find themselves in social environments that offer little hope for long-term advancement and build that into their worldview and actions. Their immediate concerns are often for their safety and getting enough to eat, concerns generally far from the minds of middle-class (even lower-middle-class) individuals.

Middle-class culture, although it has more or less condoned living together, tends to put pressure on middle-class individuals to get married if they have children or want to have children. Thus most middle-class couples choose marriage. Marriage establishes the economic responsibilities for both mother and father, and even if the parents split up, both retain legal responsibility for the children. Thus, the spouse who does not have legal custody is responsible for child support and possibly alimony. Later, when we consider divorce, we deal with these issues in more detail.

The decision to have a child is not an easy one. Children involve major responsibilities and hard work. Often it means giving up one spouse's potential income or, if both parents work, worrying about child care, education, and privacy. Moreover, parenting is no longer eighteen years and out. Many adult children are coming home to live with their parents (see Figure 8.3). This trend tends to be strongest when economic times are tough.

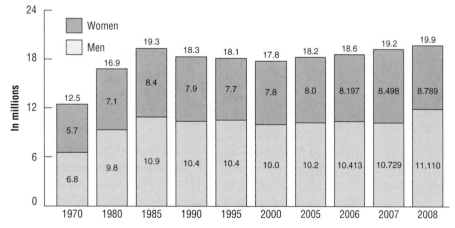

Figure 8.3

Adults ages eighteen to thirty-four living with parents. (Source: Current Population Reports, U.S. Bureau of the Census.)

In spite of the responsibility and hard work children bring to a couple, most people feel that the rewards are compensatory. The number of children that couples are willing to have, however, is smaller than two or three generations ago, and following a temporary rise in the 1940s and 1950s, the average has been dropping.

Senior Citizens

As children grow up and leave home for college, for a job, or to establish their own households, the family dwindles in size to the original two.

For the middle-class ideal family, a number of years then follow, perhaps as many as fifteen or twenty, before retirement—years in which there is time for more active participation in social and civic affairs or, for spouses who have not worked outside the home before, for employment. Companionship is now the strong bond between the couple. Shared experiences throughout the childrearing years cement this bond, but a new and satisfactory pattern of life without the children at home must be developed if the couple is to remain happy. Generally, couples are able to make the adjustment. In fact, research studies have shown that a couple's happiness declines with the birth of a child and tends to renew when the children leave. Thus, for the parents no less than for the children, maturing of the children represents a period of weaning or emancipation. When the children return on visits, their relationship is on an adult, companionable basis, and if there are grandchildren, they can provide the grandparents with a new interest in life.

The family ideal is not always reached. In the less-than-ideal family, the couple can't stand each other but stay together because they don't have enough money to live apart, or one leaves or has already left the other in order to take up with someone else or just to live alone. Whether they stay together when they want to be apart or one leaves and sets up another household, often there is a haunting loneliness for one or both members of the couple. Another less-than-ideal family type is the one in which the parents aren't speaking to the children because they have had to take second jobs to pay the kids' college loans, which the kids have defaulted on. There are countless variations of the less-than-ideal family. For the less-than-ideal family, retirement can mean being kicked out of a current job and shunted into a low-paying one that is necessary to make ends meet. As the Russian novelist Leo Tolstoy wrote in the opening sentence of his novel *Anna Karenina,* "Happy families are all alike; every unhappy family is unhappy in its own way."

When the time finally comes for the couple to retire from their regular jobs, many couples, if in good health, still have years of activity ahead. Successful adjustment to retirement also depends on personal temperament. Some individuals welcome the release from routine and responsibility; they are flexible enough to have little trouble in finding interesting ways to spend their time; others feel lost when deprived of their previous work. Health and money are also important factors.

Family Disorganization and Divorce

The preceding section described the development over time of a married couple who remain married. More and more, this is a less typical chronology. Figure 8.4 gives the marriage rate and the divorce rate since 1900. The marriage rate has fluctuated since 1900 but in 2008 has fallen to 7.0; in other words, 8.5 people out of every 1,000 get married in a given year. The divorce rate increased in the 1970s but has been decreasing since the 1980s. Table 8.2 shows the approximate ratio of divorces to marriages from 1890 to 2005. We must remember several qualifications when considering the divorce rate. For instance, if in a given year there is one divorce for every two marriages, it does not mean that half the marriages in that year ended in divorce; rather, in that year some people got married and others, who had been married for anywhere from one day to fifty years or more, got divorced.

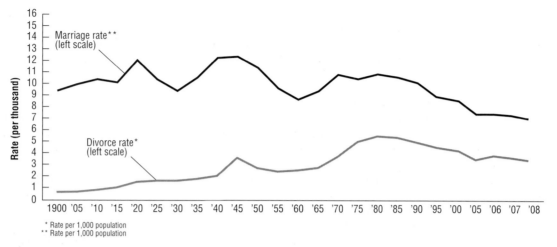

Figure 8.4

Marriages and divorces, 1900 to 2008. (Source: U.S. Bureau of the Census, *Statistical Abstract of the United States, and monthly Vital Statistics Report.*)

Statisticians have various methods for determining the number of marriages that end in divorce. One study of a group of married couples over time indicates that nearly 40 percent of first marriages end in divorce, about 80 percent of those people enter a second marriage, and almost 45 percent of the second marriages also end in divorce. Though we now have approximately one divorce for every two marriages, only about one in four households is a single-person household, because many divorced people marry again.

Why Do People Get Divorced?   There are almost as many reasons why people get divorced as there are divorces. Most can be combined into some type of incompatibility: One or both of the partners are not getting what they want out of the marriage. Sometimes a third party is involved whom one of the partners finds more attractive than his or her mate, but often the marriage would have been in trouble even if there had been no third party.

When we think about the institution of marriage, the number of divorces is not surprising. Most friendships don't last a lifetime, so why should a marriage? Those marriages that don't have serious problems often are with partners who share a common set of values and who not only love each other but also respect each other's capabilities and integrity. Not many partners fit these characteristics, so there aren't many rock-solid marriages.

Table 8.2

Approximate Ratio of Divorces to Marriages, 1890–2008

YEAR	RATIO	YEAR	RATIO
1890	1 to 18.0	1970	1 to 3.1
1910	1 to 12.0	1980	1 to 2.0
1930	1 to 5.8	1990	1 to 2.1
1950	1 to 4.3	2000	1 to 2.0
1960	1 to 3.9	2006	1 to 2.0

Source: U.S. Census Bureau the 2009 Statistical Abstract, International Statistics: Vital Statistics, Health, Education

People often marry in the hope, belief, or expectation that their partner will change. A maxim of marriage counselors is that people don't change, or if they do change, you can expect it to be in the opposite direction from what the other partner wants. In word processing, most personal computers use WYSIWYG (pronounced wizzywig)—what you see is what you get—presentations. Most courtships involve WYSIBTWYG (pronounced who knows how)—what you see is better than what you get—presentations.

Some Caution about Divorce Statistics.   Divorce statistics often are used as a measure of family disorganization, and the present high divorce rate is cited as proof that the U.S. family is in serious trouble. However, higher divorce rates today than in the past are not entirely the result of more family unhappiness. In earlier generations, many couples avoided divorce even though their married life was unhappy. They avoided it because it meant social ostracism or, in the case of women, poverty, because there were few opportunities for them to earn a good living. As the possibilities for divorced people increased and it became easier to get divorces, more unhappy couples have chosen this route.

Legal Grounds for Divorce.   There are many legal grounds for divorce, and they vary with the laws of each state. Among these are incompatibility, adultery, desertion, cruelty, nonsupport, bigamy, felony conviction, and fraudulent contract. Although the legal grounds for divorce are of some interest and significance, often they have little to do with the real reason behind a couple's desire to end a marriage. Often a husband and wife who wish to divorce cooperate to bring about real or apparent fulfillment of the necessary legal conditions.

Beginning in the 1970s, many states introduced **no-fault divorces,** in which irreconcilable differences serve as sufficient grounds for divorce. Under these laws, a marriage partner need not be declared guilty or at fault as was previously required, making the process of divorce much easier. In the 1990s, the movement shifted back in some circles. Louisiana introduced voluntary **covenant marriages,** in which divorce as an option is harder for people to get. Other states are watching this process develop and if it's successful, the idea may spread. By 2003, legal covenant marriages were available in Arkansas, Arizona, and Louisiana (bills have been put up in many other states but have not passed). In most states, you do not have to be a state resident to get married in the state, or to "upgrade" an existing marriage into a covenant marriage. So, when someone proposes marriage, he or she may now have to specify whether it is a covenant marriage proposal or a regular marriage proposal.

Breaking Up Is Hard to Do.   Even if one is not in a covenant marriage, divorce often presents serious difficulties, especially when a couple has joint property and children. The parties must decide who gets what. Some of the problems are demonstrated by the following four examples.

1. A wife has put her husband through school and has not furthered her own education. One year after he becomes a lawyer, they decide to get divorced. They have no property or children.
2. The same as (1), only it is the husband who put the wife through school.
3. A couple decides to break up after six years of marriage. They have two children, a house, a dog, and innumerable items of personal property. Both have careers but the wife's is more successful, and her income is twice that of her husband's.
4. The same as (3), only this time the husband's parents have given them the house.

In these examples as in real life, there are no easy answers to what responsibilities two divorcing people have to each other, and couples often end up in court. Generally, however, both parties are encouraged to come to a reasonable pretrial settlement.

Singles

The number of individuals choosing not to marry and the large number of divorces have created the class called singles. These people live alone or as a parent in a single-parent family. As a group, singles have increased substantially in the past twenty years. This group includes divorced people but also an increasing number of people who have never been married. As you can see in Table 8.3, more and more people are postponing marriage. As the number of singles has grown, so too has the number of activities designed for them. Health clubs for singles, singles clubs, singles bars, and video dating services have proliferated.

Not only has there been a significant increase in the number of singles, but there has also been an important increase in the number of single-parent households. Whereas in 1960 there were approximately 2 million single-parent families, in the early 2000s that number had grown to over 12 million, or about 34 percent of all families with children under age eighteen. Most of these are female-headed households. In theory, exhusbands or fathers are required to help support their children, but in practice many shirk this responsibility.

Living Together

In the 1970s, statisticians documented a dramatic increase in the number of unmarried people living together. This trend has continued and in 2008, the number of unmarried couples living together was over 6.4 million. Some of the reasons people live together without getting married are unwillingness to commit themselves to long-term relationships of any kind, desire to avoid legal complications when breakups they believe to be inevitable occur, experimentation, and the existence of an undissolved marriage of one or both partners. The practice, although traditionally frowned on, has gained acceptance, and many parents refer as casually to their children's living-together arrangements as they do to marriages.

Same-Sex Households

Although acknowledgment of homosexuality is still not the norm, a more open attitude toward this orientation, whether of men or women, is becoming increasingly common. Gays and lesbians have fought publicly since the late 1960s for specific legal rights, including the legalization of same-sex marriage. Most such efforts, though, have concentrated on essentials such as employment benefits, the right to adopt or receive custody of children, inheritance rights, and visitation rights when one member is hospitalized. Same-sex marriage is legal in the Netherlands, Belgium Norway, Sweden, Spain, South Africa, and Canada. In the United States, same-sex marriage is legal in a small number of states. In a few other states,

Table 8.3

Singles Who Have Never Been Married

	1970	1980	1990	2000	2008
Men					
25 to 29 years	19.1%	33.1%	45.2%	49.1%	59%
30 to 34 years	9.4%	15.9%	27.0%	29.5%	34.5%
Women					
25 to 29 years	10.5%	20.9%	31.1%	34.5%	45.5%
30 to 34 years	6.2%	9.5%	16.4%	20.6%	26.1%

Source: U.S. Bureau of the Census, *Current Population Reports.*

Same-Sex Marriage and Discrimination

The recent push for legalization of same-sex marriage in the United States is an interesting example of how cultural norms evolve and interact with legal structures. One of the major arguments put forward for same-sex marriage is that not to allow same-sex marriage discriminates against individuals according to sexual preference. This is true, but it is also irrelevant because laws by their very nature discriminate. A law must draw arbitrary lines somewhere, and the debate about legalizing same-sex marriage concerns where to draw an arbitrary line, not necessarily any deep-seated discrimination or homophobia.

For example, the United States has laws against polygamy in all forms, and those laws are just as discriminatory as laws against same-sex marriage. In fact, the United States actively prosecutes polygynists, and that prosecution is supported by a large majority of the population. Were there to be no discrimination based on sexual preference, all types of marriages, including cenogamy, would have to be legalized.

The point is not that same-sex marriage should or should not be given legal standing. The point is simply that laws inevitably include arbitrary lines that discriminate. Whether a law should be changed does not depend on whether the law discriminates, but on whether we, as a society, want that type of discrimination inherent in the law.

civil unions—*legally recognized commitments of two individuals, which are not technically marriage but that provide many of the same benefits as marriage*—are legal. The majority of states, however, do not recognize civil unions or same-sex marriage, and the U.S. Federal government has not recognized same-sex marriage on the federal level. Many states are, however, reconsidering their laws on marriage.

As we stated above, marriage has both religious and civil elements and some religions condone same-sex marriage, whereas others specifically prohibit it. As with any issue that has both secular and religious aspects, public debate is often rancorous as the various political parties try to stake out a position that gives them an edge in attracting voters. For example, those opposed to same-sex marriage have pushed for a constitutional amendment that would define marriage as a union between a man and a woman, even though it has little chance of passing; those in favor of same-sex marriage lobby in states and conduct same-sex marriages, even when they do not have the legal authority to do so, in order to gain publicity and to push their agenda.

The Family in Transition

The family has been and will continue to be a social institution in transition. A major reason is its interdependence with technology.

Technology's Effect on the Family

Apart from the general effects of technology on society, we can identify some specific technological developments that have affected the family. Although the medical technology of population control has had its failures, such as the intrauterine device, which led to infection and sterility in some women, as well as its social upheavals, such as that caused by the legalization of abortion and subsequent attempts to recriminalize, many safe and effective means of birth control have been developed. New ones, such as implantation of a capsule under the woman's skin, a day-after pill, and female condoms are coming along as well. A woman's ability to plan her pregnancies has revolutionized family life.

Another aspect of the revolution is technology enabling infertile women to have children. In the mid-1980s, the infertility rate among women in prime childbearing years had almost tripled since 1965, and much of the increase was attributed to smoking, pollution, abuse of recreational drugs and alcohol, and some of the means of contraception themselves. Today medical science can deal effectively with a significant number of infertility cases for both men and women. Treatments for men and women include medication and surgery. There are also various methods of fertilizing a woman's egg outside the womb and returning the fertilized egg to the womb. It is sometimes possible to use frozen sperm to fertilize the egg. Some of the medications, known as "fertility pills," are so successful that they result in multiple fertilized eggs—sometimes so many that one or more fertilized eggs must be removed from the womb so that the remaining ones can survive. A fertilized egg from one woman can be placed in the womb of another woman, usually when a woman cannot, or does not want to, go through a pregnancy herself, and occasionally when the second woman wants to give birth to a child but cannot do so without receiving a fertilized egg. There are several variations of these methods and many reasons that women use them.

Another influence of technology on the family has been the personal computer. It is not unusual for families to own several personal computers; some workers run their own businesses by way of the Internet, and some employers supply their workers with home computers. These people can work at home, and this alternative, both lucrative and attractive, has also meant flexible hours and the ability to supervise a home and children while working and earning a living.

Labor-saving devices for the home have remained essentially unchanged for thirty years, but the ingenuity of manufacturers means that we can look forward to refinements in these appliances. Some are liberating and some are not: The convenience of the work that they do is sometimes offset by the difficulty of learning to operate and maintain them. The robot that can do more than simple repetitive tasks and will clean the gutters, do the ironing, water the plants, mow the lawn, complain to the credit card company, rewire the telephone, fix the overhead door, and let the cat in is not in plain sight at this time.

The Future of the Family

The changing role of the family has left society with hard questions. Who will guide future generations? Who will be tomorrow's parents? What can prevent today's family crisis from becoming tomorrow's national disaster? Can adults please themselves as much as they hope to while producing equally happy, well-adjusted offspring who will be the solid citizen mothers and fathers we would wish for the next generation? Can both wife and husband find the satisfaction they seek at home, at work, and in their leisure hours, combining the goals of personal freedom and success so compatible with "single-blessedness" with the emotional security and commitments of wedlock?

Many individuals and groups have suggested what they believe to be effective ways to reinvigorate the family. Some of their ideas include outlawing abortion, banning busing, allowing school prayer, and prohibiting sex education in the schools. Without taking a stand on any of these issues, we doubt that they will contribute to the stability of families, although they may well be desirable for other reasons. Society changes and so too do the institutions in it. With new technologies, the optimal economic division of labor changes, and as it changes, so too do the functions of families.

Serious challenges to the family's survival are realities. With more women brought up to regard higher education and careers as their birthright, marriage will

"The family can't disappear as a social unit soon enough for me."

be only one of several paths they can choose. Many couples, deterred by high divorce rates, are deliberately opting not to marry or, if they do wed, not to have children, in view of the staggering costs of parenthood. When they do have children, those children often are left much more on their own than in the past. Consequently, rather than deriving their values from the family, these children acquire most of their values from films, television, videocassettes, magazines, the Internet, and peers.

It seems likely that changes to adapt the family to the new realities—such as flexible working hours, more shared jobs, infant care, and familial leaves for both sexes—will help achieve the goal of holding the family together. The family may take new forms as social trends demand; it may bend with the winds of change. But the diagnosis of the family unit's imminent death seems premature.

Key Points

- Four variations in family patterns are determined by the number of mates, selection of mates, family control, and reckoning of descent.
- Three functions of the family are the biological function, the psychological function, and the economic function.
- Family patterns evolve to meet these functions.
- The U.S. family today is quite different from its counterpart of fifty years ago.
- Technological change has significant effects on the family and will continue to have such effects in the future.
- The diagnosis of the family unit's imminent death is premature.

Some Important Terms

arranged marriage (148)
bilateral method (149)
cenogamy (147)
civil union (164)
covenant marriage (162)
egalitarian family (149)
extended family (147)
family (146)
gay family (147)

latchkey children (155)
marriage (146)
matriarchy (149)
matrilinear system (150)
monogamy (147)
no-fault divorce (162)
patriarchy (149)
patrilinear system (150)
personal-choice mating (149)

polyandry (147)
polygamy (147)
polygyny (147)
serial monogamy (147)
same-sex marriage (147)
single-parent family (147)
two-parent family (147)
unilateral method (149)

Questions for Review and Discussion

1. Why is the family often regarded as the most important of all social units?
2. State some important considerations in choosing a mate.
3. What are some methods of family control?
4. Why is it easier to trace your descent under a unilateral system than a bilateral system?
5. In today's circumstances, is the institution of the family really necessary for the propagation of the species? Defend your answer.
6. Monogamy is the most widespread form of marriage. Give some reasons for this.
7. What changes have the economic functions of the family undergone? Are they less important than formerly? Why or why not?
8. What changes has the physical-care function of the family undergone in the last few generations? Is it still important?
9. Describe the custom of dating as practiced in the United States, and explain the purpose it serves.

10. Describe some types of families other than the husband-wife-children household.
11. Does marrying for love eliminate consideration of compatibility and economic and social factors?
12. Can you think of some major adjustments that a newly married couple must make in their way of life? What further adjustments would be required by the arrival of children?
13. What are some of the problems a married couple must meet after the children have left home?

14. What are some of the factors that have contributed to high divorce rates?
15. What is no-fault divorce?
16. What implications does the increase in single-parent homes have for society?
17. How can family disorganization be reduced? By better marriage laws? By making divorce more difficult? Or by other methods?
18. Is the family likely to retain its present importance as a social institution? Why or why not? Could a satisfactory substitute be devised?

Internet Questions

1. According to Charlotte Allen, http://adams. patriot .net/~crouch/artj/allen.html, why did old-fashioned manners and family structure give women more freedom and fulfillment?
2. Go to the website www.answers.com/topic/ miscegenation. What does *miscegenation* mean? When did the first U.S. law appear against miscegenation? When did the Supreme Court decide *Loving v. Virginia*?
3. Go to www.youtube.com/watch?v= p2LZ1Aef7so& feature=related and watch the video on genealogy and DNA. How can DNA be used by genealogists or people interested in their own ancestry? Can DNA be used to identify specific ancestors like Alexander the Great or Genghis Khan?

4. Go to www.npr.org/news/specials/gaymarriage/ map and look at the map and the articles under related content. What is a non-Northeastern state that allows gay marriage? Which state most recently allowed gay marriage? For each state, did the courts or new legislation (voted on by the state legislatures) legalize gay marriage?
5. From www.census.gov/population/www/socdemo/ hh-fam/cps2005.html, go to Table C4. How many children live in an extended family with one or both of their parents and at least one of their grandparents? How many live with their grandparent(s) without either of their parents present?

For Further Study

Conley, Dalton, *The Pecking Order: Which Siblings Succeed and Why*, New York: Pantheon, 2004.

de Marneffe, Daphne, *Maternal Desire: On Children, Love, and the Inner Life*, London: Little Brown, 2004.

Duda, Karen, *The American Family*, New York: H. W. Wilson, 2003.

Harper, Sarah, *Aging Societies: Myths, Challenges and Opportunities*, London: Hodder Arnold, 2006.

Inglehart, Ronald, ed., *Human Beliefs and Values: Cross Cultural Sourcebook*, Ann Arbor: University of Michigan Press, 2006.

McClain, Linda C., *The Place of Families: Fostering Capacity, Equality, and Responsibility*, Cambridge, MA: Harvard University Press, 2006.

Moynihan, Daniel Patrick, *Family and Nation*, New York: Harcourt Brace Jovanovich, 1985.

Orman, Suze, *The Money Book for the Young, Fabulous & Broke*, New York: Riverhead, 2006.

Perel, Esther, *Mating in Captivity: Reconciling the Erotic and the Domestic*, New York: HarperCollins, 2006.

Schlosser, Eric, *Fast Food Nation: The Dark Side of the All-American Meal*, New York: HarperCollins, 2004.

WWW   Diversity Forum www.diversityforum.com/

WWW   Convenant Marriage Links www.divorce reform. org/cov.html

WWW   Divorcenet—Divorce Resources www.divorcenet .com

WWW   Gay Marriage News www.gaymarriagenews.com

WWW   Genealogy Sites www.cyndislist.com

WWW   National Council on Family Relations www.ncfr.org

WWW   National Family and Parenting Institute www .familyandparenting.org

WWW   Single Scene www.azsinglescene.com/library.htm

eligion

After reading this chapter, you should be able to:

- Explain why religion has existed in all societies
- State the problem that fundamentalist religions pose for the state
- List the five great religions of today and summarize their beliefs
- Discuss the role of religion in society

*The more I study science
The more I believe in God.*

—Albert Einstein

From A.D. 1095 to 1272, Europeans went to war to recapture territory, which had traditionally been controlled by Christians, from the Muslims. The Crusades, as those wars were called, changed the nature of society. As evidenced in today's problems of worldwide terrorism and fighting in the Middle East, religion is still leading to wars and still changing the nature of society. The importance of religion to society cannot be overemphasized.

If we think of religion as including all beliefs in supernatural powers, conceived of as controlling people's lives, and including various types of spirits and gods, then religion probably had its beginnings in some of the earliest human societies. The findings of archaeologists and anthropologists suggest that from time immemorial humans have sought explanations of their existence and of natural phenomena that went beyond the range of what they could learn from the ordinary experiences of life or from observation of the natural world.

An aspect of life that from very early on troubled people was the inevitability of death, and religion often promised them a life beyond death. Also, as cultures and civilizations developed, people longed to find purposes and satisfactions in life that would transcend the needs and desires of everyday living and thus give human existence greater dignity and meaning. Religion helps satisfy this longing because of the concepts common to all of its forms: the incorporation of a code of ethics; the use of myths or stories; the organization of intellectual doctrine; the display and comfort of ritual; the fostering of community and regard for others; and the hope of some intense, personal experience such as the answering of prayer.

That religious beliefs, institutions, and rituals have been a major element in the cultural patterns of most societies cannot be doubted. Even in modern industrial societies many of our oldest values and traditions are rooted in religion. In our own country, evidence of religious influence is rich. It includes the millions of people who attend religious services; the thousands of houses of worship; the celebration of holidays (holy days) such as those associated with Christmas, Easter, Passover, Yom Kippur, and Ramadan; and those ceremonies that are both private and official, such as weddings and funerals, and rites such as baptisms and bar mitzvahs.

In this chapter, our purpose is not to show the truth or falsehood of the doctrines of any particular faith. Rather, it is:

- To describe the nature of religion and the general character of certain major religions of the past and present.
- To give some attention to the role that religion has played in the development of human societies, not only to integrate and stabilize them but also, at times, to create conflicts.
- To consider the present-day influence of social change on religion and, conversely, the influence of religion on social change.

The Nature of Religion

Today, when we say that a person is religious we usually mean he or she believes in the existence of a supreme being and that this belief determines moral precepts and behavior to an important degree. Religious people believe that some things are of great value, or sacred, and they are likely to belong to a religious organization such as a church or synagogue; at the least, they attend religious services, even if on a sporadic or occasional schedule, where they commune with others whose beliefs are similar.

Religions vary greatly. Most include a belief in God or gods, some concept of an afterlife, and some theory of salvation, either by earning the right of entry into heaven or the privilege of reincarnation in a higher form of life or a higher social status. But some religions seem to have no God in any sense in which we ordinarily use that term. One of these is original Buddhism, which, unlike some later forms of this faith, is a religion without a deity, without a personal concept of God, and without any theory of salvation except the bliss of escaping perpetual rounds of reincarnation and suffering by achieving **Nirvana,** a state in which all desire and even all consciousness is lost.

Religions can have both spiritual and civil elements. **Civil religion,** a term that was first used by Rousseau, refers to religious beliefs that lead people to want to live by the laws of the land. It is a means of motivating people, out of fear of the divine power over them, to "subject themselves willingly to the governmental laws." This is in contrast to spiritual religion, which is only concerned with heavenly things and cares little what happens in this world. Neither civil nor spiritual religions are a threat to the state. However, when the two elements of religion combine, and the spiritual aspect of religion becomes interested in happenings of the world and unwilling to accept the laws of the land, the state and religion can come into conflict. Fundamentalist elements of religions, such as fundamentalist Christianity and fundamentalist Islam, often combine the two and hence come into conflict with the state. No longer does the individual subject himself or herself willingly to government laws, but is often in direct conflict with those laws. Sometimes this conflict becomes violent. We can see this in both fundamentalist Christian attacks on abortion centers and fundamentalist Islamic attacks on Western targets.

It is not easy to give a formal definition of religion that is wholly satisfactory, but the one suggested by Hans-Joachim Schoeps in the *Religions of Mankind* is useful and is the one we will use. According to him, "**religion** may be defined, in its broadest sense, as the relationship between man and the superhuman power he believes in and feels himself to be dependent upon." Such a relationship is expressed in various ways, including feelings of trust or fear, legends, myths, prayer, rituals, and the application of religious precepts to the conduct of life.

Left: Sundial, or "The Hitching Post of the Sun," in the Temple of the Sun at Machu Picchu. It is believed that the temples of the Incas did not have roofs because it was important not to obstruct the entrance of the sun, moon, and other deities. Right: The Great Sphinx and the Pyramid of Khafra.

What religions the earliest human beings practiced is a matter for speculation, but there are some tribal groups today, such as African bushmen, whose way of life is, or has been until very recently, so removed from modern technology that it is tempting to liken their beliefs to prehistoric ones. A graphic example can be seen in the classic film *The Gods Must Be Crazy.* In the first fifteen minutes of this film, Kalahari bushmen are seen living a life that we feel must have been unchanged for thousands of years. Suddenly, a Coke bottle is tossed out of a plane passing overhead and lands among them. The bushmen view the bottle as a gift from the gods, but it causes changes, including tests of faith, which themselves celebrate the imagination of primal human spirit. Ultimately, the bushmen decide they want to get rid of this "new technology" in order to preserve their way of life.

The Great Religions of Today

Today there are innumerable religions and sects, including the religions of people who still live in tribal groups. But if we are to list the great religions of the world, each of which is still a vital force in the lives of many millions of human beings, we should include at least five, namely, Hinduism, Buddhism, Judaism, Christianity, and Islam. In the world, about 70 percent of the population identifies itself with some organized religious group, although many people are only loosely affiliated. In the United States, Protestant or Catholic Christians are the largest groups, as you can see in Figure 9.1a. The Christian religion is also the largest in the world, as you can see in Figure 9.1b. Unlike in the United States, however, the largest percentage of Christians in the world is Roman Catholic rather than Protestant. Muslims and Hindus are the next two largest religious groups in the world. Were we to look at world religious affiliation over time, we would see that since 1950 the largest change has been the decreased importance of Buddhism. In large part, this decrease is due to the decline in religion in China after the communists took control in the 1950s.

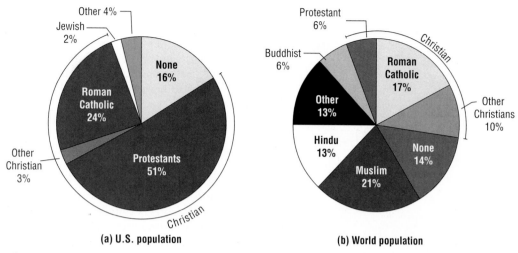

Figure 9.1

(a) Religious identification of U.S. population; (b) Religious identification of world population. (Source: *The CIA World Factbook.*)

Whether Confucianism and Taoism in China and Shintoism in Japan should be included in the great religions of today is questionable. Under the current regime, the status and future of China's ancient religions are uncertain. Furthermore, Confucianism often is said to be more a philosophy than a religion. Shintoism is the ancient religion of Japan but has had strong competition from Buddhism. In 1868 reformed Shintoism was made the official religion, but after World War II religious freedom was declared. However, some calculate that millions of Japanese still retain their faith in Shintoism. It is a mixture of nature, ancestor, and emperor worship and is closely associated with Japanese nationalism, although the concept of the emperor's divinity was officially abolished in 1945. Still, when Emperor Hirohito died in 1989, there was an outpouring of sadness in Japan and the introduction of a new era and a new calendar beginning at year zero.

Hinduism

Hinduism is the religion and social system of the Hindus, the majority of whom live in India. Since ancient times, it has had a strong hold in India, and even today it dominates the lives of the majority of its people. A minority of Indians have been converted to foreign faiths such as Christianity or Islam, or to religions such as Buddhism, Jainism, or Sikhism, all three of which developed out of Hinduism itself.

Unlike many religions, Hinduism has no founder, no distinct set of creeds, and, although it has many clear-cut paths to salvation, no unique path. It holds that the soul inhabits successive bodies in its journey through the universe, and thus all life, including insect and plant life, has a soul. All beings, even the gods, must die and be reborn in an endless cycle. Some believe that this cycle can be escaped through asceticism, in which personality is lost and the believer becomes one with the Absolute. Although Hinduism claims to be monotheistic, its High God has many forms, of which the two best known are Vishnu the creator and preserver and Siva the destroyer. There are thousands of lesser gods. No one attempts to remember all of them, but each has its place in folk affection; the believer will tell you, "They are all the same god."

In Hinduism all life is sacred because all life has a soul. The sacrifice of living creatures, a characteristic of some Hindu ceremonies, is explained by precisely this: Because life is sacred,

Siva, a Hindu god.

its sacrifice to the gods is vitally meaningful. Today, however, partly because of the economic value of animals, sacrifices are almost always represented by flowers and food (the gods eat the spiritual portion of the food; the material portion is consumed by the givers). Many animals are sacred: The cow is revered because she represents Mother Earth. She is never to be injured or killed (sick and starving cows roam the countryside and crowded city streets; they have been known to attend the movies in Calcutta). Other sacred creations are monkeys, snakes, the banyan tree, the herb known as basil, all mountains and rivers, and rocks of unusual shape.

Hindus are divided into four castes: (1) scholars and priests (Brahmans, a word meaning "source of life," or "expansive force"); (2) administrators of the state; (3) commercial and agricultural entrepreneurs; and (4) workers who perform the tasks the three higher classes shun—for example, sweeping floors, cleaning bathrooms, and repairing shoes. This **caste system,** in which individuals are differentiated in the jobs they can have, is hereditary, and although it has been officially outlawed for decades, it has proved almost impossible to eradicate and to transfer to a higher caste is very difficult.

There are hundreds of kinds of Hindus, of which the Sikhs form one of the most important in the modern world. *Sikh* is derived from a Hindu word meaning "disciple," and **Sikhs** are disciples of a group of gurus whose tenets are most easily expressed by naming principles to which they are opposed: the caste system, the priestly hierarchy and ritual, and idolatry. Sikhs are skilled farmers and shrewd businesspeople, and they are considered among the world's finest soldiers. They subscribe to such Hindu beliefs as birth and rebirth and the transmigration of the soul. In India, intense religious hatred exists between Sikhs and followers of the dominant Hinduism, and this enmity is fortified by political and regional rivalries. In 1984, after the Indian Prime Minister Indira Gandhi had ordered a military attack on the sacred Sikh temple of Amritsar (which resulted in many Sikh deaths and great damage to the edifice), she was assassinated on the grounds of her official residence; Sikhs are widely believed to have been responsible. Since then there has been ongoing tension in the Punjab region of India, where the majority of Sikhs reside.

An outward sign of Hinduism is its concentration on counting and classifying, creating categories into which to fit individual manifestations. This usually is explained as a method of imposing order on a complicated world, but it can also be seen as a means of imposing disorder, or of proving, by the endlessness of the effort, that the world cannot be categorized. This characteristic enables Hinduism to incorporate diverse and even contradictory principles if Hindus find them good.

Hinduism has been gaining popularity in the West under the auspices of movements such as Hare Krishna. Many Americans have become disenchanted with modern-day society and the principle of rationality on which it is based. They argue that rationality has led us into the mess we are in and that it is time to turn to faith and mysticism.

Buddhism

Although Buddhism, for the reasons outlined in this section, is now rare in India, it is probably the most widespread religion of the Eastern world, teaching that by right thinking and self-denial its followers can achieve Nirvana. It developed out of early Hinduism, and one of its chief objectives is to free people from the endless cycle of reincarnations that is part of Hindu doctrine. Buddhism was founded more than 500 years before Christ by a young Nepalese prince, Shakyamuni Gautama, who later became known as Buddha ("the enlightened one"). He is also sometimes called Siddhartha, "the perfected" or "completed one." After observing the

Buddha, revered in the Far East.

troubles of his father's subjects, the prince became convinced that all life results in suffering and that the only escape is to overcome desire for life and its pleasures. Therefore, he left his parents and his princely existence and became a wandering ascetic monk in order to seek a cure for suffering.

He succeeded in entering a trance in which he remembered his former incarnations and perceived himself as having already passed through so many stages that he had been ready to have himself born to his current circumstances in order to preach to others. Gautama had thus reached Enlightenment and could be called Buddha. He emerged from this state of contemplation, or Nirvana, although tempted by evil forces to remain dallying there, and went to Banaras, on the Ganges River in India, to explain how others could attain Nirvana—namely, by realizing that life is suffering, suffering springs from a burning thirst for material and spiritual riches, suffering ceases when the thirst is renounced, and we cease to thirst by passing through eight stages: right views, right aspiration, right speech, right conduct, right livelihood, right effort, right mindfulness, and right contemplation.

All of these concepts can be, and have been, divided into their own subcategories, but the heart of Buddha's teaching is gentleness, compassion, rationality, and moderation. Everyone can become a Buddha, although very few actually do so. More numerous than Buddhas are *bodhisattvas*, people who have given up or delayed entering Nirvana in order that they may stay to help others. The Buddha's preaching did not involve appeals to a higher being, because his experience of widespread suffering rendered him incapable of believing in a beneficent creator. It did involve contemplation and relinquishing; in an advanced state, one realizes "There is nothing."

The Buddha's birthplace (Kapilavastu), the place of his Enlightenment (Bodh Gaya), the place where he gave his first sermon (the deer park in Sarnath), and the place where he died (near Kapilavastu)—all in India or Nepal—are today the main destinations for Buddhist pilgrimages. Nevertheless, Buddhism is not one of the major religions of India today, having declined for many reasons, but principally because Islam overtook it both philosophically and materially, and in the eleventh century A.D. Muslims (also called Moslems) destroyed the Buddhist monasteries and dispersed the monks.

Over the centuries, as Buddhism gained converts and spread to other countries it underwent many changes, some of which greatly increased its popular appeal. Also, a variety of sects developed. It spread to Tibet, China, Korea, Japan, Southeast Asia, and Sri Lanka, taking on markedly different forms in different areas. In the south of Asia, in countries such as Sri Lanka, Myanmar, and Thailand, Buddhism is firmly established and is said to have retained more of its original character than in other regions.

Although Buddhism is primarily an Asian religion, in the 1970s small Buddhist sects sprang up in the United States. Many of these sects disbanded in the late 1980s, but a few remain. The Buddhist monastic community was founded by the Buddha himself, and its organization and character are said to be the one element in Buddhism that has changed relatively little over the centuries. Even to this day, Buddhist monks shave their heads and wear the traditional yellow robes. You are likely to see some sect members in the streets of a big city dressed in this traditional garb. Zen Buddhism, transcendental meditation, and yoga, all Buddhist practices that do not require more than several hours of practice a day, have also spread.

Judaism

We now turn to the three major **monotheistic religions** (religions with one god)—Judaism, Christianity, and Islam—which all share a common history. We begin with Judaism, which, although it has played an important role in world history, has a relatively small number of adherents. In 2008, the entire Jewish population of the world was probably only about 13.5 million, compared with about 2 billion Christians and 1.3 billion Muslims.

Judaism developed out of the religion of the ancient Hebrew tribe. According to the Bible story, a great leader of this tribe, Abraham, put his trust in a single God to guide him and his people in their migrations. During their wanderings, the Hebrews, or Israelites as they came to be called (after Jacob, or Israel, the grandson of Abraham), moved into the fertile Nile delta to escape famine. There they were eventually enslaved by the Egyptians.

During the period of their slavery, probably sometime between 1450 B.C. and 1400 B.C., there arose a great leader, Moses. He led the Israelites to freedom, as God had directed him, and came to be commonly regarded as the real founder of Judaism. After the escape of the Israelites from Egypt, Moses ascended Mount Sinai, where God appeared to him and through him made a sacred covenant with what were by then the twelve tribes of Israel. That covenant required that the Israelites acknowledge "the God of Israel" as ruler of the world and creator of heaven and earth. In return, God recognized the people of Israel as his chosen followers. Moses had been instructed by God to call him *Yahveh,* or as it is sometimes translated, Jehovah. When Moses came down from the mountain, he brought with him two stone tablets on which were inscribed Yahveh's Ten Commandments. These were later amplified into the many commandments and prohibitions set forth in the **Torah**—the Pentateuch, or the Five Books of Moses—which is part of both Jewish scriptures and the Christian Old Testament.

Judaism has several unique characteristics. First, though it makes claims to universality, it was and still is primarily the religion of a group of people who can, with qualifications, regard themselves as descendants of the ancient Israelites. Jews believe that they were chosen by God, but they do not believe that being chosen by God makes them special. They do not understand why they were chosen, and they regard it as a burden as much as a blessing. In fact, in the Book of Exodus, God suggests to Moses that perhaps he should begin again with a less fractious tribe. According to Jewish theologians, God chose the Jews simply because he had to begin somewhere. They do not see it as an honor or as a sign that they are superior, attitudes that are attributed to them by some non-Jews.

Second, Judaism has preserved much of its essential character for more than 3,000 years. It has done this in spite of the fact that for more than 1,900 years, ever since their last major rebellion against Rome was crushed by the Emperor Hadrian in A.D. 135, Jews have been a widely scattered and often persecuted minority among alien peoples. Finally, and most important, Judaism was the first great religion to develop a clear and unequivocal concept of a single God as the creator and ruler of the universe.

Although some Jews believe in the resurrection of the dead and that people must account beyond the grave for their good and evil deeds, unlike some other religions Judaism is a world-affirming, not a world-denying, faith, and it requires that Jews enjoy this life and use their abilities for the service of humankind. It looks for the coming of the **Messiah**—the expected deliverer of the Jews—and for a messianic age in which the kingdom of eternal peace will prevail and all evil impulses will be removed from the human heart. But it rejects the Christian belief that the Messiah has already come with his message of salvation.

From the Middle Ages to early modern times, the rights of Jews in Europe were greatly restricted, and they were forced to live in special sections of the cities called ghettos. The French Revolution and Napoleon did much to free Jews from the ghettos. But later there was a backlash, and it was not until after the social upheavals of 1848 that in most countries Jews received full rights of citizenship on a more or less permanent basis. But this did not end their troubles, for the very success that many of them soon enjoyed in their professions stirred up new waves of **anti-Semitism,** or feelings of hatred and dislike toward Jews.

The freeing of the Jews in the nineteenth century from their former restrictions brought about great changes in Judaism. Gradually Jews, not only in Europe but also in the United States, became divided into three major groups: the Orthodox, who resist change in beliefs and ritual; the Reform, who reject much of Jewish traditionalism and believe that Judaism should be regarded as a changing and developing religion; and the Conservatives, who cannot accept the orthodoxy but who object to an extreme break with traditions and therefore seek a middle way.

Jews sometimes are called a race, but anthropologists remind us that this term is inaccurate. Originally, they belonged to that branch of the Caucasoid race that inhabited the Arabian peninsula and spread into the fertile crescent to the north of it. They once formed a nationality, the ancient Hebrew nation. But later they were dispersed over almost the entire world, and over the centuries they interbred to some extent with the non-Jews of the countries in which they lived. Also, they converted several non-Jewish peoples to Judaism. The word *Jew* comes from Judaism, which is their religion. After World War II, some of them migrated to the ancient homeland and created the new nation of Israel.

To determine the number of Jews in the United States with any great accuracy is impossible. This is partly because many persons of Jewish ethnic background maintain no affiliation with any temple or other Jewish organization, partly because there has been an appreciable amount of intermarriage between Jews and non-Jews, and partly because Jews disagree on who is a Jew. Tradition says anyone born to a Jewish mother is a Jew. However, in the 1980s the Reform rabbinate, representing about a quarter of U.S. Jews, extended recognition to those whose only Jewish parent is the father.

There is an increasing emphasis on individual choice in Judaism, including rising numbers of conversions. Some Jews see these processes as endangering their traditional view of themselves as chosen by God, but others welcome these trends. At present, it is estimated that there are about 6 million people in this country who can be classified as Jews. More than one-third of all U.S. Jews live in metropolitan New York, and considerable numbers are concentrated in other large cities such as Los Angeles, Philadelphia, Chicago, and Miami.

Jews are sometimes considered primarily a religious group, but in a poll taken by *Newsweek* only 43 percent of U.S. Jews said they considered themselves religious. According to political scientist Daniel Eleazar of Temple University, only 20 percent of the Jewish

A Jewish family celebrates Passover seder.

population worships regularly. Of the others, 40 percent maintain nominal affiliation with a temple but usually attend services only on their high holy days of Rosh Hashanah and Yom Kippur.

On the average, U.S. Jews have markedly higher incomes than the rest of our population, though over half a million fall below the family poverty level as set by agencies of the federal government. Jews also, on average, have higher levels of education than other groups and, in proportion to their numbers, are much better represented in business and the professions.

Prejudice against the Jews, or anti-Semitism, has existed for centuries and has been strong in certain countries. Sometimes it has been tied to religion; sometimes it has been rationalized by dislike on the part of the majority of the population for certain cultural or "racial" characteristics, largely imaginary, attributed to the Jews as a group. In some parts of eastern Europe, anti-Semitism has at times gone to such extremes that thousands of Jews were killed, as in the **pogroms,** or organized massacres, that occurred in czarist Russia. But it was in Nazi Germany that anti-Semitism reached its height, and the Holocaust, in which 6 million Jews were killed, has affected Jews and everyone else in a variety of ways.

Partially because of feelings of guilt for allowing the Holocaust to occur, the Western nations supported the establishment of the state of Israel after World War II. Israel was established from lands over 50 percent of which were owned by Palestinian Arabs. After the 1948 war for control of this land, a huge number of Palestinian Arabs were displaced and moved to refugee camps in neighboring Arab states where they and their descendants still live. This area of the Middle East became a prime source of international friction.

In 1994, after almost fifty years of conflict, the Jews and the Palestinians officially agreed to become reconciled and to live in peace. That agreement was meant to culminate in a permanent peace treaty between the Palestinians and the Israelis, but disputes about

Former Nazi government women burying Jews at a concentration camp after World War II.

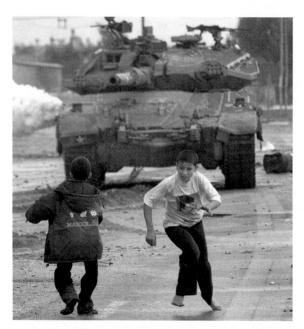

Palestinian children run for cover in front of an Israeli tank.

borders prevented any permanent agreement, and today the two sides remain engaged in fighting and serious disputes.

Christianity

Christianity, the principal religion of the Western world, developed from Judaism, and the greater part of the Christian Bible (the Old Testament) still consists of Jewish sacred writings. The ancient Jews believed that at his chosen time God would confound their enemies and set up a new Jewish kingdom under a Messiah (deliverer) descended from King David. Later, some came to believe that the Messiah would come down from heaven at the end of the world, at the time of the resurrection of the dead, and would carry out the last judgment.

Jesus of Nazareth, the founder of Christianity, was born in Bethlehem, about A.D. 1. This date in itself is an example of the power of religion. In Western cultures, events that took place before the birth of Christ are dated "B.C.," meaning "Before Christ." For instance, in Chapter 3, we said that humans first appeared in China about 20,000 B.C. The term "A.D." stands for the Latin words *anno domini*, which literally translated mean "in the year of our Lord." This term is used to begin numbering all over again, with A.D. 1 as the year of Christ's birth. The year A.D. 2000 means the two thousandth year after Christ's birth.[1]

At some point in Jesus' life, he became convinced that he was the Messiah, or Christ, and the divine son of God. Often he is called Jesus Christ, which simply means Jesus, the Messiah. Soon after he started his ministry, at about the age of thirty, he converted and gathered around him the **Apostles,** the twelve close associates who were to be his chief aides and who were to carry on his ministry after his death.

Our knowledge of Jesus' teachings comes to us indirectly. He did not write them down but depended on his disciples to preach from memory what he had taught. Our chief sources are, first, the Gospels of the New Testament and, second, the Epistles. But these were prepared long after Jesus' death. The four Gospels are thought by historians to have been written between A.D. 65 and about A.D. 100. Presumably, they were based on documents in which some of his followers had recorded his sayings as they remembered them. But how accurately his sayings and the events of his life were recorded, or how much was changed or added by successive copiers or revisers of the Gospels, historical scholarship cannot tell us with any certainty.

Jesus never doubted the reality of God or of his own special relationship to God. But he knew he had not been sent, as some of his hearers hoped, to deliver the Jews from Rome by reestablishing the earthly kingdom of David. Rather, he had been sent by his Father to show all of humanity, Jews and Gentiles alike, the way to heavenly salvation. Like many Jews of his day, he believed that the long-foretold messianic kingdom of God would come rather soon, but for him it was a kingdom in heaven, which was only for those who would believe in

---

[1]Twentieth-century scholarship indicates that Christ actually was born about 4 B.C. There will be no attempt to renumber dates, as that task would be impossible, and the Western world's dating system will continue to use A.D. 1 as a reference point. An alternative way of designating A.D. and B.C. is C.E. (Common Era) and B.C.E. (Before the Common Era).

him, who would truly repent of their sins, and who would surrender to the will of God before it was too late.

Jesus taught that the most important things are to believe in God, do His will, and believe in Jesus as the son of God. God is utterly good: supremely righteous and just, but also forgiving and merciful. Therefore, people should trust him completely and regularly seek spiritual aid through prayer. Jesus also taught that God demands we love one another, friend and foe alike, and this has been one of the most difficult teachings for devout Christians to interpret and to apply as a practical guide in daily conduct. Jesus also taught his disciples to obey the Ten Commandments, which God transmitted to Moses on Mount Sinai, and to follow the golden rule. The latter states, "Do unto others as you would have them do unto you."

Jesus' success in drawing crowds in Galilee soon attracted the attention of the leaders of the two principal Jewish sects, or parties, in Jerusalem—the Sadducees and the Pharisees. They had their own differences, but both became enemies of Jesus because his teaching and his actions did not always follow the dictates of either Judaic law or tradition. After he had been preaching for three or four years, Jesus decided to go to Jerusalem at the time of the Passover, when Jews from a wide area would be assembled for the great annual festival. This gave the enemies of Jesus an opportunity to stir up ill feeling against him among the people. Finally they seized him, made accusations against him, and denounced him to the Roman governor, Pilate, on the ground that he claimed to be king of the Jews. Pilate doubted Jesus' guilt but when the crowd demanded death, the governor acquiesced and ordered his crucifixion at Golgotha.

Three events reported in the Gospels and the Epistles are of crucial significance for Christianity: (1) the Last Supper of Jesus with his disciples on the evening before the crucifixion, (2) his crucifixion, and (3) his resurrection on the third day after his death. Even before coming to Jerusalem, Jesus had foretold his death and resurrection to the twelve apostles. A key belief of the Christian religion is that Jesus died to redeem the sins of humankind and thus opened for them the way to salvation. In the sacrament of Communion, or the Eucharist, which was first celebrated by Jesus with the twelve disciples at the Last Supper, devout communicants believe that they enter into a special relationship with Christ. The wine they drink and the bread they eat symbolize, or in Catholic doctrine actually become, the blood and body of Christ. The communicant is thus strengthened in his or her attempts to achieve salvation by the redemptive power that Christ achieved through his death and resurrection.

The Early Christians. The spread of Christianity after Jesus' death was relatively rapid, but the early Christian groups, or churches, were only loosely linked. By the end of the first

Christian worship.

century, however, administrative organization had begun to develop in Rome and elsewhere, and bishops began to assume authority not only to appoint priests to oversee local churches but also to settle disputes over doctrine. Gradually the primacy of the bishop of Rome became recognized throughout the empire, and by the end of the third century, he had taken the title of pope.

The Middle Ages and After.   Before the final collapse of the Roman Empire in the West in A.D. 476, the Church of Rome had become strong enough to prevent the complete breakdown of order and civilization that might otherwise have resulted from the successive invasions of the empire by Germanic tribes. During the Middle Ages, the church dominated the religious and intellectual life of Europe and to a great extent its politics and economics. Meanwhile, the eastern Roman Empire with its capital at Constantinople (now known as Istanbul) still survived, and the Eastern Church, later known as the Orthodox Church, became increasingly independent of Rome. The final break, or schism, between the two parts of the church occurred in 1054 and remains to this day.

The next great defection from the Church of Rome did not occur for several hundred years. In the fifteenth century, perhaps even earlier, many Christians felt that the church was undergoing moral decay. The Renaissance, which brought a renewal of interest in art, literature, and the works of classical antiquity, undoubtedly contributed to a general stir and unrest. Reformers began to urge that religion revert to its sources. The result was the **Reformation**, the Protestant revolt against traditional Catholicism, which began in 1517 when Martin Luther posted his call for reform on the door of the church in Wittenberg, Germany. Other important leaders of the Reformation included Ulrich Zwingli and John Calvin in Switzerland and John Knox in Scotland.

The Reformation led to a considerable period of religious and political turmoil, including religious wars and repression of dissident groups in various countries, and though it did not win over the majority of Catholics to Protestantism, it did result in substantial defections from the Roman Catholic Church. But the Protestants who succeeded in gaining freedom from control by Rome did not succeed in joining to form a major independent church body.

The Cathedral of Notre Dame in Paris.

Instead, they divided into a considerable number of sects, or denominations. Several of these, including the Puritans and Quakers, played an important role in the settlement of the English colonies in America.

European migration to the Americas and to areas such as South Africa, Australia, and New Zealand carried Christianity with it. In some areas, such as the United States and Canada except Quebec, Protestant settlers from northwestern Europe were in the majority. In other areas, as in practically all of Latin America, settlers came largely from overwhelmingly Catholic countries such as Spain, Portugal, and Italy. Christianity was also carried to other parts of the world by the strong missionary movement that developed in the nineteenth century, but in most non-Christian countries missionaries succeed in converting only a small fraction of the people.

Islam

Islam, like Judaism and Christianity, is a religion based on divine revelation, and its messenger, Muhammad, like Moses, made no claims to divinity for himself. He believed only that he had been chosen by God, or Allah, to receive from the angel Gabriel revelations of Allah's will. These revelations, which became frequent, he repeated in full to those who would listen, and shortly after his death they were assembled by his friend Abû Bakr to form the **Qu'ran,** the holy scriptures of the Muslims. Abû Bakr became the first successor, or caliph, to carry on Muhammad's work. The Qur'an begins as follows:

> In the name of Allah, the Beneficent, the Merciful.
>
> [1.1] All praise is due to Allah, the Lord of the Worlds.
> [1.2] The Beneficent, the Merciful.
> [1.3] Master of the Day of Judgment.
> [1.4] Thee do we serve and Thee do we beseech for help.
> [1.5] Keep us on the right path.
> [1.6] The path of those upon whom Thou hast bestowed favors. Not [the path] of those upon whom Thy wrath is brought down, nor of those who go astray.

The Qur'an is accessible on the Web in formats that are easily searchable for specific topics, and, given the importance of Islam to modern world affairs, browsing through it is definitely a worthwhile activity.

Muhammad was born about A.D. 570 at Mecca, in the western part of what is now Saudi Arabia. According to tradition, he was orphaned and became a ward of his grandfather and, later, of an uncle, both of whom were prominent members of the Koreish tribe. Later he was a merchant, and at about the age of twenty-five he became the business advisor to a rich widow, fifteen years his senior, whom he eventually married. Meanwhile, he had come into contact with the Arabian religion of his time, which was a mixture of animism and polytheism. Muhammad had also learned something about Judaism and Christianity from his acquaintances in Mecca who were followers of both religions. His contacts with Jews and Christians may have contributed to his dissatisfaction with the beliefs and practices of his fellow Arab tribesmen.

Though Muhammad himself initiated the religion of Islam, he was greatly influenced by Christianity and Judaism. He considered that he was completing and perfecting the work of Moses, Jesus, and other heavenly messengers whom he recognized as his forerunners. But Muhammad denied the Christian doctrine of the Trinity and the divinity of Christ. According to the Qur'an, God is one and God is eternal. He neither begets nor is begotten.

In Arabic, *Islam* means "submission," and Muslims are submitters to the will of God. The devout Muslim's goal is fairly simple: It is to perform one's duties as outlined in the Qu'ran and as exemplified by the acts of Muhammad in his lifetime. The Qur'an is infallible.

The so-called Five Pillars of Islam state the indispensable religious duties of a believer:

1. Acceptance and frequent repetition of the creed, "There is no God but Allah and Muhammad is his messenger"
2. The performance five times a day of prescribed rituals of prayer and devotion
3. The giving of alms to the needy
4. The fast during Ramadan, the month when the angel Gabriel appeared to Muhammad
5. The pilgrimage to the Kaaba stone at Mecca once in a lifetime by those who can afford it

From the seventh century to the eighteenth century, Islam spread as far west as Spain and as far east as the Philippines. It was able to do this through its access to trade routes from its original home in Arabia and through military conquest. Islam's influence ebbed and flowed, but by the end of World War I in 1918 it had reached a low. By the second half of the twentieth century, however, with political independence and national consciousness, Islam was enjoying a resurgence and again extending its influence. Today its principal distribution is in the Arabian peninsula, North and West Africa, the Middle East, Turkey, Afghanistan and the Indian subcontinent, parts of the former USSR, and Indonesia. In the United States, the number of Muslims is growing, and some authorities predict that there will be more Muslims than Jews in the United States in this century.

The Denominations of Islam. After Muhammad's death, Islam split into two factions: the **Shiites** (the sectarians, followers of Ali, cousin to the Prophet), who believed that Ali was the legitimate successor to Muhammad, and the **Sunni** (the traditionalists), who believed that Abū Bakr, the oldest companion of Muhammad, was the legitimate successor. Today Sunnis constitute about 85 percent of all Muslims and Shiites constitute about 15 percent. There are also smaller sects of Islam, including the Sufis and the Wahhabis, and though they are small in number, they can play important roles in the interaction between the Islamic world and the Western world.

The difference between Sunnis and Shiites concerns who should be seen as the legitimate religious authority in society. Shiites follow a system of Imamah. They believe that the existing Imam is the true leader of Muslims, and that all true Muslims must submit to his rule. Imams are appointed by existing Imams, which means there is a line of succession that always

A Palestinian Islamic family celebrates Eid al-Adha, the feast of sacrifice.

assumes a living Imam as ruler. Because Imams carry enormous power among believers to tell people what to do, Imamah can, and often does, come in conflict with governments, which also claim the right to tell people what to do. An example is Iran, which has a Shiite majority. Iran has both a religious authority—the Imam—and a democratically elected government, and there is often confusion about which authority is in charge.

Sunnis do not follow a system of Imamah. This means that Sunnis generally are more content with having a secular ruler as long as that secular ruler does not interfere with the spiritual dimension of religion. In Iraq there are both Sunnis and Shiites, with the Shiites in the majority. However, Iraq had never been a democracy, and up until 2004 the Sunnis were in charge. It was in part to keep the Shiite majority out of power that the United States had earlier supported Saddam Hussein in his war with Iran.

After invading Iraq in 2003, the United States struggled with setting up a democratic government, which the United States stated was one of the goals of the invasion, in a country with a Shiite majority whose beliefs often put religious rule by an Imam above secular democratic rule. The type of problem the Shiite sect presents today was the kind of problem that led Rousseau early on in his discussion of democracy to despair of the relationship between religion and government, and to call on government to set up a civil religion that avoided the conflict.

Islamic Fundamentalism.   In recent years, there has been much discussion of what is sometimes called Islamic fundamentalism and its connection to terrorism and **jihad.** In Arabic, jihad means "striving," but it is commonly used by the western press to denote a sacred war against the Western world. As with all fundamentalist religious groups, there is much dispute about what is meant by fundamentalist Islam and whether some groups should be considered as fundamentalist Muslims. According to the dictionary, fundamentalism consists of "strict maintenance of ancient or fundamental doctrines." The problem is that there is generally ambiguity about what those doctrines are, and the issue comes down to who is interpreting them. As interpreted by Osama bin Laden, these ancient doctrines require Muslims to fight against the Western world and to reestablish an Islamic state, regardless of the costs to society and humanity. Other Muslims interpret it quite differently, and many simply want to be left alone to follow their spiritual beliefs, leaving secular matters to government. Their concern is with religion, not government. For them, religious fundamentalism is simply strict adherence to the Five Pillars. The difference between the two views of fundamentalism has sometimes been called the difference between revivalists, who want to be spiritually devout, and fanatics and extremists, who exploit this devotion for political ends.

For some fundamentalists, the empowerment of Islam, which they see as God's plan for humankind, is a sacred end, and it can be achieved only through the establishment of an Islamic state. Ayatollah Khomeini, who led the Islamic revolution in Iran, combined fundamentalism with the Shiite belief in the role of the Imam and argued that because Islamic government is a government of law, and because a knowledge of law is necessary for anyone to rule, the person who should rule is the person whose knowledge of the law surpasses all others. Under this interpretation, it is appropriate to revolt against existing secular governments and replace them with rule by Islamic clerics, such as himself. This view fit Shiite views much better than it fit Sunni views, which preferred a separation between religion and secular government. Khomeini also claimed that the West was on a crusade to eliminate Islam from the world and that Western ways were evil. In so doing he portrayed the United States in particular as the great Satan, claiming that good Muslims would reject U.S. technology and way of life.

More recent Islamic scholars such as Hasan alt-Turai and Sayyid Muhammad Husayn Fadlallah have argued that the problem is not that the West is on a crusade to eliminate Islam, but instead that the West has dispossessed Muslims. Unlike Khomeini, these scholars argue that Islam could selectively borrow technology and institutions from the West. These debates are still going on in Islamic society, and the outcome will play an important role in the peace of the world.

The Role of Religion in Society

There can be little doubt that in primitive societies and in the earliest civilizations religious beliefs and practices were a strong integrative factor in most societies. Because of these beliefs and practices, people knew how they must behave individually and as a group to avoid the ill will of the gods and to win their favor. They knew certain things were sacred and that if the group was to avoid famine or other misfortunes, no one must be allowed to treat the gods with disrespect. Religious beliefs were tied to rules of behavior and usually gave strong support to custom and tradition.

In the early history of civilization, almost every "nation" had its own gods and sometimes, as in ancient Egypt, the king himself was regarded as divine. Even in twentieth-century Japan, up until 1945 Shinto doctrine held that the emperor was a descendant of the sun goddess. As a result, the people were drawn together not only by their common beliefs but also by their participation in common rituals of prayer, praise, and sacrifice.

Not infrequently, however, in the more highly developed civilizations of the world, differences in religious beliefs have been a source of social conflict, especially when groups with different religious beliefs have lived within the same national borders. To get an idea of the potential problem, look, for example, at Northern Ireland, where Protestants and Catholics clash, and at India, where Hindus clash with Muslims.

Religion as a Source of Moral Values and Social Change

Religion, then, can be a socially disruptive force, but it seems clear that over the years its major influence has been to integrate and stabilize nations and cultures. In the Western world, where Christianity in its various forms is by a wide margin the predominant faith, our ethical and moral values have over the centuries been modified and given greater vitality by the teachings of the Christian religion.

Religion's integrative force derives from the fact that it gives divine authority to ethical and moral principles. Without people's adherence to such principles, it would be difficult to maintain an orderly society with free elections and a wide range of personal freedoms, to produce goods with enough efficiency to hope to eliminate poverty, and in general to maintain the level of civilization we have already achieved.

Through its influence on individuals, religion also has an impact on economic and political institutions. The great German sociologist Max Weber (1864–1920) developed this thesis in his book *The Protestant Ethic and the Spirit of Capitalism.* According to his theory, the new Protestant sects that developed out of the Reformation, especially those that were influenced by the doctrines of Calvin, made a major contribution to the economic prosperity of England and western Europe and to the development of modern industrial capitalism. They did so because they believed in the **Protestant ethic**, the theory that God expects good Christians to work hard, to save, to invest their savings, and to show business initiative. The Protestant ethic also played a major role in the development of the American ideals of rugged individualism, private enterprise, and financial success.

Putting a high value on work and on the kinds of behavior necessary for material progress was never a Puritan or Protestant monopoly. It is a characteristic found everywhere among people who are determined to improve their condition, and it can be found in all societies and cultures.

Because religion is a source of moral values, it can also be a source of social change. For example, churches led the way in the civil rights battle, just as they had earlier in the antislavery movement. Churches have also been active in the push for more general economic and social equality, and for adding issues of morality to the political dialogue.

Impact of Religion on Education, the Arts, and Literature

The influence of religion on education, the arts, music, and literature is pervasive. During the Middle Ages, the church and especially the monasteries preserved ancient literature and kept learning alive. In the United States, from colonial times until well into the nineteenth century, most of our colleges and universities were started and controlled by religious organizations. Many of them are still church controlled, and some religious bodies operate extensive systems of secondary and primary schools. Many of the great works of art of ancient Greece and the European Renaissance are representations of personalities or events with religious significance. In the field of religious music, we find such outstanding composers as Bach and Handel, and in literature we have great poems such as Dante's *Inferno* and Milton's *Paradise Lost.*

Buddhism and Hinduism have inspired temples, paintings, and sculpture of great sophistication, mystery, ferocity, and beauty; Particularly in India, these represent unparalleled fecundity and vitality. In some countries such as Indonesia and China, the entire history and development of the religions are carved over acres of temple structures or wrested from vast rock-cut caves and cliffs, constituting some of the greatest artistic and historical monuments in the history of human ingenuity. In Japan, hundreds of great gardens have been created to the quiet glory of Buddhism and Shintoism. An Islamic prohibition of representations of the human figure means that the classics of their art are exhibited in architecture, caligraphy, and intricate floral and geometric patterns. Sanskrit, which means "perfect language," was developed in India to preserve religious traditions. In fulfilling this function, Sanskrit also became a great literary language and one of the Indo-European languages from which have derived most of the major languages spoken today in Europe, Iran, parts of Asia, and the Americas.

In China, the poetry of the eighth-century figure Wang Wei is one of the reasons the Tang dynasty is called the golden age. It has some Buddhist undertones, but only sixty years later the poetry of Han Shan became overtly Zen Buddhist. In India the *Ramayana* and the *Mahabharata* embody nearly all of the religious stories and myths on which the country is nurtured. In Japan we might mention the Shingon Buddhist novel of the eleventh century *Tale of Genji.*

Interfaith Efforts for Peace

Despite the many differences, significant similarities exist among religions. Religious leaders have attempted to build on these similarities by creating organizations of multiple religious denominations committed to creating better understanding among the world's population. In her book, *The Mighty and the Almighty,* former Secretary of State Madeline Albright argues that because many of the major conflicts in the world have religious roots, interfaith religious efforts are central to solving them.

The Potential Conflict between Religion and Government

The previous two sections discussed the positive elements of religion for society. But religion also plays what some consider negative roles. Specifically, it can undermine the state and lead people to fight others, all in the name of religion. The Crusades were an example of Christianity leading to war against Muslims, and recent jihad terrorist attacks are an example of Islam leading to attacks against Western countries.

Christianity and democratic government have made their peace with each other, with religion playing the spiritual role that Rousseau saw for it as a type of civil religion. The pope's decrees do not undermine Western governments, and a Catholic in government is seen as following his or her own judgment rather than the pope's decrees on issues such as gay rights or abortion. The same is true of many other religions.

This is not the case, however, with Islam, and Islamic fundamentalism poses the threat of religion to secular government that Rousseau foresaw. How those theological decisions play out will make a significant difference in what happens in the War on Terror.

Key Points

- Humans have always been troubled by the inevitability of death and the meaning of life; their interest in these issues has led them to religion.
- The five great religions of today are Hinduism, Buddhism, Judaism, Islam, and Christianity.
- In current society, religion is a source of moral values, and it significantly influences all aspects of life.

- Modern religions face serious questions. Disputes arise both within religions and among religions.
- Religion has played a central role in society for thousands of years and is likely to do so for thousands of years in the future.
- Religion presents a potential problem for secular government if religion extends its influence beyond the spiritual realm.

Some Important Terms

anti-Semitism (175)
Apostles (177)
caste system (172)
civil religion (169)
jihad (182)
Messiah (174)

monotheistic religions (174)
Nirvana (169)
pogroms (176)
Protestant ethic (183)
Qur'an (180)
Reformation (179)

religion (169)
Shiites (181)
Sikhs (172)
Sunni (181)
Torah (174)

Questions for Review and Discussion

1. Why has religion had a strong appeal to human beings from earliest times?
2. To Westerners, Hinduism seems a strange faith. Why?
3. How did Prince Shakyamuni Gautama found Buddhism?
4. What are the unique characteristics of Judaism?
5. How did Islam begin? What was the origin of the Qur'an?
6. State some of the similarities of Islam to Judaism or Christianity; also state some of the more important differences.
7. What are the Five Pillars of Islam?
8. What potential problems does fundamentalist Islam pose?

9. Why is our knowledge of Jesus' teachings indirect?
10. List as many as you can of the more important teachings of Jesus.
11. Explain how Islam spread from Arabia to other parts of the world from the seventh to the eighteenth century.
12. Why are religious beliefs likely to strengthen the moral and ethical principles of a society? How are they likely to create dissension and war?
13. On balance, has religion been an integrative or divisive factor in today's society? Defend your answer.
14. Why did Rousseau believe that governments needed to create a civil religion?

Internet Questions

1. Go to www.tibet.com. What is a Dalai Lama? Who is the current Dalai Lama?
2. Using information found in www.infoplease.com/ipa/A0193627.html, explain what the Dead Sea Scrolls are. Who wrote them?
3. Who were the Knights Templar, according to www.knightstemplar.org? What was their original purpose?
4. Go to www.pbs.org/mormons/etc/genealogy.html. Why are Mormons so interested in genealogy?
5. Using the list of countries' religious makeup, http://worldfactsandfigures.com/religion.php, what countries have indigenous beliefs as their largest percentage?

For Further Study

Albright, Madeline, *The Mighty and the Almighty*, New York, HarperCollins, 2006.

Eagleman, David, *Sum*, New York, NY: Pantheon, 2009.

Evans, Michael D., *The American Prophecies: Ancient Scriptures Reveal Our Nation's Future*, Nashville, TN: Warner Faith, 2004.

Hecht, Jennifer Michael, *Doubt: A History: The Great Doubters and Their Legacy of Innovation*, San Francisco: HarperSan Francisco, 2004.

Mailer, Norman, and John Buffalo Mailer, *The Big Empty: Dialogues on Politics, Sex, God, Boxing, Morality, Myth, Poker and Bad Conscience in America*, New York: Nation Books, 2006.

Mishra, Pankaj, *An End to Suffering: The Buddha in the World*, New York: Farrar, Straus & Giroux, 2005.

Paine, Jeffrey, *Re-Enchantment: Tibetan Buddhism Comes to the West*, New York: Norton, 2004.

Scafi, Alessandro, *Mapping Paradise: A History of Heaven on Earth*, Chicago: University of Chicago Press, 2006.

Slifkin, Nosson, *Mysterious Creatures: Fantastic Animals in Torah and Scriptures*, Brooklyn, NY: Yashar Books, 2005.

Stewart, Matthew, *The Courtier and the Heretic: The Fate of God in the Modern World*, New Haven, CT: Yale University Press, 2006.

Yusa, Michiko, *Japanese Religions*, London: Routledge, 2002.

WWW Academic Info Religion Gateway www.academicinfo.net/religindex.html

WWW Adherents.com www. thearda.com

WWW American Religion Data Archive www.thearda.com

WWW Buddhist Education and Information Network www.buddhanet.net

WWW Christianity Today www.christianitytoday.com

WWW Islam Online www.islamonline.net/english/index.shtml

WWW Judaism 101 www.jewfaq.org

WWW World Council of Churches www.wcc-coe.org

Education

After reading this chapter, you should be able to:

- Explain how schools serve as agents of social control
- Give a brief history of the development of U.S. education
- Discuss the main problem facing our school system
- Summarize the evolution of the college curriculum
- Explain why the methods of funding education contribute to unequal education

A human being is not, in any proper sense, a human being till he is educated.

—Horace Mann

Everything you do involves, or should involve, learning or education. Education is a never-ending process that begins with the socialization of the child and continues through all of adult life. In common usage, however, the term *education* has a more limited meaning. **Education** refers especially to efforts, usually by the more mature members of a society, to teach each new generation the beliefs, the way of life, the values, and some portion of the knowledge and skills of the group; it also refers to efforts to learn on the part of those who are the objects of teaching.

In modern society, there is so much to learn that any one person can acquire, at most, only a very small part of the total knowledge. Therefore, individuals must specialize in particular fields. Furthermore, in many fields, such as medicine and engineering, the knowledge and skills required have multiplied until they not only take years to learn but also require highly specialized educational arrangements in colleges, universities, and research institutions. Thus, as our modern industrial society increases in complexity, it becomes more and more dependent on formal education—that is, on a system of schooling—both for transmitting and for developing its cultural heritage. In the United States, we have created a school system that provides more opportunities for more people than any the world has ever known. In 2008, we spent well over $800 billion to meet the needs of more than 75 million students at all levels of the educational ladder.

In the early 2000s, there was enormous concern about what we are getting for that money. Are we simply **credentializing** individuals, which means using school diplomas as a way to limit entry into jobs but not to train people appropriately? Why do U.S. students rate so poorly when compared internationally? Should we be providing "schooling"—the teaching of knowledge and skill—or should we be providing broader educational and social skills—the teaching of critical thinking and multicultural topics? And, finally, how can we get more for less?

Schools as Agencies of Social Control

In her book, *Miss Manners' Guide to Rearing Perfect Children,* Judith Martin writes that "every child is born ignorant . . . and is civilized by two things, example and nagging." In many ways, example and nagging are education, and it is education that civilizes us. Put more formally, it is through education that society transmits to individuals the knowledge dealing with the ways of life of the group. Education is a prime agency of social control, and decisions made about how to educate play crucial roles in deciding the direction society will take.

The Dual Thrust of U.S. Education

In the United States, such socialization is deeply embedded in the schooling process, but it is modified by attempts to foster individuality and to maintain individual and **academic freedom**—the freedom of students and teachers to pursue, discuss, and teach knowledge without hindrance or censorship. In other countries, education concentrates more on instilling discipline; individuality is frowned on (see box on "Real Education in Pakistan"). For example, in Japan and in other Eastern countries students face strict disciplinary codes, and according to international tests, they learn more.

The **dual thrust of U.S. education**—both the development of individuality and the socialization of students—leads to a tension in our attitude toward education. The tension shows itself in many ways. For example, some educational philosophies emphasize teamwork and cooperative learning, whereas others emphasize competition and individualism. The tension between these two approaches inevitably leads to debates: How much freedom should students be given? Should government determine what is taught, or should teachers and parents decide at the local level? Should private schools be subsidized with government money? And if they are, should they be subject to government control? Private schools have pushed for government financial support without control; public education advocates have resisted such moves.

"It's one thing for the National Commission to comment on the quality of teaching in our schools. It's another thing entirely for you to stand up and call Mr. Costello a yo-yo."

Education and U.S. Democracy

The dual thrust in education exists because the education system not only educates people but also prepares them to fit into society. It makes the many disparate parts of our population fit together. For that reason, education serves as a fundamental building block of U.S. democracy. It does so in the following four ways:

1. *By teaching the masses of our citizens to be literate,* public education makes it possible for them to communicate with one another more effectively beyond the local community and to learn something of politics and public policy by reading newspapers, magazines, and books. This enables people to vote more intelligently and to choose leaders more wisely.

2. *The public schools teach children to get along with different kinds of people.* In many areas, the students who attend these schools come from widely varied social, economic, national, and racial backgrounds. Also, extensive efforts have been made to integrate children who have special learning,

The Thinker, by Auguste Rodin.

physical, or emotional problems into the mainstream classrooms. Though going to school together will not necessarily make all children love one another, it does tend to create better understanding and to give all groups a keener sense of their common U.S. heritage.

3. *Our system of public support for education reduces inequalities of opportunity at all educational levels.* The masses of our people, even at the lower income levels, are now receiving an education up through high school. Large numbers are going on to college or technical and professional schools, in part because they can attend publicly supported schools with low tuition and in part because there are many government loan and grant opportunities.

4. *Finally, and by no means least important, our public school system has enabled us as a nation to make much more effective use of our human resources.* In the public schools, we discover many students who have unusual ability, including those who come from unfavorable social backgrounds. The talents of most such students would never be brought to light if it were not for free public schools. Once discovered, they often can be encouraged and helped to develop their capacities to the maximum. Thus, not only do they themselves lead fuller lives, but as scholars, scientists, or leaders in other fields, they also make a contribution to the welfare of the nation. Our public school system is by no means a perfect instrument, either for achieving complete equality of educational opportunity or for enabling us to make maximum use of our human resources, but it has helped us to take great strides toward both of these objectives.

The Development of U.S. Education

American interest in education goes back to earliest colonial times. Within about fifty years after the first settlement at Plymouth, Massachusetts, in 1620, all the New England colonies except Rhode Island had passed legislation making it mandatory for parents and the masters of apprentices to ensure that their charges learned both a trade and the elements of reading, writing, and religion. Before long, laws were passed making it compulsory for towns to establish elementary schools. These early schools received some public support, but they also charged tuition.

In spite of early beginnings in New England, the idea that all citizens of a democracy should be taught at least reading, writing, and arithmetic was slow to take hold. The founders of our republic were not thoroughly democratic in all senses of the word. Although the Declaration of Independence pronounced that all men are created equal, most of our early leaders had limited faith in the ability of the common citizen either to vote wisely or to profit from education. Everywhere, the right to vote was restricted to the few by property and other qualifications, and except perhaps in New England, only a small minority of the people even learned to read and write.[1]

This situation did not change radically until well into the nineteenth century, when a new spirit of democracy began to be felt. It permeated the entire country but was especially strong in the recently settled regions west of the Alleghenies and along the rapidly advancing western frontier.

This new surge of democratic sentiment brought about the election of Andrew Jackson to the presidency in 1828. Jackson was a product of the frontier, and he represented the new democracy of the expanding West. In the period from Jackson's election to the Civil War,

---

[1]Women were not allowed to vote in national elections until 1920.

"Real" Education in Pakistan

Education in Pakistan reflects the country's hierarchically structured society. In Pakistan, the concept of individual freedom is subordinated to the demands of self-discipline and obedience to elders. When your father (men are given more respect than women) says to do something, you do it, or you get beaten. (Physical punishment is quite acceptable in Pakistan.)

When you enter school, normally at the age of four, you have already been thoroughly indoctrinated by your parents to give the teacher that same respect and unquestioning obedience. The school day is rigidly organized; it has none of the free-form organizational structure that permeates U.S. schools. School begins with a general assembly in which all students line up in rectangular formations to recite the Qur'an and sing the national anthem. If you refuse to sing, you're beaten—but nobody refuses.

The dress code is strictly enforced, and improperly attired children are either punished by their teachers or sent back home with a note telling the parents to turn up the next day with their child. Students up to the thirteenth grade (the final year of high school) are required to stand up when a teacher enters the classroom, greet him—the teachers are mostly men, especially in the senior classes—and sit down only when allowed to do so by the teacher. Throughout the lecture, all students are expected to sit in an upright position and preserve utter silence. Troublemakers (i.e., noisy kids) are caned (i.e., beaten). Students are not to question what the teacher says; the teacher's word is supposed to be almost as sacrosanct as the Qur'an.

After the eighth grade, students normally split up into two streams, the science group and the arts group. The students have little choice in this matter; their grades and parental pressure are the two most important determining factors. Generally, the brighter students are channeled into science and the second-raters are channeled into the arts.

Most Americans wouldn't like this system; they would see it as demeaning to the students and inconsistent with U.S. cultural mores. But in Pakistan, it works. It instills in students a work ethic and discipline that serves them well at the university level, both at home and abroad, and most Pakistani university students are glad they went through it, rather than through what they would describe as the namby-pamby U.S. educational system.

public elementary education became firmly established. In the 1830s, Alexis de Tocqueville, a French author, visited the United States and expressed astonishment at the ever-growing belief in and commitment to public education. In Europe, education was still restricted to members of the wealthy class and the clergy.

By 1860, tax-supported elementary schools had opened in many states. During these years, some publicly supported high schools were also established, but for the most part secondary education continued to be provided by the private academies that had succeeded the early colonial Latin grammar schools. These academies increased rapidly in number, but not until some time after the Civil War did the idea of publicly supported high schools begin to gain wide acceptance.

The Country School, 1871, by Winslow Homer.

Since 1865, there has been a phenomenal expansion of education in this country. In 1870, five years after the end of the Civil War, the number of children attending elementary schools was less than 7 million, and enrollment in public high schools was only 80,000. Some children were also attending private grade schools and academies. In 2007, total enrollment in elementary schools, public and private, was 32.2 million, and enrollment in secondary schools was 17.1 million. In 1870, less than half the children five to seventeen years old were attending school, and the average number of days attended by each child was only 50. In the early 2000s, almost 100 percent of children from the ages of five to seventeen were in school at least some days every school year, and on the average, children attended school for about 165 days a year.

The most striking expansion of education in the twentieth century was in the colleges and universities. In 1920, fewer than 600,000 students were enrolled in all of our institutions of higher learning. Enrollment in colleges and universities was less than 25 percent of high school enrollment. By 2007, the number of students in colleges and universities had increased more than twenty times, to nearly 18 million.

The overall trends since 1970 are shown in Figure 10.1. Until 1970, school enrollment rose at all levels. Then, in the 1970s, school enrollment began to decline. This trend was in large part caused by the completion of schooling of the children of the World War II baby boom. Enrollment in elementary schools started to rise again in the late 1980s due to the secondary baby boom (baby boomers' children). As the children of this secondary boom grew older, the enrollment in later grades also rose. Through all these trends, college education enrollment has risen as higher percentages of students go on to college and as older individuals decide to attend college.

Democratic Structure of the U.S. School System

The school structure of the United States is quite different from what is traditional in most countries. Before World War I, nearly all European countries had a dual school system, and in spite of some changes since, European schools still retain much of this dual character. A **dual school system** separates, at an early age, the children who expect to go on to a college or a university from those who do not, and provides a different type of education for each group. In Mexico, all children are given an exam at about the age of twelve, after completing six years of primary education. Students who do well are sent to special "secondary" or university preparatory schools; others are sent to vocational, agricultural, or technical schools after completing

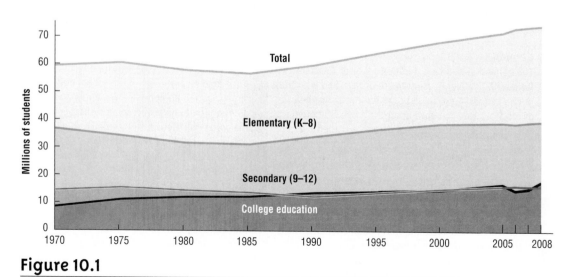

Figure 10.1

School enrollment by level of instruction, 1970 to 2008. (Source: National Center for Education Statistics, Digest of Education Statistics Tables and Figures, 2008.)

their elementary education. This holds true in most European countries, too, although the age and grade level at which children are segregated varies from country to country. In Germany, the age at which the examination is usually taken is ten; in Great Britain, it is twelve.

In the United States, we developed in the late nineteenth century a so-called unitary system. In a **unitary school system,** most children (unless they have dropped out along the way) attend the same type of school and follow a course of study that eventually leads to graduation from high school after twelve years. They are then ready, supposedly, to go on to a college or university. The door to further education is, so far as possible, kept open all along the line.

Of course, not all courses prepare students to enter a college or university. Even so, our school system is fairly successful in keeping open the doors to further educational advancement because the student who has not taken a college preparatory course can often qualify for some type of college training by merely making up a few required admission courses. Also, many colleges are flexible in their entrance requirements for students who give evidence, by test scores or otherwise, that they have the ability to do good work in college.

Education in Some Other Countries

In this chapter we focus on the U.S. educational system. Our system is not the only way to educate. Let's take a brief look at how educational systems work in some other countries.

Germany

Schools are divided into three categories: grammar, technical, and vocational. The system grooms the gifted students and tests the abilities of those who will become skilled workers. Equal emphasis and status are accorded the sciences and the arts. Adolescents are treated like adults, and students see how success in education is connected to earning a living. Some weaknesses are that the grading system is not as disciplined as it is in some countries and that vocational training is seen by some as being too traditional, without encouraging future entrepreneurs.

Denmark

The general structure is similar to that of Germany. In Denmark, however, if parents are dissatisfied with their public school, they can get together to set up their own school, and the government will pay 90 percent of the cost. At the university level, where students used to be able to take as long as they wanted to get a degree, there are now detailed schedules to discourage students from wasting time.

France

Scientific and technical schools enjoy a high status. Adolescents understand the tradition of spending most of their time working for a rigorous general examination. Vocational training has been weak, but recently the government has mandated employers to spend 1 percent of their sales receipts for training workers. Simultaneously, the government has encouraged vocational schools to expand, setting forth clear, ambitious goals.

Britain

Britain has a national curriculum, tested by national exams. Parents can send their children to the best available school, and the government finances schools on the basis of how many students they are able to attract. Exam results are published and schools are ranked comparatively, so parents can make informed decisions about which school to choose. Schools are encouraged to escape from supervisory bureaucracies and run themselves independently. As in some other European countries, vocational schools need improvement, but Britain is working on this task.

Japan

Japan has what some call "a cult of education." Students attend for long hours. Even after regular school hours, many attend evening, holiday, and weekend "cramming" schools to get extra education. Schools are run economically. Most of the school buildings are shabby and ill-equipped by Western standards. Students are required to help with some tasks, such as serving in the cafeteria. These tasks are believed to improve character, and they help keep school costs low. Competition is intense because students know their adult careers depend on how well they do in school. Also, the importance of education is demonstrated by the parental pressure exerted on children to excel. Parents endure financial and other sacrifices to pay for extra schooling. In recent years, the Japanese Ministry of Education has tried to discourage overly long hours, as they have been embarrassed by the statistics on teenage suicide and nervous breakdowns attributed to overwork at school.

Formalization of the School System

An institution as important as education quickly acquires a formal structure, and by 1880 the structure of schools in the United States had evolved into the 8-4-4 system—a graded eight-year elementary school, a four-year high school, and a four-year college. As inevitably as a formal structure developed, so did the criticism and evolution of that structure. Increasing criticism of the 8-4-4 system after World War I led initially to the establishment of junior high schools in many communities. These schools took over the seventh and eighth years of schooling from the grade schools and the first year from the senior high schools. The junior high school made it possible to begin secondary education earlier and facilitated the introduction of new types of courses. In the 1970s, the evolution continued, and elementary school was reduced to five years, junior high was changed to three years of middle school, and high school was extended to four years, making the 5-3-4-4 system common for most communities in the early 2000s.

Education prior to the grade school years also changed. For example, in most U.S. communities a year of kindergarten was added at the bottom of the scale, preceding the first grade. Later still, private nursery schools became common for very young children, and in more recent years, programs have been introduced for young children from disadvantaged backgrounds. For example, **Head Start** is a federal program that seeks to enhance the social and intellectual development of students as young as three years old.

*H*ow Much Does It Cost?

Some countries spend more on education than do other countries. The graph below shows the percentage of total spending that selected governments devote to education.

The amount of money spent doesn't necessarily measure the effectiveness of an education system.

What does seem to matter is the students' understanding that success in education leads to economic success, parents' determination that the students do well, and government support for choice and innovation combined with insistence on consistent standards.

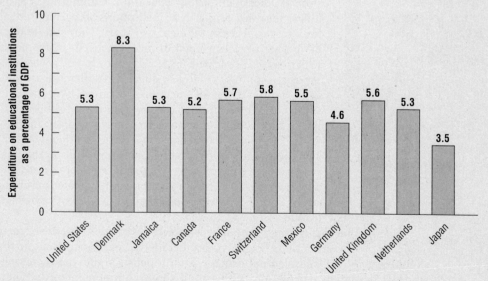

Source: CIA World Factbook

Reprinted by permission of OECD

The Decline of Standards

A big city school system requires a student in the seventh grade to be able to read as well as a fifth grader, who, by the way, must be able to read as well as a fourth grader, who, in turn, must be able to read as well as a third grader. What's wrong with demanding that a seventh grader be required to read like a *seventh* grader? How would you like to be operated on by a brain surgeon who graduated from a school that allowed its students to be a year and a half behind in their skills?

United Technologies advertisement.

Evolution has also occurred at the college level. A good example is the community college movement, which developed slowly at first. In the early 1920s, only a few such schools existed throughout the country. The first public community colleges were usually established by school districts as a kind of extension of high school. Often, they were begun in high school buildings and their classes were taught by high school teachers, preferably those with some graduate school training. Just as some educators had argued earlier that the first two years of college should be moved down to the secondary level, some now regarded the community college as an extension of secondary education. In fact, however, most of the early community colleges followed rather closely the curricula of the first two years of the four-year colleges and universities, and they were chiefly concerned with preparing their students to enter such institutions in their junior year. By the end of the 1930s, the number of community colleges had substantially increased, and because most of them were established in areas where college education had not earlier been available, they gave many young people a better opportunity for getting at least some college training.

After World War II, in response to the increased demand for higher education, the number of two-year colleges, both private and public, rose rapidly. In the early 2000s there were about 1,650 in the United States, with a total enrollment of nearly 6 million students, among whom were 38 percent of all undergraduates. Community college enrollments account for 45 percent of all black students and 52 percent of all Hispanic students.

Gradually, as community colleges multiplied and more and more students crowded into them, their function changed to parallel more closely the initial concept of such colleges as an extension of high school. Now **community colleges** are colleges designed to meet the diverse needs of students who could benefit from some extension of their high school education. Community colleges are no longer regarded primarily as institutions preparing students to enter four-year colleges in the final two years. They still do this, but their design has been expanded to meet the needs of the community in which they are located. Especially for students who want to save money, community colleges, dollar for dollar, are a wonderful bargain. Various types of vocational training have been introduced, some of them technical. Courses are offered to train auto mechanics, beauty shop operators, salespeople, medical and dental assistants, laboratory technicians, and various other types of workers. The community college has become an institution that seeks to provide training that not only will produce better citizens but that also will meet the needs of our economy for a greater number of trained workers and the needs of young people for jobs that will yield both satisfaction and a reasonable level of income.

Exactly what that training should be is subject to debate. Some advocate traditional academic studies and others favor a vocational focus. Vocationalists argue that courses should provide skills needed in business. Traditionalists argue that there is a danger of students becoming narrow job specialists without common interests. They feel that job-specific skills can be learned on the job and that colleges should be designed to teach people to think and understand the world around them. The debate is likely to continue.

Examining the School System

The preceding history of the school system should give you a good sense of the U.S. educational system and how it developed. It is a compulsory system through age eighteen, usually the last year of high school, and it is a broad-based college system. It is also an expensive system costing hundreds of billions of dollars. Given education's significant role in modern society, it should not be surprising that there is a constant examination of the school system: how it delivers its services, how it is paid for, what it teaches, and what its results are. These continuing efforts to understand and improve the system will inevitably introduce changes.

Technological Change and Teaching

As with other institutions, technology changes both the method of teaching and what needs to be taught. With the development of computers, for example, the process of writing is changing. Computer programs are now available that correct grammatical, spelling, and stylistic mistakes. It is predicted that some time in this century these programs will expertly translate onto paper the words and ideas that a person speaks into them, making obsolete much of what is now taught in grammar and composition classes. Such changes would parallel those already accomplished in math by calculators, which have made nearly obsolete the necessity to do arithmetic mentally or on paper. Books will move online, and where full on-line bibliographies have become available through computers, many library skills are no longer necessary; we simply need to know how to use the relevant search program.

What the long-range future holds is limited only by our imagination. Perhaps with the advance in the analysis of the brain, by 2040 teachers and schools may be obsolete, and students may simply hook up their brains to various data banks that directly translate knowledge from computer memory to student memory. Luckily for teachers, that time is not yet here.

Private Schools and Home Schooling

Private schools have always been a part of the U.S. educational system, and their total enrollment includes about 10 percent of all schoolchildren. Schools defined as private or independent include religious schools, private nonsectarian schools, and home schools. In the early 2000s, there were about 30,000 independent schools. Of the country's 53 million school-age children, over 6 million attended independent schools and about 1.5 million were home-schooled, together representing about 14 percent of total school enrollment. Figure 10.2 gives you a sense of how public school enrollment has compared to private school enrollment.

A large number of these private schools have religious affiliations. Instruction in some of the religious schools is based on systematized programs, such as the one published by Accelerated Christian Education, Inc., of Lewisville, Texas. The pool of students in religious schools is estimated to be more than 1 million, and about half of these use the Accelerated Christian Education method of silent, individual study using workbooks and cassette recorders. There are several thousand different workbooks compiled to be "distinctively Christian," and each student goes through as many as sixty-five different workbooks in a school year.

These systems are inexpensive and easy to set up. They use church space and incur no additional expenses for heat, utilities, and most equipment. Students from these schools who have taken the California Achievement Test have, on average, scored above the national norms in every subject.

Despite the significant amount of such activity and the fact that the choice of independent schools is growing rapidly, the total number of students in and from these schools is still statistically small. There is speculation that such schooling may lead to

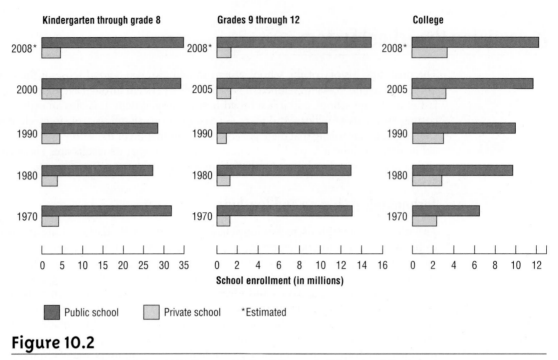

Figure 10.2

School enrollment from 1970 to 2008. (Source: National Center for Educational Statistics.)

isolation, narrow interests, poor socialization, and alienation from the mainstream. These conclusions have not been subjected to testing. The results from the California Achievement Test provide at least some evidence that alternate systems of schooling are providing acceptable academic results. As educators gain more experience from work with these types of schools, we are likely to see many studies, reports, and recommendations on the subject.

An alternative to private schools is home schooling, in which parents teach their own children at home. As concern about public schools has increased, so too has home schooling, but it remains uncommon.

Charter Schools, Privatization, and the Problem of School Finance

Good schooling costs money, but it is not surprising that the taxpayers who pay for it often try to pay less. Historically, education in the United States has been paid for largely by local property taxes—taxes on land, houses, and businesses in the school district. Because many property owners do not have children in school, some of them object to increases in school taxes. This leads to periodic community dissension and failure of the voters to pass school budgets. A second effect that local financing of schools has is significant differences in tax burdens among school districts. School districts with large amounts of valuable taxable property find that they can support schools with a much lower tax rate per property owner than can districts with little valuable taxable property. The result is significant differences in availability of funds for schools.

The inequity in this funding method has come under attack in the courts, and a number of states face legal mandates to change school finance methods by instituting some

First-graders pass through the hallway in a charter school.

method of equalizing tax burdens and available resources. In Michigan, for example, the school property tax was eliminated a few years ago and replaced with a sales tax. Recently, Vermont and New Hampshire were both forced to deal with state court decisions mandating major changes in the way property could be assessed for school purposes.

Attempts to change these financing methods have led to more dissension and to calls for privatizing education so that it is no longer supplied by government, but is instead supplied by private, for-profit businesses. Under the typical privatization plan, students are given a voucher worth, say, $5,000, which they can use to attend whichever school they want. Advocates push for such privatization programs using the phrase "school choice," because students would have a choice of schools. Opponents of such schemes argue that the private schools would "skim the cream," taking the easy-to-educate students and leaving the difficult and expensive-to-educate students in public school. They also argue that it would significantly change the socialization function of the public schools and, hence, change the nature of U.S. society. Although a number of privatization initiatives have been put forward, in the early 2000s none had passed.

One initiative that has passed in about thirty states is **charter schools**—decentralized schools based on a charter between an individual or group (usually teachers, parents, and others in a community) and its sponsor (usually the local or state school board). Charter schools are designed as an alternative to private and public schools. Although largely controlled by parents and teachers, their financing usually is provided by the state in which they're located. About 10 percent of charter schools are run by businesses, most of whose hopes to make a profit are fixed on the vague future. Their structure minimizes bureaucracy and promotes innovative approaches to learning by empowering teachers and parents to create the curriculum. Accountability is achieved by performance tests that determine whether the charter is renewed. Over the next few years, these schools will be watched closely so that the quality and breadth of the programs that emerge can be measured.

Textbooks

After systematic testing had been developed as a research tool beginning in the 1920s, educational testers reached the conclusion that the elementary curriculum was too hard, and they targeted the textbook. Since then, textbooks for elementary schools have tended to become less and less rigorous. Long words and complex grammatical constructions are frowned on, as are connective words. According to Harriet Bernstein, textbook expert of the Council of Chief State School Officers, the word *because* does not appear in most U.S. schoolbooks before the eighth grade. Some believe these simple books continue to be used because overworked, undertrained teachers need something easy to teach from.

The situation is complicated by the claims of various ethnic, religious, political, and other pressure groups. For instance, nutritionists who believe that refined sugar is a health hazard have succeeded in some states in having removed from children's textbooks most references to cake and candy. The results can sometimes be unintended; in one case, these omissions resulted in stories about a child having a birthday—with no birthday cake.

Textbooks developed for high schools and colleges have some of the same characteristics. Open several and stand back so that you cannot read the print: You will find that they all tend to look alike. Popular strategies include frequent subheads, charts and pictures, boxed material appearing in the middle of a page to relieve the blocks of print, and glosses in the margins that enable the student to get the gist of the chapter without reading the main text. Publishers demand these devices because that is what sells, and textbook writers comply.

In our view (yes, it is true that textbook authors have views), textbooks coddle students too much. We make learning too easy, so students don't have to think. Nevertheless, we coddle (a word that probably shouldn't be used because it is too unusual), although less than other textbook writers do, because teachers and publishers say that a truly thought-provoking (and therefore painful) textbook wouldn't get published and wouldn't get read.

School Dropouts

When education becomes too painful, students drop out. According to data compiled by the U.S. Bureau of the Census, as many as 50 percent of high school students in some major cities drop out before graduating. The dropout rate has fallen somewhat over the past decades, from about 14 percent nationwide in the 1970s to less than 10 percent in the 2000s. It remains higher for Hispanics at about 22 percent and blacks at about 11 percent. This lower number for blacks may look good, but this is partly because so many black male teenagers have ended up in jail and are not counted as being eligible for school or as dropping out. Boys drop out at a higher rate than girls (10 percent to 8 percent). The total number of students not graduating from high school is somewhat lower because many students who drop out go on to earn a GED (General Educational Development) degree, which is considered a high school equivalency degree. In the early 2000s, about 63 percent of dropouts obtained a GED within eight years of dropping out.

A number of programs have been established to deal with dropouts. In New York City, for example, workers for Operation Far Cry contact dropouts from high school by phone and attempt to persuade them to return to school. Other areas have tried flexible school scheduling, work-study plans, and identification and counseling programs. In a cash-for-class project, one California school paid students to attend school.

The high dropout rate is a problem not only for the individual student but also for the entire community. Education has a direct relationship to crime, and in the long run the higher the average level of education, the lower the crime rate. Dropping out of high school also affects one's ability to get a job; the unemployment rate among dropouts is roughly twice as high as the unemployment rate for high school graduates.

Multiculturalism, Collaborative Learning, and Institutional Fairness

People learn in different ways, and various groups respond differently to alternative learning environments. Much of our current learning environment is what Peggy McIntosh, an education specialist at the Center for Research on Women at Wellesley College, calls "winner-killer competitive," which she argues is not conducive to some minority cultures' and women's backgrounds. The current system, she argues, is biased toward white males and does not provide a **collaborative learning environment,** in which students learn to work together, helping each other excel rather than competing with others to beat them down.

McIntosh's theories are highly controversial, but aspects of them are making their way into mainstream educational practices in what is called the **multiculturalism movement,** the movement to make social institutions unbiased with respect to all ethnic and cultural groups.

One example of this multicultural movement is Uri Treisman's work with black college math majors. Treisman is a mathematics professor at the University of Texas at Austin who has studied in depth the reasons why black students made up a disproportionately small number of college math majors, whereas Asian students made up a disproportionately large number.

Together with a number of social scientists, he conducted research to find out why. He found that the cause had nothing to do with ability. The groups he was looking at (students at the University of California at Berkeley) had equal ability in math in their high schools and on standardized tests. The difference was more in the institutional structure of the program. He found that Asian students tended to work on problems together in informal social groups, so studying math became part of their social interaction. On the other hand, he found that black students' social activities did not include any such interaction, as they were drawn to black cultural centers that did not include other math majors. Thus, they did not experience the type of collaborative learning that the Asian students did. He set about to change that and successfully instituted collaborative learning exercises that, together with other institutional reforms, significantly increased the percentage of black math majors at the University of Texas.

There are many more such examples at all levels of the educational system, and over the next ten years we can expect to hear much more about how institutional structure affects learning behavior.

The ways in which discrimination occurs can be subtle, although sometimes when pointed out they are not so subtle after all. For example, Gary Mitchell, a New Jersey attorney, sent his child to a progressive school and was struck by the awards given out in the child's kindergarten class. The awards given to students of one gender were for best thinker, most eager learner, most imaginative, most enthusiastic, most scientific, best friend, best personality, hardest worker, and best sense of humor. The other gender's awards were for all-around sweetheart, sweetest personality, cutest personality, best sharer, best artist, biggest heart, best manners, best helper, and most creative. I leave it to you to figure out which gender got which list of awards.

How Good Are U.S. Schools?

Probably the most important questions we can ask about our educational system are: Does it deliver? and, Are students receiving a good education? The answers are not a unanimous yes. Many argue that there has been a marked decline in the effectiveness of education over

---

*A*re Boys Discriminated against in School?

Discrimination takes many forms, and as one type of discrimination is corrected, others are created. Take the discrimination against girls in education alluded to in the text. In the 1970s and 1980s, this topic was much discussed, and a large majority of the population felt that the educational structure discriminated against girls. That view led to the passage of the Gender Equity in Education Act in 1994, which specifically banned discrimination against girls in school. Fifteen years later, it is not girls whom social scientists feel are being discriminated against; it is boys. The signs of discrimination are many. Girls, on average, get higher grades than boys; girls are more likely to be in advanced placement and honors courses; and girls attend college in higher percentages than boys.

The suggested reasons are varied. Some include:

- Teachers tend to choose "feeling" books that appeal to girls rather than "action" books that appeal to boys, so boys don't learn to read.
- Math is being taught with words, with which girls excel, rather than with numerical algorithms, with which boys excel.
- Competition, which boys thrive on, is portrayed as bad, and "cooperative learning," a learning style that girls do better with, is portrayed as good.

Also varied are the suggested solutions. Some want to make boys more like girls, so that they relate to feelings rather than to action. Others want to make school more conducive to masculine ways of learning. Still others say we should simply get rid of the Gender Equity Act, which was too much, too late; it went into effect when women had already achieved equity.

Whatever the answer, we can expect to hear more about the issue in the future.

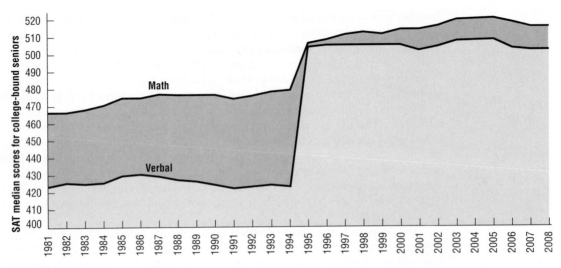

Figure 10.3

SAT scores for college-bound seniors, 1981–2005. In 1995 the scores were normed at a higher level. There was no large, sudden increase in unnormed scores. (1981–1994 scores are median scores; 1995–2008 scores are mean scores. There are only small differences between the mean and the median scores; the jump is caused by the renorming.) (Source: Based on information from the College Entrance Examination Board.)

the last few decades; students graduate without knowing the fundamentals of reading, writing, spelling, and arithmetic, especially in depressed inner-city areas. Starting in 1995, SAT scores rose substantially, as you can see in Figure 10.3. This was not because students were doing better, however, but because the test scores were **normed,** that is, adjusted to fit a predetermined scale. Whereas previously 450 had been the median score, after norming, 500 was the median score. Thus someone who in 1997 received a verbal score of 505 would have received only a 428 in 1995. In other words, the scores were simply raised, on average for both math and science, by 45 points. Why do this? Cynics suggest it is the only way to raise scores. The SAT administrators say it is to give students a better sense of where they stand in relation to other students. We leave you to decide which answer is the most persuasive. (To be fair to the SAT, in reporting the scores, they also raised recent previous scores.)

Starting in 2004, the SAT tests changed significantly:

- Instead of two sections, there are three, with a two-part writing test being introduced. This means that the highest score will be 2400, rather than 1600.
- The verbal reasoning section was renamed "critical reading," and analogies will be dropped.
- The math section added higher-level math problems.

The hope in making these changes was that the test would better reflect what colleges are looking for and give those students who take harder courses an edge.

Educators justify the shortcomings in our schools in a variety of ways. They argue that many modern-day students do not want to learn and have little ability to master traditional academic subjects. Teachers are then under pressure to lower standards. It seems unreasonable to give failing grades to, say, 50 percent of a class, no matter how poor it is; naturally, many principals and parents would blame the teacher. In addition, teenagers with little schooling now have trouble getting jobs. If they leave school, they may just wander the streets and get into trouble. So in many schools most marginal students are promoted regardless of their lack of achievement.

The tendency to pass students from grade to grade on the basis of little or no achievement is strengthened in some schools by the policy of social promotion. This means promoting students along with their classmates regardless of whether they reach a minimum standard of achievement in their studies. The theory is that it is better for social reasons to keep them with their own age group, whether they learn anything or not, and at all costs to avoid stigmatizing them as failures. However, promotion on this basis does not help matters much. Students who have not learned elementary mathematics in the lower grades become completely frustrated or indifferent if they must attend math classes in the upper grades. Thus, so-called education consists only of going through the motions of attending classes. Not only do these students become a problem to the teachers and hinder the other students from learning, but they also often feel their own inadequacy more keenly than if they had been held back. Whether under these conditions students gain anything by remaining with their own age group or by staying in school at all is open to question. If this problem is to be solved, we probably must address it early in a child's life.

The Search for Excellence

In response to many criticisms of the U.S. educational system, measures to stem what critics call a tide of mediocrity have been instituted. The reforms have been mostly on the state and local level and have increased salary scales, lengthened the school day, improved teacher certification standards, given teachers more responsibility, and put in place frequent standardized testing in a variety of grades and subjects so that students' performance will be monitored in a measurable way.

On July 1, 1994, a federal law about national education standards was passed. This law, called the Goals 2000: Educate America Act, recommends academic standards for grades 4, 8, and 11 and encourages states to design new ways to measure student performance. The goals included the following six:

1. All students will arrive at school ready to learn.
2. The nation's high school graduation rate will be at least 90 percent.

Can You Read This?

About 9 percent of adult Americans whose native language is English can't read English. That's what the U.S. Bureau of the Census says. If we're talking about people whose native language is not English, then the Census Bureau says 48 percent can't read English. Put these two groups together and they add up to about 27 million people.

Here are a few of the test questions that many people couldn't answer:

1. Pick another word for *sickness:*
   The patient has the right to ask for information about his sickness.
   benefits/payments/expenses/illness
2. Pick the best fill-in for the blank:
   Don't allow your medical information card to
   —————— by any other person.
   be used/have destroy/go lose/get expired

3. Choose the answer that means the same as the phrase with a line under it:
   We cannot see you today. <u>When can you return?</u>

   When was the last time you came?
   Who should you call when you come?
   On what date can you come again?
   Are those the papers you can return?

Of course, no test is perfect. For instance, all the preceding questions seem to imply that the person taking the test is sick. Some authorities have challenged the Census Bureau study by criticizing the test. But as one of the critics said, "What does it matter if there are 10 million or 20 million? We're not even taking care of a small fraction of them. There are too many."

3. Students will be competent in English, history, geography, foreign languages, and the arts.
4. U.S. students will lead the world in math and science.
5. All adults will be literate.
6. Every school will be free of violence and drugs.

The year 2000 came and went and the goals were not met, although spending on schools increased and there were pockets of improvement. In 2001, Congress passed the No Child Left Behind Act, a sweeping reform that redefined the federal government's role in K–12 education. It was based on four principles: stronger accountability, increased local control, expanded parental options, and emphasis on proven teaching methods. The most expensive and controversial aspect of this program was its emphasis on standardized testing. One side saw high-stakes tests as defining accountability, the other as stifling broader learning and forcing teachers to teach to a test, not to teach for understanding. The debate about this program is ongoing, with no definitive results about its effectiveness.

Changes in the College Curriculum

Until the middle of the nineteenth century, higher education consisted chiefly of learning the ancient languages, mathematics, philosophy, and theology. Some attention was also given to modern foreign languages and the social sciences, but these held a place of less importance. After the Civil War, however, the curriculum began to show the effects of new developments in science, technology, and other fields of knowledge. As enrollments increased and the interests of students became more and more diverse, scientific, technical, and vocational training were increasingly introduced at the college level. Subjects and courses of study multiplied until it became impossible for any student to take more than a very small portion of the total offerings.

The Development of the Elective System.   To meet this problem, the elective system was adopted. This permitted students, with some restrictions, to determine their own courses of study. But the results were not always satisfactory, for often students chose a hodgepodge of unrelated subjects, and at the same time they frequently missed entirely any acquaintance with some of the basic fields of human knowledge.

The shortcomings of the elective system led to two developments. First, colleges began to require students to major in one field of knowledge by taking a substantial proportion of their work in this field. At the same time, they began to require students to spread some of their courses in such a way that they became acquainted with at least several of the basic fields of knowledge. The expression *liberal education* came to be associated especially with the attempt to give students breadth of understanding.

This attempt led to the rapid spread in the 1930s of survey courses covering broad fields of knowledge such as physical science, biological science, social science, and the humanities. Sometimes all students were required in their freshman and sophomore years to take a core curriculum consisting of several of these survey courses. After World War II, courses of this type continued to spread; this book originally was written for such a survey or basic course in the social sciences.

To this period belong terms such as **general education,** college programs intended to broaden students' intellectual horizons. Sometimes the term is used merely as a substitute for the older term *liberal education.* Both expressions refer to a type of training designed to go much beyond narrowly practical or vocational objectives. But although liberal education emphasizes the desirability of learning something about a variety of subjects, general education puts more stress on the importance of not missing completely any of the major fields of human knowledge.

Following the Fads.   In the late 1960s and throughout the 1970s, colleges and universities restructured their curricula to be relevant. Students in the 1960s were interested in the social issues of their times. As the 1970s progressed, students became less interested in social issues and more interested in money and how to get it. As a result, institutions of higher learning experienced a demand for courses related to business and the professions such as law, medicine, engineering, and banking. Since 1985, the majority of college students have been majoring in business or business-related subjects.

From 1950 to the early 2000s, college enrollments quintupled, which contributed to the relaxing of standards, the dropping of course requirements, and the introduction of courses such as family food management and automobile ownership. In the early 2000s, slightly less than half of the students who entered college as first-year students failed to get degrees.

Almost as soon as colleges began to allow flexible requirements and courses of study, and instituted courses and even whole departments in response to trendy demands, they started thinking about making the curriculum more rigorous. By the late 1970s, some colleges and universities were experiencing the equivalent of the back-to-basics movement in elementary and secondary school practice. This took the form of eliminating superficial survey courses, returning to requirements of Greek and Latin, asking students to take more math, and trying to ensure that students had at least some knowledge of fields that are considered part of a broad liberal education but that many students would not study unless they were required to.

These tendencies were at once summed up and endorsed in 1984 when the National Endowment for the Humanities (NEH) made its report *Excellence in Education.* This report argued that colleges had not made good on "promises to make you better off culturally and morally," and that "colleges have been ripping off students." It attributed this to poor management and ill-conceived curricula, and suggested that the money invested in a college education would serve a more useful purpose if the parents would instead give that sum to a child to buy a small business.

That report reinforced the existing tendency to make curricula more rigorous. Some colleges have thrown out their entire catalogs and redesigned their curricula from scratch; others have reshaped curricula to deal with both content and structure.

For instance, responding to the report's complaint that colleges fail to give students "an adequate education in the culture and civilization of which they are members," some schools have set up curricula in terms of fields of knowledge, which they variously designate as "perspectives," "ways of looking at the world," or "modes of inquiry"; the specifications for perspectives might include "science, society, and human values." Because employers want employees who can write and think, colleges are placing more emphasis on composition and math. It has now become acceptable to assert that faculty, not students, know more when it comes to deciding on course content.

$\mathcal{S}$ocial Science: No Fad

Social science has been around a long time; it is no fad course. It is one of the courses that provides students with an education in their culture and civilization. Various incarnations of this particular book have been a staple of social science courses since the 1930s when nine Chicago professors put their notes together and created a selection of readings for their students. It has since been revised many times to keep it current. It has been "Hunt and Colander" since the early 1980s.

As the social sciences have split into their various components, it's been harder and harder to find professors with training and inclination to teach the course, but because it provides a necessary and broad overview of social science thinking, it is precisely the type of course that reformers are advocating.

Is the U.S. Educational System Equal?

Although the U.S. educational system provides greater opportunities for the masses than any other country, it still perpetuates inequalities that are difficult to justify. The most striking of these is found in comparing the situation of blacks with whites, as we already discussed in earlier chapters.

Figure 10.4, which shows the percentage of black adults compared to the total number of adults who have completed four years of high school, demonstrates some of the strides we have made since 1950, but also shows our need to make further gains.

As discussed, a second inequality in education is based on wealth and income. Because most localities finance their education with property taxes, variations of taxable wealth in different regions and localities cause significant variations in educational opportunities. In many poor areas, residents find it impossible to provide adequate school facilities for their children. In the 1970s, a Supreme Court case determined that the use of the local property tax to support education perpetuated inequality, and states were directed to explore alternative ways of financing. Thus, over the past decades, we have seen some states shift from local property taxation as their only school financing tax to statewide property taxation or state income or sales taxes as additional sources of funding for schools. We can expect further change over the coming decade.

Even if all localities received equal support for education, inequality would still exist. There is a close correlation between the amount of schooling received by children and the income status of their families. The higher the family income, the greater the likelihood that a child will finish high school or go to college.

How Much Education Should the Average Citizen Receive?

How far should the formal education of the average citizen be carried? Grade school? High school? Junior college? This basic question must be answered as our school system changes and develops, but there is no simple response. For every person, there is certainly a limit to

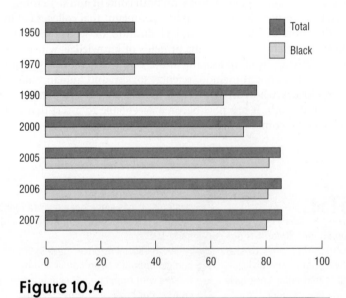

Figure 10.4

Percentage of adults who have completed four years of high school or more, 1950 to 2007. (Source: U.S. Bureau of the Census, *Statistical Abstract of the United States.*)

the time that can be spent in acquiring a formal education. Where this limit is depends on the temperament, abilities, interests, and purposes of the individual, on the kinds of education available to the person, and on the costs that must be met by the student, the parents, and the community.

Today, few people would question that a grade school education is worth the cost for almost everyone. Also, there is general agreement in this country that a high school education is desirable and worth the cost for the majority of young people, though perhaps for many of them we are not providing the most helpful kind of curriculum. The situation with respect to higher education is somewhat different, and we may well question whether it is desirable for the great majority of young people to complete four years of college. Many people believe we should set admission standards that would limit enrollments in four-year colleges and universities. But there seems to be increasing support for the point of view that eventually most young people should have at least the equivalent of a two-year community/junior college degree. As you can see in Figure 10.5, the percentage of our population receiving a high school and college education has increased substantially since 1960.

With junior colleges and community colleges becoming more adaptive to current needs, high school graduates today can more easily find the kind of further education that suits their abilities and needs. For those who have no liking for it, the indefinite extension of formal academic education holds no magic. But it is increasingly difficult for adolescents without training to find jobs. This largely explains the increasing emphasis on providing more vocational schools and more vocational courses in community colleges. However, this may also reflect both the recent conservative trend that has swept the country and a return to concern with developing skills that make the U.S. competitive in the world economy.

But what of individuals who are not interested in further schooling and who in some cases may have little ability to benefit from a high level of vocational training? There is still a great deal of relatively unskilled work that needs to be done and for which people would pay if willing workers could be found at reasonable wages. One difficulty is that we have been downgrading the dignity of commonplace work, of jobs that are useful but provide only small or moderate pay and offer no glamorous future. In doing this, we have robbed many young people with limited ability of the chance to learn how to work and, by gaining confidence and experience, to find a useful and independent place in life.

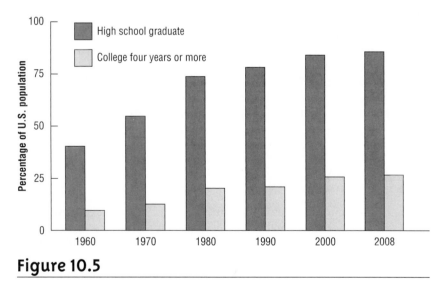

Figure 10.5

Educational attainment (persons age twenty-five years and over).
(Source: U.S. Bureau of the Census.)

Interaction of Economics, Politics, and Social Institutions

Most subjects in social science can be isolated for purposes of study, but in reality they are not isolated. So it is with the educational system. Our educational system includes cultural values and thereby plays an important role in shaping other social, economic, and political institutions, but simultaneously it is shaped by them. The state of education in the 2000s is a case in point. All agree that school systems could and should do a better job. The question is, how? Some argue that the answer is to spend more—for instance, to improve teachers' pay and to provide schools with the latest technological equipment. Others argue that the ideal answer is to become more efficient—for teachers to work harder, for students to study harder, and for administrators to decide that schools do not need so much administration and to eliminate their own jobs. But don't hold your breath waiting. Individuals in educational institutions are likely to opt for the easy path. Students aren't going to be motivated to study harder unless provided with incentives to do so. It's the same with teachers. And there is almost no way administrators are going to eliminate their own jobs.

The response of many parents to the problems in public education is to move their children to private schools, thus circumventing the culturally integrating role of the public school system. Different groups become more inwardly self-sufficient, and political divergences widen. Those differences, in turn, lead to even less money being spent on public schools.

To offset the reduced flow of federal money into the system, some people have advanced ideas such as tuition tax credits to parents of children attending private schools or federal income tax credits for certain education situations. But to the degree that tax credits for private schools work, they further reduce the nation's pool of common experiences; and there is disagreement as to whether targeted income tax credits would reach their targets or would turn out to be economically insignificant.

Another area in which the interaction of economics, politics, and social institutions can be illustrated is that of setting teacher standards. The concepts of setting standards, certifying competence, and mandating the teaching of certain basic subjects are admirable, but all are liable to abuse. Teachers are divided in their view on certification. Teachers who have been teaching for years feel it is unfair for their competency suddenly to be questioned and tested. New teachers feel that their own recent educations qualify them in the latest methods and believe that if the older teachers had nothing to fear, they would not protest competency tests. Both groups can unite in their scorn of agencies that set educational standards when the staffs of the agencies have no professional educational training. Yet taxpayers do not want to leave certification in the hands of the very people who are to be certified.

The point of these discussions is twofold: (1) There are no easy answers to difficult questions, and (2) what we do in one area of society is likely to have significant effects in other areas. Only by considering all those effects and recognizing the pitfalls in implementing the easy solutions can we hope to develop wise social policy.

Key Points

- The U.S. educational system has a dual thrust: It attempts to develop students' individuality and to socialize students.
- U.S. educational institutions are a product of their history.
- The main problem facing our educational system is how to provide excellent, equal education efficiently, inexpensively, and in a manner that appropriately socializes the students.
- The college curriculum has evolved from a rigid system that taught specific subjects to an elective system with significant freedom and varied courses.
- An important reason why our educational system is not equal is the methods used to fund it.

Some Important Terms

academic freedom (188)
charter school (197)
collaborative learning
   environment (198)
community college (194)

credentializing (187)
dual school system (191)
dual thrust of U.S. education
   (188)
education (187)

general education (202)
Head Start (193)
multiculturalism movement (198)
normed (200)
unitary school system (192)

Questions for Review and Discussion

1. Explain the difference between education and socialization.
2. How does free public education contribute to the development of U.S. democracy?
3. Discuss the development of U.S. education since colonial times.
4. What factors have contributed to increasing enrollments at the primary and secondary levels?
5. How does the structure of the educational system in the United States differ from that of Europe?
6. Discuss the history of community colleges.
7. Discuss the changes that have taken place in school curricula over the past hundred years.
8. What differences in educational opportunities exist?
9. How can multiculturalism and collaborative learning improve the effectiveness of schools?
10. Discuss some types of schools that are alternatives to public schools.
11. What conclusions can be drawn concerning the progress made in U.S. education over the past hundred years? What still remains to be done?
12. Give an example of a political issue influencing an educational issue.

Internet Questions

1. According to www.ericdigests.org/1995-1/multicultural.htm, what are the three basic types of multicultural education programs and what is the focus of each?
2. Go to www.amshq.org. What is the Montessori approach to education?
3. The National Center for Policy Analysis, www.ncpa.org/pub/ba602 finds Hispanic dropout rates extraordinarily high; what is blamed?
4. Go to www.notonthetest.com and watch the video or just listen to the song. What current education policy is being criticized? Name three criticisms of this policy.
5. Go to www.edreform.com. According to the Center for Educational Reform, what are charter schools?

For Further Study

Bloom, Allan D., *The Closing of the American Mind: How Higher Education Has Failed Democracy and Impoverished Souls of Today's Students,* New York: Simon & Schuster, 1987.

Dwyer, James G., *Vouchers within Reason: A Child-Centered Approach to Education Reform,* Ithaca, NY: Cornell University Press, 2002.

Johnson, Cynthia, *Caffeine Will Not Help You Pass that Test,* New York: Simon & Schuster, 2005.

Keogh, Barbara K., *Temperament in the Classroom: Understanding Individual Differences,* Baltimore: Brookes, 2003.

No Child Left Behind, Public Law 107-110, Washington, DC: U.S. Department of Education, 2001.

School for Tomorrow: Think Scenarios, Re-Think Education, Centre for Educational and Resort and Innovation, Paris: Organization for Economic Cooperation and Development, 2006.

Stern, Sol, *Breaking Free: Public School Lessons and the Imperative of School Choice*, New York: Encounter Books, 2005.

Wagner, Tony, *Making the Grade: Reinventing America's Schools,* New York: Routledge/Falmer, 2002.

Wolff, Edward N., *Does Education Really Help? Skill, Work, and Inequality*, New York: Oxford University Press, 2006.

WWW   American Association of Community Colleges www.aacc.nche.edu

WWW   Educational Resources Information Center www.eric.ed.gov

WWW   Home Education Research Institute www.nheri.org

WWW   Institute for Higher Education Policy www.ihep.org

WWW   National Center for Education Statistics www.nces.ed.gov

WWW   United States Department of Education www.ed.gov

WWW   United States Distance Learning Association www.usdla.org

Social and Economic Stratification

After reading this chapter, you should be able to:

- List three types of social stratification
- Discuss the role of social mobility in making some social stratification acceptable to society
- List three sources of income inequality
- State what the poverty threshold is in the United States
- Discuss six issues that any practical program for meeting the problems of economic inequality must take into account
- Explain what is meant by the U.S. class system and how it relates to class consciousness

> *. . . all the animals are equal here, but some are more equal than others.*
>
> **—George Orwell**

The people of every society can be divided into groups—sometimes along clear-cut lines, sometimes only roughly. **Stratification** is the grouping of people according to differences in income, occupation, power, privilege, manner of living, region where they live, age, gender, or race; you can probably think of other categories. Stratification, in the sense of differentiation, is not necessarily bad. People differ and that difference adds diversity to life. But when there is a **hierarchy**—when one group considers itself better, or maintains privileged access to society's resources—questions of social equity are raised. Many systems of social and economic stratification do create a hierarchy of superior, intermediate, and inferior groups; that hierarchical stratification is our primary concern in this chapter.

Social stratification appears to be unavoidable. Some activities and some kinds of work are more important to a society than others. Some can be carried on only by people of outstanding ability with special training or experience. Political offices must be filled, economic activities must be organized, medical services must be provided, and military forces must be commanded. Those who play important roles in such activities acquire power and prestige. Usually they also acquire larger than average incomes and various special privileges. In addition, because these individuals tend to associate principally with one another, they develop common attitudes and modes of living. Sometimes they entrench themselves in their positions by means of legal and religious sanctions, but even without these safeguards, they can often pass their superior status along to their children.

When firmly established, social stratification contributes to social stability. It means general acceptance of the fact that certain groups perform certain functions, as do their children after them. Competitiveness is reduced because people know their place in society and the paths they are expected to follow. When social stratification is less rigid and there are more opportunities for an individual to change status, dissatisfaction and conflict may be more evident, even though the situation is objectively fairer in the sense that there is more social mobility. Thus a lessening of stratification often is accompanied by social unrest because that reduction focuses attention on the unfairness of the system.

Types of Social Stratification

There are three principal types of social stratification: estates, castes, and social classes. We are chiefly interested in the last type because social classes represent the major form of stratification found in modern industrial societies. However, some knowledge of estate and caste systems will contribute to our understanding of the nature of social classes.

Estates

When used in a discussion of stratification, the term **estate** refers not to land but to groups such as the nobility, the clergy, merchants, artisans, and peasants. The estate stratification system developed in Europe under feudalism. The estate to which a person belonged and its place in the social hierarchy were determined chiefly by custom, occupation, rights and obligations with respect to land, and other legal sanctions.

In an estate system, the position of an individual in society is nearly always inherited from parents; the lines between groups are clearly drawn, and almost everyone knows just where he or she belongs. They may even be required to dress in a particular way to indicate their station in relation to others. The opportunity for mobility is small, but it is entirely possible within the framework of law and custom. In feudal times, a noble could free a serf from bondage to the land in return for a special service, or a king could bestow a title of nobility (the Queen of England still bestows titles today). Military service and the priesthood are also possible avenues of upward mobility in an estate system.

The medieval estate system, with its relatively rigid social categories, was better suited to a static than to a dynamic society. It gradually disintegrated under the impact of changes such as the decline of feudalism, the Industrial Revolution, and the rise of democratic ideology, with its strong emphasis on freedom and equality.

Castes

Caste is a rigid class distinction based on birth, wealth, or some other distinguishing characteristic. Within a discussion of stratification, the caste system is usually associated with India, where until recently it had prevailed for about 3,000 years. In the 1980s, the legal underpinnings of the caste system were removed in India, but the cultural legacy remains and caste still plays an important role in Indian life. Under the caste system, an individual acquires a social position at birth. The great vitality of the caste system seems to arise from the fact that, besides being firmly established by custom, it is an integral part of the Hindu religion. It is based on the doctrines of karma and transmigration. **Karma** is the belief that every person should fulfill in this life the duties associated with membership in a caste. The doctrine of **transmigration** holds that if a person fulfills duties sufficiently well in this life, that person will in a future life be reborn or reincarnated into a higher caste. A caste system is even more rigid than an estate system because in theory there is no way of moving to a higher status except through death and reincarnation. In practice, a very limited amount of upward shifting occurs. Recently, the Indian government attempted to increase the upward shifting by creating a quota system, which holds places open in universities for members of the lower castes. This move has been controversial as the higher-level castes argue that such a quota system is unfair to them.

Poor, low-caste Indian farmers.

Social stratification systems having some of the characteristics of the one in India have been found in other societies. In the United States, blacks, especially in the South, have been called a caste by some writers. To support this designation, they point out that blacks belong by birth to a socially underprivileged group and that, at least in the past, it was very difficult for them to enter groups predominantly occupied by whites. Until 2000, it was technically illegal in some states for blacks and whites to intermarry. Alabama, in 2000, was the last state to repeal its law. (The law had not been enforced since the 1960s.)

Despite these similarities, most observers believe the position of U.S. blacks differed considerably from that of the members of a low Hindu caste. In the first place, even before recent reforms, blacks were subject to no rigid occupational limitations, and some achieved high positions in government, business, and the professions. Even more important, their inferior social position was not based on religious sanctions; rather, it was and is contrary to most Americans' religious teachings and democratic ideals of freedom and equal opportunity for all human beings.

A closer analogy to the caste system than the U.S. situation is the **apartheid system**—a separation of the races—in South Africa, where until recently blacks could not hold the same jobs or live in the same places as whites, and their interrelations with whites were severely limited. Apartheid was condemned by most other countries; in the early 1960s, it was overthrown altogether in the southern African country of Zimbabwe, and in the 1990s it was abolished in South Africa.

Social Classes

Although most modern industrial societies do not have formal stratification systems, they do have a type of social stratification called a social class system. Unlike estates and castes, these social classes are not supported by any legal or religious sanctions, and they are not clear-cut, definitely delimited, groups into which every person in the community can be placed. The fact that social classes are not perfectly clear-cut entities is proven by the inability of social scientists to come to any general agreement on just how many of them should be recognized as existing. In a democratic industrial society, social status is a continuum, with individuals and families scattered along it from top to bottom. If we divide people on this social scale into two, three, or more social classes, we must do so arbitrarily.

Social scientists also have difficulty deciding just what criteria should be used in determining social status. Some would place an individual (or family) in a given class entirely on the basis of economic considerations. Those who take this point of view usually put their chief emphasis on income. Others, probably the majority, would determine the status of an individual by general social standing—that is, by whether the community, on the basis of various criteria, places the individual high or low on the social scale. Income would be only one factor. Some of the common stratification

A symbol of apartheid in South Africa.

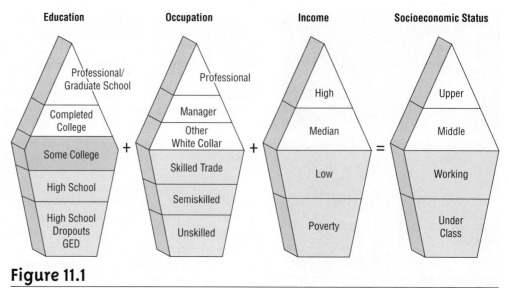

Figure 11.1

Socioeconomic hierarchies.

hierarchies are shown in Figure 11.1. The combination of hierarchies—education, occupation, and income—forms an individual's socioeconomic status.[1]

Notice that the hierarchies shown in Figure 11.1 are drawn as pentagons with a sharp point at the top and a somewhat wider base. This shape represents a change from the way earlier editions of the book have presented this material. Back in the 1930s when this book was first published, the shape was a pyramid—narrow at the top and wide at the bottom. This reflected the way social scientists had talked about income inequality for hundreds of years because the social stratification of European societies of the seventeenth and eighteenth centuries, with most people at the bottom and very few at the top, could be reasonably well represented by a pyramid.

In the 1950s and 1960s, that began to change; the lower classes decreased in relative size as more people moved into the middle class. The pyramid no longer was appropriate to represent the situation. To capture that change, we shifted to a diamond shape, suggesting that the majority of people fell in the middle class, with smaller upper and lower classes. We made the change to the diamond shape in the expectation that the lower class would continue to shrink as the members moved up the social ladder. Those expectations were wrong; the lower classes have stopped shrinking as upward social mobility has slowed and as immigration has increased. Hence, the need to expand the bottom of the hierarchies led to the pentagon shape.

Social Class Defined. A **social class** consists of those people in a community who are somewhat similar in their economic status, their attitudes and beliefs, their educational attainments, their ways of living, the regard in which others hold them, and their power or lack of power to influence community affairs. According to this definition, social class is, to some degree, a subculture. People whose social statuses are similar are not only likely to live in the same neighborhoods, associate largely with one another, and marry one another, but they are also likely to show similarities of speech, manners, and moral standards as compared with people who are higher or lower on the social scale.

---

[1]There are many ways to classify the population. One imaginative survey undertook to see if "You are what you eat" is a defensible statement. The survey, covering some 13,000 households, identified five strata: (1) meat and potatoes households (30 percent); (2) child-oriented households: hot dogs, peanut butter, and soft drinks (25 percent); (3) seriously concerned over diet (15 percent); (4) natural-food enthusiasts (15 percent); and (5) sophisticates: quiche, raspberry tofu, and instant gourmet dinner (15 percent).

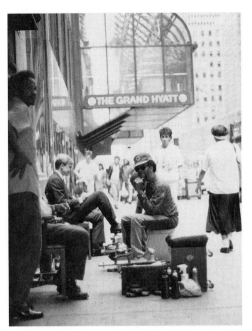

Class structure in the United States. Shoe shines are almost invariably given by minorities. Some argue that this is because society fails to offer better opportunities.

Because social classes, like other types of stratification, represent superiority/inferiority relationships, some writers have compared the class structure of society to a layer cake. At the top of the cake is a thin layer consisting of a small group of people who have the highest economic and social status. At the bottom of the cake is another thin layer representing those whose economic and social status is very low and whom the community regards as of little account. Between these two extremes, at various levels, lie thicker layers, which represent the great majority of the population. The chief objection to this analogy is that the divisions between social classes are not as definite as those between the layers of a cake.

Social classes are not organized groups like families or communities. Rather, they are useful concepts. They are also social realities, but only in the sense that the people of any complex society can be divided roughly into a few large groups in such a way that those in each group have about the same general social standing and other similarities. Because the lines of division among classes are both vague and arbitrary, many individuals are difficult to place. The more class layers, the greater the difficulty of distinguishing between them and determining just where individuals fit.

In order to classify individuals into socioeconomic classes, it is generally necessary to average a variety of characteristics. This is normally done by a weighting system; points are allocated for various characteristics, these points are added up, and individuals within certain ranges of points are assigned to certain categories. For example, people with advanced education may get many points, but high income also confers many points, so somebody with high income and low education and somebody with low income and advanced education may fall into the same socioeconomic group after the weighting process. Using the weighting system allows us to organize people into upper class, upper middle class, middle class, lower middle class, and lower class. Some of the characteristics looked at are occupation, sources of income, type of housing, and the area within which the subject lives. Figure 11.2 presents typical class divisions and characteristics.

Most people do have some idea of the social class to which they belong, though they may not give it the same name that a sociologist would. For example, a family may think of themselves as ordinary people; a sociologist might classify them as belonging to the lower middle class. Members of a social class recognize that they have more in common with others at a similar social level than they do with those above or below them. Also, as we have noted, they are likely to live in those areas and do those kinds of work that bring them into especially close association with people like themselves.

The Family Basis of Social Class. The primary unit of stratification is the family, for except in rare cases all members of a family are regarded as belonging to the same stratum, or layer. The same social status is shared by all members of the immediate family group. As a rule, the most important factors in determining social class are the occupation and the wealth and income of the breadwinners in the family.

Such occupations as law and medicine, high government positions, and the management of large business enterprises yield considerable prestige because they require more than average ability and training; other occupations, such as keeping small stores or working at skilled trades, are regarded as respectable; but some occupations, especially those that require unskilled manual labor, are looked down on by many members of the community. In general, the regard in which an occupation is held is closely correlated with the income it yields, although there are exceptions to this rule. A federal judge, for example, may have more prestige but less income than the owner of a catering service.

Class levels	Approximate percentage of population	Likely occupation	Likely education	Approximate annual income (some overlap between classes)	Residential neighborhood	Newspaper reading
I. Upper class	5	Independently wealthy Lawyers Professionals Doctors Accountants	Seventeen or more years of school, elite college, and beyond	Over 400,000 Some extremely high Much inherited wealth	Very elite neighbor- hood Expensive houses Gated communities	*Wall Street Journal New York Times*
II. Upper middle class	20	Small businesspeople Teachers Lawyers Professors Managers of small firms	Around sixteen years High-ranked college	Between 125,000 and 500,000 Most earned income by salary	Good neigh- borhoods Moderately expensive homes	*Wall Street Journal New York Times*
III. Middle class	35	Administrative Clerical Chain store managers Technicians Salespeople	High school and lower- ranked college	Between 30,000 and 125,000 Salary Some wages	Private homes, medium sized Some tract homes	Local paper
IV. Lower middle class	25	Skilled labor Industrial workers	Ten to twelve years GED	20,000 to 40,000 Hourly wages	Apartments Small tract homes Trailers	*National Enquirer*
V. Lower class	15	Unskilled labor Unemployed	Eight to twelve years	Under 20,000 Poverty and welfare	Blighted areas Poor apartments	None

Figure 11.2

Social classes: Sociologists do not completely agree about how many classes there are in the United States because classes overlap considerably and there are not sharp breaks between them. It is generally possible, however, to identify five or six basic social classes. (Source: Authors' modification of U.S. Bureau of the Census, "Money Income and Poverty Status of Families and Persons in the United States.")

Membership in social classes tends to be transmitted in the same family line from generation to generation because children are likely to acquire much the same attitudes and modes of living as their parents, to receive similar educational advantages, to enter similar occupations, and to inherit whatever wealth their parents may possess.

Social Mobility

Any class system is somewhat inconsistent with the democratic ideal of equal opportunities for life, liberty, and the pursuit of happiness. Certainly, lower-class children do not have the same opportunities as those in the upper classes. In the United States, we try to avoid thinking in terms of "low class" and "high class," but there is no escaping the fact that some people are economically and socially better off than some other people. What made this situation acceptable to most Americans was that the United States had an **open class system**—a system in which class lines are not definite, and for many people the possibilities of moving up are excellent. The important element was not the size of the various groups or the disparity, but the ability of individuals to move among the groups. The degree of **social mobility**—the comparative ease with which a person in a society can improve (or worsen) his or her social and economic status—was considered quite large in the United States, so people at the bottom could imagine their kids moving to the top. Until recently, most observers viewed the United States as having significant social mobility. This view of a socially mobile U.S. society was captured by a nineteenth-century U.S. novelist who gave his name, Horatio Alger, to stories of ordinary Americans who have improved their social and economic status through commitment, dedication, hard work, education, thrift, moral rectitude, and, very often, help from family, friends, teachers, employers, and scholarships and government programs.[2] Downward mobility is also a possibility, and although there is not much proof, many believe that the spoiled children of the idle rich will eventually land in the gutter.

Fifty years ago, social scientists found that Alger was generally correct. In a 1960s study, Gerhard Lenski found that 33 percent of all males in the period from 1945 to 1965 were upwardly mobile. Downward mobility at that time was clearly present but its incidence was not well documented. However, in the 1970s, the U.S. expectation of upward mobility began to erode. A study by Featherman and Hauser in 1978 found that one-fourth of all persons age twenty-one to fifty-three had slid to an occupational level below their first jobs. A study by Greg J. Duncan and colleagues compared mobility between the 1968–1979 and 1980–1987 periods and found that the incidence of upward mobility for those in the lower class declined while upward mobility for those at the upper income levels rose, leading to a shrinking middle class.

In the early 2000s, social scientist Brent Bratsberg and his colleagues found further erosion, and discovered that Europe had more social mobility than did the United States. Specifically, they ranked countries on a scale of 0 to 1, with 0 meaning perfect mobility (a child's income bears no relation to parental income) and 1 meaning no mobility (a child's income is identical to parental income). They found that for sons Sweden scored a .2; Britain scored a .36 and the United States scored a .54, suggesting that the United States had only about half as much social mobility as did Sweden and Britain. The situation was worse at the bottom; children born to families in the bottom fifth of the U.S. income distribution were the least likely to move up. Further, this situation was exacerbated by the large increase in income and wealth inequality in the United States, where the rich have been getting much richer and the poor have been essentially treading water. Their incomes have hardly increased, or have even fallen. These changes in social mobility have the potential to undermine the political and social stability of the United States because much of that stability is based on a belief that although there are large inequalities in the United States, such inequalities are acceptable since they reflect effort on the part of the rich. With hard work, people with low incomes can move up. In 2010, these findings had not become a political issue in the United States, but many social scientists expect that they will become one in the next decade.

Who Are the Upwardly Mobile?

While overall upward mobility has decreased, it is still possible to move up if a person has certain traits. Studies of people who have achieved upward mobility have identified certain related traits: race, gender, being an only (or first) child, and a belief in deferred gratification, which is when a person is willing to trade off an immediate pleasure for a future goal. The first and second of these are so important that we treat them in a separate chapter under the subject of

---

[2]Horatio Alger was born in 1834. He wrote hundreds of stories with titles such as *Ragged Dick* or *Luck and Pluck* in which his young heroes went "from rags to riches." Alger worked hard, saved up a fortune, and gave his money away. He died poor in 1899.

Up, Down, and Out

If you pay $25,000, can you get your name in the *Social Register?* If you drop your subscription, can you get your name out of the *Social Register?* Should you let people know you are in the *Social Register?* Do you use the *Social Register* for a phone book? Do you know anyone who knows what the *Social Register* is?

To some people, these are important questions. The book comes out annually and tries to limit the number of names to around 33,000. Some people get into it without trying; some people have always been there and can't get out; some people are in it by virtue of their office (U.S. presidents, for instance). Marrying up won't get you in and might get your spouse deleted. If you get in and want to be sure to stay in, don't get divorced, start an acting career, or go to jail.

discrimination. The third is probably related to income (it has been found that rich people are more likely to have only one child) and is not within an individual's control. The last trait, however, can be and is probably the most important. How much a belief in deferred gratification can be fostered is debatable. Your beliefs are, in large part, transmitted from your parents through continually supportive feedback, and by the time you reach college age, these beliefs are probably set.

Thus, for most of you, whether you are to be upwardly mobile may have already been determined and is partially built into your personality. Of course, luck (such as being in the right place at the right time for a job) plays an important role, and many people who have the traits associated with being upwardly mobile may find themselves disappointed. For example, if you had a crisis the night before you took the college boards, you may have done poorly on them, which may have played a role in whether you won a scholarship. Bad luck is not pleasant, but it is a fact of life and should not be considered unusual. No one ever said life is fair.

Discussions of mobility often overlook one simple fact: Room at the top is always limited. When we talk about social mobility, we are apt to think of opportunities to move upward on the social scale, but we must remember that as some people, or their children, move up, others, or their children, are likely to move down. Assuming no increase in the proportionate size of the upper class, a high degree of mobility means only that it is fairly easy for some citizens who have ambition, energy, and intelligence to move up the social ladder and displace those who are less ambitious or less capable.

What are the conditions that contribute to social mobility? Probably most important of all is social change. In a changing society, the old order is always being disturbed, and new ways of achieving wealth or position keep appearing. For the past 200 years, industrialization, with its ever newer methods of production and types of business organization, has provided opportunities to climb the economic and social ladder.

What's changing now for people is globalization. From a global perspective, U.S. workers, even poor ones, are on the high end of the income distribution ladder. People want to immigrate to the United States even if it means accepting a "low-wage" job because that low-wage U.S. job is a "high-wage" job for them. With U.S. companies increasingly willing to (or forced to because of global competition) shift production to low-wage countries throughout the world, and with low-wage countries increasingly developing their own companies that compete with U.S. companies, the avenues for U.S. citizens at the bottom of the income/social scale to move up are decreasing. Thus we can expect that social mobility will be of increasing concern over the coming years.

Education and Social Mobility

One of the best ways to advance from one class to another is through education (see Table 11.1). Education allows individuals access to job possibilities that otherwise would not be open to them, and in doing so it raises their income.

One method that *doesn't* lead to class advancement is to increase income without attention to other issues. Social scientist Susan Mayer developed a statistical model that predicted what would happen to a child's prospects for success in life if the annual income of the child's family were doubled. She found that if the increased income were the only factor in the life of a child in that family, the child's chances of becoming a successful adult would

Table 11.1

**Starting Salary Offers to New College Graduates in 2009,
by Selected Fields of Study**

BUSINESS	
Accounting	$48,377
Finance	$49,754
Marketing	$43,628
HUMANITIES, SOCIAL SCIENCES	
English	$32,733
History	$37,606
Psychology	$34,942
ENGINEERING	
Chemical	$65,403
Computer	$61,017
Electrical	$57,600
HI-TECH	
Computer science	$57,693
Information systems	$49,334

Source: NACE Salary Survey.

hardly improve at all. Intelligence, determination, good health, and a willingness to cooperate were far better predictors of advancement.

Class Consciousness in the United States

Most Americans are not highly **class conscious**, that is, overly concerned about their status in society and the standing of other people in relation to them. Ambition usually takes the form of a desire for a more satisfying job, more income, or more personal prestige. Any resulting change in social status usually is secondary or wholly incidental. Relatively few Americans have a strong desire to move into a higher social class except insofar as this may help them to achieve other objectives.

Why are Americans so comparatively free of class consciousness? Partly, the reasons are historical. We never did have a hereditary nobility, and throughout our early history rapid growth and expansion resulted in considerable social mobility. It is more than a coincidence that, although a number of our presidents have come from wealthy or aristocratic families, some have had very humble origins.

Throughout the 1980s, other factors tended to keep class consciousness at a low level. One was the general rise in standards of living. Even though people were not changing their position in the social scale, they felt they were making progress when their incomes rose and when they could improve their way of life.

Another factor that has tended to reduce class consciousness and discontent is **horizontal mobility**, the opportunities that exist for moving from one job to another, and often to a better-liked job. Horizontal mobility is important because while U.S. citizens are not especially class conscious, they are group conscious and their desire to be in the "in group" is strong. This desire begins early in life as cliques form in schools, and students are classified as nerds, druggies, preppies, and jocks, for instance. Advertising takes advantage of our group consciousness, portraying goods as providing group cachet to the buyer. Celebrity endorsements are common in advertising, under the assumption that if some movie or sports star uses the product, if you also use it you will fit in with the group to which they belong. Take a look at the shoes or clothes you are wearing. Did you buy them because they were the least expensive but still comfortable clothes you could find? Or did you buy them because they made you feel "in"? This horizontal mobility gives people the feeling of making progress, even though the change has little effect on income or social status.

With globalization, the factors mitigating against class consciousness have been somewhat reduced. Wages for lower-income individuals are not rising, and horizontal mobility is getting harder. To date, these changes have not led to an increase in class consciousness, but they may well do so in the future.

Class Consciousness, Marx, and Weber

In his criticism of capitalist society, Karl Marx, the nineteenth-century father of communism and one of the founders of the field of sociology, divided the populations of industrial societies into two classes—**capitalists**, or owners of the means of production, and the **proletariat**, or workers, who were exploited by the capitalists. The proletariat's labor was used to further the capitalists' own profits, without consideration of the workers' needs. Marx felt that the increasing exploitation of workers would lead to an increasing class consciousness among the proletariat.

Marx believed that under capitalistic exploitation the condition of the workers would become worse and worse. Eventually they would rise up in revolt, seize the means of production, and establish a socialist state under the "dictatorship of the proletariat." Actually, the standard of living of the working people in most industrial countries, quite contrary to Marx's prediction, tended to rise.

Marx's division of the classes is not the only division. Max Weber, an outspoken critic of Marx's views, argued that property is not the sole basis of class. Instead class is determined by the three *p*'s—property, prestige, and power. Weber's more general concept of class is accepted by numerous sociologists, but their views of how to quantify prestige and power often differ substantially. We shall use Weber's concept.

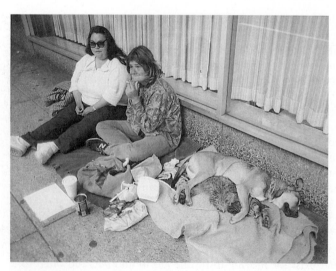

Homeless women on the streets.

*E*conomic and Social Inequality

We focus on an individual's money income because that is what we collect figures on. True inequality depends on much more. For example, say you have a choice of poor health and an income of $100,000 per year or good health and $25,000 per year. Which would you choose? Probably the latter, for people's true income includes all aspects of their position. Because we cannot measure true income, most studies focus on monetary income and individuals' standard of living.

Even if we focus on money income, we still have difficulty in determining how

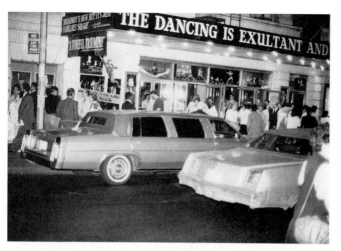

Riches in the United States.

much of a problem income inequality is. For example, how much poverty do we have in the United States today? That depends on how the word is defined. In terms of what poverty means in India or China, or even in terms of what it meant in this country or Europe a hundred years ago, we have very little poverty. Almost no one here literally dies of starvation, but tens of thousands do in Africa.

It is true that homeless persons sleep on the streets or in all kinds of makeshift shelters such as large packing cartons in the cities of the United States, but this is most often because of other kinds of social problems (a spirit of independence carried to psychotic extremes, for instance, or policies of releasing marginally competent people from mental facilities). It is not because there are no programs or funds available to shelter this population.

On the other hand, large numbers of people depend on public assistance to live, and many who do not receive such payments have incomes so small that they must live in depressing or unsafe surroundings, wear shabby clothes, and buy cheap food. They cannot afford to spend money for travel, entertainment, or education, and if they are out of work or if an emergency such as serious illness arises, their only recourse is public aid or charity.

In 1996, Congress passed a welfare reform law designed to drastically reduce the number of people on long-term public assistance and to help them improve their economic status through measures such as education, job training, child care facilities, and medical assistance. Two results of this law have been to put millions of low-income people in jobs and to reduce public assistance rolls significantly. However, some of the people who have found jobs still do not make enough money to support themselves and their families; many people are somewhat worse off than they were under the previous system; and there is still a large population of low-income people. Although its effects are continuing to be monitored, most observers see public assistance reform as a success in reducing the number of people on welfare and in channeling them into more productive activities, especially if it is fine-tuned to eliminate some of its harshest effects, and is accompanied by labor market reforms that increase the upward potential for those who work.

Causes of Income Inequality

Differences in income arise directly from three sources: variations in earnings from personal services, differences in the amounts of property owned, and variations in transfer payments from government. Differences in the earnings of individuals are the most important. These differences are based partly on occupation and partly on the personal qualities of those engaged in each occupation. The most basic of the factors that determine income variations between occupational groups is demand and supply.

Hotel maids often are poorly paid.

In general, occupations that are not easy to enter because they require special aptitudes and long training are highly paid because the supply of workers is small relative to the demand. On the other hand, occupations classified as common labor, which anyone can enter with relatively little ability or training, tend to be poorly paid. But within each occupational group, there are often great differences in individual earning power, especially at the higher professional and managerial levels.

For example, in 2007, average hourly earnings of construction workers were about $21.00, whereas the average hourly rate for retail trade workers was only about $13.00. Although in recent years the average annual pay in New York was about $55,000, in Mississippi, it was only about $31,000. The differences persist, in part, because of differences in the cost of living. Farmers' average annual income (about $30,000 in the late 2000s) is lower because it is cheaper to live in the country; the average pay in New York is higher, but so is the cost of a meal or an apartment.

Tables 11.2a–11.2d show the distribution of income by percentage of families; by regions of the country; by representative states; and by race, gender, and household status. As you can see, income is distributed unequally in the general population and also by place where one lives, by race, by gender, and by occupation.

Measuring Poverty

In order to measure poverty in a country, we must define the term. It isn't easy to do so. In the United States, the Social Security Administration and the Bureau of the Census attempt to do this by determining the **poverty threshold**, that is, the minimum amount of income

Table 11.2a
Money Income of Families by Percentage in the United States, 2006

Under $15,000	8.4%
$15,000–$24,999	9.1%
$25,000–$34,999	10.0%
$35,000–$49,999	14.6%
$50,000–$74,999	20.9%
$75,000–$99,999	14.3%
$100,000 and over	22.7%

Table 11.2b
Median Family Income by Region, 2007

Northeast	66,687
Midwest	62,874
South	56,538
West	63,423

Table 11.2c
Median Family Income in Four States, 2008

Hawaii	67,214
New York	56,033
Oklahoma	42,822
West Virginia	37,989

Table 11.2d
Household Median Family Money Income by Race, Gender, and Household Status, 2006

White	61,280
Black	38,269
Hispanic	40,000
Single Male householder	41,844
Single Female householder	28,829
Married couple	69,404

Source: U.S. Bureau of the Census. *American Community Survey.*

needed to maintain a living standard above the poverty level. Obviously, the poverty threshold will be lower for an individual than for a family, and it will differ for families of different size. It will also change with fluctuations in the cost of living.

To be above the poverty level, an individual or family must have enough income to obtain food, clothing, and shelter that will maintain health, plus some margin for other necessary expenditures. Just what minimum income is essential at any given time and place cannot be determined with any great precision, and hence any specific poverty threshold is to some degree arbitrary. However, after a careful and objective weighing of the facts, the determined cutoff can have enough meaning to be useful. Each year, the Bureau of the Census publishes poverty thresholds for single ("unrelated") individuals and for families of various sizes. The level at which the poverty level is set is important because that level determines which families receive government assistance.

According to census estimates, the total number of Americans who lived in poverty in 2008 was about 39.1 million, or 13.1 percent. For a family of four (excluding Alaska and Hawaii), this represented an annual income of $21,050 in 2009. For a single person, it is about $11,000. As you can see in Figure 11.3, the percentage of people in poverty depends on race and ethnicity. Blacks and Hispanics are much more likely than whites to be poor.

These measures of the number of Americans who live in poverty should be accepted with some reservations. Undoubtedly, many of those included had incomes that were only temporarily extremely low, or had savings with which to supplement current income, or owned homes and lived in communities where they could get along reasonably well on a small income, or were young people getting help from parents. However, after all such allowances are made, it is clear that a substantial amount of poverty exists in this country.

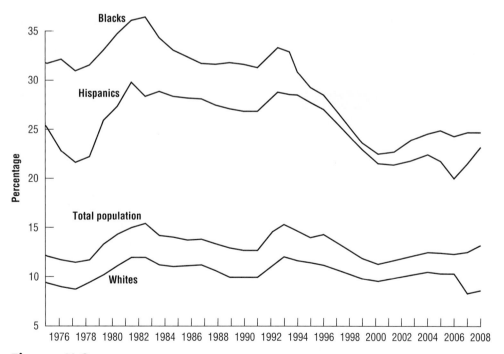

Figure 11.3

Percentage of poverty by race. (Data after 1992 are not strictly comparable to earlier data.)
(Source: Based on statistics from U.S. Bureau of the Census, *Current Population Reports, and Statistical Abstract of the United States, 2009*).

Increasing Social and Economic Inequality

It would seem that a country as rich as the United States should be able to eliminate poverty, if what we mean by that is simply providing everyone with enough income for physical comfort and security.[3] To do so, the United States has instituted a variety of programs including public assistance, unemployment insurance, Medicare, Social Security, and Supplemental Security Income (SSI). In many ways, these programs have succeeded, but they have also introduced new problems.

Being poor in the United States is quite different from being poor in a developing country; it is consistent with having air conditioners and cable TV. That said, it should also be noted that most people view their positions in society relatively, not absolutely. And relatively, over the past twenty-five years inequality has been increasing substantially. Median family income has risen by about 20 percent over those twenty-five years, but the median income of the top 1 percent has increased by 200 percent over that same period. Moreover, the median income of most families has risen over that period only because women have entered the workforce in increasing numbers. The wage (adjusted for inflation) that a worker makes has actually fallen.

Table 11.3 gives you an idea of how U.S. income distribution has changed over time. In it you can see that the number of households earning over $100,000 has increased in proportion, and the low-income groups have shrunk, but nowhere near as much as the high-income group's wealth has risen. In terms of wealth, the situation is even more unequal. The top 15 percent of the population controls 85 percent of the nation's wealth. The bottom 50 percent controls only 2.5 percent. In the early 2000s wealth became much more unequal, but the recession that began in 2007 reversed that as the rich found that they lost wealth, while the poor didn't have any to lose.

The reasons for these changes are both structural and policy related. Structurally, global competition has hit low-income, nonspecialized workers hardest. They were presented with a difficult choice: lower your wage or your job will be **outsourced**—transferred

Table 11.3

Distribution of Money Income of Households in Constant Dollars, 1971–2006

	UNDER $15,000	$15,000– $24,999	$25,000– $34,999	$35,000– $49,999	$50,000– $74,999	$75,000– $99,999	$100,000 AND OVER
1971	18.0	13.3	13.7	19.5	21.1	8.3	6.0
1976	16.8	14.0	13.3	17.7	21.7	9.6	6.9
1981	17.0	13.8	13.0	16.8	20.7	10.2	8.5
1986	16.1	12.6	11.8	16.2	20.2	11.4	11.8
1991	15.8	12.8	12.1	15.8	19.6	11.2	12.7
1996	14.8	12.9	11.9	14.8	19.0	11.8	14.7
2001	13.7	11.7	11.5	14.7	18.3	12.1	18.1
2006	13.4	11.8	11.5	14.6	18.2	11.3	19.1

Source: U.S. Census Bureau.

---

[3]If we define poverty in relative terms, as many sociologists do, then to some degree the problem will always be with us. No matter how much incomes rise, if we assume the continuance of substantial inequalities, people with relatively low incomes will continue to be deprived of various things that the rest can enjoy.

to a low-wage worker outside the United States, or transferred to a low-wage recent immigrant willing to do the same work for much lower pay. High-wage workers with specialized skills are also now beginning to feel the pressure of global competitiveness, as new technologies have allowed more and more of their jobs to be outsourced.

These structural forces pushing for inequality have been compounded by policy changes—the progressivity of the U.S. income tax has been significantly reduced, the inheritance tax has been reduced, and the capital gains tax—a tax on the increase in value of assets that falls mainly on the rich—has been reduced. Advocates for these policy changes claim that they kept the U.S. economy expanding, and that the focus of attention should not be on inequality, but on the overall health of the U.S. economy. Critics see the policy changes as giveaways to the rich—taking from the poor to give to the rich. With the election of Barack Obama as president in 2008, most observers believed that the progressivity of the U.S. tax structure was likely to increase in the coming years.

Policies to Reduce Inequality

The view that economic inequality should be reduced is widely shared. While there is nothing inherently correct about this view, it is prominently held, which raises the question of how to do it. High progressive taxes are one way, but they tend to hurt entrepreneurial incentives. Moreover, they are hard to enforce and they tend to create numerous evasion and avoidance schemes that misdirect resources and cause economic inefficiency. As government tries to prevent this evasion and avoidance, the taxes often become bureaucratic and legal nightmares. These serious problems with highly progressive taxes have led to the **supply-side argument** that in some cases lowering tax rates actually can raise tax revenues. That said, most economists believe it is technically possible to have an effective, more progressive tax system in the United States than we currently have, although the political process of implementing the system usually so distorts it from the ideal that the end result is often problematic. The bottom line: What can be achieved with a progressive tax system is limited.

Another way for government to redistribute income involves government programs to help the poor, but these too tend to have serious negative incentive effects—for example, they usually have a cutoff so if you work or earn above a certain amount, you are no longer eligible. That cutoff discourages work—to stay eligible for the program, people don't work. It was such negative incentive effects that led to the welfare reforms in the 1990s, which limited public assistance eligibility to a five-year window and placed a work requirement on those collecting public assistance benefits.

Both these government approaches attempt to redistribute income after it has been distributed by the market. But because the government sets the laws that govern the economy, it can equalize income in other ways. Specifically, it can directly affect the way in which income is distributed through legislation. For example, patents, copyrights, and intellectual property rights tend to create income inequality. Shortening the length for which these are given out would lead to less inequality, although it would also reduce the incentive to innovate. All economists agree that an appropriate trade-off must be found between equity and incentives to innovate, but many economists believe that the current trade-off leans far too heavily toward those with intellectual property rights protected by government patents and copyrights. In developing countries, economist Hernando de Soto found that the lack of capitalizable property rights (property rights that can be used as collateral for loans) was a major reason why the poor stayed poor, and that a key element to reducing inequality would be for government to reduce the number of permits and restrictions on the poor's activities. He also argued that governments should simultaneously formalize the titles to property of the poor.

Some Conclusions about the U.S. Class System

In spite of the statement in the Declaration of Independence that "all men are created equal," everyone knows that in many ways people are not equal. They are not born with equal potentialities for learning and achieving, nor are they born into equally favorable social environments. Nevertheless, equality before the law and equality of opportunity are strongly cherished democratic ideals. Over the years, we have been striving in the United States to come closer to these ideals, and since the Declaration of Independence was written, we have made considerable progress toward them. Recent structural changes in the U.S. economy have led some to be concerned about whether the country is providing equality of opportunity, and this issue may well become an important one in the next decade.

Key Points

- Three types of social stratification are estates, castes, and social classes.
- The existence of social mobility allows people to move from one class to another and makes the social and economic stratification more acceptable to society.
- Three sources of income inequality are variations in earnings from personal services, differences in the amounts of property owned, and variations in transfer payments from government.
- The poverty threshold in the United States is that level of income needed to maintain a living standard above the poverty level. In 2009, the poverty level was set at $20,050 for the average family of four.
- Any practical program for meeting the problems of economic inequality must take into account the poorest people, the need for health care, justice, children's rights, and the need for savings and incentives.
- The U.S. economic class system is not strongly developed, in part due to historical factors and in part due to the market economy, the government, and the underlying U.S. ideology that sees class consciousness as a negative trait.

Some Important Terms

apartheid system (211)
capitalists (218)
caste (210)
class conscious (217)
estate (210)
hierarchy (209)

horizontal mobility (217)
karma (210)
open class system (214)
outsourced (222)
poverty threshold (220)
proletariat (218)

social class (212)
social mobility (215)
supply-side argument (223)
stratification (209)
transmigration (210)

Questions for Review and Discussion

1. Name the three principal types of social stratification and briefly describe the nature of each.
2. How has the position of blacks in our society resembled, and how has it differed from, the position of a low Hindu caste?
3. Societies can be stratified in a variety of ways. What is the major form of stratification in modern industrial societies?
4. Why has the kind of class conflict Karl Marx predicted never developed anywhere?
5. Why are Americans not highly class conscious?
6. What difficulties are encountered when we attempt to divide the people of an industrial society into clear-cut social classes?
7. Why is social class a family matter rather than an individual matter?
8. What are some of the principal factors that may contribute to class mobility?
9. Why is upward social mobility necessarily limited in any society?
10. What factors have been operating in the United States in recent years to reduce class distinctions?

Can you name any factors that, in your opinion, have had the opposite effect?

11. Characterize the U.S. class system from the standpoint of (a) the sharpness of class distinctions, (b) the degree of class consciousness, and (c) the amount of social mobility.

12. Is U.S. society becoming more stratified? Defend your point of view.

*I*nternet Questions

1. Using www.hindunet.org/varna, list the four social orders in India's caste system. In ancient India, were people born into their caste?

2. Looking at the U.S. Department of Health and Human Services' poverty guidelines, http://aspe.hhs.gov/poverty/index.shtml, what is the most recent poverty threshold for a family of six? In Alaska?

3. Go to www.doi.gov/hrm/pmanager/st3f.html, the site of the Department of the Interior, Upward Mobility Program. What is the purpose of this program?

4. Go to www.salary.com and use the Salary Wizard. In your area, what is the income range for the middle 50 percent of teacher's aides? What is the range for associate professors of economics?

5. Using the information found at www.census.gov/did/www/saipe/, what is SAIPE? What statistics does the program produce for all individual counties of the United States?

*F*or Further Study

Adams, Nick, *Making Friends with Black People,* New York: Davina Press, 2006.

Ehrenreich, Barbara, *Nickel and Dimed: On (Not) Getting By in America,* New York: Holt, 2004.

Harford, Tim, *The Undercover Economist: Exposing Why the Rich Are Rich, the Poor Are Poor and Why You Can Never Buy a Decent Used Car,* New York: Little Brown, 2005.

McCarthy, Nolan, Keith T. Poole, and Howard Rosenthal, *Polarized America: The Dance of Ideology and Unequal Riches,* Cambridge, MA: MIT Press, 2006.

Shipler, David K., *The Working Poor: Invisible in America,* New York: Knopf, 2004.

Toffler, Alvin, and Heidi Toffler, *Revolutionary Wealth: How It Will Be Created and How It Will Change Our Lives,* New York: Knopf, 2006.

Underhill, Paco, *The Call of the Mall,* New York: Simon & Schuster, 2004.

Wilson, William Julius, *Being Black and Poor in the Inner City,* New York, NY: Norton, 2009.

WWW   Bureau of Labor Statistics www.bls.gov

WWW   National Association of Colleges and Employers www.naceweb.org

WWW   National Center for Children in Poverty www.nccp.org

WWW   Occupational Outlook Handbook www.bls.gov/oco

WWW   U.S. Bureau of the Census, Income www.census.gov/hhes/www/income.html

WWW   U.S. Bureau of the Census, Poverty www.census.gov/hhes/www/poverty.html

WWW   U.S. Department of Health and Human Services www.os.dhhs.gov

Stratification, Minorities, and Discrimination

After reading this chapter, you should be able to:

- List four reasons for ethnic and racial prejudice
- Distinguish between minority and dominant groups
- Discuss the race problem in the United States today
- Distinguish Chicanos from Latinos and explain the problem of illegal Mexican immigration
- Discuss briefly the problems of religious minorities
- Discuss briefly the problems of sexual minorities
- Give arguments for and against age discrimination

Wrong never lies in unequal rights, it lies in the pretension of equal rights.

—Friedrich Nietzsche

In Chapter 11, social stratification was considered primarily along economic and social lines. Societies are also stratified along racial, ethnic, and cultural lines. Questions of discrimination based on a person's race, religion, ethnicity, age, gender, or even sexual preferences, and issues of busing, job quotas, and right to jobs—these issues are not of the past, but rather appear daily in the media.

Many of you may feel that you are well aware of the problems, either because you have lived them or because they have been extensively discussed at home or in school. This chapter is necessary, nonetheless, both to provide you with a sense of the history and dimension of the issue and to give you a standard by which to judge your own views. The issues of equality and discrimination are as pertinent today as they were fifty or sixty years ago, when social scientists first considered these issues.

Race and Ethnicity

Although all human beings belong to the same species, *Homo sapiens*, they exhibit many physical and cultural variations, including differences in height, weight, skin color, and the shape of the head and face. Any group of people, if isolated from others over a long period of time, will develop differentiating physical characteristics. Thus it is possible to distinguish groups of people by these characteristics and to call those groups a race.

To classify the peoples of the world by race is problematic; there are few natural dividing lines and those dividing lines are arbitrary. In addition, a range of gradations within races can be found. One classification has divided most people into three groups based on physical variations—Caucasoids, Mongoloids, and Negroids. The problem with this classification is twofold. First, it reflects social constructions loosely based on biological differences. However, the biological differences between so-called races often are far fewer than the biological differences between individuals of the same "race." What do we mean by social construction? Consider hair color: There are redheads, brunettes, and blonds, yet because our social system doesn't distinguish among them, hair color does not delineate race. But skin color does, not because blacks and whites are inherently different, but because our social system differentiates them.

Second, over time migration has led to a mixing of the races, and ranges of gradation within races can be found. Thus race as a classification system is losing significance. The U.S. Bureau of the Census dealt with this classification problem when it prepared the 2000 census forms by listing a large number of ethnicities, such as black, white, Hispanic, of Hispanic origin, Pacific Islander, and many others, including "Other," leaving people to classify themselves in any way they pleased. Golf star Tiger Woods, who is of Thai and African American descent, tried to devise a unique term for his heritage, and this may mark a trend. The year 2000 is not the first time the Census Bureau has changed its race classification system, and you should not be surprised to see more changes in the terminology used to describe race. Some even argue that the government should be prevented from collecting information on race because having that information leads the government to be less race-neutral in its policies than many believe it should be. Why should the government care how many people consider themselves black or Hispanic? We are all Americans.

A concept closely related to race is ethnicity, which is a more defensible way of classifying groups of people. It is important to distinguish between race and ethnicity. The reason for doing so is the following: Whereas race is a biological classification system, ethnicity is a cultural classification. An **ethnic group** is a group of people who identify with each other on the basis of common ancestry and cultural heritage.

In popular usage, ethnic differences often are confused with racial differences. Ethnic differences between groups in matters such as nationality, language, and religion are important, but they do not constitute differences in race. It would be incorrect, for example, to speak of the French race or the German race. France and Germany are adjacent countries, and the people who live on one side of the border are physically little different from those who live on the other side. It is also misleading to call the Jews a race. They have no physical characteristics by which they can be dependably distinguished from non-Jews in our population. What holds them together as a group primarily is religion, history, and social tradition—that is, ethnic ties.

Racial and ethnic differences fall into distinct categories and largely are independent of each other. The frequently made assumption that race determines culture has little scientific or factual basis. Where different racial groups have lived in close association for some time, as in Hawaii, they are likely to have much the same culture; on the other hand, members of the same race living in different parts of the world often exhibit cultural patterns that are radically different. To see the truth of this last statement, we need only compare the culture of black Americans with that of blacks living in the Congo basin of Africa.

Questions of Ethnic and Racial Superiority

Some people believe that one race or one ethnic group is innately superior to others in intelligence and creativity, and that this superiority largely explains the high degree of civilization certain groups have been able to achieve. This may seem superficially plausible because many of the recorded scientific and social advances (or at least the ones familiar to whites of European descent) in the last several hundred years have been made by the European-descended ethnic groups.

Such a view would be extremely shortsighted. Over the centuries, the particular groups who have taken the lead in the advances of civilization have changed. First it was the Sumerians and the Egyptians; later the people of India and China, the Jews, the Phoenicians, and the Persians; still later the Greeks and Romans; then for a while the Arabs; and finally the peoples of northern and western Europe. But we need go back only 2,000 years or less to find Roman writers who looked on the then-primitive Britons and Germans as not only crude and uncivilized but also stupid. In other parts of the world, well-organized societies developed but they either disintegrated or were destroyed by invaders, disease, or natural disasters. These include the Maya and Inca civilizations in the Americas and various kingdoms in black Africa south of the Sahara.

There is no convincing scientific evidence to support the contention that some races biologically inherit a greater capacity for development than others. Which society leads the world development of civilization is the result of a combination of other factors such as favorable climate and soil, migrations that stimulated change by bringing together peoples with different cultural backgrounds, and fortuitous discoveries and inventions. Such advances tend to lead to further advances, a gradual accumulation of technical skills, an increase in food output, a slow growth of population, and the development of towns and cities. Every group of people has its bright and dull individuals, its great intellects and its idiots.

It is possible that, on average, there are some inherited mental and psychological differences between ethnic groups, just as there are physical differences. Statistics collected by Richard Herrnstein and Charles Murray in a controversial book entitled *The Bell Curve* suggest that in the United States, on average, Americans of Asian descent score a few points higher than whites on IQ tests, and blacks score about 15 points lower than whites. These statistics, and the usefulness of IQ tests in measuring mental abilities, have been challenged on a variety of levels. But even if the statistics are correct and IQ tests actually measure mental ability, it is not clear whether the difference in scores is inherent in ethnic groups or is socially determined. Moreover, averages say nothing about individuals, so most social scientists say that no policy inference can be drawn from such statistics.

Even if some inborn mental and psychological differences exist, they do not necessarily mean superiority or inferiority any more than do differences in skin color, hair texture, or head shape. In any case, such differences are minor compared with the great differences that exist among individuals in every ethnic group.

Some social scientists argue that the concept of race is so socially determined that such discussions do not belong in social science. The problem is that discussions of race are often emotionally charged and emotion is anathema to good science. We agree. The reasons not to discuss race include:

■ The term *race* is a social, not an important physical, construction.

■ Biological differences within a race tend to far exceed biological differences among races.

■ The race concept has a history of being inappropriately used.

These reasons lead most social scientists to focus on other ways of classifying people. We discuss the issue of race here not because we believe races are distinguishable in any meaningful biological way, but simply because race is much discussed in our society and we believe it is necessary to address issues of societal concern. Regardless of whether the concept of race is a meaningful concept in a democracy, the important thing is to treat all people as human beings, to judge people on their individual merits, and to provide every opportunity for people to develop and use whatever capabilities they possess.

Ethnic and Racial Prejudice and Discrimination

Ethnic relations vary greatly in different societies and in different social situations. In some cases, relatively little friction exists among members of different ethnic groups. **Prejudice**—an adverse judgment or opinion formed beforehand or without knowledge or examination of the facts—exists, but ethnic barriers are not sufficient to prevent considerable social

Ethnic Cleansing

Ethnic divisions affect every country, and in many ways they are worse abroad than they are in the United States. Let's consider two cases where they are particularly bad: Bosnia and the countries of central Africa.

Bosnia

In Bosnia, significant hatred exists among the many different factions that make up the population of the country. The most numerous are Bosnians, Serbs, and Croatians. Bosnians, who are primarily Muslims, make up about two-fifths of the population; Serbs, who are mainly Eastern Orthodox Christians, make up about one-third of the population; and Croats, who are primarily Roman Catholic, make up about one-fifth of the population. This diversity in the area has existed for over a thousand years and has been the cause of continuing tension. When Yugoslavia collapsed in 1991, widespread and devastating political, economic, and religious fighting broke out.

The various factions embarked on programs of "ethnic cleansing." As one side or another was temporarily victorious, the temporarily defeated were killed, tortured, or driven from their homes, causing most of the rest of the world to worry about the stability of the country and the fate of its people. Efforts by many countries, including several European powers and the United States, resulted in an international conference held in Dayton, Ohio, in 1995 that ended the worst of the incidents. However, the hatred aroused and intensified by the ethnic cleansing has persisted as the factions flare up and violate the Dayton Accords. The political, economic, and religious situation in Bosnia remains highly unstable.

Central Africa

In the early 1990s, the world became aware of a fierce tribal war in the central African country of Rwanda, where two principal tribes, the Hutu and the Tutsi, tried to exterminate each other. In 1994, a group of militant Hutus massacred over one million ethnic Tutsis (and moderate Hutus). Hundreds of thousands more managed to escape into the neighboring country of Burundi. Burundi could not support such a huge number of refugees, and worldwide assistance was only partially effective. In Burundi, the Hutu were in the majority but the Tutsi controlled the military, and so the warfare continued. This led to hundreds of thousands of refugees escaping to the neighboring countries of Zaire and Uganda.

The influx of refugees into Zaire upset the ethnic and political balance there between Hutus and Tutsis, and hundreds of thousands of members of both tribes were killed. In 1997, a radical change of government took place, and even the country's name was changed (from Zaire to Democratic Republic of Congo). While international organizations tried to find solutions, in 1997 the situation in Zaire became so intolerable for the Rwandan refugees that those who had survived the warfare made their way back to Rwanda.

Because large numbers of members of these tribes live in all of the countries of central Africa, the Hutu–Tutsi conflict is not confined to any one of these countries. The Congo is mineral rich and the competition for the land and its resources exacerbates the rivalries in this politically unstable area. Political alliances shift often. In 2002, the first Tutsi president of Rwanda signed a peace accord with the Congo, which agreed to a disarming of Hutu militiamen. The conflict is far from resolved and will continue to warrant international concern into the indefinite future, but in the early 2000s the ethnic ferocity had diminished from the heights it reached in the mid- and late 1990s.

Mass graves of victims of genocide in Bosnia.

contact and frequent intermarriages. This seems to be the situation today in Hawaii, where the principal ethnic classifications are Caucasian and Asian/Pacific Islander. Though the various ethnic groups have not yet lost their sense of identity, residentially, economically, and educationally they are nearly integrated. But there are other places in the world where prejudice and **discrimination**—actions, behavior, or treatment based on prejudice—are intense and where racial segregation is the accepted pattern.

What is the explanation for these great variations? Many people feel that prejudice is inevitable, that it is an inherited aversion. But the belief that human beings inherit attitudes has long been discredited by psychologists, and racial prejudice cannot be accounted for by any such simple explanation. Moreover, attitude and prejudice need not necessarily lead to discriminatory actions.

Writers have suggested various reasons for ethnic and racial prejudice. Prominent among these are the following four:

1. Influence of tradition
2. Psychological need of individuals to belong to a particular, identifiable group
3. Building up of the ego by cultivating a feeling of superiority
4. Usefulness of prejudice as an economic and political weapon

Each of these could be expanded enormously, but we will leave that to sociology courses. Here, we simply want you to consider your own attitudes, to ask yourself whether they reflect prejudice, and if so to consider the reasons behind that prejudice. After you've done that, take the next step and ask yourself whether your prejudices show up in discriminatory actions. If they do, evaluate whether you find those actions justified.

The Melting Pot

Because of its heterogeneous population and the tendency of immigrant groups ultimately to become assimilated, the United States often has been called a melting pot. Although the white colonial population was predominantly British, other nationalities were also represented. During the nineteenth century, this country received 30 million immigrants, and in the early twentieth century millions more arrived. A few came from almost every section of the world, but the great majority were Caucasians from Europe. In the last thirty years, immigration from Asian countries to the United States has been high and will likely continue to be high through the early 2000s.

Groups whose basic patterns of life were not too unlike those of the early British settlers became assimilated in a relatively short time; others were assimilated more slowly. But from the

Stratification in the Former Soviet Union

The United States is not the only country that has problems with prejudice and discrimination. These problems are universal. Take the former USSR, for example. It was a country with more than a hundred nationalities. The Russian nationality was the largest (about 50 percent of the population), and it controlled about 90 percent of the top posts in the Soviet Union. Many of the other nationalities were not happy about that Russian dominance.

Until the late 1980s, the Soviet Union dealt with its minority problem by refusing to allow any dissent and by maintaining a secret police force to ensure stability. Joseph Stalin, for example, moved the Crimean Tatars from their native lands when he became displeased with their actions. The communist government kept the nationalist groups under control. When the communist structure collapsed in the late 1980s, so did the communist government's solution to the nationality problem.

The problems surfaced in the late 1980s, when Russia reduced the police-imposed limitations on individual action. The result has been unrest among a number of Soviet minority groups, such as that between the Armenians and the Azarbaijani. There was fighting and rioting between the two groups, but the Azarbaijani retained their domination over the Armenians, who, however, continued to grumble. In the 1990s, so many minority groups demanded recognition that the entire political structure of the Soviet Union broke apart into a number of different countries. The Soviet Union was no longer a union and a major reason was the nationality problem. Ethnic conflicts persist in the 2000s in many of the former Soviet republics, especially Chechnya, Armenia, Azerbaijan, and Tajikistan.

beginning there were non-Caucasian groups whose assimilation seemed impossible because they differed not only culturally but also racially from the majority of the American people. Today there are still unassimilated groups. The best known of these are blacks, but they also include Hispanics, who are largely Caucasian but who have come to this country rather recently; Asians, whose physical characteristics set them apart from white Causasians and who sometimes find themselves the subjects of economic and educational discrimination; and individuals of Middle Eastern descent, whose connections with Islam have subjected them to discrimination as the United States struggles to balance the "War on Terror" with individual liberties.

*M*inorities

If various groups were different but essentially equal, prejudice and discrimination probably would not be a central concern of social scientists. But as was the case with social and economic stratification, racial and ethnic groups are not viewed equally: **minority groups** are groups of people singled out for unequal negative treatment and who regard themselves as objects of collective discrimination, and **dominant groups** are groups of people singled out for positive treatment. The term *dominant group* is used rather than *majority* because the dominant group may be a minority, as was the case with whites in South Africa.

In the remainder of this chapter, we introduce you to the important minority groups in the United States.

Native Americans

The Native Americans were the first settlers of what is now the United States. Although the date is uncertain, most anthropologists believe they came from Asia about 30,000 years ago. After Europeans began to colonize North America, Native Americans were slowly outnumbered and eventually conquered. Today, they are a relatively small minority, and for a long time they were the most isolated of all minority groups and perhaps the most deprived in education. Recently, Native Americans have taken the initiative in efforts to increase ties with the dominant U.S. culture, to improve their educational and employment opportunities, and in some cases to restore lands taken in the eighteenth and early nineteenth centuries by procedures that Native Americans have attacked in the courts.

The policies of the dominant white population toward Native Americans have undergone changes in the past century from (1) enforced isolation and segregation; to (2) forced integration into U.S. society, with almost disastrous results for the Native Americans culturally, economically, and physically; to (3) a policy of much more gradual assimilation. The present government policy toward them is based on the Indian Reorganization Act of 1934, which was designed to encourage Native American tribes to revive their traditions and to manage their own political and economic affairs. Although many Native Americans choose to live on land designated as Native American homeland, they can live where they like; they are U.S. citizens and can vote; they pay certain taxes, and they receive Social Security benefits; they may own private property; and they are free to seek employment anywhere they wish. But they sometimes encounter prejudice and have difficulty in adjusting to the dominant U.S. culture outside of areas designated as Native American lands. Also, some of them are handicapped by poor health, a lack of education and skills, and the language barrier. Each of the tribes has its own language or dialect, which usually is very difficult for a person who is not a member of the particular tribe to learn. According to the federal Bureau of Indian Affairs, there were originally about 300 different languages spoken by Native Americans in what is now the United States, and possibiy as many as 200 still survive. If in addition the tribe is isolated, the processes of education and assimilation are extremely slow. For instance, it is still the case that many Navajos, one of the largest tribes in the United States, do not yet speak English.

Blacks (African Americans[1])

Blacks constitute approximately 38 million people, or 13 percent of the U.S. population. American blacks are for the most part descendants of slaves brought over to the United States in the seventeenth, eighteenth, and early nineteenth centuries. According to one estimate, at least 14 to 15 million black slaves were landed in the Americas, North and South, from 1600 to the latter part of the nineteenth century.

The African Origins of U.S. Blacks. The main source of slaves in the seventeenth and eighteenth centuries was the Gulf of Guinea in Africa. This area was more densely populated than most of Africa, and as merchants had already established trade with the outside world in ivory and gold, it was easy to provide slaves as well. The trade routes of the Guinea people were evidence of a relatively advanced culture. Although they were a nonliterate people, the inhabitants of this area were among the leaders of black Africa in agriculture, metalwork, pottery, and sculpture.

Slave trading has a long history. Muslim Berbers and Arabs exported black slaves from Africa as far back as the early 900s. In the fifteenth century, Spain and Portugal imported slaves from Africa, which they bought from other Africans. The first ship of slaves did not arrive in America until 1619, when it landed blacks in Virginia for labor in the English colonies. Plantation owners needed a large force of controllable workers, and black slaves were the answer to this need.

Although importation of slaves into the United States became illegal in 1808, the need for a workforce did not subside, and thousands of slaves were smuggled in despite the laws. These practices continued until the Civil War, when, in 1863, Abraham Lincoln signed the Emancipation Proclamation. Abolitionists were a strong force in the North, but aside from humanitarian concerns, political leaders also saw emancipation as a way to further cripple the South during the war.

The Emancipation Proclamation and the 13th Amendment to the U.S. Constitution changed the legal status of slaves but not their social status. The systematic legal segregation of blacks was promoted by what were called Jim Crow laws,[2] and the voting rights of blacks were effectively blocked in the southern states. White supremacy propaganda became intense and was often accompanied by violence.

Continuing Discrimination against Blacks. The problems of blacks in the United States today differ from those of any other minority group in this country. To begin with, blacks in the United States are so far removed from their African homeland that much of their cultural heritage is difficult to identify today. Though their cultural patterns may differ

An illustration shows the cramped quarters on a slave ship.

---

[1]Debate continues about whether "African American," "Afro-American," or "people of color" should be substituted for "black."

[2]The name Jim Crow is thought to have come from a character in a popular minstrel song written by Thomas D. Rice in 1832.

Ivory and Ebony or Evory and Ibony?

Over the years, there has been a considerable amount of mixing of the black-skinned and white-skinned people, just as there has been mixing of people with many other different physical attributes. Much of this mixing occurred under slavery when slave owners fathered children by black mothers. The great abolitionist leader Frederick Douglass was the son of a white father and a slave mother. Just how much white ancestry U.S. blacks have cannot be determined with certainty, but some geneticists have attempted to make an estimate.

Most of the ancestors of U.S. blacks came from certain areas in West Africa. By comparing the percentages of the West African natives who carry a certain gene (the rhesus-factor allele R^0) with the percentage of U.S. blacks and U.S. whites who carry it, geneticists estimate that, on the average, the ancestry of U.S. blacks is probably about 30 percent white. Other researchers have estimated that about 75 percent of all U.S. blacks have at least one white ancestor.

Similarly, it is estimated that about 25 percent of whites have at least one black ancestor. As intermarriage continues, these percentages will increase, making black- and white-skinned physical characteristics less noticeable. Perhaps, someday we will arrive at a society in which skin color will not comprise an ethnic grouping and will instead be just another physical characteristic on a par with hair color, eye color, and height, and in which it will be just as strange to think of a person as "black" as it is to think of a person as "green-eyed."

somewhat from those of other Americans, they essentially are American by culture, as reflected in their language, customs, education, and religion. But the position of the black minority still is influenced unfavorably by the fact that it is the only minority in this country whose ancestors once served a long period of slavery to whites. No other minority groups have experienced the social and psychological upheavals caused by slavery, followed by sudden emancipation and then by a long period of discrimination and segregation, some of it enforced by law. In addition, blacks tend to differ from whites in skin color, hair, and features more than other minority ethnic groups, and this has contributed to the strong personal prejudice that sometimes exists between whites and blacks.

Although the status of blacks has advanced in many ways in recent decades, they still suffer from prejudice and discrimination and from handicaps that are the legacy of past discrimination.

Legal Discrimination and Segregation.   We have already described briefly the rise of legal segregation in the South. The constitutionality of the state laws on which it was based was long a matter of dispute because the Fourteenth Amendment to the Constitution of the United States, adopted in 1868, provides that no state may deny any person equal protection under the laws. The question was whether segregation constituted denial of equal protection. Those who attempted to challenge these laws in the courts had no important success until 1954, when the U.S. Supreme Court, in the case of *Brown v. Board of Education,* outlawed segregation in public schools.

The *Brown* decision reversed a decision made by the Court in 1896, when, in the case of *Plessy v. Ferguson,* it had issued a decision approving segregation of blacks and whites by state legislation. The decision in *Plessy v. Ferguson* was based on the so-called **separate-but-equal doctrine**, that is, the theory that providing separate educational, recreational, and other public facilities for blacks was not denying equal protection under the laws if these facilities were equal to those for whites. In practice, this equality proved to be a myth.

The *Brown* decision outlawing school segregation opened the way for challenging other segregation laws, and within a decade or so it became clear that they were all unconstitutional. However, the breaking down of segregation, especially in the case of schools, has proved to be a slow and difficult process. Some confusion has resulted from disagreement about whether court decisions and civil rights acts passed by Congress merely annul laws and public policies that require or encourage attendance at segregated schools, or whether they also place an obligation on communities and school boards to take positive measures

Martin Luther King, Jr., at the 1963 civil rights march in Washington.

to eliminate **de facto segregation**—segregation that occurs because of social and cultural, not legal, reasons. **De jure segregation** is segregation based on actual segregation laws. Do these decisions and acts make illegal the segregation that results because some residential areas are wholly black and others wholly white, or make illegal the segregation brought about partly because some parents, black as well as white, may prefer to have their children attend segregated schools?

Since 1954, many major pieces of civil rights legislation have been passed. For example, the Civil Rights Acts of the 1950s and 1960s enforced the voting rights of blacks and prohibited discrimination on the basis of "race" (as was then the terminology), sex, or national origin in public accommodations, federally assisted programs, and housing.

Causes of Blacks' Frustration.   Despite all of this legislation, for many blacks there has been little progress, and the frustration level has at times led to riots and civil disturbances. Blacks' frustration is grounded in both social and economic conditions. Though the economic condition of blacks has, on the average, improved greatly, it has by no means caught up with that of whites. In the early 2000s, blacks earned a median income that was only about 60 percent of that earned by whites.

The reasons for this lower income are complicated and varied. They include discrimination, family structure, age structure, occupation, and education. Blacks make up a higher proportion of the labor force for low-skilled jobs than their numbers would predict, and a lower percentage of managerial jobs. Additionally, their unemployment rates are higher. Table 12.1a shows that black unemployment rates have consistently remained at higher levels than those of the other major groups (whites and Hispanics). The unemployment rate is especially high among young black males, as can be seen in Table 12.1b.

Much of the problem can be attributed to past and present discrimination against blacks. Discrimination has robbed some blacks of the incentive to acquire the necessary education and training to fill jobs that require not only willingness to work but also more than average skill, training, and education. They believe they will not be given such jobs even if they are qualified to fill them. As a result, to them it makes no sense to acquire marketable skills. To make matters worse, especially in the North, a large proportion of blacks live in neighborhoods where crime is rampant and housing substandard.

Progress toward Equality.   Notwithstanding these problems, the average economic condition of blacks has improved. Many blacks have moved into career-level and skilled

Table 12.1a
Unemployment among Races, 1975–2008

YEAR	ALL ETHNIC GROUPS (%)	WHITE (%)	BLACK (%)	HISPANIC (%)
1975	8.5	7.8	14.8	Not available
1980	7.1	6.3	14.3	10.1
1985	7.3	6.5	14.0	10.6
1990	5.5	5.1	12.0	8.7
1995	5.6	4.9	10.4	9.3
2000	4.0	3.9	8.5	7.0
2005	5.1	4.4	10.0	7.1
2008	5.8	5.2	10.1	7.6

Source: U.S. Bureau of Labor and Statistics, *Employment and Earnings.*

Table 12.1b
Unemployment by Age Group, 2008

AGE GROUP	WHITE MALES (%)	BLACK MALES (%)
16–19	19.1	35.9
20–24	10.2	19.3
25–34	5.3	11.8
35–44	4.3	7.7
45–54	3.8	7.7
55–64	3.4	7.1
65 and over	4.1	9.5

Source: U.S. Bureau of Labor and Statistics, CPS.

jobs. The major credit for the job advancement of blacks should probably go to those individuals among them who have had the ambition and the willingness to acquire education and training. But they have been helped by organized efforts to give blacks far greater opportunities than were available to them in the past. These efforts are made by government agencies, colleges and universities, corporations, and various other private groups including some organized by blacks themselves. They range all the way from trying to train the hard-core unemployed for specific jobs to providing qualified blacks with scholarships or fellowships for advanced study.

In the past, a significant factor in restricting the economic progress of blacks has been discrimination by labor unions, many of which refused to accept them as members. Some still strongly resist admission of blacks, but the number of such unions that discriminate is declining. Building trade unions in large cities have been especially slow in accepting black apprentices except in token numbers, but under pressure they are adopting more liberal policies.

In the past, black business or professional people were generally limited to their own community for a market for their services. Today the situation is changing. Many corporations are actively seeking qualified blacks to fill professional or administrative positions. This is not always easy, because there are still relatively few blacks with good college training and even fewer with degrees from graduate or professional schools, and the competition to hire them is sometimes intense. But progress is being made, and black enrollment in college and professional schools has risen significantly in the past decades.

From 1960 to 2008, the percentage of blacks completing four years of college rose from about 3.5 percent to almost 20 percent. The percentage of blacks completing high school rose from 23 percent in 1960 to about 83 percent in 2008. In addition, as black political power has grown and the demands for equality have mounted, more and more professional and administrative jobs have been opened to blacks in public institutions such as hospitals, schools, and state and local government agencies.

Part of the reason for this increase was **affirmative action programs**, programs designed to favor minority groups. Such programs came under attack beginning in the late 1990s and early 2000s. For example, in California and Texas, affirmative action programs were overturned by the courts and replaced by need-based and race-neutral programs. As a result, the number of blacks in higher education decreased. This decline has led to the development of programs that seek diversity in other ways, such as admitting a certain percentage of the top students from public high schools. Though this has boosted minority enrollments, many college officials remain opposed to ending affirmative action.

Affirmative action continues to be much in the news. Much of the debate concerns precisely what is meant by affirmative action and how it translates into policies. Does it justify numerical quotas, and if so, what is the nature of those quotas? Does it require that race be the major factor in decision making, or does it simply allow race to be considered as one of the factors in decisions? And if it allows a consideration of race, how much weight can be given to race? Does it require or allow that specific preferences be given to minority groups (and if so, how strong can those preferences be), or must all groups be treated equally?

As an example of the issues that can arise, let's consider the college admission program at the University of Texas. That program was changed after its affirmative action program, which gave specific preferences to blacks, was one of the programs that the courts struck down. (Its program giving specific preferences to football players or to legacies—children of alumni—in admissions was not struck down.) In response, the University of Texas decided to allow automatic admission to the top 10 percent of all Texas high school students. Because many of the inner-city high schools in Texas are predominantly black and, on average, score low on standardized tests, whereas suburban high schools are predominantly white and, on average, score high on standardized tests, this new program gave blacks an advantage compared to their chances of admission if only test scores had been considered. Was this new program allowable under an affirmative action plan that used a "top 10 percent" standard, or did it represent a strategy to avoid the accusation that the schools were still giving preference to blacks? Even if it were allowable, is it desirable? (There were stories about some whites transferring into inner-city schools so that they would get admitted to the University of Texas.) The bigger question is, What is reasonable discretion in admissions (discretion similar to the allowable attempt of colleges to have a geographic diversity in their student body) and what is unreasonable discretion when it comes to race? Many such issues will have to be dealt with over the next decade.

Another example involved the University of Michigan, where applicants were selected on the basis of points. Applicants were given 20 points for being black and 20 points for attending a predominantly minority high school, out of a total of 150 points. (SATs accounted for only 12 points.) Was this too much of a preference, and if so, what would not be too much? When thinking about an answer to this, consider also that legacies, who are generally white and well-off, were given 1 to 4 points for their alumni relationships. Was that too much, and if so, what would not be too much? The U.S. Supreme Court, which has the ultimate power to make these decisions in the United States, decided that, at an undergraduate level, the points for black students were too much like affirmative action. However, it held that colleges could take race into account in their admission decisions, thereby legalizing affirmative action. Future decisions may, however, be different. The reason it is difficult to predict what the Court will decide is because the Court's composition changes over time, as judges retire, and are replaced by others with different judicial philosophies. For example, the replacement of David Souter with Sonia Sotomayor in 2009 may make a difference. While both have liberal persuasions—since he was a white male from New Hampshire, and she was a Hispanic woman from the Bronx—many expect her to take different views on some discrimination issues.

A field in which blacks have as yet made limited progress is business ownership or control. Though corporations are more willing than formerly to hire those who qualify for administrative positions, as yet blacks control comparatively few enterprises of any size. Principal exceptions are some insurance companies, banks, and publishing concerns that chiefly serve the black community. But even the larger black communities such as New York City's Harlem neighborhood are served for the most part by concerns owned and operated by whites.

Eliminating the Vestiges of Discrimination. When we consider the extent to which discrimination against blacks prevailed throughout this country from early colonial times to World War II, the progress toward equal treatment since that war has been substantial, even though it has fallen far short of the hopes and expectations of many. Segregation in the armed forces, formerly the unchallenged rule in all branches of the service, was completely abandoned as a policy by the mid-1950s. Discrimination against blacks in hotels, motels, restaurants, and other public places has been virtually eliminated, partly because of changes in public attitudes and partly because of laws forbidding it. To be sure, not all the subtler forms of discrimination have disappeared, but at least they are on the defensive.

Another area in which discrimination against blacks has been reduced is in the right to buy property. Formerly, the purchaser of a house might be required to sign a restrictive covenant in which he or she agreed not to rent or sell to members of specified racial or cultural groups. This covenant sometimes made it impossible for blacks to buy or rent housing except in overcrowded black neighborhoods that were often slums. But in 1948, the Supreme Court ruled that restrictive covenants are contrary to public policy and may not be enforced by the courts. In 1968, Congress passed an Open Housing Act prohibiting racial discrimination in the sale or rental of about 80 percent of all housing, and in the same year the Supreme Court interpreted an 1866 federal law as banning racial discrimination in the sale or rental of any housing. Although these actions have not completely eliminated discrimination in the sale of housing, they have made it difficult, especially for real estate firms.

One place where social scientists have found significant discrimination against blacks is in entry-level jobs and low-skilled positions. Researchers had young high school graduates with similar job histories apply for the same jobs. Thirty-four percent of the white applicants were called back; 14 percent of the blacks were called back. In another experiment, social scientists had fictitious individuals apply for jobs on-line. Some had white-sounding names, such as Greg Kelly, and some had more African American names, such as Jamal Jackson. They found that the white-sounding names received many more callbacks and that the white-sounding name was worth approximately eight years of experience. Thus a person with a black-sounding name had to have eight years more experience to have the same callback rate as an otherwise similar white. The discrimination was even greater when both black and white applicants had criminal records; in the first experiment, a black with a criminal record had only a 5 percent chance of getting a callback, whereas a white with a criminal record had a 17 percent chance of getting a callback. Since almost one in five of all black men have served some time, this presents a serious problem for integrating them back into the community.

Black–White Social Relations. In his classic book, *An American Dilemma,* economist Gunnar Myrdal observed that the area of strongest white prejudice against blacks had to do with intermarriage and other intimate social contacts. This seems still to be true. The great majority of whites believe that blacks should have equality of opportunity in employment, housing, education, health facilities, and legal rights, but many of them are still uneasy about intermarriage (just as many blacks are) and often are awkward in developing close social contacts.

Among some groups, especially in the younger generation, there is a trend toward breaking down the obstacles to social contacts between the races, including those to interracial

The Obama family.

marriages. After World War II, more than half of our states had laws prohibiting marriage between a white person and anyone defined legally as a "Negro," but in 1967 the Supreme Court ruled that no state may ban interracial marriages. Still, today interracial couples constitute only about 4 percent of all couples, and only 18 percent of those are between blacks and whites. Opposition to these marriages, whether from blacks or whites, is diminishing, but it is still strong.

Discrimination occurs not only between blacks and whites but also among blacks, with darker-skinned blacks called derogatory names and treated differently by lighter-skinned blacks. Moreover, the discrimination that does occur by whites seems to be more pronounced the darker the skin the other person has. In a study of brothers from the same family who differed by skin color, it was found that the lighter-skinned brothers tended to have higher incomes and experience less discrimination.

In 2008, the United States made a major step forward in race relations with the election of a light-skinned black president with a very African name—Barack Obama. That election was, to many, an indication that the United States has come a long way in solving the race problem. But it has a long way to go.

Ultimately, we will know that the race problem has been solved if bringing home a black fiancée to a white family, or bringing home a white fiancée to a black family, raises no more eyebrows than bringing a blond fiancée home to a brunette's family, or a brunette fiancée to a blond's family.

The Future of Black Americans.   In the early 1960s, some twenty years after he had completed *An American Dilemma,* Myrdal was asked if he foresaw any solution to our race problems. He replied, "Well, you can find solutions to technical problems; but in social problems, particularly those that are so intrinsically difficult and mixed up as the [black] problem, there is no solution in an absolute sense."

In his study, Myrdal called the race problem in the United States a white problem because the whites are the great majority and hold the bulk of wealth and power. He saw progress by blacks to be dependent on white cooperation, on a lifting of the bars of discrimination. But it is clear that even if all whites (and blacks) could quickly and completely rid themselves of ethnic prejudice, it would still take time for blacks as a group to overcome completely all the effects of generations of slavery followed by decades of extreme discrimination.

Some have even argued that blacks are owed reparations for the injustices of the past, and that such reparations are necessary to achieve equality. They have collected information about companies' and universities' pasts and have shown that a number of them profited from the slave trade and oppression of blacks. Others argue that reparations are precisely the wrong way to achieve equality since reparations are unlikely to achieve significant results from a practical point of view. To hold people today accountable for wrongs of their ancestors is a highly tenuous proposition. Trying to do so will move the debate away from the more important issue of how to provide better opportunities for blacks now and in the future. Regardless of what is decided about reparations, no group can give equality to another group except in the sense of treating its members fairly and sympathetically and helping to provide them with opportunities. Neither disadvantaged blacks nor disadvantaged whites will achieve equality with the average citizen merely by being given jobs for which they are not qualified or by being admitted to colleges whose academic standards they cannot meet. They can, however, be offered opportunities for job training and, if they have the will and ability, chances to make up academic deficiencies.

The debate over what to do about inequality has manifested itself in the debate about affirmative action programs. Advocates of affirmative action programs argue that they are necessary to offset past discrimination. Critics charge that such programs are unfair both to the minorities and to whites. They say that affirmative action programs place blacks in situations for which they are unqualified and that preference for blacks discriminates against needy whites.

As we stated earlier, in response to criticism some states such as Texas and California have started substituting need for race and gender as the determining factor for preferential treatment. For instance, in 1996 California passed a law designed "to abolish affirmative action." According to this law, "The state shall not discriminate against, or grant preferential treatment to, any individual or group on the basis of race, sex, color, ethnicity, or national origin in the operation of public employment, public education, or public contracting." This statement demonstrates neutrality, and it abolished previous legislation that had favored preferential treatment for minorities and women. Some other states are considering similar legislation.

Eliminating affirmative action on the basis of skin color will not necessarily mean an end to giving preference to blacks; it will simply be preference not solely based on skin color, so a white child and a black child of upper-middle-class families will be treated equally. However, because many blacks are poor and come from backgrounds without a strong focus on education, they, along with whites from similar backgrounds, can be given preference in admissions and hiring because, to achieve what they have, they had to overcome greater obstacles than a person from a rich, pro-education background.

It is doubtful whether ethnic prejudice and discrimination can be completely eliminated as long as blacks constitute a distinct ethnic group in our society. Discrimination is inherent to some degree in most social relationships all over the world. It occurs in the contacts between individuals, between individuals and groups, and between groups of many types, including families. But, in the view of the textbook authors, to deny to an entire ethnic or cultural group equal civil rights and equal educational, political, and economic opportunities is a type of discrimination that a society should not tolerate.

Hispanics

The largest minority group in the United States is **Hispanics,** or individuals of Spanish-speaking origin. These include **Latinos,** who have historical and cultural ties to Latin America, and **Chicanos,** who have historical and cultural ties to Mexico. From 1988 to 2000, the Hispanic population in the United States more than doubled and it has grown even faster since. About 46 million U.S. citizens (more than 15 percent of the population) identify themselves as being of Spanish origin. Of the total number, about 67 percent gave Mexico as their place of origin, about 9 percent gave Puerto Rico, about 4 percent gave Cuba, and the remainder gave other Latin American countries. However, of all who considered themselves of Spanish origin, about 63 percent were actually born in the United States or in Puerto Rico, all of whose natives have U.S. citizenship. Immigration, both legal and illegal, has been an important part of Hispanic population growth, and in 2008 there were an estimated 9 million undocumented Hispanics in the United States, 76 percent of all undocumented immigrants.

The proprietor lends a hand in the kitchen of his Mexican restaurant.

Chicanos. The Chicanos are of special importance because they are the largest of all Hispanic minority groups. But they differ from other Americans of

Spanish origin not only in their national origin but also in their racial background. "To be a Mexican," says Philip D. Ortega, "is to be a member of la raza, the race of Montezuma's children. More than two-fifths of the Mexican population are pure-blooded Indians; more than half have some Indian blood in them. Yet, despite Indian resilience, the language of the conquerors dominated."

Besides Native Americans, Mexicans, or Spaniards from Mexico, were the first settlers of what is now the southwestern part of the United States. All of this area was a part of Mexico before the United States annexed it in 1848 after the Mexican War. When the first settlers from the United States began moving into the Southwest, Mexicans were already there, and many of their descendants can be found there today, especially in Colorado and northern New Mexico, where a few villages are still composed almost entirely of descendants of Mexicans.

The modern influx of Mexican immigration came after 1900. It was not affected by the quota restrictions, passed by Congress in 1921 and 1924, that greatly reduced the inflow of immigrants from eastern and southern Europe, because these did not apply to the Western hemisphere. Most Mexicans came as common laborers. Many were employed as seasonal migratory workers in agriculture; others found jobs on road-building projects or as railroad workers. However, up until 1964 many of our Mexican migratory workers were not citizens or residents of the United States. Rather, they were *braceros,* Mexicans who were allowed to enter this country seasonally as contract workers in agriculture. The law permitting these contract workers was allowed to expire in 1964, but it was reinstated in 1986.

In addition to contract workers, a number of Mexicans are in the United States illegally. They come to the United States to find jobs offering wages and working conditions better than they can find in Mexico. Given the 2,000-mile-long border between Mexico and the United States, limiting the flow of illegal immigration from Mexico is very difficult.

In 1986, Congress passed a law that was meant to deal with this problem. Among other things, it allowed certain illegal aliens who had been in the United States for at least five years to receive amnesty and to apply for U.S. citizenship. The requirements of this law were quite strict, but millions of Mexican illegal aliens came forward to apply. The 1986 law did not resolve the problem. In 2007, a new immigration bill was proposed that would provide a path toward legalization for the millions of Mexicans living in the United States who were still illegal and would establish a guest worker program but would also increase border security and increase penalties imposed on employers who hire illegal aliens. The bill did not even make it far enough to get voted on. In 2009, the Obama administration considered submitting its own immigration bill, which stirred up even more debate on the issue.

Today, Chicanos are one of our most rapidly growing groups. Because of their high birthrate, a large proportion of them are young. Four out of five Chicanos live in the Southwest. The great majority are concentrated in Texas and California, but substantial numbers are found in Arizona, New Mexico, and Colorado. They go where the work is, and the U.S. economy's high demand for workers in states such as Iowa, Kansas, and Georgia has meant that in the 1990s and early 2000s many moved to those states. In fact, many farms throughout the United States have come to rely on illegal Mexican immigrants because of the Mexicans' willingness to work for lower wages and do harder jobs than U.S. workers. Although some are of Spanish descent, most are of mixed Spanish and Indian ancestry. They tend to live in segregated residential areas, to retain their own customs, and to continue to speak Spanish. They often lack the level of education of their U.S. neighbors, and the parents often do not speak English fluently (although the children who were born here do). In states where they have previously been sparsely represented, they sometimes are discriminated against not only by the long-established population but also by Mexicans who have been in the country longer than the newest arrivals. All these factors contribute to slow their economic and social progress.

Though many Chicanos still live in the Southwest and are employed in agriculture, and a relatively small number of them are still migrants, the great majority—close to 85 percent—

live in urban areas, where they sometimes form small colonies. In cities, Chicanos work in many job areas, but as yet relatively few are found in high-ranking occupations. As a group, their incomes are much lower than those of white Americans of European descent, and about 22 percent live below the poverty level. But like the descendants of earlier immigrant groups, some are finding their way up the social and economic ladder, and today about 34 percent of them hold white-collar jobs.

Latinos.   Another ethnic-culture group of Hispanics are Latinos. The largest subset of this group are Puerto Ricans who have come to the United States in the last fifty years. Though most Puerto Ricans are Caucasians, a substantial proportion of them are of black or mixed ancestry. There are now more than 4 million Puerto Ricans scattered throughout the United States, although most live in New York City.

Because Puerto Ricans are U.S. citizens, they have the same rights as all other U.S. citizens, but because of language difficulties, lack of skills, lack of education, and discrimination, those living in the United States often earn low wages and are forced to live in blighted areas where health conditions are poor and crime rates are high. Also, many social difficulties arise because their cultural patterns are so different from those they encounter in the United States. Some return home, disappointed. Others "commute," staying only long enough to earn whatever amount of money they need to sustain them for a while.

Another subset of Latinos are Cuban immigrants. Immediately after Fidel Castro came to power in Cuba in 1959, several hundred thousand refugees came to this country under special congressional legislation that created a Cuban refugee program. These first-wave Cubans have done well in the United States and make up a large percentage of the middle class in Miami, for example. From 1960 until 1980, the influx of refugees declined; in 1980 another large group of Cuban refugees was admitted into the country as political refugees.

Asians

In the early 2000s, over 12 million Asians lived in the United States. They have spread throughout the country, but most live in large cities. Despite prejudice against them, many of them have done well both financially and socially.

Chinese Immigrants.   The Chinese first came to this country in large numbers when gold was discovered in California. In the single year of 1852, some 20,000 were admitted. They worked as cooks and launderers and as laborers in the mines. When the gold rush was over, many of them were employed in building the western portion of the transcontinental railroad. They also spread out into occupations such as agriculture and fishing. But to the white settlers, they were strange and unwelcome. As their numbers grew, antagonism increased and they endured many types of discrimination. There were even riots in which they were chased through the streets and beaten or lynched. Part of this antagonism resulted from the competition for jobs. The Chinese were willing to live on very little and, if forced to do so, would work for extremely low wages. Finally, in 1882 Congress passed the Chinese Exclusion Act, which virtually suspended all Chinese immigration until 1943.

In 1965, a revision of immigration laws ended discrimination against the Chinese and the immigrants from all other countries by abolishing quotas based on national origin. Due in part to U.S. response to the upheavals in Southeast Asia that began at least as early as 1970, immigration laws have undergone several subsequent liberalizations, especially for highly trained individuals. Immigration law is complex, but at the present time we can say that it has permitted a significant increase in the number of Chinese and Southeast Asian immigrants to the United States.

A U.S. Gulag?

On February 11, 1942, U.S. authorities began rounding up Japanese Americans and shipping them to internment camps simply because of their Japanese heritage. Fear that these Americans would support Japan in that country's war with the United States was the ostensible cause, but anger at the Japanese attack on Pearl Harbor in Hawaii on December 7, 1941, and ethnic prejudice were major unstated reasons. Although these internment camps were far more humane than the Soviet Gulag, in which prisoners were inhumanely treated and in which millions died, the fact that the U.S. government created these camps at all is considered a travesty by many. Just as angry people often strike out in vengeance without thinking, angry societies sometimes strike out in revenge and thoughtlessness.

Japanese Immigrants. After Congress passed the Chinese Exclusion Act, the Japanese began arriving on the West Coast in increasing numbers. Most of them settled in California, and before long they, like the Chinese before them, began to encounter prejudice and discrimination. As with the Chinese, the feeling against them was partly based on conflicting economic interests. Many Japanese became truck gardeners (growers of fresh vegetables), and because whole families were willing to work hard and live on very little, the native California truck gardeners complained that they could not meet Japanese competition. Also it was argued that the strong loyalty of the Japanese to their homeland made assimilation impossible.

During World War II, anti-Japanese feelings increased. The U.S. government forcibly moved 117,000 people of Japanese birth or ancestry away from the West Coast to relocation centers further inland. This move was explained as a security measure, but it is now generally recognized as an inexcusable injustice, for removal was not based on disloyalty but only on national origin, and it meant gross discrimination against thousands of loyal U.S. citizens. In 1945, the evacuation order was rescinded, but many Japanese did not return to the West Coast, preferring to live in areas where prejudice against them was less marked.

In recent years, prejudice against the Japanese has disappeared or greatly diminished. In 1988, the U.S. government finally apologized to the surviving Japanese Americans who had been interned and agreed to pay each of them $20,000.

Other Asian Immigrants. Over the years, there have been varying numbers of other Asian immigrants. In the 1970s, hundreds of thousands of Vietnamese immigrants were allowed into the United States to escape political oppression in their native country. More recently, many highly trained Indians, Pakistanis, and other Southeast Asians have been allowed in because of a shortage of workers in high-tech fields. In a number of high-tech companies, foreign-born workers outnumber U.S.-born workers.

Asian American immigration has been highly self-selective. It has primarily consisted of highly educated individuals who have found it relatively easy to succeed in the United States. Often they have taken low-level jobs that were only loosely controlled as to minimum wage and hour requirements, and they have worked hard to advance. For example, many Indians worked in motels and then bought the motels, providing jobs for new Indian immigrants. Once they learned the business and saved enough money, the new immigrants went out and bought their own motels. Today, many local motels are owned by Indians. The same is true of doughnut shops and some other occupations; for example, most doughnut shops in California are owned by Indians.

The success of Asian Americans has led to the stereotype of them as a "model minority." Thus, even though they are a minority, they are not seen as being discriminated against in work opportunities and education, and thus not in need of affirmative action. If anything, they are discriminated against in education because they attend school in greater numbers and often achieve better results than other groups, including whites. Thus, to maintain diversity some colleges, especially those located in areas with a large Asian population, discriminate against Asian Americans by making it more difficult for them to get accepted into those colleges. Not all Asian Americans are rich, educated, and successful, however, Asian Americans still have higher poverty rates than whites.

Arab Americans and Americans of Middle Eastern Descent

The last minority we will discuss is Arab Americans, of whom there are over 3 million, more than 90 percent of whom live in urban areas. As a group, Arab Americans have done relatively well, and their average incomes are 22 percent higher than the U.S. national average. Traditional multicultural efforts often overlook this ethnic group, though they face stereotyping and prejudice. The first wave of immigration of Arabs from the Middle East took place between 1875 through 1920. Most of these early Arab immigrants were from Lebanon and Syria; most were Christians seeking economic opportunities. Immigration then slowed as the United States began imposing restrictions. The second wave began in the 1940s because of the Arab–Israeli conflict and civil wars; this group came from a much more diverse area, and many practiced Islam. But like the earlier group, most were more financially secure when they came.

The 2000s have been particularly difficult for Arab Americans. Because the 9/11 terrorists were of Middle Eastern descent, many Arab Americans have been subject to discrimination and prejudice, even though almost all of them strongly condemn the terrorists and consider themselves Americans. Although they may feel that U.S. policy in the Middle East is tilted in Israel's favor, that is a feeling shared with many other Americans, and with many individuals throughout the world, and is in no way unpatriotic. New Arab American immigrants are especially singled out. The U.S. government has implemented a mandatory registration for nonimmigrant aliens from the Arab and Muslim world. They are also profiled and subject to special surveillance by law enforcement. Thus, the "crackdown" on terrorism created discrimination toward Arab Americans in travel, housing, and educational and work opportunities. Whether that discrimination was a necessary side effect of the government's need to provide security, or was an unacceptable form of discrimination, is currently debated.

Immigration and Minorities

In the early 1900s, when immigration into the United States reached its peak, some 1 million persons were arriving every year, the great majority from Europe. Nationalities tended to group together. For a while, they became isolated islands of culture, continuing among themselves to speak their own language and to perpetuate their own traditions. At first, most immigrants took the unskilled jobs and occupied the lowest place in the class structure, consequently pushing into the upper classes a larger proportion of older immigrant residents than might otherwise have been found there. These older residents had the advantage of being on high ground earlier, as a result of which they not only knew the language and customs, but also in many cases had accumulated property.

In some ways, the situation of European immigrants was like that of a minority ethnic group. The difference lay in the fact that although most second- and third-generation individuals from ethnic groups were still set apart and considered unassimilable no matter how Americanized they became, those from the Caucasian nationality groups had little trouble, in a generation or two, in identifying with the major group.

Restrictions on Immigration.   Until 1890, most immigrants to the United States were from northwestern Europe. Then immigration from southern and eastern Europe began to grow, and Mexican immigration also increased. Many "old" Americans, and even some of the earlier immigrants, were strongly prejudiced against southern and eastern Europeans. Demands for restrictive legislation led to laws limiting immigration.

In 1921, the first **Immigration Quota Act,** designed to reduce immigration to specified annual quotas for each national group, was passed. The quota for each country was 3 percent of the number of people living in the United States in 1910 who were of that national origin. The effect of this legislation was a sharp reduction in immigration from the countries of central, eastern, and southern Europe. Later, the quotas were reduced,

Illegal immigrants sometimes die during their attempts to sneak into the United States.

and in 1924 the maximum total number of immigrants to be admitted annually was cut to 150,000. The quota laws did not apply to countries in the Western hemisphere.

During the years following World War II, Congress passed various immigration acts to admit considerable numbers of immigrants over and above the quotas. Most of these were Europeans displaced from their homes by World War II or by the 1956 Hungarian rebellion against communist rule. Later, as we have already mentioned, Cuban and Asian refugees were admitted under special legislation.

But in 1965, under pressure from people who considered our immigration laws discriminatory, Congress passed an act that provided for the complete abandonment of national quotas by mid-1968. Under this act, admittance is based not on national origin but on the U.S. need for the training or skills of a would-be immigrant. Various special immigration laws applying to groups such as Cubans, Southeast Asians, Irish, and political refugees have been passed since 1965. In addition, many classes of immigrants are exempt from any numerical limitations—such as immediate relatives of U.S. citizens. The change in the composition of immigration can be seen in Figure 12.1.

In 1989, the United States again changed the quotas, cutting the number of Asians allowed and increasing the number of Soviets. These actions created a political stir. In 1990, Congress overhauled the immigration laws, raising the quota of immigrants by nearly 50 percent and allowing entry for a larger percentage of immigrants who were not related to U.S. citizens. It also created 30,000 slots for wealthy foreigners of any origin who would guarantee that they would invest at least $1 million in the United States. This led to charges that the United States was selling U.S. citizenship.

In 1997, the Illegal Immigration Act went into effect. It substantially deliberalizes the conditions under which a U.S. citizen or legal resident can sponsor a would-be immigrant and makes permanent residency much harder to achieve than under the older laws. It also increases the requirements for various formal certificates, such as birth and marriage, that an immigrant has to meet. This legislation makes it harder for immigrants to comply with the formalities that the law directs employers to investigate before giving a job to an immigrant.

The effectiveness of our immigration laws, especially when we consider that some seem to conflict with others, has been questioned. First, their application and enforcement have not been consistent: leverage can and has been exerted for individuals or small groups. Second, the crucial task of controlling illegal entry along our long northern and southern borders and the approaches by sea (not to mention exotic tactics, such as parachuting) is a formidable one for the available authorities. Even legal admissions are difficult to enforce

Figure 12.1

Legal immigrants by continent, 1820 to 2008. The large jump in 1990 is due to the legalization of many Mexican immigrants (later years on the time axis are extended for easier viewing of recent changes). (Source: U.S. Bureau of the Census, Statistical Abstract of the United States; BCIS, Yearbook of Immigration Statistics.)

because there is insufficient monitoring of students and other visitors to see that they comply with the restrictions of their visas or do not outstay their permissions.

Dealing with Undocumented Aliens.   The **Immigration and Naturalization Service (INS)** estimates that about 12 million undocumented aliens live in the United States, a number that had increased by more than 500,000 a year for several years, but finally peaked in 2007. About 40 percent of undocumented aliens have entered the country legally but outstay their visas; the others primarily are unauthorized Mexicans. This 12 million does not include those immigrants folded into the population when in 1986 the United States passed legislation imposing more restrictions on new illegal immigration while at the same time making provisions for legitimizing the status of some of the 2.7 million aliens already illegally living and working in the United States at that time. This law legalized a large group of formerly Undocumented aliens, but also made employers subject to penalties for employing illegal aliens. The resulting large one-time jump in Mexican immigration is evident in Figure 12.1.

The 1986 law was not highly successful. After the passage of the law, illegal Mexican immigration initially held constant. However, until the 2007 recession, it increased as the demand for low-wage workers in the United States was high. In the 2000s, there has been much debate about illegal immigration. There was a push for legislation that would establish a guest worker program and allow many undocumented workers to stay in the United States, while at the same time increasing border enforcement. The basic structure of that legislation had much in common with the 1986 law. Since that time, similar legislation has been debated, but none has passed.

Religious Minorities

A number of religious groups in this country espouse beliefs that lead them to follow ways of life somewhat different from the general pattern of U.S. culture. These include sects such as the Amish, the Seventh-Day Adventists, and the Jehovah's Witnesses. But their total number is small. At one time, Mormons could have been included, but after they officially abandoned polygamy they became, in their relation to U.S. culture, not very different from any other Christian sect.

Jews, however, form an important minority group whose influence on our society is greater than their numbers alone would seem to indicate. We have already considered the nature of Judaism in Chapter 9, but we will take up here a brief discussion of anti-Semitism. Prejudice or severe discrimination against Jews, called anti-Semitism, has existed for centuries and has been strong in certain countries at certain periods. Sometimes it has been tied to religion; sometimes it has been rationalized by dislike on the part of the majority of the population for certain cultural or "racial" characteristics, largely imaginary, attributed to Jews as a group. In some parts of eastern Europe, anti-Semitism has at times been taken to such extremes that thousands of Jews were killed, as in the pogroms, or organized massacres, that occurred in czarist Russia. But it was in Nazi Germany that anti-Semitism reached its height, for Jews constituted 6 million of the more than 10 million people who were murdered in Hitler's concentration camps.

Anti-Semitism continues to exist, although in the United States it has slowly diminished, perhaps in part because it was overshadowed by the greater problem of black–white relations. But in recent years, some Jews have felt that the level of prejudice was rising. Two factors may have contributed to this. First, when the new nation of Israel was established and conflict with the Arabs began, the majority of Jews were drawn together by a sense of pride, and many gave their full support to Israel. Often non-Jews do not share their sentiments. Second, as blacks have increased their demands for equality, some of them have tended to identify the Jewish merchant in the black ghetto as the symbol of white oppression.

In spite of such developments there is no clear evidence that in the country as a whole anti-Semitism is increasing. The long-run trend appears to be in the other direction. Intermarriage seems to be more and more common, although according to polls taken in recent years, Jewish opposition to it has fluctuated. Whether Jews in the United States will, after a few generations, lose their identity as a separate cultural group remains to be seen. But under modern conditions in our society, this may happen. At least there are no ethnic differences of the kind that make the complete assimilation of the blacks relatively difficult.

Another religious minority that has been experiencing discrimination is the Muslim population. Although we discussed discrimination against some Muslims earlier, it is important to remember that not all Arabs are Muslims and not all Muslims are Arabs. The U.S. Muslim population, estimated to be more than 5 million (estimates vary significantly from 3 million to 9 million), is diverse, with only about 12.5 percent ethnically Arab. A large percentage of Muslims are also blacks; they make up over 40 percent of all U.S. Muslims. The next largest percentage is South Asians at about 25 percent. Muslims can be found in every U.S. state, with the largest numbers in California and New York. Since 2001, many U.S. citizens have associated Islam (the religion of Muslims) with terrorism, even though only a small percentage of Muslims are terrorists. But all too often in recent times Muslims are judged guilty by association.

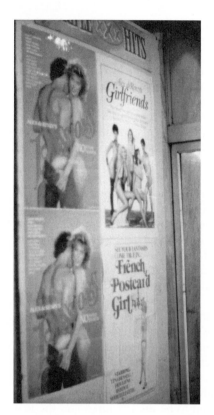

Pornography treating women as objects.

While discrimination on the basis of religion exists in the United States, relative to many other countries, the United States has a relatively good record. In China, a Christian is subject to persecution by the state. Even more severe persecution occurs in some Islamic countries. In Iran, for example, a person who converts from Islam to another religion may be subject to the death penalty.

Women

In today's society, the roles of men and women differ: Women are in some ways subordinated to men. Thus, although women make up a majority of the U.S. population, given this subordinate position they still are often referred to as a minority. Whether this subordinate position is acceptable is up to each one of us to decide, but in making that decision, we must be aware of the facts.

One fact is that our society has decided that discrimination is not legally allowed on the basis of sex, age, ethnicity, or national origin. Despite the law, there is discrimination against women. This discrimination takes many forms. Sometimes it is disguised as protection: Women are not allowed to do things because they are perceived as *the weaker sex;* the prohibition against women serving in combat in almost all of the armed forces is an example. Other times, the discrimination is built into the way men treat women—as objects rather than as human beings; pornography is a good example. Still other times the discrimination is in women's access to jobs: The perception that firms have of women's abilities often differs from the reality. The list goes on. We cannot provide a comprehensive list of the various practices of discrimination, partly because our space is limited and partly because the perception of discrimination varies from individual to individual.

To deal with this complex, subtle discrimination, many people supported a constitutional amendment, the **Equal Rights Amendment (ERA),** which stated simply: "Equality of rights under the laws shall not be denied or abridged . . . on account of sex." It needed ratification by three-fourths of the states, which it did not receive. Supporters point out that the state legislatures that defeated this amendment were all overwhelmingly staffed by males.

History of the Women's Movement. We can trace the women's movement, sometimes called feminism, at least as far back as the early nineteenth century. In the late 1800s and early 1900s, the suffragist movement continued its work. Women whose primary aim in the women's movement was to win the right to vote were called suffragettes. The women won this campaign in 1920. During World Wars I and II, women were called on to assume many of the tasks that had been assigned to men until the men were called into military service, and the women reaped many of the satisfactions. They found it difficult and, indeed, absurd to give up the freedoms they had won just because the wars ended and the men came home. But, as can be seen in the movie *Rosie the Riveter,* the government exerted strong pressure on women to resume their so-called proper role at home and to give up their jobs to men.

The principal permanent achievement marking women's contributions in World War I is the passage of the Nineteenth Amendment to the U.S. Constitution (1920) that gave them the right to vote. During World War II, women's performance in the civilian economy and their actual service in the armed forces gave them confidence to assert claims for greater equality. Their performance in the Persian Gulf War was superb, and following that war Congress passed a law authorizing women pilots to take part in combat. In the latest Iraq war, women have served honorably in combat roles, and women have been captured and held as prisoners of war. Still, the army is far from sex-neutral, and it allows only limited combat roles for women. Additionally, all men are required to sign up with the Selective Service System and thus may be drafted should the need arise. Women are not required to sign up and under present law cannot be drafted.

The fact that women were in the past and are now an actual majority of our people but yet have had a subordinate status similar to that of a minority makes their situation paradoxical. They are not a minority, but they are treated as one. In 1848, Lucretia Mott and Elizabeth Cady Stanton organized the first U.S. women's rights convention at Seneca Falls, New York. Then in 1869 Stanton, together with Susan B. Anthony, founded the National Woman Suffrage Association, which became known as the suffragist movement. More recently, the push for women's equality has been known as women's liberation.

Women have made significant gains in many areas. There are now more women in better-paying jobs; more women in colleges and graduate schools, in government office, in corporate boardrooms, in the highest ranking positions of financial institutions; and more women in professions such as medicine, the law, and engineering. Yet when we examine the record more closely, in many areas these gains seem to have little overall effect on equality. For example, only 20 to 25 percent of state legislators are female. In 2009, only 77 out of the 435 members of the House of Representatives were women, and there were only 18 female senators. Thus, primarily men are both the lawmakers and the law enforcers.

The average earnings of a woman are still less than the average for a man, even when equal work is performed. At managerial levels, women usually rise only to middle management jobs, and they tend to stay there. Many women tend to be segregated into "pink-collar jobs" such as teaching, nursing, and library work, which pay less than white-collar jobs. To see how women's earnings compare with those of men, see Table 12.2.

In addition, as women have comparatively recently entered occupations such as construction work, firefighting, and police forces, they tend to be the last hired and the first fired. None of these acts is necessarily discriminating on the individual or firm level. For example, many companies have established a seniority system that governs their hiring and firing. Thus they are required by the system to fire the last one hired, of which women constitute a larger percentage. With respect to pink-collar jobs, the schools, hospitals, museums, and libraries that offer these positions say they merely hire from the pool of those who apply and that they are not directing women to take the jobs.

Much of the gender discrimination occurs too early and is too subtle and built into the system to attribute to specific individuals. If you take a poll in your class, you may find that the men have higher career aspirations than the women. Why?

It might be that in childhood the boys were pressured harder; it was made clear to them that they would be ultimately responsible for their own lives. When a girl had difficulty completing a project, she might have been treated leniently. Or it may have been a career counselor who guided girls in a different direction from boys. A woman who was, say, a brilliant mathematician and a straight A student may have been counseled into education courses rather than to professional schools of business, finance, or international relations. Frustrated with teaching, she may leave that occupation to marry and have children. The fact that she made that decision does not mean she is unhappy or that her life is any less fulfilling (it may be more), but it does show the process by which women are channeled into certain careers.

Table 12.2

Earnings for Men and Women by Occupation, 2009

MEDIAN EARNINGS FOR VARIOUS FULL-TIME WORKERS BY OCCUPATION IN 2009 (WEEKLY, IN DOLLARS)

Occupation	Male	Female
Managerial, professional, and related	1258	907
Office and administrative support	664	601
Service	516	411
Farming, fishing, and forestry	413	404
Installation, maintenance, and repair	772	743
Production	660	450

Source: Bureau of Labor Statistics, *Economics News Releases.*

Reasons for Women Entering the Workforce.   Former Congresswoman Patricia Schroeder pinpointed one of the most important reasons for women to enter the workforce when she argued that the primary reason they do so in such unprecedented numbers is that they have to maintain their families. Many family women work because they must work. For others, although families have become smaller, wants have become larger. Therefore, for these family women, work is not an actual necessity but it is a social need: It is the only way the family can meet its desires. However, for black and other minority females, work has been a necessity for much longer than for white females. Women in the workforce as a percentage of total women of working age rose from 32 percent in 1972 to over 70 percent in the early 2000s. According to the 2000 census, 64.5 percent of two-parent families with children under age eighteen had both parents working. (This percentage had risen from 33 percent in 1976.) Analysts who study such trends say that the percentage of working women with children is expected to continue to grow even though some very high-income women may choose to stop working and stay home with their children.

It is sometimes argued that for many women the decision to work is not as important as that for men because they work only to provide "extras," often listed as a second car, a vacation home, restaurant meals—items that can be seen as frivolous or self-indulgent. If this is so, then women can be paid less because their earnings are not essential and their attachment to the labor force is intermittent. Others argue that this argument is wrong for two reasons. First, not all women are one-half of a couple, and approximately half of all families headed by women live below the poverty level. Their need for income is as great as, or greater than, a man's. But, more important, the argument is wrong because it is both immoral and illegal to pay one individual less than another individual for the same work.

The breakdown of the family has had its most telling impact on women. The outlook for women and their children who do not have their father living with them is not bright—many absent fathers make no child support payments, or do so at a level substantially lower

One Woman's Struggle

Stratification is millions of personal stories. What breaks down stratification is individual fortitude and initiative. Here's one of those stories.

Burnita S. Matthews, who was born in 1894, was the first woman ever appointed as a judge to a U.S. federal court. She had to wait until she was sixty-four years old to get that judgeship.

Her father sent her brother to law school and Burnita to a music conservatory. On her own, she went to law school at night, graduating in 1919. She then applied to the U.S. Veterans Administration for a lawyer's job; the Veterans Administration told her they would never hire a woman. She sent her membership dues to the Bar Association; they returned her check. She opened her own law office anyway.

In 1949, President Harry S Truman appointed her to the judgeship. All the other judges in her court were men, of course. One of them made a public announcement: "Mrs. Matthews would be a good judge, but there is one thing wrong—she's a woman." The other judges agreed among themselves to give her the most boring work the court had. She did the work and stuck

to her job. In fact, she never officially retired. She heard her last district court case in 1983, when she was eighty-eight.

As the years went on after her appointment, things got better for women. Matthews eventually got important cases on which to work. For instance, she ruled that Black Muslims had a right to attend religious services of their choice even though they were in jail. She ruled that people who receive disability benefits from Social Security can't have the money suddenly cut off just because the government decides they aren't disabled anymore. The people are entitled to a hearing and a chance to show that the government is wrong, and they are allowed to keep their checks unless the government can justify stopping the money.

A federal judge has younger lawyers working for her (or him). Matthews always employed women lawyers. She said, "I always chose women because often when a lawyer does well, the authorities say that some man did the work. I wanted everyone to know that when one of my lawyers did well, the work was done by a woman."

Burnita Matthews died in 1988, her life a symbol of overcoming barriers of stratification.

More and more women are doing "male" jobs.

than the amounts ordered by the court. In the last thirty years, laws have been passed to improve the situation. For example, in 1984 Congress allowed attachment of wages in certain cases, and in 1991 a federal law authorizing wage attachment for all absent parents who did not live up to their child support obligations was passed. Subsequent adjustments to federal law have mandated additional measures such as that employers must report newly hired employees to a national data bank to find out whether any of them owe child support payments. But it is still difficult for most single parents (generally women) to collect.

The situation for divorced women is also precarious. It has been said that for a woman the surest road to poverty is divorce. The majority of women who should receive alimony payments often do not, as many men who are supposed to make these payments default (some, in all fairness, cannot meet these financial demands). The tendency to give child custody to women still prevails, although more recently judges have been awarding custody either jointly or solely to the father. Because most women earn less than men, the financial burden of a divorced woman with children can be overwhelming.

We have been saying that women work for the same reasons men do: to make a living and provide for their families. But there are other reasons, which women share with men, for their desire to work: self-fulfillment and personal satisfaction. Apart from the basic satisfaction of seeing their work rewarded with money—the symbol of reward in our society, whatever opinion we may have of that symbol—women want to accept the challenges of competition and the acquisition and manipulation of new skills, to associate with peers, and to make contributions to the success of projects and enterprises.

Many men feel threatened or inconvenienced by the changes at home and at work caused by new attitudes and conditions. Men who were raised by traditional patriarchal fathers are baffled and confused by what has amounted to a kind of social revolution.

Yet the women's movement has affected men in several positive ways. Large numbers of men, either married or divorced, have become househusbands, taking on household and child care tasks and finding a new joy in being closer to their children. Although many women still end up with a larger share of the housework and the care of the children, men for the most part are beginning to appreciate the burdens and drudgery that women have long handled alone. Significant numbers of men have found themselves liberated from ancient stereotypes that barred them from kitchens and nurseries at home and nursing and clerical work in the workplace. Some men have begun to realize that to equalize duties is also to free males from the superman image of sole provider and family mainstay, reducing their tension.

Not all men are willing or able to take on the duties of child care. Good day care is hard to come by, and although some firms have established on-site day-care facilities, these companies represent a tiny minority. One solution has been the classic method of changing the problem instead of finding the answer: namely, to reduce the number of children. Especially among professional women earning high incomes and enjoying the exhilaration of the competitive business or professional world, childbearing has been postponed or even specifically declared to be completely outside their plans.

This tendency has been countered in recent years by a number of women finding that the desire to have at least one child is strong, resulting in an upsurge in the number of children born to mothers between the ages of 35 and 45. Such a development brings us full circle: Trying to work at a full-time job while simultaneously caring for a house and family, even if the family work is shared, is demanding, requiring almost a superwoman to achieve it. As one woman said in a *New York Times* interview, "People say to me, 'You go to school, you have a great job, a wonderful child and a wonderful husband, and your house looks clean. Wow!' But what's interesting is that I'm not planning to do that anymore. I've done the superwoman thing. And now that I know that I can do it, my question is: Do I want to do it? Do I want to live like that? Do I want to set the alarm for two and study until four? And the answer is absolutely not!"

Despite the problems, the issue of women's rights will not disappear—their proportion of the total workforce and their need to work and earn a decent wage cannot be denied. Many men remain unconvinced that helping women surmount the obstacles still in their path will probably be good for men. It is, however, quite possible that both sexes can gain from a more equitable policy toward women and that both men and women can find, through their less traditional roles, a new sense of trust, mutual respect, and cooperation.

Discrimination Based on Sexual Preference.   People are also discriminated against based on sexual orientation. Members of the Lesbian, Gay, Bisexual, and Transgendered Coalition argue that they experience enormous discrimination, both in the way people think about them and in finding work. For example, the U.S. armed forces had a rule that all homosexuals must resign from the army. Some homosexuals who have been discharged from the armed services have gone to court to try to gain reinstatement. In 1991, there were signs from the Secretary of Defense that this discriminatory barrier would be reconsidered. In 1994, the Department of Defense agreed to a compromise policy allowing homosexuals to serve in the military—known as the "don't ask, don't tell, don't pursue," rule which effectively allows those who do not reveal their sexual preference to serve in the military. In 2009, that policy was found to be in violation of the U.S. Constitution by a lower federal appeals court, so we may see some change in it in the future.

Other instances in which people with same-sex sexual preferences have tried to overcome discrimination by going to court include the case of the Boy Scouts of America. The Boy Scouts refused to let a scoutmaster continue in that work when they found out he was gay. He sued on his own behalf and on behalf of other gays, but he lost in every court to which he appealed, including the U.S. Supreme Court, which in 2000 decided that as a private organization the Boy Scouts had a right to exclude persons based on their sexual orientation.

To try to counteract that discrimination, gays have been pushing for explicit gay rights laws and hate-crime bills. Some of the proposed gay rights laws specifically prohibit discrimination on the basis of sexual orientation, and the proposed hate-crime bills make crimes that reflect underlying prejudice subject to stronger than normal penalties. More recently, a number of states, including Massachusetts, Connecticut, Vermont, Iowa, New Hampshire and Maine, began allowing state sanctioned same-sex marriage. California courts allowed it, but in response a referendum modified the California constitution disallowing it. A number of other state legislatures and courts are reviewing the issue, so we are likely to see more changes in the future.

Senior Citizens

A final characteristic that plays an important role in our society is age. Age stratification must be considered on a slightly different basis from the other characteristics we have been discussing. Whereas we are born either male or female, the characteristics of aging are universal for both sexes. Aging is inevitable, and Ponce de León's fountain of youth remains a legend.

Some stratification according to age is inevitable. As children, we are unable to care for ourselves and are thus separated from older age groups who productively contribute to society. As we grow old, our physical abilities decline and we are not able to do all that we once could, again creating a group separate from others. There is, however, no clear demarcation line as we move from youth to middle-age to being elderly. **Chronological age,** or age measured in years, often does not reflect a person's mental age or capacity to work and contribute to society.

Senior Citizens' Role in Society. In primitive societies, few individuals live to an old age because of poor health care systems and their difficult lifestyle in general. The few who do live to old age are venerated as sources of information and wisdom. In modern industrial societies, because of advanced technology life expectancy has almost doubled since 1900, and the elderly are not a scarcity. Because in these societies, great value is placed on physical achievement, grace, and agility, the normal physical slowdown that characterizes aging has been accompanied by decreased status for the elderly. Sometimes the output of senior workers has not been thought to be worth their wages. Even though it is against federal law for employers to discriminate against older workers, businesses often have been successful in finding ways around the law to get rid of these workers. Most of the elderly live productive and active lives, but when they can no longer do so they have retreated to retirement communities if they can afford them, or, if they need a lot of care, they have had to enter nursing homes, some of which have been described as "waiting rooms for death."

As medical technology advances, the perception of what it is to be an older person, and what an older person can do, has changed. In the early 2000s, a significant number of older people are reaching their mid-eighties or older in good health. The proliferation of knowledge about DNA and gene function has fostered so much research that previously unheard-of increases in life expectancy have been predicted, although today the work is highly theoretical and practical results, if any, are probably decades in the future. But it is not outside the realm of possibility that in the coming decades life expectancy could increase by 20 or 30 percent should the "aging gene" be found and science discover how to modify it.

The Growth in the Proportion of Senior Citizens. As you can see in Figure 12.2, the proportion of the elderly population has been growing. In 1900, less than 4 percent of the total population was sixty-five years of age or older. In 2010, they numbered about 39 million, about 13 percent of the total population. Projections are that their number will rise to about 70 million by the year 2030, or about 20 percent of the projected population. The growth is more substantial for those over eighty-five. In 1985, there were more than 2 million people over age eighty-five; in 2000, there were more than 4 million, and it is projected that by 2050, there will be about 21 million, or about 5 percent of the projected population.

This growth of the elderly population is beginning to present significant economic and social problems. For instance, the amount of Social Security benefits, including medical insurance payments, for the elderly has placed a strain on the Social Security system, and as the proportion of mostly nonworking elderly grows in relation to the number of younger, working contributors, fewer and fewer workers will be supporting more and more elderly. This causes anxiety about the solvency of the fund and resentment on the part of younger workers.

In the early 2000s, over 35 percent of the federal budget was spent on the elderly, and federal spending on the elderly is projected to be 42.8 percent of the 2010 budget, yet some studies show that the over-sixty-five group is financially better off than younger groups, partly because of relatively generous Social Security benefits and partly because of various tax advantages. Many younger workers believe they will find the Social Security fund empty when it is their turn to seek benefits as elderly

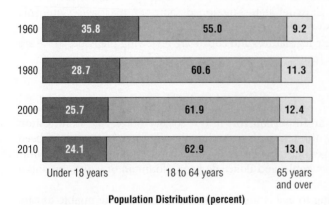

Figure 12.2

Resident population: age distribution. (Source: U.S. Bureau of the Census, Statistical Abstract of the United States.)

persons; in the meantime, they are making high Social Security tax payments—in many cases higher than their income tax liability—and some are bitter about this mix. They ask why they should pay for all of these giveaways.

The problem of care for the elderly is increasing, along with the difficulty of providing older people with opportunities for a meaningful life. These problems have been worsened by changing family structures. With the decline of extended families, children often do not include their parents in social activities. These changing family structures are likely to continue for many years, and as they do the problems of finding a role for grandparents and great-grandparents in the family are likely to increase. To argue that a role for grandparents in the family is desirable does not mean that parents should be considered an appendage of their children's family. On the whole, the elderly prefer to live independently, yet at the same time contact with family and friends remains a vital part of their lives.

Age Discrimination.   In reaction to the problems facing older people, the gerontological set has turned to political and social activism, demanding their rights as individuals and as workers. They have formed groups such as the Gray Panthers, who play an active role in the political arena. These groups helped to win passage of the Age Discrimination Act of 1967, which prohibits discrimination against persons between the ages of forty and sixty-five. Moreover, in the Age Discrimination in Employment Act of 1978, the mandatory retirement age was raised from sixty-five to seventy, and in 1986 it was eliminated for most occupations. The elderly are an effective political force; when the AARP (American Association of Retired Persons), which has more than 35 million members, speaks, lawmakers tend to listen. Because their numbers are expected to continue to grow at such an impressive rate, their influence can only increase over the next few decades.

The issues involved in age discrimination are not simple ones. For example, a sixty-year-old person differs from a twenty-five-year-old person; each relates to people in a different way. If a store believes customers prefer to have younger salespeople, should it be against the law if it "discriminates" on the basis of age? Under current laws, it is. Alternatively, some firms used the sixty-five or seventy retirement age to ease out employees who were unable to keep up, without having to state explicitly the reason for their release. Under the Age Discrimination in Employment Act, they cannot blame the change on a general rule and thus save face for both. Training older persons as new employees presents another problem. Many jobs require years of training, and in order to recoup an investment in a worker, a firm counts on that employee working for the firm for a sufficiently long period of time.

The argument can, of course, be reversed. Some firms have fired workers right before retirement in order to save pension payments. Others have merely fired older workers in order to have a better image, using "training" or "customers' perception" as an excuse. Age group conflicts are beginning to appear as the percentage of wage earners goes down and the number of pension recipients increases. The dilemma in many firms is in deciding whether to keep on older workers, who have had much experience, or to hire in their place a younger workforce with more energy and newer ideas. In fact, in the early 2000s as worker shortages developed, some firms began to welcome workers at and above retirement age because of their reliability and their work ethic. In the future, we are certain to hear more about the employment issues of age, whether discussing a young workforce or an older workforce, because, as discussed here and earlier in the chapter, they are indicative of an ongoing change in the structure of our society.

Senior activists march against age discrimination.

Conclusion

At this point we end our discussion of stratification and the issues it raises, but not because we have exhausted the topics—we have only touched on many of them. We end it because of the pressure of space and the variety of other topics to be covered. Most of these other topics—social institutions, economics, and politics—deal with some of the same issues from a different perspective, and each perspective provides yet another insight into the problems of society and the workings of social scientists' minds.

Our discussion of stratification was designed to encourage you to draw your own conclusions. Obviously, merely in the way the chapters are written, certain biases became clear, although we worked hard to keep the analyses as objective as possible.

We can, however, conclude that stratification and discrimination do exist. Of that there is little doubt. It also seems fair to say that the issues are far more complicated than the advocates of either side generally present, and we must be careful not to focus too strongly on one side's argument. We raise the methodology issue at this point because most of us are involved in some type of discriminatory action—either discriminating or being discriminated against. It is at precisely such instances when our objectivity leaves us and we find the fairness or unfairness of the situation clear and beyond question. At this point, rational discourse breaks down. Whenever you seem to have such a strong belief, count to ten and try to "walk a mile in the other person's shoes."

Key Points

- Four reasons for ethnic prejudice are the influence of tradition, psychological needs, ego, and economic advantages.
- A minority group is a group of people singled out for unequal, negative treatment, whereas a dominant group is singled out for positive treatment.
- Although the United States has made progress in dealing with the problem of prejudice against various ethnic groups, it still has a long way to go.
- Hispanics with historical and cultural ties to Latin America are called Latinos, whereas those with ties to Mexico are called Chicanos.

- Undocumented Mexican immigration continues to be a problem despite several recent laws meant to deal with it.
- Anti-Semitism has been reduced, but it remains a potential problem.
- Anti-Islamic discrimination is on the rise in the United States.
- Women have made strides toward equality but still have a way to go before they achieve full equality.
- Senior citizens are likely to be a major political force in the twenty-first century.

Some Important Terms

affirmative action programs (236)
Chicanos (239)
chronological age (251)
de facto segregation (234)
de jure segregation (234)
discrimination (229)

dominant groups (231)
Equal Rights Amendment (ERA) (247)
ethnic group (227)
Hispanics (239)
Immigration and Naturalization Service (INS) (245)

Immigration Quota Act (243)
Latinos (239)
minority groups (231)
prejudice (228)
separate-but-equal doctrine (233)

Questions for Review and Discussion

1. Why are racial and ethnic differences largely independent of each other?
2. Has it been proved that some ethnic groups are superior to others in their capacity for mental development? Has it been proved that all ethnic groups are alike in their inborn capacities for mental and emotional development? Explain.
3. How would you explain the existence and the extent of ethnic prejudice in the world?
4. What is the relationship of prejudice to discrimination?
5. Why is the position of the black minority different from that of any other minority group?
6. What effect did the Supreme Court cases of *Plessy v. Ferguson* and *Brown v. Board of Education* have on legal segregation?
7. What are the obstacles to the elimination of de facto school segregation?
8. How does the economic position of blacks compare with that of whites? List the major factors that have brought economic gains to blacks.
9. What advances have been made in protecting the civil and political rights of black Americans? Which do you think have been most significant? Discuss what still needs to be accomplished.
10. Are blacks continuing to improve their social, political, and economic position? Defend your point of view.
11. What does Gunnar Myrdal mean when he says that no social problem as complex as the U.S. race problem is ever solved in an "absolute" sense?
12. Why are friendly relations between ethnic groups important to both the dominant and the minority groups?
13. What is the social and economic status of Latinos and Chicanos in U.S. society?
14. Discuss the history of Asian migration to the United States.
15. How do you account for the existence of anti-Semitism in both Europe and the United States?
16. Is discrimination against Muslims acceptable because of national security needs?
17. What might be some of the reasons the average earnings for a woman are lower than the average earnings for a man? Does this necessarily imply discrimination by individuals or firms?
18. What determined your career aspirations? Do those aspirations reflect institutional discrimination?
19. How is the growth in the proportion of people over age sixty-five in the population likely to affect our society?
20. What differentiates age discrimination from other types of discrimination?
21. If a store prefers to hire younger salespeople, should it be allowed to do so? Why or why not?

Internet Questions

1. What is the National LGBT Bar Association (www.lgbtbar.org)?
2. Go to www.eeoc.gov, the website of the U.S. Equal Employment Opportunity Commission. What is their latest news announcement?
3. Go to www.newsweek.com/id/141165 and read the article. What group is the most satisfied in the military? How does this compare to civilian occupations? What is the likely reason for these results?
4. The Arab American Institute (www.aaiusa.org) identifies some famous Americans of Arab descent. List the names familiar to you, perhaps through sports or entertainment.
5. Based on www.hrw.org/news, what does the Human Rights Watch organization list as one of the issues involving the United States and human rights?

For Further Study

Dreisinger, Baz, *Near Black: White-to-Black Passing in American Culture,* Cambridge, MA: University of Massachusetts Press, 2009.

Eberstadt, Mary, *Home-Alone America: The Hidden Toll of Day Care, Wonder Drugs, and Other Parent Substitutes,* Seabrook, MD: Sentinel, 2004.

Ephron, Nora, *I Feel Bad about My Neck: And Other Thoughts about Being a Woman,* New York: Knopf, 2006.

Gates, Henry Louis, Jr., *America Behind the Color Line,* New York: Warner Books, 2004.

Malcomson, Scott L., *One Drop of Blood: The American Misadventure of Race,* New York: Farrar, Straus & Giroux, 2000.

McWhorter, John, *Winning the Race: Beyond the Crisis in Black America,* New York: Gotham, 2006.

Myrdal, Gunnar, *An American Dilemma,* 2 vols., New York: Pantheon, 1975.

Obama, Barack, *Dreams from My Father: A Story of Race and Inheritance,* New York: Crown, 2004.

Pelzer, Dave, *A Child Called "It,"* Deerfield Beach, FL: Health Communications, 2004.

Smoak, Gregory, *Ghost Dancers and Identity: Prophetic Religion and American Indian Ethnogenesis,* Berkeley: University of California Press, 2006.

Suárez-Orozco, Carola, and Marcelo M. Suárez-Orozco, *Children of Immigration,* Cambridge, MA: Harvard University Press, 2001.

Williams, Lena, *It's the Little Things: The Everyday Interactions That Get under the Skin of Blacks and Whites,* New York: Harcourt, 2000.

Yalle, Victor M., and Rodolfo D. Torres, *Latino Metropolis,* Minneapolis: University of Minnesota Press, 2000.

Young, Cathy, *Ceasefire! Why Women and Men Must Join Forces to Achieve True Equality,* New York: Free Press, 1999.

WWW   American Association for Retired Persons www.aarp.org

WWW   Anti-Defamation League www.adl.org

WWW   Human Rights Watch www.hrw.org

WWW   National Association for the Advancement of Colored People www.naacp.org

WWW   National Organization for Women www.now.org

WWW   Public Broadcasting Service Race www.pbs.org/race

WWW   U.S. Citizenship and Immigration http://www.uscis.gov

WWW   U.S. Department of Justice www.usdoj.gov

The Functions and Forms of Government

After reading this chapter, you should be able to:

- List five primary functions of government
- Identify three contrasting views of government
- Explain the liberal, conservative, radical, reactionary, and anarchist philosophies of government
- Distinguish a democracy from an autocracy
- List some distinguishing characteristics of a democracy
- Explain the democratic concept of the individual
- List the common justifications for an autocracy
- List four characteristics of an autocracy

Government after all is a very simple thing.

—Warren G. Harding

There never was a more pathetic misapprehension of responsibility than Harding's touching statement.

—Felix Frankfurter

Are governments necessary? To answer this question, all we have to do is look around the world to what happens when an effective government does not exist: to Iraq, where, after the U.S. army moved in, the country was left without an effective government, and anarchy and looting were widespread; and to Somalia, where in 2009, because no effective government existed, competing factions fought for control, spreading devastation throughout the countryside—looting, raping, and murdering almost indiscriminately. The list could go on, but these two examples make the point: Effective government is necessary.

Government is the set of institutions by which a society is ruled. People often disagree violently about the role that government should play in society, which accounts for many of the political conflicts within a nation. Much of the controversy over the proper role of government in society arises from different conceptions of society and government, and any discussion of political and governmental concepts requires some common agreement on the meaning of these terms.

In the first part of this chapter, we look at the various functions of government. Then in the second part we consider the various forms of government and how they operate. Finally, in the third section we examine various views of government.

As with all social institutions, there is a presumption that if an institution exists it serves some function. Government is no exception. The **functionalist approach** to government argues that what exists must exist as it is and not be tampered with because it serves a necessary function. That is too rigid a position for most social scientists but that does not mean that the Functionalist approach is not important. In this book we have emphasized change and how change modifies the role that institutions play in society. Thus we may find that institutions that once played a functional role may now play a quite different role, maybe functional, maybe dysfunctional. To decide that, we have to consider carefully the functions government serves in our society.

The Primary Functions of Government

In every society of any size, some form of organized government develops due to the need for an agency capable of exercising overall social control. The role of government can be better understood if we examine the specific functions most governments perform or claim to perform.

Maintaining Internal Order and External Security

Though the functions of government are many and varied, its basic job is to protect its citizens from internal and external enemies. The highest value in every political society is self-preservation, and the government is the one agency equipped to protect a nation. It alone possesses the power to enforce obedience to the rules of life that the society has established, and it alone has at its disposal all the military might that the nation can provide to repel aggression.

Government, as the guardian of internal social order, employs police, prisons, and courts in its attempts to protect persons, property, rights, and whatever society designates as worthy of preservation. None of our other social institutions could exist without the "domestic tranquility"—the peace and safety—that government provides. Wherever law and order break down, the government is unable to perform its other functions; the people become fearful, and all aspects of society begin to disintegrate. **Anarchy** is a society without government or law.

Anarchy generally is so injurious to society that, after a period of social confusion, people sometimes welcome as a blessing a dictator who can restore peace and order. Recognition of this fact led Thomas Hobbes, the seventeenth-century English philosopher, to conclude that government results from a contract among free men desirous of preserving life and of increasing its contentment—"that is to say, of getting themselves out from that miserable condition of war" that necessarily results from the absence of effective government.

Most advanced modern nations have eliminated internal warfare and reduced internal violence to such a low level that nearly all the conflicts that arise among their citizens are settled in an orderly and peaceful manner. When countries have not succeeded in doing this, bloodshed, destruction, and agony tear them apart, as we have seen clearly in places such as Iraq, Somalia, Rwanda, Sudan, the Republic of Congo, and others on a sad list.

Ensuring Justice

The belief in justice appears to be universal, and every modern government professes devotion to it. **Justice** is the maintenance or administration of what is considered fair—by law or by judicial proceedings. It is a concept that involves the relationships of individuals (and groups) both to society and to one another. Though justice means different things to different people and no one definition has been agreed on that describes its content, nearly every society considers it to mean "to everyone their due."

Not all governments strive for justice, although most generally profess to do so. All governments based on popular support aspire to convince the people that they are being treated justly. In fact, justices of the peace, sheriffs, judges, and courts exist in some form almost everywhere, and their main function is to administer justice.

People have confidence in their governments to the extent that they deal out rewards and punishment in accordance with the popular conception of justice. People willingly submit their private disputes for public settlement when they have faith that justice will be done. For example, a person whose home has been burglarized is generally willing to have the burglar prosecuted in a court of law, rather than attempting to secure personal revenge,

Somalia: A failed State and Modern Day Pirates

Somalia has been essentially a stateless society since the dictatorship of Siad Barre was overthrown in January 1991. It was not replaced with an effective government and the result has been anarchy and civil war. While a transitional federal government is in place, it has no ability to collect taxes and no real power base and is only kept in power by support from the Ethiopian government. That government has to contend with the Islamic Courts Union, which is another group vying for power, as well as with local warlords.

The results have been disastrous for Somalia, which has had no effective economy and no legal structure. Many now long for the stable days of the old dictatorship. Life in Somalia is difficult; if you have money, you have to pay protection to a warlord, and foreign aid workers have been kidnapped so many times and only let free when a ransom was paid that many aids groups have stopped operating there even though the needs are enormous. Trying to drive 30 miles from the airport to Mogadishu can mean stopping at seven or more "checkpoints" and each time paying a toll or an entry fee of up to $300, depending on the value of the goods you are transporting. Most schools have stopped functioning, and only about 15 percent of the children now go to primary school.

About the only business that is thriving is crime such as kidnapping and piracy, and ships are now avoiding the coast of Somalia to prevent their being taken over by pirates, as happened to the Saudi oil tanker, the *Sirius Star*, which was taken over by Somali pirates even though it was more than 50 nautical miles out at sea. Eventually, after the ships owners paid a multimillion dollar ransom, the ship was released. Political philosopher Thomas Hobbes wrote that "life is solitary, poor, nasty, brutish and short" without government. Somalia seems to be making his point.

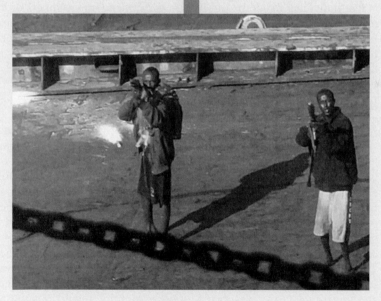

Somali pirates.

as long as that person is convinced the courts will deal fairly with the matter. When government fails to perform this function adequately, or loses the ability to enforce its decisions, lawlessness begins to spread, and revolution may even result.

Safeguarding Individual freedoms

Without some kind of government there can be no organized, stable society, and without a stable society there can be little real freedom for individuals. All governments profess to try to safeguard certain freedoms by maintaining law and order. But like the case of ensuring justice, not all governments actually do so. Democratic governments go further than nondemocratic governments; they have come to accept the defense of individual freedoms as a primary function. For example, the Constitution of the United States declares that a fundamental purpose of the union is to "secure the Blessings of Liberty to ourselves and our Posterity."

But in past times, when modern democracies were in the early stages of their development, government was often considered the enemy of freedom. Faith in government as the defender of individual freedoms has developed slowly over the years, until now in modern democracies there is a trend to look toward government for protection. Our federal government, for example, has taken action against monopolies, corrupt political practices, and discrimination against ethnic minorities and women.

There are, to be sure, two sides to this picture. Sometimes government regulations unjustly or needlessly restrict personal freedom, and there is always the danger that government may fall under the influence of special interests and fail to reflect the will of the majority. There is also likely to be debate about how much individual freedom should be infringed on to protect society. For example, after the 9/11 attacks, the U.S. Congress passed the **Patriot Act,** which gave the government the right to detain people it felt might be terrorists or others who might support them. The act greatly broadened the circumstances under which surveillance was permitted, especially with on-line activities. It required financial institutions to provide information on client transactions and bookstores and libraries to provide information about what books individuals checked out or bought. Some felt this law went too far; others felt it didn't go far enough. These debates are healthy. The reality is that individual freedoms can be safe only when large numbers of individuals, and also organized groups, are dedicated to their defense. The preservation of these freedoms necessitates an active and responsible vigilance on the part of the people who enjoy them. Individual freedoms are responsibilities as well as rights, and as such, they must be defended to ensure their continued strength and legitimacy.

Regulating Individuals' Actions

In the growth of modern societies, many institutions and groups have developed to perform various functions. Some of these institutions and groups provide important social services, but often they also have selfish interests that are contrary to the welfare of society. Where this is true, government may find it necessary to regulate their activities. Our great public utility enterprises illustrate this well. Because of the nature of their business, they tend to be monopolies, and, in the past, when they were left to themselves they often charged excessive prices and gave poor service. Therefore, to protect the public the government established procedures for controlling them. Since the 1980s, both in the United States and in other countries, many public utilities have been privatized—that is, sold by the government to private companies. Along with this has come some lessening of government regulation. However, some of the consequences of privatization and deregulation have been unexpected and undesirable. Examples include loose accounting regulations that played a role in the Enron and Worldcom accounting scandals, and electricity deregulation in California that led to an energy crisis and financial deregulation that contributed to the financial crisis of 2008. In such areas, governments are reinstituting controls and regulation.

Promoting the General Welfare

Government as the agency for overall social control cannot escape the task of promoting the general welfare in a variety of ways that go beyond the functions we have discussed. The general welfare activities of government have multiplied many times in recent decades, but governments have always to some degree undertaken by positive means to promote the material well-being of their citizens. Even the governments of antiquity carried on some welfare activities. At times they gave aid to farmers, subsidized other private enterprises, and even controlled prices.

The Bible relates how Joseph in Egypt supervised an extensive government program of buying and storing surplus grain to provide food in times of famine. The modern state extends and intensifies this ancient function of government.

Government provides the institutional structure within which economic and social interaction can take place. It regulates the economy; levies taxes; and prohibits, protects, and provides services to benefit individuals, groups, and the whole of society. Whether we think about it or not, every person every day is affected by the demands of government and by the benefits it provides. Whenever citizens leave home in a car, they drive on streets and roads provided by government; they can enjoy parks set aside by government; they can send their children to government-supported schools; they can travel abroad on government-issued passports, and in case of trouble can go to the consular or diplomatic agents of their government for aid; they can receive help from the government when they are unemployed or disabled; and if accused of breaking a law, they can be heard in a court established by government. These are only a few of the ways in which individuals are taxed, controlled, or benefited by government, all for the purpose of promoting the general welfare.

Welfare activities of government include health services, education, Social Security, and various other benefits. In the United States today there is debate about what kind of health insurance coverage the federal government should provide citizens, or about how to restructure the way it provides welfare services.

Governments furnish these benefits to meet public demands and to increase their own strength. Even dictatorships find it in their interest to provide workers with vacations and pensions on retirement. People who are deprived of their liberties are less likely to revolt against a government that appears to show consideration for their welfare. In democracies, where the political system makes public policy more directly responsive to public opinion, government has greatly broadened its welfare activities in response to the wishes of an enlarged electorate.

For centuries, students of politics have believed that if the masses were given the right to vote they would demand a redistribution of wealth and privileges. In modern democracies, wealth and income have been redistributed by such means as progressive income taxes, inheritance taxes, Social Security benefits, public assistance payments, and public housing projects. This redistribution has happened to varying degrees. For example, in the 1960s, the income tax was highly progressive, inheritance taxes were high, and there were numerous government programs to help the poor. In the 1980s and 1990s that tendency toward redistribution was reduced. For example, the degree of progressiveness of the income tax was lowered. Many of these changes were supported by the lower middle class, even though it did not help them economically. This support can be explained by a belief, held by many in the United States, that more effort should go into increasing total outputs—raising everyone's income—and less into redistribution of income. More recently, with new government programs such as health care expansion, the pendulum has been swinging the other way.

Debates about the Nature of Government

The preceding brief discussion summarized the various functions of government and debates about those functions. As you can see, although a government serves definite functions, there are spirited debates about these activities. In the evolution of the state over the centuries, the nature of government functions has in many ways remained the same. However, as other social institutions, such as the family and social mores, have evolved in response to technological change, the ways that governments carry out these functions have changed and so have the forms of government. Differences in culture have led different states down different paths and, therefore, to differing forms of government. We now turn to this issue.

Political Theory and Government

Government is by far the most powerful of all social institutions. It controls resources of extreme physical coercion, and it has taken over countless functions and responsibilities that once resided in the family, religion, and business enterprises, such as education and various social services. For example, in earlier times children took care of elderly parents; today, the government often does this through social programs such as Medicare. Although government today is in a position to regulate and control all other social institutions, it is in turn controlled by them. People's beliefs and attitudes and the ways they behave in the family, religion, and business enterprises determine the kind of government they develop, and often the expansion of government functions results from the failure of other institutions to meet social needs.

Politics is the means by which individuals affect government. Because of the importance of government and politics, an immense area of study, called political theory, has developed to study governments and politics. **Political theory** is that area of inquiry dealing with the nature of government and politics. Political theory has its origins in the writings of Aristotle, but our current systems of government are founded more on the writings of political theorists John Locke or Thomas Hobbes. Their alternative views of the relationships between the individual and the state form the basis of many modern **political ideologies**, deeply held beliefs in an idea—held so deeply and with such conviction that a person is willing to die for those beliefs. For example, **democracy**—the rule of the people—is the ideology of the United States, and it is rooted in the writings of John Locke. An alternative ideology, **fascism**—the belief in the rule of an elite whose members have special abilities—is the basis for what some people have argued is a preferable form of government as compared to democracy.

When two political ideologies meet, there often is conflict. For example, World War II was in some ways a conflict between fascism and democracy. Ideologies are closely related to various views of the nature of government. If we believe that there is no role in society for government, we will likely have a significantly different ideological position than someone who believes that government has a positive role.

Three Views of the Nature of Government

To organize our thinking about these issues, it is helpful to differentiate the following three views of the nature of government: (1) government as a necessary evil; (2) government as a positive good; and (3) government as an unnecessary evil.

Government as a Necessary Evil.   Government follows us all through life, telling us what we can and cannot do. If we want to drive a car, we must first pass a government examination and buy a government license; then government forbids us to park in convenient places and fines us for exceeding the speed limit. It forces us to stay in school when we want to go to work. (We are told that we are too young to work.) It has the right to take us out of school and compel us to enter military service. We can only become a lawyer or a doctor by securing a license from the government. If we earn any money, government claims a share in taxes. If we are fortunate enough during our lifetime to accumulate enough wealth to leave to our children, government may impose an inheritance tax. Such activities as these make government the object of complaint and abuse and cause many people to feel that, at best, government is a necessary evil.

The very essence of government is to prohibit, to restrain, to regulate, to compel, and to coerce. For example, government possesses the authority to pass laws and the power to enforce them. Parents, therapists, and employers may cajole and condemn, but only government can legally imprison. It regulates the affairs of family and economic enterprise in accordance with its conception of public security, morality, and welfare. Of all institutions of social control, government is the most inclusive and the most powerful. Here, indeed, is a power so great that no one can safely ignore it.

Government as a Positive Good.   Another picture of government can also be painted. Many years ago, Supreme Court Justice Oliver Wendell Holmes was asked by a young law clerk, "Don't you hate to pay taxes?" Justice Holmes is reported to have answered, "No, young man, I like to pay taxes. With taxes I buy civilization."

Some years later, when taxes were much higher, Supreme Court Justice William O. Douglas made another classic statement about government. He wrote,

> Government is the most advanced art of human relations. It dispenses the various services that the complexities of civilization require or make desirable. It is designed to keep in balance the various competing forces present in any society and to satisfy the dominant, contemporary demands upon it. As a result it serves a high purpose; it is the cohesive quality in civilization.

People such as those we have quoted think of government as a positive good. They realize there is some truth in Thomas Paine's contention that government is necessary "to supply the defect of moral virtue," to force us to do right when our moral weakness would lead us to injure one another. For these people, government is more than a "punisher"; it is a promoter of the common good. It is the proper social instrument for positive action to bring the essentials of the good life to all the people.

Government as an Unnecessary Evil.   Writers of communist doctrine offered another picture of government. **Communism** is a theory of social organization based on the holding of all property in common, actual ownership being ascribed to the community or state. Marx, Lenin,[1] and Stalin,[2] for example, portrayed government as an instrument of oppression, "special machinery for the suppression of one class by another." All capitalist governments, so the argument runs, are tools of the rich used to enforce the exploitation of the poor. Capitalist democracy allows the people "once every few years, to decide which particular representatives of the oppressing class should be in parliament to represent and oppress them." In communist theory, the **bourgeoisie** is the class that, in contrast to the proletariat or wage-earning class, is primarily concerned with property values.

In this way of thinking, machinery for suppression will be necessary only until the internal and external enemies of communism are converted or destroyed. In general, communist theory pictures government, or at least the coercive powers of government, as an unnecessary evil, to be abolished as soon as possible.

In this respect, communist theory resembles that of the anarchists. Communists have always considered government to be an unnecessary evil and have advocated the eventual abolition of all political authority and all instruments of coercion. It should be noted, however, that although Karl Marx, the early communist theoretician, wrote that there should be an end to the "coercive powers of government" and a "withering away" of the state, the former USSR and other communist nations found it difficult to follow their own ideology. Communist governments in the Soviet Union and a number of eastern European countries ended not because they withered away, but because they were removed by the very people whose interests, in theory, they were serving. Today there are very few purely communist governments. In China the Communist Party still rules, but it is reducing its pervasive role in the economy. The two countries that come the closest to having pure communist governments are Cuba and North Korea. In both, there are signs of change.

How Powerful Should Government Be?   Another way to classify people's views of government is by how strong a role they see government playing. Figure 13.1 represents various classifications of people's views, starting with those who see the least role for government and ending with those who see the strongest.

---

[1]V. I. Lenin, *State and Revolution*. A good edition in English is the revised edition, New York: International Publishers, 1932.

[2]Joseph Stalin, *Foundations of Leninism*, New York: International Publishers, 1939.

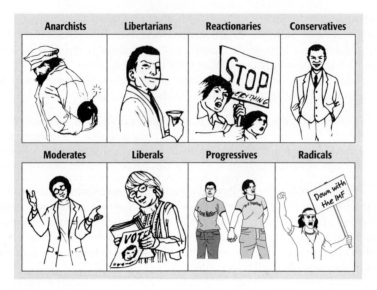

Figure 13.1

Views of the role of government: Some exaggerated characterizations.

Individuals who believe in the least role for government, such as anarchists and libertarians, argue that government necessarily limits individual freedom in an unacceptable way. **Anarchists** are people who believe that the institutions of society, such as private property and the state, exploit and corrupt humans. If these authoritarian structures were removed, people would be free to realize their intrinsic goodness and establish the communal lifestyle instinctive to all human beings. **Libertarians** are people who advocate greater freedom for individuals. They dislike arbitrary authority and argue for active freedom and the free expression of the individual personality. Libertarians, such as the philosopher Robert Nozick, see a role for a minimal state. They disagree with the anarchists, arguing that we need the state to provide defense against other states, but that much of what modern states do is harmful.

Next in our classification system come reactionaries. **Reactionaries** believe that more than a minimal government is necessary, but that the role government currently plays in society is much too large. They prefer turning back the clock and organizing under the smaller role they believe the government played in earlier times.

Anarchist, libertarian, and reactionary views are not widely held in the United States. Most individuals accept the need for government in a form similar to that which we now have. They differ primarily in degree and in the role they see government playing. The most commonly used terms, with their generally accepted descriptions, are the following: **Conservatives** favor a smaller role for government than currently exists; **moderates** favor about the same role for government as exists; and **liberals** favor a broader role for government than exists. These views of government are the predominant ones in the United States.

By considering the three different views of the role of government, you can see that the distinction between liberals and conservatives is not as clear-cut as the listing in the previous paragraph implies. In actuality, liberals tend to see government as a necessary evil and thus they favor limiting government's role of infringing on individual rights, emphasizing concepts such as freedom of speech and freedom to worship as one wishes. When liberalism was founded, its focus was on limiting the role of government—the position we now call conservatism. But over time, liberalism became associated with government establishing a framework within which individuals' freedoms have real meaning, and thereby it became

*R*epublicans, Democrats, and Political Ideologies

In the text, we develop a number of classifications of views of government, distinguishing conservatives, liberals, and moderates. Most of the political discussion in the news does not relate specifically to these groups, but instead to two political parties—Republican and Democrat. Democrats are often classified as liberals and Republicans as conservatives, but those classifications are misleading. The parties actually are coalitions of groups developed to win elections, not to espouse a particular political ideology, unless doing so will help them win elections. Thus, there is no close relationship between the two parties and the classifications, the meanings of which are themselves changing. Because of the difficulty of equating a political party with a particular ideology, more and more people in the United States are classifying themselves as political independents, who will support whichever candidate espouses positions most consistent with their overall views at a particular time.

This tendency of moderates to pull away from the party affiliations has let small groups of political activists increasingly control the agendas of the two parties—social conservatives in the case of the Republicans and social liberals in the case of the Democrats. These groups often combine with private interest groups, who have no specific political ideology other than to design laws to channel more money to themselves, to control the parties. This leads candidates on both sides to pander to the social activists and private interest groups during primary elections in which candidates are chosen. Then, once they win the primary, candidates portray themselves as more moderate in the general election as they try to put together a winning coalition.

We saw this happening in the 2008 election where initially both John McCain and Barack Obama "played to their base" with McCain emphasizing his conservative views and Obama emphasizing his liberal views. Then, after Obama won the primary, he moved toward more moderate positions that were much closer to middle ground policies than his positions in the primary.

associated with increasing the size of government, even though liberalism maintained its view of government as a necessary evil.

When conservatism was founded, its focus was on a strong government because conservatives saw the government as a keeper of the public morals and, hence, as a potential public good. Therefore conservatives felt that it was proper for government to legislate morality and to tell people what was right and what was wrong. With the rise in the 1980s of the Christian Coalition political groups in the United States, we can see some of these conservative positions being taken up again. The conservative viewpoint in the United States is also associated with policies such as lower taxes; elimination or reduction of regulation, both of public and private activities; highly structured elementary and secondary education, with frequent tests to be sure students are learning the basics; and an emphasis on the family values of stable marriage and careful rearing of children by the parents.

To illustrate, it is the conservatives who generally support the government's right to legislate whether certain sexual activities such as sodomy are legal. Liberals generally oppose the government's right to control an individual's intimate life. In this example, liberals support less, not more, government. New Right conservatives generally support the government's right to control individual sexual practices, because these conservatives see the government as a positive good—as the keeper of the society's moral code. Therefore, on such issues conservatives favor a stronger government role whereas liberals favor a weaker government role. Over such issues the commonly accepted distinctions break down.

Not all groups fit this classification. For example, you may often hear the term *radical.* **Radicals** believe that the existing government must be changed from what it is to something else. They do not necessarily favor a larger or smaller role for government—just a change from the existing situation. Progressives also advocate for change and reform of government, but are considered less "radical" than radicals. Theodore Roosevelt was one of the United States' most prominent progressives, and when he ran as a Progressive Party candidate in 1912, he won the largest share of votes for a third party candidate in U.S. history.

Elements of Truth in Each of the Views

All of these views of the role that government plays in society contain elements of truth. Differences of opinion arise in part from differences in governments and in part from the different functions that every government performs. Governments have been oppressive and have exploited the masses; they have at times been almost exclusively concerned with restraining the unruly elements in human society; they have also been used by society to promote by positive means the common good. A rational evaluation of government must be based on many considerations, and important among these is an examination of the primary functions of government common to all modern societies.

Forms of Government

Of the many ways to divide governments, none is perfect. The first distinctions we draw are democratic, nondemocratic, and partially democratic countries.

Both the word and the concept of *democracy* come from the Greeks: *demos* means "people" and *kratos* means "rule." Thus democracy means rule of the people. Democracies are governments based on a popular vote; elections decide who will be in power.

The map on this page shows one way in which the countries of the world could be divided in the early 2000s. About 30 percent were democracies, 25 percent were partial democracies, and 45 percent were autocracies. (The lines between the various characterizations are sometimes vague.) In later chapters, we discuss each in more detail. Here we simply present a basic overview.

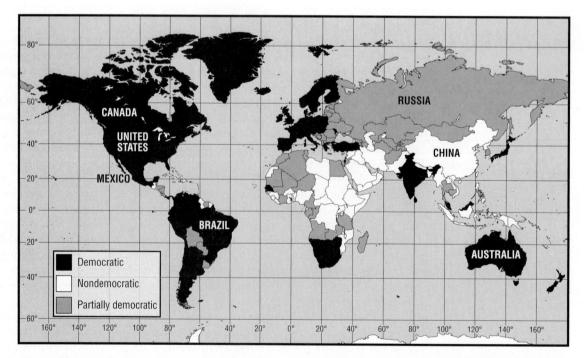

Democratic, partially democratic, and nondemocratic governments of the world. There is some ambiguity about how democratic a number of countries are, and this list reflects judgments of the author over the last decade. Countries can change quickly if there is a coup. Almost all countries call themselves democratic. For example, North Korea calls itself the Democratic Peoples Republic.

Democracies

Democracy is a word that means different things to different people. To the ancient Greek philosopher Plato, it meant mob rule, or anarchy. To some people today it means capitalism; to others it means socialism. Before the nineteenth century, few people in the world considered democracy desirable. But today, comparatively few people will admit opposition to democracy. Now almost every important nation, including the republics of the former Soviet Union, claim to be democratic. In pre-1990 Soviet terminology, communism, in which individuals' rights to undertake actions within the economy were limited, was the only true form of democracy. Soviet and some U.S. scholars argued that in capitalist countries control is actually in the hands of a small group of people—sometimes called the power elite (the wealthy and the autocracy)—and that the so-called democratic states of the West are in reality states serving the interests of the power elite.

These arguments may have been correct, but they were discredited by the reality of most of these communist states. In these states, the communist parties were not the protectors of the workers; often they were the exploiters. With their inefficient economic systems, to live well they had to exploit a lot, creating enormous animosity among the people. That's why most people in the Western democracies believed that the communist states were dictatorships. Some people in the West even went so far as to maintain that democracy and any form of extensive governmental interference in the economy, such as they had in the Soviet Union, are in the long run incompatible—that we have one or the other, but not both. That's debatable, but what happened in the communist countries has been an enormously positive advertisement for democracy. As Winston Churchill aptly noted, "It has been said that democracy is the worst form of government except all the others that have been tried."

Characteristics of a Democracy.   Obviously, democracy cannot be defined in any precise way that satisfies everyone. However, we can clarify some of the concepts and opinions involved. For instance, we can distinguish between democracy as a form of government and democracy as a theory of economic and social relationships. We can describe the characteristics that the West includes under the term *democracy* and, having done this, we can distinguish between profession and practice and between democratic ideals and democratic realities.

In thinking about a democracy, the first thing that usually comes to mind is the concept of popular sovereignty. **Popular sovereignty** is the right of individuals to select their leaders by voting for them. A state that does not have popular sovereignty cannot be a democracy. We use the complicated term *popular sovereignty* rather than *voting* because the mere act of voting does not guarantee that the people decide who will be their leaders. In deciding whether a government is really democratic, we must consider whether popular sovereignty prevails, or whether the voting is simply a matter of form. Universal adult suffrage is not sufficient to make a political system democratic if the voters have no real choice among candidates.

The essential requisite for political democracy is that the people (not a king, an elite, or a class) are ultimately sovereign. Not only are the people the source of all political power, but they also are the masters of any government they establish to serve their interests. The "consent of the governed" means more than passive acquiescence; it means the power to control. In order for the people to control the government, there must be

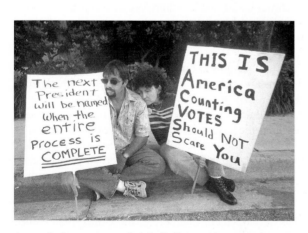

A couple demonstrates their belief in popular sovereignty as they demand a complete vote count in the 2000 U.S. presidential election.

(1) freedom of speech, (2) effective legislative organs to represent the people, and (3) free elections in which the people may change the government by legal and hence peaceful methods.

Most modern democrats in the West consider freedom or liberty to be an essential element of democracy. But popular sovereignty means, in effect, majority rule, and there is always some tension or conflict between majority rule and the ideal of individual liberty. There is no way of completely resolving this conflict, but if the ruling majority is reasonably tolerant, it attempts to limit personal freedom only in situations in which such freedom would seriously interfere with the freedom and rights of others.

Key words that indicate important aspects of the democratic method are *free discussion, accommodation, compromise, moderation, tolerance,* and *reconciliation.* If these aspects exist to a sufficient degree, the definition of democracy as majority rule is perhaps acceptable. But democracy really means more than majority rule, for in the absence of these methods of resolving conflict, a majority can be just as tyrannical as any absolute monarch or modern dictator. It means that the majority will respect and guarantee the rights of the minorities, and that it will allow the minorities the right to try to become the majority. Democracy means that the end, no matter how noble, cannot justify the means. It holds that no goal, however desirable, is worth the price of sacrificing democratic methods.

Democratic Concept of the Individual.   Every philosophical, social, and political system is based on certain assumptions about the nature of human beings, and no political system can be understood without a knowledge of the assumptions it makes about humans and their relationship to society and government. Democratic assumptions are worlds apart from those made by dictatorships. Not all democratic assumptions can be scientifically demonstrated, but they are part of the democratic faith and the democratic ideal. In the absence of these assumptions, democracy could not operate successfully, for no other system of government puts so much faith in the average person or depends so much on the average person for its success. Democracy demands that the common people exercise sovereign authority over themselves, maintain freedom, and employ the judgment needed to secure the blessings of good government.

Rationality and the Democratic Way of Life.   Democratic theory assumes that people are capable of developing a culture in which individuals will have learned to listen to discussion and argument, and in which they will try to discover the truth by a rational weighing of the evidence. It assumes that a human society is possible in which the people will realize that they cannot get all they want from government, and that it is therefore in everyone's interest to make compromises. In a successful democracy, every important group must be willing to make such concessions to the interests of others as are necessary.

Equality.   Democratic theory holds that all humans should be regarded as equal, not in ability or in achievement, but in legal status and in their right to seek the good life. It does not insist that people are equal in beauty, brawn, and brains; in money and morals; or in power and prestige, but it does assert that all are equal before the law. It may even be said that the basic assumption underlying democratic government is that all—or at least most—citizens potentially are capable of reaching wise political decisions. It follows, therefore, that all should be given equal opportunities to participate in the political process: to vote, to hold office, to have opinions, and to strive to make their opinions prevail. No individual group is regarded as having a monopoly on political wisdom. Equality implies that public laws apply equally to all and that they will be impartially administered.

The democratic ideal of equality has developed considerably in the United States since the Declaration of Independence was written and has played an important role in eliminating slavery, in expanding educational opportunities, and in stimulating efforts to eliminate extreme poverty. Its work is still unfinished and necessarily always will be, but the widespread sharing of respect and power that democracy implies depends on a broad distribution of economic goods and the means of intellectual enlightenment. Further movements toward equality of opportunity will bring closer to full realization the ideal of popular control of government and should improve the quality of popular political decisions.

Primacy of the Individual.   Democratic philosophy and democratic government put primary emphasis on the dignity and worth of the individual. Government and society are considered to exist for the individual. The best organization of society—the best form of government—is regarded as the one that enhances the dignity of the individual and provides for the fullest and richest development of personality. The individual is considered to be the primary unit, one whose interests should be served by all social institutions. Individuals are not to be considered as means; they are the ends, for which all else exists.

The primary values of liberal democracy are freedom for and respect for the individual personality, and these values provide the basis for resolving the apparent contradictions between other democratic values. For example, freedom and equality are permitted and promoted insofar as they create the best environment for the development of individual personality. Freedom that disrupts social order is prohibited because order in society is necessary for the fullest exercise of the kind of freedom that promotes the development of wholesome personality. Individual or group freedoms that seriously limit the freedoms of either the majority or minorities are curtailed because the goal is as much freedom as possible for all, in order that all may lead full and satisfying lives. Complete social equality is not enforced, because such enforcement would destroy the individual freedom required for personality development. The line between freedom and order is a difficult one to draw, and inevitably there will be differences of opinion.

At times democracies may have exaggerated the value of individualism and failed to give full recognition to the value of social cooperation for the common good. In a world in which many nations glorify the state and tend to subordinate the individual completely, the democratic emphasis on the value, freedom, and dignity of the individual personality serves as a powerful bulwark to protect the social progress made in Western societies through centuries of struggle.

Where Democracy Works Best.   Democracy is a Western ideology, and we often think that it is the solution to all political problems. Unfortunately, it is not. For democracy to work, one needs the right environment. The right environment includes a tradition of respect for individual rights, a commitment to solving problems peacefully, a relatively homogeneous population (in which subgroups of the population are not antagonistic to one another), a commitment to minority rights, a commitment to democracy over other obligations such as religion, a generally acceptable distribution of income and wealth, an educated population, a free press, and a commitment to law. In many countries of the world, this environment does not exist, making the establishment of a well-functioning democracy difficult if not totally impossible.

Alternative Forms of Democracy.   The fundamental requirements of democracy are not to be confused with any precise type of governmental organization. Students of government agree that political democracy exists in many forms. It may be direct (as in a New England town meeting, which every citizen can attend) or representative (as it must be in all units with large populations). It may be presidential (as in the United States) or parliamentary (as in Britain, Canada, and Italy). It may be unitary (as in Britain and France) or federal (as in the United States). It may exist where there is either a written or an unwritten constitution, but there must be in some sense a constitution or fundamental law that the government respects. It may exist in a republic (as in the United States and France) or in a constitutional monarchy (as in Sweden and Britain).

*L*etting a Guilty Person Go Free

The primacy of the individual can be seen in various aspects of life in the United States. One example is Miranda rights, which were established by a decision of the U.S. Supreme Court in 1966 (*Miranda v. Arizona*). In that case, Ernesto Miranda had been convicted of kidnapping and rape after appearing in a police lineup, being questioned, and signing a statement. The Supreme Court held that the courts cannot use statements obtained by the police while a suspect is in custody unless the suspect has been warned of the protection against self-incrimination provided by the First and Fifth Amendments to the Constitution. The Court laid out the points that must be covered. You may have heard them on television crime stories.

The Miranda Warning: *You have the right to remain silent. Anything you say can be used against you in a court of law. You have the right to the presence of an attorney. If you cannot afford an attorney, one will be appointed for you prior to the questioning if you so desire.*

If these individual rights are not read to the suspect, or are not understood by the suspect, the individual's statement cannot be used as evidence against him or her. Other examples of our concerns for the rights of the individual include limitations on how evidence is obtained: For instance, illegal wiretapping and unwarranted search may also be grounds for letting a person who may be guilty go free.

Autocracy

In the preceding discussion, you saw that the term *democracy* was far more complicated than you might have thought. The same is true of the term **autocracy,** a government in which a single person or a small group of people has or claims unlimited power. Like democracies, autocracies come in many varieties. Antiquity had rulers in the clan, tribe, city-state, and empire. The names of some of the great Roman dictators are well known: Julius Caesar, Augustus Caesar, and Marcus Aurelius. The short-lived and limited democracy of the Greek city-states was replaced by autocracies under men such as Pisistratus, the Athenian tyrant.

The absolute monarchies that emerged from the disintegration of feudalism in the Middle Ages constituted the type of authoritarian rule commonly found before the emergence in the twentieth century of fascism and communism. Like many twentieth-century autocracies, these earlier absolute monarchies were marked by arbitrary rule, which at times tended to become irresponsible. Nevertheless, many of their rulers provided "popular" or "benevolent" government. Unlike most contemporary autocracies, the absolute monarchies were fairly stable because usually one hereditary ruler followed another without introducing any basic changes in society. In modern societies, we generally do not have absolute monarchies. Instead, we usually have limited monarchies in which the monarch plays a ceremonial role but has little to say in the governing of the country. Despite the trend away from monarchies, especially absolute monarchies, more than 25 national monarchs still remain, holding varying degrees of governing power. British Queen Elizabeth II can claim over 15 countries as her kingdoms, although her real power is effectively none. On the other side of the spectrum, Swaziland, Brunei, Oman, Qatar, and Saudi Arabia are still ruled by almost monarchs.

In the twentieth century, various types of autocracies developed in accordance with different conditions in different countries. The two basic types of autocracies that remain are the authoritarian and the totalitarian.

An **authoritarian autocracy** is one in which the society is ruled by a dictator or clique that forbids all activities that threaten its position. Although this group ruthlessly guards its power, it generally is indifferent to activities that do not threaten its rule. It wants to rule because it likes ruling or because it likes the benefits of ruling, such as the enormous potential income. The societies of the eighteenth-century empress Catherine the Great of Russia and, in the twentieth century, Francisco Franco of Spain are examples of past authoritarian autocracies, and the military juntas in a number of countries of Africa are examples of current authoritarian autocracies.

A **totalitarian autocracy** is one that wants to control all aspects of an individual's life. A totalitarian ruler is different from an authoritarian ruler who does not care who teaches in a school as long as he or she takes no political stand and does not threaten the ruler's power. Put simply, "an authoritarian wants obedience; the totalitarian wants worship." The concept of totalitarianism was not formally introduced until the twentieth century. The reason is that overwhelming dominance of the political authority emanating from a totalitarian nation was not possible until twentieth-century technology succeeded in significantly increasing the scope of the state's control.

Most totalitarian autocracies are based on an ideology. With this ideology, they can justify their actions in terms of the goal of a better world. Nazism and Marxism are two examples of ideologies underlying totalitarian rule.

An authoritarian autocracy is not necessarily better or worse than a totalitarian autocracy. For example, authoritarian autocrats often plunder their countries' wealth, living in splendor while the people they rule may starve. Because totalitarian autocracies are generally based on ideology, totalitarian leaders are often far less interested in wealth for themselves and are more interested in seeing that individuals in their society share their own ideology. Thus, in a totalitarian autocracy people can be better off financially but have fewer personal freedoms.

Justifications Given for an Autocracy.   Because most of the countries that we classify as autocracies claim to be democracies, to gain a better sense of an autocracy we must consider their arguments about why they do not allow free elections. Here we find ongoing debate about what is meant by *free*. For instance, some communists argue that when workers depend on businesses for jobs they are not free to express their own will—that their will is just an expression of the capitalists' and power elite's will. They argue that the control of a government by the Communist Party is a temporary expedient necessary to prevent the existing vested interests (the bourgeoisie) from thwarting the state's movement to a higher, freer stage. The theory is that only by accepting some limitation on freedom in the present can citizens under communism achieve true freedom in the future. Given the

A despot giving orders.

upheavals that ended communist rule in most former communist countries, this justification did not satisfy many of those who lived under communism.

In similar fashion, the autocracies of many underdeveloped countries claim that they are merely caretakers, that if they were not in charge, some other group far less benevolent and far less committed to democracy would take over and eliminate any possibility of the country ever becoming a democracy. They argue that because the environment of their country is not suitable for democracy, they must preserve order so that the environment can be made safe for democracy. They argue that they are not antidemocratic; on the contrary, they are protective of democracy. An example of a relatively beneficent caretaker autocracy is the African country of Uganda, where the president, Yoweri Museveni, has led Uganda back from chaos and created the stability needed for economic growth while at the same time maintaining a relatively uncorrupt government. He has tried to be inclusive in his government, but nonetheless has not allowed significant political opposition, arguing that with the ethnic hatreds that are so pervasive in Uganda, the country is not yet ready for Western-style democracy. This lesser-of-two-evils justification for autocracy goes back to the political philosophy of Thomas Hobbes, who justified monarchy in this fashion.

Each of these arguments has some validity. Democracy has its weaknesses. Modern democracies were developed to reflect Western cultural values and social institutions, and these may not flourish when transplanted. The will of the people is not well defined and so the concept can be manipulated. Moreover, democracies operate within certain legal frameworks that restrict individual liberties in certain areas. As recently as the 1950s here in the United States, during what is called the McCarthy era,[3] a congressional body, the House Committee on Un-American Activities, summoned people suspected of being communists or of being "fellow travelers" (having friends who are communists). As a result of their testimony, or refusal to testify, some lost their jobs or could not find work in their professions, and some were even arrested and jailed. More recently, as part of the war on terrorism, individuals of Islamic beliefs or origin are being singled out as possible terrorist supporters. They can lose their jobs, even be arrested or jailed for having contact with suspected terrorists. Some believe that this treatment is a reasonable price to pay to root out terrorism. Others believe it has trampled on the rights of individuals that are supposed to be sacrosanct.

Similarly, developing countries often have problems making democracy work. In a country with two (or more) separate and opposing cultures, democracy is almost doomed to failure. Examples include Nigeria, with its many tribes and deep divisions between the Christians and Muslims; Iraq, with the Kurds, Shiites, and Sunnis; Afghanistan, with its many tribes; and the Republic of the Congo, with its many ethnic divisions.

Western countries have been frustrated with recent efforts to promote liberal democracy in Asia, Africa, and Latin America. However, the leaders in the West need to realize and accept that it is difficult to impose the typical Western model of democracy on non-Western societies, which possess distinct (and often contrary) cultural and sociopolitical characteristics. Therefore, classifying a country as an autocracy does not necessarily mean it is bad; it means it is not responsive to the will of the people in the same way as Western democracies.

Autocracy and Power.   As we stated earlier, an autocracy is a government that exists independently of, or beyond, the will of its citizens. It may or may not act contrary to the wishes of those it governs. It is important to note that in an autocracy, the people have limited means of calling the government to account. Its right to rule does not depend on majority support but, rather, derives from power that for authoritarian autocracies can be an end in itself. However, even in an autocracy, a leader who has lost the support of the people may find it difficult to stay in power.

A dramatic overthrow of an autocratic dictator occurred in Romania in 1989. Nicolae Ceauşescu had ruthlessly governed Romania during the cold war and was responsible for

---

[3]This era takes its name from a U.S. senator of the time, Joseph McCarthy, who conducted an infamous campaign against communists in government and in influential positions throughout U.S. society.

numerous human rights violations. When the tide of the pro-democracy movement engulfed eastern Europe in the late 1980s, Romania was the stage for a massive revolt against the incumbent dictatorship. On December 16, 1989, Ceaușescu declared a state of emergency after hundreds of protestors died during demonstrations in the city of Timisoara. The wave of protest spread rapidly throughout Romania and people openly marched into the capital, Bucharest, demanding Ceaușescu's dismissal. Army units joined the rebellion and on December 22, 1989, a group calling itself the Council of National Salvation announced that it had overthrown the government. A bloody conflict followed between security forces still loyal to the dictator and the new government. The Council of National Salvation gained control and Ceaușescu and his wife were captured. After a speedy trial, they were found guilty of genocide and were executed on December 25, 1989. On the same day, Ion Iliescu, the leader of the rebellion, was sworn in as the new president of Romania. In 1991, a new constitution set up a system by which the president and the legislature are elected by popular vote.

Whereas for authoritarian autocracies power is an end in itself (and possibly a tool for personal enrichment), and they need claim no other justification, for totalitarian autocracies the power is nearly always a means to a higher ideological end. There generally is some belief that the ruling elite possesses the "best brains," the "best blood," the "highest political insight," and the "capacity to rule."[4] Autocrats do not expect people to know what is good for them; they tell the people what is best and hope the people will believe it. If the people do not believe it, the autocrats can try to do what is good for them anyway. Of course, they can also listen to the people and carry out popular wishes, either because they believe that is the right thing to do or because they fear an uprising or a coup. Thus, we can have autocracies that are responsive to the general will. They remain autocracies because the decision to be responsive rests with the ruler, not the people.

"Frankly, it's no better or worse than any other form of government."

---

[4]For example, the classic totalitarian autocrat, Adolf Hitler, wrote, "A philosophy of life which, by rejecting the democratic concept of the mass-man, endeavors to give this earth to the best nation, the highest type of human beings, must in turn, logically, obey the same aristocratic principle within that nation and must secure leadership and greatest influence for the best brains. It rests on the basis of personality, not on that of majority." Translated from *Mein Kampf,* Munich, 1938, p. 493 (earlier editions in 1925 and 1927).

Characteristics of an Autocracy. The central characteristic of the totalitarian autocracies that came into power after World War I was their policy of controlling the total life of individuals and private groups. They employed whatever devices they could to make possible the effective control by the state of all social activity. The sphere of private freedom, which democracy attempts to maximize, is narrowly restricted by totalitarianism. Totalitarian government attempts to regulate all of life for state ends. Capital and labor, press and religion, family and fraternal organizations, work and play, individuals and society—all are subject to strict controls designed to promote the general welfare and to enhance the power and prestige of the state.

Loyalty to the Party and the State. Totalitarian autocracies demand complete loyalty and obedience to the party and the state. Fascist theory glorified and exalted the state. Some forms of communism exalt the social revolution and require of the individual complete dedication to the objectives of the Communist Party. But under both systems, the political party has direct control of the government and determines what government policy will be. Totalitarian communist states, for example, are the instrument for carrying out the policies of the Communist Party. Both fascism and totalitarian communism demand that individuals, where there is any conflict, subordinate their own interests to those of the party and the state.[5]

In the 1990s, there were signals of a possible resurgence of fascism in Europe, with the relative success of extremist parties in France, Germany, Italy, and Russia. These movements exist, but at least by the early 2000s they have generally remained without effective power.

Rule by Leaders. Democracy emphasizes constitutionalism and rule by law; an autocracy is often characterized less by the rule of law and more by the rule of leaders. Until 1215, England was a complete autocracy and no rule of law limited the ruler's power. In that year England adopted the **Magna Carta,** or "great charter," which forced King John to agree that free men had rights and liberties that could not be trampled on. After King John accepted the Magna Carta, his rights were limited, and England took a step from autocracy to democracy. As we have stated, autocracies differ from one another, and so do countries. However, where the power of the autocracy is strong and the ruler or ruling party unresponsive to the wishes of the citizens, the autocrat can change the political rules arbitrarily to meet the purposes of the moment; no law or established procedure is permitted to interfere with the continued existence and absolute rule of the power holders. Under such circumstances, life, liberty, and property are insecure, for a person may be found guilty on false charges without any genuine trial.

One-Party Monopoly. Autocracy desires a monopoly on control; it generally tolerates no organized opposition, but it sometimes makes use of a political party. The one highly disciplined party that exists may have begun as a traditional political group struggling for parliamentary control. Once in power, however, it loses its private character and becomes the official control agency of the state. The purposes it serves are very different from those served by parties in a democracy. It offers the people no alternatives and it gives them no opportunity to participate in the formulation of public policy. Its purpose is to serve the organizational needs of the autocratic leaders and their followers. It provides for close contact between the rulers and the people, for the dissemination of the party line, and for the control and regimentation of the people in the interest of the rulers. It may, as in China, possess a legal

---

[5]Benito Mussolini, the fascist leader of Italy between the two world wars, wrote: "For Fascism the State is an absolute before which individuals and groups are relative. . . . When one says Liberalism, one says the individual; when one says Fascism, one says the State. . . . The Liberal State does not direct the interplay and the material and spiritual development of the groups, but limits itself to registering the results; the Fascist state has a consciousness of its own, a will of its own." "The Doctrine of Fascism" quoted in William Ebenstein, *Great Political Thinkers: Plato to the Present,* New York: Holt, 1951, pp. 597, 598.

Hitler's Germany embodied fascist theory.

monopoly on the power to nominate candidates. Regardless of its legal position, the state party carries out the will of the autocratic leaders and prevents the people from forming a legal opposition party to challenge the present rulers. Thus the party becomes in practice synonymous with the state; its personnel, policies, and programs become those of the state.

A Controlled Press.   If a leader is to maintain control without resorting to elections, she or he often finds it necessary to control the press and the other media to ensure popular support for the regime. **Propaganda** is the product of the state controlling the press and structuring the flow of information to the people in order to make the state look good. Totalitarian autocracies often employ an elaborate propaganda machine designed to secure mass support through intellectual conformity. The people are denied the privilege of hearing any other side of an issue. For these reasons, autocracies often have strong public support, but without a free press and freedom of expression for individuals, it is difficult to say whether that support would exist if people were offered a wider range of choices.

Communism, Fascism, and Autocracy.   When thinking of autocracy, we often think of communism and fascism because the terms *communism* and *fascist Nazism* have sometimes been used synonymously with *totalitarian autocracy.* This is somewhat misleading because communism and fascism are not really types of government. Rather, they are different systems of social, economic, and political theory that have produced totalitarian governments of a similar character. The differences between them are largely matters of detail and ideology, but as we stated at the beginning of the chapter, ideological differences are important.

Under communism the totalitarianism is meant to be temporary, and rule by the Communist Party is said to be a transition toward a higher stage of society in which "the State will wither away" because true equality and freedom have been achieved and totalitarian rule no longer has any function. Fascism, originally developed as an ideology to combat communism, does not see itself as a mere stage; it sees itself as a complete system capable of withstanding all assaults. (Adolf Hitler, the German founder of fascist Nazism, proclaimed that the Third Reich, which he established, would last a thousand years—it lasted less than twenty.)

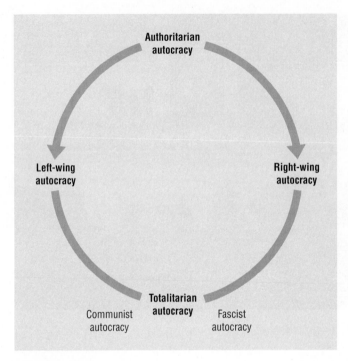

Figure 13.2

Continuum of autocracies.

The development of fascism in reaction to communism shows the problem that ideologies present to society. The goals of communism (to each according to his needs; from each according to his abilities) sound noble, but when that ideology conflicts with a democratic ideology, one or the other must give. In the 1930s, communist ideologists argued that the democratic ideology must give. Once one group in a democracy no longer accepts the democratic ideology, it becomes more and more difficult for other groups to accept the limitations democratic ideology places on them. For example, if you're playing cards and the person you're playing with cheats, at some point you are likely either to cheat too or quit playing. In the 1920s and 1930s, fascists argued that because communists were not playing by the rules, fascists didn't have to play by the rules either. In Germany that argument carried the day, and Germany became a fascist state to "protect itself from the communists." The ultimate result was World War II.

Often fascism and communism are seen as opposite ends of the spectrum—communism on the left and fascism on the right. It is better to think of a circle, as depicted in Figure 13.2. At the top of the circle are autocracies without any ideological commitment. Traveling all the way around the left side of the circle to the bottom would bring us to communism, and tracing around the right side would end in fascism. Thus, almost at the bottom, but not quite touching, are communists and fascists.

Governments Are Far from Simple

Having come to the end of this first chapter on political systems, we are in a better position to see why a former Supreme Court justice, Felix Frankfurter, attacked President Warren Harding's view that government, after all, is a very simple thing. Government is far from simple. Understanding the role of government is not like understanding mathematics or logic. There is an art to government, and although the goals of government may remain constant, the means of achieving those goals may vary with the temper of the times.

We could go on about the nature of governments, but you'll learn far more by considering examples. In the next chapter we look at five governments, some of which are autocracies and some of which are democracies; in Chapter 15, we consider the U.S. government more carefully.

Key Points

- Five primary functions of government are maintaining internal order and external security, ensuring justice, safeguarding individual freedoms, regulating individuals' actions, and promoting the general welfare.
- Three contrasting views of government are government as a necessary evil, government as a positive good, and government as an unnecessary evil.
- The liberal, conservative, reactionary, and anarchist philosophies of government differ in their view of how strong government should be.
- The two primary forms of government are democracy and autocracy.

- Three distinguishing characteristics of a democracy are freedom of speech, effective representation of the people, and free elections.
- The democratic concept of the individual is that he or she is rational, equal to all others, and primary.
- Common justifications for an autocracy include the repressiveness of markets, the need for a temporary caretaker, and the lack of the requirements for a democracy.
- Four characteristics of an autocracy include loyalty to the party and state, rule by leaders, one-party monopoly, and a controlled press.

Some Important Terms

anarchists (264)
anarchy (258)
authoritarian autocracy (270)
autocracy (270)
bourgeoisie (263)
communism (263)
conservatives (264)
democracy (262)
fascism (262)

functionalist approach (257)
government (257)
justice (258)
liberals (264)
libertarians (264)
Magna Carta (274)
moderates (264)
Patriot Act (260)
political ideologies (262)

political theory (262)
politics (262)
popular sovereignty (267)
propaganda (275)
radicals (265)
reactionaries (264)
totalitarian autocracy (271)

Questions for Review and Discussion

1. What are some of the functions of government that make it such a powerful institution?
2. Distinguish between anarchists and libertarians.
3. What three different attitudes toward government are predominant in the United States?
4. What are some of the reasons people disagree over the role government ought to play?
5. What does equality mean to you?

6. How do you think a government can administer the ideal of individual freedom without infringing on the freedom of other individuals?
7. Some forms of government advocate individual liberty; some others advocate individual control. Name one or two ideologies on each side and describe what you think each would mean for a citizen under such a government.

8. What are some of the differences between an authoritarian autocracy and a totalitarian autocracy? Name a state governed under each of these systems, and give reasons for your choices.
9. In what ways can communism be said to advocate liberty? In what ways can democracy be said to lead to repression?

10. What kind of government provides open elections but with only one candidate on the ballot? What kind might give voters a choice of candidates but have soldiers stationed at the polling place?

Internet Questions

1. Go to the Frontiers of Freedom website, www.ff.org. What is their mission statement?
2. May 4 marks two different riots/protests in the United States that ended in tragedy. What were the two riots? In each riot, who was protesting, and why were they protesting? What went wrong?
3. Looking at the Homeland Security threat and protection information at www.dhs.gov, what alert status are we in right now, and what does that mean?

4. Who was Idi Amin? Go to http://video.aol.com/video-detail/last-king-of-scotland-the-real-idi-amin/285855676 and watch the video.
5. Take the "World's Smallest Political Quiz" on the Libertarian Party website, www.theadvocates.org/quizp/index.html (accessed June 10, 2009). How do you score?

For Further Study

Aristotle, *Politics,* trans. H. Rackham, Cambridge, MA: Harvard University Press, 1944.

Arsenault, Raymond, *Freedom Riders: Beyond the Crisis in Black America,* New York: Gotham, 2006.

Diamond, Jared, *Guns, Germs and Steel: Why the West Triumphed,* New York: Norton, 2006.

Ericson, Richard V., and Nico Stehr, eds., *Governing Modern Societies,* Toronto: University of Toronto Press, 2000.

Friedman, Thomas L., *Longitudes and Attitudes: Exploring the World after September 11th,* New York: Farrar, Straus & Giroux, 2002.

Hayek, Friedrich A., *The Constitution of Liberty,* Chicago: University of Chicago Press, 1960.

Hitler, Adolf, *Mein Kampf* (1927), Boston: Houghton Mifflin, 1962.

Hobbes, Thomas, *Leviathan* (1651), Baltimore: Penguin, 1982.

Holzer, Harold, and Joshua Wolf Shenk eds., *In Lincoln's Hand: His Original Manuscripts with Commentary by Distinguished Americans.* New York, NY: Bantam, 2008.

Locke, John, *Of Civil Government, Second Essay* (1690), Chicago: Henry Regnery, 1960.

Marx, Karl, and Friedrich Engels, *The Communist Manifesto* (1848), ed. Samuel H. Beer, New York: Appleton- Century-Crofts, 1955.

Micklethwait, John, and Adrian Wooldridge, *The Right Nation: Conservative Power in America,* New York: Penguin, 2004.

9/11 Commission Report: Final Report of the National Commission on Terrorist Attacks Upon the United States, Philip Zelikow, Commission Executive Director, New York: Norton, 2004.

Roberts, Cokie, *Founding Mothers: The Women Who Raised Our Nation,* New York: Morrow, 2004.

Tocqueville, Alexis de, *Democracy in America* (1835), Garden City, NY: Doubleday, 1969.

WWW   Advocates for Self Government www.theadvocates .org

WWW   American Civil Liberties Union www.aclu.org/

WWW   The Christian Coalition www.cc.org

WWW   Department of Homeland Security www.dhs.gov

WWW   Directory of U.S. Political Parties www.politics1.com/parties.htm.

$\mathcal{G}$overnments of the World

After reading this chapter, you should be able to:

- Give a history and describe the key features of the French government
- Give a history and describe the key features of the Mexican government
- Give a history and describe the key features of the Nigerian government
- Give a history and describe the key features of the Russian government
- Give a history and describe the key features of the Saudi Arabian government

If the gods should hand down to mortals, as mortals now are, a perfect system, it would be all banged up and skewed twistways inside of ten years.

—Don Marquis

The idea behind governments is one thing—how the ideas work in practice is another. In this chapter we try to give some concreteness to the ideas in the previous chapter by providing a brief description of five governments: France, Mexico, Russia, Nigeria, and Saudi Arabia. Our goal in doing so is not to make you an expert on these governments, but to show you the diversity that exists in governments and to show how the historical context within which each country developed has shaped its specific form of government and how much variance there is among autocracies and among democracies.

$\mathcal{F}$rench Government

France, the country where democracy was reborn, is a good country with which to begin our consideration of governments besides our own. The current system of French government developed in reaction to the absolute monarchy that had become nonresponsive to the changing social conditions—specifically, the emerging middle class. **Bastille Day** is the equivalent of our Fourth of July and commemorates the storming of the Bastille prison in Paris. The French celebrate it every year on the fourteenth of July.

The storming of the Bastille in 1789 marked an uprising of the people, the **French Revolution**—the revolt in France against the monarchy and aristocracy, lasting from 1789 to 1799—and led to a decade of chaos and terror, with the revolutionaries tearing down the political structure and other social institutions of the country but not replacing them. This chaos ended when dictator Napoleon Bonaparte took control. Although Napoleon reversed the process of democratization and returned France to an autocracy, after his reign there was a gradual evolution away from autocracy and toward a liberal parliamentary system that characterizes the French government today. In 1871, after France was defeated in a short war with Germany, the Franco-Prussian War, all vestiges of autocracy were ended, and the democratic French republic was established.

Although the republics of France have always had a written constitution, the French constitution has never been as firmly established as the U.S. Constitution. In fact, there have been sixteen constitutions since the revolution of 1789. There is some continuity, however, and their present constitution refers to the Declaration of the Rights of Man, part of the preamble to the original constitution written in 1789.

The lack of a stable constitution has made the French people regard laws differently than they are regarded in the United States, where for many people the law is the law; the law is right. For the French people, laws are simply technical rules under which they live. The difference is not so much in what actually happens in each country—in both some people break the law. In the United States, if you break the law (for example, by evading taxes) you probably feel guilty about it. In France, people often are proud of having broken what they regard as mere rules made by people who made different ones last week and will make still different ones next month.

The French Parliamentary System

France is now organized under what is called the Fifth Republic. Each of its republics has had a different constitution. Ever since the Third Republic, established in 1871, France has had a modified parliamentary system, modeled after the British parliamentary system. Perhaps the most distinctive aspect of French government and politics has been their instability. During the seventy years of the Third Republic (1871–1940), France had more than a hundred prime ministers, each one holding office less than eight months. This occurred because of the many political parties and the unwillingness of the members of the legislature to compromise. The Fourth Republic, established in 1946 after World War II, was even worse than the Third Republic. In response, on September 28, 1958, with the country on the brink of civil war, the Fifth Republic was instituted. In the Fifth Republic, it is much more difficult for the parliament to vote on a **censure motion,** a motion that, if successful, means the prime minister does not get a vote of confidence and must resign or call for a new election. A **vote of confidence** is a formal and constitutionally binding expression of preference in favor of the prime minister by the parliament.

The legislative branch of French government is elected every five years and consists of two houses: the National Assembly, whose members are elected directly by all citizens over age eighteen, and the Senate, which is chosen by an electoral college and provides stronger representation for rural areas than does the other house. When there is disagreement between the two houses, the National Assembly takes precedence. Compared with the U.S. Congress, however, neither of these legislative bodies has significant power. Once having elected executive officers, the executive branch can in many cases both legislate and carry out the laws. The strength of the executive branch was a change made in the Fifth Republic and accepted because the previous governments had been so unstable.

The French Executive Branch

The executive branch of the French government has two leaders: a prime minister and a president. Unlike many parliamentary systems, in France both leaders wield considerable power. The president is the head of state and the executive head of government. He or she is elected every five years by direct popular vote. The president appoints the prime minister and together they choose the cabinet.

In the 2007 election, Nicolas Sarkozy beat the Socialist party nominee, Segolene Royal, and Sarkozy began implementing his pro-market reform. However, the contracting GDP

Declaration of the Rights of Man and of the Citizen

Adopted by the National Assembly during the French Revolution on August 26, 1789, and affirmed by the constitution of 1958.

Preamble

The representatives of the French people, formed into a National Assembly, considering ignorance, forgetfulness or contempt of the rights of man to be the only causes of public misfortunes and the corruption of Governments, have resolved to set forth, in a solemn Declaration, the natural, unalienable and sacred rights of man, to the end that this Declaration, constantly present to all members of the body politic, may remind them unceasingly of their rights and their duties; to the end that the acts of the legislative power and those of the executive power, since they may be continually compared with the aim of every political institution, may thereby be the more respected; to the end that the demands of the citizens, founded henceforth on simple and uncontestable principles, may always be directed toward the maintenance of the Constitution and the happiness of all.

In consequence whereof, the National Assembly recognizes and declares, in the presence and under the auspices of the Supreme Being, the following Rights of Man and of the Citizen.

Article 1—Men are born and remain free and equal in rights. Social distinctions may be based only on considerations of the common good.

Article 2—The aim of every political association is the preservation of the natural and imprescriptible rights of man. These rights are Liberty, Property, Safety, and Resistance to Oppression.

Article 3—The source of all sovereignty lies essentially in the Nation. No corporate body, no individual may exercise any authority that does not expressly emanate from it.

Article 4—Liberty consists in being able to do anything that does not harm others; thus, the exercise of the natural rights of every man has no bounds other than those that ensure to the other members of society the enjoyment of these same rights. These bounds may be determined only by Law.

Article 5—The Law has the right to forbid only those actions that are injurious to society. Nothing that is not forbidden by Law may be hindered, and no one may be compelled to do what the Law does not ordain.

Article 6—The Law is the expression of the general will. All citizens have the right to take part, personally or through their representatives, in its making. It must be the same for all, whether it protects or punishes.

All citizens, being equal in its eyes, shall be equally eligible to all high offices, public positions and employments, according to their ability, and without other distinction than that of their virtues and talents.

Article 7—No man may be accused, arrested or detained except in the cases determined by the Law, and following the procedure that it has prescribed. Those who solicit, expedite, carry out, or cause to be carried out arbitrary orders must be punished; but any citizen summoned or apprehended by virtue of the Law, must give instant obedience; resistance makes him guilty.

Article 8—The Law must prescribe only the punishments that are strictly and evidently necessary; and no one may be punished except by virtue of a Law drawn up and promulgated before the offense is committed, and legally applied.

Article 9—As every man is presumed innocent until he has been declared guilty, if it should be considered necessary to arrest him, any undue harshness that is not required to secure his person must be severely curbed by Law.

Article 10—No one may be disturbed on account of his opinions, even religious ones, as long as the manifestation of such opinions does not interfere with the established Law and Order.

Article 11—The free communication of ideas and of opinions is one of the most precious rights of man. Any citizen may therefore speak, write and publish freely, except what is tantamount to the abuse of this liberty in the cases determined by Law.

Article 12—To guarantee the Rights of Man and of the Citizen a public force is necessary; this force is therefore established for the benefit of all, and not for the particular use of those to whom it is entrusted.

Article 13—For the maintenance of the public force, and for administrative expenses, a general tax is indispensable; it must be equally distributed among all citizens, in proportion to their ability to pay.

Article 14—All citizens have the right to ascertain, by themselves, or through their representatives, the need for a public tax, to consent to it freely, to watch over its use, and to determine its proportion, basis, collection and duration.

Article 15—Society has the right to ask a public official for an accounting of his administration.

Article 16—Any society in which no provision is made for guaranteeing rights or for the separation of powers, has no Constitution.

Article 17—Since the right to Property is inviolable and sacred, no one may be deprived thereof, unless public necessity, legally ascertained, obviously requires it, and just and prior indemnity has been paid.

France

Population: 62 million (2009)
Area: 211,209 square miles (547,030 square km)
Distribution: 77 percent urban; 23 percent rural
Capital city: Paris
National anthem: "La Marseillaise"
Government leaders: President Nicolas Sarkozy (since 2007) Prime Minister Francois Fillon (since 2007)

Ethnic divisions: Celtic and Latin with Teutonic, Slavic, North African, Indochinese, and Basque minorities
Literacy rate: 99 percent
Religion: 83–88 percent Roman Catholic, 5–10 percent Muslim, others include Protestant and Jewish
GDP: 2.097 trillion; per capita: 32,700 (2008)
Currency unit: Euro
Monetary conversion rate: 1 euro = $1.41(Jun. 2009)
Internet users: 30.8 million (2007)
Cell phones: 55.4 million (2007)

France

and rising unemployment starting in 2008 led to large labor strikes and demonstrations against the pro-market reforms and forced the Sarkozy government to examine the political ramifications of economic reforms.

Mexican Government

The government of Mexico is particularly interesting for two reasons: It reveals the blurred line between democratic and autocratic governments, and it demonstrates that governmental systems still are in the process of change.

The Difference between a Parliamentary and a Presidential System

Democracy has many forms. To hold meetings where everyone in the country can come and be heard is impossible when countries have millions of people. Therefore, every democracy must establish systems of representation. The United States has a presidential system, but most democratic countries in the world use a parliamentary system. The difference is found in who elects the leader of the country. In a presidential system, the people elect the leader, called the president, by direct election or indirectly through an electoral college. In a parliamentary system, people elect the members of the legislature and the legislators elect the executive leader, generally called a prime minister. Thus, in a presidential system, the legislature and the executive can be of opposing parties (as

happened in the United States in the 1990s when Bill Clinton, a Democrat, was president but Congress was controlled by the Republicans). In a parliamentary system, the majority in the legislature and the executive are of the same party or collection of parties. If the prime minister loses the support of the parliament, the government is said to fall and the prime minister must call for a new election or resign.

Parliamentary systems also often have presidents, whether elected by the legislature or by popular vote. The job of a president in such a system usually is to be a functionary—that is, to attend receptions and play a largely ceremonial role. In Great Britain, the king or queen serves the function that a president serves in other parliamentary systems. France presents an exception to both the parliamentary and the presidential system. In France, the president is elected by popular vote and then appoints the prime minister from the party or coalition of parties that rules the legislature.

Mexico is ostensibly a democracy—it has multiple parties and holds popular elections—but until 1988 the nature of those elections left no doubt as to who would be the chosen leader, and Mexico was ruled as an autocracy. But in 1988 this changed, and in 2000 Vicente Fox, a politician from a non-ruling party, won the general election for president.

To understand the current political situation in Mexico, we need to consider its history. Mexico won independence from Spain in 1821 and initially set itself up as a monarchy, but the monarchy was quickly overthrown and replaced with a republic marked by political and social confusion. In 1848, Mexico lost the Mexican-American War to the United States, and with that loss went about half its territory, including Texas, New Mexico, and parts of what are now eight other states. The loss of that war led to a civil war in Mexico and ultimately to the country's annexation by Napoleon III of France. In 1867, Mexico again won its independence, and Porfirio Díaz established a liberal dictatorship known as the Porfiriato. It was conducted under the general ideas of the liberals who had won the civil war: the rule of law, a strong federalist government, and the separation of church and state. These ideas are reflected in Mexico's current constitution as well.

What the 1867 constitution did not provide was equity, and the growth of the Mexican economy at that time was marked by a major transfer of land from the peasantry to a group of rich landowners and by a labor force with few rights. This transfer resulted in significant social unrest, characterized by strikes and revolts that were suppressed by the government.

Although Mexico called itself a democracy during this time, while Díaz was in power no one ever ran against him. However, the repressive measures of the early 1900s resulted in the growth of an opposition party that looked as though it had a chance of winning until the opposition leader was thrown in jail. The

President Felipe Calderon of Mexico.

jailing of this leader led to a revolution, the establishment of the modern Mexican state, and a new constitution in 1917. This new constitution reflected the social problems of the previous period. Specifically, the new constitution followed the old in maintaining a federal republic, but it took strong, definite social steps. For example, private ownership of land was no longer a right—it was a privilege that could be revoked by the state at will when land ownership did not serve a positive social function. Labor was given the right to strike, an eight-hour working day, and a minimum wage. Compared to the U.S. Constitution, this Mexican constitution was much more specific and dealt more extensively with social and economic concerns.

Mexico

Population (approximate): 111 million (2009)
Area: 761,605 square miles (1,972,550 square km)
Distribution: 77 percent urban; 23 percent rural
Capital city: Mexico City
National anthem: "Mexicanos, al grito de Guerra" ("Mexicans, to the Cry of War")
Government leader: President Felipe Calderon (since 2006)

Ethnic divisions: 60 percent Mestizo (Indian-Spanish); 30 percent Amerindian or predominantly Amerindian; 9 percent white or predominantly white; 1 percent other
Literacy rate: 91 percent
Religion: 76.5 percent Roman Catholic; 6 percent Protestant
GDP: $1.559 trillion; per capita: $14,200 (2008)
Currency unit: Peso
Monetary conversion rate: 1 peso = $.076 (Jun. 2009)
Internet users: 23 million (2007)
Cell phones: 68 million (2007)

Mexico

Politically, the constitution created an extremely powerful president who came close to choosing his or her successor. The legislative body consists of a Chamber of Deputies and a Senate, both of which are elected by popular vote. The president can serve only one (six-year) term.

To end the political turmoil that existed under the former constitution, the 1917 constitution gave the president enormous power. The president has the **line-item veto,** which means the power to veto any part of a bill, leaving the rest of it intact. This line-item veto makes legislative compromises difficult because the president has the power to accept part of the compromise and reject another part of it. The president also has the power to declare a state of siege, which gives him enormous police power, and he can appoint a cabinet without consulting the legislative body.

Although the constitution guarantees a strong president, the actual bureaucracy and institutions have given the president almost dictatorial authority. With the government controlling so many economic rights, individuals are indebted to the president for their jobs. For example, to pick through garbage you must belong to a union, the leader of which is appointed by the president. The union leader's job is to deliver the members' votes to the government.

As we stated earlier, the constitution gives individuals significant social and economic rights and gives the government—and hence the president—power to implement these rights. The result is a large, bureaucratic government structure with deep involvement in most aspects of economic and social life. The members of this bureaucratic structure are appointed by the government, to which they owe their allegiance.

After the revolution, the **Institutional Revolutionary Party (PRI),** the political party that was by far the most important, took control of the bureaucratic apparatus and used it to stay in power. The PRI remained the ruling party for more than seventy years. It instituted **land reform**—the redistribution of land from the large landholders to the middle-sized farmers and the peasantry—that was carried out under Lázaro Cárdenas, one of the most famous presidents of Mexico. He redistributed almost 50 million acres of land from rich landlords to peasants, but instead of giving ownership of the land directly to the peasants, he gave it to a communal *ejido,* or cooperative, the leader of which got much of his power from the government. The *ejido* leader delivered the votes and could maintain his or her little fiefdom. Similar fiefdoms existed in most industries, and there are about 200 decentralized joint government/private agencies such as Pemex, the agency that controls Mexico's oil industry.

The dominance of the PRI began to wane in the late 1980s amid scandals, accusations of corruption, and even blatant electoral fraud. Politics in México entered a transition period to a more American form. A severe recession in 1995 along with domestic unrest forced México to adopt many financial and social reforms. These measures, meant to encourage international investment, further weakened the PRI.

President Ernesto Zedillo, the PRI president in the late 1990s, made significant political concessions to the opposition. Congress was given a much greater role in the political process while the role of the presidency was significantly reduced. Electoral and judicial reforms were enacted to boost confidence in the Mexican political system. In recent years, Mexican elections have been fiercely competitive, the PRI, National Action Party (PAN), and the Party of the Democratic Revolution (PRD) are the three main parties. The very fact that elections have become competitive means there have been major changes in the Mexican bureaucratic structure.

The 2006 election represented a turning point in Mexican politics. It marked the first time Mexican politicians utilized mass media and an "American style" campaign to reach voters. It was a true election and suggested a shift away from a "who you know" system of government to a "how well you can campaign" system of government. The election represented a turning point because it was accepted as legitimate and all parties ultimately accepted the results. For a while, it didn't seem as if this would be the case. Specifically, when Felipe Calderon, a conservative PAN candidate, defeated Lopez Obrador, a liberal PDR candidate in a close election, Obrador supporters initially tried to overturn the results with sometimes violent demonstrations, riots and protests. Ultimately, these demonstrations

Supporters of Mexican presidential candidate Andres Manuel Lopez Obrador demand a ballot-by-ballot recount of the 2006 election.

ended, and Calderon was accepted by the large majority of the Mexican public as the legitimate president. The acceptance of the vote was seen by many outside observers as a great triumph for the Mexican electoral system and a testament to the progress they made since the days when the PRI controlled government.

Nigerian Government

The next country we consider, the African country called the Federal Republic of Nigeria, provides a good example of the problems faced by many of the former African European colonies. To understand the problems and government of Nigeria, it is helpful to take a brief look at the nation's precolonial and colonial history. The roots of Nigeria lie in its tribal foundations, with each tribe representing a unique blend of language, religion, and culture. The three main tribes occupied separate geographic areas in the region: Muslim tribes in the North and Christian tribes in the south, but in Nigeria these religious differences are tied to major cultural differences as well.

Before British colonization, there were three distinct tribal regions with many subregions. But for administrative ease, the British grouped together these three regions—Lagos, the Niger Coast, and the Northern Protectorate—into the area that came to be known as Nigeria. Today, it remains a country of more than 250 ethnic groups with varying languages and customs. Its official language is English, which was chosen to facilitate cultural and linguistic unity. Nigeria's other major languages are Hausa, Yoruba, and Igbo.

Since its early beginnings, through colonization, to the emergence of its first democratic republic, to now, the history of Nigeria has been marked by ethnic conflict, civil war, and military rule. Since gaining independence from the British in 1960, Nigeria has progressed through three separate republics and survived the aftermaths of their collapses. With intervention from Western powers, the most recent—the fourth republic—hopes to mark the final chapter in the history of this important African country.

The British Influence

The British became interested in West Africa at the time of the slave trade. British-based companies such as the Royal Niger Company occupied the region. As the companies slowly gained influence, so did the British Empire. This growth eventually climaxed in the establishment of the Protectorate of Nigeria at the beginning of the twentieth century. Despite the revocation of the charters of several of the British companies, the influence of the British government in the region continued to grow. With colonization under way, an influx of Christian missionaries brought churches and schools to the predominantly Muslim region. Within the first few years of the new century, several protectorates had been established, growing outward from the original stronghold in Lagos on the southern coast.

Each protectorate came under the authority of a lieutenant-governor, whose job was to keep order and generate revenue for the British government. Slow steps toward unification of the separate regions were taken in 1906, with the incorporation of Lagos into the Southern Protectorate. Several ideas were proposed to unify the remaining regions, and

Population (approximate): 149,229,090 (2009)
Area: 356,668 square miles (923,768 square km)
Distribution: 48% urban; 52% rural
Capital city: Abuja
National anthem: "Arise O Compatriots, Nigeria's Call Obey"

Government leader: President Umaru Musa Yar'Adua (since 2007)
Ethnic divisions: 29 percent Hausa and Fulani; 21 percent Yoruba; 18 percent Igbo; 10 percent Ijaw; 4 percent Kanuri; 3.5 percent Ibibio; 2.5 percent Tiv
Literacy rate: 68 percent
Religion: 50 percent Muslim; 40 percent Christian; 10 percent indigenous beliefs
GDP: $338.1 billion; per capita: $2,300 (2008)
Currency unit: Naira
Monetary conversion rate: 1 naira = $.0068 (Jun. 2009)
Internet users: 10 million (2007)
Cell phones: 40 million (2007)

Nigeria

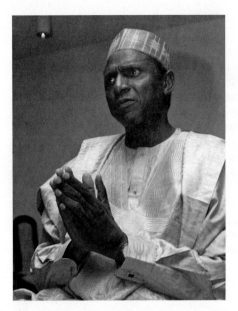

President Olusegun Obasanjo of Nigeria.

by 1914 the British had established the unified modern foundations of Nigeria with Sir Frederick Lugard serving as its first governor. He set up an advisory body known as the Nigerian Council that featured representation from each former protectorate and limited input from the African natives.

Meanwhile, the National Congress of British West Africa established itself as a growing force in the region. Though ongoing fights with the British government failed to establish this group as part of the legislative council, native Africans slowly gained more representation. In 1922, the British Empire ratified the first constitution of Nigeria. However, the constitution failed to give equal weight to all of the former protectorates, and it continued the strategy of indirect rule of the northern and predominantly Muslim areas by the Christian southern areas. Over the years, Britain made numerous efforts to unite the northern and southern regions of Nigeria. At the same time, changes to the constitution combined with growing nationalism led to a push toward national sovereignty.

The sixty years of British rule were marked by continual fights for independence. With each of these fights, Britain allowed greater local Nigerian self-government, and created various constitutions that were meant to demonstrate the efficacy of self-rule. Ultimately, Nigeria was given its independence in 1960, and it established a republican parlimentary system of government. However, just as Britain found it difficult to govern the diverse cultural areas that made up the country, so too did the elected Nigerian government. It faced fighting among political parties, uncompromising religious division, and a lack of cohesiveness between the former protectorate regions. These problems set the stage for subsequent upheavals and constant transitioning through various governmental structures. A military coup in 1966 overthrew the first republic, which led to civil war and enormous turmoil. Eventually, in 1979, a second republic was created, this time as a presidential system, but in 1983 it too ended in a coup and military rule.

At about that time, Western countries become interested in Nigeria, in large part because it was becoming an important oil-producing country in the world. They played a role in the establishment of a third republic, which resumed elections and attempted to establish a two-party system.

Nigeria emerged as a somewhat stable democracy in 1999 with the creation of the fourth republic. While this republic has been marred by a pattern of violence and civil unrest that undid the first three republics, it has survived even though it is characterized by many of the inefficiencies and problems that plagued previous republics. Still, it is working and in the 2007 election Umaru Yar'Adua of the People's Democratic Party (PDP) was elected president, even though his election was marred by claims of electoral fraud and criticisms from both candidates and from international observers.

A couple of points are worth noting in this history. First, the geographic area that became Nigeria did not develop organically, but was imposed by the British to make colonial rule easier. The combination of diverse cultural regions is problematic because Nigerians often see themselves first as tribal members, then as Nigerian citizens. Second, Nigeria has oil wealth, which one would think is a blessing, but which, in many ways, is a curse. The problem is that the oil wealth creates a prize to fight for, making it difficult for Nigeria's non-oil-producing regions to accept a breakup in the country, because then they would get none of the wealth. At the same time, that oil wealth provides a strong reason for the oil-producing regions to support a breakup because then they would reap the financial benefits from the oil. Oil wealth also means that outside interests will fund the side that promises them some of that wealth. Consequently, the civil unrest that has marked recent Nigerian political history may continue for a long time.

Modern Nigeria's Government: The Fourth Republic

Though British rule was not especially successful, the constitutions that Britain created to govern Nigeria became important guides for the development of the modern state of Nigeria. First, the legacy of British rule led to the creation of a government with both a legislative and executive branch; second, it led to the establishment of a system of common law based on British common law; and third, it spurred the creation of political parties. In short, the constitutions embodying British ideas became integrated with domestic Nigerian traditions to create the modern structure of the Nigerian government.

In addition to the national government, Nigeria has various regional governments, and is divided into 36 states and 774 local governments. This large number of local governments is an attempt to provide a degree of home rule to the many different tribes that make up Nigeria.

The fourth republic can be considered a transition republic as control has shifted from the military rule of the third republic to civilian rule. Nigeria uses a presidential system in which the president serves as both chief of state and head of the government.

Nigeria has a bicameral legislature. The Senate has 109 seats—three from each state plus one from Abuja, and its members are elected by popular vote to serve four-year terms. The House of Representatives has 360 seats with its members also elected by popular vote for four-year terms. There are two main parties, the People's Democratic Party (PDP) and the All Nigeria Peoples Party (ANPP). In the 2007 election, the PDP won the majority of the seats in both houses. Also in 2007, PDP candidate Umaru Yar'Adua was elected in a disputed election. He was the first civilian and university educated leader of Nigeria and has looked to increase development programs, establish peace in the Niger delta, and fight corruption.

Nigeria's legal system is composed of four distinct systems of law: English law, common law, customary law, and Sharia'ah. Sharia'ah is a form of Islamic law that gets significant press in the West because its punishments are often considered harsh by Westerners. Sharia'ah is practiced primarily within the northern states of Nigeria, but it is being slowly introduced elsewhere in the country. The judicial system has a Federal Court of Appeals appointed by the federal government, and a Supreme Court whose members are appointed by the president.

The history of the Nigerian government demonstrates the problems that multiculturalism presents for democracy. For a democracy to work, its people must share certain values, one of the most important of which is that people will not resort to armed conflict even when they feel they have been wronged. That value depends on a level of goodwill and belief that others will not take advantage of situations when they are in power. Because of the diversity in Nigeria, that goodwill often doesn't exist, and Nigeria continues to struggle with the problems imposed on it by its colonial history. It is trying; on its website the Nigerian Embassy concluded its discussion of its government with the statement:

> The administration is determined to transform the country, in line with democratic principles, into a land of opportunity, equity, of government's use of dialogue and progress and prosperity for all.

Outside observers can only hope that they succeed.

ussian Government

In 1991, the Union of Soviet Socialist Republics (USSR) ended and the republics that made it up each became independent states, connected by history and a loose commonwealth. To understand the current government in Russia, we need to consider the history of the former Soviet government, which began in 1917. Before that time, the Soviet Union, then known as the Russian Empire, was a centralized autocracy ruled by czars. World War I created severe economic difficulties for the Russian Empire and led to political confusion and civil war. In 1917, the **Bolsheviks,** members of the more radical majority of the Russian Social Democratic party, under the leadership of Vladimir Lenin took over the Russian government and, after winning the civil war, established control over the country. In 1922, Lenin designed a federal type of constitution that incorporated republics surrounding Russia, republics that had previously been part of the Russian Empire. The constitution marked the beginning of the USSR. Although it was revised in 1936 and again in 1977, this constitution was, in many of its parts, the same one in force until the 1991 breakup of the Soviet Union.

A key element of that constitution and the government of the Soviet Union was the relationship between the government and the Communist Party. Article 6 of the earlier Soviet constitution stated: "The Communist party of the Soviet Union is the leading and guiding force of the Soviet society and the nucleus of its political system and of all state and public organizations."

The Communist Party's dominant control of the Russian government meant that the government was largely a rubber stamp and administrative institution for carrying out policies made by the party. There was a radical change in the Russian political system in the late 1980s when Soviet leader Mikhail Gorbachev introduced a number of liberalizing reforms. These reforms reduced the power of the party and unleashed a wave of nationalistic and economic upheaval.

The chaos preceding the breakup of the union upset a number of communist leaders, and in 1991 a group of them attempted a **coup d'état**—an extraconstitutional takeover of a country. That coup failed because the military and a majority of the people in the former Soviet Union resisted, and leaders such as Boris Yeltsin, the head of the Russian republic, refused to accept the coup and began a struggle against it. The coup leaders were arrested and the Soviet Union ceased to exist. Each of the republics claimed its independence. In the 1990s a number of the republics joined together in the Commonwealth of Independent States, but it was primarily a symbolic organization.

Chaos reigned in the early 1990s in all the countries that made up the former Soviet Union. After the aborted coup, the Soviet Union broke apart. The legislative branch of the government, the Congress of People's Deputies, dissolved itself, and the republics declared themselves independent. Russia, the largest of the republics, took control of most of the former Soviet government.

Russia created a governmental system consisting of a president and a legislative branch, called the Congress of People's Deputies. The two branches of government shared roughly equal powers, causing many gridlocks in policy decisions in the early years. A new constitution in 1993 created a stronger president but also maintained a Federal Assembly composed of an upper Chamber of the Federation and a lower State Duma with checks on presidential power.

In 1999, Vladimir Putin was elected president. Throughout his eight years in office, he was an extraordinarily popular president, in part because he brought stability back to Russia, and in part because he brought pride back to being Russian. Because of a two-term limitation on service as president, he could not run for election in 2008, but his handpicked successor, Dmitry Medvedev, won in a

Prime Minister and former President Vladimir Putin of Russia.

Russia

Population (approximate): 140,041,247 (2009)
Area: 6,592,800 square miles (17,075,200 square km)
Distribution: 73.3 percent urban; 26.7 percent rural
Capital city: Moscow
National anthem: "Hymn of the Russian Federation" (formerly "The Patriotic Song" and "God Save the Tsar")
Government leaders: President Dmitry Medvedev (since 2008); Prime Minister Vladimir Putin (since 2008)
Former Soviet Union: Russia is the largest country of the former Soviet Union. The other new countries are Armenia, Azerbaijan, Belarus, Estonia, Georgia, Kazakhstan, Kyrgyzstan, Latvia, Lithuania, Moldova, Tajikistan, Turkmenistan, Ukraine, and Uzbekistan.
Ethnic divisions: 80 percent Russian; 4 percent Tatar; 2 percent Ukrainian; 1 percent Bashkir; 1 percent Chuvash; 12 percent other
Literacy rate: 99 percent
Religion: 67 percent atheist; 15–20 percent Russian Orthodox; 10–15 percent Muslim; 2 percent other Christian
GDP: $2.2 trillion; per capita: $15,800 (2008)
Currency unit: Ruble
Monetary conversion rate: 1 ruble = $.032 (June 2009)
Internet users: 30 million (2007)
Cell phones: 170 million (2007)

Russia

The Russian Federation

The Constitution

The current Constitution of the Russian Federation came into force in December 1993, following its approval by a majority of participants in a nationwide plebiscite. It replaced the Constitution (Fundamental Law) originally passed on April 12, 1978, but amended many times after 1990.

The Principles of the Constitutional System

The Russian Federation (Russia) is a democratic federative, law-based state with a republican form of government. Its multiethnic people bear its sovereignty and are the sole source of authority. State power in the Russian Federation is divided between the legislative, executive, and judicial branches, which are independent from one another. Ideological pluralism and a multiparty political system are recognized. The Russian Federation is a secular state and all religious associations are equal before the law. All laws are made public and in accordance with universally acknowledged principles and with international law.

Human and Civil Rights and Freedoms

The basic human rights and freedoms of the Russian citizen are guaranteed regardless of sex, race, nationality, or religion. The Constitution declares the right to life, to freedom, to personal inviolability. The principles of freedom of movement, freedom of expression, and freedom of conscience are upheld. Censorship is prohibited. Citizens are guaranteed the right to vote and stand for election in state and local elections and to participate in referendums.

The Organization of the Federation

There are eighty-nine members (federal territorial units) of the Russian Federation. Russian is declared the state language, but all peoples of the Russian Federation are guaranteed the right to preserve their native tongue.

The President of the Russian Federation

The president is elected to office for a term of four years by universal, direct suffrage. The same individual may be elected to the office of President for no more than two consecutive terms. The president may appoint the Chairman of the Government of the Russian Federation, with the approval of the State Duma, and may dismiss the Deputy Chairmen and the federal ministers from office.

Source: Eastern Europe and the Commonwealth of Independent States, London: Europa Publications, 1994.

landslide after hardly campaigning. After the election, Medvedev appointed Putin as Prime Minister, and together they have been popular in Russia. They have remained less popular in the West, as they have tried to exert Russia's influence on the world political scene.

Saudi Arabian Government

Unlike the other four countries we have considered, all of which are, to varying degrees, democracies, Saudi Arabia makes no such claim. It is a monarchy, and it provides us with an example of an authoritarian autocracy.

The Saudi Arabian government is relatively modern; the present kingdom was established in 1932. Before that time, what is now Saudi Arabia, like the other countries in the Arabian peninsula, was a collection of tribes generally following Islamic religious traditions. Life in the individual tribes and among the various tribes was governed by those traditions and by the **Qur'an,** the primary Islamic religious body of writings. Until the twentieth century, no single, long-term leader emerged from this collection of tribes.

That changed in the early 1900s when Ibn Sa'ūd conquered most of the tribes in central Arabia and became the political and spiritual leader of the Bedouin tribe. He extended his authority during the first third of the twentieth century and created the kingdom of Saudi Arabia in 1932.

The kingdom has no written constitution, relying instead on historical precedent, the Qur'an, and royal decrees as its guides. There are no legislative bodies and no political par-

King Abdullah of Saudi Arabia.

ties. It is in a very real sense an absolute monarchy. But even absolute monarchies have their limits. Although the Saudi state has no constitution and no laws that restrict the king's powers, the Qur'an and historical custom limit what the king does, and over time a quasi-constitutional system has developed. The ruler is chosen by members of the royal family from among its members, subject to the approval of a group of Muslim leaders (the *ulema*). The *ulema* can remove the ruler, and he is also dependent for support on tribal leaders and, more recently, on important businessmen. Notice that there is no question of female rule in Saudi Arabia, because Islam's view of women precludes them from taking any such role.

Running a government is too much for any one person, and in 1953 King Sa'ūd created a Council of Ministers to assist him, with a prime minister playing a significant role partially independent of the king. The prime minister appoints the Council, along with other advisory councils who assist him in both legislative and executive matters. This dual power base created a tension between the king and the prime minister that was temporarily resolved when the prime minister, Prince Faisal, became king in 1964. King Faisal was assassinated in 1975 and the tension returned. King Faisal's successor was King Khālid, who died in 1982. Khālid was followed by King Fahd, who solved the tension by naming himself as prime minister. When King Fahd's health became frail, his cousin, Crown Prince Abdullah, was named prime minister. King Fahd died in 2005 and Abdullah became King.

As is the case with many governments, especially those established in the twentieth century, the Saudi system of government is still evolving. In 1980, a committee was established to define a basic system of rule based entirely on Islamic principles. In 1992, the committee reported to King Fahd, who set up a sixty-one-member *Majlis Al-Shura*, or Consultative Council. This council could make recommendations to the king and prime minister but would have no ability to make law (the king retained that right). He also reorganized provincial administrations and formalized the existing system of government, keeping the throne in the al-Sa'ūd family in perpetuity.

Although King Fahd announced that the political system would be directed by *Sharia* (Islamic law), he recognized that the public expects the *Majlis* to be more than another rubber-stamping institution with the sole purpose of legitimizing the regime. Upon taking office, King Abdullah declared that he would like to see the *Majlis* and the thirteen regional councils (composed of 210 appointed ministers) play a more influential role in policymaking in the future. However, it is still uncertain how responsive the royal family will be to the advice of these ministers.

People tolerate strong autocracies in which they have little or no power for numerous reasons including military force wielded by the government, historical precedent, fear of the chaos that a change would bring, or satisfaction with the existing state of affairs. In the Saudi case, despite the enormous income taken by the Saudi monarchy, the Saudi people are relatively satisfied. The reason is the huge amount of oil income received by the government that allows it to undertake numerous social projects for the people. For example, all Saudis are entitled to free medical care. These projects are financed without significant taxation, even while providing lavish lifestyles for the Saudi royal family.

The Persian Gulf War of 1991 eroded the ability of the monarchy-led government to "buy its legitimacy." Low oil prices squeezed the government budget and led to severe austerity measures in the mid-1990s. Although those measures were somewhat relaxed by 1997, agitation against the absolute monarchy of the al-Sa'ūd family has continued to increase. King Abdullah has continued modernizing and is in negotiation for member-

Saudi Arabia

Population (approximate): 28,686,633 (2009)
Area: 830,000 square miles (2,150,000 square km)
Distribution: 82 percent urban; 18 percent rural
Capital city: Riyadh
National anthem: "As-salaam al-malaki as-Saud"
   ("Royal Salute of Saud")

Government leader: King and Prime Minister
   Abdullah bin Abdul Aziz al-Sa'ud (since 2005)
Ethnic divisions: 90 percent Arab; 10 percent
   Afro-Asian
Literacy rate: 79 percent
Religion: 100 percent Muslim
GDP: $583 billion; per capita: $20,700 (2008)
Currency unit: Riyal
Monetary conversion rate: 1 riyal = $0.267 (June
   2009)
Internet users: 6 million (2007)
Cell phones: 28 million (2007)

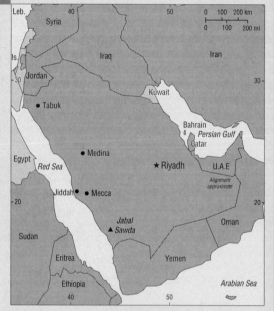

Saudi Arabia

ship in the World Trade Organization (WTO) and is trying to liberalize Saudi Arabia's policy toward foreign investment. The country's oil revenues constitute more than 75 percent of its annual budget, and therefore its economic health goes up and down with oil prices.

The Saudi government finds itself in a difficult position. Internally, the ultra-religious Sunni Muslims advocate a return to more strict Islamic tradition while externally it faces intense criticism from human rights groups and Western-oriented Saudis who call for increased democracy, less strict punishments for criminals than the Shariah, and equal treatment for women under the law. In 2005, municipal elections were held, and were seen by some outside observers as a first step toward democracy in the kingdom.

The westernization of Saudi Arabia has infuriated a number of Saudis, such as rich businessman/terrorist Osama bin Laden, who masterminded the 9/11 attacks on the United States. What makes it so difficult for Saudi Arabia and other Islamic states to be friendly with the United States is the United States' strong support for Israel, which has fueled anti-American feeling in Saudi Arabia and throughout the Middle East. If Saudi Arabia does evolve into a democracy, which the United States has stated that it ostensibly wants, the result will likely be a government far less supportive of U.S. policy than the current government.

Some Lessons about Governments

This survey of governments of the world should give you a sense of the variety and diversity of governments—both democratic and autocratic. From it you can see that there are many types of democracy and autocracy and that it is difficult to compare one with the other.

A number of general points about governments can be made:

1. Governments reflect their history (for example, the Nigerian government reflects its British heritage, and the strong French government reflects its unstable history).

2. Governments are evolving. France, Nigeria, and Saudi Arabia do not have the same governmental structure they had fifty or sixty years ago, and the Soviet Union no longer exists. These countries are unlikely to have the same governmental structure fifty years from now as they have today. The rate of change depends on the historical tradition as current government practices become embodied in society and place limitations on change.

3. Autocracies are more likely to change than long-standing democracies. The reason is that the process of change is easier. When the former Soviet Union decided to change governmental form, it could do so relatively easily compared with the United States. Saudi Arabia would be able to do so even more rapidly.

4. Changes in autocracies occur from within as much as from without. The changes in the Mexican and former Soviet governments are examples. Often the process of liberalization brings about opposition that otherwise would have been silent or suppressed.

More rules and insights are embodied in the examples, but we leave them for you to draw out.

Future Changes in Governments

What does the future hold for these and other governments? As usual, it is unclear. We are likely to see significant changes in the structure of government of the republics of the former Soviet Union and some Middle Eastern autocracies such as Kuwait and Saudi Arabia, as well as many eastern European countries. If the coming years hold prosperity and countries manage to avoid all-out war, the present forms of most other governments are likely to continue. If the economic and social conditions worsen, however, more changes can be expected. And if there is a major nuclear war, who knows what will remain of government, culture, or society? Obviously, we hope such major changes will not occur because of war, but current troublesome social and economic conditions could dash those hopes.

Some of these social and economic conditions are high unemployment rates in many countries, including much of industrialized Europe; the proliferation of destructive weapons systems in areas of the world where social, political, economic, and religious quarrels are already disrupting ordinary life; repression and denial of opportunity to large populations in some countries; widespread financial hardship in some countries burdened with heavy debt they owe to more prosperous nations; and environmental pollution that threatens to change whole areas of the world. Fortunately not all of these conditions exist in any one country, and it is always possible that diplomacy and, ultimately, good sense exercised by governments will enable the compromises and adjustments necessary for peacekeeping to prevail.

Key Points

- The French government is a parliamentary democracy with both a president and a prime minister.
- The Mexican government has been a partial autocracy ruled by the PRI, but it is moving toward a competitive democracy.
- The Nigerian government is a republic whose political instability in large part reflects its colonial heritage.

- The governments of republics of the former Soviet Union are in a state of transition.
- The Saudi government is an autocracy based largely on Islamic principles.
- Some lessons about governments that can be drawn from these examples include the following: governments reflect their history, governments are changing, autocracies can change quickly, and autocracies often change from within.

Some Important Terms

Bastille Day (279)
Bolsheviks (290)
censure motion (280)
coup d'état (290)

French Revolution (279)
Institutional Revolutionary Party (PRI) (285)
land reform (285)

line-item veto (285)
Qur'an (292)
vote of confidence (280)

Questions for Review and Discussion

1. What is the relationship between the Declaration of the Rights of Man and the French constitution?
2. How can the French prime minister be removed from office?
3. Is Mexico a democracy or an autocracy?
4. What are some differences between the Mexican constitution and the U.S. Constitution?
5. What is a line-item veto?
6. Explain how *ejidos* in Mexico worked to maintain the power of the PRI.
7. Why is it harder for Nigeria to maintain political stability than it is for many other countries?
8. What is the official language of Nigeria? Why was it chosen?

9. What was the relationship between the Communist Party and the former Soviet government?
10. How does the new Russian Federation differ from the former Soviet Republic?
11. What are some concerns about Russia's ability to deal with its problems? What are some causes of optimism?
12. Does the Saudi autocratic government have unlimited power?
13. Why do the Saudi people tolerate the Saudi autocracy?
14. State five lessons about government that can be derived from this chapter.
15. What do you believe would be the ideal system of government?

Internet Questions

1. Look at the composition of the French government on the embassy site www.ambafrance-us.org/spip.php?article615 (accessed June 11, 2009). What are the fourteen minister posts under the prime minister?
2. Go to www.nigeriaembassyusa.org/history.shtml. In terms of population, how does Nigeria rank

compared to other African countries? How does it rank in terms of physical size?
3. According to www.saudia-online.com/saudi_arabia.htm what does the legislative branch of Saudi Arabia's government consist of?
4. Go to www.time.com/time/specials/2007/personoftheyear/ and watch TIME's interview

with Vladimir Putin. According to the reporter, why was Putin chosen as the 2007 TIME Person of the Year? According to Putin, what is a country's sovereign right?

5. Using the CIA World Factbook, https://www.cia.gov/library/publications/the-world-factbook/, what are the administrative divisions of Mexico?

*F*or Further Study

Anderson, N., *The Kingdom of Saudi Arabia,* rev. ed., London: Stacey International, 1986.

Bronson, Rachel, *Thicker Than Oil: America's Uneasy Partnership with Saudi Arabia,* New York: Oxford University Press, 2006.

Levy, Daniel C., Kathleen Bruhn, and Emilio Zebadúa, *Mexico: The Struggle for Democratic Development,* Berkeley: University of California Press, 2001.

Lippman, Thomas W., *Understanding Islam: An Introduction to the Muslim World,* New York: Penguin Putnam, 2002.

McPaul, Michael, Nicolai Petrov, and Andrei Riabov, *Between Dictatorship and Democracy: Russian Post-Communist Political Reform*, Washington, DC: Carnegie Endowment for International Peace, 2004.

Preston, Julia, and Samuel Dillon, *Opening Mexico: The Making of a Democracy,* New York: Farrar, Straus & Giroux, 2004.

Soyinka, Wole, *The Open Sore of a Conflict: A Personal Narrative of the Nigerian Crisis,* Oxford, UK: Oxford University Press, 1996.

WWW   CIA World Factbook www.cia.gov/library/publications/the-world-factbook/

WWW   The French Prime Minister www.governement.fr/en

WWW   The Government of the Russian Federation www.gov.ru/main/page8.html

WWW   Mexico Online www.mexonline.com

WWW   Nigeria Direct www.nigeria.gov.ng

WWW   Partido Acción Nacional (National Action Party) www.pan.org.mx

WWW   The Royal Embassy of Saudi Arabia www.saudiembassy.net

Democratic Government in the United States

After reading this chapter, you should be able to:

- Give a brief account of the development of the U.S. government
- List the five key elements in the Declaration of Independence
- Outline the structure of the U.S. federal government
- Explain the distribution of powers as set out in the U.S. Constitution
- Describe the political process in the United States
- Summarize the role of the fourth estate, the political elite, the military-industrial complex, and PACs in the political process

An oppressive government is more to be feared than a tiger.
—**Confucius**

In the previous chapter, we briefly considered the governments of five countries. In this chapter, we look specifically at the U.S. government and how it works. As you will see, government, like other aspects of your life, is in an ongoing process of evolution.

Historical Development of U.S. Government

Because the United States started as a colonial possession of Great Britain, it is natural that our government reflects a British heritage. Initially, ties to Britain were strong, but when Britain tried to tighten control over colonial trade and to levy taxes on the colonists without obtaining the consent of the colonial legislatures, the colonies took action to end British rule and set up their own state. The most important event in the formation of the U.S. government took place when the Second Continental Congress met in 1776, issued the Declaration of Independence, and resolved to draw up a plan for the United States of America. (The Declaration of Independence can be found at www.usconstitution.net/declar.html if you want to read the full text.)

The Declaration of Independence states that:

- The people have the right to revolt against oppressive government.
- Legitimate government must be based on the consent of the governed.
- Both the ruler and the ruled are obligated to preserve a government that pursues legitimate purposes.
- All men are created equal.
- All men are endowed with certain inalienable rights, including life, liberty, and the pursuit of happiness.

These principles became the foundation of the U.S. form of government.

The Declaration of Independence formalized the war that had begun with the Battle of Bunker Hill in April 1775. It proclaimed the colonies "free and independent states." Having declared themselves independent, the states faced the problem of establishing a workable form of government. This was done in a Constitutional Convention held in Philadelphia in May 1787.

The Constitutional Convention succeeded because the delegates were willing to compromise. The decision to have a federal government was probably the biggest compromise. It satisfied both supporters of a **unitary government**—a government in which all the power is centralized in the national government, and the central government is absolutely supreme over all other government within such a nation—and supporters of a **federation,** a number of separate states, each of which retains control of its own internal affairs. The federal system of government had aspects of both. States retained control of some issues; the central government retained control over others.

Other important compromises included:

- The differential representation in the House (by population) and Senate (two per state).

- The establishment of an Electoral College to choose the president. The **Electoral College** is a body of electors chosen by the voters in each state to elect the president and the vice president. In the Electoral College, each state is allowed to have as many electors as it has representatives and senators in Congress, and each state can determine the method of choosing its electors.

- The direct election by all the people of a particular state of its House members and the selection by state legislatures of the two senators allowed each state.[1]

In addition to those just mentioned, compromises on many other issues were necessary because of the extensive conflict of interests and opinions. In essence, the Constitution can be characterized as a bundle of compromises.

The U.S. Constitution—the foundation of the U.S. government and legal system—was signed on September 17, 1787, and forwarded to Congress with the recommendation that it be submitted to state conventions for ratification and that it become effective on acceptance by nine states, which it was after much struggle. (The U.S. Constitution can be found at www.usconstitution.net/const.html if you want to see the full text.)

Many of the states ratified the Constitution on the condition that amendments protecting private rights be adopted as soon as the new government was formed. The first ten amendments, adopted in 1791, accomplished this insofar as the national government was concerned. This **Bill of Rights**—a formal statement of the fundamental rights of the people of a nation—forbade the national government to invade basic private rights.

The Structure of U.S. Government

Because of the compromises in the Constitution, the United States has a federal government. It operates on three levels: national, state, and local. Over time, the relative strengths of these various levels have changed. Specifically, the national government has been strengthened in part by wars, in part by advances in communication and transportation, and in part by the increasing complexity and nationwide scope of social problems. Nevertheless, state and local governments are still of great importance both to the individual and to our entire society.

---

[1]The election of senators by the people is one change that has taken place in the Constitution.

Each of the fifty states, with its independent constitution, its own supreme court, and its own governmental agencies, exercises jurisdiction over most personal relationships, such as those of husband and wife, parent and child, and employer and employee, and also over property and business matters, including contracts, deeds, wills, corporations, and partnerships. Each state regulates commerce within its borders; establishes and controls local government; protects health, safety, and public order; conducts elections; and provides education.

Local governments are subdivisions of the state, are incorporated by the state, and possess varying degrees of autonomy. They include the county, city, town, township, village, borough, and school district and also include special agencies such as park districts, sanitary districts, and planning and zoning boards. Local governments are close to the individual, who can hardly escape noticing the services they provide. The sidewalks, lights, schools, public health service, police and fire protection, parks, beaches, and libraries are largely provided by local governments.

Structure of the National Government

Because the national government has become most important, we describe it in some detail. The national government of the United States as established by the Constitution is divided into three branches: the executive branch, the legislative branch, and the judicial branch. Figure 15.1 is worth careful study; it provides an outline of the structure of our national government.

The **executive branch,** the branch of government charged with the execution of laws and the administration of public affairs, is headed by the president, who is in charge of enforcing or executing the laws. Under the president, to whom all members of the executive branch are directly responsible, are the vice president, who would become president if the president were unable to serve, and the **Cabinet,** the heads of the major administrative departments of government. These Cabinet members, called secretaries, are appointed by the president, subject to approval by the Senate. Within the executive department there are also a number of agencies and commissions such as the Environmental Protection Agency. The extent to which these are responsible to the president is determined by law. The executive branch of the government is primarily concerned with enforcing the laws and with carrying on daily the many activities in which a modern government must engage. However, the president also plays an important role in determining governmental policies.

The **legislative branch** is the branch of the government vested with the power to enact and legislate the law. It consists of the two houses of Congress: the House of Representatives and the Senate. The legislative branch is chiefly the policymaking agency of government. It determines government policies by passing laws, or statutes. See Figure 15.2 and the box on page 308 for a better understanding of how a bill becomes a law.

The **judicial branch** is the branch of government that interprets the laws as they apply to particular cases that may arise. It consists of the Supreme Court and of the various lower and special federal courts. Once the meaning of a law has been decided in its application to a case, a precedent is said to have been established, and similar cases are likely to be decided in the same way. The federal courts interpret not only the laws passed by Congress but also the Constitution itself. For legal purposes, the Constitution of the United States means whatever the Supreme Court says it means. If the Court should obviously and persistently misinterpret the Constitution, the primary redress would be for the House of Representatives to impeach the justices responsible. Then the Senate would try them and, if they were convicted, remove them from office. In the more than 200 years of its existence, this has never happened to the U.S. Supreme Court.

We now turn to the broad issues, clarifying our national government.

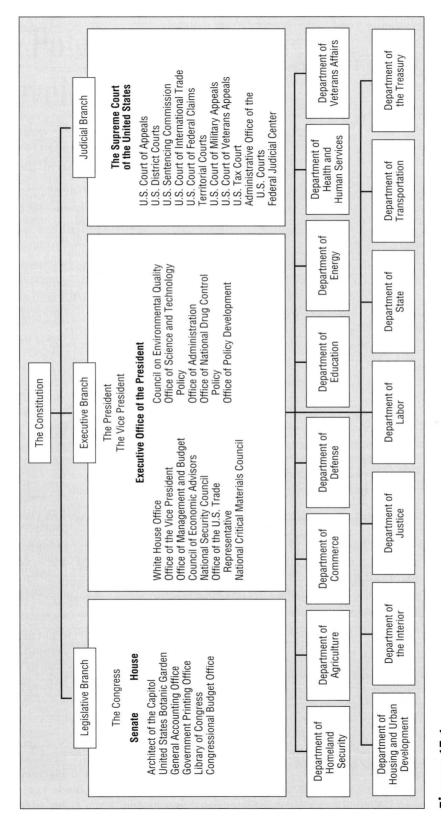

Figure 15.1

Diagram of the government of the United States as of 2009. The U.S. government is organized into three branches: the legislative, executive, and judicial. (Source: U.S. Bureau of the Census, Statistical Abstract of the United States.)

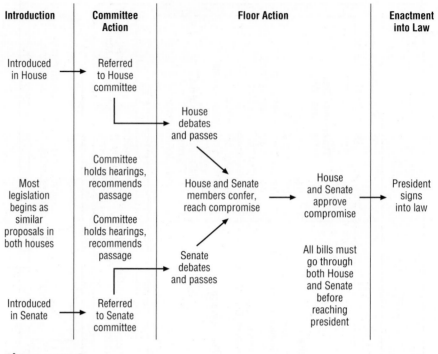

Introduction	Committee Action	Floor Action	Enactment into Law

Figure 15.2

How a bill becomes law. This diagram illustrates the most typical way in which proposed legislation is enacted into law. There are more complicated, as well as simpler, routes. Most bills fall by the wayside and never become law.

The Nature of Our National Government

A short answer to the question, What kind of national government do we have? would contain as few as four words: democratic, republican, federal, and presidential. Our national government is democratic rather than dictatorial or oligarchical; it is republican rather than monarchical; it is federal, in contrast to most of the governments of the world, which are unitary; and it is presidential rather than parliamentary. It should be noted that the governments of all the fifty states have the same basic characteristics as the national government except that they are unitary rather than federal.

Why Our Government Is Both a Democracy and a Republic. There is an old but fruitless argument as to whether the United States is a democracy or a republic. Actually, the nation has the essential characteristics of both of these forms, and therefore it may be described as both democratic and republican. A **republic** is a form of government in which the head of the state, the president, does not inherit the office but is elected by those citizens who are qualified to vote. The United States is a republic according to this definition. Our Supreme Court has expressed the American concept of a republic as follows: "The distinguishing feature of the republican form of government is the right of the people to choose its own officers." This makes *republic* synonymous with *democracy,* which is the kind of government we have. Technically the United States has a **representative democracy,** a form of government in which the people make most governmental decisions not directly but through elected representatives, rather than a **pure democracy**, a political system under which all citizens vote directly on every piece of legislation. Pure democracy is possible only in very small communities.

The Meaning of Presidential Government.   We have noted that the U.S. national government is presidential. In a **presidential form of government,** the chief executive (usually called the president) is elected for a definite period of years independent of the legislative or lawmaking body and has certain powers derived directly from the Constitution. In contrast, under the **parliamentary form of government,** the executive branch is a committee, or cabinet, that represents the majority party in the legislative body and holds office only as long as it can command a majority in that body.

Great Britain presents a good example of parliamentary government. There the cabinet and its chief, the prime minister, are responsible to Parliament, and they can hold office only as long as Parliament supports their policies. The Parliament may withdraw its support for the prime minister by approving or introducing a vote of no confidence against the government. This system makes for close coordination of the executive and legislative departments. Under the presidential system, as exemplified in the United States, it is possible for the president and the majority in Congress to represent different parties and therefore fail to cooperate. On many issues, however, party lines are not sharply drawn.

In practice, the president usually takes the leadership in developing a legislative program, and insofar as this lead is effective, our system of government operates somewhat like the parliamentary system. Unfortunately, there are times when the president and the majority in Congress clash on major issues and are unable to resolve their differences. This may make it difficult for the president to take decisive and effective action to meet problems as they arise both at home and abroad.

Clashes were the rule in the 1990s as Congress was controlled by one party and the presidency by another. These clashes led to the impeachment of President Bill Clinton in 1998. In 2000, in an extraordinarily close election, President George W. Bush narrowly won the election but lost the popular vote. The election was heavily contested as only a few thousand votes separated Bush and Albert Gore, his opponent, in Florida, and all knew that whoever won Florida would win the election. After much legal wrangling, the Supreme Court issued a decision that essentially made Bush the winner. Many Gore supporters saw the election as unfair, but they accepted the outcome. Thus, in 2000, the Republicans won control of both houses of Congress and the presidency, and there were fewer clashes. In the 2004 elections, the Republicans again won control of both houses of Congress and the presidency, but in 2006, the Democrats won control of both the House and the Senate, and in 2008, the Democrats increased their majorities in Congress and won the presidency with the election of Barack Obama.

Democratic candidate Barack Obama celebrates victory in the 2008 presidential election.

The president has two major functions: to take the lead in formulating policies and proposing legislation to Congress, and the administrative task of keeping the vast and unwieldy government organization operating smoothly and efficiently to perform its various normal duties. The latter involves many important responsibilities including acting as commander in chief of the nation's armed forces. Thus, when the United States went to war against Iraq, it was President Bush who ultimately was responsible for making the decision to do so.

Distribution of Powers by the Constitution.   A broad view of the national Constitution as originally devised and as it stands today reveals a wide distribution of political power. The founding fathers, though desiring a central government strong enough to govern, feared too great a concentration of power and therefore attempted to devise means for preventing the abuse of power. Broadly speaking, power is distributed in accordance with four constitutional principles:

1. **Federalism**—power is divided between the national government and the separate states.
2. **Separation of powers**—legislative, judicial, and executive powers are divided among three separate branches of the national government, each with its own duties and limitations of power.
3. **Checks and balances**—the decisions of one branch must be ratified by different branches of government. This system is designed so that no one branch of government can become too powerful.
4. **Limited government**—power is divided between the people and the government. This fourth principle includes the democratic doctrines of popular sovereignty, the inviolability of personal rights, and constitutionalism.

Division of Powers between the Nation and the States.   One of the great problems under federalism is how to divide powers between the central government and the states. In the United States, the national government theoretically possesses only the powers delegated to it, and all others belong to the states. Powers delegated to our federal government are of two kinds, enumerated and implied. The **enumerated powers** are expressly delegated by the Constitution and include the grant of legislative powers to Congress (Article I, Sections 1 and 8), executive powers to the president (Article II), and judicial powers to the Supreme Court and other federal courts (Article III). In general, the enumerated powers delegated to the national government deal with all international affairs and domestic affairs of a national, rather than merely state, concern. The **implied powers** can only be inferred from the Constitution and have no explicit provision. They have, however, provided the flexibility necessary for the national government to meet the new problems arising over the years from economic and social change. They have also, as some critics of expanding federal powers put it, enabled the central government to encroach on the rights and functions of the states. The implied powers are based on the so-called **elastic clause** (Article I, Section 8), which gives Congress the power "to make all laws which shall be necessary and proper for carrying into execution the foregoing powers, and all other powers vested by this Constitution in the government of the United States, or in any department or officer thereof."

The constitutional provisions for the division of powers also distinguish, though not very clearly, between exclusive and concurrent powers. **Exclusive powers** belong only to the national government or only to the states. **Concurrent powers** belong to both the national and state governments, such as the power to tax, borrow, and spend. Many government powers were not mentioned in the original Constitution, and the general understanding was that these belonged to the separate states. The Tenth Amendment made it plain that these reserved or residual powers "are reserved to the States respectively, or to the people."[2]

---

[2]In some federal systems (Canada, for example), the reserved powers belong to the national government.

In the final analysis, however, it is clear that in spite of a careful attempt to separate powers, national supremacy has become a principle of the U.S. constitutional system. This principle grows out of the supreme-law-of-the-land clause, which states that the Constitution, laws of Congress in pursuance thereof, and treaties are the supreme law of the land, despite anything to the contrary in state constitutions and laws. In case of conflict, the states must make the necessary changes to conform to national law. Moreover, a branch of the national government, the Supreme Court, decides the issue when a conflict exists, so that in effect the national government judges its own case.

Separation of Powers of the Branches of Government.   As an additional safeguard against tyranny, the founding fathers divided governmental powers on a functional basis in accordance with the principle of separation of powers. James Madison wrote,

A United States of Europe?

The European Union as of 2009.

In 1958 a few western European states formed together into a common economic market. In 1967 they strengthened their mutual ties and forged the European Community, also establishing a European legislature called the Council of Europe. Over the years, the common market evolved into the European Economic Community (EEC), and after the historic Maastricht Treaty of 1992, it formed the European Union (EU), a confederation of sovereign member states. When formed, the EU contained approximately 350 million people from twelve member countries: Belgium, the Netherlands, Luxembourg, Italy, Germany, Greece, France, Spain, Portugal, Denmark, Ireland, and Great Britain. On May 4, 1994, the European Parliament voted in favor of enlarging the EU's membership to sixteen to include Austria, Finland, Norway, and Sweden, but the voters of Norway voted against joining. In 2004,

ten new countries joined the European Union: Cyprus, the Czech Republic, Estonia, Hungary, Latvia, Lithuania, Malta, Poland, Slovakia, and Slovenia. Two more countries, Bulgaria and Romania, joined in 2007. These additions brought the total membership to twenty-seven countries with a total population of almost 500 million. Other countries are negotiating for membership, so that number may well increase.

The goals of the EU are virtually unprecedented for any regional organization in the international community. The Maastricht Treaty established a tariff-free Europe; created a central bank to oversee banking in all member countries by 1997; and introduced a common currency, the euro, in some of the countries. In 2002 euro notes and coins went into circulation, with twelve of the member states adopting the currency. Further, the EU had two other long-range objectives: first, the formation of a European Political Union (EPU), which would harmonize the foreign policy interests of the member states and give the union a common voice in international relations, including matters of defense and security; second, a joint action plan to regulate agriculture, education, energy, the environment, public health, tourism, trade, and so on. Essentially it was a call for a far-reaching economic and political union that would eventually become the United States of Europe.

In an attempt to implement that vision in 2004, European leaders created a European Defense Agency, which was meant to coordinate their defense policies. They also signed a revised Constitutional Treaty which would have further unified Europe. However, voters in both France and the Netherlands rejected that proposed constitution. In response, the EU leaders created the Treaty of Lisbon, which contained many of the changes in the Constitutional Treaty, but which was formulated as amendments to the original treaty, and thus did not have to be ratified by the voters. It went into effect December 1, 2009.

> No political truth is certainly of greater intrinsic value, or is stamped with the authority of more enlightened patrons of liberty, than that … the accumulation of all powers, legislative, executive, and judiciary, in the same hands … may justly be pronounced the very definition of tyranny.

The overconcentration of power in the colonial royal governors and the exalted position of the legislatures in the state governments of the Revolutionary War era had both proved unsatisfactory. The founding fathers feared tyranny by a majority of the electorate as well as by a strong executive. Most of the fathers were conservatives who wanted, among other things, to safeguard property against the "ill-humor" of popular majorities. They decided to place legislative, executive, and judicial powers in three different branches, each independent of the others. Each of the three branches of government was designed to be not only independent of the others but also directly dependent on different sources for office. The president was to be chosen by the electors in the Electoral College for four years; senators by state legislatures for six years; representatives directly by the people for two years; and judges by the president and Senate for life. As a consequence, it would be difficult for even the majority of citizens to "seize" complete control of the government and "tyrannize" over the minority, even though these constitutional mechanisms might not frustrate the will of the majority forever.

Checks and Balances. Supplementing and modifying the principle of separation of powers is that of checks and balances. Because of this principle, there has never been in practice a complete separation of executive, legislative, and judicial powers. Broadly speaking, the separation of powers is part of the checks-and-balances system, for it fulfills Madison's dictum, "Ambition must be made to counteract ambition." Strictly speaking, however, checks and balances refer to restraints placed on each branch by requiring it to divide some of its powers with the others so that it cannot exercise independently the major functions allotted to it. Despite some popular opinion to the contrary, the authors of the Constitution never intended the three branches to be completely independent of each other. What they wanted to prevent was all legislative powers and all executive powers from falling into the same hands.

The Constitution clearly provides for interdependence between the three branches, which Madison also said was essential to free government.[3] Each branch of the government has some responsibility and power to influence the functions of the other two. Congress enacts laws, but they are subject to the president's veto, and that veto can be overridden by a two-thirds majority in each house. The Supreme Court can declare acts of Congress void, but Congress determines the appellate jurisdiction of the Court, and the president and the Senate appoint the judges. The president can make treaties, but only with the advice and consent of the Senate, and presidential appointments to government offices must receive Senate confirmation. The president and two-thirds of the Senate can make a treaty, but the House of Representatives must approve if any money is involved. The president administers the laws, but Congress must establish the departments and agencies and provide for their support. Many of the regulatory commissions (which are administrative agencies) created by Congress actually exercise executive, legislative, and judicial powers. Congress, by investigative committees and other means, attempts to secure the faithful administration of the laws. In a very real sense, all three branches participate in the making and the administration of public policy.

The extent of the power of the various branches is continually being tested. For example, the Constitution (in Article I, Section 8, paragraph 11) specifically gives Congress the right to declare war, yet presidents have often entered government forces into battle without

---

[3]He wrote that "unless these departments be so far connected and blended as to give to each a constitutional control over the others, the degree of separation which the maxim requires, as essential to free government, can never in practice be duly maintained."

The Capitol building in the early 1850s.

having Congress declare war. When they do this, presidents say it isn't really a war but a "police action." The Vietnam conflict is the most vivid example.

In response to the Vietnam "police action," Congress passed the War Powers Act, which was meant to define clearly when the president must consult Congress about a warlike action, but it hasn't worked out that way, as you can see by considering the invasion of Grenada, the actions of U.S. ships in the Persian Gulf off Iran in the war between Iraq and Iran, and the bombing of Kosovo in 1999, all of which were done without congressional approval. In the Persian Gulf War of 1991, President George Bush (the father of George W. Bush) maintained his right to commit forces to war unilaterally, as did President Clinton in Kosovo. However, usually presidents do try to get congressional approval before entering into war (as President George W. Bush did in the 2003 Iraq war), even though they argue that they don't need it.

An Independent Judiciary and Judicial Review.   U.S. tradition places great faith in an independent judiciary, one free of all pressure and all fear of political reprisal. Democratic theory has not demanded that the courts be directly subject to popular control. The U.S. Constitution provides for a Supreme Court relatively free of the executive and legislative branches, and once the judges are appointed, they can be removed only by impeachment and conviction by Congress. The function of the courts is to interpret the law and apply it in individual cases. For this task, independence is necessary in order to avoid decisions influenced by public sentiment or thoughts of job security and patronage.

The power to interpret the law is an enormous power. As you have seen throughout this book, concepts are often vague and somebody must give them specific meaning. Does "equal rights for all" require busing students to particular schools? Are segregated private clubs violating the rights of nonmembers? Do we have a constitutional right to doctor-assisted suicide? How much newly presented evidence, and what kind, is necessary to over-turn a death sentence? Making these decisions and others like them is the main function of the courts.

As the Supreme Court has evolved, it has become a protector of the rights of the people (as it interprets those rights). Every law passed in the United States is subject to judicial re-view by the Supreme Court of the nation or the supreme court of the state in which it was enacted. Under **judicial review,** the Supreme Court passes judgment on the constitutionality of a legislative or executive act. If the Court decides a law is unconstitutional, it is no longer a law. This independent judicial review, the third in our system of checks and balances, is a

Funny Things Happen to an Idea on Its Way to a Law

So that you can get a sense of how the national government functions, let's briefly follow a fictional idea through the various stages from conception to law. Let's say the idea begins with a social science professor who figures out that if the government establishes a new reform of the public assistance system everyone will be better off. At a cocktail party, she meets a legislative assistant for one of the congresspeople (congresspeople have a number of assistants who analyze potential bills for them). The legislative assistant hears the idea, likes it, and decides to talk it over with some friends who work as assistants at the White House. If the White House staff like it, they may make it part of their proposals; if the White House doesn't like it, the congressperson or a senator may introduce it as a bill (a proposed law) on his or her own. If it is to get any further than that, other congresspeople or senators must be interested in it, and often, if they like it, several will become joint sponsors.

If possible, a similar bill will be introduced in the other legislative body. Then the bill will be sent to the appropriate committee, which will decide whether to consider the bill. The committee chair has significant flexibility in deciding which bills to consider. The bill might also be sent to subcommittees. By now, if the committee has chosen to, it will consider the bill for a formal vote and bring it up to the House or Senate with its recommendation (many bills die in committee). At this stage, it is important that the bill have

other backers. For example, if the bill is part of the president's program, the president can probably generate significant pressure to bring the bill to the floor—that is, to introduce the bill to the full House and Senate. Let's say one of the legislative bodies passes the bill. Then it is sent to the other legislative body. At each stage, the bill is subject to debate and can be amended. Thus, even if the bill passes both houses, it will probably be different from the originally proposed bill.

If both houses of Congress pass the bill in some form—say, simple majority vote—it is sent to a resolution committee that irons out the differences between the two versions (the one passed by the House of Representatives and the one passed by the Senate). Once that's done, the bill is sent to the president, who can either sign it, at which point it becomes law, or veto it. If the president vetoes it, Congress can override that veto with a two-thirds majority. But that is a rather hard thing to come by, and usually the politicians will try to compromise on a bill so that the president will agree to it in the first place.

Now the professor's idea is a law. But it's still subject to judicial review—an examination by the Supreme Court to determine whether the law is in accordance with the Constitution when a case relevant to that law is brought before it. If the Supreme Court holds that it is unconstitutional, that idea is no longer law.

This is a fairly succinct description of how an idea becomes a law. In reality the process is more complicated, but this summary should give you some idea of what happens to a bill on its way to becoming a law.

---

unique U.S. contribution to government and it has served us well. The national Constitution does not expressly grant or deny the Supreme Court the power of judicial review, but the Court has exercised it since 1803, when Chief Justice John Marshall concluded in the case of *Marbury v. Madison* that the Court must do so to fulfill its expressed duty of exercising jurisdiction over all cases arising under the Constitution.

Whether the founding fathers intended it to be so is uncertain, but our system of government required that this function be performed by some agency, and the Court was the logical choice. Marshall's opinion may have been partially political, but it was logical and has proved expedient. His basic assumption, which democratic theory endorses, is that the Constitution is superior to ordinary law.

The necessity for judicial review arises from federalism, the separation of powers, and the inviolability of private rights. The Court decides whether the national government has encroached on the powers reserved to the states, whether the states have exceeded their constitutional powers, whether the president or Congress have encroached on the rightful sphere of the other, and whether the national or state governments have violated constitutionally guaranteed private rights. This, of course, provides no safeguards against encroachment by the Court on the allotted spheres of the other agencies, including the states.

The aspect of judicial review that has provoked the greatest opposition is the voiding of acts of Congress. To nullify acts of Congress is to frustrate the will of the people expressed by democratically elected representatives, or so the critics have argued. There is truth in this accusation, but most Americans prefer having the majority will occasionally frustrated to having a system of government in which the majority is free of constitutional restraints. If a measure really has powerful public support, the people can always resort to a constitutional amendment or new legislation, adjusted to meet the Court's objections.

Over the years, the Supreme Court has gained great prestige by the manner in which it has protected the constitutional rights of national and state governments, Congress, the president, and individuals. However, its prestige has fluctuated greatly from time to time, and its decisions have never, of course, pleased everyone. In the 1960s, the Court was regarded as liberal. It found legal justification for giving the federal government greater power to deal with national problems, to expand its real or alleged welfare activities, and to protect individual rights when the states fail to do so. Then in the 1970s and 1980s, the Court became more and more conservative and tended to limit federal governmental powers and follow a more conservative view of the role of government. In the early 1990s, the movement of the Court to the right increased with the appointment of conservative justices such as Clarence Thomas. Many felt that his appointment would ensure a conservative majority in the courts for decades. President Clinton attempted to redress this perceived imbalance with his nominations to the Supreme Court; but President Bush shifted it back toward a more conservative stance and President Obama's appointment of Sonia Sotomayor swung it back to liberal.

Federal judges, however, do not sit in an ivory tower rendering their decisions completely apart from public opinion. When the Court reverses a previous decision, this almost invariably reflects a basic change in public opinion. In 1954, the Supreme Court rendered a long-awaited decision on the constitutionality of "separate-but-equal" public school facilities. It reversed a fifty-six-year-old decision and found segregation in public schools to be a denial of "equal protection of the laws." Some people of the South accused the Court of playing politics, but in this case the justices were making a reasonable interpretation of the Constitution that agreed with the contemporary evaluation of majority opinion in the United States.

Limited Government.   Our national government under the Constitution has limited power. First, it shares power with the states. Second, at fairly frequent intervals, the voters, in free elections, may reject those in office or extend their tenure. Third, every citizen has certain inalienable rights recognized by our Constitution. These include freedom of speech, assembly, and religion, and they also include the right not to be tried, convicted, and punished for crimes without due process of law—that is, without being given the benefit of certain procedures and privileges that the law provides for an accused person in order to assure a fair trial.

Two characteristics of U.S. government, both of which are closely related to the subject of judicial review, require special comment at this point. One is the recognition by our laws and Constitution that every citizen has certain inalienable rights. The second is the fact that, though our federal Constitution is difficult to amend, the meanings ascribed to many of its clauses change gradually, as new situations arise, through the process of reinterpretation by the courts. For this reason it has sometimes been called a living constitution.

Individuals' Inalienable Rights.   The Preamble of our Constitution contains the declaration that one of the great purposes of government is "to secure the blessings of liberty to ourselves and our posterity." The U.S. concept of limited, constitutional government is based on the proposition that the people reserve to themselves certain areas of freedom that government may not invade, that people have inherent rights no political authority may either give or take away, "and among these are life, liberty, and the pursuit of happiness." Democratic government assumes that the majority will rule but also that the minority has the right to dissent. In the United States, as in any democracy, the majority rules legitimately only so long as it respects minority rights.

The founding fathers considered government to be largely an enemy of freedom rather than a friend. As stated earlier, the original Constitution and its Bill of Rights provided safeguards against the national government, and the Fourteenth Amendment extended most of these to the states.[4] We have learned through experience that government can be both the enemy and the friend of freedom. Most of us do not regret that our government was forbidden the right to invade a wide sphere of private rights, though we may no longer believe that government is a necessary evil. We know that liberty and security are inseparable and that without the security provided by stable, effective government, there would be few freedoms to enjoy. Thus the trend for more than a hundred years has been toward popular dependence on government to promote basic human rights.

Rights versus Duties.   Rights are never absolute. Furthermore, rights involve duties. The right to freedoms involves the duty of respecting the freedoms of others, whether these concern their choices of religion, political party, economic philosophy, or place of residence. Our freedoms are guaranteed only so long as we exercise them responsibly and refrain from using them as a cloak for obscenity, slander and libel, murder, public nuisances, incitement to riot and insurrection, and other unlawful acts. It is always the duty of the courts to draw a line between the legitimate and the illegitimate exercise of freedom, between controls essential for the welfare and safety of society and controls that unnecessarily invade the area of protected personal freedoms. No duty of government is more important or more difficult than this one.

Symbol of a dream, Abraham Lincoln, the president who freed the slaves, was present symbolically as participants in the 1963 March on Washington massed at the Lincoln Memorial to hear Rev. Martin Luther King, Jr.

---

[4]All responsible U.S. citizens would do well to acquaint themselves with the Bill of Rights and its significance for their welfare. These rights include (1) substantive rights, such as freedom of religion, of the person, of speech and the press, and of peaceable assembly; and (2) procedural rights, such as due process of law, just compensation for property taken for public use, specific warrant for arrest or search, writ of habeas corpus, speedy and fair trial by jury, and freedom from excessive bail, unusual punishment, bills of attainder, double jeopardy, compulsory self-incrimination, and ex post facto laws.

There is no simple way of drawing a hard and fast line between the inalienable rights and freedoms of the individual and the controls required to protect the rights and freedoms of others. Many people, including a number of respected lawyers and judges, feel that in recent years the Supreme Court, in its efforts to guard the civil rights of individuals, has shown more concern for the rights of those accused of crime than for the rights of their alleged victims. Other critics, equally respected, defend the Court's decisions on the ground that protection of accused persons who may be innocent requires strict adherence to correct legal procedures. Since 1985, however, the Supreme Court has begun to crack down on criminals by giving the police more rights. That push has been strengthened by new laws, such as the Crime Act of 1994, which imposed mandatory life imprisonment for three-time convicted felons. The 9/11 terrorist attacks on the United States led to the passage of the Patriot Act, which gives the government significant power to detain individuals suspected of terrorist motives. Under this law, it is possible to keep these detainees for an indefinite period without charging them with a specific crime nor allowing them to speak with a lawyer. The reviews on the Patriot Act are mixed. Some see it as undermining the basic rights of individuals; others see it as a necessary deterrent to terrorism.

Figure 15.3 shows the basic rights that, under our U.S. system of government, are designed to protect an accused person against an unfair trial. One great protection is the right to trial by jury. In criminal cases, conviction requires a unanimous decision. (Some states do not require unanimity for deciding civil cases.)

Growth of the Living Constitution.   U.S. government is constitutional government, and we Americans are proud of our written Constitution. In Great Britain, democratic government and the fundamental principles on which it is based developed slowly, so that no need was

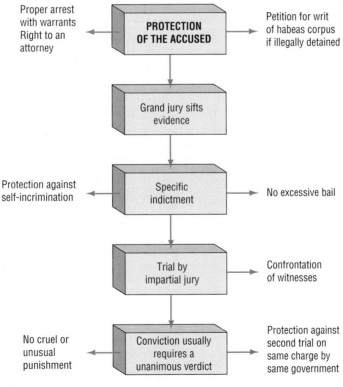

Figure 15.3

Civil liberties: An American heritage.

felt for a formal written document expressing these principles. But in the United States, a new nation had to be suddenly created out of thirteen independent colonies or states, and the only solution for this problem was to draw up in writing a formal agreement describing the structure and powers of the new government and also expressing the principles on which it was based. Because of our long and successful experience with this written Constitution, we have perhaps come to feel that fundamental political principles cannot be trusted to provide a framework for government unless they have been formally agreed on and duly recorded.

A written constitution is, however, rigid in that it cannot be easily amended. The amendment procedure stated in Article V of the U.S. Constitution provides for two methods of proposing and two methods of ratifying amendments. They may be proposed by two-thirds of both houses of Congress (the only method ever used to date) or by a constitutional convention called on the petition of two-thirds of the states. A number of states have called for such a constitutional convention, although most observers do not believe as many as two-thirds of the states would agree to petition Congress to call such a convention. Once proposed, amendments may be ratified by legislatures in three-fourths of the states (the method used all but once) or by conventions in three-fourths of the states (the method used to ratify the Twenty-first Amendment). The procedure was set up to ensure that the integrity of the document will not be violated by frequent revisions prompted by transient shifts in public and governmental opinion.

In spite of the difficulty in amending it, the Constitution has been a flexible instrument. It has changed, not so much through amendment as through reinterpretation by the courts, to meet new practices and new situations that those who drew up the Constitution could not have foreseen. It has thus become a living constitution in the sense that it has been able to adjust in many ways to the changing beliefs and needs of the people. For example, through custom the undemocratic elements of the Electoral College were largely eliminated. Originally, the people elected leading citizens to the college and these then selected the president. But the practice soon evolved for candidates to the Electoral College to pledge themselves to a presidential candidate in advance, so that for all practical purposes when a citizen voted for an elector, the vote was for a certain person for president.

The rise of national political parties has helped bring about unity to our national government in spite of the separation of powers provided for in the Constitution. Also, the growth of nationalism, the need for giving the executive great powers in times of crisis, and other influences have resulted in the emergence of the president as a strong unifying element in government. Much expansion of government functions has also been made possible by new interpretations of the Constitution. When the people wanted the government to play a more vigorous role in the regulation of business activity, they and their Supreme Court found the necessary authority implied in the enumerated powers of the Constitution. When new social problems arose and the people demanded more government services, the needed authority was again found to exist, by implication, in the original document.

If you look again at Figure 15.1 and note the major agencies of the executive branch of the federal government, you will have some idea of the vast expansion in government functions that has taken place over the years. Whether that expansion should continue or whether it should be reduced is a major issue that must be faced in the coming years.

The Political Process

Earlier, we described democracy as it works in theory. We also touched on some examples of its workings in practice. We would be remiss in stopping there because, as with just about everything else, practice is different from theory. In our large country, decisions cannot be made by the institutions of democracy alone. Instead, they are made by a political process that

President Barack Obama.

includes numerous influences, some of which have no lofty goals—only the goal of establishing and using a power base. Others play a more beneficent role, but it is a role that was not foreseen by the early proponents of democracy. Political pressure groups and elites that have direct influence on governmental decisions are prime examples of practices deviating from theory.

Individuals influence government in our democracy through the political process. This political process includes numerous factors that determine policy formation, including public opinion, political pressure groups, the military-industrial complex, political parties, nominations and elections, and, finally, legislation. We can't give a complete discussion of each of these, but we can mention the most important.

Political Parties

Although political parties in the modern sense did not begin to develop until the middle or later part of the eighteenth century, today they are universal in democracies. George Washington advised the new American nation to avoid dividing into parties, and they are not mentioned in the U.S. Constitution. But as democratic government developed, political parties came into existence because they fulfilled two important functions: interest aggregation and policy-making. They are not the result of theory but of practical experience, and they are necessities in representative democracies.

Compromising Conflicting Interests.   Probably the most important role of political parties is in compromising conflicting interests. In a dynamic society, many conflicting interest groups compete for control of the government and for favorable legislation. The majority of these sincerely believe that their programs represent justice, progress, and the general welfare, but they cannot all have their way. No government can provide at the same time for prohibition of and the right to manufacture, sell, and consume marijuana; for outlawing strikes and the freedom to strike; for the complete separation of church and state and publicly supported church schools. If all the conflicting groups that arise from differences in race, nationality, social class, creed, economic interest, and geographic location refused to accept any compromises, a unified national policy would be impossible. In the United States and other countries with two-party systems, most of the necessary compromises are brought about within each political party.

The political party, especially in the two-party system, acts as a mediator and cushion between, on the one hand, the individuals and groups that belong to it and, on the other hand, the government. Individuals and interest groups can bring pressure to bear on the party to adopt policies they favor. The organized party then seeks to reach compromise agreements and to convert them into legislation.

The Two-Party System.   Although the number of parties is not determined in the Constitution, the United States has generally operated on a two-party (Republicans and Democrats) system. Most observers believe that this provides a more workable system than the alternative multiparty system. However, because of the necessary compromise on issues, a two-party system seldom shows sharp and clear-cut differences in program or principle, and often differences that appear to exist before an election tend to disappear once a party gets into power. The need of each of the two major parties to appeal to a large segment of the population contributes to the development of relatively moderate philosophic orientations. Moreover, in their attempt to attract people from all interest groups, the two parties tend to promise everything to everybody. Voters who want to influence some particular policy (such as extension of civil liberties, more public housing, gradual elimination of farm price supports, or a planned reduction of foreign aid) often feel frustrated because they cannot make their voices heard in the party. Periodically, there have been attempts to establish a third party. The Reform Party's candidate won significant votes in the 1992 presidential election and Ralph Nader, the Green Party candidate, won about 3 percent of the votes in the 2000 election. Although these votes were far from the number needed to win those elections, they were sufficient to influence the outcome, and some Gore supporters argued that Nader was responsible for Bush's victory.

The argument in favor of two parties is that in a nation as large and diverse as the United States, unity is essential, and each of our major parties performs the valuable function of bringing together under one umbrella a number of groups whose interests vary considerably. If a portion of the population is not happy with the policy alternatives presented by the two major parties, however, it is at liberty to create an alternative party. This potential for the development of an alternative party helps keep the two major parties responsive to the needs and demands of the people.

An important trend in party affiliation that has been increasingly evident is the decline in the number of people who identify themselves with one or the other major party. Today, more than one-third of the voters in the United States describe themselves as independents. Some of the reasons for this are (1) people do not need to rely as much on favors extended to them by their party as they did seventy-five or one hundred years ago, when formal support systems were less common; (2) they wish to split their votes among candidates of different parties; (3) they are disillusioned with the party system or with some kinds of government activities; and (4) they have so many social and professional interests that they no longer see a political party as a kind of club. Relaxation of party ties does not mean, however, that people have given up the privilege of voting, and of voting within the choices offered by the two-party system.

Elections

Democratic government implies the wide extension of the **franchise**—the right to vote. Citizens of modern dictatorships also enjoy this privilege, though for them it is a privilege stripped of power. The right to elect government officials and to vote on public policies has been achieved by centuries of effort. We have already noted how suffrage was restricted in early America by property and religious qualifications. Because of such requirements, in 1790 only about 15 percent of adult white males, and no women, could vote. Thus, women were not included in the suffrage at all.

Over time, the United States has done away with property, religious, racial, and gender qualifications. The gradual trend throughout the world has been to extend the franchise and make it universal for all responsible citizens. In the United States, black males won the right to vote in national elections in 1870, when the ballot was awarded them by the Fifteenth Amendment to the Constitution. It was not until 1920, when the Nineteenth Amendment to the Constitution was ratified, that women won the right to vote in U.S. national elections, although some individual states had granted them local rights much earlier. The most recent such movement in the United States was to reduce the voting age from twenty-one to eighteen, which was accomplished by the ratification of the Twenty-sixth Amendment to the Constitution in 1971.

As we discussed earlier, one of the important compromises of the original Constitutional Convention was the establishment of the Electoral College. The people elect members of the Electoral College, which then elects the president. In a number of elections, the most recent example being in 2000, the popular vote and the Electoral College vote differ. This led to calls for the elimination of the Electoral College, but we are unlikely to see any such change because constitutional change comes very slowly, and small states, who would lose power, are likely to block any effort to abolish the Electoral College.

Obstacles to Effective Popular Control.   The right to vote is not equivalent to the power to control the government. The electorates in democracies throughout the world have had their ballot power weakened in many ways, including the following:

- Overburdening voters with a long ballot
- Permitting voters to participate only in indirect elections
- Forcing voters to declare their choices publicly
- Providing inadequate voting facilities
- Allowing nominations to be controlled by the privileged few
- Limiting categories of those who can hold office
- Conducting corrupt elections
- Use of psychological methods to guide people to vote in certain ways
- Placing on the ballot only candidates sponsored by the official government party

Some of these limitations have existed and still exist in the United States and other democracies. In the early 1990s, some electorates, such as those of Colorado and California, limited their own power by voting to limit the number of terms their elected representatives could serve. They did this because they disliked the idea that the representatives, once elected, tended to get reelected indefinitely. However, the voters were also preventing themselves from constantly reelecting individuals if they liked them well enough. The debate over whether term limits should be repealed or whether more electorates should adopt them is likely to be discussed well into the present century.

The Nonvoter.   In the United States, perhaps 60 percent of the civilian population of voting age exercise their franchise in presidential elections; in the off-year congressional elections, only about 40 percent participate; and in local elections, a mere 15 percent is not uncommon. In Britain and the other democracies, the percentage is considerably higher (it is over 75 percent in Britain). Why do Americans fail to vote? The many reasons include the long ballot, the belief that politics are irrelevant to contemporary concerns, lack of interest, or feelings that one vote can't matter.

Probably the most important reason is indifference produced by lack of political education and experience. People simply feel no compulsion to participate in the electoral process. Many of them come from homes with a long tradition of nonparticipation in political affairs. Such people are often considered selfish and unpatriotic, but in many cases ignorance of issues and candidates is the main reason for not voting. Only increased education can improve the percentages of voters.

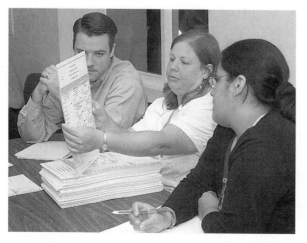

In the 2000 presidential election, every vote counted.

One of the reasons people don't vote is the belief that their vote cannot make a difference. Generally, they are right—one vote does not swing an election, but in the 2000 elections numerous votes were extremely close, and a few votes either way could have changed the result in various House and Senate races. In the U.S. presidency race, the election came down to who would get Florida's twenty-five electoral votes. After initial recounts of the votes, only about 900 out of 6 million votes separated the candidates, and there was much legal wrangling about which votes could be counted. The number of partially punched ballots in those counties that had punch card ballots far exceeded the 900 vote difference, so the presidential election hinged on decisions made about these ballots. Ultimately, George W. Bush was declared the winner, but only after a Supreme Court decision. Had a few more

Gerrymandering and the U.S. House of Lords

Current
32nd Congressional
District

Proposed
32nd Congressional
District

Gerrymandering.

The U.S. democracy doesn't work perfectly. Incumbents use their powers—PAC money,* free use of the postal service, perks of office, the large support budgets they are given to pay for staff—to vest themselves in office. These powers are sufficiently great that in the last forty years, 80 percent of all members of the House of Representatives who have run for reelection have indeed been reelected. In 1986, 98 percent of such members were reelected; in 1988, 99 percent were reelected, leading the *Wall Street Journal* to call this body "The House of Lords." More recently, the benefits of incumbency have been less clear, but the large majority of incumbents who decided to run did retain their seats.

One of the ways incumbents win reelection is to have the districts from which they are elected gerrymandered, or drawn up in such a way that it is difficult for them to lose. For example, consider the strange shape of the Thirty-second District of California, shown on the left side of the drawing. Why does it have that shape? Why isn't it shaped like the proposed district on the right side of the drawing? Answer: Because demographic characteristics make the odd-shaped district a safe district for the incumbent; the "reformed" district wouldn't be safe.

Shaw v. Reno (1993) illustrated some of the problems that plague democracy in the United States. In that case, white voters claimed that a long, skinny North Carolina district was unconstitutional because it was drawn to include blacks and exclude whites. The Supreme Court sent the case back to the lower court for a review of the issues: the meaning of the constitutional "right" to vote and

the propriety of racially motivated state legislation designed to benefit members of historically disadvantaged racial minority groups. The lower court then said that the district was constitutional because it helped remedy past discrimination and that its odd shape alone was not enough to void the legislation. The white voters appealed the decision by going back to the Supreme Court in 1995, this time in a case called *Shaw v. Hunt.*

When the Supreme Court decided *Shaw v. Hunt* in 1996, it said that the legislation was indeed unconstitutional because North Carolina had not overcome the presumption that the use of race as the "predominant factor" in drawing district lines is unconstitutional. In response, North Carolina wrote a new version of the statute, and the case again worked its way up to the Supreme Court, where it appeared in 1999 as *Hunt v. Cromartie.* This time, the Court said that to think that states must absolutely eliminate the use of race in drawing up their electoral districts was to misinterpret the 1996 decision. Instead, the Court said, a state might have other reasons, besides focusing on black voters, for drawing a district that happened to have large numbers of black voters, and that anyone challenging such a law must be prepared to prove that the state's main motive was to isolate or favor black voters. Boiled down, the Court meant: "Case not proved." North Carolina was left to ponder yet again the reasons for the shape of the district. In 2001, the case was ultimately decided, and the Supreme Court ruled that race could be used in redistricting, as long as it was not the predominant factor.

With the significant redistricting that came with the 2000 census, this issue will remain contentious. Just how contentious can be seen in Texas. In 2006, the Supreme Court ruled that a mid-decade redistricting in Texas, done specifically to increase the likelihood of maintaining a Republican majority, was legal as long as that redistricting did not violate the rights of Hispanics and blacks. This ruling led to more redistricting attempts by both Democrats and Republicans but it also led to a bipartisan bill to eliminate such gerrymandering, through the creation of an independent federal commission that would make all redistricting decisions, instead of having the state legislature make them.

*For a further discussion of PACs (political action committees), see p. 319.

Gore supporters voted, or even had they been more careful when they voted, Al Gore might have won. So individual votes do matter.

Referendums, Recall Elections, and Direct Democracy. In the United States, most elections are indirect—we elect a governor and a legislature and they then determine the laws. Decisions can, however, be more directly related to the voting public if a referendum is held and the people decide directly what the law will be. These referendums avoid the governmental structure and allow direct voter input into a law.

The direct approach is used most in California, which allows voter initiatives on a large number of issues, and these voter initiatives often play an important role in the laws that are passed. For example, property taxes are limited due to a referendum, and in 2003 Governor Gray Davis was recalled and actor Arnold Schwarzenegger was elected.

The California experience demonstrates both the benefits and the problems with direct democracy. To pass an issue by referendum requires large spending on advertising and organization, and this means that some special interest is usually behind those referendums that pass. So, whether these referendums lead to better government, or simply to another means through which special interests can achieve their desires is much in debate.

The Fourth Estate

Most politicians now acknowledge that what is often called the **fourth estate**—the journalistic profession or its members, including the print and broadcast media—is equal in importance to the president, Congress, and the judicial system. *Public opinion* is a general term that everyone talks about, but no one is quite sure what it is or what determines it. Nonetheless, it is extremely important, and political leaders keep a close watch on the mood of the public by listening to feedback from their local representatives and through opinion polls. Politicians try to shape public opinion by giving speeches, selectively granting interviews, and allowing information leaks. As they do this, they must listen to the press and television because these institutions control the information that flows to the general population. The ease of publicizing one's individual opinions by means of the Internet can also affect public opinion, but unlike print or television the Internet is not a good medium for political control because it doesn't organize concentrated action.

Inherent in our Constitution is the guarantee of freedom of the press, but the press is not free from influence by private pressure groups and businesses. The media are important because they play such central roles in influencing public opinion. For example, consider our earlier discussion of the process by which a bill becomes a law. If the social scientist who had the idea has good contacts with the media and can get it to cover stories on how wonderful the idea is, she will probably be much more effective in getting her idea considered by the political process. Similarly, if the media doesn't like the idea, the idea will probably disappear quickly.

Despite the time, energy, and skill they devote to obtaining favorable media coverage, politicians are often not pleased with the results. For example, Presidents Nixon, Carter, and Clinton felt hounded by the press. Both Nixon and Carter believed it to have played an important role in their political defeats. On the other hand, President Reagan, whose career until well into middle age was based in radio announcing and film and television acting, was called "the Teflon president" because press criticism would not stick to him. His personality and experience served him well in politics, where he was also called "the great communicator" because he could get his points across to the American people so effectively.

The Political Elite

A basic assumption in the United States is that all individuals are created equal, but it would be a mistake to assume that practice follows that ideal. In practice, there is an elite in the United States whose feelings, aspirations, and influence carry more weight than those of other groups, either because they can use money or power to influence events or because they have direct access to those in power. If they don't like what is going on, they contact a high-ranking U.S. official to let him or her know their concerns.

Who are the political and economic elite in the United States? Any list would have to include the president, U.S. senators and representatives, governors, state senators, state representatives, and high executives in government, which, using U.S. civil service rankings, would be Grade Service Level 15 and above. To these we would need to add approximately 15,000 to 20,000 executives who hold most of the power afforded by their positions as heads of manufacturing and e-commerce enterprises; the executives of the top financial organizations, law firms, universities, and religious bodies; judges; and independent professionals such as writers, doctors, and scientists. Roughly estimated, we would arrive at about 100,000 people who would have to be considered the political and economic elite of our society.

Does the political elite rule our country and thwart democracy? That's debatable. For example, consider the two presidential candidates in the 2000 election—one was the son of a former famous senator; the other was the son of a former president. That suggests that the elite tend to pass on their control to their children. The authors' view of the elite is that it certainly doesn't rule our country directly, but indirectly it holds a considerable degree of power. All agree, however, that there are limits to that power.

The Military-Industrial Complex and Pressure Groups

In a living democracy, the division among the various groups is often not as clear-cut as it seems. A good example of this is what is often called the **military-industrial complex,** the nexus between the armed forces, the Pentagon, and defense industries. The term was originated in 1961 by President Dwight D. Eisenhower, who had just ended his term of office. In his farewell radio and television address, he said,

> This conjunction of an immense military establishment and a large arms industry is new in the American experience. The total influence—economic, political, even spiritual—is felt in every city, every statehouse, every office of the federal government. We recognize the imperative need for this development. Yet we must not fail to comprehend its grave implications. Our toil, resources, and livelihood are all involved; so is the very structure of our society.
>
> In the councils of government, we must guard against the acquisition of unwarranted influence, whether sought or unsought, by the military-industrial complex. The potential for the disastrous rise of misplaced power exists and will persist.
>
> We must never let the weight of this combination endanger our liberties or democratic processes. We should take nothing for granted. Only an alert and knowledgeable citizenry can compel the proper meshing of the huge industrial and military machinery of defense with our peaceful methods and goals, so that security and liberty may prosper together.

Eisenhower's warning is no less relevant today than it was in 1961. The simple reality is that there is money to be made in defense (in 2008, defense spending totaled about $700 billion), and when there is, firms and individuals will try to make money by expanding their particular areas, using whatever political means they can to ensure political support. This has continued to be true in the early 2000s even though most observers believe that the enormous changes in the former Soviet Union have significantly reduced the need for defensive arms. Thus it is possible to have weapons systems that serve little purpose other than to make profits for defense firms, jobs for their workers, and votes for congresspeople. This means that once the building of such a weapons system is begun, it is extremely hard to stop.

Of course, it is not only industry and the military that combine to create pressure groups for continuation of their programs. Advocates of other kinds of programs also form pressure groups. But the potential damage from weapons systems is so great that the military-industrial complex deserves special mention.

Another way in which groups interact is by means of **pressure groups** that have organized to influence the political process. Pressure groups play an important role in trying to shape public opinion. In addition to exerting indirect influence, they often try to influence legislators directly. Thus pressure groups fill a gap in a two-party system, enabling people with common interests to petition government for redress of grievances and to make their will known on many specific issues. Through the use of lobbyists, they keep national and state legislators and executives informed about what the people they represent really want from government. They also present a threat to well-functioning democracies in that certain special interests may become so powerful that, unless the public is alert, they frustrate the will of the majority and thus obstruct government by and for the many.

Fortunately, one powerful interest group (such as organized labor) is often balanced by another powerful interest group (such as business). However, certain interest groups that lack effective organization, such as hired farm labor and consumers, tend to suffer from pressure-group government. But to say that consumers are likely to suffer from the activities of pressure groups is only one way of saying that the public interest is likely to suffer, for everybody is a consumer.

Political Action Committees.   The problems presented by special-interest pressure groups have surfaced in a new way with the advent of political action committees (PACs). **PACs** essentially are campaign committees established by individuals to raise money for particular political purposes. They sprang up as a result of the revised 1974 federal election laws that limited the amount of money individuals were allowed to contribute to a candidate. Under the law, an individual contributor could give only $1,000 to a candidate's primary and general election campaigns, whereas a PAC could give $5,000 to each.

In 2002, the Congress passed the Bipartisan Campaign Reform Act (BCRA). This law eliminated all soft money donations to the national parties; however, it doubled the allowable hard money contribution. The act also addressed issue ads, placing a limit on advertisements paid for with **soft money**—money contributed to political parties rather than to individuals. The act requires that any ad which supports a specific candidate aired within thirty days before a primary election and sixty days before a general election must be paid for with hard money. However, parties are free to spend whatever they want before that cutoff. Although the BCRA was challenged in the Supreme Court the following year, the law was upheld there by a majority vote.

Other recent advancements in campaign finance reform include the passage of "Clean Money" bills in several U.S. cities. A Clean Money election proposes to publicly finance candidates who can show enough public support through signatures and small donations. These candidates must agree to additional stipulations that limit outside donations or use of personal money to finance the election campaign.

A voluntary funding system is in place for presidential elections in which taxpayers are allowed to check a box on their tax returns that allows a small amount of their tax payments to support presidential campaigns. In return for public money, candidates are required to adhere to spending limits. In the 2008 election, Barack Obama, who, as a primary candidate, had promised to abide by the limits and accept the federal money, decided not to accept the money when it became clear that he could raise far more through private donations. His challenger, John McCain, accepted the federal campaign money and the spending limits that went along with it. Obama won the election decisively, and the additional money he had may well have played a part in his election. Thus, we are likely to hear more about campaign finance reform in the future.

Some writers maintain that the most effective defense against special-interest groups is the organization of still other groups to check and balance those that now exist. The weakness of this theory is that if great numbers of people cannot organize effectively to protect themselves, the general interests of the public—which may constitute the most vital interests of every group—often are neglected.

Evaluation of the Democratic Political Process

The political process in the United States is complex, confusing, and challenging. To win election to a major office takes time, work, money, and patience; from an idea to the enactment of a law often is a long journey. To reach such goals, mountains of obstacles must be scaled and arid deserts of electoral inertia must be crossed. Compromises are necessary, and concessions must be made by many conflicting interest groups, each of which has a somewhat different destination in mind. Ignorance and other human limitations must be taken into account all along the route. Fraud and favoritism are constant dangers. But democracy offers ordinary people the challenge of the opportunity to rule themselves.

In the United States, the democratic way of life has become so firmly embedded in our culture and has brought us so many personal and social advantages that few of us can really conceive of living under any other social system. No other system can give us such a high degree of personal liberty or protect our individual rights so well. If at times we complain about the faults of democracy and its failure to achieve perfection, we are only being human. When we consider the alternatives, most of us believe that our U.S. brand of democracy is providing us with benefits that can be matched in few other countries, and we believe that if we meet our responsibilities, democracy will provide these benefits in greater measure in the future. Most Americans believe that, on balance, our government is and will continue to be a government of the people, by the people, and for the people.

Key Points

- The United States revolted from Britain in 1776 and became a new nation in 1787.
- The Declaration of Independence declared that the right to revolt is reserved by the people, consent to be governed is necessary, governmental action is limited, and all people are created equal and are endowed with certain inalienable rights.
- The national government of the United States as established by the Constitution is divided into three branches: the executive, the legislative, and the judicial.
- The Constitution provides for federalism, separation of powers, checks and balances, and limited government.
- The political process in the United States is a mess that works.
- The fourth estate, the political elite, the military-industrial complex, and PACs all play an important role in the political process.

Some Important Terms

Bill of Rights (299)
Cabinet (300)
checks and balances (304)
concurrent powers (304)
elastic clause (304)
Electoral College (299)
enumerated powers (304)
exclusive powers (304)
executive branch (300)
federalism (304)
federation (299)

fourth estate (317)
franchise (314)
implied powers (304)
judicial branch (300)
judicial review (307)
legislative branch (300)
limited government (304)
military-industrial complex (318)
PACs (319)
parliamentary form of government (303)

presidential form of government (303)
pressure groups (319)
pure democracy (302)
representative democracy (302)
republic (302)
separation of powers (304)
soft money (319)
unitary government (299)

Questions for Review and Discussion

1. Is the United States a democratic society? Explain your answer.
2. In what positive ways did British politics and government influence the U.S. Constitution?
3. What important decisions were made by the Constitutional Convention?
4. What major compromises were made at the Philadelphia convention?
5. Compare federal government with unitary government.
6. What are the three levels of government in the United States, and how are they related to one another?
7. What are the three branches of our national government, and what is the function of each?
8. What are the four basic characteristics of the U.S. system of government?
9. Compare presidential government with parliamentary government.
10. In what ways does the Constitution distribute power?
11. How does the principle of checks and balances modify that of separation of powers?
12. What is the meaning and significance of judicial review?
13. How is the "living constitution" related to the written one, and how does it keep pace with changing conditions and new problems?
14. What role do political parties play in a democratic system?
15. What are the primary reasons people do not vote?
16. What is the "fourth estate"? How does it influence our government?
17. What is the military-industrial complex? How does it influence our government?
18. What role do PACs play in shaping legislation? Is it a positive or negative role?

Internet Questions

1. Go to the Federal Election Commission website, www.fec.gov/pages/elecvote.htm. Which states have more than twenty electoral votes? Which states have fewer votes now than in 1990?
2. Who are your present senators and in what year were they first elected? Check www.congress.org.
3. Use www.supremecourthistory.org to find out: Who are the nine justices on the Supreme Court today?
4. What is the Preamble to the United States Constitution? See www.usconstitution.net/const.html.
5. Using www.whitehouse.gov who is in the president's advisory cabinet?

For Further Study

Kobrak, Peter, *Cozy Politics: Political Parties, Campaign Finance, and Compromised Governance,* Boulder, CO: Lynn Rienner, 2002.

Kryssar, Theodore, *The Right to Vote: The Contested History of Democracy in the United States,* New York: Basic Books, 2000.

McDougall, Walter A., *Freedom Just Around the Corner: A New American History, 1585–1838* (vol. 1 of proposed 3 vols.), New York: HarperCollins, 2004.

Philbrick, Nathaniel, *Mayflower: A Story of Courage, Community, and War,* New York: Viking, 2006.

Rothkopf, David, *Running the World: The Inside Story of the National Security Council and Architects of American Power,* New York: Public Affairs, 2006.

U.S. Constitution and Fascinating Facts about It, full text of the U.S. Constitution with supplemental facts by Robert F. Tedeschi, Jr., 5th ed, Green Farms, CT: Oak Hill Publishing, 1995.

United States Government Organization Manual, Office of the Federal Register, National Archives and Records Service, Washington, DC: Government Printing Office, issued annually.

Wood, Gordon S., *Revolutionary Characters: What Made the Founders Different,* New York: Penguin, 2006.

WWW   Reform Party www.reformparty.org

WWW   USA.gov www.usa.gov

WWW   The U.S. Constitution www.usconstitution.net

WWW   The U.S. House of Representatives www.house.gov

WWW   The U.S. Senate www.senate.gov

WWW   The U.S. Supreme Court www.supremecourtus.gov

WWW   The White House www.whitehouse.gov

The Organization of Economic Activities

chapter 6

After reading this chapter, you should be able to:

- Define the great economic problem
- Discuss the evolution of our economy from feudalism, to mercantilism, to a market economy, and to a pragmatic market economy
- Summarize the historical development of socialist thought
- Distinguish between a planned and an unplanned economy
- Explain the terms *supply* and *demand*, and use them to explain how a market economy works
- Explain why all modern economies are pragmatic market economies

The ideas of economists and political philosophers, both when they are right and when they are wrong, are more powerful than is commonly understood. Indeed, the world is ruled by little else.

—John Maynard Keynes

Traditionally, economics was that branch of social science concerned with the ways in which people provided themselves with material goods and services. More recently, economics has broadened its scope and sees itself as the science of choice. It considers how people and societies allocate resources among alternative ends to achieve their wants. Thus, we will define **economics** as the study of the social organization through which people satisfy their wants. In the process of satisfying these wants, economic institutions develop that govern individuals' economic interactions in the same way that social institutions govern individuals' social interactions. These economic institutions include government organizations, business firms, unions, and the laws that facilitate the production, distribution, and consumption of goods. To understand how an economy operates, we must be well acquainted with these institutions. In this chapter, we consider how economies are organized. Before we do that, because economists tend to play a more active role as policy advisers than do other social scientists, let's briefly consider how economists approach problems.

Economists bring a unique analytical approach to looking at social problems, an approach that emphasizes rational choice and costs and benefits. They take as a starting point that everything has to be paid for by someone and argue that society should take explicit account of costs and benefits so that it can make rational decisions. Economists picture a world populated by individuals doing precisely that—they search out benefits, and they weigh those benefits relative to the costs. If the benefits exceed the costs, they do it; if not, they don't do it. Economists define rationality in relation to this cost/benefit approach: Rational individuals are individuals who weigh the benefits and costs of decisions and make decisions that have the largest benefits at the lowest costs. Economists extend that reasoning when they analyze social problems, arguing that government and society need to establish rules and institutions that require decision makers to take the costs of laws and regulations into account as well as the benefits.

The Nature of an Economy

In modern industrial societies, economic relationships are complex. Almost nothing can be produced and made available to the final buyer without the help of a variety of economic institutions and the conscious or unconscious cooperation of great numbers of workers. This is true of almost every commodity, whether it be a shirt, a computer, a ballpoint pen, or frozen yogurt. Our ability to satisfy our daily economic wants depends on the existence of many highly systematized social arrangements. Without these organizations, our economic efforts would be largely futile, and most of us, especially in the cities, would soon starve to death.

Taken together, all the complex social arrangements by which we satisfy economic wants constitute an economic system, or an economy. An **economy** may be defined as the social organization by means of which the people of a given society produce and distribute economic goods.

Functions of an Economy

An economy must perform at least four basic functions, and ideally it should perform them in such a way as to confer maximum benefits on the community. It must determine:

1. The kinds of goods to be produced
2. The amount of each good to be produced
3. The resources that are to be allocated to a good's output
4. The ultimate division of the goods among those who are to enjoy them

In addition, an economy should provide a favorable environment for economic progress.

Economics and the Social Sciences

Before we consider these issues, we need to consider how economic issues fit in with other issues in social science.

Some economists argue that economic issues are at the center of all social science issues. We disagree. While economic issues are important, we would not argue that they are the central elements of our lives. Often economic goods are wanted for only social and cultural reasons (if you have enough money to buy that sports car, that cute girl or guy will go out with you; otherwise, she or he won't give you the time of day). Ultimately, it is not money or economic goods that we desire—it is happiness, and recent research on happiness has found that after society has reached an annual income threshold (of about $15,000 per capita), additional income does not seem to make a society happier.

Although economic wants are not the *most* important, they are important. If you're hungry or lack adequate clothing or shelter, you're probably not happy; and if all your friends have new cars, you probably aren't happy unless you have a new car, too. Thus, it is important to study economic needs and wants, and how societies fulfill them.

Economic Wants and Economic Goods

Economic wants are desires for things that can be obtained by labor or through exchange and on which, in a modern society, a money value can be placed. Not all wants are economic. People want love and affection, respect, health, happiness, and many other things that cannot be measured in money. These things may be affected by the economic circumstances of the individual, but they are not primarily economic. A certain amount of money and the things that money can buy are necessary to sustain life and to make it worth living, but beyond that the relationship between money and happiness is not so clear.

Economic goods are the things that money can buy and that are the objects of our economic wants. If we possess such goods, we can obtain money or other valuable things in exchange for them. If we wish to acquire them, we can do so by offering enough money to pay the price demanded. In some cases we can produce them for ourselves if we are willing to invest the necessary labor.

Economic goods have monetary value because they are desirable and because they are scarce. By scarce, we mean that if the goods were free, the amount that individuals want would exceed the supply, the amount available. Because the whole supply is owned or controlled by people, if we want more of such goods than we already have, we must either produce them for ourselves or offer something valuable in exchange to induce others to part with them.

Economic goods are not necessarily material. They may consist of services such as those of a housekeeper or a doctor, and, more and more, services are becoming the most important economic goods in the United States. Anything that offers benefits in exchange for a definite sum of money is an economic good. Economic goods in the form of services can be obtained from things as well as from people. If people want to enjoy the benefit of a house, they usually have a choice: They may buy the services of one in return for a monthly payment called rent, or they may buy one outright, thereby obtaining all the benefits the house is capable of yielding until it wears out or falls down. But when we wish to enjoy the benefits of a housekeeper or a doctor, we can't buy this choice; we have to rent it, because slavery is illegal.

Wealth is what we call the material economic goods—the kind we can see, feel, and accumulate. All economic goods take the form of either wealth or services.

The Economic Aspects of Culture

We have already emphasized many of the economic aspects of culture in earlier chapters. People's problems in adjusting to their physical environment are largely economic. The solutions require producing the kinds of goods that the environment demands; for example, in a cold climate, warm clothing, fuel, and well-insulated housing are necessary goods. Our attempts to improve our economic situation motivate technological progress.

Economic factors also play an important role in shaping the mores and the institutions of every society. Many of our most firmly held beliefs of what is right and wrong have to do with property and property rights, as illustrated by our strong condemnation of theft, robbery, cheating, and embezzlement. Most of our social institutions, even those that are not usually regarded as primarily economic, have economic aspects of major importance. The family is an excellent example. When two people marry, they not only signify their intention of living together and establishing a family, but they also undertake important economic obligations to care for each other and, if they have them, their children.

The Great Economic Problem

Producing economic goods to satisfy human wants requires resources. **Factors of production** are all the human and nonhuman resources that go into the production of material goods. These resources are of three principal types: first, **labor,** or the efforts of human beings; second, **natural resources,** resources such as land, raw materials, and so on that are the basis of all the material products that humans make; and, third, **capital,** or productive equipment, which includes tools, machines, factory buildings, and all the things that human beings have made to help them produce more easily and efficiently the kinds of goods they ultimately require to satisfy personal wants. Goods in the form of capital do not *directly* satisfy human wants. Their importance is that they ultimately enable us to produce a much greater quantity and variety of consumer goods than would otherwise be possible, and often goods of a more desirable kind or quality.

However, all productive resources—labor, natural resources, and capital—are limited in quantity, whereas in modern societies human wants seem practically unlimited. Our own society may be affluent in comparison with others, and a very small minority of its members may have few wants of consequence that remain unsatisfied, but the vast majority find it difficult to stretch their incomes enough to provide all the things they desire. The **great economic problem** facing every modern society is how to make scarce resources satisfy as fully as possible the ever-expanding wants of its members. But, as we have noted in earlier chapters, we cannot continue indefinitely to satisfy greater and greater economic wants for an ever-increasing population without encountering shortages of resources and more and more environmental pollution. In the 1970s, the trend in thinking was that economic growth is undesirable and that "small is beautiful." By the 1980s and continuing into the twenty-first century, most people were seeking ways to have increasingly higher levels of economic growth without diminishing efforts to master pollution and conserve and extend resources. This led to serious concerns that the energy consumption associated with economic activity was causing the global temperature to rise, which was bringing about some major physical changes to our world.

Economizing—making the best possible use of the resources that we employ at any time, regardless of what we think of growth—is one of the most important functions of an economic system. Determining the best mechanism for economizing, or allocating resources, is the fundamental task of economic policy.

The Evolution of Economic Systems

Throughout the Middle Ages, markets grew as trade among diverse areas expanded. Governments were not well developed in those times, and for the market to exist it was necessary to work out agreements with leaders of the various towns. As the Western political system evolved, first controlled by local lords or nobility and then by monarchs, all individuals who wanted to undertake economic activities were required to get permission from the noble or the royal head of state. Those who did not have permission were not allowed to undertake such economic activities.

Open-air trading continues today, as this scene of a person selling fish in New York City's Chinatown demonstrates.

From Feudalism to Mercantilism

As we discussed in Chapter 3, early on the economic system of the Western world was **feudalism,** in which tradition ruled and most people were peasants tied to the land and their feudal lord. A few individuals escaped this pattern; these included the workers who built the great medieval cathedrals of Europe (and who gave the term *Freemason* to our vocabulary) and traders who traveled in caravans they set up as temporary markets in or near feudal estates. These traveling workers and traders played a pivotal role in spreading culture and ideas from one estate to another and in establishing the political geography that evolved into our modern states. For example, many of the temporary markets became permanent and formed the centers around which towns and cities grew. Traders brought ideas as well as goods, providing peasants with a view of the wider world. As trade progressed, people began living in towns and producing goods full time for the market.

As people moved into the city, the economic system evolved into the **mercantilist system,** in which manufacturing or processing was favored above agriculture, and governments determined who could do what. The important aspect of the mercantilist system was that permission to engage in economic activity had to be obtained from local authorities, and as increasing trade fostered the development of the nation-state, traders soon found they had to obtain permission from the evolving governments.

From Mercantilism to a Pragmatic Market Economy

Beginning in the eighteenth century, the Industrial Revolution brought about a change from artisan production to machine production, which required a large number of individuals to work at specific manufacturing tasks in a common place (instead of scattered around in small enterprises). The Industrial Revolution was characterized by specialization of individuals in their work tasks. It unleashed an engine for material growth through growth in technology that transformed not only the economy and economic institutions, but also the social institutions of society.

The Industrial Revolution placed an economic strain on the mercantilist system, which had incorporated so many limitations on individual enterprise that many who might have been very good at some economic activity were simply not allowed to undertake that activity; this created tension and opposition to the existing social structure. By the mid-eighteenth century, opposition to the limitations of the mercantilist system had grown important. In 1776, moral philosopher Adam Smith wrote *The Wealth of Nations,* in which he expressed the underlying economic ideas that became central to the development of modern Western economic institutions.

Smith argued that for the government to prevent individuals who were good at something from doing it was not beneficial to society. Individuals, he held, should be free to do what they want, and he argued that such freedom would not lead to chaos. Instead, the market's **invisible hand**—the rise and fall of prices that guide individuals' actions in a market—would guide individuals' choices, so that each individual pursuing his or her own self-interest would simultaneously help society and create the greatest wealth for the greatest number of people in that society. For example, Smith argued that bakers will supply bread to people when they can make a profit, and this bread will satisfy people's hunger. If the baker charges too high a price, as long as there is competition others will enter and drive the price down to its cost of production. Alternatively, say there is too little bread. The price of bread will rise, and as it does, as long as individuals are free to become bakers, more people will become bakers, more bread will be produced, and there will no longer be too little bread. Then the price of bread will fall. People's needs are met by the market not because people are nice or concerned about others' welfare, but because people are selfish and pursue profit. But the market, through changes in prices, guides individuals' choices like an invisible hand, so that what helps them personally also helps society.

Laissez-faire is a policy that allows the market to operate with a minimum of government regulation. The policy of laissez-faire was quite different from the mercantilist economic system in which the government played an important role in determining who could and could not produce certain goods. The debate that began between mercantilism and laissez-faire has continued. On a

Adam Smith.

global scale, it is tied to the debate between planned and unplanned economies. Within the United States, we see it surfacing currently in the debates about how much government involvement in, and regulation of, the market should exist. Laissez-faire advocates argue that the government should stay out of economic activities except to provide the framework within which individuals can themselves carry out those activities.

Historically, opponents of the market have argued that the market causes people enormous pain, and that government has to enter in to alleviate that pain. During the Industrial Revolution, wages were low, living conditions were poor, and often people were thrown out of work and left starving on the street. Whereas individuals under feudalism had a society with built-in supports to fall back on, they had none under capitalism. Many industrialists liked it that way: The fear of starvation kept wages low and profits high.

The arguments against the market offered two alternatives. One was that the government should intervene in the market to alleviate the worst problems and to see that the market interactions achieved a degree of equity. They argued for keeping the market, but keeping it under control with laws and regulations. The second was much more radical. It called for an overthrow of the market economy and the establishment of socialism or communism.

The Push for Socialism.   The complaints about laissez faire capitalism increased through the early 1800s, and by the mid-1800s when laissez-faire capitalism was at its peak, there were many groups devoted to exploring and instituting alternatives. Those interested in socialist alternatives turned to the writings of utopian socialists such as Charles Fourier and Robert Owen, who favored establishing new communities where all members would contribute to the output of the community and use whatever community resources they needed. There, the decision of the community rather than the decision of the market would be the determinant of the allocation and distribution of goods. Utopian socialists believed that the market system was flawed, but they did not see a need for revolution against the system, nor did they see the development of an inevitable class struggle between workers and the owners of the means of production.

More radical reformers did see such needs and developments. These radical social reformers, such as Karl Marx and Friedrich Engels, saw the market system as inherently flawed. They argued that as the capitalists, or the owners of the means of production, exploited the workers, the workers would unite and establish a new form of economic organization called *communism,* under which each person would work according to his or her ability and each would consume according to his or her needs. Thus communism would evolve into somewhat the same type of economic system as that envisioned by the utopian socialists, but the path by which society would reach its destination was different. Under socialism, the path would be peaceful, with everyone joining in for the good of society; under communism, the path would be one of revolution against the existing social structure.

Socialism and Communism.   The terms *socialism* and *communism* are not easy to define; they developed slowly over time, and the nature of the concepts themselves has changed and is continuing to change. From the 1930s until about the late 1980s, both were associated with what we now call **Soviet-style socialism**—an economic system in which the government, rather than the market, makes decisions about the allocation and distribution of goods. Communism was a type of Soviet-style socialism in which the Communist Party played a key role in the economy. In the 1990s, as the former Soviet-style socialist countries underwent tremendous upheavals, some socialists were suggesting different definitions under which socialism was compatible with the use of markets to distribute goods. Most people, however, still used the definition that associates socialism with government decisions about the allocation and distribution of goods. But a change in that definition would not be surprising; the definition of socialism has continually changed.

In the mid-1800s, for example, the French writer and reformer Louis Blanc, one of the originators of socialism, argued that all individuals had an inherent right to a decent job.

Capitalism failed to achieve that goal and, therefore, violated individuals' rights. Initially, the right to a job was a central tenet of socialism.

Having a right to a job means that somehow jobs must become available, and quickly the principle expanded to include not only the right but also the means by which government would supply jobs to all—through government ownership of the means of production. As this happened, government ownership of the means of production became a key element in the definition of socialism. The focus on jobs also switched to a focus on equality of income, and the advocacy of equality of income became another key element of socialist thought. Thus, programs designed to equalize income in a country are often called socialistic.

Given this evolution, there is no unambiguous description of socialism. Because we need some definition, however, we define **socialism** in the traditional way, as an economic system under which society as a whole takes the primary responsibility for producing and distributing economic goods. Using this broad definition, Soviet-style socialism is a particular type of socialism. Although there is no inherent political system associated with socialism, the focus on society as a whole as the producer and distributor of economic goods quickly linked the theory of socialism to a comprehensive plan of government and hence, autocracy, although the relationship is subject to debate.

In practice, socialism has taken on a variety of forms, and elements of socialist thought have influenced the evolution of capitalist societies. For example, the establishment of social security systems was originally a socialist goal, as were many of the social welfare programs that we now regard as part of our capitalist economic system.

We formally define **communism** as a type of autocratic or state socialism in which the Communist Party is the small group of people—not subject to elections—that determines society's goals. But communism also includes specific political elements and thus must be differentiated from socialism. Communism includes a set of beliefs following from communist writers such as Karl Marx and Vladimir Lenin. As we stated earlier, Marx's criticisms of capitalism were more widely focused than those of the socialist writers; he saw capitalism as being doomed by the laws of history. He argued that history progressed in stages and that each stage had two opposing elements—thesis and antithesis. Each stage played a role in history, but once the role was played, society would progress to the next stage.

Karl Marx.

In capitalism, Marx saw one of the opposing forces as the bourgeoisie—the capitalists who brought about growth by exploiting the workers. This exploitation, he argued, played an important role in causing the economy to grow, but once that growth had brought society enough income, he believed that the workers would unite to overthrow the capitalists who were no longer needed. Then the workers would constitute a communist form of economic organization, with the following creed: From each according to his ability, to each according to his need.

Marx had little to say about how a communist economy would operate. In practice, it involved the same key points as socialism—a stated belief in the equality of income and a centralized system of distribution and production. Marx also argued that under communism the state would wither away, which might be interpreted to mean not the complete disappearance of an administrative mechanism but the complete disappearance of any need for controlling people by force. Presumably, after the state had withered away, production would be carried on by cooperative groups of workers in complete harmony and without any need for coercion. But in no country that we called communist has the state withered away.

The following list summarizes five reasons why Soviet-style socialism was abandoned:

1. Soviet-style economies weren't delivering goods.
2. Communist Party members were using their position to obtain desired goods and favorable treatment.
3. Socialist economies were significantly lagging behind capitalist economies.
4. New technological developments made it more difficult for the government to repress information and ideas that were contrary to the interest of the ruling parties.
5. Long-standing ethnic and cultural differences undermined the ability of the societies to form a national consensus.

In response to these problems, socialism and communism underwent enormous changes. Most Soviet-style socialist countries dumped Soviet-style socialism completely; others, such as China, attempted to integrate the market into their socialist institutions, freeing up certain areas of the economy while keeping others under government control. Still others talked about following some as yet undefined third way—an alternative path that was neither socialist nor capitalist. As this occurred, the repressive nature of the Communist Party was made clear to all, and most pretense to maintaining a higher moral ground was lost. The Communist Party was not the protector of the working people; it was simply another group vying for political control.

Planned and Unplanned Economies

In the past, economies were differentiated by whether they were unplanned or market economies or planned socialistic economies. **Unplanned economies** were economies that relied primarily on the market to control economic decisions. Because they relied on private capital markets to raise money for building production facilities such as factories, and because any profits or losses from production accrued to the owners of those facilities, these societies were also sometimes called *private enterprise* or *capitalist economies*. In an unplanned or market economy, individuals have significant freedom to own and operate productive enterprises, to produce economic goods, and to develop specialized institutions, such as banks and insurance companies, to fulfill their needs. The U.S. and Western European economies were given as examples.

Planned economies were economies that relied on government-controlled production and distribution systems. In a planned economy, the money for building the production facilities came from government, and any profits or losses from production accrued to government. In a totally planned economy, some central governmental authority has the power to plan, own, and operate directly all productive activities. The former Soviet Union and China were given as examples.

How Planned Economies Are Supposed to Work

To understand the difference between planned and unplanned economies, let's consider how they are meant to work in theory.

Let's start by considering how bread is produced in a planned economy. Wheat is raised on government-owned farms. The central planners decide on a set of production goals for a five-year period and determine what they will need in the way of equipment, seed, money, and other efforts to meet those goals. Once those decisions are made, the farms and central planners are responsible for meeting the goals. The farms do not calculate profit or loss (although the central planners do consider such issues), nor is there any necessary relationship between the costs of production and the price of the wheat. Production goals are set in terms of quantities, not economic value.

After the wheat is produced, the flour is sent to a bakery, which has also negotiated with central planners about its own five-year plan. Wheat is one of the "inputs" for which the bakery planned. Thus, the bakery's goal might have been to produce 5 million loaves of bread with 4.5 thousand tons of wheat. Having baked the bread, the bakery sends it to a government-owned retail store, which sells it to the consumer at whatever price the government tells the retailer to charge. In the Soviet planned economy in the 1980s, the price set for bread was far lower than the price of a loaf of bread in the United States because the Soviet government wanted to make this essential food widely available.

There is one other element, or input, in the production that we should mention, and that is labor. Each of the government production facilities needs a certain number of workers. Once the planning commission has determined the labor requirements of the firm, the government assigns individuals to various jobs in that facility. Thus, in the pre-1990 Soviet economy, when a Soviet citizen graduated from school, she or he was assigned to a job. However, students in the top 2 percent of their class were allowed to choose their jobs. The government also set the wages that workers received.

Why Central Planning Did Not Meet Its Goals

The goals of socialist or communist economies are admirable. In the ideal society envisioned by communist theorists, citizens would be completely free of coercion by the state and would be happy enough to accept all their social responsibilities. Social classes would disappear. Everyone would work, the entire product of the economy would go to labor, and all workers would have equal rights to share it. They would share, however, not equally but according to need. If money were used as a medium of exchange, presumably wages would be paid to workers according to their needs. In any case, certain basic essential goods would be provided free to all citizens.

To some degree, communist countries achieved their goals. Basic necessities were relatively much cheaper in the former Soviet Union and China than they are in market economies; however, luxuries were much more expensive. For example, in 1986 an average

The cities in China have become modern, as this picture of Shanghai demonstrates.

two-room apartment in the former Soviet Union cost approximately $24 per month, and all workers were guaranteed a one-month holiday. Similarly, medical care and education were free. In China, the communist government made the provision of health care a top priority. It instituted a "barefoot doctor" program that sent doctors out to teach paramedics the basics of sanitation, hygiene, preventive medicine, and birth control. It similarly embarked on an educational program for all its people.

Despite these impressive showings, both the Chinese and the Soviet systems often fell short. The $24-a-month apartments often required a ten-year wait, and consumer goods were generally rationed or impossible to get except on the black market, where they were enormously expensive. The medical care was inept. There were serious shortages of goods of all kinds. Productivity—the amount of output per worker—lagged and economic growth slowed. New technologies were not developed because no one had an incentive to develop them.

One goal they did not meet was equity and fairness. The shortages did not fall on all people equally. Through special commissaries, government leaders and Communist Party members easily got the goods that were in short supply, while other people had to wait in long lines. By the 1980s, the general view of most social scientists and of many citizens in communist countries was that the planned economy was not delivering the goods. The people were becoming dissatisfied.

In response, China introduced major modifications in its economic system, allowing the development of private markets while maintaining overall political control. The former Soviet Union and a number of the countries of eastern Europe took much more drastic measures. They essentially abandoned the socialist planned economy.

How Market Economies Are Supposed to Work

As you can see, planned economies have many problems. But so too do market economies. We can see some of the problems of the market economy in the United States by considering the recent plight of farmers who, in the recent recession, have lost their farms. In the planned economy, there might be losses, but they would not be suffered by the farmer, and the farm operation would continue uninterrupted. In the United States, some people graduating from (or dropping out of) school cannot find a job, and they join the ranks of the unemployed. In the planned economy, all graduates have jobs. The complaints about market economies that led people to search for alternatives did not come from nowhere. As we stated previously, the complaints were rooted in suffering the market caused that people were unwilling to accept. To better understand how market economies are supposed to work, let's briefly consider economists' theory of a market economy.

A **market economy** is an economic system that relies on the initiative of private citizens for the production of economic goods. In the market economy, no production quotas are assigned. Farmers, bakers, and retail stores individually decide how much they want to produce on the basis of expected prices and costs of input. If they make a mistake, they—not the government—are responsible for the loss, and if they make a profit, they—not the government—receive that profit. Workers are not assigned to jobs; they seek their own. Those who organize and control production must have incentives, and in a market economy the chief incentive is the possibility of making profits.

Planned economies were characterized by significant food shortages, causing people to line up to buy scarce goods.

Subject to the law of the land, anyone who chooses to is free to undertake the establishment of almost any kind of business enterprise. Businesspeople can choose both the products to be produced and the methods to be employed in their production; they can buy materials, labor, they managerial services; they can sell their products wherever people will buy them and at any price that customers are willing to pay. The chief problem in getting started is likely to be finding sufficient capital. If the new business is small, the owner's capital plus personal credit or borrowing power may be sufficient. But if the business is larger, the owner must interest other people and induce them to contribute capital as partners or, if a corporation is formed, as stockholders.

Institutional Foundations of a Market Economy.   There is no such thing as a pure or absolute free market economy in which the government plays no part at all—because freedom itself is always relative. When we sometimes describe the U.S. market economy as a free enterprise system, we do not mean that anybody can establish just any kind of business without meeting obstacles. We mean that in most cases it is quite feasible for people who can obtain capital, and who have the necessary personal qualities, to organize and operate new business enterprises, and that they have a wide range of freedom in making the decisions involved. But in some industries, certain obstacles are difficult to overcome. In the automobile industry, for example, the capital required to establish a new company is huge, and the risk of failure is great, and in the public utility industries, local monopolies are sometimes supported by law because this is believed to be in the public interest. Free enterprise, however, means more than the right to start a business. Fully as important is the right of those who already own business enterprises to operate and control them—to determine policies—subject only to laws and restrictions deemed necessary and reasonable by government.

The government must provide the legal and economic framework and the general rules within which private enterprises operate. Although government participation in economic affairs may be great or small, no government follows a complete policy of laissez-faire with respect to the economic activities of private individuals.

Figure 16.1 provides an example of the interrelationships within a market economy. In it we see that producers (firms) and consumers relate through the market. Workers earn income from firms and, in turn, spend their income on goods that the firms produce. What the workers don't spend they save in financial institutions that, in their turn, lend money to firms. The government enters the picture in two ways. It establishes the laws and regulations that govern the interaction of individuals and producers, and it collects taxes and provides services for firms and consumers.

Supply and Demand

In a free enterprise system, markets and prices play a dominant role in organizing and controlling economic activities. Any commodity that cannot be sold in the market at a profitable price will not be produced, at least not for long, whereas any commodity that can be sold at a profit is probably going to be produced by someone sooner or later.

When prices are not regulated and when markets are highly competitive, price changes keep adjusting production to consumption and consumption to production. For simplicity, let us assume that by a competitive market we mean one in which there are many small independent sellers of the same product and many independent buyers. Under these conditions, if people wish to increase their purchases of a commodity, the resulting increase in demand will cause the price to rise and production to be stimulated. Simultaneously, the rise in price will restrict the increase of market demand.

On the other hand, if people decide to decrease their purchases, the price will fall and this will discourage production, but the lower price will tend to limit the decline in sales and consumption. As long as more of the commodity is still being produced and offered for

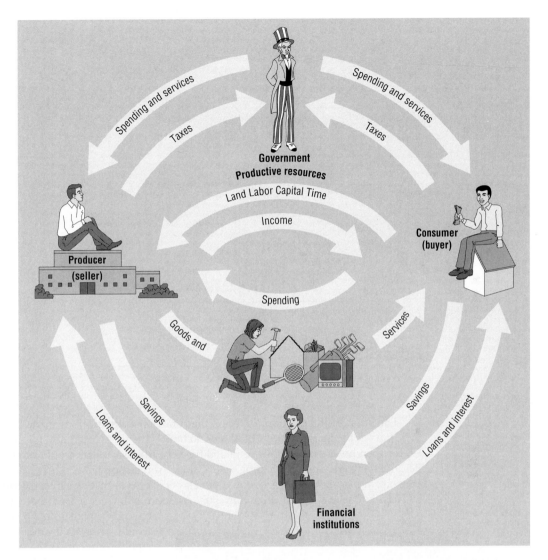

Figure 16.1

Model of a market economy.

sale than people are willing to buy, the price will continue to drop. In competitive markets, the price always tends to rise or fall until the amount of a commodity that is being produced and offered for sale is equal, at the market price, to the amount that consumers are willing to buy. This determines the **equilibrium price,** or the price at which demand exactly equals supply.

Figure 16.2 is far too simple to take into account all the conditions in a real market, but it does illustrate the tendency under competition for the price of a commodity to rise or fall until **demand,** the amount of a product that people are willing to buy at a given price and time, equals **supply,** the amount that others are willing to sell. The vertical *y*-axis measures the price of potatoes per bushel; the horizontal *x*-axis measures the number of bushels. The **demand curve,** *DD,* shows the amount of a good buyers would be willing to purchase at different prices in the market on a certain day. The **supply curve,** *SS,* shows the amount of a good sellers would be willing to offer at different prices on the same day.

Figure 16.2

Determination of equilibrium price.

The point of intersection, *P*, shows that under the assumptions made in constructing these curves, the market price would tend to be $6. The price could not, for example, stay at $7, for then buyers would take only 300 bushels, whereas sellers would offer 600 bushels. Because there are many competing sellers, some would soon reduce their prices as they saw sales lagging. Likewise, the price could not stay at $5, for in that case buyers would want 700 bushels, but sellers would offer only 300. As soon as buyers sensed that there were not enough potatoes to go around, some would raise their offers. Only at the equilibrium price of $6 would the forces of supply and demand be in balance, for at that price, buyers would be willing to purchase 500 bushels, just the amount that sellers would offer.

To see the way markets work, it is useful to consider two important historical events: an oil "crisis" and the computer revolution. Five times in the last fifty years, there has been a sudden dramatic decrease in the supply of oil. In each case, the market's reaction has been a rise in the price of oil. The resulting price rise hurt consumers, and it made them change their consumption habits. For instance, smaller, more energy-efficient cars were developed. The result was a decrease in the quantity of oil demanded, induced by the higher

The floor of the New York Stock Exchange.

price. The higher price acted like a stick, leading people to decrease the quantity of oil they used. Simultaneously, the higher price acted like a carrot, encouraging oil-producing firms to produce more and explore for more oil.

Now let's consider the computer revolution, which represents a more pleasant side of the market for consumers. Major technological breakthroughs in the development of computers increased supply, quality, and capacity. In response, prices of computers fell, and individuals, firms, and schools developed new ways to use computers, increasing the quantity demanded. This revolution is continuing and will be an important phenomenon well into the twenty-first century. An increase in supply causes prices to fall, giving individuals more for less. Thus, not only does the market act as a stick as individuals are forced to change their ways because of higher prices, but it also acts as a carrot, causing individuals to find new uses for goods and services whose prices have fallen.

*M*odern Economies Are Pragmatic Market Economies

The preceding discussion should make it clear that the distinction between planned and unplanned economies has broken down. First, those countries that had a planned economy in the strict sense of the word abandoned it. The Soviet Union dissolved, and its component countries adopted markets. Similarly, China abandoned large portions of central planning and adopted markets as well. So, planned economies in the traditional sense are no longer of central importance. Second, the United States and western European countries adopted significantly more planning and government involvement in the economy than anything envisioned by the theory of a market economy. In the U.S. economy today, government is involved in all levels of economic activity—either directly or indirectly. Consider the 2008 financial crisis. When large U.S. banks and automobile companies were on the verge of going under, the government stepped in and bailed them out. It poured trillions of dollars into the economy to support these companies.

Our point is that, today, the distinctions among countries are much more nuanced than planned or unplanned. All modern economies, whatever their history, have evolved into **pragmatic market economies**—*economies that use markets as a central way of allocating resources, but which also regulate and control those markets and change market outcomes to varying degrees.* Along with the downplaying of the differences in the planned and unplanned nature of economies has gone a downplaying of the differences between capitalist economies and socialist economies. Modern economies are blends of both and are guided more by what works than by a strong ideological commitment to either. Today's economies reflect pragmatism more than the other "isms." Pragmatism, not ideology or economic theory, has become the primary driving force in determining how modern economies operate and the degree of government involvement.

What really differentiates modern economies is their institutional and historical settings, which affect how government interacts with markets. For example, in China, most people expect that the government will step in and change the results of markets if it does not favor those results.

In China and Russia, property rights and the rule of law are far less established than they are in the United States, which means that the Chinese and Russian governments can more easily step in and change a market outcome they do not like than can the U.S. government. People's property rights are determined by the government, and a change in government can change these property rights. In the United States, greater reliance on what is called the "rule of law," which stands above whatever government is in power, places restrictions on what government can do. Specifically, the rule of law limits any government's ability to change property rights. This limitation allows businesses to plan ahead more easily than they otherwise could.

Although we have also seen many examples of government intervention in the United States, the law under which businesses are run is largely independent of who constitutes the government in power and therefore can be relied upon to be relatively stable. That is far less so in China and Russia. Because the rule of law is less established, the law and property rights can be more easily changed by the specific government in power, if it chooses to do so. So, one's ownership of property is seen as at the will of government. This makes longer term planning more difficult and gives government a more important role in the economy than in the United States. So, even though both China and Russia are now market economies, they are different market economies than the United States. In China and Russia, there is an implicit government control on economic activities that is stronger than in the United States. The difference is, however, nuanced, not the stark difference that was sometimes conveyed in the past.

Conclusion

Fifty years ago, there were enormous debates about whether planned or unplanned, market or nonmarket, socialist or capitalist economies were better. Some said that the collapse of many Soviet-style socialist planned economies showed that the market is definitely preferable to other ways of organizing economies and used that event as an argument for laissez faire and against regulation. That argument is wrong. While the market certainly has its advantages, the history of the U.S. economy reflects the serious problems markets can create, and that what has survived is not a pure market economy, but a pragmatic market economy with enormous government involvement. The United States has government-sponsored unemployment insurance, government-regulated retirement programs (Social Security), government-owned schools, and an enormous number of government regulations that limit our actions in the market. We have a pragmatic market economy rather than a pure market economy.

Today's economies in the world are almost all pragmatic market economies where government and the market interact in nuanced ways to solve problems that present themselves. There are problems with markets and there are problems with government regulation and government planning, and societies make pragmatic decisions about how to handle these, at times relying more on markets, at other times relying more on government.

In short, there is no perfect economic system. Organizing the economic affairs of millions of people is a difficult process and will be continually marked by problems. As new problems are faced, it is likely that economies will continually evolve, perhaps into types we have not yet classified. Economic systems, like culture and human beings, adapt to changes and evolve as new ways of coordinating behavior are tried and as those new ways create new problems.

Key Points

- The great economic problem that faces every modern society is to make the scarce resources available satisfy as fully as possible the ever-expanding wants of its members.
- Our economy has evolved from feudalism to mercantilism to a market economy and finally to a pragmatic market economy.
- Socialist thought developed in reaction to the problems caused by a nonregulated market economy.

- Unplanned economies rely on markets to control economic decisions; planned economies rely on government.
- All modern economies have market economies that involve different amounts of government involvement and planning. Pragmatism has become the primary driving force in determining the nature of the economy.
- Soviet-style socialism was abandoned because its economies weren't delivering the goods. Many of

the goods were distributed unfairly, economic growth lagged behind that of capitalist countries, technology in communications promoted dissent, and ethnic and cultural differences undermined national unity.

- Markets create carrots and sticks when supply differs from demand, leading the invisible hand to get people to do what is in society's interest.

Some Important Terms

capital (324)
communism (328)
demand (333)
demand curve (333)
economic goods (324)
economics (322)
economic wants (323)
economizing (325)
economy (323)

equilibrium price (333)
factors of production (324)
feudalism (325)
great economic problem (325)
invisible hand (326)
labor (324)
laissez-faire (326)
market economy (331)
mercantilist system (326)

natural resources (324)
planned economies (329)
pragmatic market economy (335)
socialism (328)
Soviet-style socialism (327)
supply (333)
supply curve (333)
unplanned economies (329)
wealth (324)

Questions for Review and Discussion

1. Economics studies the social organization through which people satisfy their wants for scarce goods, including services. Give some examples of economic wants.
2. What four important functions must every economy perform?
3. What are economic goods? What are economic needs? What are economic wants?
4. What economic aspects does the family have?
5. What three factors of production are necessary to produce economic goods?
6. What is the great economic problem facing every society?
7. How did the Industrial Revolution contribute to economic growth?
8. In 1776, Adam Smith published the book *The Wealth of Nations.* How did he believe a nation could become wealthy?
9. In a planned or socialist economy, who is responsible for building the factories and distributing the goods?
10. In an unplanned or market economy, who raises the money and builds the factories? Who gets the profits or suffers the losses?
11. If the government controls the means of production, what is produced, and how the goods are distributed, what are the advantages? What are the disadvantages?
12. In a planned economy, if weather and plant disease caused an agricultural disaster, would farms go out of production? Why or why not?
13. What are some of the reasons that some consumer goods are scarce and of poor quality in a socialist economy?
14. If the price of Coca-Cola went up to $5 a can, what would you expect to happen to the quantity of Coca-Cola demanded?
15. Do you believe that everyone has a right to a job? If so, whose responsibility is it to provide that many jobs?
16. Give an example of how a socialist idea has been adopted in a market economy.
17. Give an example of how a capitalist idea has been adopted in a socialist economy.
18. In market economies, such as the United States and Sweden, taxes are quite high. How does this blur the distinction between the terms *capitalist* and *socialist*?
19. Why is the distinction between a planned and an unplanned economy less relevant today?

Internet Questions

1. To construct a market economy, R. Vernon, at www.cipe.org/publications/ert/e20/E20.D2.pdf, states three lessons to learn from history. What are they?
2. Using information found at www.auburn.edu/~johnspm/gloss/index.html, what is the definition of a black market?
3. Go to www.res.org.uk/society/mediabriefings/pdfs/1996/november/agell.asp and read about the welfare state. What lesson can be learned from Sweden's experience?
4. Using http://news.nationalgeographic.com/news/2002/10/1002_021002_indiabirds.html, what are the seven practices determined to be reasons for the large black market in exotic birds in India?
5. Go to: www.economist.com/displaystory.cfm?story_id=13743310. What does the article mean by the visible hand, and how does it relate to a pragmatic market economy?

For Further Study

Bishop, Matthew, *Essential Economics*, New York: Bloomberg/Economist Books, 2006.

Eichenwald, Kurt, *Conspiracy of Fools: A True Story*, New York: Basic Books, 2006.

Friedman, Milton, *Capitalism and Freedom*, Chicago: University of Chicago Press, 1962.

Galbraith, John Kenneth, *Economics and the Public Purpose*, Boston: Houghton Mifflin, 1973.

Gilder, George, *Wealth and Poverty*, New York: Basic Books, 1981.

Hayek, Friedrich, *The Road to Serfdom*, Chicago: University of Chicago Press, 1944.

Jaffe, Adam B., and Josh Lerner, *Innovation and Its Discontents: How Our Broken Patent System Is Endangering Innovation and Progress, and What to Do about It*, Princeton, NJ: Princeton University Press, 2006.

Prahalad, C. K., *The Fortune at the Bottom of the Pyramid: Eradicating Poverty through Profits*, Philadelphia: Wharton School Publishing, 2006.

Prestowitz, Clyde, *Three Billion New Capitalists: The Great Shift of Wealth and Power to the East*, New York: Basic Books, 2006.

Prins, Naomi, *Other People's Money: The Corporate Mugging of America*, New York: New Press, 2006.

Roberts, John, *The Modern Firm: Organisational Design for Performance and Growth*, New York: Oxford University Press, 2004.

Schumpeter, Joseph A., *Capitalism, Socialism and Democracy*, New York: Harper & Row, 1962.

Simmons, Matthew R., *Twilight in the Desert: The Coming Saudi Oil Shock and the World Economy*, New York: Wiley, 2006.

Walter, David Moberg, *The Wal-Mart Effect: How the World's Most Powerful Company Really Works—and How It's Transforming the American Economy*, New York: Penguin, 2004.

Weber, Max, *The Protestant Ethic and the Spirit of Capitalism* (1904), New York: Scribner, 1958.

WWW   Capitalism.org   www.capitalism.org

WWW   The Economist   www.economist.com

WWW   Freedom Network   http://thefreedomnetwork.org

WWW   Informal Communist Discussion   www.communism.com

WWW   Max Planck Institute of Economics   www.mpiew-jena.mpg.de

WWW   Organization for Economic Cooperation and Development www.OECD.org

The Economy, Government, and Economic Challenges Facing the United States

After reading this chapter, you should be able to:

- Distinguish government's indirect and direct roles in the economy
- Summarize the costs and benefits of regulation, and explain why regulation should be seen as a continuous process
- Discuss two contentious roles of government
- Give examples of two ways the government influences the distribution of income
- Define monetary policy and fiscal policy
- Give a short summary of economists' view of the fiscal crisis, globalization, and global warming
- Define globalization, and explain the importance of the law of one price

If you don't know what you are doing, for God's sake, do it gently.

—William Brainard

As we discussed in the last chapter, our economic system is best thought of as a pragmatic market economy. That means we are continually searching for the right mix of government and market control to meet society's desires. In this chapter, we explore that mix and the challenges facing the U.S. economy in the coming decades.

In talking about the government's role in the economy it is useful to distinguish government's indirect role—its role in specifying what individuals and businesses can and cannot do through laws and regulation—from its direct role—its role in the economy as an institution that spends and taxes. Let's begin with government's indirect role.

Government's Indirect Role in the Economy

The government's indirect role in the economy is to provide a legal and institutional setting for the workings of the market by establishing and enforcing laws that regulate actions of individuals and businesses. Such laws have significant influence on who gets what, how people spend their money, and how people conduct economic activities.

Let's first consider government's influence on who gets what. Say the government passes a law that people can freely share downloadable songs and movies, or even that they can provide a site that allows other people to share songs and movies. Such a law will transfer income away from the producers of songs and movies to consumers of songs and movies.

Alternatively, if the government establishes laws that prevent someone from practicing law or from teaching without a license—even if other people want to hire them despite their lack of a license—that law will transfer income to licensed lawyers and teachers and away from consumers. The list of ways in which the government indirectly determines the distribution of income with such laws of regulation is long and can be extended almost infinitely. In other words, what someone earns reflects not only his or her efforts but also the rules the government establishes that govern how the income is earned.

The government's influence on how we conduct economic activities is just as pervasive. For example, if you want to drive a car, most states require you to have car insurance. You must wait until you are a certain age to begin to work, and when you do work, you must keep certain records and file tax returns. Firms must abide by certain nondiscriminatory practices when hiring, provide proof of insurance, and ensure their products meet certain standards. It is because of government's large indirect role that we called our economic system a pragmatic market economy rather than a free market economy as it is sometimes called. A free market economy would be anarchy. The U.S. economy is far from anarchy; it is a highly regulated market economy where the regulations reflect pragmatic considerations that reflect attempts to correct problems caused by markets and problems caused by government. Both are problematic, and all societies continually search for the right combination.

The Problem of Regulating the Economy

All individuals agree that some regulation is needed. The questions are: How much? And what type? One type of regulation that has come under specific attack is **unfunded mandates,** or regulations by the federal government that impose significant costs on individuals and states but do not provide the funds to pay those costs. One example of an unfunded mandate is the law passed by the federal government to make all public buildings in the United States accessible to all individuals, including people with physical and mental disabilities. Passing the law was easy and seemed right to many Americans. But the law imposed serious costs on many businesses, and the law did not provide those businesses with a way to pay for them. Governments pass many such laws and regulations every year that impose large costs on individuals and firms in the economy—costs that someone, either the firm or their customers, must pay.

The debate over regulation is ongoing. Supporters of a particular regulation generally argue that the regulation serves an important purpose of protecting individuals and of ensuring that economic activities are carried out in a way that the legal system considers fair. Opponents of a particular regulation generally argue that the costs of the regulation are too high, citing examples such as the following, which appeared in the *Wall Street Journal.* An upstate New York nursing home had been cited by state officials as "a shining example" of what such an establishment ought to be. However, not long afterward, the owner of this home closed it down with the following explanation: "It was just impossible. There were eighteen state and federal agencies putting forms, questions, and statistical requests across my desk. Medical reports…census figures…Social Security…unemployment insurance…workers' compensation…withholding taxes…daily time sheets…work plans…It was just one thing after another." According to the owner, she sometimes spent eighteen hours a day just handling the government paperwork required for only twenty patients and fourteen employees. The weight of the regulatory burden on firms is given a stark representation in Figure 17.1. Such large-scale regulations have brought about a reaction on the part of some people supporting the doctrine of **laissez-faire,** the theory that government should interfere with business as little as possible.

The problem for strong advocates of laissez faire is that while there are many examples of large-scale and intrusive regulation, there are also many examples of regulations that have helped society, and there are parts of society that most observers would consider under-regulated—areas of the economy where the lack of regulation has caused significant problems for the economy. Let's consider a couple of them. The first involves pollution. In

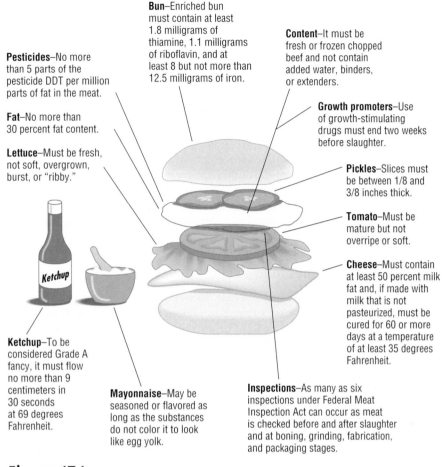

Pesticides–No more than 5 parts of the pesticide DDT per million parts of fat in the meat.

Fat–No more than 30 percent fat content.

Lettuce–Must be fresh, not soft, overgrown, burst, or "ribby."

Bun–Enriched bun must contain at least 1.8 milligrams of thiamine, 1.1 milligrams of riboflavin, and at least 8 but not more than 12.5 milligrams of iron.

Content–It must be fresh or frozen chopped beef and not contain added water, binders, or extenders.

Growth promoters–Use of growth-stimulating drugs must end two weeks before slaughter.

Pickles–Slices must be between 1/8 and 3/8 inches thick.

Tomato–Must be mature but not overripe or soft.

Cheese–Must contain at least 50 percent milk fat and, if made with milk that is not pasteurized, must be cured for 60 or more days at a temperature of at least 35 degrees Fahrenheit.

Ketchup–To be considered Grade A fancy, it must flow no more than 9 centimeters in 30 seconds at 69 degrees Fahrenheit.

Mayonnaise–May be seasoned or flavored as long as the substances do not color it to look like egg yolk.

Inspections–As many as six inspections under Federal Meat Inspection Act can occur as meat is checked before and after slaughter and at boning, grinding, fabrication, and packaging stages.

Figure 17.1

Your hamburger: More than 41,000 regulations.

the past, firms and people have been able to pollute without facing any limitations on their actions. That pollution has often made streams unusable, the air unbreathable, and has destroyed beautiful areas and public lands. In economists' parlance, such problems are caused by **externalities**—the effects of a firm's actions or decisions that negatively affect others but that the firm does not consider when undertaking the action. When there are externalities, the situation is made worse for the majority of people by the action that caused the externality. Economists agree that even in a primarily market-based economy, regulation is needed to see that those creating negative externalities stop doing so at least to the degree that others would be willing to pay them not to undertake those activities.

Another example of an area where lack of regulation causes problems involves financial firms that made loans and took in deposits without regulation. The lack of regulation allowed these firms to borrow enormous amounts of money to buy highly speculative mortgage backed securities (bonds backed by risky mortgages). When the value of those bonds fell, the firms could not pay back the loans, and they would have collapsed without government intervention. Many felt that these financial institutions deserved to collapse. Unfortunately, their collapse would have brought down the entire United States, and probably world, economy along with it, which would have made the situation worse for everyone. They were considered "too big to fail," which means that the U.S. government felt it necessary

342 chapter 17   The Economy, Government, and Economic Challenges Facing the United States

to enter in and bail out the firms. The bailout, which occurred in 2008 and 2009, could cost the U.S. government trillions of dollars. The problem here is the fact that if a firm is too big to fail, it is too big *not* to be regulated; and in 2009 and 2010, the United States was exploring ways to increase the regulation of financial firms in an attempt to avoid another financial crisis in the future.

There are huge differences of opinion about how much and what kind of regulation is desirable. It is clear that many government regulations have served the public interest, but it seems equally clear that some intended to do so have not. What makes finding the right mix of regulation so difficult is that the problem of regulation cannot be solved once and for all and then forgotten. Technology and social situations are continually changing, which means that regulations appropriate in the past may no longer be appropriate. People also figure out ways to get around regulations, so that the regulations become less effective over time. Thus, regulation must be seen as a continual process, which requires regulators to stay ahead of the firms and the individuals regulated. Successfully doing so requires enormous expertise and commitment—expertise that is expensive and often beyond the budget of governments.

Whose Desires Does the Government Reflect?

If government always reflected "society's will," there would be far less debate about regulation and government's role. But it doesn't. "Society's will" is an artificial construct; there is no society that has a will of its own that can be specified separately from the collective will of the individuals within the society. Whose desires will be reflected by government as society's desires is subject to enormous political infighting; it reflects the political power of various groups—those with political power get their desires met, while those without political power do not.

Often, from many outside observers' perspectives, government laws and regulations are not designed to help the general public, but instead are designed to help special interests. Consider the issues of patents and copyrights. All agree that some patent and copyright protection is useful because it creates incentives for the development of new technologies and products, but many argue that the length of time that patents and copyrights last is far longer than necessary to encourage such developments and that the length of patents and copyrights in the United States could be shortened significantly, thereby benefiting the general public with minimal negative effects on incentives.

Why don't governments shorten these times? Critics claim that the reason is that it would reduce the patent and copyright owners' income—and those owners lobby Congress hard to prevent that from happening. An example of this is the Copyright Term Extension Act of 1998, often called the "Mickey Mouse Protection Act" because the Disney Corporation was a big beneficiary of the law. Disney's copyright on Mickey Mouse was about to expire after 75 years. That would have let anyone produce Mickey Mouse goods without paying Disney. Disney lobbied Congress hard, and Congress extended the copyright for decades longer, essentially transferring billions of dollars from consumers to Disney. Many similar examples exist.

So while most people agree that in principle, regulations can improve the workings of an economy, there is far less agreement whether in the real world regulations can improve the workings of the economy or whether regulation simply provides an alternative method through which special interests can improve their position.

Fluctuating Attitudes toward Regulation

U.S. attitudes toward regulation have fluctuated. In the 1960s and early 1970s, regulation was seen as a necessary limit to private powers. About the mid-1970s and well into the 1980s, the pendulum of public opinion shifted, and many believed that the U.S. economy was suffering from overregulation. This led to a belief that deregulation or the removal of those excessive regulations would improve the workings of the economy. Then, in the 2000s, the pendulum swung again as first accounting scandals, and then the financial crisis of 2008–2009, rocked the economy and brought it to the verge of collapse because of financial risktaking by large banks and insurance companies. In response, public opinion shifted to favor more, or at least better, regulation.

Government's Direct Role in the Economy

Besides its indirect role of making laws and regulations for the economy, government also plays a direct role in the economy. By that I mean that it is an active participant in the economy and that it collects and spends trillions of dollars a year. The reason government has a direct role in the economy is because some things are better done collectively than individually, and government is the natural institution in our society to carry out collective action. Let's consider one example of something best done collectively: defense. If each of us provided for our own defense for attack from another country, our country would likely be taken over by another country—each individual in our country couldn't afford to provide even one plane or one battleship. These collective consumption goods, sometimes called **public goods,** are more efficiently supplied by government than by individuals.

Where the Government Spends Its Money

Each year, the federal government spends over $3 trillion to finance its activities, and state governments spend more than $1 trillion to finance their activities. Figure 17.2a shows the division of federal government expenditures; Figure 17.2b shows the division of state government expenditures.

As you can see, the federal government spends the largest percentage of its tax revenue on income security programs. By contrast, after administration, state governments spend most of their money on education and income support. In addition to federal and state governmental activities, there are also local government activities. Local governments spend most of their budgets on education and roads.

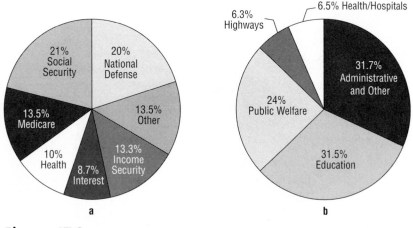

Figure 17.2

(a) Federal outlays by use, 2008. (b) State outlays by use, 2007. (Source: U.S. Department of Commerce, U.S. Department of the Treasury.)

Where Government Gets Its Money

If government is to supply a good, it has to pay for it. The three main options for paying are voluntary contribution, taxes, and borrowing. The most prominent of these is taxes. To have a government is to have taxes. Why not pay for those goods through voluntary contributions? The reason is that people have a natural tendency to avoid contributing toward public goods, even when they are receiving the benefits. Therefore, all governments have the power to tax—to force people to pay for the goods that government supplies. Borrowing is also used by government, but borrowing does not eliminate the need for government to pay for the goods or for taxes; it simply puts it off until later. Moreover, borrowing means that the government not only has to pay the money back; it also has to pay interest on the loan.

Each year, the U.S. federal, state, and local governments together collect over $4 trillion in taxes. Figures 17.3a and b show the divisions of tax revenues for the federal and state governments. As you can see, the federal government's primary sources of revenue are Social Security taxes, individual income taxes, and corporate income taxes. State and local governments' primary sources of revenue are a combination of two sources—sales taxes and transfers from the federal government. Local governments get most of their income from property taxes.

Alternative Methods of Supply in a Pragmatic Market Economy

Once a government exists, the political process can decide which goods the government should provide, which goods should be supplied privately through the market, and what other roles the government should have. Many different arrangements are possible. Consider education. It could be supplied privately with individuals paying for the education they want, in the same way that people pay for their cars. But this is not the way most societies provide education. Most societies provide education for all students by paying for it with money collected in taxes. Why? Because they feel education benefits the society as a whole as well as the individuals getting the education. In the United States, tax-paid public education ends with the completion of high school, although most states have colleges and universities that receive part of their budgets from tax money.

Currently, there is a debate about whether public schools are doing an adequate job of providing a quality education and whether their costs—more than $10,000 per student per

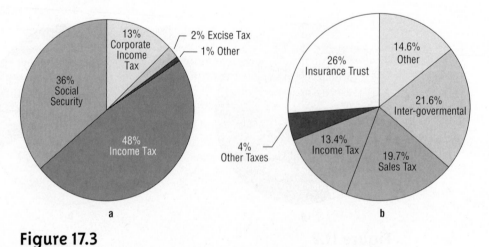

a   b

Figure 17.3

(a) Federal revenue by source, 2008. (b) State revenue by source, 2007. (Source: U.S. Department of Commerce, U.S. Department of Treasury.)

year—are excessive. Some reformers advocate a hybrid system—public funding but private provision—through vouchers given to parents, allowing families to choose which school to send their children to and to pay for at least part of the school cost with the government vouchers.

Education is not the only good that can be paid for and supplied either by government, individuals, or private firms. For instance, health care and prescription drugs are goods that could be paid for and supplied privately but are actually paid for in part by the government, although in the United States, supply remains private. Some reformers are advocating a much larger role for government in paying for and supplying these goods.

The direct role of government in the economy will always be an important issue of debate in a pragmatic market economy. Economics gives guidance about problems that will likely develop if certain methods of supply are chosen over other methods, but economic theory does not say that one approach is better than another. Economic theory, and social science theory generally, provides insights into the consequences of adopting certain policies, but not the answer to the question of which policy should be adopted. That is a choice society must make.

Some Controversial Roles of the Government

Let's now turn to some roles of government in the economy that combine the government's indirect and direct roles. First, we will look at income redistribution through government; and, second, we look at government's macroeconomic role.

Income Redistribution through Government

Perhaps government's most controversial role involves the redistribution of income. Redistribution of income is achieved both through the government's direct and indirect roles. We have spoken of the indirect role's effect on distribution above. By allowing long-term patents and copyrights, the government redistributes income from consumers of books and music to people who own those copyrights and patents. Another example of such indirect redistribution involves the allocation of the broadcast spectrum, which the government has given to a small number of corporations, providing billions of dollars in wealth for them and higher costs for the public. A third example concerns the recent proposed allocation of CO_2 rights for the cap and trade policy by which the government is attempting to help fight global warming by reducing CO_2 emissions. Ignoring the advice of almost all economists, the government has proposed to give the majority of these rights to existing polluters rather than auctioning them off. The existing polluters will then be free to "sell" those rights if they cut their pollution. By allocating the rights in that manner, the government is creating a transfer of hundreds of billions of dollars to these companies and to the people who buy their outputs—and away from the government that would have received the income from auctioning off these rights.

A final example involves the licensing of professions such as lawyers, medicine, and real estate. Those licenses force suppliers of these services to go through an often expensive schooling before they are allowed to practice that profession. In doing so, the government limits certain activities to those who have gotten the credential. That limitation raises the price of the service considerably from what it would be if entry had been free. Consider a couple of examples—a person (even a medical doctor) is not allowed to charge for administering a rabies shot to a dog, even though he or she might know how to do so from his or her training. Similarly, a person who has specialized in writing wills is not allowed to charge for writing a will for a friend. Doing either would be practicing a profession without a license, which is against the law. There are, of course, benefits of people having qualifications, but often the training doesn't really make someone qualified; it simply serves as a hurdle that people must meet to enter a profession. Government could let people know who has qualifications with a certification program, rather than a licensing program. Then people could decide if they wanted to hire a "certified" lawyer or an uncertified lawyer. Through such a program, it would be possible to have much more freedom of entry into professions than there currently is, while still giving people the option of hiring a certified professional. Alternatively, government could provide narrower sublicenses in which a non-lawyer could be licensed to do particular types of activities—such as writing a will—but not other types of activities, such as defending a client in court.

Government also directly influences the distribution of income through its use of its taxing power and its spending functions. Generally, this involves imposing relatively higher taxes on people who have high incomes and using that tax money to provide additional income to people whose income would otherwise be much lower. There are three ways this is done in the United States:

1. We have a **progressive income tax system**—people who earn high incomes are taxed at a high rate so that the government can use tax money to provide programs for lower-income people. Although our income tax is progressive, it is far less progressive than it has been in the past. During World War II and for a short while thereafter, the top federal tax rate on high-income individuals was over 90 percent. Today, top federal tax rates on earned income such as wages are about 35 percent. Some other income, such as increases in the value of stock and stock dividends, is taxed at a lower rate. Even at these lower rates, however, there is still some redistribution of income.

2. We have low-income tax credits. Low-income people are given a tax credit, so instead of paying taxes, they receive a direct payment from the government.

3. We have entitlement programs that favor the poor. The majority of income support our government provides is through entitlement programs such as Social Security, Medicare, and Medicaid, which are designed to favor the poor somewhat. For example, the federal government pays the Medicare (health insurance) premiums for many low-income people.

Each of these programs is complicated, and we could write a book about each one just trying to explain their intricacies; we won't do that here. We focus our discussion on one example, the Social Security program, the largest government expenditure program.

The U.S. Social Security System   The first comprehensive government-administered social insurance system was enacted by imperial Germany in 1889, sponsored by the famous German chancellor Otto von Bismarck, who apparently conceived of it as a plan for allaying social unrest. Over the next three decades, similar plans were adopted by most other major industrial nations. It was not until the Great Depression of the 1930s that the United States passed the Social Security Act of 1935, a broad program of social insurance. Under pressure from President Franklin D. Roosevelt, Congress enacted the **Federal Insurance Contributions Act (FICA)**, a plan providing a broad program of social insurance funded by a tax levied half on employers and half on employees. The plan was a compromise between liberals who wanted a much larger guarantee of government income support and conservatives who opposed any such plan.

Social Security Is Not Insurance   Because of the debate surrounding it, Social Security was described to the public as a type of contributory insurance plan, even though it really did not meet that definition. A true insurance plan would collect money, invest it, and out of the proceeds pay people who found themselves in the circumstances against which they were insuring themselves. As it developed, the Social Security system paid out the money almost as soon as it took it in. Thus, it was not funded like an insurance plan but was a system in which there was only a small reserve; benefits were paid from current contributions. Such a procedure does not necessarily mean the system is unsound. As long as new contributions at least equal expenditures, the system can continue forever. However, by calling it an insurance plan when it was actually something quite different, the government laid the foundation for future problems.

Initially, the problems were not evident: The plan was a modest one, contributions were very small, and monthly benefit levels were very low. In those initial years, it was not planned as a retirement system but, rather, as a cushion against destitution in old age and as a supplement to whatever other plans workers made for retirement income. Through the 1980s, the law was amended many times, almost always to increase the amount of an individual's benefit and sometimes to increase the number of people who could become eligible. As legislated expenditures of the program have increased, the tax has greatly increased as well. Beginning in the 1980s, fear about the stability of the system led to some cutbacks such as computing current benefits at slightly lower amounts and, for the future, setting the retirement age higher.

Social Security Benefits and Taxes   How much do people pay for Social Security? In 2009, individuals paid a tax of 6.2 percent on their wages up to $106,800 and an additional tax, dedicated to health benefits, of 1.45 percent on their total wages. Businesses that hired them paid an equal amount. This is in addition to the income tax that individuals pay.

How much do people get back for what they put in? That depends on how long they worked, how much they earned when they worked, and when they started claiming benefits, along with a variety of other factors. To give you a rough idea of how much someone would get, say a worker earned $50,000 a year when he or she retired, and worked consistently most of his or her life. That worker would receive about, $1,400 a month in 2009. (You can figure out what you might get when you retire by going to http://www.retirement-income.net/social-security-calculator.html). That amount is indexed for inflation, so it will increase as inflation increases.

The Future of the Social Security System   Because Social Security is a pay-as-you-go system, not an insurance system, how solvent it is depends on how many people are paying into it and how many are drawing out of it. When the program began, many paid in and few took out. In 1950, for every one person drawing benefits, 16.5 people were paying in. In the early 2000s, that ratio had changed to about one person drawing out for every three people paying in, necessitating a much higher tax rate applied to a much higher base (in 1937, the tax was just 1 percent and applied only to the first $3,000 of income). But the real crunch will come between 2020 and 2030, when a large majority of the baby boomers retire. At that time, the ratio of people paying in to people drawing out will be two to one.

The Social Security Trust Fund, which has been built up by raising the FICA tax above what is necessary to fund the current benefits, provides some cushion against the future imbalance between the number of people paying in compared to the number of people drawing out. But the United States cannot escape the fact that in ten to twenty years, the Social Security system will be supporting many more retirees than it does now, while at the same time having many fewer contributors per retiree.

Government's Macroeconomic Role

Another important, but controversial, form of government involvement in the economy involves its **macroeconomic role** which involves protecting and increasing society's welfare based on a consideration of society's welfare as a whole. To understand government's macroeconomic role, it is useful to contrast it with government's **microeconomic role**—a role that involves protecting and increasing society's welfare based on the consideration of individuals' welfare. Both roles consider society, but microeconomics builds up from the individual, and macroeconomics starts with the whole and then breaks the whole down. The reason is it called macroeconomics is that it focuses its concerns on the aggregate (macro) society—whereas microeconomics focuses its concerns on the individual. Both categories consider the welfare of society, but they approach it differently.

Thus, for economists, government's microeconomic role is concerned with individual problems such as health care or old-age pensions. Government's macroeconomic role is concerned with the economy as a whole—seeing to it that the overall economy remains stable, does not fall into a depression, or experience runaway inflation.

Stabilizing the Economy.　Over the past hundred years, there has been significant fluctuation in unemployment, inflation, and output. These fluctuations in aggregate output are called business cycles. A typical business cycle is shown in Figure 17.4; it has a boom period and a recession period.

Up until the 1930s, most economists thought such business cycles were inevitable. Society should put up with them just as one endures minor aches and pains in one's body. So there was felt to be little macroeconomic role for government in stabilizing the economy. Fluctuations and unemployment were seen as inevitable parts of life. Economists believed that government should be concerned with preventing inflation, and figuring out how to control its tendency to spend without taxing to pay for that spending. To do that, most economists of the time supported government running balanced budgets—except in periods of wartime—and in limiting increases in the money supply.

That view of the role of government changed in the 1930s when the economy fell into a deep depression. A **depression** is a period of drastic decline in an economy, characterized by decreasing business activity, falling prices, and unemployment. Most Americans, judged by today's standards of income and consumption, were relatively poor in the middle and late 1920s, but we must be cautious in judging the past by the present, for in comparison with anything they had known before, people were enjoying a period of unprecedented prosperity. True, some groups, including farmers, did not share in this prosperity, but most Americans had achieved higher incomes than ever before. Furthermore, a great speculative rise in the prices of real estate and stocks had helped to create a general feeling of optimism.

This feeling was soon dissipated by some rude shocks. In October 1929, there was a spectacular break in the stock market, and this was only the first of a series of developments that, by 1932, brought the country to the greatest depths of depression in its entire history. From 1929 to 1932, industrial production and national income dropped by about half, and unemployment rose from about 3 million to between 12 and 15 million, or about a quarter of the nation's labor force. These developments brought losses, discouragement, and great hardship to millions of people.

In response to that depression, in the 1930s the government instituted many of its income security programs. It also took a much greater role in maintaining the level of employment in the economy and in stabilizing the economy. This change was closely tied to

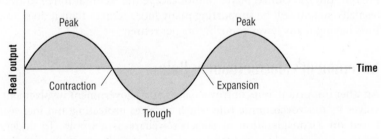

Figure 17.4

Idealized business cycle.

what has become known as the **Keynesian view**—the view that government can and should play a stabilizing role in the economy. It is named after John Maynard Keynes, the English economist whose work played a big role in bringing about the change. The widespread adoption of the Keynesian view of the economy created the field of macroeconomics as distinct from that of microeconomics.

Monetary and Fiscal Policy.   Government's macroeconomic role is performed by both the executive branch of government, which has responsibility for fiscal policy, and by the Central Bank of the United States, the Federal Reserve Bank, or Fed—a type of banker's bank that has responsibility for monetary policy. Let's discuss each in turn.

Fiscal policy is a policy of using the government budget surplus or deficit to influence the level of spending and income in the economy. The economist's standard rule of thumb for fiscal policy is that if total spending in the economy is too low, the government should run a budget deficit; this deficit adds spending to the total flow of income and has a multiplied effect on the total level of spending. If total spending is too high, the government should run a budget surplus; this surplus subtracts spending from the total flow of income and has a multiplied downward effect on the total level of spending.

This rule of thumb allows that some government budget deficits can be useful in stimulating the economy out of a recession. Therefore, if the U.S. economy falls into a recession, we are likely to hear calls for increases in government spending or decreases in taxes in order to stimulate the economy. That is precisely what we heard in 2008 when the U.S. economy seemed to be in freefall. In response, the government ran a massive deficit and in doing so likely avoided a depression. But it also created an enormous problem—how to wean the U.S. economy from the deficit spending and the bailouts.

A second macroeconomic tool to control the economy is monetary policy. **Monetary policy** is a policy in which the Central Bank (in the United States, the Federal Reserve Bank, or Fed) varies the level of money and credit in the economy to affect the level of income. The **Federal Reserve Bank (Fed)** is a semiautonomous agency that is only indirectly responsible to Congress and the president. It is run by a Board of Governors appointed by the president and serves as a bank to banks. It issues IOUs (also called notes) that serve as the basis of our money supply. (If you look on a dollar bill, you will see that it is a Federal Reserve note.) Whereas at one time gold backed the dollar, presently only trust in the fact that others will accept this dollar backs it. The government provides no backing for the dollar except its ability to tax. What gives money its value is that the Fed is committed to issuing only a limited quantity of its notes, or IOUs.

Credit and the financial sector are the equivalent to an economy's heart. They are essential to the economy because a failure of the financial sector means its heart stops beating; if that happens, firms and individuals cannot borrow or pay their bills, and they have to cut production. These cuts in production can push the economy into a downward spiral that ends in a depression.

The discussion of the technical operation of monetary policy is best left to economics courses. What you should know now is that monetary policy does not affect the level of income directly; rather, it affects the interest rate by making it easier or harder for individuals and firms to borrow. When the Fed increases the money supply, it is called expansionary monetary policy. Expansionary monetary policy makes credit easier to get and lowers interest rates; as interest rates fall, investment increases, which in turn has a multiplied effect (upward) on the level of income. When the Fed decreases the money supply, it is called contractionary monetary policy. Contractionary monetary policy makes credit harder to get and raises interest rates. As interest rates rise, investment decreases, which in turn has a multiplied effect (downward) on the level of income.

Government's Role in the Financial Crisis of 2008–2009.   We can see the macroeconomic role of government in action in the 2008–2009 financial crisis. The crisis began with a sustained rise in housing prices, leading people to see home ownership as a way of making money. People reasoned that if housing prices are rising by 30 percent a year, and they could borrow $100,000 at 6 percent interest to buy a house, that they would pay $6,000 in interest, get a house to live in, and after a year they could sell it for $130,000. They could earn $24,000 minus commission by "flipping" that house. They then would do it again—this time borrowing $130,000. With prices of housing rising at 30 percent per year, owning a house was even better than a free lunch. It was a money machine.

The housing boom was fueled by a relaxation of bank and government regulations on how much money people could borrow on a house. The relaxation of these regulations reduced the down payments and reduced the income they had to have in order to qualify for a loan. In some instances, outright fraud was encouraged by mortgage brokers who told individuals to put much higher incomes on their application forms than they actually had so that they could qualify for a higher loan. For example, a grocery clerk checkout person might list her income at $2,000 per week, and the loan would be approved without checking up on the income. (These loans became known as liar loans.)

As the boom continued, housing price rises became expected; more and more people entered the housing game—moving to bigger houses, taking equity out of their existing houses with home equity mortgages, and buying two or three houses and renting them out. "Flip That House" became a popular TV show.

The process worked as long as housing prices kept rising. But when housing prices stopped rising and started falling, the free money disappeared. Now the people who bought the house discovered that they had a house worth $90,000 and a mortgage of $130,000, which they couldn't pay. They faced foreclosure. Someone, of course, had to pay, and much of the discussion after the housing bubble burst concerned who should pay. Everyone wanted someone else to pay.

The financial problems of the United States in 2008–2009 were not confined to the housing sector. The problems spread, like a cancer, through the entire financial system. The reason why was that when the housing boom was in full progress, the mortgages on these houses were combined together into **financial derivatives**—financial assets whose value is derived from another financial instrument—and sold as safe, secure assets that paid higher interest than other safe assets. Investment banks and large commercial banks bought large numbers of these financial derivatives, paying for them with borrowed money. This meant that highly insecure mortgages—many of which were going into default—were serving as security for significant amounts of financial assets held by banks, individuals, and pension funds. In turn, these financial institutions held people's savings and checking accounts, which meant that the financial system was like a house of cards with defaulting home mortgages on the bottom line. When they crashed, the rest of the house of cards collapsed as well.

When housing prices stopped rising, it became clear that many of these mortgages were not going to be paid back. This meant that investment banks and commercial banks that held these assets were holding assets worth far less than they had paid, and that they actually might go bankrupt. Because of fears of that happening, other firms did not want to do business with those banks and financial institutions. Financial flows in the economy, which make trade possible, came to an abrupt halt. It was as if the economy's heart stopped beating.

As the effects of the financial crisis affected more and more sectors of the economy, the entire U.S. economy began moving into a recession, and possibly a depression, with production falling, people losing their jobs, which meant they bought less, which meant production fell more. . . . .

In response, the U.S. government stepped in and did two things. First, it instituted a massive financial bailout of banks and financial institutions—buying some of the derivatives that no one wanted, and guaranteeing many of the banks' loans. This quick action saved the U.S. banking system from collapse. Second, the government instituted a massive fiscal stimulus package, increasing its spending enormously, while cutting taxes. In 2009, the U.S. government ran a $1.4 trillion deficit, which meant it spent $1.4 trillion more than it took in taxes. Those actions kept the U.S. economy going, and prevented a depression, but it left it in a weakened condition to meet important challenges in the future.

Economic Challenges Facing the U.S. in the Future

In the remainder of this chapter, we introduce you to economists' thinking about three current and future challenges, the fiscal crisis, global warming, and surviving in a globalized economy.

The Fiscal Crisis

As discussed in the previous section, the government responded to the financial crisis by increasing spending and cutting taxes. This created a huge fiscal deficit that is so large that it can reasonably be called a **fiscal crisis**—an increase of deficits and debt of a country to a level that can threaten the financial stability of the government. You can see the problem that the government faces in Figure 17-5a, which shows U.S. budgets as a percentage of U.S. total output. Figure 17-5b shows the size of the U.S. total debt relative to its total output.

As you can see, the United States has run an almost continual deficit over the years, and that deficit has increased enormously in recent years. This means that even though total output has been increasing, total U.S. debt, which had declined as a percentage of total output after World War II, has been increasing for the last thirty years and has increased enormously in recent years. To solve the fiscal crisis in the coming years, the government must figure out a way to eliminate much of that deficit and start paying back some of the debt it has accumulated.

The reason it will have to eliminate that deficit is that in order to finance it, it must sell bonds; and, if it accumulates too much debt, people will not be willing to hold government bonds. We're a long way from that now, but if the greater than trillion dollar deficit continues, we will get there relatively quickly. So the government will have to figure out a way to cut spending or to raise taxes. Economic theory does not say which must be done, but it does say that one, the other, or some combination of the two must be done for us to find a solution to the financial crisis.

The accompanying box captures the key element of any solution to the fiscal crisis—there's "no free lunch" and government's activities will have to be paid for. The **"no free lunch" problem** (everything has a cost and must ultimately be paid for) facing government is the same problem facing individuals and businesses. One of the central policy propositions that economics has come to is that successful societies are those that have figured out

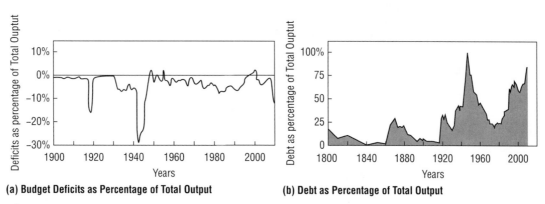

(a) Budget Deficits as Percentage of Total Output   (b) Debt as Percentage of Total Output

Figure 17-5

Source: The Economic and Budget Outlook, Congressional Budget Office, 2009 (www.cbo.gov) U. S. Bureau of the Census, historical Statistics, and estimates.

There Is No Such Thing as a Free Lunch

It is sometimes said that economics is simply the application of some tautologies (statements that are true by definition) to a consideration of social issues. One of those tautologies is captured by the following apocryphal story about a tyrannical king who decided that he wanted all economic knowledge summed up in a ten-volume work, so that he could read it and better rule his country. He assembled the best economists in the nation and told them to complete the task in four years. They set to work, and at the end of four years they had all ten volumes completed.

Unfortunately, the king had become busy with affairs of state in the interim, and he no longer had time to read ten volumes. So he told the economists to reduce it all to one volume within the next year. They dutifully set to work doing so. But at the end of one year, the king became much busier and felt he no longer had time to even read a book. Moreover, he had become a tyrant, so he ordered the economists to reduce the information in the book to one sentence within the next week. He told them he would put them to death if they did not complete the task.

After lamenting their fate for a couple of hours, they decided the task was hopeless and that they might as well order one last meal before they were put to death. They called in their order for a thick-crust, super-veggie pizza. When the delivery man came with their pizza asked for his money, the economists realized that they didn't have any. The king had taken away their checkbooks and credit cards. When they told the delivery man that, he took the pizza back and walked away, saying "you guys are economists; you should know that there ain't no such thing as a free lunch." Upon hearing this, the hungry economists looked at each other with a grin, saying in unison, "We're saved; that's it—that's economic knowledge summed up in one sentence." They ran and told the king, who thanked them, and sent them back to their respective universities, where they began teaching social science.

TANSTAAFL! It is a fact of life that you don't get something just for nothing. That's all!

ways to build that tautology into the decision-making process for all decisions makers so that it occurs almost without thinking. That's an important reason why economists tend to like markets: Markets let people make voluntary trades that improve their lot. So when someone trades in the market, they believe that the benefits they get from the trade exceed the cost, which means that they are made better off by the trade; but, the trade also takes into account that something must be given up. So in the market, people are made better off even as the "no free lunch" principle is maintained.

While the "no free lunch" proposition is a tautology for the entire system, it is not always true for an individual, government, or business. Someone can eat a lunch and leave the paying to others. Government, people, and businesses have a strong incentive to do precisely that, and much of economists' advice about the economic challenges facing the United States involves instituting measures that build the "no free lunch" proposition into society's decisions.

Of course, there are ways around the "no free lunch" tautology, and individuals, firms, governments and countries have figured out ingenious ways to get around that proposition, at least temporarily, by borrowing or running deficits. Thus, when you or government runs a deficit, you get to consume now but pay later. Because you are paying later, you are not actually getting around the "no free lunch" proposition, but you are getting around it temporarily. Alternatively, if you can consume the good and get someone else to pay the tab, you get a free lunch and they end up paying. This happens all the time. Consider your or your kids' decisions as to what to buy. When we're shopping, my kids tell me they want this and that—they just have to have it. And if I'm paying, they actually do want it. But if they go shopping with their own money, somehow what they need or want changes.

The same reasoning occurs in medical care. When we are talking about what we "need" in medical care when an insurance company or the government is paying, only the best medical care will do. But when people are paying out of their own pocket, they often decide a generic drug will do fine, or they didn't really need some surgical procedure, or that a medical test is superfluous. The reality is that more health care is demanded when it is provided by government, or by insurance, than when it is not.

Notice that this is not an argument specifically against government provision of a good; it is simply an argument that says that whenever the payer is a different person than the person receiving the benefit, the amount demanded increases enormously, and the costs go up. So a policy proposition in economics is that, whenever possible, keep the beneficiary and the payer the same, because only the actual payer will make the hard decisions, building the "no free lunch" proposition directly into their decision. If you don't have the market to do it, then you need some other institutional structure that does. For example, there could be a constitutional requirement that whenever the government spends on a new project or takes on a new obligation, it will have to simultaneously pay for that new project by increasing taxes or by cutting other programs. The United States has such a law (it is called the pay-as-you-go (PAYGO) law). Unfortunately, it is structured in such a way that it can easily be avoided, and it has not forced government to face the "no free lunch" tautology. If it were significantly tightened, government would be forced to make the hard decisions about costs that will have to be incurred to deal with the fiscal crisis.

To summarize: economists' suggestion for the fiscal crisis is that whatever is decided politically, the true economic solution will involve some mechanism that forces society to recognize that the costs cannot be passed on forever, and that a true solution will include a matching of the costs and benefits. That solution will include making some hard decisions, which will involve less spending than desired by some and more taxes than desired by others.

The Globalization Crisis

The U.S. is a rich country due to a variety of reasons—its institutional structure that encourages initiative on the part of its people, its natural resources, its political cohesiveness, and its luck. For whatever reason, in the beginning of the twentieth century, the

U.S. became the world's dominant economic power; throughout the twentieth century, it had higher wages and much more industrial power than any other country in the world.

That is in the process of change as industrial power is shifting from the U.S. to newly developed countries. This shifting of production that is occurring in the world economy goes under the name **globalization,** which can be defined as the integration of world economies. While the name, globalization, is fairly new, the phenomenon is not. It is a process that has been ebbing and flowing for centuries. For example, in the colonialization period of the 1600s and 1700s, colonial "possessions" were integrated into the economies that controlled them, and there was much trade between the home country and the colonies. In 1914, World War I ended the era of colonial globalization. Global trade did not begin to recover until the end of World War II. Since then, it has re-expanded greatly, but it is important to understand that globalization is not new to our generation, and the world's economies have been in a continual process of integration, segregation, and re-integration.

During the twentieth century, it became taken as given by many Americans that U.S. per capita income would be higher than world per capita income. In the period immediately after World War II, U.S. power grew and U.S. wages rose far above those of other countries; U.S. technology also was far above others and U.S. economic might was unchallenged. The globalization crisis involves coming to grips with the realization that U.S. economic dominance is not inherent and that very likely in the coming decades, its dominance will decline. The reason why U.S. dominance will decline is because this dominance was not a stable situation to begin with. It violated what might be called the economic **law of one price,** which states that if a free flow of resources and technology exists, equally productive factors will tend to earn equal amounts, and tradable goods will tend to have the same price.

According to the law of one price, eventually—assuming they are equally productive— a Chinese, Indian, or African engineer will earn the same as a U.S. engineer. This law holds because if it isn't the case, firms will relocate production to areas with lower-cost workers. This process of equalizing wages of equally productive workers is called factor price equalization. It has been occurring since the end of World War II—first with the growth of the European, Japanese, and Korean economies and more recently with the growth of India and China's economies relative to the U.S.

An important condition to note is that the law of one price is dependent on a free flow of resources and technology, and in many sectors of the economy that does not hold. For example, an American cannot get a haircut from someone in China or India, so haircuts are not tradable, which means that a Chinese haircutter can receive less than a U.S. haircutter without the U.S. haircutter worrying about losing his or her job. Similarly, if U.S. firms have access to better technology than Chinese and Indian firms, which they did for much of the Twentieth century, they could earn higher profits and pay higher wages than Chinese and Indian firms.

In the late twentieth century and the beginning of the twenty-first century, those qualifiers—which made it possible for U.S. incomes of many U.S. workers to significantly exceed those of workers in other countries' incomes—have been fading away. One reason is because technology has opened up new areas where trade can take place that did not exist before. This expansion of trade has occurred in both goods and services. It has expanded in terms of goods because of enormous technological changes in shipping and transportation. Modern containers allow much lower cost shipping of bulky items than was previously possible. Today, the oceans are filled with gigantic containerized ships that are unloaded at ports and sent on their way by computerized systems that have significantly lowered the cost of shipping.

Computers, the Internet, and modern communications technology have also allowed instant contact with firms all over the world, which reduces much of the advantage of producing for U.S. consumers in the U.S. Simultaneously, countries previously hostile to markets have adopted markets and thus have become trading partners, creating billions of additional potential workers competing for a job. This has added enormous competition to the manufacturing sector in the U.S. and has changed its very nature, from one where most manufactured goods consumed by U.S. consumers were produced in the U.S., to one where most U.S. manufactured goods consumed by U.S. customers are produced abroad. Today, U.S. manufacturing specializes in certain niche and high-tech consumption goods and on research and development. China is now the factory for the world much more than is the U.S.

It is not only in goods that this movement has taken place. It is also in services, and the loss of service jobs to other countries goes under the name **outsourcing**—the shifting of jobs from the United States to lower-wage developing countries. Thus, while U.S. haircutters do not face competition from abroad, people working in service support positions do. For example, call centers now are typically found in India, and when you call for technical support on your computer or with a question about your bill, the telephone call will likely be handled by someone in India.

Similarly, accounting and bookkeeping for firms is more and more done in India. The areas of competition are expanding. Say you need some tutoring. Now you can go on-line and hire an Indian tutor to help you with your homework. We can expect much more such competition in the future.

To maintain its dominance in a globalized economy, and the higher wages that go with that dominance, the United States will have to maintain a technological edge over other countries. Doing so will likely become increasingly difficult as India and China move up the technological ladder—just as Japan, Korea, and the European countries did earlier. This doesn't mean that U.S. income must fall from where it is now; it only means that the largest growth in income and output will likely be in countries such as China and India, and that the United States and Europe will experience relatively slower growth.

What do economists have to offer to meet the globalization crisis? If you are looking for an easy fix, the answer is not much. They see globalization as an inevitable process, not a crisis. They argue that the best a country can do is to learn to live with it. It must concentrate on producing as efficiently as possible and must learn to no longer see itself as special. In an economy, you're only special to the degree that you can produce goods people want at a lower cost than others.

Why shouldn't the U.S. impose tariffs to project our jobs? As we will discuss in Chapter 19, economists argue that imposing tariffs would lead to other countries imposing tariffs, which would reduce demand for U.S. goods, and which could enter the world economy into a trade war. With the globalization process, the market is doing precisely what it is designed to do—channeling production to the lowest-cost area so that goods are produced as efficiently as possible. It is this globalization of goods and services that has allowed the United States to develop the high standard of living it enjoys today. So, economists' solution to the globalization crisis is that the U.S. should learn to live with it and compete as hard as it can to maintain its standard of living.

Global Warming

Let's conclude with a consideration of a third problem—one that not only the U.S. but the entire world, is facing—global warming. Global warming is occurring because too much economic production is using carbon-based fuels, which increase the level of CO_2 in the atmosphere. In the words of economists, the use of carbon-based fuels is creating an externality, which, as we stated above, is the result of a decision that is not taken into account by the decision maker. Thus, while the private decision maker balances the costs and benefits facing him or her, those private costs do not match the social costs that the action imposes on society. This is occurring so much in the consumption of carbon-based fuels that it is changing the world's atmosphere by increasing CO_2 levels and thereby increasing the average world temperature. The result is a rising sea level and significant weather changes for many areas. Low-lying areas face flooding, if as predicted, the sea rises by 3–5 feet over the next century.

The economic answer to the problem of global warming is to see that the costs of the decision to use carbon-based fuel are taken into account by the decision maker. This can be done either by placing a tax on carbon-based fuel so that people face the true social cost, or by creating a cap-and-trade system—essentially creating property rights in pollution.

Given the fiscal problems the U.S. government faces—and the need for additional revenue—the tax-based approach is the one most economists favor, but imposing taxes is difficult politically, and the U.S. chose the market-based approach. As they set it up, the question is: Who would get the property rights? Most economists favored government receiving the property rights to the pollution rights because it would have meant hundreds of billions of dollars in revenue that the government needs. Initially, the U.S. government was following the economists' suggestion, but it soon backed away from that and gave most of the rights to existing polluters. This made the implementation of the cap and trade system politically feasible, but problematic, because it would entrench existing companies, and make creating new firms more costly.

U.S. companies argued that they would lose their competitive edge if they were not given the rights to pollute. What that argument misses is that new companies starting in the U.S. will have to buy pollution permits from existing firms who reduce their CO_2 output, which will place them at a competitive disadvantage. Because new firms often develop new technologies, this can actually work against the U.S. in its efforts to maintain a competitive edge.

Economists also point out that the solution to global warming must occur at the global level because, otherwise, firms will simply move to where restrictions are weakest, and there will be a flight to the lowest level of regulation. Thus, without a strict international agreement, that all countries of the world abide by, it is almost inconceivable that a global warming solution will be achieved. So, the economists' perspective on global warming is that you should expect a warmer world because effective solutions are beyond our current international institutional structure, and voluntary measures do not work when dealing with problems that involve costly solutions.

Conclusion

Much more could be discussed on all of these issues, but we don't have time. However, despite the cursory structure, this chapter and the preceding chapter should give you a sense of economists' thinking and of the economic challenges facing the U.S. economy. Such thinking involves an explicit consideration of both the costs and benefits of government policy and actions. The goal is to minimize costs while maximizing the benefits that laws and policies achieve. Imposing those policies is not easy, and is often politically difficult, which is why economics alone does not provide answers to problems. It simply provides a framework. The answers have to be found in the realm of politics.

Key Points

- Government plays both an indirect role in the economy—setting the rules and regulating the economy—and a direct role—spending and taxing to pay for its spending.
- Regulation has both benefits and costs. It helps limit people from activities that might hurt others, but in doing so restricts people's actions and often stops them from activities that would be beneficial to others.

- Regulation is a continuous process because technologies change and people learn how to get around existing regulations.
- Two contentious roles of the government are its income redistribution role and its macroeconomic role.
- An important federal government expenditure is the Social Security program, and financing the program may present problems in the future.

- The government influences the level of activity in the economy with fiscal policy—using the government budget surplus or deficit to control the level of spending in the economy—and by monetary policy—allowing the Federal Reserve Bank to control the level of money and credit in the economy.
- The United States faces a number of economic challenges in the coming years, including a fiscal crisis, globalization, and global warming

- To solve the fiscal crisis, the United States must come to grips with the reality that there is no free lunch. It is going to have to see that revenues match spending, either by cutting spending or by raising taxes.
- Globalization is the natural process of economic integration and is driven by the law of one price.
- To deal with global warming, the costs of activities that contribute to global warming will have to be raised considerably.

Some Important Terms

depression (348)
externalities (341)
Federal Reserve Bank (Fed) (349)
Federal Insurance Contributions
   Act (FICA) (346)
financial derivatives (350)
fiscal crisis (351)

fiscal policy (349)
globalization (354)
Keynesian view (349)
laissez-faire (340)
law of one price (354)
macroeconomic role (347)
microeconomic role (347)

monetary policy (349)
"no free lunch" problem (351)
outsourcing (355)
progressive income tax
   system (346)
public goods (343)
unfunded mandates (340)

Questions for Review and Discussion

1. About how much does the federal government spend each year to finance its activities? As a result, does it run a deficit or a surplus?
2. What has the U.S. government done so far in response to the issue of global warming, and why does this issue require an international solution?
3. While spending more money on manufacturing goods is looked upon favorably, why do people feel uneasy about additional spending in health care and education?
4. On what major category do state governments spend the most money per year?
5. What is fiscal policy, and what entity conducts it?
6. What is monetary policy, and what entity conducts it?
7. What problems is the government likely to face in paying Social Security benefits in the future?

8. What is the Keynesian view?
9. Should the federal government allow an unlicensed lawyer to practice law? Why or why not?
10. What problem will most likely arise when tariffs are imposed?
11. What two measures did the U.S. government take to stop the 2008–2009 financial crisis? What effect will they have in the long run?
12. Will outsourcing ultimately lead to a shift of all U.S. manufacturing to lower-wage countries?
13. Give two examples of how government laws can indirectly influence the distribution of income.
14. What is the law of one price, and what does it mean for the wages of U.S. workers?
15. What is the Mickey Mouse Protection Act? Is it good public policy?

Internet Questions

1. Go to www.taxadmin.org, the website of the Federation of Tax Administrators. Does your state have an income tax? Using the latest figures, what is the lowest and highest income tax rate for your state? Is it a progressive tax system? Explain.
2. Go to www.cbo.gov, the site of the Congressional Budget Office. How much has been spent on

Social Security benefits for the current fiscal year thus far? What percentage is that of the total government outlays?
3. Go to www.publicdebt.treas.gov, the site of the Bureau of the Public Debt. What is the current amount of the national debt? What is the interest expense for the latest month? For the last complete fiscal year?

4. Using a quick calculator, www.ssa.gov/planners/calculators.htm, estimate your Social Security benefits with the information you have now.

5. According to the Federal Reserve, www.federalreserve.gov/faqs.htm, what are its responsibilities?

For Further Study

Baumol, William J., Robert E. Litan and Carl. J. Schramm, *Good Capitalism, Bad Capitalism, and the Economics of Growth and Prosperity,* New Haven, CT: Yale University Press: 2007.

Bernstein, Jared, *Crunch: Why Do I Feel So Squeezed? (And Other Unsolved Economic Mysteries),* San Francisco: Berrett-Koehler Publishers, 2008.

Blinder, Alan S., *Hard Heads, Soft Hearts: Tough Economics for a Just Society,* Reading, MA: Perseus Publishing, 1988.

Citizens Against Government Waste, *Pig Book: How the Government Wastes Your Money,* New York: Viking, 2004.

Friedman, Milton, *Capitalism and Freedom,* Chicago: University of Chicago Press, 1982.

Heilbroner, Robert, L., *The Worldly Philosophers: The Lives, Times and Ideas of the Great Economic Thinkers,* London: Allen Lane, 1969.

Landsburg, Steven E., *Armchair Economist: Economics & Everyday Life,* Free Press: New York, 1995.

Levitt, Steve D., and Steven Dubner, *Freakonomics: A Rogue Economist Explores the Hidden Side of Everything,* London: Allen Lane, 2005.

McKibben, Bill, *Deep Economy: The Wealth of Economies and the Durable Future,* New York: Henry Holt & Co, 2007.

U.S. Bureau of the Census, *Statistical Abstract of the United States,* Washington, DC: U.S. Government Printing Office, 2010.

WWW Antitrust Division of the Department of Justice www.usdoj.gov/atr/overview.html

WWW Federal Reserve www.federalreserve.gov

WWW Internal Revenue Service www.irs.ustreas.gov

WWW Medicare www.medicare.gov

WWW Office of Budget Management www.access.gpo.gov/usbudget

WWW Social Security Administration www.ssa.gov

WWW U.S. Treasury www.treas.gov

International Political Relations

chapter 8

After reading this chapter, you should be able to:

- Explain the role of the state in international relations
- Define power and explain why nothing is more basic to an understanding of international relations
- Define foreign policy and discuss five issues that policymakers must heed when forming foreign policy
- List the three ideologies that have been prevalent since World War II
- Summarize the role of Congress and the president in conducting foreign policy

> *We are trying to make a society instead of a set of barbarians out of the governments of the world.*
>
> —**Woodrow Wilson**

As transportation technology has improved, the world has shrunk. Whereas only a hundred years ago our community meant our town, today it means the entire world. To understand this community, with its component states and their objectives, its problems and their possible solutions, its history, its economy, its wars, and its processes of order and stability—all this is the task of those who aspire to understand contemporary international relations. Real as this world community is, you should be warned that it differs greatly from communities of individual persons because its units—states—are so different from the men and women who inhabit towns, cities, and nations.

The State in International Relations

The term *state* has a number of different meanings. In this country, it is most commonly used to refer to any one of the fifty members of our national union. But as the word is used in discussing international relations, and as we are using it in this chapter, a **state** is a body politic organized for civil rule and government. It is an independent political unit that can carry on negotiations or make agreements with other such units. In this sense, the United States qualifies as a state, but political entities such as Alabama, California, and Michigan do not.

Consider the map of the world on pages 360–361, on which you can count a total of about 190 states. Not all of these states are completely sovereign or independent, nor are they fully comparable. There are extreme variations among them in both physical characteristics and in cultural matters such as religion, education, ethnic background, industry, standards of living, and government.

For instance, in area they range from Russia, with an area of 6.6 million square miles, down to Monaco, with less than 1 square mile, and tiny Vatican City, with a mere 106 acres of land; only eight states possess more than a million square miles of territory. In population

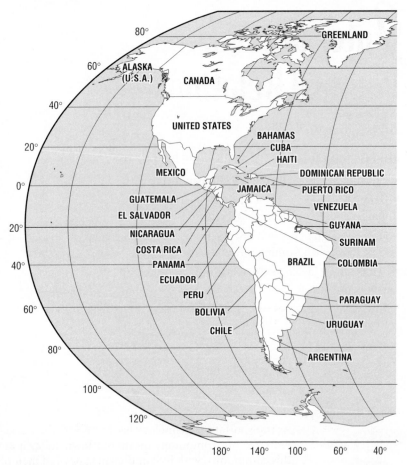

Nations of the world. A few of the smaller countries have been left out. See how many of them you can name.

the largest states are China (over 1.3 billion people) and India (over 1.1 billion); the smallest are Tuvalu (12,000) and Vatican City (under 1,000). Some states are overwhelmingly Roman Catholic in faith (such as Spain and France); some are almost entirely Protestant (Denmark and Sweden); others are both Catholic and Protestant (Germany); some accommodate a wide variety of faiths (the United States). There are also states in which other religions prevail, including Islam, Buddhism, Judaism, and Hinduism. Income per capita ranges all the way from more than $100,000 per year in Liechtenstein and Qatar to estimates of less than $500 per year in some African countries.

The Nation-State

In this chapter, we use the terms *state* and *nation* more or less as synonyms. Strictly, however, they carry different meanings, and in the precise language of international law and diplomacy, only "state" is employed; this is true, for instance, in the Charter of the United Nations, in the Statute of the International Court of Justice, and in treaties generally. The characteristics of a **state,** according to the Charter of the Organization of American States (1948) are (1) a permanent population, (2) a clearly defined territory, (3) a government, and (4) sovereignty that requires a capacity for international relations. The term **nation** was originally applied to groups of people with the same ethnic background, such as the Germans or the French, each of whom could point to a common language and a common cultural heritage.

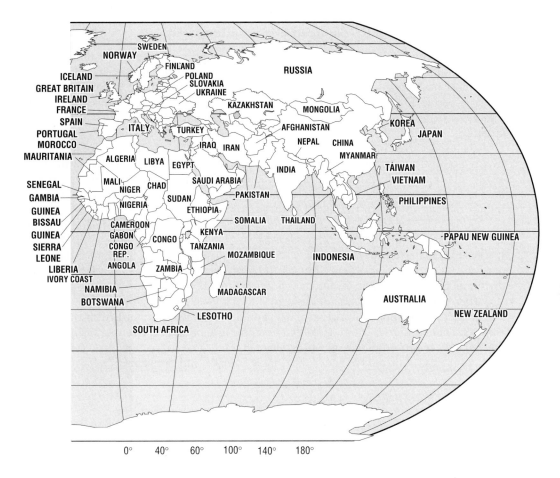

The explanation of the modern popular practice of using state and nation as synonyms lies in the fact that for some centuries now the **nation-state**—a state that has tended to include substantially the same people as the ethnic nation—has been one of the most prominent forms of state in existence. The French state, for instance, is for the most part made up of a French-speaking people with a common historical and cultural background. There are some nation-states, however—including Switzerland, India, Russia, and Canada—that do not have a common language or cultural background. These differences in language and in cultural and ethnic background can cause problems, as we have seen in recent years in Belgium, Sri Lanka, India, the emerging African states, the republics of the former Soviet Union, Nepal, and Kosovo.

As we saw in Chapter 3, the structure of the modern nation-state was constructed on the ruins of feudalism in western Europe. In the conflicts among feudal lords, a certain lord within an area would emerge as victor, and eventually large areas where the people spoke similar dialects were brought together under a ruler who called himself king.

England was one of the first nation-states, and by the latter part of the twelfth century, the authority of King Henry II extended over almost all of the country as well as over parts of what is now France. Most of France was unified a little later; by the middle of the fifteenth century, English authority had been forced off the continent. By the end of the reign of the French king Louis XI (1461–1483), France could claim to be a new nation-state. Other nation-states gradually emerged, so that in time the map of Europe showed a substantial group—England, France, Spain, Denmark, Hungary, Russia, Poland, Norway, and Sweden. The Treaty of Westphalia (1648) put its stamp of approval on the new system by recognizing that the political authority of the pope and of the old Holy Roman Empire was dead.

The Establishment and Disappearance of Nation-States

Since 1648, many new nation-states have sprung into being, and from time to time old ones have died out. For example, during the nineteenth century, Turkish authority was expelled from most of Europe, and new states took its place on the Balkan peninsula: Greece, Bulgaria, Serbia, Romania, Albania, and Montenegro (later included in Yugoslavia). By the mid-1990s, several of these nation-states were again in political turmoil. Yugoslavia broke apart.

Change occurred in the western hemisphere in the 1800s. For example, approximately twenty new states were formed from the old holdings of Spain and Portugal in the New World. About the middle of the nineteenth century, China and Japan, ancient countries of the Far East, opened their doors to Western trade. They, too, were admitted into the community of nation-states, in 1842 and 1854, respectively.

World War I tore down the old multinational state of Austria-Hungary and built up several new states: Poland, Czechoslovakia, Austria, Hungary, Latvia, Lithuania, and Estonia. It also added to the territory of already existing states such as Romania. World War II snuffed out Latvia, Lithuania, and Estonia, but it led directly to the establishment of Israel and the divisions of Korea and Germany into new political units.

After World War II, a surge of nationalism took place in the colonial areas of Africa, and in the 1960s a number of African and Asian states emerged from the British and French empires. These countries combined different ethnic groups and experienced turmoil at the turn of the century, not all of which has subsided. Their structure may yet change. Significant areas of turmoil included the Congo, Somalia, and Zimbabwe.

The Rise of the European Union

As you can see, states are constantly evolving. Another aspect of this evolution involves the building up of states through combinations of previously existing states. An example is the on-going development of the European Union (EU). The beginnings of the EU go back to 1951 when Belgium, West Germany, Luxembourg, France, Italy, and the Netherlands set up a European Coal and Steel Community. In 1957, this same group of countries expanded the organization into the European Economic Community (EEC), and the countries began to remove trade barriers between them, forming a common market. In 1967, a European Parliament was created, and with it the beginnings of a political union, but the union was still primarily economic. In 1979, direct elections for members of the European Parliament were held, and in 1992 the Treaty of Maastricht was signed. This changed the EEC to the EU, which was not only an economic union but also a political union. The countries were still independent, but there were forms of cooperation in defense, justice, and home affairs. Work toward common regulations and policies began, and European laws started to replace, override, and sometimes conflict with laws within the countries. You can see the effect of these changes when you travel among most European countries—you no longer have to go through a border check.

In 1992, the EU made another move toward greater cooperation when twelve countries adopted a common currency—the euro. Now, when you go to Germany, for example, you no longer use German marks as your currency; you use the euro.

As these changes occurred, membership expanded. Denmark, Ireland, and the United Kingdom joined in 1973, followed by Greece, Spain, Portugal, Austria, Finland, and Sweden in the years up until 1995. In 2004, ten new members joined and in 2007 two more countries, Bulgaria and Romania, joined. Currently, other countries including Croatia and Turkey are negotiating membership.

All these changes, however, leave the EU a long way from being considered a state. Attempts at consolidation have floundered. For example, a number of countries, such as Denmark and Britain, chose not to adopt the euro. Another example is the 2003 Treaty of Nice, which laid down new rules governing the way the EU would work; it was to be a stepping-stone

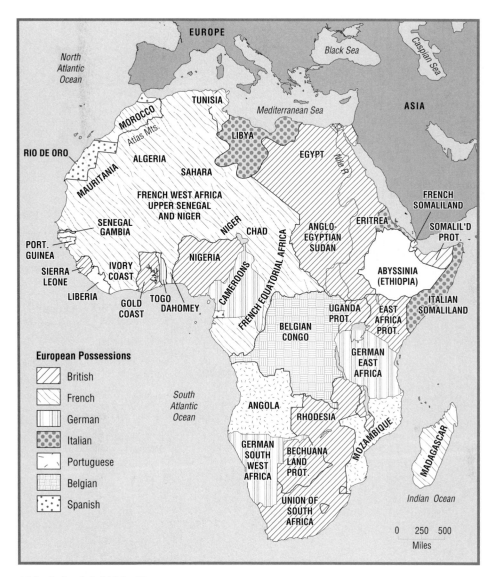

Africa before World War II.

to a new EU constitution. But voters in France and the Netherlands, two of the original members, did not ratify the treaty. In response, the European Parliament instituted many of the provisions of the proposed constitution in a treaty called the Treaty of Lisbon, which did not require voter approval. The Treaty of Lisbon was signed in 2007 and went into force in 2009.

Sovereignty of States

All states are legally sovereign, which means they are not legally subordinate to any other state. In practice, however, their sovereignty is limited by economic and political realities. For example, some Latin American countries rely on aid from the International Monetary Fund and the United States. Therefore, they generally consider carefully the probable reaction of the United States and the Western "alliance" in determining their international position.

Similarly, after the 9/11 attacks on the United States and former President Bush's war on terrorism policy of preemption—in which the United States claimed the right to attack a

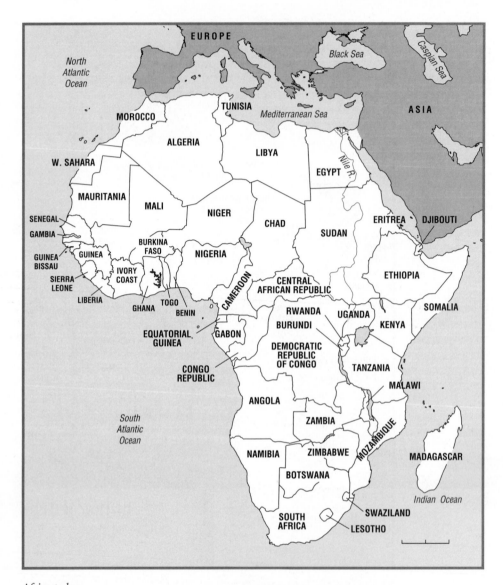

Africa today.

country believed to be harboring, aiding, or abetting terrorists—countries such as Pakistan or Syria needed to carefully consider the United States' views before undertaking any policy. With the strongest military power in the world threatening you, it is hard to consider yourself fully sovereign and independent.

Power in the World Community

Nothing is more basic to an understanding of international relations than an appreciation of the role of **power**—the capacity to compel another party to commit an action contrary to its explicitly stated will. Countries have national goals, and to achieve those goals they need power. Current expressions such as "power politics," "the great powers," the "small powers," and the "balance of power" all attest to the importance of that role. Power has

Power has almost inevitably been based on military might, as this monument to El Cid memorializes.

many dimensions: military, economic, moral, geographic, and political, and in the next sections we discuss some of them.

The Nature and Sources of National Power

In the final analysis, the power of a state consists of the means it possesses for promoting its vital interests by influencing or controlling the behavior of other states. Although military force is the most obvious type of power, it is not the only one. The principal forms of pressure available to states in their dealings with each other are military power, power over opinion at home and abroad, economic power, and geographic power. Possession of any of these attributes tends to augment the power of an individual nation and thus increase its ability to realize its political, social, economic, and military goals.

Of all the sources of power, military power is the most important. The parallel to individual relationships is clear: If you can beat up everyone on the block, you are free to do pretty much what you want. There are, of course, limits if you want to maintain friendly, rather than fearful, relations with others, but a nation with clear military superiority can generally boast control of its destiny. It is seldom the case, however, that one country emerges as indisputably superior militarily. Instead, competing spheres of military power develop, leading to a standoff.

In historical terms, the beginning of the twenty-first century was unusual in terms of military power. The United States was a **hegemon,** a country with almost indisputable military superiority. That military might gave it enormous power, and its desires became much more important than those of other sovereign countries. It had the power to say: If you don't like it, tough—we're going to do what we want. Thus, when the United States wanted to use military force because it believed (incorrectly) that Iraq had **weapons of mass destruction** (biological, chemical, and nuclear weapons) and it wanted to rid Iraq of those weapons, it did so even though a majority of the world's countries felt that military force was not yet called for.

There was no overwhelming cry for the United States to apply its mandate equally— Israel had significant weapons of mass destruction, but when Arab countries tried to raise that issue, they were ignored by the United States. In fact, the very definition of weapons of mass destruction was itself a reflection of the U.S. point of view. Cruise missiles and Big Brother bombs, which the United States used against Iraq, were not classified as weapons of mass destruction, but chemical and biological agents, which the United States accused Iraq of developing, were.

The United States (and some other countries that joined the U.S.) attacked Iraq and found no evidence of these weapons. After doing so, the U.S. was not condemned by the U.N. for an inappropriate preemptive war. Instead, the UN Security Council officially recognized the United States and Great Britain as legitimate occupying powers. Such is the power of a military hegemonic state.

Military power depends on far more than weapons. Military power is also limited by social and cultural conventions. In its war with Iraq, the United States could have used nuclear weapons to achieve its objective much more quickly, but it was prevented from doing so by cultural, social, and political pressures. Thus, military power depends on the will to use that military power and the will to accept the losses that the use of military action entails.

A country's will to use military power depends, in part, on its ability and willingness to accept criticism of its actions. By showing that the United States was willing to use its military might on grounds that it determined, and that it would not accept outside limitations on its power, including UN limitations, the United States changed the international political landscape. Thereafter, all countries were a bit more careful in their interactions with the United

Israeli infantry troops march in southern Lebanon.

States. Thus, the war initially extended the power of the United States. But the U.S.'s "go it alone" attitude also undermined much of the world's view about its commitment to fairness. The failure of the United States to bring about peace in Iraq, and the loss of popular support for the war by the U.S. population, has undermined U.S. power. Some of the hostility toward the United States has subsided with the election of President Barack Obama. But his use of military power will necessarily reflect the lessons from the Iraq War. Today, few countries believe that in the future the United States will act as independently and unilaterally as it did in Iraq.

The importance of social and cultural factors means that the structure of government plays a role in determining the military power of a country. In Western liberal democracies, in which the press and individuals enjoy extensive freedoms, public opinion plays a significant role in determining governmental policy. Public opinion plays less of a role in the policies of autocratic governments. Such governments can partially shape public opinion through tight control of the media. If, in spite of such control, dissent develops, they can use secret police or other repressive organizations to ferret out and kill or imprison its leaders and, in some cases, whole groups of dissenters. Saddam Hussein used this power ruthlessly in Iraq. Just how strong the control of the press was in Iraq is shown by the briefings of the Iraqi Ministry of Information during the final days of the U.S. invasion. As U.S. tanks were driving through the city of Baghdad, the minister of information was briefing reporters on how Iraq was winning the war and driving back the Americans.

We should point out that while democracies have less control over public opinion, they can still influence it, and during times of war they directly control the flow of news that reaches reporters. In the 2003 Iraq war, members of the press were "embedded" within military units, giving them a much closer look at the war. Critics pointed out that embedding was a way of shaping the reporter's view, because it is difficult to criticize individuals who are protecting you. The difference in control of the press in an autocracy and in a democracy is one of degree. In an autocracy, the control over the press is often direct; in a democracy, it is generally indirect, with the government relying on creating an appropriate "spin" on the reporting.

Although the government of an autocratic state may be able to shape public opinion at home, it has no direct control over foreign opinion. In their attempts to influence opinion abroad, both autocratic and democratic governments are likely to resort to propaganda, and though there are no very dependable ways of measuring its results, it is safe to assume that the large-scale propaganda campaigns conducted by all strong nations

Anti-Iraq War protesters in England.

Why Do So Few Americans Have Access to Al Jazeera?

Western countries have numerous news sources that provide news from a Western slant. While there are differences—Fox News provides a more conservative view than CNN, which provides a more liberal view than the BBC, which provides a more European liberal view—the overall view is definitely Western. These news sources broadcast around the world, and people in all countries have access to these news sources. There are other views, and a good source for those other views is the Al Jazeera English language news network, which has offered its network free to numerous U.S. cable companies. Because one of the pillars of U.S. democracy is free access to all viewpoints, it would seem that the United States would support widespread access to Al Jazeera. Yet, as of 2009, only three cable providers in the United States—in Burlington, Vermont; Toledo, Ohio; and Washington, DC—carried the network. The question is why?

Satellite and cable systems cite limited channel capacity as a reason for not providing the Al Jazeera network, but many Arabs see political and social pressures as the true cause. Former Secretary of Defense Donald Rumsfeld called its broadcasts of the Iraq war "vicious, inaccurate and inexcusable." Many in the United States agree. The difficulty for the United States in maintaining that position and informally or formally restricting access to the Al Jazeera network is that the United States is also committed to free speech. To many observers, Al Jazeera, while providing a significantly different slant on the news, does not deviate from the truth significantly more than other networks. Thus, Europeans have wide access to the Al Jazeera network, and many Arabs see it as much more objective than their state television networks and Western networks.

Because the Internet is open and does not rely on a cable company to provide it, Al Jazeera is available in the United States on the Internet. You might want to take a look at its news coverage at http://english .aljazeera.net/news and decide for yourself if it is objective.

would not be undertaken unless they were thought to be effective, either in strengthening home morale and winning support abroad or else in undermining the morale of potential enemies.

Following World War II, the United States enjoyed the confidence and respect of most other Western nations. This confidence reflected not so much propaganda and military might (although the United States had a good deal of the latter) but the appreciation of most countries for the U.S. role in the war. That confidence gradually eroded through the 1980s. This erosion reflected the impact of issues such as our role in Vietnam and dissension at home. With the downfall of the Soviet Union, respect for U.S. military power returned, but the confidence that the United States would use that military might for the benefit of the world, and not for itself, did not. The 2003 Iraq war reinforced that reduced confidence. It remains to be seen whether that confidence can be restored by the Obama presidency.

Other Sources of Power

The usefulness of economic power in international relations has often been demonstrated. During the struggle against Napoleon Bonaparte in the early 1800s, it enabled Great Britain not only to expand its own military forces but also to provide money and supplies for its allies. More than a century later, it enabled the United States to do likewise in both world wars; after World War II, it enabled the United States to make an important contribution to rebuilding the economies and the military forces of the countries of western Europe that had been over-run by the Nazis and that later felt threatened by the expanded military power of the former Soviet Union.

Though the sources of a nation's power are varied, some of them are more basic than others. For a state to generate great national strength, it helps to be large, both in area and population. Size is an advantage enjoyed by both Russia and the United States, and that size helps explain their importance. On the other hand, Japan is geographically small, but it is a major economic power. Industrial might is another vital source of power, for in its factories a country must produce the equipment for modern warfare, including tanks, ships, planes, missiles, and nuclear bombs. The high industrial output of the United States is a great asset in the power game, and Japan's industrial output is what its strength is based on. It must also be noted, however, that Japan's power is limited by its dependence on foreign oil. Japan's industrial needs require that it maintain friendly relations with the United States and the Organization of Petroleum Exporting Countries (OPEC), and its power is partly conditional on the hold other countries have over its fuel supply.

Another major source of economic power is dependable access to adequate supplies of raw materials because without these no nation can develop and maintain a large and efficient industrial complex. Yet another condition that is still a factor in national power is geographic location. This can, among other things, affect both access to raw materials and the degree to which a nation is vulnerable to a military attack. Geographic location is one element of U.S. strength. We are separated by oceans from any other major power, and though these can be crossed in a few minutes by nuclear missiles, there are, as we have pointed out, strong deterrents to the use of such weapons. Meanwhile, the oceans still protect us against attack by great armies using conventional weapons.

However, given size, a well-developed industry, and dependable access to adequate raw materials, probably the most important source of a nation's power is the characteristics of its people. Among the people there should be a substantial number of able scientists, artists, educators, businesspeople, military leaders, politicians, and many highly skilled workers of all types. In a democracy, perhaps the characteristic of a people that, if they have it, contributes most to the power of the nation in dealing with others is a strong sense of patriotism and loyalty that makes them willing to support their government in any policy they consider reasonable. But in dealing with foreign countries, the governments of democracies can face difficult problems at home. Negotiations cannot be carried on by all the people; they must be conducted by those who represent them in government.

This creates no great problem if those who represent the country are following policies with which the vast majority of the people agree. Frequently, however, there are large dissenting minorities, or there may even be an almost equal division of public opinion on the wisdom of government policies. When such differences of opinion concern issues about which people have strong emotions, the power of a government to formulate clear foreign policies and to make satisfactory agreements with other countries is likely to be impaired.

Maintaining Security

In a world community of sovereign nation-states, there are several ways in which a state could conceivably attempt to achieve security from attack without war and at the same time gain some of its other international objectives.

If it is a large state, such as the United States, with adequate resources and industrial development, it might attempt to make a **unilateral**—independent or one-sided—buildup of its military power to such a degree that no other state or probable combination of states would dare to challenge it. In the contemporary world, this would be a difficult achievement for any nation. First, it would mean diverting to military uses vast amounts of resources badly needed to improve the living conditions of its people and needed to meet various other social problems. Second, other nations, fearful for their safety and their power to control their own affairs, might form alliances to protect their interests. Thus, after the start of the 2003 Iraq war—a war that a majority of U.S. allies strongly opposed—a number of European nations began reconsidering their alliance with the United States and began exploring the creation of a separate European defense organization that would operate independently of the United States.

Another conceivable approach to the problem of security, one that a group of cooperating states could attempt to implement, would be to organize all the states of the world into a system of world government. To have much chance of success, such a system or organization would have to include most of the states of the world, especially the more powerful ones. It would have to be a kind of federation or superstate, with courts for settling disputes between nations and with a military establishment capable of forcing a recalcitrant nation to accept court decisions. The chances of establishing such a system in the foreseeable future are small because most power is in the hands of several very large countries, many of whose interests appear to be in opposition.

Furthermore, few nations seem willing to give up much of their sovereignty or their right to adopt any foreign policies they please. The United Nations, which we discuss in Chapter 21, may be regarded as a first step toward a system of world government, but actually it has very little power to protect its members or to prevent war. It does, however, perform many useful international services.

The most common way of preventing or at least indefinitely delaying a disastrous war between the world's most powerful nations is to develop and, if possible, maintain a stable balance of power. The term **balance of power** means an equilibrium or adjustment of power that for the time being no nation is willing to disturb. The power of one nation prevents the other nation from using its power. During the century that followed the Congress of Vienna (1815), a fairly effective power balance was maintained, for though that era did witness some adjustments of power and even several sizable wars, until World War I no state attempted to radically challenge the existing balance. After World War I, the United States became a major power, and its power significantly increased during and right after World War II. After World War II, the balance of power was between the Western bloc (the United States, western Europe, Japan, and their allies) and the Eastern bloc (the Soviet Union, eastern Europe, and their allies). This balance was structurally indicated by their membership in formal alliance organizations.

In the 1990, that balance of power became unbalanced. The United States was the world's strongest military power, much stronger than any other country. Given that reality, there was talk of a **new world order**—an international order in which the United States would follow the dictum of right rather than might in its conduct of external and internal affairs—replacing the balance of power.

As social scientists discussed the emergence of a new world order, a political theory emerged to fit the changing order. It is called the **theory of complex interdependence,** in which the largest nation's powers are limited by a variety of interdependencies. This new theory is in contrast to the **realist theory,** in which a balance of power with two competing nations was necessary to maintain the peace. As the world gradually moved toward a unipolar system, with the United States as the primary superpower, without an equally as strong offsetting balancing force, the theory of complex interdependencies has gained acceptance. The question political scientists were asking was what interdependencies were limiting the United States' use of power.

The emerging international realities are bringing into question the purpose of some international organizations. One example is the **North Atlantic Treaty Organization (NATO),** the organization responsible for the collective defense and protection of the West. Members of NATO included Belgium, Britain, Canada, Czech Republic, Denmark, France, Germany, Greece, Hungary, Iceland, Italy, Luxembourg, the Netherlands, Norway, Poland, Portugal, Spain, Turkey, and the United States (see Figure 18.1). In the 1990s, NATO lost much of its former purpose. But, like many organizations that have lost their purpose, it continued in existence, searching for a new purpose. As it searched, it expanded, adding some states that it had previously been established to counterbalance, such as Poland, Hungary, and the Czech Republic in 1997. Other states were also asking for membership, and NATO even worked out a cooperative agreement with Russia. In 2010, NATO had twenty-eight member states.

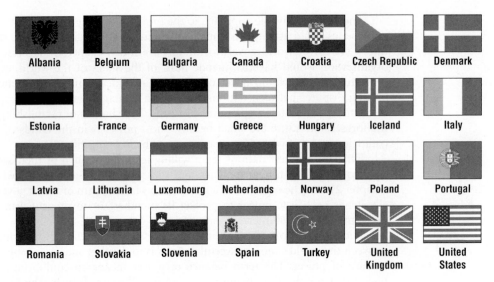

Figure 18.1

The members of NATO (as of 2010).

In light of recent events, NATO faces many challenges. Because of the 2003 war in Iraq, a war that many NATO countries opposed, NATO scaled back its mission and began refashioning itself as an "all-purpose military and political toolbox that can be tapped at short notice by ad hoc clusters of NATO counties." This change means that NATO can commit its NATO forces to peacekeeping activities even if all NATO countries don't agree.

The Berlin Plus Agreement in 2002 also saw the European Union further enhance its military capabilities; it gave the European Union access to NATO resources should the latter decline to intervene in a crisis. The expansion of the EU's military role poses serious questions about NATO's future. Unless NATO's members can find consensus in formulating and pursuing a shared security policy, NATO's future remains uncertain.

Whereas with a balance of power each country limits its actions for fear of upsetting that balance, in the new world order it is foreseen that each country will limit its actions according to "what is right." How is "what is right" determined? It is determined by the major power who, for the new world order to work, must interpret "what is right" in a way that seems right to most people regardless of what is in the countries' individual interests. Making the new world order work is a tall order, an issue that we discuss further in Chapter 21.

Foreign Policies

Relationships between states that affect the national security or general welfare of each are the core of international relations. The **foreign policies** of a nation are the courses of action a nation uses to achieve its international objectives. As a rule, the nation's primary purposes are to increase its own security and its own general economic welfare. Sometimes, however, a foreign policy may further the interests of some politically powerful pressure group rather than those of the nation as a whole. When this is so, those who support it usually attempt to convince the majority that it benefits the entire nation.

Generally speaking, the foreign policies of a state are designed to serve the national interests as these are conceived by the public or by those in direct control. Security and prosperity are always major objectives; other objectives may include the spread of an ideology such as the expansion of national power and prestige. Unfortunately, there is no simple formula guaranteeing that the right foreign policy decisions will always be made. Debate is, therefore, inevitable.

An example of the problems of foreign policy is the first Persian Gulf War of 1991. Here, Iraq, which the United States had supported in the Iran–Iraq war, invaded Kuwait, which was also a U.S. ally. In response, the United States aligned itself with Syria, which had been one of its major enemies, and kept its close ally, Israel, a country that was hated by Kuwait and Syria, out of the war while the United States simultaneously tried to establish closer ties with Iran. And who knows what secret agreements were made between the countries? The intrigue of soap operas pales in comparison with the intrigue of foreign policy.

Geography and Foreign Policy

Conspicuous among the facts and forces that act as determinants of foreign policy is, as we have pointed out, the geographic position of a nation. For the promotion of the country's security and prosperity, policymakers must give heed to matters such as the following:

- The defensibility of the state's boundaries
- The effects of distance on its powers of offense and defense by means of long-range missiles
- The availability of ports for useful trade and for naval bases
- The attitudes of neighboring states and their size and power
- The state's own size and natural resources

If a state is satisfied with its geographic lot in life, it can direct its efforts toward protecting what it has; if it is dissatisfied, it will, if possible, maneuver its policies toward the elimination of its alleged handicaps, asserting itself dynamically, perhaps even aggressively, in order to get from others what it believes it needs.

The term **geopolitics** refers to the relation between geography and security that foreign policymakers attempt to take into account. According to Nicholas Spykman, geopolitics is "the planning of the security policy of a country in terms of its geographic factors." No nation pursued the subject as seriously as did Germany in the 1930s. Under the Nazis, Germany embraced the theories of earlier geopoliticians, and it worked out a "scientific" policy of expansion calculated to secure Germany's position as a master power for an indefinite future, all at the expense of "decadent" neighbors.

Without constructing a complicated theory of geopolitics comparable to that of the Nazis, most states nevertheless have exhibited their geographic aspirations in their foreign policies. Russia for centuries has sought good warm-water ports; it has wanted control over the Dardanelles, and it has tried to get buffer territory on its western frontier to make up for its lack of defensible boundaries there. Its activities in Iran and Afghanistan in the 1970s and 1980s reflected that desire. France long felt that its geographic position required it to seek a frontier on the Rhine River and to undermine the strength of its dangerous neighbor, Germany, which had several times invaded France's territory. In the Far East, Japan attempted before World War II to add to the security of its position by absorbing Korea, Manchuria, Taiwan, and many islands of the Pacific and by controlling China. Iraq's 1990 invasion of Kuwait was in part an attempt by Iraq to gain control of two of Kuwait's islands, which would give it better control of the shipping lanes out of the Iraqi port of Basra, and the 2003 Iraq invasion was seen by some observers as an attempt by the United States to gain a strong military presence in the Middle East so that it could protect its oil interests and provide better protection for Israel.

Values, Ideologies, and Foreign Policy

A term that one often hears when discussing foreign policy is **ideology**—a deeply held vision of what the correct form of government should be. Since World War I, the three ideologies that have been prevalent are the fascist ideology, the democratic capitalist ideology, and the communist ideology.

Fascist Ideology.   The fascist ideology holds that a natural leader will arise in a country to tell the people what they want. It gives enormous power to a small group of leaders, which means that it tends to overlook the rights of individuals and minority groups. Under fascist ideology, the leader will make the people, the nation, and their culture great. With the defeat of Hitler in Germany and Mussolini in Italy in World War II, fascism has declined as an ideology, but you can still see support for fascist ideology in the small Nazi Party in the United States and in some countries where significant social turmoil exists.

Democratic capitalist ideology.   The dominant ideology today throughout the world is the democratic capitalist ideology. It is an ideology that sees the people as making society's decisions through democratic elections of their government. The will of the people is dominant, and subject to the preservation of certain inalienable individual rights such as the right to hold property and the right to free speech. The working of the elections and the inalienable rights are spelled out in either a formal or informal constitution which is the core of the laws of the country. In democratic capitalist ideology, all leaders are subservient to the laws. Thus, democratic capitalism is supposed to involve a combination of the rule of law and the rule of people.

Communist Ideology.   Communist ideology is an ideology that sees people as making society's decisions through a set of leaders who have the best interests of the people at heart. Thus, it places a small group of leaders above the political will of the people and above the law. It gives less weight to inalienable rights, private property, and the law than does democratic capitalist ideology.

The meaning of communist ideology is changing. When Karl Marx wrote *Das Kapital* and *The Communist Manifesto,* he spent almost no time discussing how a communist society would be implemented or would operate. It was only through the experience of the Soviet Union under its communist government after World War I and in the writings of the Soviet leader and practical theorist Vladimir Lenin, that the nature of what we now call communist countries became clear.

Because, according to Marx, communism involves the eventual withering away of the state, even so-called communist countries would agree that they are in a transition stage. For many people, it is not communism that goes against these values; it is the transition stage. During the Stalin era, large numbers of Soviet people were liquidated. Stalinist justification for that policy—that the end justifies the means—was, and is, unacceptable to most outside observers. They felt that nothing justifies such wholesale killing.

The 1980s and 1990s saw an enormous change in communism. Many states, including the formerly communist eastern European states such as East Germany and Poland and many of the republics of the former Soviet Union, have simply abandoned it, and in others, such as China, communism has evolved both economically and politically. This evolution, to some, suggests a victory of capitalist and democratic ideology, and in many ways, it is. People in the former Soviet Union focused their demands for reforms on achieving markets and democratic elections. Clearly, the totalitarian nature of Soviet communism and the favoritism the Soviet Union showed to Communist Party members were highly problematic.

But other observers point out that the Communist Party itself should also have been opposed by true communists. The party was meant to protect the rights of the working class, not to become the class of people with special privileges that it became. These other observers argue that communism failed because it abandoned communist ideals.

Most social scientists accept the argument that communism abandoned its ideals. They differ, however, on the question of whether that abandonment was inherent in the structure of communism—no society can ever give that much power to any group—or whether the communists simply didn't try hard enough to preserve their ideals. Whatever the answer is to that question, the reality is that communism is not yet dead. For example, communist parties still control the governments of China, North Korea, Venezulia, and Cuba.

Ideologies and Foreign Policies.   By emphasizing certain aspects of decisions, ideologies can be made to seem more or less desirable. A supporter of a certain ideology will likely provide a different spin on an ideology than an opponent of that ideology. If that supporter has rhetorical abilities, he can likely convince others to support it as well. Thus, a supporter of communism is likely to emphasize cases when property rights have led to what to most people would seem to be undesirable outcomes while a supporter of democratic capitalism is likely to emphasize cases when the small group of leaders have brought about undesirable outcomes. That's why societies generally come to share a certain ideology, and its implications for what is an acceptable form of government and action by government. We must, however, be extraordinarily careful about letting our emotions affect our considerations of those issues so that we do not become **ideologues**—individuals who are so fixated on certain ideologies that they cannot reasonably consider opposition arguments; they tend to insist on everyone looking at the world as they do.

As I stated previously, the dominant global ideology today is democratic capitalism. It is an ideology that most people in the U.S., including myself, support. While there is much to be said for the democratic capitalist ideology, care must be taken to see that we supporters do not become ideologues, and that our support is based on reasoned argument and that we are open to the weaknesses of democratic capitalism, and the positive aspects of other ideologies. Doing so is especially important in deciding on foreign policy. For example, often when I hear of what occurs in other countries, my immediate reaction is one of abhorrence, and I wish our country would "do something." There have been numerous examples: the restriction of Soviet Jews' right to emigrate from the former Soviet Union; the practice of Idi Amin, former ruler of Uganda, of arbitrarily killing opponents (probably by the thousands); South Africa's apartheid policy; Latin American right-wing death squads; the systematic killing of millions in Cambodia under the Khmer Rouge; and the mass genocide and ethnic cleansing in Bosnia and Rwanda, and more recently the terrible atrocities in the Darfur region of Sudan.

These actions go against my ideological beliefs about what is acceptable action by a state. The question each of us must answer is: Do these actions rise to the level of contradicting our values such that we would support the United States using its power to stop and prevent such activities occurring in another supposedly sovereign country? And if so, what powers should we use?

Unfortunately, there is no easy answer to these questions. Not all cultures have the same regard for human rights as we do, and I also believe that we generally do not have the right to impose our personal values on others. In all cases, it is proper to use diplomatic channels and public channels to do what can be done to support human rights, but in doing so a country must apply the same criteria to friendly countries as to unfriendly countries, recognizing that countries have different social values. For instance, if a country has a mandatory military draft, that draft may violate the concept some have of human rights, but it would be wrong to assume that such opposition is a universally agreed-on human right.

More difficult choices than one about a military draft confront us when issues such as forced labor camps for large minorities within a population, involuntary abortion, infanticide, and apartheid surface. There comes a point when the offenses against human rights become too great to sit back and accept. Again, this is based on my particular value judgments, which are not universally shared. Examples include the annihilation of the Jews in Germany in the 1930s and 1940s (to which the United States initially responded by restricting immigration visas for Jews) and Pol Pot's massacre of millions of his fellow citizens in Cambodia in the 1970s (which the United States ignored, at least officially). The U.S. changing position in regard to Iraq shows the difficult choices. When Iraq used chemical weapons against Iran and the Kurds in the 1980s, Iraq was a U.S. ally and the United States said nothing; in fact, it shipped Iraq more weapons. However, in 2003 it used Iraq's previous use of chemical weapons as one of the reasons it should liberate Iraq from Saddam Hussein.

The United States in the World Community

The separation-of-powers doctrine, modified by a system of checks and balances, was embodied in the U.S. Constitution of 1787 to prevent tyranny, and it applies to the field of foreign affairs as well as to domestic politics. Although the judiciary has no hand in policy-making and is confined in its work to the interpretation and application of treaties and statutes, the other two branches of the government—the president and Congress (especially the Senate)—are both equipped with far-reaching authority to determine foreign policy.

The President and Foreign Policy

The president derives great power in foreign affairs from the right to appoint diplomats (with the consent of the Senate) and to receive the diplomats of other countries, and has ultimate responsibility for the diplomatic messages our government transmits abroad and for the operations of the Department of State generally. Presidential control of diplomacy gives the president a strong initiative in foreign affairs, for diplomatic correspondence can be a vehicle of policy, as in 1899 when Secretary of State John Hay originated the Open Door policy in China by messages to selected governments. The president's prerogative in diplomacy confers, too, the right to deny or to extend recognition to a new government or state, for it is usually by establishing diplomatic relationships that recognition is accorded. President Carter demonstrated that policy when he established formal relations with the People's Republic of China as the appropriate representative of the Chinese people and cut relations with Taiwan.

The president has the initiative in treaty making, too, but here these actions require the approval of two-thirds of the senators present when a vote is taken. This arrangement, indeed, is a good example of the system of checks and balances that pervades all of government in the United States. Much criticism has been aimed at the Senate for its obstructive tactics in its consideration of treaties—notably the Treaty of Versailles (1919)—and several proposals have been submitted to amend the Constitution to substitute a majority of both houses of Congress in place of two-thirds of the Senate in treaty making, but such proposals have never had much support. Some of the problems that can develop from this dual responsibility can be seen in the Law of the Sea Treaty negotiated between 1974 and 1980 under UN auspices. This treaty was signed by President Carter but was never approved by the Senate. When President Reagan was elected, he specifically disavowed the treaty, leaving the United States in an ambiguous position.

Former President George W. Bush took a strong position against U.S. involvement in international treaties, opposing multilateral cooperation, in which countries attempt to negotiate their differences through international treaties and organizations, and favoring unilateralism, in which each country goes it alone. Soon after being elected, he withdrew from or rejected numerous international treaties and organizations, including the Biological Weapons Convention, the Kyoto Protocol, the Anti-Ballistic Missile Treaty, and the International Criminal Court. These actions convinced many that under president George W. Bush, the United States saw itself as above the international community and was willing to rely on its military power to achieve its ends.

The president's authority in foreign affairs is augmented by some more general powers. As commander in chief of the armed forces, the president can dispatch the Army, Navy, Marines, or Air Force to any part of the world to carry out a policy and can conclude executive agreements by which bases abroad are placed at the disposal of the services. This gives the president enormous power, in effect, to enter into war without Senate approval. For example, during President Kennedy's administration, the U.S. government supported the Bay of Pigs invasion of Cuba with no Senate approval. Similarly, in 1964 President Johnson

A scene from the Vietnam War, which challenged U.S. beliefs about the United States's role in the world.

began the direct U.S. military role in Vietnam by ordering attacks on North Vietnamese military targets following attacks on U.S. warships in the Gulf of Tonkin.

In response to the latter incident, Congress passed a series of laws that placed stricter limits on presidential actions. Because the Constitution explicitly gives Congress the powers to declare war and control military and naval expenditures, it was argued that the president's discretionary powers as commander in chief had become too broad. These laws removed the president's power to "wage war, sell arms, conduct covert operations, or enter into executive agreements with foreign governments." According to these laws, a president can deploy troops to protect our interest only for a limited time without the consent of Congress.

In 1986, the president's National Security Council sold arms to Iran without informing Congress and used the proceeds to fund the Nicaraguan contras, thereby violating these laws and creating a scandal for the Reagan administration. In the 1980s, when President Reagan considered increasing the U.S. military presence in trouble spots in Latin America, the Senate played an active role. The reduced power of the presidency has led some to suggest that the president no longer wields any power at all.[1]

Such suggestions were exaggerations, as was made clear by the first President George Bush's actions in the 1991 Persian Gulf War, President Clinton's actions in the bombing of Yugoslavia, and President George W. Bush's decision to go to war against Iraq. In each case, some members of Congress argued that the president had to get congressional approval before actually starting a war, but the presidents denied that they were required to do so. The issues became academic when in each case Congress, faced with initial widespread public approval of the president's actions, authorized the president to use force. Thus, this question of war powers remains unanswered.

With such ambiguous divided powers between the presidency and Congress, cooperation between the two branches of the government is essential to avoid paralyzing deadlocks. On occasion, cooperation has not been forthcoming and the nation has found itself seriously embarrassed. The president has signed treaties that the Senate would not approve,

---

[1]Such complaints are not totally new. Harry Truman, who normally said what he thought, described the problem as follows: "People think I sit here and push buttons and get things accomplished. Well, I spent today kissing behinds."

and the president has dispatched troops overseas and then taken a broadside of criticism from Congress. Such conflicts are likely to continue, however, owing to the fundamental structure of the U.S. democratic system.

U.S. Foreign Policies

Throughout much of the nineteenth century, the United States was deeply committed to a policy of isolation. **Isolationism,** a policy according to which the United States made no alliances abroad and kept as free as possible from the political embroilments of Europe, reigned supreme. Even after the Spanish-American War (1898), the nation remained aloof, though the acquisition of scattered dependencies such as Hawaii as a result of the war had widened U.S. interests a great deal. Isolationism broke down when the United States in 1917 became a belligerent in World War I, but it was revived in 1919–1920, when the Senate rejected membership in the new League of Nations. Although under attack in the 1920s and 1930s, isolationism continued to have strong support, as shown by U.S. neutrality legislation (1935 and later) and by the efforts from 1939 to 1941 to keep the United States from becoming involved in World War II.

But the Japanese attack on Pearl Harbor in 1941 changed all this and moved us from a period of isolationism to internationalism. **Internationalism** refers to the belief that world peace can be realized by the friendly association of all nations. As a result, the United States quickly became enmeshed in world politics and has continued to be deeply involved ever since.

Since World War II, the United States has made or affirmed a number of alliances and maintained troops or military outposts in various parts of the world, especially in Europe and the Far East. The United States has committed large military forces to the fighting of four local undeclared wars: Korea, Vietnam, Iraq, and Afghanistan.

Much of our foreign policy in the postwar era has been dedicated to the protection of capitalism and "liberal" democracy. For example, our foreign policy immediately following World War II revolved around the Truman Doctrine of 1947. Essentially, the **Truman Doctrine** stated that if any country threatened by communist aggression was willing to resist that threat and asked for help, the United States would come to its aid. This was often referred to as a policy of containing communism and was part of what was called the **cold war,** the tension between communist countries, such as the former Soviet Union, and the United States and its allies following World War II until the 1990s. During the cold war, the United States believed that if it did not take the lead in resisting the aggressive moves of the Soviet Union and the other communist nations, there would probably be no effective opposition, and a domino effect would occur, with one country after another falling to the communists.

The basis of the peace in the cold war was a **nuclear standoff**—a position of stalemate brought about by the recognition that if attacked, the other party possesses sufficient ability to launch a devastating nuclear counterattack. In a nuclear standoff, because each country has the ability to destroy the other many times over, the concept of military superiority becomes difficult to define. This was especially apparent in the 1980s when the United States and the former USSR negotiated a reduction of the arms buildup. Both sides claimed that the other had military superiority; which side actually did was unclear.

The containment approach to U.S. foreign policy lost favor following our involvement in Vietnam in the 1960s and early 1970s, and a period of **détente**—an easing or relaxation of strained relations and political tensions between countries—replaced the cold war. Under détente, the U.S. involvement in world political affairs decreased, and the United States reduced its expenditures on defense as a percentage of total output. That changed in September 2001, when terrorists attacked the United States and the United States declared a war on terrorism.

That war on terrorism pitted the United States not against a particular country, but against an ambiguous enemy who could be anywhere. A new Homeland Security

An Outline of U.S. Foreign Policy*

1789–1897: Isolationism/unilateralism, with the following examples showing how we followed this policy:

1796—Washington's Farewell Address: "Beware of entangling alliances" (balance-of-power entanglements in today's words).
1834—Monroe Doctrine. U.S. promises not to interfere in European affairs and demands that Europe not interfere in Latin America.

1898–1918: Interventionism.

1898—Spanish-American War: events leading to it and results/fruits of this interventionism.
1917—U.S. intervention into World War I.

1919–1941: Return to isolationism/unilateralism as the nation sees the result of interventionism.

1919—U.S. Senate rejects joining the League of Nations.
1930s—Neutrality Acts of 1935, 1937, and 1939 as we see Europe heading toward war.
1941–1945: No special change in policy necessary; United States simply responds to attack. Any nation follows a similar policy of defending itself.

1945–1999: Internationalism. Actually starts with the Truman Doctrine (1947), even though we join UN in 1945.

1949—NATO.
1950—Korean conflict (even though UN sponsored).
1961–1973—Involvement in Vietnam (really following tenets of the Truman Doctrine).
1972—Nixon Doctrine (so called, although it should rightfully be called a corollary to the Truman Doctrine).
1990—Foreign policy directed at working with rather than against Russia.
1991—Persian Gulf War; beginning of new world order, or at least Western control.
1993—U.S. tries to enforce its will with UN backing in a variety of states such as Haiti, Somalia, Bosnia, North Korea. The results are questionable.

2000–2008: Unilateralism and preemption

2001—9/11 attacks on United States and beginning of war on terrorism.
2003—Bush Doctrine of Preemption: President Bush declares the United States has the right to wage preemptive war against countries that allow terrorists on their soil.

2009—Barack Obama becomes president, and moves toward a more multilateral foreign policy and moves away from preemption.

*We are grateful to Prof. W. K. Callam for supplying an initial draft of this outline.

Department was established in the United States, and military expenditures increased substantially. But exactly how this war on terrorism was to be fought remained open. Does the United States have the right to fight terrorism anywhere? Are preemptive wars truly justified? What limitations on individual rights are acceptable trade-offs for increased security? Does the United States have the right to eliminate governments it feels are harboring terrorists and developing weapons of mass destruction? What proof does it need to carry on such preemptive wars? And, finally, will fighting such a war do more harm than good, creating hatred for the United States that will lead to more terrorism?

In 2009, Barack Obama became president and signaled to the world that his administration would be less belligerent to other countries and work with them to arrive at a multinational solution to problems. However, at the same time, he promised that the United States would be vigilant against terrorism and would carry on and even expand the war against the Taliban in Afghanistan; further, he vowed to continue to attack the Taliban in Pakistan even though Pakistan was a sovereign country that publicly opposed such action by the United States. Thus, while the rhetoric was considerably different under Obama than it was under Bush, it was unclear to what degree the policies will differ when it comes down to the difficult issues that all presidents must address.

Key Points

- The state is the institution empowered to conduct international relations for its citizens.
- Power is the capacity to compel another party to commit an action contrary to its explicitly stated will. Ultimately, power determines whether a foreign policy will be successful.
- Governments use foreign policy to achieve their international objectives, but they must take geography and other nations' strengths into consideration when they make policy.
- In the past century, the three most prevalent ideologies have been the communist ideology, the democratic capitalist ideology, and the fascist ideology.
- The president is responsible for foreign policy and is commander in chief of the armed forces, but only Congress can declare war.
- In the early 2000s, the United States adopted a policy of unilateralism and preemption.

Some Important Terms

balance of power (369)
cold war (376)
détente (376)
fascist ideology (372)
foreign policies (370)
geopolitics (371)
hegemon (365)
ideologues (373)

internationalism (376)
isolationism (376)
nation (360)
nation-state (361)
new world order (369)
North Atlantic Treaty Organization (NATO) (369)
nuclear standoff (376)

power (364)
realist theory (369)
state (360)
theory of complex interdependence (369)
Truman Doctrine (376)
unilateral (368)
weapons of mass destruction (365)

Questions for Review and Discussion

1. In what sense do the nation-states of the world form a community?
2. List the more important differences between nations and states.
3. As the term is used in this chapter, which of the following are states: Alaska, Luxembourg, Scotland, Bavaria, Australia, Michigan, Hong Kong? On what basis did you make your selection?
4. Historically, how did nation-states develop?
5. Would the European Union have been a state if the Treaty of Nice had been ratified? Why or why not?
6. The effectiveness of a nation's military power in supporting its foreign policies depends on what factors in addition to the size, training, and equipment of its armed forces?
7. Why are democratic governments more restricted in their actions by public opinion than are totalitarian governments?
8. What is a hegemon?
9. What factors make up a nation's economic power?
10. What are three possible approaches to the problem of achieving some degree of national security? Explain each.
11. Explain how the theory of complex interdependence is becoming a substitute for the balance of power in maintaining the peace in today's world.
12. How may foreign policies be influenced by (a) geography and (b) an ideology?
13. What powers does the president of the United States have in foreign affairs? What powers are held by Congress? Point out the advantages and disadvantages of this division of responsibility.
14. Do you believe that the president of the United States should have more power or less power to determine and carry out foreign policies? Defend your answer.
15. Was the 1991 Iraq war justified? Was the 2003 Iraq invasion justified? Why or why not?
16. What is the U.S. policy of preemption, and is it justified?
17. Explain the shift of U.S. foreign policy away from an attitude of aloofness to one of active participation in world affairs.

Internet Questions

1. Pick a country to which you have never traveled. Using http://projectvisa.com/, find what type of travel visa you can get to enter the country and how to do so.
2. Go to http://www.archives.gov/exhibits/charters/charters.html. What does Article II, Section 2, clauses 1 and 2 of the United States Constitution state?
3. Watch the YouTube video at http://www.cnn.com/video/#/video/world/2009/03/26/starr.china.military. cnn?iref=videosearch. What references to geopolitics can be found in the video? Do you think this video demonstrates a return to a balance of power? Defend your answer.
4. Using the website of the American Foreign Policy Council, www.afpc.org, describe one of their latest news stories.
5. Using the NATO site, www.nato.int, what is the Euro-Atlantic Partnership Council, and how many members are there?

For Further Study

Andrews, Peter, *Border Games: Policing the U.S.–Mexico Divide,* Ithaca, NY: Cornell University Press, 2000.

Ash, Timothy Green, *Free World: America, Europe and the Surprising Future of the West*, New York: Random House, 2004.

Epstein, Joseph, *Friendship*, New York: Houghton Mifflin, 2006.

Khalidi, Rashid, *The Cold War and American Dominance in the Middle East*, Boston, MA: Beacon Press, 2008.

Kissinger, Henry, *Years of Renewal,* New York: Simon & Schuster, 1999.

Nicholson, Philip Yale, *Who Do We Think We Are? Race and Nation in the Modern World,* Armonk, NY: Sharpe, 2000.

Reynolds, David, *One World Divisible: A Global History since 1945,* New York: Norton, 2000.

Sloan, Stanley R., *NATO and Transatlantic Relations in the 21st Century: Crisis, Continuity or Change?* New York: Foreign Policy Association, 2002.

Smith, Rupert, *The Utility of Force: The Art of War in the Modern World*, New York: Penguin/Allen Lane, 2005.

Zunes, Stephen, *Tinderbox: U.S. Foreign Policy and the Roots of Terrorism,* Monroe, ME: Common Courage Press, 2003.

WWW   Council on Foreign Relations   www.cfr.org

WWW   The Electronic Embassy   www.embassy.org

WWW   Foreign Policy Association   www.fpa.org

WWW   Global Geopolitics http://globalgeopolitics.net

WWW   International Information Programs   www.state.gov/r/iip/

WWW   League of Nations Archives   www.unog.ch/library/archives/archives.htm

WWW   NATO   www.nato.int

$\mathcal{I}$nternational Economic Relations

After reading this chapter, you should be able to:

- Differentiate between the balance of payments and the balance of trade
- Compare the advantages and disadvantages of international trade
- State the arguments in favor of and against protective tariffs
- Distinguish between a fixed and a flexible exchange rate
- State whether the United States is a debtor or a creditor nation and explain what that means
- Discuss the advantages and disadvantages of limiting imports to protect U.S. jobs from the threat of globalization

One of the purest fallacies is that trade follows the flag. Trade follows the lowest price current. If a dealer in any colony wished to buy Union Jacks, he would order them from Britain's worst foe if he could save a sixpence.

—Andrew Carnegie

Can we be frank? Once we cut through many of the high-sounding moral positions nations (and individuals) take, often there is a crass materialistic or economic motive underlying those positions. Therefore, to understand international relations, we must understand international economics, which includes the study of international trade, determination of foreign exchange rates, and foreign investment.

In Chapter 3, we discussed the rise and importance of international trade in the development of society and the evolution of cultures. As nations developed, trade transferred culture and made merchants rich, which helped break up the feudal system and led to the modern nation-state. The modern role of international trade is no less important, but without the perspective of history we are less likely to see it.

In the 1930s, the United States followed an isolationist policy toward trade. Since that time, the importance of international trade for the United States has grown significantly, particularly over the last few decades, and now accounts for well over 10 percent of our total GDP. But even this percentage underestimates its importance. It fails to take into account the fact that once export industries become established, people employed in them furnish a part of the market for industries producing products for domestic consumption. Hence, if exports decline, production and employment, in accordance with the multiplier principle, also fall off in other industries.

That figure also does not take into account the importance of imports to us. A number of our imports are necessary or desirable commodities that we cannot produce ourselves, or cannot produce as much of as we would like, such as coffee, bananas, natural rubber, nickel, tin, and oil. The crisis and shortages in the U.S. economy as a result of the Arab oil embargo in the 1970s demonstrate the importance of international trade. Similarly, the fear that an unfriendly government would control a large portion of the world oil supply was a significant factor in the quick reaction of the United States to the invasion of Kuwait by Iraq in 1990, and its continued strong role in the Middle East. International trade is fundamentally important to the U.S. economy.

The Terminology of Trade

The expanding importance of international trade has led to the introduction of new terms and the increasing importance of others. For example, many corporations have become **global corporations** (also called multinational corporations), which have production and distribution facilities in a variety of countries. Another term that has become important is **cartel,** an organization of countries that produce a specific good and that agree to limit production of that good in order to increase the price the countries in the organization get. Probably the most well known of these cartels is the Organization of the Petroleum Exporting Countries (OPEC), which played a significant role in international trade in the 1970s and 1980s and again in the early 2000s.

The Balance of Trade and the Balance of Payments

In discussing international trade, two terms are used frequently: the *balance of trade* and the *balance of payments.* **Balance of trade** refers to the relation of our total exports to our total imports. It tells us the dollar difference between exports and imports. Figure 19.1 shows that the U.S. balance of trade significantly worsened in the mid-1980s as the country ran

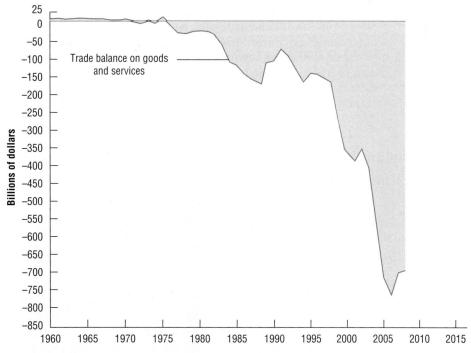

Figure 19.1

U.S. trade balance (including services), 1950–2008. (Source: Bureau of Economic Analysis.)

large deficits. The deficits improved somewhat in the early 1990s, but worsened again in the late 1990s and early 2000s.

Balance of payments refers to the relation of total payments made abroad to total payments received from abroad. It includes not only traded goods and services but also currency flows, such as loans and investments, among countries. Even though the balance of trade has been in deficit recently, the balance of payments has not, because the trade imbalance is being offset by large foreign capital inflows into the United States.

The difference between the balance of payments and the balance of trade can be seen by considering the U.S. position in 2008 when it was running a significant balance-of-trade deficit of over $700 billion. However, at that same time, foreigners were investing heavily in the United States, largely in the form of bonds. Therefore, because the balance of payments includes flows of investment, even though the balance of trade was in deficit, the balance of payments was not.

That does not mean we don't have to worry about the international trade deficit. When foreign money is invested in the United States, foreigners acquire U.S. assets and will take profits from them and will control them in the future. They also can decide to no longer hold their assets in the United States, in which case the value of the dollar can fall substantially, as it has over the last few years.

Visible and Invisible Trade

Many people, when they think of imports and exports, have in mind only the **visible items of trade**—material goods such as wheat, pianos, or machinery. But to think of foreign trade as consisting of these alone is misleading, because the so-called invisible items may be just as important.

Invisible items of trade consist of services of all sorts for which the people of one country pay those of another. For example, in normal years, we pay British citizens and other foreigners large amounts in freight charges for carrying U.S. goods on their ships and planes. U.S. tourists also pay British citizens, French citizens, Italians, and others large sums to buy hotel accommodations and transportation in their countries. Such items represent purchases abroad just as truly as do imports of coffee or shoes. Another important invisible item of trade is the interest Americans receive from foreign investments. This is payment for permitting foreigners to use our capital, something that is just as truly a service as their permitting us to use their hotel rooms.

The Changing Nature of International Trade

In the 1960s, 1970s, and 1980s, international trade expanded in the developing countries, mainly in the area of manufacturing. One after another U.S. manufacturing plants moved abroad to take advantage of cheaper labor, and today the majority of goods you consume are manufactured abroad. The 1990s marked a new dimension in the expansion of international trade. Companies began dividing up their production processes into components and looking for ways to shift the various subcomponents of production abroad. Each aspect of production was separated—such as bookkeeping service, maintenance service, and advertising—and ways to achieve lower costs by outsourcing—contracting out for others to provide that activity for the firm rather than having someone in the firm do it—were explored.

Beginning in the 1990s, services began moving abroad. For example, accounting for some firms is done in India, where labor costs one-tenth what it does in the United States. Likewise with telephone service: When you actually reach a service representative, it might well be a person in India, Pakistan, or Bangladesh who has been trained to speak "American" and who receives a wage that is a fraction of what a U.S. citizen would get. Such movement overseas of subcomponents of production is likely to continue and even increase in the coming years.

As far as the visible items of trade are concerned, before World War II we normally exported much more than we imported. But in respect to the invisible items, the reverse was true. Therefore, for the most part imports equaled exports, so that our money payments to other countries were offset by their payments to us. However, this balance was upset by World War II. From then until the 1960s, the United States ran a substantial balance-of-trade surplus that was offset by foreign aid and loans that the United States made to other countries. Since the end of the 1960s, the flow has been reversed, and the United States has been running large balance-of-trade deficits that we have paid for by our previously accumulated reserves. In the 1980s, the deficit became so large that the United States became a net debtor nation (a country that owes more than it is owed). The deficits continued in the early 2000s, and the United States now owes trillions of dollars more than it is owed.

Advantages and Disadvantages of International Trade

Trade is the lifeblood of a modern economy, and the benefits of international trade are so great that it is inconceivable that a modern nation should adopt a policy of complete economic isolation. The full utilization of machinery, with its attendant specialization, requires mass production, and mass production calls for extensive trade in very wide markets. To limit the market of an industry to one country would often mean reduced efficiency and higher costs. Also, modern society requires a great variety of goods, both for consumption and as raw materials for its industries, including tea, coffee, cotton, rubber, petroleum, iron, manganese, aluminum, nickel, coal—a complete list would be long indeed. No country has or can produce all of these products. The missing ones can be obtained only through trade. When trade flows freely between countries, the world tends to become more prosperous. When trade languishes, production lags, unemployment increases, and the world's income shrinks.

Three Advantages of Trade

There are three primary advantages of international trade. The first is that it enables a country to obtain products that cannot be produced at home at all or that cannot be produced in adequate quantities and at acceptable costs. Sometimes the inability of a country to produce certain things is a matter of climate, such as the difficulty in growing tea and coffee in the United States. In other cases, it is a lack of certain natural resources. Italy, for example, has no good coal deposits, and Britain does not have enough good farmland to meet its demands for food.

The second advantage of international trade is that it often enables a country to get a better product than can be produced at home. This may be due to differences in climate and soil or to differences in natural resources. Sometimes, however, it is owing to the fact that the people of some foreign countries have, over a long period of time, acquired certain techniques that are not easily transferred. English factories for years produced finer woolens than most U.S. factories because they had specialized in fine woolens for generations.

A third advantage of international trade is that it often makes products available at a lower price than would be possible if they were produced at home. This raises standards of living by increasing consumer purchasing power. Consider a country that, like Great Britain, produces only about half of its needed food supply. Conceivably, Britain might be able to raise enough food within its own borders to feed its people. However, any attempt to do this would mean inadequate amounts of many foods and the absence of commodities such as oranges, tea, and coffee. It would also mean high prices for the foods that could be produced. Britain has a large population relative to the amount of land available for cultivation. To raise all of its food, it would have to cultivate its good land more intensively, in spite

U.S. exports being loaded onto a Panamanian-registered South Korean ship.

of the tendency toward diminishing returns; it would also have to resort to inferior land not really suitable for agriculture. Both methods are expensive and result in high prices. In the long run, Britain can provide its people with better standards of living by selling industrial goods and buying a substantial portion of its food supply abroad.

Disadvantages of Trade

If international trade had only advantages, there would be free trade among nations and little debate over what to do about international trade. There is significant debate, however, so obviously there must be some disadvantages to international trade. To see these disadvantages, let's consider some examples. Say, for instance, that China began building automobiles that would sell in the United States for $4,000. This would benefit the Chinese who make the automobiles and U.S. consumers of automobiles, but it would hurt one group of producers—U.S. automobile companies—and one group of workers—U.S. automobile workers—a lot. Other examples abound. Importing potatoes helps U.S. consumers but hurts Maine and Idaho potato producers; importing textiles from Bangladesh helps U.S. consumers but hurts textile firms here in the United States.

When we look at both groups together, we see that the benefits of international trade almost always outweigh the costs, but the benefits are spread over a large group of people, whereas the costs are imposed on a few. Those few who are hurt express their opposition to international competition loudly, and so in the United States, as in most countries, there is often a tendency to encourage exports and discourage imports. The complainers argue something like the following: Just as it seems plain that exports give profits and wages to U.S. producers, so it seems equally plain that imports rob U.S. producers of the profits and wages they might have received had these goods been purchased at home.

Why Economists Generally Support Free Trade

The notion that U.S. producers as a group are injured by foreign purchases is a fallacy. In the long run, the United States can sell goods to other countries only if it also buys goods from them. Though we may gain home markets for the products of some U.S. workers, we do this only at the expense of losing foreign markets for the products of other U.S. workers. For the country as a whole, these two things cancel each other out, and the long-run net result is that U.S. consumers pay higher prices or receive inferior goods.

Why You Can't Get the Advantages without the Disadvantages

Why is it that we can sell goods to other countries only if we also buy goods from them? Briefly, the reason is that, in the long run, foreign countries can pay for what they buy only with the goods they sell. Let us explain as simply as possible how imports pay for exports, and vice versa. For simplicity, we first assume that trade takes place only between Britain and the United States.

Suppose that at a certain time a British importer wishes to buy $1 million worth of U.S. machinery. The U.S. firms that have this machinery for sale are unlikely to want British money, or pounds sterling. Rather, they want dollars. Therefore, in order to buy the machinery, the British importer must find some way to change British money into dollars—that is, to find someone who has dollars and who is willing to sell them in exchange for pounds.

Who will have dollars and be willing to exchange them for pounds? For the most part, they can be found in two groups: (1) Americans who want pounds in order to buy goods or services from Britain, and (2) British exporters who have accepted checks or drafts in dollars for British goods that they have sold to Americans. In either case, the source of the dollars available to the British to buy American goods is the payments Americans have made, or plan to make, for British goods.

If for any reason U.S. imports of British goods should decline, the British would be forced to curtail their purchases of U.S. goods because they could no longer obtain sufficient dollars to buy in the previous volume.

The preceding explanation disregards certain complicating factors. Actually, British importers do not go directly to British exporters to obtain U.S. money. The banks act as middlemen. If British exporters accept in payment dollar-value checks drawn on U.S. banks, they do so because they can take them to their own banks and there exchange them for pounds sterling and deposit them to their own accounts. Their banks can then deposit these checks in New York banks and sell dollar drafts to British importers who need them in order to pay for U.S. goods.

Another factor that our explanation disregards is that trade does not take place just between Britain and the United States. Other countries come into the picture. For example, British exporters might receive dollars for textiles sold in the United States, and British importers might in turn use these dollars to buy beef in Argentina. The dollars would then be available to Argentine importers to buy machinery in the United States. In this case, the dollars we spent for British textiles made it possible for Argentines to buy our machinery.

A final qualification is the time dimension. In the long run, any country's imports must equal its exports. In the short run, however, this statement must be qualified. Over considerable periods of time, one country may be able to buy substantially more from another country than it sells, or vice versa. This can happen for two reasons: (1) countries may have stocks of gold, other reserve currencies, or financial assets that they are willing to send us in payment for their purchases, and (2) countries may be willing to sell goods on credit. This is the position that the U.S. has been in for the last two decades. People outside the U.S. have been willing to hold dollars and dollar-denominated assets, which has allowed U.S. imports to greatly exceed U.S. exports. However, this cannot continue indefinitely, and we can expect the situation to change in the coming years, probably with a major international currency crisis.

Restrictions on International Trade

We have seen that there are significant advantages to international trade, and in most cases nations would derive the greatest economic advantage from international trade if they allowed free trade. This, however, is not the usual practice; instead, numerous controls are applied. These controls include subsidies on exports, tariffs, quotas, exchange controls, and bilateral barter agreements. In the past, tariffs have been the principal device for regulating trade, but in recent years other methods of control, especially quotas, have assumed greatly increased importance.

The reason for these controls has to do with how economics relates to politics. The benefits of trade are spread widely among consumers, who simply take these benefits for granted. The costs fall on a relatively small group and often affect them rather severely, causing firms that can't compete to go out of business and workers to lose their jobs. Even though the total costs are less than the total benefits, politicians will listen to, and make laws to protect, the few who are hurt. Therefore there is continual pressure for trade restrictions. We now consider some of these.

Tariffs on Imports

A **tariff** is a tax, or duty, usually on an imported commodity. When tariff duties are levied as a fixed charge per barrel or yard, they are said to be *specific.* When they are levied as a percentage of the value of a commodity, they are said to be *ad valorem* (value-added). A tariff generally has one of two purposes: either to raise revenue or to protect the market of a domestic industry by keeping out the products of foreign competitors. To a degree, these two purposes are incompatible because a tariff that would keep the foreign product out entirely would raise no revenue at all. In practice, however, protective tariffs are seldom high enough to exclude imports completely and hence do raise some revenue. But if the chief purpose of a tariff is to raise revenue, it should not be high enough to discourage most imports. Further, instead of being levied on a commodity produced both at home and abroad, it should, if possible, be levied on one that cannot be produced at home. This eliminates the possibility that imports and revenues may fall off because buyers turn to home producers.

Although tariffs for revenue interfere with trade to some extent, that is not their purpose, and such interference is usually kept at a minimum. Their use is in no sense incompatible with a policy of free trade. Whether they represent a desirable kind of tax is another question, and we might point out that, unless they are levied chiefly on luxuries, they have the same drawback as a sales tax—namely, their burden falls more heavily on people of low income than on the well-to-do. On the other hand, the only justification for a protective tariff is a belief that it is in the public interest to keep people from buying goods abroad and to force them to buy at home.

Most economists oppose the levying of protective tariffs and the setting up of other trade barriers designed to limit competition and maintain or raise prices. Studies of congressional hearings and debates indicate that protective tariffs are nearly always enacted as a result of political pressure from business and labor groups interested in the production of a certain product, and who expect to benefit from a reduction of foreign competition.

The Case against Protective Tariffs.   The basic argument against protective tariffs is that, by restricting international trade, they rob us of part of its benefits. Further, we emphasize again that free admission of imports is one of the most effective ways of expanding the foreign markets of home industries because it is payments for our imports that furnish foreigners with most of the funds with which to buy our exports.

When one country institutes tariffs, it is likely that other countries will follow. The result will be a contracting spiral of trade, making all countries worse off. That is precisely what happened in the Great Depression from 1929 to 1933 (see Figure 19.2). As one country after another instituted tariffs to protect jobs at home—the United States instituted the infamous Smoot-Hawley tariff—trade declined, and the entire world fell into a serious economic depression.

The Arguments in Favor of Protective Tariffs.   The advocates of protective tariffs support their point of view with a number of plausible arguments: the home-market argument, the high-wages argument, the infant-industry argument, and the self-sufficiency argument.

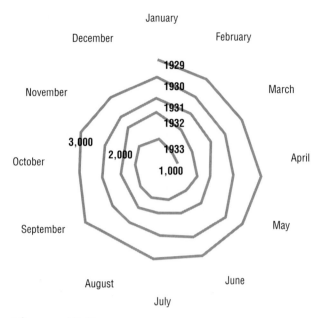

January
February
December
1929
1930
March
November
1931
1932
3,000
1933
October
2,000
April
1,000
September
May
August
June
July

Figure 19.2

The contracting spiral of world trade, 1929 to 1933. Total imports of seventy-five countries (monthly values in terms of old U.S. gold dollars in millions). (Source: Original diagram by League of Nations.)

Home-Market Argument. One of the most effective of the claims made by the protectionists is the home-market argument. According to this reasoning, a tariff that keeps out foreign goods increases the market for U.S. goods and thereby increases home profits and employment. Undoubtedly, there is some truth in this contention if we consider only short periods of time, but, as we have already pointed out, the final result is that a home market is created for some goods at the expense of losing a foreign market for others. This loss of the foreign market comes all the faster because, when we raise our tariffs on their goods, other countries retaliate by raising their tariffs on our goods. Meanwhile, as we have seen, U.S. consumers pay higher prices or receive inferior products.

High-Wages Argument. A second claim that protectionists make is expressed by the high-wages argument. They assert that the tariff maintains the U.S. wage level and the U.S. standard of living by protecting our workers from having to compete with cheap foreign labor. This argument is also plausible, but a little analysis and observation robs it of most of its force. In the first place, if a tariff makes possible higher wages, it does so only by enabling producers to sell their products at a higher price. This may benefit one group of employers and workers, but it reduces the purchasing power and standard of living of all others who must buy the product. If this kind of price raising were applied to a great many products, the general reduction in standards of living might be serious.

Infant-Industry Argument. A third defense of the protective tariff is the infant-industry argument. Those who advance it often disclaim any wish to give permanent tariff protection to an industry not able to survive without it. But, they say, a small new industry in the United States cannot hope to produce at as low a cost as an old, established industry abroad. Let us give it protection until it can get established and grow. Eventually, it may become more efficient than its foreign competitors. If so, it can provide consumers with goods at reduced prices, and it will no longer need tariff protection.

The infant-industry argument has been advanced in the United States at one time or another in support of tariffs to protect various industries. In theory it is sound, but it is difficult to find any clear case in which it has been successfully applied—that is, where an industry has been established as a result of tariff protection and then has continued successfully without such protection.

Self-Sufficiency Argument. A final argument for protective tariffs is that they make a country more self-sufficient and thus less dependent on foreign countries for essential commodities in time of war. This argument is sound in theory, but the situations to which it can usefully be applied in practice are probably rather limited. Though our experience in World War II emphasized the importance of having dependable supplies of vital raw materials, to keep such products out of the country by tariffs would not always result in building up home production. Moreover, many products once deemed essential are less so today because of greatly improved substitutes. Familiar examples are wool, tin, and natural rubber.

When there is real danger of a shortage of strategic materials in time of war, the best solution is probably to build up stockpiles. The U.S. government has followed this policy with a number of minerals and with oil, but many students of the problem believe that much of this stockpiling has been unjustified and is a waste of the taxpayers' money.

Import Quotas

Another device for protecting home industries is the import quota. An **import quota** limits the quantity or the value of a commodity that can be brought into a country in a given period of time. For example, the government may decide to limit sugar imports to 2 million tons a year, and it may decide to assign definite parts of this quota to specified foreign countries. Usually, import quotas, like protective tariffs, are imposed to keep out foreign goods for the benefit of domestic producers, but sometimes they are imposed chiefly to limit payments to foreign countries in order to conserve limited supplies of foreign currency.

Many advocates of freer trade consider quotas more objectionable than tariffs. For one thing, though quotas restrict trade, they bring no revenue to the government of the importing country as a tariff would. But for those who wish to restrict imports, quotas have certain advantages over tariffs. Often, they do not require special legislation but instead may be imposed or changed by administrative decrees. Moreover, a quota can be fixed to admit a definite amount of a commodity, whereas if a protective tariff is levied, there is no way of knowing just how much of it will enter.

Removing Trade Restrictions

Most economists believe that if trade could flow freely and securely through the world, there would be a great expansion of its total volume and that in the long run all nations would be more prosperous. There would be less talk of have-not countries and less need for foreign aid because every country would have free access to the markets and raw materials of the world. The average price of consumer goods would be lower everywhere. Nothing would contribute more to the expansion of world trade than removal of the great mass of restrictions that have been placed on it by government action. But as we saw earlier, decreasing these restrictions will be a slow and tortuous process.

Some steps have already been taken. The Reciprocal Trade Agreements Act of 1934 empowered the president to make reciprocal trade agreements and to reduce tariff duties by as much as 50 percent in return for trade concessions by other countries. This act was extended in 1947 through the **General Agreement on Trade and Tariffs (GATT)**, an agreement in which most Western nations agreed to a mutual effort to reduce trade barriers. Countries met every so often under GATT in order to reduce trade restrictions. In the mid-1990s, GATT was replaced by the **World Trade Organization** (WTO), an international organization designed to foster trade among countries.

Every two years, a ministerial conference is held in which all the WTO member countries, close to 150, make decisions on all matters of trade agreements. This includes launching negotiations for new agreements, which begin when members see limits to their existing rules. Member countries negotiate, during a certain period of time, on many trade issues simultaneously; this period of negotiation is called a "trade round." The ninth round, the Doha Development Round, was started during the fourth WTO conference, held in Qatar in 2001. This round is specifically meant to help poor countries; for the first time, development issues are at the core of a round. Negotiations in this round have been contentious and the successful completion of it looked doubtful in 2009.

The slow going in decreasing world trade restrictions was accompanied by the creation of a number of free trade areas, the most prominent of which are the **European Union**

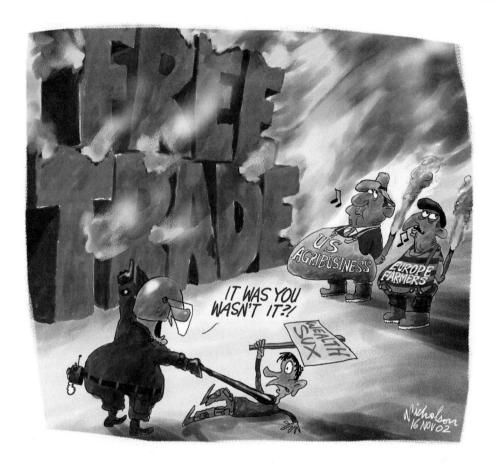

(EU)—the economic and political union of a number of European states (see box, p. 391)—and the North American Free Trade Agreement (NAFTA) involving the United States, Canada, and Mexico. These agreements eliminate trade barriers among member countries and establish common barriers against nonmember nations. Economists, who generally favor free trade, are of two minds about these associations. They favor associations because they reduce barriers among countries, but they fear that the associations make it harder to achieve a worldwide reduction in barriers.

Globalization and Trade Restrictions

The late 1990s and early 2000s were marked by significant demonstrations against **globalization**—the integration of various world economies in terms of production, distribution, and finances. In a fully globalized world, global firms can move across national borders with ease. We are a long way from this, but global firms have played a major role in expanding international trade, and in doing so they have significantly changed the international economic environment. When workers in one country demand wages that are too high, these firms are in a position simply to transfer production to another country where workers are willing to work for lower wages. For instance, IBM closed many of its production facilities in the United States and moved them to Asia where labor costs were significantly lower. Then, in 2004, it sold its entire personal computer business to a Chinese company, Lenovo. Many other companies have done the same, and manufacturing in the United States has languished over the past decades. In the early 2000s, it was not only manufacturing industries that were transferring jobs abroad, but it was also service industries. When you phone a company for technical assistance or to buy something, you are likely to speak to an operator in the Philippines or India.

Global corporations affect the trading environment in another way. Say, for instance, that the United States were to establish unilateral quotas for Japanese cars. By becoming a global company and establishing production or assembly plants in the United States, a Japanese company could avoid the quotas and sell as many cars in the United States as it wished. That is exactly what happened in the 1980s when a number of foreign-car producers established assembly plants in the United States. In the late 1990s and early 2000s, it was U.S.-based global firms that were establishing production facilities elsewhere. This upset some U.S. workers who felt they were losing their jobs and others who felt that the firms were being imperialistic and paying unacceptably low wages to their foreign workers. These beliefs led to demonstrations against globalization.

To prevent the job loss from globalization, critics of globalization argue that we should protect domestic jobs by establishing tariffs on imports, or limiting imports directly by quotas. Most economists oppose such policies, pointing out that job losses and other disadvantages of trade go along with the advantages of trade—the lower cost of goods. Were it not for trade and globalization, many of the goods we buy—the computers, shoes, shirts, telephones, and so on—would cost two, three, or four times as much, making us much poorer. On average, trade benefits both countries involved; otherwise they wouldn't enter into the trade.

The political difficulty for trade proponents is that the benefits of trade are often stealth benefits—benefits affecting large numbers of consumers a little bit—but the costs of trade are often localized in an industry or a region, and hence are more apparent. That said, economists' argument that trade is better on average for us does not mean that globalization does not present serious potential difficulties for the United States. The reality is that with our large trade deficit over the last decades, the United States has consumed not only the immediate benefits of trade but also many of the future benefits of trade. We have transferred to the world trillions of dollars of future trade benefits in the form of money, bonds, and other future promissory notes. Moreover, we continue to run trade deficits of hundreds of billions of dollars per year. At some point, other countries are going to stop accepting those promissory notes in return for goods and services and are going to ask for payment. At that point, a difficult adjustment for the U.S. economy will occur. Before we can discuss it, however, we must discuss foreign exchange markets.

Foreign Exchange

When the balance of payments is in imbalance, actual transfers of wealth from one country to another can usually be made only in the form of goods or an **international reserve currency**—a currency that all countries are willing to accept as final payment for obligations owed to it—such as the U.S. dollar. If for any reason a country cannot export enough goods to pay for its imports, it must settle the balance with a reserve currency or by borrowing abroad. When a country cannot meet its international obligations, it will be forced to depreciate its currency, which means it must lower the foreign exchange price of its currency. In the 1990s, the dollar was the only reserve currency, but in the early 2000s the euro was becoming an alternative reserve currency.

The Meaning of Foreign Exchange

Foreign exchange refers to the process of exchanging the money of one country for that of another and to the monies themselves. Thus, the Japanese yen is called foreign exchange in the United States. Goods are generally paid for in terms of money, but in international trade the buyer uses one kind of money and the seller another, so the price that one pays and the

The European Monetary Union and the Euro

Countries in the EU, including new members.

The land mass known as Europe contains numerous countries, and usually the little group of islands off the western coast of France known as Great Britain is also included when we use the term *Europe.* These countries have joined together economically, and to a limited degree politically, to form the European Union (EU).

The EU began as an economic union in 1958. At that time, several governments of Europe, to expand their markets and increase competition, decided to form a common economic market, or customs union, in which the members agreed to allow free trade among themselves. In 1992, the EU attempted to increase cooperation among its member countries by having the countries that chose to, and that met appropriate criteria, join the European Monetary Union (EMU) and adopt a common currency—the euro. This common currency means that you can travel between these countries without changing the money you use. That seems an advantage, and it is, but it also involves costs for the countries. Specifically, the countries are no longer able to use a separate monetary policy to stimulate their economy if they feel it needs stimulation. For example, say that Italy's economy is lagging. Before, the Italian central bank could lower interest rates and increase the money supply, expanding the Italian economy. Now that it is a member of the European Monetary Union, it cannot do that; all it can do is ask the European Central Bank to lower interest rates. Such concerns have kept a number of countries in the EU from joining the EMU. Presently only sixteen of the twenty-seven countries in the EU are members of the EMU.

other receives depends in part on the rate at which their two currencies exchange. For example, in 1980, when the price of a British pound in terms of dollars was $2.20, a setting of chinaware selling for 10 pounds in London would have cost a U.S. tourist $22. In 1985, when the pound had depreciated to $1.20, the same setting of chinaware would have cost a U.S. tourist only $12. In 2009, a pound cost about $1.60, so the chinaware would cost that tourist about $16.00.

In studying foreign exchange, we are concerned first of all with exchange rates and how they are determined. It is desirable for exchange rates between two countries to be at a level that will encourage trade. They should also be reasonably stable. Erratic fluctuations in exchange rates are a handicap to trade because they increase the uncertainty and risk involved in transactions that require time for their completion.

Fixed and Flexible Exchange Rate Systems

For many years before World War I, the principal trading countries of the world maintained monetary systems based on **fixed exchange rates,** exchange rates in which the relative values of the various currencies are established by agreement. (Under **flexible exchange rates,** in contrast, the government allows the market forces of supply and demand to fix the exchange rate of that country.) A fixed exchange rate system was achieved during this time by using the **gold standard,** a fixed exchange rate system in which the prices of the various currencies are set in relation to the price of gold. During the war, this standard broke down in most countries, and though it was revived for a time after the war, it suffered a second general breakdown with the coming of the Great Depression in the early 1930s.

When two or more countries are on the gold standard, only very small fluctuations can take place in the exchange rates between their currencies. Under the traditional gold standard, each country will exchange its paper money freely for a fixed amount of gold. When paper money and gold are freely interchangeable in each of two countries, the relative values of their currencies depend almost entirely on the relative amounts of gold they represent.

Let us suppose that the French franc once represented 4 grains of gold and the U.S. dollar 20 grains of gold.[1] Then a dollar would always exchange for approximately 5 francs. Slight variations in the exchange rate could still occur because of the cost of shipping gold. For example, though under the gold standard Americans could always exchange dollars in this country for a fixed amount of gold, in order to use this gold to obtain francs in Paris they would first have to pay the cost of shipping it to France.

The weakness of the gold standard was that, in order to maintain it, a government had to keep on hand enough gold to meet all demands for redeeming its currency. The advantage of this standard was that, as long as there was a determination to maintain it, it was an effective check on inflation. It forced a government to limit the expansion of bank deposits and the issue of paper money. Otherwise, demands for conversion of paper into gold would soon reach such a level that the government would be forced to stop redemption, thus automatically placing its money on a paper, or fiat, standard.

Paper Standards and the Gold Exchange Standard.   A **paper standard** is a system under which the basic monetary unit of a country is represented by engraved pieces of paper. These have value only because they are limited in quantity and, in the country of issue, are legal tender and acceptable in trade.

After World War II, the Western world initially went on a modified gold standard, under which countries were allowed to adjust their exchange rate (devalue) slightly (by no more than 10 percent), but no major devaluations were allowed without approval from other countries. The approval came from the **International Monetary Fund (IMF)**, an international organization set up just after World War II, both to aid in the adjustment and stabilization of exchange rates and to bring about the development of free exchange markets. The IMF could help its members meet temporary exchange difficulties by lending them limited amounts of gold or redeemable foreign currency.

Though the IMF has not entirely lived up to the hopes of its founders, it has helped stabilize foreign exchange markets. The system worked well until 1958, when the United States stopped running a balance-of-payments surplus and began running a balance-of-payments deficit. This led to runs on the dollar in which foreign holders of dollars wanted gold for them.

From a Fixed System to Our Current System: The Dirty Float.   In 1971, the foreign demand for gold was so great that the United States stopped convertibility, and our international exchange mechanism moved from a fixed exchange rate and a gold standard to flexible exchange rates. Under the new system, our reserves are no longer held only in gold, but are instead held in reserve currencies and a type of paper gold, or special drawing rights. These special drawing rights can now be used, within limits, for meeting international obligations, and they can be lent by the IMF to countries whose other reserves are being rapidly reduced by an adverse balance of payments.

Other countries can no longer get gold for dollars from the United States, but they can exchange dollars for U.S. goods. As the supply and demand for U.S. goods fluctuates, the

---

[1]Under the gold standard as it existed before World War I, U.S. gold coins actually contained 23.22 grains of pure gold per dollar, and French gold coins contained slightly less than one-fifth of this amount per franc. (A grain is equal to 1/7,000 of a pound.)

supply and demand for U.S. currency fluctuates also, changing its relative price. Thus, one month you might be able to buy an English pound for $1.90, and the next month it might cost $2.00. If that happens, we say the exchange rate of dollars for pounds has fallen from 1.9/1 to 2.0/1. In a perfectly flexible exchange rate system, the balance of payments must always be in equilibrium. Put another way, the supply of currency must always equal the demand for that currency. This follows from the definition of balance of payments as the relation of total payments made abroad to total payments received from abroad.

Actually, although the U.S. exchange rate system is generally a flexible rate system, it is not perfectly flexible. Every so often, the United States and other countries enter into the foreign exchange markets to attempt to raise or lower the value of the dollar. This makes our exchange rate system a **dirty float**—a partially flexible exchange rate system through which every so often the government enters into the foreign exchange market to affect the exchange rate.

Problems of Flexible Exchange Rates.   One of the problems facing the international flexible exchange rate system is the pressure of what can be called *hot money.* In the past, long-term investment has predominated, and capital flows among countries tended to be rather stable. With the continued development of computer technology for transfer of funds, however, in the last ten years short-term investments have become far more important. These short-term investments—hot money—will flow in or out of a country at the slightest change in relative interest rates. On an average day, more than $200 billion may be traded in this way.

The last part of 1997 provides us with a vivid example of the problems hot money can present to countries. At that time, investors lost confidence in a number of Pacific Rim countries, such as Thailand and Korea, and moved their money out of those countries. This created a currency crisis in those countries. Emergency loans were arranged to prevent their exchange rates from falling precipitously, but these loans came with conditions that slowed growth in these countries for the remainder of the twentieth century. In 2003, the hot money was leaving the United States, increasing the demand for foreign currencies and decreasing the demand for dollars. The result was a significant fall in the value of the dollar. Fluctuations in the value of the dollar can be seen in Figure 19.3. You can see that the value of the dollar has recently been on a roller coaster ride.

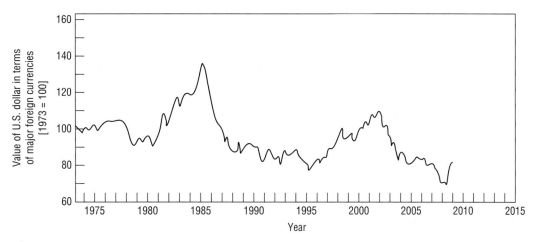

Figure 19.3

Fluctuations in the value of the dollar. (Source: Federal Reserve System.)

Globalization, Trade Imbalances, and Exchange Rates

Now that we've discussed exchange rates, we're ready to address the question of the future adjustment that the United States will experience due to globalization and the trade imbalances it has been running. Currently, countries are accepting dollars (U.S. promisary notes) for their goods and services. As discussed earlier, their willingness to do so has allowed the United States to run large trade deficits over the past few decades. At some point in the future, countries will stop accepting these U.S. dollars and promissory notes and instead want goods and services from the United States. When that happens, the value of the dollar is likely to fall substantially, especially in reference to the Chinese currency, the yuan, and the Indian currency, the rupee. At that point, Chinese- and Indian-produced goods will become more expensive in this country (making U.S. citizens less well off) and U.S. goods will become cheaper in India and China (making their citizens better off). As we buy fewer Chinese and Indian imports, and as they buy more U.S. exports, the trade balance will disappear, but in the process the United States will no longer have the enormously higher standard of living over the rest of the world that it currently enjoys.

Conclusion

As you can see, there is much to be learned about international economic relations, and we have only touched the surface. The international economy is complicated and operates on faith and goodwill among nations. If countries each try to go their own way, instituting protective tariffs and other forms of protectionism, the entire world will likely suffer. Therefore, cooperation is as essential in the international economy as it is in the domestic economy.

What makes international economic issues all the more important is their close relationship to international political relations. Countries that trade together generally do not fight wars. Thus, international economic and political relations will probably determine the direction the world takes in moving toward peace or moving toward war.

Key Points

- Balance of trade refers to the relation of our total exports to our total imports. Balance of payments refers to the relation of total payments made abroad to total payments received from abroad.
- Trade enables a country to obtain better products cheaper, but trade can hurt the domestic producers of those products.
- Protective tariffs restrict international trade and rob us of part of its benefits. This argument is countered by the home-market argument, the high-wages argument, the infant-industry argument, and the self-sufficiency argument.

- In a fixed exchange rate system, the relative values of currencies are set by agreement; in a flexible exchange rate system, the relative values of currencies are set by the market.
- The United States is the largest debtor nation in the world; we owe trillions of dollars more to foreigners than foreigners owe to us.
- The large U.S. trade deficit will likely lead to a fall in the value of the dollar, which will eliminate that trade imbalance.

Some Important Terms

balance of payments (382)
balance of trade (381)

cartel (381)
dirty float (393)

European Union (EU) (388)
fixed exchange rate (391)

flexible exchange rate (391)
foreign exchange (390)
General Agreement on Trade
   and Tariffs (GATT) (388)
global corporation (381)
globalization (389)

gold standard (391)
import quota (388)
International Monetary Fund
   (IMF) (392)
international reserve currency
   (390)

invisible items of trade (382)
paper standard (392)
tariff (386)
visible items of trade (382)
World Trade Organization
   (WTO) (388)

Questions for Review and Discussion

1. What are the three main advantages of international trade? What are some disadvantages?
2. Exports depend on imports, and vice versa. Why is this true?
3. Is it more desirable for a country to build up its visible or its invisible trade? Explain.
4. Is a favorable balance of trade possible? Is it desirable? Explain.
5. State and evaluate the principal arguments for protective tariffs.
6. The use of quotas to limit imports has been spreading recently. Are import quotas less damaging to consumers than tariffs? Why or why not?
7. Explain the impact of the formation of OPEC on the international economy.
8. In what ways can a country meet an excess of foreign payments over foreign receipts? Can it meet such an excess indefinitely? Explain.
9. Besides the example of Japanese car assembly given in the text, can you think of some examples of foreign investment in the United States?
10. What is the nature and purpose of the European Union?
11. Why were foreign exchange rates stable under the gold standard?
12. What is the purpose of the International Monetary Fund?
13. Why will the value of the U.S. dollar likely fall in the future, and what will that fall do to the relative standard of living in the United States and developing countries such as China and India?

Internet Questions

1. Look up the exchange rate at www.econo magic.com/fedstl.htm for U.S. dollars to the euro for the latest date and then for a year before. How did the rate change?
2. From U.S. census data at www.census.gov/foreign-trade/balance/index.html, pick a country and find the U.S. trade balance with that country now, in 2008, and in 2000.
3. Using http://dataweb.usitc.gov/scripts/tariff.asp, the U.S. International Trade Commission's database, find out what the tariff is per liter of beer. Why are there two different tariff rates?
4. Using www.worldbank.org/data/countrydata/countrydata.html, pick a country under Profile Tables. What are its exports and imports as a percentage of GDP for the latest year? What is the trend for the last three years? Compare it to another country.
5. Go to http://newsweek.washingtonpost.com/postglobal/america/2007/07/inside_an_indian_call_center.html, read the article, and watch the video. In a typical day, how many sales does a sales representative make? Would you be willing to work for $10 per day?

For Further Study

Bhagwati, Jagdish, *In Defense of Globalization*, New York: Oxford University Press, 2004.

Cameron, Maxwell A., and Brian W. Tomlin, *The Making of NAFTA: How the Deal Was Done*, Ithaca, NY: Cornell University Press, 2000.

Clissold, Tim, *Mr. China: A Wall Street Banker, an Englishman, an ex-Red Guard and $418,000,000 Disappearing Day by Day*, New York: HarperBusiness, 2006.

DeSoto, Hernando, *The Mystery of Capital: Why Capitalism Triumphs in the West and Fails Everywhere Else*, New York: Basic Books, 2000.

International Bank for Reconciliation and Development, annual reports, Washington, DC.

Kunstler, James Howard, *The Long Emergency: Surviving the Emerging Catastrophe of the Twenty-First Century*, New York: Atlantic Monthly Press, 2005.

Milner, Chris, and Robert Read, *Trade Liberalisation, Competition, and the WTO*, Cheltenham, UK: Edward Elgar, 2002.

Pomeranz, Kenneth, and Stephen Topik, *The World That Trade Created: Society, Culture, and the World Economy, 1400–the Present*, Armonk, NY: Sharpe, 2000.

Schmidt, Vivien, *From State to Market? The Transformation of French Business and Government*, Cambridge: Cambridge University Press, 2005.

Steger, Manfred B., *Globalism: The New Market Ideology*, Lanham, MD: Rowman & Littlefield, 2002.

United Nations: Various agencies of the UN from time to time publish reports and statistics on world economic conditions in particular nations. Write to United Nations Office of Public Information, New York, NY 10017.

Yergin, Daniel, and Joseph Stanislaw, *The Commanding Heights: The Battle between Government and the Marketplace That Is Remaking the Modern World*, New York: Simon & Schuster, 1998.

Zachary, Pascal, *Global Me: Comparative Edge and the New Cosmopolitans*, New York: Public Affairs, 2000.

WWW   Bureau of Economic Analysis   www.bea.gov

WWW   The European Union   www.eurunion.org

WWW   Foreign Trade Statistics   www.census.gov/foreign-trade/

WWW   The International Monetary Fund   www.imf.org

WWW   Universal Exchange Rate Converter   www.xe.com/ucc

WWW   U.S. International Trade Commission   www.usitc.gov

WWW   The World Trade Organization   www.wto.org

$\mathcal{T}$he Political Economies of Developing Countries

After reading this chapter, you should be able to:

- List six problems facing all developing countries
- Explain why each of those problems is so difficult to solve
- List three suggestions you might give to a potential leader of a developing country
- List and discuss the various policy options of developing countries
- Discuss developing countries' problems with specific reference to the cases of China, Mexico, and Uganda

A poor country is poor because it is poor.

—**Ragnar Nurske**

A country becomes rich because it is already rich.

—**P. Chaunu**

There are over 190 countries in the world; of these, about 56 might be considered developed. Others are called **developing countries**—countries still in various stages of economic and political development. Developing countries are called developing because they have far lower incomes than developed countries. As a group, they make up about 80 percent of the world's population but consume only about 25 percent of the world's output. Table 20.1 shows some other dimensions of the schism between developed and developing countries. As you can see, people in developing countries live shorter lives and earn less money.

Developing countries can be divided into a variety of groupings. The position of many Latin American countries, such as Mexico, Brazil, and Argentina, which have developed to some degree, is better than that of some others. A second group of developing countries, primarily those in the Pacific Rim, have managed to maintain rather rapid economic growth. These include South Korea, Taiwan, Singapore, and Hong Kong, which have had high growth rates (over 7 percent) over the last forty years. More recently China, India, and other neighboring countries have been experiencing fast growth. Because these countries have grown, they are sometimes considered to have left the developing country classification and entered the "newly industrialized country" classification. The worst performers in terms of economic growth have been the countries of Africa, which for the most part have not grown. Some have even seen their total output per capita decline. To differentiate these less developed countries in the early 2000s, the United Nations created a new category, **least developed country,** which includes countries with per capita GDPs of under $900. The fifty countries on page 398 below fall into this category. For a profile of these countries, go to www.un.org/special-rep/ohrlls/ohrlls/countryprofile.htm.

Table 20.1

The Schism between Developed and Developing Countries in the Early 2000s

	HIGHER-INCOME DEVELOPED COUNTRIES	LOWER-INCOME DEVELOPING COUNTRIES
Population	1 billion	5.5 billion
Per capita GDP	$37,000	$2,500
Life expectancy	79 years	67 years
Literacy rate	99%	61%

Source: Projections and estimates based on World Bank data.

Afghanistan	Djibouti	Malawi	Sudan
Angola	Equatorial	Maldives	Timor-Lesté
Bangladesh	Guinea	Mali	Togo
Benin	Eritrea	Mauritania	Tuvalu
Bhutan	Ethiopia	Mozambique	Uganda
Burkina Faso	Gambia	Myanmar	United Republic
Burundi	Guinea	Nepal	of Tanzania
Cambodia	Guinea Bissau	Niger	Vanuatu
Cape Verde	Haiti	Rwanda	Yemen
Central African	Kiribati	Samoa	Zambia
Republic	Lao People's	Sao Tome and	
Chad	Democratic	Principe	
Comoros	Republic	Sierra Leone	
Democratic	Lesotho	Senegal	
Republic of	Liberia	Solomon Islands	
Congo	Madagascar	Somalia	

The different performance of these various groups is a result, in part, of their contrasting policies. Asian countries, such as China and India, have generally adopted policies to promote exports and have worked hard to maintain competitive exchange rates. Many of the African countries have not. Another difference concerns the government and political structure. Asian governments have been strong and stable; African governments have been weak and unstable; Latin American governments' stability has generally fallen between the two. Stable governments are a requirement of economic growth.

The economic growth of developing countries has varied. Figure 20.1 shows the growth rates of developing countries compared with those of industrialized countries. Since 1965, developing countries have grown at a faster rate than industrial countries, but the gap between the two in absolute terms has grown larger.

Developing countries were once called "backward," but, on belated recognition of the value judgment inherent in that term, we began to call them "underdeveloped," and, on belated recognition of the value judgment inherent in that term, we now call them "developing." Although developing is preferable to backward, even the current term embodies a value judgment and suggests that some day developing nations will turn into, or that they want to turn into, developed nations. That is not necessarily the case—it is possible that some countries may not want to "develop." One of the reasons is that the term *developing* refers primarily to economies, not cultures. So-called developing countries can have highly refined cultures that are inconsistent with modern economies. It would be ethnocentric of

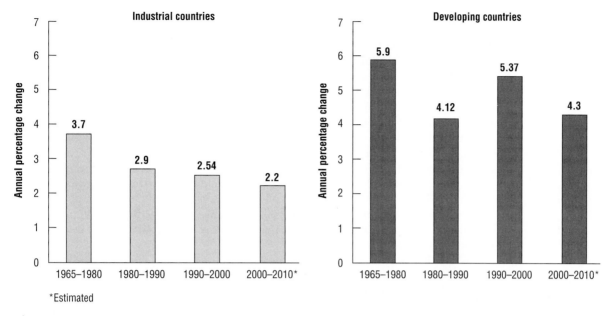

Figure 20.1

Economic growth rate among regions of the world. (Source: International Monetary Fund.)

us to think that their cultures are any less refined than ours, or that they should want to become like us.

What is less developed are their economies and their systems of government. Those developing countries that do not develop do not have the stable governments and social systems that hold a country together. In another world, that would not necessarily present a problem, but in today's world, without stable governments it is unlikely that they will be able to maintain their culture or their society as they currently exist. They will simply be overrun by U.S. and other Western cultures. That is not good or bad; that's just the way it is. Thus developing countries find themselves at a point of choice.

Problems of Developing Countries

To summarize and review much of what we have previously written on politics, economics, and their interrelationship, in this chapter we consider some of the problems facing developing countries, both in terms of their choice of social, economic, and political systems and of their attempts to maintain whatever such systems they have chosen. Although these problems are not unique to developing countries—many of the same problems are faced by developed countries—their severity in developing countries makes them worth emphasizing.

In looking at their choices, we would like to consider the full range of possibilities open to developing countries. Given that there are over 190 countries in the world, it would seem they have a wide range to choose from existing societies, but that is not the case. The various societies have not developed separately; they have been influenced by the other societies. Thus we now have two main economic systems, capitalism and socialism, and two main systems of government, democracy and autocracy. These systems do not necessarily span the range of possibilities, and probably many forms of society have not been tried. So we must keep an open mind about new possibilities.

The Political Consensus Problem

The central problem facing nonindustrial nations is what might be called the political consensus problem. **Political consensus** means sufficient political order and government efficacy so that the leaders of the state are able to rule. The political consensus problem is the following: Any state that is to operate as a nation-state must have a political consensus. The ability to rule can be derived from military might, force of personality, or cultural and social mores, but it must exist if the country is to develop.

In the United States, we have information availability, an educated public, cultural unity, and a long tradition of democracy. That tradition limits individuals' actions and holds our society together. For example, when a political party loses an election, it does not declare the election null and void; it accepts the election results. Developing countries seldom have all of these qualities, and they often do not have any of them. In those countries, it is unlikely that the democratic model will serve them well in the present, although it may provide a goal for the future. Generally, the developing state evolves into, at best, a partial democracy, or an autocracy.

When the ability of autocracy to rule is based on military might, the military has a final say on what is and is not to be done. Haiti is an example. The regime of President François Duvalier lasted for twenty-five years, and when he died in 1986 he was followed by his nineteen-year-old son, J. C. Duvalier, who called himself "President for life" but was overthrown by the army within a year. The military tolerated a temporary government until 1988, when a new president was chosen, who was overthrown the same year. From then until 2007, Haiti has had more than ten presidents, including Jean Bertrand Aristide, who has been in and out of office as political winds shifted and as he gained and lost favor with the United States. Throughout this period, Aristide supporters regularly clashed with their opponents. Almost all the presidents were members of the military, or were initially chosen through strong military influence, and were overthrown by the military when the army found them unsatisfactory. Aristide was a civilian, but it was through significant military influence that he was chosen, overthrown, replaced, returned, and again replaced.

Both autocracy and democracy present problems for developing countries. Democracies often lead to continual changes of government, and the general population's will is not always what is best for a country. Autocracies often lead to arbitrary and capricious rule. The old saying that power corrupts is not without merit. However, when leaders are not strong, power bases often develop outside the state framework. These power bases have their own means of enforcement; they might require payment for protection and make their own rules. Drug dealers in Colombia are an example. In 1985, when the Colombian Supreme Court cracked down on drug dealers, the head of the Supreme Court in that nation was killed. Then one of the many terrorist groups in Colombia invaded the Hall of Justice, and in a shoot-out with the military, twelve more justices were killed. Under President Alvaro Uribe, the situation has improved and the terrorist rebels have been largely defeated. However, the government's association with paramilitary groups and corruption of some politicians have led to difficulties. In 2008–2009, for example, more than sixty members of congress were under investigation and thirty lawmakers were in jail—for corruption.

The Corruption Problem

Closely associated with the lack of an established government, one that has inherent legitimacy, is the problem of corruption. Corruption is a way of life in developing countries. For example, in Mexico City, when you park your car, a police officer might ask you for a protection payment. If you want to import an item, you often must bribe the appropriate authorities to obtain permission. No bribe, no importing. In the Philippines, former President Marcos amassed a fortune estimated at $5 billion to $10 billion, although his presidential salary was

Political Instability in Africa

One of many victims of internal political strife being removed from the shores of Lake Victoria.

African countries have experienced the slowest growth and a major reason for this is political instability. If a government does not offer effective control or protections for its citizens, its economy will not grow. Consider just some of the African political crises that existed in 2010.

Sudan Pro-government militias begin ethnic cleansing campaigns beginning a humanitarian crisis in 2004. The Darfur region is in serious trouble.

Somalia Collapse of the military government in 1991 led to a civil war that killed thousands of citizens. Warlords continue to fight for power in a country of essential anarchy. In 2006 an Islamic leader declares a jihad on the Somali government, leading to civil war.

Republic of Congo A series of wars between ethnic and military powerhouses has marked the country's history. All elections are contested and the country remains mired by ethnic disputes and civil strife.

Rwanda In the early 1990s, economic collapse led to an outbreak of war. The country is still trying to come to grips with genocide that killed hundreds of thousand of citizens.

Zimbabwe This formerly prosperous country has been marked by human rights abuses, political instability, and economic collapse. Hyperinflation has made the currency useless, and elections are marked by killing and violence.

only about $6,000 per year. Either he was an awfully shrewd investor, or he was heavily involved in skimming money from the Philippine economy and government.

The examples of the corruption problem are wide ranging and are not tied to any particular country or party within that country. What we call corruption here may be simply accepted practice there. We see no easy answer to the problem of corruption, or even a complicated answer.

No system clearly offers a way around corruption. Only a deep-seated conviction built into the social mores offers some help, a conviction that regardless of the temptations, the leader will not take advantage of the situation to amass power and wealth. This is a bit like sitting you in a room of a hundred beautiful people of the opposite sex and telling you not to talk to any of them.

The Economic Problem

When income is below the starvation level, some form of economic development seems necessary. At that point the question is not, Should a country develop? but, how? The answer is unclear. To develop, a country requires savings and investment, but when you don't have enough to eat, how can you save or invest? Therefore, at below a certain level of income, societies find themselves in a vicious cycle from which there is no easy escape—and sometimes no escape at all. They must try, somehow, to pull themselves up by their own bootstraps to reach a point where they begin to grow.

In Cambodia in the late 1970s, the Khmer Rouge government killed millions of people as it attempted to force resettlement to bring about economic and social change.

To achieve takeoff into economic growth, a country needs to raise the level of investment to a certain minimum proportion of the national income. What is also essential, and what must develop along with any substantial increase of savings and investment, is an understanding on the part of the people of how a successful industrial society operates. The citizens must then be able and willing to develop the attitudes, the patterns of behavior, and the initiative required for vigorous economic growth. Simply pouring in capital is not enough.

Sometimes because of lack of understanding, or to satisfy the pride of politicians, countries striving for economic growth spend their available capital on the wrong things. They may, for example, produce impressive government projects such as national airlines or power dams, when what would help most, initially, might be greater production of food. Economic growth will proceed faster if it is balanced, if a foundation is gradually laid for a broad expansion of output. Before too many new airlines are founded or power plants are built, increased provision should be made for certain types of education and training; basic transportation, communication, and banking facilities should be provided; and efforts should be made to raise standards of living in order to increase both the welfare and productivity of workers and also to make possible a significant amount of saving and investment.

As is always the case, social, political, and economic factors interact. For example, many companies simply will not invest in certain foreign countries because of the unstable governments there, and they are unwilling to pay the bribes necessary to carry on business in such countries. Here, we can see the clash of two different cultures. U.S. firms would be breaking U.S. law if they were to pay bribes to foreign government officials, yet without paying bribes they could not operate in some countries.

Foreign Aid and Trade Barriers.   When countries cannot pull themselves up by their own bootstraps by developing internal savings and investment, they have another option. They can seek foreign infusion of investment, which can come in the form of private foreign investment or governmental **foreign aid,** which consists of financial and practical assistance

The World Bank

Various international institutions have been developed to assist developing countries. One of these is the World Bank. The **World Bank** is an international organization whose goal is to foster development by making loans and giving out economic advice. It receives funds primarily from developed countries, and makes loans primarily to developing countries. The World Bank was formed in 1944, and since that time it has provided low-interest loans to many developing countries. It has a staff of about 11,000.

The World Bank's initial loans focused on large projects such as dams and power plants. The World Bank received strong criticism in the early 1990s for the nature of its loans. Critics said that the loans were too heavily focused on large projects that hurt the environment. In 1994, when the bank celebrated its fiftieth anniversary, it responded to the criticisms by saying that it would change its lending practices. It reiterated its basic goal of promoting broad-based economic growth that benefits the poor, but it said that to achieve that goal it would increase its investment in human, as opposed to physical, resources. Specifically, it would increase its support of educational, nutritional, and family planning programs. It also stated that it would concentrate on environmentally sound physical investments, and that it would help fund programs that build on and expand the role of women in development. Since that time, it has changed its lending practices, but it has continued to be the target of criticism because of its association with free trade and because protestors feel it is still not doing enough.

Anti-WTO protests provide an example of how social, political, and economic factors interact.

given by one country to another, especially by a technologically advanced country to a less developed one.

Over the last sixty years, in response to the developing world's need for assistance, the United States has given foreign aid at the rate of about one-half of 1 percent of our total output. The results of that aid have been mixed. Much of it has not gone for humanitarian purposes; rather, it has had political and military purposes.

The biggest recipient of U.S. foreign aid is Israel, and that aid has been provided out of blatantly political motives. Even aid that was given for humanitarian purposes has undergone strong criticism. Much of that aid was eaten up in bureaucracy and skimmed by foreign politicians; thus, it never reached its intended recipients. In response to these criticisms, more and more aid is flowing to *nongovernmental organizations,* or **NGOs**—privately established agencies that attempt to help countries and channel aid to those who need it.

Foreign aid and investment are only part of the answer. An equally, or even more important, part of the economic answer is removing developed countries' trade barriers. The reality is that developed countries are not very open to exports from developing countries. For example, the EU provides enormous subsidies to its farmers who then export subsidized farm products to countries that could have produced them, but which can't compete with subsidized prices. In addition, the EU maintains tariffs against many farm imports. This combination of policies makes it difficult for developing countries to develop or expand their farm exports, countering much of the benefit of EU foreign aid. The United States is not as bad as the EU in this regard, but it still has significant trade barriers built into its farm policy. Combining all policies that help or hurt developing countries, the Centre for Global Development ranked twenty-one rich countries in a "Commitment to Development Index." The United States came in next to last.

The Historical Legacy of Colonialism. When Western governments' budgets are tight, the amount of foreign aid they give often comes under attack. Opponents of aid argue that the developed countries owe nothing to the developing countries. Supporters of aid, on the other hand, point to history in providing justification not only for giving aid, but also for giving even more than we do. The historical argument goes as follows: Western countries colonized the developing countries, creating artificial political entities that brought together incompatible ethnic groups and extracted what they could from those countries. These developing countries were not allowed to develop in their own way. In following these policies, the West created the problems that developing countries face today. Given the West's role in creating many of the problems that developing countries face, supporters of foreign aid argue that the West has a moral obligation to assist them.

The Debt Problem

The reliance on private investment, including loans from U.S. and other banks, has created a new problem for many developing countries: the debt problem. Private investment and loans must be serviced, which means that interest must be paid.

In the 1980s, the problem of the **international debt**—the amount of outstanding loans among different nations—grew in importance. The large borrowings of the developing countries throughout the 1970s, together with high-interest rates, made it almost impossible for a number of developing countries to meet their debt obligations.

In the 1990s, that debt problem was greatly reduced by **debt restructuring**—allowing repayment of debt over extended periods of time—and a fall in the world interest rate. In 2001, the IMF granted debt relief for twenty-two countries, continuing the trend of debt restructuring.

In 2005, the Group of Eight agreed to cancel more than $40 billion in debt owed by the poorest countries, in part due to pressure from U-2's lead singer, Bono. It allows nations to use the money they save to provide health care, education, and other social improvements. However, in order to qualify for the program, the countries must comply with good governing practices and transparency. Despite these restructurings, particular developing countries had large debt overhangs, and paying off that debt will remain a problem through the early decades of the 2000s.

The Population Problem

Even if they begin to grow, developing countries will not necessarily escape the vicious cycle we have discussed, because they face another large problem. Put simply, as long as population continues to grow at current rates, these countries are going to have enormous, perhaps insurmountable, difficulties in increasing their **per capita output,** the total output divided by the country's population. The vicious cycle that Thomas Malthus[1] wrote about is very real to many developing countries. Although with sufficient technological development there is no limit to the amount of production one can get from land, one must overcome the initial investment hurdle that will provide them with the means to make that technological progress.

The Brain Drain Problem

As bad as the preceding problems are, they do not leave developing countries without hope. The emergence of nation-states and their development show that the transition to developed states is possible. But before we say, We grew, why don't you? we should consider that the nation-states of Western society enjoyed significant advantages over currently developing countries.

In the 1700s, when Western economies developed, travel was limited and individuals tended to stay home and to consider their life in relation to their society. The bright, dynamic individuals modified their society, but because their lives were in their society, their modifications were generally small and consistent with that society's culture. That is often not the way it happens in developing countries today. Developing countries have a **brain drain,** a process in which the individuals who could make a country develop leave that country.

---

[1]See Chapter 5 for a discussion of Thomas Malthus and his theories.

Having attended school in Great Britain and Germany, one of the authors came to know a number of the brightest and best students of a variety of developing countries. They were sent away to school because they were so outstanding. They often do well, but in doing so they become immersed in the developed culture.

When they finish their studies, these students often are presented with a choice between two totally different economies and cultures. One offers enormous amounts of material goods, intellectual challenge for which their training has prepared them, and excitement. The other offers traditional values from which their foreign education has taught them to escape, material shortages, and enormous intellectual challenges for which they have no preparation. Faced with such choices, many decide to remain in the developed country or to join an international agency that pays as well as a good job in the United States. The result is the brain drain.

Consider the brain drain problem from the perspective of an outside observer. Doctors trained in India, where doctors are in short supply, are constantly immigrating to the United States where there are many more doctors per capita; the same is true with engineers and computer experts. The United States benefits enormously from this immigration, and immigrants constitute nearly a fifth of all doctors and Ph.D.s. The UN estimates that India loses $2 billion a year just from computer expert emigration to the United States. In addition, many of the brightest students are going abroad for higher education, causing a foreign exchange outflow of $10 billion annually. Removing the best and the brightest from a society makes it that much harder for the society to develop.

Mission Impossible: Advice to a Potential Leader

What, then, should a developing country do?

Neither we nor any other social scientist knows what to do. Advice has run the gamut of possibilities. The results have been so bad that we are going to deviate from standard textbook policy: We do not tell you what the experts think should be done. Instead, we are asking you what you think should be done. So, we hereby appoint you as social advisor to Hopelandia. (If you have foreign students in your class, you might find that the exercise is not so far-fetched. Many of them are the future leaders of their countries.)

Your task, should you decide to accept, is to prepare a development plan and determine what set of policies a developing country should follow to solve the problems mentioned earlier. To make the assignment easier, we begin by providing you with some general advice that we would give a potential leader, a set of policy options to help formulate your thinking about the problems, and some initial background information on three developing countries.

Keep an Open Mind.   The first piece of advice to an advisor to a developing country is don't rule out options arbitrarily and do use all available knowledge of the interrelationships of various aspects of social science. Don't try to emulate any specific developed country. Do what is right for your country, because what works for one country might not work for another. For example, in Uganda there are enormous tribal differences, and individuals' allegiance is to their tribe rather than to the larger society or to their country. Voting almost invariably means voting for whichever candidate is from one's tribe. Within such a situation, democracy is unstable. For democracy to succeed, the allegiance must be to the entire country, not to an individual subsection of that country.

Recognize the Difficulties.   The second piece of advice is to set goals and priorities with full recognition of the difficulties that the development plan will encounter. Should a country grow economically, or should it instead set different goals, such as maintaining its tradition and furthering its religion? In the Middle East, many Shiite Muslims tend to be more fundamentalist in their beliefs; they fear that economic growth means the infusion of Western values into their society and a worsening, not an improvement, of the society.

Therefore, the goals they choose have little to do with economics other than as a means to the end of preserving their religion and their way of life. In other countries, economic growth is weighted more heavily, and although maintaining tradition always plays some role, when faced with the inevitable trade-off, these countries, such as South Korea, will make choices based on economic development.

Maintain Your Idealism.   A final and most important piece of advice is to maintain your idealism. Unless you love your country and are willing to use whatever power you have for the good of the country as well as you understand that good, and not for your own gain or that of your friends, then forget about being a leader and give your support to an individual who will.

Options of Developing Countries

Developing countries have a variety of ways to deal with their almost impossible problems. Let's briefly consider their options.

Political Options

Political options include democracy, autocracy, and various shades in between the two. Somehow the system chosen must be one that combines the various ethnic and regional groupings into a complete whole and makes them feel that they belong together, rather than that they are blood rivals who must continuously fight with each other. The policies you suggest to meet this necessity will determine the type of policies you can advocate in regard to the economic problem.

Economic Options

The range of economic options goes from (1) a type of unfettered capitalism, in which the government enters into the economy as little as possible; to (2) socialism, in which individuals can operate in certain areas, but the government plays a much stronger role in guiding the choice of each individual decision; to (3) some new kind of economic organization that you think of. The choices are interrelated.

Foreign Policy Options

Countries do not develop in a vacuum. Other countries play a role, at times stabilizing a regime, at other times destabilizing a regime, depending on whether the individuals guiding these regimes are following the other country's goals, and on whether the particular major power can live with the operation of the regime to which it has lent support. Therefore, you have to choose a foreign policy.

During the cold war, developing countries could play the former Soviet Union against the United States. With the breakup of the Soviet Union, this strategy ended. The United States and its allies were about all there was left to flirt with. That's why in the early 2000s most development plans have been democratic, market-oriented plans. However, the significant economic growth in China, and China's increasing international presence, is beginning to present developing countries with a variation of the "flirting" option.

Population Options

You need to ask yourself some questions about population. First, do you have a population problem? Facing this issue is one of the most difficult tasks confronting human beings, whether on a personal level, a national level, an international level, or—now that space colonization is not just a wild, science-fiction dream—a cosmic level. Second, if you have an overpopulation problem (and in the countries we are talking about here, let us hint that you may likely have overpopulation problems), do you then go in and direct people not to have children, or at least to limit the number to one or two? How would you do this? Third, having made the decision which way to go, and how to go that way, what consequences can you foresee will have to be dealt with when the results of your policy begin to show up in the census figures?

The Brain Drain Option

Should you encourage your top students to go abroad? If you do, how can you be sure they'll come home again to use their new skills in the country that sent them to be educated? Suppose you decide the other way, that is, to keep your most promising youth at home. In that case, how will you foster new ideas, youthful enthusiasm, and the importation of valuable ideas and methods that have already been developed in other countries (you don't want to reinvent the wheel)?

Who Will Be the Next Leader?

What qualities do you want and what qualities does your country need in a leader? Should there be a committee or coalition of some kind, rather than a single leader? In either case, how will leadership qualities be developed? How will leadership qualities be recognized? What will the leader, or leaders, do once in power? How should the leadership be controlled, if it should be controlled? How can you search for and pick out the leaders in your country? Perhaps that search won't be fruitful, or not as fruitful as you expect. Should you look for imported talent? Where should you look for it, if this is your choice? Ask the same questions about the imported talent that you asked about possible homegrown leaders.

You could, of course, ask many other questions, but these few should start you on the way.

Case Studies

To really get a sense of the problems facing developing countries and their options, we need to look at specific experiences of real-world countries. Thus, we conclude this chapter with three case studies.

China

Of all the case studies to consider, China is a must. It is the largest and most populous developing country in the world, and it has approximately as large an area as the United States. Its main language is Mandarin Chinese, although there are eight separate dialects. Ostensibly, it is a federal republic with twenty-three provinces, five autonomous regions, and, since July 1997, Hong Kong. Its political regime rules a socialist state, with the Communist Party of China specifying the state ideology.

In 1989, strong student pressures for democracy were crushed, and political control by the Communist Party has held firm into the early 2000s. The box on page 409 gives an overview of the statistics relevant to China.

Since the late 1980s, China has undergone enormous economic liberalization with the introduction of markets and market incentives to try to encourage individual production without generating what China believes are the negative side effects of markets. It has moved away from central planning, although in what it considers key goods, government production still rules.

The freeing of the market in many sectors has led to China becoming the world's fastest-growing economy at the turn of the century, creating a substantial middle class and many "newly rich" people. This income growth has been highly skewed, and the large majority of Chinese remain poor.

The key to China's future will be the manner in which the Communist leadership reconciles political reform and liberalization with economic progress. If China can sustain its economic performance, it will become a vital player in the international system: Given the present trajectories, it seems set to join the United States as a genuine international superpower in the next twenty-five years.

Background of China.　China is surrounded by a variety of natural barriers: the sea to the east, mountains and desert to the southwest and north. There are three natural regions: the west, an area of high plateaus and desert; the north, an area of fertile plains; and the south, mostly hills and valleys. The two main rivers, the Yangtze and the Yellow, are both of extreme economic importance. Most of the population of China belongs to the Mongolian race, and 95 percent are Chinese speaking, although there are many dialects and a variety of other languages.

Though now officially atheist, most Chinese practice variants of Buddhism, Taoism, or Chinese folk religion. Even before that, Confucianism, based on patriarchal dominance, had established extraordinarily strong family and social ties based on male supremacy. As one result of the communist takeover in the 1940s and the establishment of communes, many

China.

of these ties were significantly deduced. As that occurred, the status of women in Chinese society improved greatly.

The key to recent Chinese economic history is the communist takeover of the government in 1945 and its attempt to introduce socialism into the Chinese system and culture. Then, in 1978, a change in leadership gradually introduced market-oriented reforms and decentralized economic decision making.

China's Population Problem.   Population growth remains a key problem, and the government has introduced a variety of rather strong policies to limit that growth. Birth control has been a national priority in China since 1971, when the government instituted a new program—an edict pronouncing as a norm the two-child family. Because of improved health and longer life spans, even this was projected to result in an enormous increase in population. In 1979, the two-child limit was cut to a one-child limit, and the system is backed by a variety of economic rewards for those who comply and penalties for those who do not. Families having more than one child lose rights, lose income, and are counseled by most of the leaders of their community that they are not doing the right thing.

The initial results were significant. By 1982, the majority of newly formed families in the cities were having only one child. This was not the case, however, in the countryside, where the desire to have several children and, above all, to have boys, meant that families ignored the limit or, in some cases, killed newborn female babies. Recognizing the difficulty of policing these vast rural areas, in the late 1980s the authorities relaxed their one-child policy for those areas.

In the largest cities, such as Shanghai and Beijing, the one-child policy prevails, but by the early 2000s economic conditions in parts of China had become so favorable that many families wanting to have more than one child simply do so and willingly risk having to pay

China: Selected Statistics

Population: 1.3 billion (2009)
  Urban: 43%
  Rural: 57%
  Sex distribution
    1.1 males/females
  Age distribution
    Under 15: 19.8%
    15–64: 72.1%
    Over 64: 8.1%
Household size
  Rural: 4.6
  Urban: 3.4
Birthrate per year per 1,000 population: 14
Death rate per year per 1,000 population: 7.03
  (world average: 9.3)
Infant mortality: 20.25 per 1,000
Life expectancy at birth
  Male: 71.61
  Female: 75.52
Marriage rate per year per 1,000 population: 7.0
Divorce rate per year per 1,000 population: 1.5
Hospital Beds: 1 per 220 persons

Religions
  Nonreligious: 59.2%
  Chinese folk: 20.1%
  Atheist: 12.0%
  Buddhist: 6.0%
  Muslim: 2.4%
  Christian: 0.2%
  Other: 0.1%
Educational attainment among those aged 25 and older
  No schooling: 29.3%
  Incomplete primary: 34.3%
  Completed primary school: 34.4%
  Postsecondary: 2.0%
Literacy rate among those aged 15 and older: 91%
  (2002)
GDP per year: $7.8 trillion (2005)
  GDP per capita: $6,000 (ppp)
Number of radios: 195 per 1,000
Number of television sets: 400 million
Number of telephones: 312 million
Cell phones: 335 million (2004)
Personal computers: 60 per 1000
Internet users: 253 million (2007)
Website: www.china-embassy.org

The old Shanghai overshadowed by the new Shanghai.

a large fine. In some localities, government officials, eager to have the income from such fines, even propose that families have a second or third child. This trend is thought to be sufficiently offset by the vast numbers of families sticking to the one-child limit or opting to have no children at all. In 2008, China's population was about 1.3 billion, remaining stable at that level since the early 2000s, and is well within the goal of less than 1.4 billion by 2010. As the population ages China has even relaxed its one-child policy, allowing many couples who were single children to have two children of their own.

Even though it is the third largest food producer in the world, because of its enormous population China still produces barely enough to feed its own people. All available land is already under cultivation. One bright side of the Chinese economy is that it has relatively rich mineral resources, and in recent years, with its introduction of a market economy, it has expanded production enormously.

China's Political Problems.   Politically, China remains controlled by the Communist Party, although it is moving more and more toward a market economy. The way to its present state has been a zigzag path. From 1966 until 1976, China was governed by a radical faction that engineered a **Cultural Revolution** and encouraged the youth to purge the economy and society of excesses and external influences that it felt had adverse consequences for China. Universities were torn apart and strong attempts were made to break down the vested ruling interests. It is estimated by some that millions of people were killed in this movement. In 1976, after the death of Mao Ze-dong, the group that brought the Cultural Revolution to China was thrown out of power, and moderates, headed by Deng Xiaoping, took over. They started developing economic incentives and economic modernization.

After Deng retired in 1986, Zhao Ziyang and Li Peng shared China's leadership. They cautiously continued Deng's economic modernization policies, while maintaining communist control. Economic modernization led to demands for political liberalization as well, and in 1989 the world saw millions of students and ordinary citizens clashing with China's government. The uprising was repressed, and Zhao lost his post while Li retained leadership. In the late 1990s, President Jiang Zemin emerged as the leader of China and in 2003, he was replaced with Ju Jintao. They have continued the economic reform process and have been quick to suppress political dissension.

Economically, since the early 2000s China has been growing at over 10 percent per year, which means that the changes China is undergoing are incredible. Millions of people are moving off farms and into cities. Much of the growth has been focused on China's eastern seaboard, especially in the urban areas and in the southern part of China. The growth has been accompanied by an enormous increase in inequality. Local governments have often seized what was communal land from rural farmers, frequently with little compensation. The result has been significant unrest in the rural areas. The 2008 financial crisis threatened China's economy with stagnation. As the United States' and other countries' disposable incomes were washed away, China's export market slowed considerably. They saw a 17.5 percent drop in year over year exports and nearly 20 million migrant workers lost their city jobs. These workers, who may be forced back to their rural jobs, may see a halving of their wages as they revert back to farming and other occupations. The Chinese response was quick. They ran large deficits and expanded the money supply, creating internal demand to offset much of the loss in exports.

Uneven economic growth has widened the gap between the rich minority and the millions of poor workers and peasants. Some observers believe it is likely that growing resentment among the poor will have substantial repercussions in the near future. Official corruption has rapidly grown to become one of China's major problems.

Another potential problem is China's relationship with Taiwan, an island off the coast of China, where the anti-communists fled in the 1940s and which once saw itself as the legitimate government of China. China claims it as part of China, and thus there is always the chance for trouble if the differences cannot be resolved through diplomatic means.

In 2008, the Beijing Summer Olympics was widely interpreted as a showcase of Chinese progress and ingenuity to the world. Many factors obscured this fact and demonstrated that China is still in the process of becoming a global leader. For example, both Taiwan and Tibet criticized the Chinese government for their political and social repression. In summary, China is emerging as a full-fledged superpower, but it remains to be seen whether its "market socialism" ideology—involving concurrent political repression and economic liberalization—will be viable over the long haul.

Mexico

Mexico is the third largest country in North America. It is bounded on the north by the United States and on the south by Guatemala and Belize. About 75 percent of Mexico is a

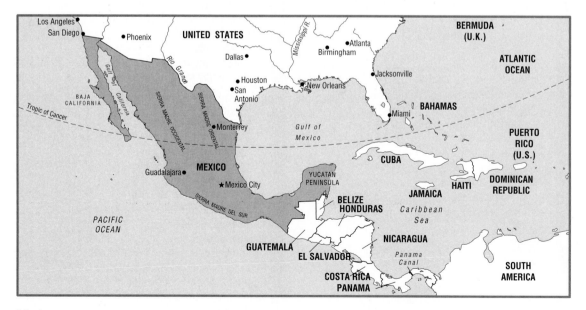

Mexico.

central plateau with low hills, basins, and mountains bounded by the Sierra Madre Occidental and Sierra Madre Oriente. The southern edge has many volcanoes, and the region is subject to earthquakes. Much of southern Mexico is laced with swamps and lagoons, and northern Mexico is arid and has few rivers.

Mexico's population is about 111 million in an area of 761,605 square miles, for a population density of about 140 people to a square mile. The language is primarily Spanish, although there are some Indian languages. The religion is overwhelmingly Roman Catholic. Population has been increasing rapidly, and 77 percent of the population lives in towns and cities. About 60 percent of Mexicans are Mestizos (of mixed Indian and European ancestry), 30 percent are pure Indian, and 9 percent are Caucasian. About 9 percent of the population is illiterate.

The Mexican economy has expanded significantly since World War II. In addition, it has changed from an agricultural to an industrial and service economy.

The present system of government in Mexico was established by the revolution of 1910, in which most large estates were expropriated and land was redistributed among peasants organized into landholding communities. A federal republic was created in 1924, and the Madera Revolution of 1910 had already established the political forces that are there currently. The central party, the National Revolutionary Party, was formed from all major political groups in 1929. It was later renamed the Institutional Revolutionary Party (PRI) and goes under that name today. In recent times, Mexico has had a stable government. The Mexican economy has expanded significantly since World War II during its transition from an agricultural to an industrial and service economy. The system of government remained unchanged for nearly eighty years under stable PRI control. The long ruling period for the PRI, along with its strong government control of industry, established an entrenched bureaucracy that fostered corruption and bribery.

In 1998, Carlos Salinas was elected and began the road to economic liberalization and democratic reform. He lessened government control of the economy, instituted anticorruption measures in business and the government, and instituted a controversial free trade

Mexico: Selected Statistics

Population: 111 million (2006)
　Urban: 77%
　Rural: 23%
　Sex distribution　1.05
　　males/females
　Age distribution
　　Under 15: 29%
　　15–64: 65%
　　Over 64: 6%
Household size
　Average household size: 5
Birthrate per year per 1,000 population: 19.7
Death rate per year per 1,000 population:
　4.78
Life expectancy
　Male: 73.25
　Female: 79
Marriage rate per 1,000 population: 7.7
Divorce rate per 1,000 population: 0.4

Religions　(2000 census)
　Roman Catholic: 77%
　Protestant: 6%
　Other: 17%
Educational attainment among those aged 15 and older
　No primary school: 14%
　Some primary school: 22%
　Completed primary school: 21%
　Some secondary school: 10%
　Completed secondary school: 24%
　Some postsecondary school: 8%
Literacy rate among those aged 15 and older: 91%
GDP: $1.143 trillion (2005)
　GDP per capita: $10,000
Number of radios: 329 per 1,000
Number of television sets: 25.6 million
Number of telephones: 19.754 million
Cell phones: 68.254 million (2007)
Personal computers: 140 per 1000
Internet users: 22.812 million.
Website: www.inegi.gob.mx

agreement, NAFTA. These programs dramatically accelerated Mexico's economic modernization but created many short term negative effects with Mexico's poor and working class citizens.

The PRI slowly lost their grip on Mexican politics, and in 2000 the first non-PRI candidate, Vicente Fox, was elected president. However, partisanship in the congress limited Fox's ability to enact further reforms that were desperately needed. In 2006, another opposition PAN (National Action Party) candidate, Felipe Calderon, was elected president. Through 2009, Calderon's approval rating has stayed quite high. He implemented an anticorruption policy designed to reform the police and military. One of his first acts as president was to increase police and military salaries to combat bribes and corruption. As part of this policy, he declared a war on drug cartels and their ability to flaunt the laws. This has led to significant conflict between the cartels and government, creating an enormously violent situation in some areas.

Uganda

Uganda has an area of 93,070 square miles and a population of about 32 million. A variety of languages are spoken, including Bantu, Swahili, and English. Its religions are Christian, Muslim, and a variety of tribal sects. Uganda lies on the equator and has an average elevation of 4,000 feet above sea level. The fertile plateau is bounded by the Great Rift Valley. Annual rainfall is about 40 inches, and temperatures generally remain between 60°F and 85°F.

Uganda's biggest problem is a lack of political coherence; it comprises a dozen major tribes, of which the Bantu-speaking groups form the majority. The Ugandan tribes, in the south, are now the most numerous and have given their tribal name to the whole country. Most people depend on agriculture for a living, although some of the northern tribes are also wandering herders. Illiteracy is extremely high. Most agriculture consists of subsistence and livestock farming, although Uganda remains one of the world's largest producers of coffee, which accounts for almost all of its export earnings.

Africa (left); Uganda (right)

President Yoweri Museveni of Uganda.

Uganda developed, in its current form, as a British protectorate in 1894, and was extended to its present boundaries in 1914. It became independent in 1962, and in 1971 Idi Amin deposed President Milton Obote in a military coup. In 1972, Amin expelled Uganda's Asian population and launched a rule of terror.

In 1979, Uganda was invaded by Tanzania, and Amin fled. (In 2000, he died in exile in Saudi Arabia.) With Amin's exile, the ex-president, Obote, returned to rule the nation. Obote ruled for five years but favored his own tribe, the Langi, and in mid-1985 was again deposed, being replaced by a military man, Tito Okello, a member of the Acholi tribe.

In 1986, Okello was replaced by Yoweri Museveni, who turned what seemed to be a hopeless situation—a country that existed more in name than in reality, a country that earlier editions of this book described as a basket case—into a more politically stable country that since 1987 has continued to grow impressively.

How did he do this? First, he kept his idealism; he did not appropriate large amounts of the country's wealth to himself and his followers. Second, he opened his government to other tribes and built a political alliance among tribes that, although tenuous, allowed the fighting to stop. Third, he reduced major corruption in government while leaving minor corruption in place to maintain the support of the government workers. Fourth, he established a sufficiently stable system of laws that allowed international and domestic investment to occur. Fifth, although he is a socialist, he established free markets and reduced the number of government monopolies and government-controlled businesses. And finally, he maintained a strong army under his control.

Uganda still has serious problems. Northern Uganda cities, such as Kitgum, are caught up in a civil war; more than 200,000 people have died since 2000, and a large majority of the population is afraid to leave the refugee camps to which they have fled. The reason is the "Lord's Resistance Army" led by Joseph Kony, which has been trying to overthrow Museveni. It has abducted an estimated 25,000 children and used them as soldiers, forcing them to kill a parent or sibling, or to serve as sex slaves. In 2005, the International Criminal Court indicted Kony and other leaders of the Lord's Resistance Army, but he remained in hiding in the Democratic Republic of the Congo, which has almost no government.

*U*ganda: Selected Statistics

Population: 32 million (early 2006) 369558
   Urban: 13%
   Rural: 87%
   Sex distribution
      1.03 male/female
   Age distribution
      Under 15: 50%
      15–64: 47.9%
      65 and over: 2.1%
Household size: 5 people
Birthrate per year per 1,000 population: 47.84
Death rate per year per 1,000 population:
   12.32
Infant mortality: 64.82 per 1,000
Life expectancy
   Male: 51.66
   Female: 53.81
Religions

Roman Catholic: 41.9%
Protestant: 42%
Muslim: 12.1%
Other: 4%
Educational attainment: Percentage of population age 25 and over having
No formal schooling or less than one year: 46.9%
Primary school: 42.1%
Secondary school: 10.5%
Higher: 0.5%
Literacy rate among those 15 and higher: 66.8%
GDP: $35.88 billion (2008)
   GDP per capita: $1100 (2008)
Number of radios: 5 million
Number of television sets: 500,000
Number of telephones: 162,300
Cell phones: 4.795 million
Personal computers: 20 per 1,000
Internet users: 2 million (2007)
Website: www.ubos.org

In 2007, he gave an interview in which he stated that he wanted peace and that he was willing to face trial in Uganda, but the fighting has continued throughout 2009.

It should be noted that the commendable economic performance in Uganda has not led to political reform. In the elections of 1989, the ruling party, the NRM, was the only party. Museveni argues that while multiparty democracies suit Western societies, which divide horizontally by class, they only deepen divisions within African societies, which are vertically split along ethnic or regional lines. He says that given the ethnic problems Uganda faces, Western-style democracy is not appropriate for Uganda or most other African nations and that Western countries should consider the results of his rule and not worry about whether it has a Western-style democracy. Uganda's arrangement of severely restricted, though not banned, political parties is known as the **"Movement" system.**

Ten years after he came to power following the 1986 coup, Museveni was elected to a five-year term as president in 1996 amid complaints that he was virtually assured of victory because of the resources and apparatus of the Ugandan government backing him. In 2001, Museveni, though faced by a major challenger calling for political pluralism, won the presidential election. In 2003, Museveni indicated support for a multiparty system in the name of peace building, although in the election of 2006, which he won handily, his main opponent, Besigye, was arrested and charged with treason and rape just months prior to the election.

Museveni's "Movement" system is a challenge to western scholars who support democracy as it is practiced in Western countries. The problem is that in developing countries with many competing ethnic groups, Western-style democracy often leads to enormous corruption and civil war. Museveni argues that given that reality, developing African countries need an idealistic broad group committed to state stability and preventing corruption to oversee the playing out of political democracy. He sees his Movement as providing that for Uganda, and after he leaves office, he has called for the Movement to remain—not as a political party but as an organization overseeing state stability and preventing corruption. The problem is whether any group will be able to provide checks on the Movement if they lose their idealism.

Conclusion

In considering the choices a developing country must make, you will see the game of society played in its entirety. The individuals who succeed in making the right choices launch their countries into prosperity and political stability. Those who make the wrong choices leave their countries in poverty.

The preceding descriptions have been necessarily brief. You can find more information in the library, and you'll need a lot more information before you can make reasonable choices. Even if you don't take that step-for-social-science into the library, keep your eyes and ears open for stories about these and other countries in the newspapers; in news-magazines such as *Time, Newsweek,* and *U.S. News & World Report;* and on television and the Internet—because these countries will be in the news. The issues of social science surround you and will continue to surround you all your life.

Key Points

- Six problems facing all developing countries are the political consensus problem, the corruption problem, the economic problem, the debt problem, the population problem, and the brain drain problem.

- Each of these problems is interrelated with the others and is deeply ingrained in the culture of the society.
- Reasonable suggestions for a potential leader of a developing country include keeping an open

mind, recognizing the difficulties, and maintaining your idealism.
- Policy options for developing countries include political options, economic options, foreign policy options, population options, and brain drain options.
- To truly understand the problems of developing countries, we must do case studies of specific countries.

Some Important Terms

brain drain (404)
Cultural Revolution (410)
debt restructuring (404)
developing countries (397)

foreign aid (402)
international debt (404)
least developed country (397)
"Movement" system (415)

NGO (403)
per capita output (404)
political consensus (400)
World Bank (402)

Questions for Review and Discussion

1. What is the chief characteristic that identifies a country as developing?
2. Name three groups of developing countries, and state briefly what distinguishes one group from another.
3. If a developing country cannot find a way to hold itself together, what is likely to happen to it?
4. Why might democracy not be the best choice of political system for a developing country?
5. Are there any good things to be said for autocratic government? If so, what are some of them?
6. What are some of the abuses a corrupt government indulges in?
7. A poor country might solve its problems by becoming richer. How can a poor country save and invest?
8. Aid to developing countries from the governments of developed countries has been decreasing. Give some of the reasons.

9. Some developing countries have borrowed so much money from foreign banks that they are having great difficulty paying it back. What is likely to happen in such countries?
10. What problems does rapid population growth present to a developing country? Are there any advantages to rapid population growth in developing countries?
11. How can a developing country acquire the human skills, training, and valuable ideas it needs in order to compete in modern industrial society?
12. Are there guaranteed solutions to the problems of developing countries? If so, describe some of the solutions.
13. What were your proposals for the development of the country of Hopelandia?

Internet Questions

1. What countries does the World Bank, http://web.worldbank.org/WBSITE/EXTERNAL/COUNTRIES/0,,pagePK:180619~theSitePK:136917,00.html, identify as developing in the South Asia region?
2. After watching Lennart Bage's (President of the International Fund for Agricultural Development) video, http://www.youtube.com/watch?v=i-S-Oe3WoJI, what are the main reasons for supporting IFAP? Can you think of any costs?
3. According to the World Bank, http://web.worldbank.org/WBSITE/EXTERNAL/COUNTRIES/

LACEXT/JAMAICAEXTN/0,,menuPK:338341~pagePK:141159~piPK:141110∼theSitePK:338335,00.html, what are three of Jamaica's economic problems?
4. What three criteria does the United Nations Conference on Trade and Development look at when determining whether a country is an LDC? http://www.unctad.org/Templates/Page.asp?intItemID=3618&lang=1
5. Go to the International Monetary Fund page, www.imf.org/external/np/exr/glossary/index.asp. What is the HIPC Initiative?

For Further Study

Akyuz, Yilmaz, ed., *Developing Countries and World Trade Performance*, London: Zed Books, 2003.

Boyce, James, and Robert Pollin, eds., *Human Development in the Era of Globalization*, Cheltenham, UK: Edward Elgar, 2004.

Epstein, Gerald, *Capital Flight and Capital Controls in Developing Countries*, Cheltenham, UK: Edward Elgar, 2005.

Guest, Robert, *The Shackled Continent: Power, Corruption, and African Lives*, Washington, DC: Smithsonian Books, 2004.

Isefawa, Moses, *Snakepit* (Uganda), New York: Knopf, 2004.

Lomborg, Bjorn, ed., *Global Crises, Global Solutions*, London: Cambridge University Press, 2004.

Michalopoulos, Constantine, *Developing Countries in the WTO*, New York: Palgrave, 2002.

Pollin, Robert, et al., eds., *An Employment-Targeted Economic Program for South Africa*, United Nations Development Program, Cheltenham, UK: Edward Elgar, 2006.

Roberts, Adam, and Joe Thioloe, eds., *Soweto Inside Out: Stories About Africa's Famous Township*, New York: Penguin, 2004.

Stiglitz, Joseph E., *Globalization and Its Discontents*, New York: Norton, 2002.

Wolf, Martin, *Why Globalization Works*, New Haven, CT: Yale University Press, 2004.

WWW   The Chinese Embassy   www.china-embassy.org

WWW   Economy and Environment Program for Southeast Asia   www.eepsea.org

WWW   International Monetary Fund   www.imf.org

WWW   Mexico Online   www.mexonline.com

WWW   NAFTA   www.mac.doc.gov/nafta

WWW   Uganda   www.government.go.ug

WWW   United States Agency for International Development   www.usaid.gov

WWW   The World Bank Group   www.worldbank.org

International Institutions and the Search for Peace

After reading this chapter, you should be able to:

- Explain the statement, "War is merely a continuation of politics by other means"
- Define the Bush policy of preemption and explain its implications for international harmony
- Describe the usefulness and limitations of international law
- List the five principal organs of the United Nations
- Summarize the United States' position on the United Nations
- Summarize the current outlook for peace
- Give a history of the Arab–Israeli conflict

> *Nothing is more important than the war on war.*
>
> **—Pope Leo XIII**

September 11, 2001, changed the way the United States relates to the rest of the world. After **al Qaeda** (a fundamentalist Islamic terrorist group) highjacked airliners and crashed them into the New York World Trade Center and the Pentagon, the United States declared a war on terrorism. This war was different from previous wars in that it was not aimed at specific countries, but against an ambiguous foe—terrorists. Soon after, the nature of that war was determined. Then President Bush decided that the United States would follow a **policy of preemption**—a policy in which the United States would attack terrorists wherever they were before they commit acts of terrorism. This policy of preemption became known as the Bush Doctrine. Two aspects of this change were highly controversial—the first was that the United States declared that it had the right to go into any sovereign country and fight terrorists, and if the country harbored terrorists, that country would be considered a terrorist country and thus subject to U.S. attack. Second, those attacks could be based on suspicions and clandestinely gathered information, which would be hard for any other country to verify.

President Bush singled out four countries as an "Axis of Evil"—Iraq, Iran, Syria, and North Korea—and implied that if these countries did not change their ways, they would be made to do so. The United States invaded Afghanistan to root out the Taliban from power in retaliation for the 9/11 attack, and because of their support of terrorism, replacing it with a government more friendly to the United States. In 2003, he implemented that policy by attacking Iraq (assisted by what he called the "Coalition of the Willing," the most important country of the coalition being Great Britain) and deposing Saddam Hussein, even after the United Nations refused to directly sanction the attack. The "war" ended in a month, but that left the United States with the problem of winning the peace, and establishing a government in Iraq that would be friendly to the United States but not be seen as a U.S. "puppet" government by the Iraqi people and the world.

Winning the peace and establishing a functioning government in Iraq has been much more difficult than overthrowing Saddam Hussein. Since his overthrow, Iraq has experienced enormous civil strife, with different Iraqi groups vying for power. Trying to maintain order in Iraq has cost thousands of U.S. lives and hundreds of billions of dollars. Similarly with Afghanistan. While the ouster of the Taliban was fairly easy, establishing an effective democratic government in Afghanistan has not been easy, and the country remains in turmoil, and that turmoil has spilled over in neighboring Pakistan, creating major instability in that region.

In the 2008 presidential election, Barack Obama made getting the United States out of Iraq one of his major campaign planks, and his election was seen as a popular endorsement of a U.S. pullback from Iraq.

The United States' difficulties in Iraq and Afghanistan led Iran and North Korea to take stronger stands against the U.S. demands. North Korea announced that it had nuclear weapons, and Iran looked to be developing them, despite protests from the United States and other countries. As the United States struggles in Iraq and Afghanistan, the world order is changing. U.S. economic and political hegemony (dominance), which developed with the breakup of the former Soviet Union in the 1980s, is ending, and China and the European Union are beginning to fill the void. Even relatively small nations, such as Venezuela and Bolivia, have felt able to thumb their noses at the United States—calling it a paper tiger whose time has passed. These issues quickly become complicated by nuances, so we will stop the discussion here by drawing two likely conclusions: (1) the United States failed to take advantage of its role as the dominant superpower; and (2) the future world political scene will be one of highly complex interdependencies.

In this chapter, we consider issues of war and peace in specific relation to the international institutions that have developed to help maintain international relations and to alleviate the primary trouble spots of the world. We also consider how the change in U.S. foreign policy challenges those institutions, whose main purpose is to prevent war and maintain the peace. Before we consider the role of these international institutions, let's consider the problem of war.

The Problem of War

Besides the thousands of lives and billions of dollars that are lost, war brings about enormous social and cultural changes. World War I paved the way for the success of communism in the former USSR, it helped to bring on the Great Depression of the 1930s, and it unleashed forces that produced fascism in Italy and national socialism (Nazism) in Germany. Similarly, World War II changed the nature of the world, bringing an end to the colonial empire system. Similarly, the U.S.–Iraq wars led to quite different results than anticipated by most in the U.S. government when they began them, and the full effects of those wars will not be known for many years.

The Causes of War

Few things are certain about war, but it seems that inevitably it is the other side who started it and that the stated cause of the war will mask other underlying causes. Analyzing the causes of war is not a task about which a person can afford to be dogmatic. We can point to many forces at work and can reason as to how the forces work, but we cannot with exactitude draft any formula that will fully explain, evaluate, and relate the many pressures, conditions, emotions, ambitions, and practices behind international discord. Karl von Clausewitz, an influential German general and military strategist of the nineteenth century, argued that "war is merely a continuation of politics by other means." When peaceful methods don't accomplish their objectives, countries consider force.

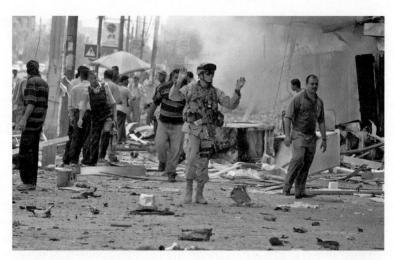

U.S. soldier tries to maintain peace after a car bomb explosion in Baghdad.

Generally speaking, identifying forces that tend to bring about war is easier than explaining or evaluating them. Factors that may contribute to bringing on war include the desire of a nation for power, economic rivalries, religious and political divisions (such as those in Northern Ireland or India), social unrest, the ambitions of political and military leaders, fanatical devotion to revolutionary ideologies (as in some Middle Eastern countries), intense ethnic rivalry among various groups, the desire for security or territory (as in Israel), the need to protect a country's national honor, or simply mistaken ideas about another country's intentions.

Because states are the work of human beings, inquiry into the causes of war goes back to the nature of human beings. Although psychologists and biologists admit that war may seem to reflect the impulses and emotions of humans—anger, fear, suspicion, and frustration—the general opinion is that people are not so made that they require war for the satisfaction of their basic drives. Their war making is believed to depend more on acquired attitudes, beliefs, and points of view than on their inherent nature.

The nation-state, as typified by public opinion and by its leaders, may be sensitive, quick to take offense, and hasty to retaliate. In the 2003 Iraq war, once the United States had decided that Saddam Hussein was harboring "weapons of mass destruction," negotiations proved fruitless, even though in the end it was clear that Iraq had no such weapons.

Within states or within the community of states as a whole, certain conditions often add to the chances of war at any given time. Poverty in a nation may produce a restlessness that breeds civil strife, and this in turn may result in international war or lead to dictatorships that foster warlike conditions. Dissension or economic depression within a state may cause governments to welcome war in order to establish national unity or to create a diversion from internal problems incapable of solution. When a spirit of militarism has been developed within a nation, as it had in Germany in the 1930s, touching off a war is relatively simple. That same spirit of militarism exists, although to a lesser extent, in the Middle East today, which is one of the reasons that area has been the site of numerous wars and is also why it is likely to be the site of more trouble in the future.

Among conditions in the international community conducive to war is a sharp ideological split, like the one that, up until the early 1990s, existed between the former Soviet Union and its allies on the one hand and the United States and its allies on the other. In the early 2000s, the religious differences among certain secular societies are turning into ideological splits that are highly conducive to war.

The existence of a power vacuum of sizable proportions is another hazardous condition in the world community, and it is frequently found when an empire has just been demolished or an alliance has broken down. Thus, the breakup of the Soviet Union, while reducing the ideological friction between the former Soviet Union and the United States, produced numerous tinderboxes in eastern Europe and in the former Soviet Union itself. It also changed international political dynamics, and there was no effective counterbalance to the United States, allowing the United States to enter into small wars without any expectation of serious reprisals from other countries, although, in many observers' eyes, the United States's unbridled use of power has contributed to terrorism and to the scattered support that terrorism gets in a number of countries. Thus, terrorism may be seen as a type of reprisal.

Approaches to the Problem of War

Throughout history, most people have probably desired peace, though in some tribal societies war, in combination with customs such as war dances, head hunting, and scalp collection, became an integral part of the group culture. War helped to give life meaning by providing danger, excitement, and opportunities for winning prestige. Nevertheless, the quest for peace goes back at least to the biblical prophet Isaiah's long look ahead to the time when "nation shall not lift up sword against nation, neither shall they learn war anymore."

Ever since nation-states began to develop in the late Middle Ages, various poets, philosophers, and politicians have presented plans for maintaining peace. These peacemakers include Dante, King Henry IV of France, William Penn, and Immanuel Kant. But none of the plans were practical, nor did they reach the masses or receive serious consideration from governments.

Diplomacy.   Disputes are, or at least seem to be, inevitable among people, bullies and ninety-pound weaklings alike. The alternative to a slugfest is reasonable discussion, which on the international level is called diplomacy. The problems of states are first of all handled by diplomats, usually with success. Occasionally, however, diplomacy fails. Because a serious dispute that gets out of hand can result in war, states genuinely anxious to stay at peace will keep their diplomats at work as long as any hope of a solution exists. Throughout the history of the nation-state, diplomacy has done much to avoid war.

The contributions of diplomacy to peace include the efforts of third states as well as the parties to disputes. A disinterested state may try to get disputants together for further negotiations when they reach a deadlock and when unfortunate developments appear imminent; or, injecting itself a little further into a controversy, a third state may attempt **mediation,**—a procedure that calls on the mediating government to make suggestions for solutions, thus concerning itself with the merits of the issues involved. For example, European countries tried to mediate a dispute between the United States and Iran about Iran's nuclear power program. Similarly, the United States has been trying to mediate the ongoing dispute between Israel and the Palestinian Authority.

In recent years, a number of countries such as East Timor, Kenya, Nepal, Somalia, Sudan, and Nigeria—both independently and through the United Nations—have relied on outside mediation activities. When mediation breaks down, the mediators must choose whether to become actively involved by providing peacekeeping forces or military force to achieve what they consider to be a fair resolution to the problems, or, less frequently and very reluctantly, to give up, admitting that some situations are, at least for a time, immune to outside influence.

International Government.   As we have seen, governments, for all their problems, generally maintain order within their boundaries by providing alternative mechanisms for settling disputes. Thus, it is only natural that some of the proposals for preventing war between nation-states have involved an international government, or at least some option other than war, for settling disputes on an international level. These include the international courts and the **United Nations (UN),** an organization of independent states that debate, and sometimes does something about, international problems. Together, these institutions comprise the rudimentary beginnings of world government, although when nations don't like the decisions, they generally disregard them. Thus, when the United Nations failed to officially sanction war against Iraq, the United States attacked anyway, with some U.S. government officials declaring the UN irrelevant. However, later when it wanted Iran to end its nuclear program, the United States relied on the authority of the UN as providing a reason why Iran had to comply.

International Law and International Courts.   For centuries, the ideal of a world ordered by a unified system of law has persisted. The ancient Greek city-states applied among themselves an elemental body of rules relating to matters such as diplomacy, treaties, and war. In Rome there was a *jus gentium,* or forum, to regulate the relations of the diverse peoples within the empire. As soon as the system of nation-states got under way centuries ago, it began constructing for itself a body of law. Hugo Grotius, a Dutchman, usually is referred to as the founder of modern **international law**—the system of rules on rights and duties of states in their mutual relations— because of his systematic organization and discussion of the law of his day in his famous book entitled *The Law of War and Peace* (1625). Often, however, emphasis was put on what nations ought to do rather than on their customary behavior.

By the nineteenth century, the actual practices of states in their relations to one another began to be stressed more and more in discussions of international law, and less attention was paid to what they ought to do from the point of view of abstract justice. Today, established procedures in the form of custom, treaties, conventions, and formal agreements are the chief basis of international law. Its subject matter is extensive, embracing items such as the recognition of new states and governments, diplomatic privileges and immunities, the acquisition of territory, nationality, extradition, the treatment of aliens, commerce, the jurisdiction of states, the responsibility of states, the beginning of war, the conduct of war, and the effect of war on treaties.

The Usefulness and the Limitations of International Law.   The usefulness of international law in the maintenance of order and peace among nations has always been limited. No international system of criminal law and prosecution has been established to date, although the UN has established an International Court of Justice (commonly known as the World Court), an International Criminal Court, and a War Crimes Law, under which international tribunals can hold proceedings. War crimes in the former Yugoslavia were prosecuted under one such tribunal.

A country's submission to an international court's justice is voluntary, and there are no effective means available to the community of states for the enforcement of the law. A violator may be threatened by the injured party, it may be the object of retaliatory measures, and in the last analysis it may be challenged in war. But these are not orderly procedures comparable to the methods possessed by a state for enforcing laws internally. For example, in the mid-1980s, when the United States was found to be in violation of international law with its policy in Central America, and especially in Nicaragua, it simply ignored the ruling. However, in the 1990s and early 2000s, the United States argued that Iraq was violating international law and should be punished for its violations. When in 2003 the UN punishment was insufficient from the U.S. point of view, the United States declared that it could attack Iraq on its own. The moral: A country's view of international law depends on which side of the law it finds itself.

Despite these deficiencies of the community of states, the usefulness of international law should not be underestimated. Nations may be able to violate the law and get away with it, but they much prefer not to do so, for they do not like to be regarded as lawbreakers.

A bad reputation can be harmful to a state, even a powerful one such as the United States. The fact that nations constantly appeal to the standard of the law in their communications and negotiations with each other, both in claiming rights and in meeting their obligations, is evidence that they at least like to appear law abiding.

In recent history, many states discovered the high costs of having a bad reputation (due to a consistent violation of international law). For example, South Africa finally ended over four decades of apartheid in response to significant pressure that included economic sanctions and condemnations. Similarly, in 1999 Indonesia let one of its components, East Timor, declare independence after significant pressure from the international community. More recently, Burma and North Korea have undertaken actions that have led to international condemnation and UN sanctions.

A major issue recently has been how the United States will be seen by the world due to its disregard for the views of other countries in its conduct of foreign policy. To some degree, the successful use of military power generates its own support—countries recognize they must live with the power realities. But the United States' recent use of military power to achieve its objectives, regardless of the views of other countries, has left a wake of hostility toward the United States throughout the world, not only among countries regarded as somewhat hostile to the United States, such as many of the Muslim countries, but also among states generally considered U.S. allies, such as Germany and France. With the election of Barack Obama, and his more cooperative foreign policy, observers are hoping for improved relations.

$\mathcal{T}$he United Nations

The United Nations is the closest institution we have to a world government. The UN was formed in reaction to a surge of enthusiasm after World War II for a world organization able to keep the peace. On August 4, 1941, Prime Minister Winston Churchill of Great Britain and U.S. President Franklin Roosevelt announced in the famous Atlantic Charter the need for a "permanent system of general security." On January 1, 1942, soon after the United States entered the war, a United Nations Declaration was signed confirming the objectives of the Atlantic Charter. This declaration gave the United Nations, which was established on October 24, 1945, its name. The primary purpose of the United Nations, according to Article 1 of the Charter, is maintaining "international peace and security."

The United Nations is not the first attempt at a worldwide organization designed to keep the peace. The first comprehensive approach to the problem of war by a group of states was written into the Covenant of the League of Nations in 1919 following World War I. This organization failed, however, to receive the international support necessary to make it a viable world organization. Although the United States was cooperative, it never became a member, and in 1939, after numerous ineffective attempts to use the League as an arbitration tool, it folded.

The most important organs of the United Nations are the Security Council, the General Assembly, and the Secretariat. The **Security Council**—the legislative body that has "primary responsibility for the maintenance of international peace and security"—is the most powerful organ of the United Nations. The council deals with international disputes and decides when aggression is taking place or when there is a threat to the peace. It is composed of fifteen nations, of which five—the People's Republic of China, France, Russia (which took over the seat of the former Soviet Union), the United Kingdom, and the United States—are permanent members. The other ten members are nonpermanent and are elected by the General Assembly for terms of two years, with the elections staggered so that five new countries come into office each year.

The Security Council must have the affirmative vote of nine of its members. When an issue is procedural in nature, any nine suffice, but in all other matters, the nine must include

The Security Council of the United Nations adopting a resolution.

all five permanent members of the council. On major questions, each of the five permanent members has a **veto,**—a vote that forbids or blocks the making of a decision. This veto has been used relatively often, reducing the Security Council's ability to make decisions on controversial issues. For example, in 2009, the United States wanted a resolution imposing strong sanctions on North Korea for its testing of nuclear weapons, so it turned to the UN Security Council. However, it could not get the support of the other four permanent members, any one of which had veto power, so it had to modify its resolution and settle for weaker sanctions.

The **General Assembly** is a UN legislative body that includes representatives of all the member states. It meets annually and concerns itself "with any questions or matters within the scope of the present charter or relating to the powers and functions of any organs provided for in the present charter." It has no legislative power, but it discusses a wide variety of international problems. When it arrives at a decision, it is in the form of a recommendation, either to states or to other organs.

The **Secretariat** is the UN executive arm. It is headed by the secretary-general, who is elected by the General Assembly and traditionally holds the post for a period of five years. The Secretariat carries out a variety of organizational, research, publication, and communication functions, and the secretary-general plays an important role in diplomacy among states.

Is the UN Worth It?

When the UN began, there was great hope for using it as a vehicle for resolving disputes among nations without resort to violence, and for discussion that could prevent war in the future. Initially, the UN was dominated by the United States and its allies, with the former Soviet Union the odd country out. Because it had different views, the Soviet Union used its veto to stop a wide variety of activities. As the UN expanded from its initial 55 members to its approximately 191 members today, the general tenor of the organization changed. The new states tended to disagree with the United States, and in the 1970s and 1980s the UN was often at odds with U.S. policy.

This change was reflected in U.S. voting in the Security Council. Whereas in the early years of the UN the United States never used its veto, in the 1970s and 1980s the United States used its veto power relatively often to prevent action by the UN. In the late 1980s, the nature of the UN changed from what it was in the 1970s and early to mid-1980s. Changes in the former Soviet Union and China made agreement in the Security Council more likely, and the UN more often reflected U.S. desires. This agreement within the UN with regard to U.S. desires gave more legitimacy to U.S. actions in maintaining the peace and achieving its international goals.

During the presidency of George W. Bush, the UN was not supportive of many U.S. positions, and the U.S. reaction was to withdraw, if not in fact, at least in principle, and look to other means of handling international disputes. That's precisely what it did in 2003. When it was clear that the UN would not sanction war against Iraq to eliminate weapons of mass destruction, but instead wanted to give UN weapons inspectors more time to determine whether Iraq had such weapons, the United States simply went to war on its own together with what it called the Coalition of the Willing.

The United States also chose not to sign the Law of the Sea treaty developed by the UN, and it withdrew from the United Nations Educational, Scientific, and Cultural Organization (UNESCO) in 1984, claiming extraneous politicization and "an endemic hostility toward the institutions of free society, particularly those that protect the free press, free markets, and, above all, individual human rights." An assistant secretary of state said, "When UNESCO returns to its original principles, the United States would be in a position to return to UNESCO." Since that time, UNESCO has reformed some of its practices, and the United States rejoined UNESCO in 2003. However, the funding for its membership has remained politically contentious. With the election of Barack Obama in 2008, the U.S. attitude toward the UN has become much more supportive and cooperative, and perhaps, in the next few years the United States's relationship with the UN will improve.

Because the U.S. contribution is about one-fourth of the UN's budget (see Figure 21.1), the UN was forced to take notice of the U.S. position, and over the past twenty years, the UN has modified its organization in order to be more in accordance with U.S. desires. Despite this change, U.S. support for the UN has been only lukewarm in recent years.

The United States is not alone in its concern about financing the UN. Japan is as well because it pays 20 percent of the costs, but has no permanent seat on the Security Council. Japan has argued that all permanent members of the Security Council should pay at least 3 percent, or even 5 percent, of the UN's costs. China and Russia do not meet that criterion.

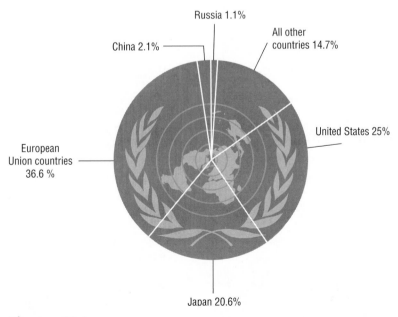

Figure 21.1

Approximate assessments for paying for the United Nations, 2009.

Not surprisingly, both China and Russia oppose Japan's proposal, and oppose Japan being given a permanent seat on the Security Council. Japan has said that it will ask for a large reduction in its UN dues unless it is given a permanent seat on the Security Council.

The UN's Role in Keeping the Peace

Supporters of the UN point out that for all its problems, the UN is still the only world force for peace that we have, and therefore it is worthwhile considering how it has kept peace and how it can continue to do so.

In the event of a "threat to the peace, breach of the peace, or act of aggression," the Security Council may invoke **sanctions**—diplomatic, economic, or military punitive actions undertaken through a collective security system—against the state that is to blame. The charter lists three types of coercive measures:

1. Severance of diplomatic relations
2. The complete or partial interruption of economic relations with the dissident state
3. The use of armed forces

The amount of pressure that diplomatic sanctions produce would ordinarily be limited. The more powerful economic sanctions are seldom tried, although in 1990 economic sanctions were imposed against Iraq after its invasion of Kuwait. All countries were forbidden to trade with Iraq, and the use of force was condoned. Because Iraq did not comply with the terms of the peace treaty, these sanctions continued until the beginning of the 2003 Iraq war, when the United States invasion led to the establishment of an alternative government in Iraq. These sanctions caused considerable hardship for the Iraqi people but were not successful in leading to the end of Saddam Hussein's rule, as some had hoped they would be.

The military sanction is supposed to be the final recourse of the UN in its peacemaking efforts. To make the system function more smoothly, the charter imposes on each member of the organization the duty of contributing to the UN military force, with the Security Council responsible for defining each member's contribution to the joint effort should an occasion for military sanctions arise.

Bombed-out UN Headquarters in Iraq.

Impressive as the charter provisions regarding military sanctions may appear at first glance, in fact they have been of limited value. When the North Koreans attacked South Korea on June 25, 1950, the Security Council had no force on which it could draw because no agreements had been reached about what members were expected to provide. The failure to make those agreements had resulted from the inability of the Military Staff Committee to specify the general principles that such agreements should embody; no nation had yet undertaken a definite obligation with respect to any possible joint military action.

When the report came that South Korea had been invaded, a meeting of the Security Council was immediately called to deal with the problem. The council urgently asked for a cessation of hostilities and a withdrawal of the invading troops. Because two days later the cease-fire order had not been respected, the Security Council set to work to apply military sanctions against North Korea. This action would undoubtedly have been vetoed by the former Soviet Union had its delegates been present, but months earlier they had withdrawn from the UN meetings in anger because Taiwan, rather than China, had been given the Chinese seat in the organization. Because the Soviet delegate was not present at the ensuing Security Council meeting, the council was able to call for a cease-fire and authorize a UN-led military action—the Korean War, which lasted from 1950 to 1953.

Since then, the UN has had some successes in keeping the peace—the Suez Canal Crisis, helping to end the Iran–Iraq war, and helping to end the internal conflict in Angola; it has also had failures. The largest of these failures involves its diplomatic attempt to keep the peace in the Middle East. When Iraq invaded Kuwait, the UN imposed economic sanctions against Iraq and authorized military force to achieve Iraq's withdrawal from Kuwait. These authorizations occurred in the Security Council and were supported by the former USSR and accepted by China (both of whom had veto power). The UN hoped the economic sanctions and the threat of war would bring about a diplomatic solution. No diplomatic solution was found, and in 1991 the UN authorized the use of force to achieve the directives. However, instead of establishing a UN military force, the UN simply authorized the United States to lead a coalition in a war against Iraq. The U.S.-led forces quickly won the war, and the UN played a key role in establishing the framework under which Iraq surrendered. It also played an important role in assisting refugees from the war and in undertaking weapons inspections.

The UN did not maintain those weapons inspections, and in the early 2000s, Iraq expelled the UN inspectors, leading to intense diplomatic negotiations. In fall 2002, the United States pushed the UN to give Saddam Hussein an ultimatum, and in spring 2003, Hussein let the weapons inspectors back in to Iraq. Despite this concession, the United States was not satisfied with the progress made in finding weapons of mass destruction. The United States pushed the UN to declare Iraq in material breach of the earlier peace accord agreements and to allow the use of military force to assure compliance.

When it became clear that the Security Council was not going to authorize force at this time, the United States, together with Great Britain, declared that a UN mandate was unnecessary and attacked Saddam Hussein to "eliminate weapons of mass destruction" and thereby help protect the world from terrorism. Initially, there were significant antiwar activities, especially in Europe, where a large majority of the population opposed the U.S. unilateral action.

Once in control, the United States found little in the way of weapons of mass destruction—the given reason for the war. Despite this, because the initial attack went well, and because Saddam Hussein was deposed, even many who opposed the war felt the outcome was a good thing because Hussein had been a brutal dictator. Immediately after Hussein's overthrow, a large majority of the U.S. population supported it—the "it dussint matter why we dundit as long as we wunnit" approach to war.

After starting the war without UN approval, the United States took major control of the establishment of a new government in Iraq, freezing the UN out of much of the process. Essentially, it told the UN, "We will do what we want; if you condone it, we will let you play a role; if you don't, we will do what we want anyway."

UN peacekeeping force in Lebanon.

That U.S. attitude did not sit well with the rest of the world, and there were significant anti-U.S. feelings outside the United States. But there was also an acceptance of the "realpolitik"—the United States has unsurpassed military power—and thus there was little that other countries could do if the United States decided to use that power. In many people's eyes, the UN had lost any effective role in providing for peace and security in the world. The United States had usurped it. However, as the difficulties of maintaining the peace have become enormous for the United States, the United States has gone back to the UN, asking for its help and conveying a willingness to consider giving up some control. Barack Obama's election win in 2008 has reinforced that more cooperative U.S. attitude.

The United States again turned to the UN when it wanted to limit Iran's nuclear program to ensure that Iran did not develop nuclear weapons. Although it had to modify its demands, the United States pushed through a resolution for Iran to end its nuclear program, with possible sanctions resulting if it did not. However, when Israel bombed Lebanon in 2006 in response to Hizballah's militant (a political group within Lebanon) capture of two of its soldiers, and most countries of the world wanted a resolution to stop the bombing and introduce a cease-fire, the United States delayed, giving Israel additional time to achieve its objectives. Eventually, even the United States and many in Israel became so concerned about the Israeli bombing that there was a general feeling that it should end, and there was a call for UN peacekeeping. This led to an Israeli withdrawal and the introduction of a limited UN peacekeeping force.

The failure of many UN peacekeeping attempts has led to a UN report calling for a permanent UN-controlled army so that the UN will have "the tools" to address any conflict situation. Because countries are reluctant to give up autonomy to the UN, there may be some increase in and modernization of the UN peacekeeping department, but the troops will likely remain "on loan" from individual nations. The problem is one of control. The UN does not have the high-level military structure to successfully direct the operations even if it gets the troops. Therefore control generally falls to one country. And, if a peacekeeping state becomes unhappy with the action, it can simply recall its troops, as India did with its troops in Sierra Leone in 2000.

In considering the UN, a key point to remember is that the UN is not a superstate. It cannot force individuals or states to accept its decisions, and often it simply lacks the ability to impose its will on the member states. All it can do is impose sanctions, which are methods of exerting pressure on recalcitrant states. In imposing sanctions, two basic handicaps limit its effectiveness: (1) its member states retain their sovereignty and (2) much of the power of the world is concentrated in a few powerful states, and unless these states concur and choose to use the UN as a vehicle to achieve their ends, the UN will not be effective.

Other UN Approaches

Some of the other approaches the UN has tried include the following:

- Registration of treaties in order to avoid obstructive secret treaties
- Further development of international law
- Promotion of education through the programs of UNESCO

- Encouragement of regional arrangements devoted to the preservation of peace
- International control of nuclear energy
- Regulation of national armaments, including missiles and nuclear weapons

The practice of having treaties registered and published by the Secretariat has become firmly established, and although it does not guarantee that secret agreements will be eliminated, it does reduce the chances of their existence. An International Law Commission has tried to promote the progressive development of international law, and it has made headway slowly. The programs of UNESCO have aimed at the furtherance of fundamental education, technical and vocational education, the exchange of books between nations, the exchange of students, and many other objectives, all designed to produce a better international outlook on the part of people everywhere. However, these methods for advancing the cause of peace are necessarily slow and their results somewhat uncertain.

Efforts to establish international control of nuclear energy and national armaments began in 1963 under the direction of President Kennedy, and they were formalized in 1968 with the Treaty on Nonproliferation of Nuclear Weapons (NPT), which provided for nonnuclear nations to forgo nuclear bomb development in exchange for aid in building peaceful nuclear power programs. Nations with the bomb were ordered to reduce armaments. Despite UN efforts, about fifty nations failed to sign the agreement. The UN's International Atomic Energy Agency (IAEA) has supervisory power over this treaty, but its authority and capabilities are limited. Thus, in 2003, when North Korea decided to develop a nuclear bomb, it simply expelled the UN observers who had been there expressly to ensure this did not happen. In 2006, Iran threatened to follow North Korea's lead.

Given its limited sanctions and tools, the UN has not been especially successful in stopping even small wars, and it certainly has not been capable of coercing the largest and most powerful members of the international community. Even when dealing with small conflicts among member nations, the UN currently has no facility to force anyone to follow its policy. Thus, in the Iran–Iraq war in the mid-1980s, the UN was unable to enforce a cease-fire for years simply because the countries refused to obey the order. Only in 1988, when both countries chose to have a cease-fire, could the UN "enforce" its policy. In the Kosovo conflict in the late 1990s, it was not the UN that organized the air campaign against Serbia. Instead, that task was undertaken by the **North Atlantic Treaty Organization (NATO).** NATO is an alliance of Western nations, one of whose purposes is joint military and economic cooperation. Finally, in the 2003 Iraq war, the United States went to war without UN authorization.

Loyal supporters of the UN still hope that in time it will develop into an organization capable of maintaining international law, order, and justice. As the world grows smaller and smaller and as the range and deadliness of weapons increase, the need for such an organization becomes ever greater.

The Outlook for Peace

The beginning of the new millennium was marked by the end of the cold war and the beginning of a period of U.S. domination in the world militarily and politically. This changes the nature of the outlook for peace. The fears associated with the cold war and the "communist threat" that filled the United States in the 1950s and 1960s are gone. Today, the communist threat seems a long way behind us, and it is hard to believe that in the 1950s and early 1960s, U.S. schools conducted air raid drills in which students practiced what to do in case of a Russian attack and U.S. families built and stocked air raid shelters. For the United States, at least, such imminent threats are gone, but other threats have replaced them. Ironically, the decline of fear of a global nuclear disaster has increased the likelihood of regional conflicts and the possibility that those regional conflicts could be nuclear. Why? Because a decreased fear that any regional conflict will pit two superpowers against each other in unreconcilable positions frees nations from automatically expecting a small war to lead to a large war. But simply because the expectation of a large war is reduced, it is not necessarily the case that the actual probability of a large war is reduced, and regional conflicts might, in fact, lead to such unreconcilable positions and the possibility of World War III. Just as fights between siblings can erupt at any time, so too can disagreements among supposedly friendly nations.

The rise of U.S. dominance has also provoked an anti-U.S. backlash and the development of terrorists cells throughout the world whose goal is to inflict harm on the United States and make it pay for its "bullying ways." This is particularly true among Arab and Islamic individuals who feel that the United States has been biased in its support of Israel in the Israeli–Palestinian war. The power of these groups was seen in the 9/11 attacks on the Pentagon and the World Trade Center and in the terrorist bombing of the United States and U.S.-ally institutions around the world. To fight such threats, the United States has established a war on terrorism, an ongoing war in which the United States claims the right to attack terrorists with preemptive strikes. Unfortunately, each of these strikes convinces others of the United States' bullying ways and leads more to join the terrorist cause, or at least to implicitly or explicitly support the terrorist cause. What the right mix of strength and understanding is for the United States to follow is still much in debate.

Those countries that have been accused of harboring terrorists and of being part of President Bush's Axis of Evil fear attacks by the United States, which leads them to aggressive policies that might prevent attack. In the case of North Korea and likely of Iran, this meant trying to increase its nuclear bomb capabilities, under the assumption that such a capability, and a willingness to use it, would prevent a U.S. attack. The 2008 election of Barack Obama, who supported a more conciliatory and diplomatic approach to other countries, will give us a sense of whether reliance on diplomacy will reduce the tensions.

The breakup of the Soviet Union has been marked by substantial ethnic unrest, and significant political shifts are still possible. For example, in early 1993 an ethnic region in Russia, Chechnya, declared its independence, and in 1995 a long-lasting war between Chechen independence supporters and the Russian army created havoc not only in Chechnya but also in Russia, where many opposed the Russian army's use of force to subdue the independence movement. That use of force also created tension between the United States and Russia. Still, in the early 2000s, the United States and Russia see eye to eye on many issues, and both are committed to peaceful coexistence. It is, however, an uneasy alliance, and it is possible that a fight between Russia and some of its ethnic regions, or between Russia and some of the former republics of the Soviet Union, could break down that alliance or create tension between the United States and a former republic. A republic could have significant nuclear power, and the United States could find itself in a position in which it felt compelled to stop the republic's leader. The result could be a war. Therefore it is vital to be vigilant in keeping the peace.

Whatever happens, it is important to recognize that "right" is almost inevitably a gray area, and each side will often do what is politically and economically in its own interest. We can expect that any government with the power to do so will attempt to impose its will on its people and on the world. It is a maxim of politics that power corrupts and absolute power corrupts absolutely. The only way peace will have a chance is if those possessing power do not interpret to their advantage what is "right" in the large number of gray areas. Unfortunately, there haven't been many examples of such objective interpretation of what is "right" in history. Instead, history has contained many more examples of the view that "might makes right."

At the end of the 1990s there was much talk of a **new world order,** a relationship among the nations of the world governed by what all countries believe is right and enforced primarily by the military superiority of the United States. If this new world order was to succeed, it depended on the United States being seen as an objective and fair arbiter. Without that perception of fairness, the new world order is doomed. Given the recent actions of the United States, this is not the way it has worked out, and the United States is currently seen as a country willing to unilaterally impose its will on other countries. Moreover, the failure of the U.S. military intervention in Iraq, and the difficulties it is experiencing in Afghanistan, has reduced U.S. power. Few nations believe that the United States will try another such invasion soon, unless it is directly attacked. That has left a power void in the world, which will likely see other countries pushing hard to achieve their goals, thereby bringing them into direct opposition with the United States.

Trouble Spots of the World

Recent events have changed the way the United States thinks of trouble spots and of war. The war on terrorism has less of a geographic component than did previous wars. Terrorists could be anywhere—they could be living right next door to you. Similarly, the damage from terrorism is not limited to some far-off country. It could be right here in the United States. Still, terrorism often has its roots in conflicts in particular geographic areas; thus, a consideration of these conflicts is important to any consideration of the search for peace.

African Stability.   During the post–World War II period, many African countries won their independence from European colonial nations, but that independence has been marked by bloody internal strife, coups d'état, and disputes over borders with neighboring countries. Few of the countries have the underlying social infrastructure necessary for a democratic government, so the governments have generally been autocracies, and the fights have been over which and what type of autocracy will rule.

With the transfer of power to blacks in South Africa, most African nations are controlled by blacks, but because of the historically imposed boundaries that combine competing ethnic groups, there will likely be continuing internal wars and fights throughout

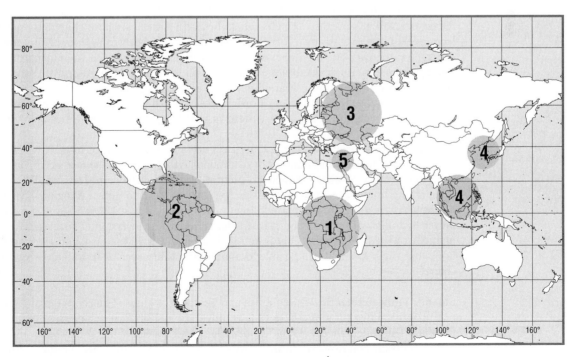

Some potential trouble spots. 1: African stability. 2: Latin American and Caribbean Basin stability. 3: Former Soviet Republics and eastern Europe stability. 4: Far East stability. 5: Middle East stability.

the 2000s. Examples include Somalia, where fighting between competing groups has led to famine and civil war; Rwanda, where fighting between the Tutsi and Hutus has torn the country's social fabric apart; the Sudan, where rebel groups and government-backed militia have been involved in a bloody conflict; as well as in Zimbabwe, where the government of Robert Mugabe has clung to power through the use of intimidation and violence on opposition leaders.

Latin American Stability.   Latin America is no longer the troubled region it was twenty or thirty years ago, when it was a location for a proxy war between the competing superpowers. An example of the problems caused by that competition between superpowers were the bloody civil wars in Nicaragua and El Salvador in the early 1980s as both the United States and the former Soviet Union jockeyed for position.

Significant problems remain, however. Some of these problems are simply leftover antagonisms from the earlier conflicts. Others result from the large disparities in income within countries, the weak democratic traditions in many of them, and the powerful drug cartels.

In the mid-2000s, Latin American countries are trying to figure out how to deal with these problems. The majority are following the U.S. suggestions, liberalizing their economies and relying on market forces to lead those economies forward. However, two oil rich countries, Venezuela and Bolivia, are trying to follow the example of Cuba, the one country in Latin America that remained tied to the Soviet Union before its breakup, and which was founded on the principles of communism, not capitalism. With the downfall of the Soviet Union, Cuba was left on its own, and the trade embargo imposed on it by the United States prevented it from growing. Many thought it was just a matter of time until its aging leader, Fidel Castro, passed away and Cuba would either give up communism or succumb to turmoil in a post-Castro struggle for power. But despite being ill, and ceding power to his brother, Raul Castro, as of 2009, Fidel Castro remained an outside-the-government power, and little rapprochement with the United States has occurred.

With Hugo Chavez's victory in Venezuela's presidential elections, and Ivo Morales' victory in Bolivia's presidential elections, the Latin American calm changed. Both these leaders professed admiration for Fidel Castro, and set about to nationalize their oil industries and to institute policies similar to Cuba's. This has led to internal tensions among Latin American countries as well as with the United States, and these turmoils could escalate in upcoming years. Venezuela also faces a major problem at its border with Colombia, an area of cross-border violence, kidnapping, smuggling, and drug trafficking. Given these problems, there is real potential for strife between the two countries.

Despite these problems, Latin America is not a major hotbed of instability relative to other parts of the world. A number of countries have had peaceful transmissions of power from one democratically elected government to another, and a democratic tradition seems to be taking hold. Whereas before coups d'état would lead to political regime changes, in recent years elections have replaced violent overthrows. Thus, Hugo Chavez did not take power by military force; he won it in an election, and the losers, after some serious complaints, accepted his victory. That is definitely a positive step forward, and gives observers hope that Latin America will be able to maintain stability even as it undergoes significant change.

Stability in the Former Soviet Republics and Eastern Europe.   The 2000s remain a time of potential instability for a number of the countries of eastern Europe and the former Soviet republics. Although in the 1990s explicit fighting between Croats, Muslims, and Serbs ended in Bosnia and Kosovo, ethnic hatreds remain high. Nearby Albania remains unstable. The situation in Russia and the republics of the former Soviet Union remain tenuous as they struggle with transformation problems; the Chechen war is just one example there.

Before the U.S. war on terrorism, the United States had strongly opposed Russian military action in Chechnya. After the war on terrorism began, Russia pointed out that the Chechen's were allied with terrorists, and U.S. opposition to Russian military action there decreased, allowing Russia to significantly reduce the fighting there.

Other former Soviet republics, such as Uzbekistan and Turkistan in Central Asia, are also highly unstable politically, which make them potential threats to world peace. Of special concern for the rest of the world is what is happening to the nuclear arsenal and nuclear weapons experts of the former Soviet Union. Some of that arsenal has been secured through careful monitoring by joint Russian and world groups, but if even a small part of that arsenal ends up in the hands of terrorists, the probability of nuclear war or nuclear terrorism may have turned out to increase, rather than decrease, with the breakup of the Soviet Union and the end of the cold war.

Stability in the Far East and Indochina.   In the early 2000s, the border between North and South Korea still remains a trouble spot. Observers believe that the North Korean leadership worries that the United States will launch a preemptive war against them. To try to prevent such a war, North Korea has tried to increase the number of nuclear bombs it has, creating difficulties for the détente approach that South Korea has been following. Because most observers believed North Korea was willing to use nuclear weapons, they also believed that a preemptive war by the United States would lead North Korea to retaliate with an attack on Seoul, the capital of South Korea, killing hundreds of thousands of people. Unlike its approach to Iraq in 2002 and 2003, the United States has so far used diplomacy to achieve its ends even as North Korea has conducted nuclear tests as well as tested missiles that have the potential for reaching the United States. Because the United States has thousands of U.S. troops stationed in Korea, the Korean peninsula will likely remain a trouble spot.

The status of China is also of some concern. In China, there are significant pressures for political reform, which are kept under control by repressive actions of the government. The United States opposes those repressive measures, but wants to stay friendly with the Chinese government.

Politically, China remains a communist state, but economically it is turning increasingly to the market. Significant concern exists in the United States about political repression of groups such as the Fulong Gong. The Fulong Gong asserts that it is an "exercise club," but the Chinese government claims it is a subversive group and has outlawed it and jailed some of its members. Whether the political repression and liberal economic activity can both continue remains to be seen. Once the war on terrorism began, the concern about China diminished because the United States saw its main threat from small countries with weak governments where terrorists could operate. Because China opposed terrorists, the United States found itself closer to China after the war on terrorism began than before the war.

Economically, China has become a market economy, and is growing enormously fast— at about 10 percent per year. This growth means that China will need resources such as oil and metals, which means that it will be extending its economic reach throughout the world in an attempt to ensure supplies of these resources. Thus, it has developed ties with both Latin American and African countries—extending aid to them and developing long-term commercial contracts with them. Eventually, the economic competition between the United States and China will likely lead to political strife between the two.

The relationship between China and Taiwan also remains a hot international issue. The United States has accepted a one-China policy, which states that Taiwan is part of China, not a separate country. At times China has suggested that it might try to forcibly take control of Taiwan. If that happened, the United States would probably extend aid to Taiwan because the Taiwanese have close ties with the United States despite the one-China policy. Most believe the issue will eventually be settled peacefully.

The Middle East and surrounding countries.

Stability in the Middle East.   Despite the problems and potential instability in other areas of the world, none of them is considered the major trouble spot of the world. This dubious honor goes to the Middle East.

Practically since the beginning of history, the Middle East has been a virtual hotbed of warring peoples. The countries of the area, such as Libya, Syria, Iraq, Israel, and Iran, have periodically fallen under the influence of rulers from many different nations. During World War I, the area was occupied by French and British troops, and between 1922 and 1939 the Jewish population in Palestine (now Israel) rose from 84,000 to 445,000. The land they bought and occupied had been previously owned by absentee landlords, and the displaced Arabs who had previously rented the land remained hostile to the new settlers. The land became disputed territory.

As the Jewish population increased, so did **Zionist**—individuals who support the establishment of a Jewish homeland—activities. During World War II, Zionist forces fought on the side of the Allies, but continually reminded the Allied forces that their own central motive was to seek independence for a Jewish nation. The area in which the nation was proposed was a British protectorate, and in 1942 Britain passed the Biltmore Resolution, which called for the first steps to be taken to secure Palestine for the Jews. It provided for unrestricted Jewish immigration into Palestine and eventual establishment of a Jewish commonwealth.

Palestinian Arabs, meanwhile, did not put up a united resistance to the Zionists. Therefore, at the end of World War II, the Palestinian Arabs had only the League of Arab States (Egypt, Syria, Lebanon, Transjordan, Iraq, Saudi Arabia, and Yemen) to turn to. They voiced opposition to the Biltmore Resolution. Britain, undecided about how the situation should be handled, called for the establishment of a binational state in Palestine, and refused to admit some 100,000 European Jewish refugees to the area. Another outbreak of violence caused the UN to intervene. On September 1, 1947, the UN commission of inquiry called for the division of the territory into two states—one Arab and one Jewish.

The Arabs, who constituted a majority in both the "states" the UN had created, re-fused the order and thus the Palestinian War began. The well-organized Zionist forces overcame the Arabs, and by May 1948 they had obtained control not only of the Jewish

Palestinian demonstrators throw stones at Israeli soldiers during a clash in the West Bank of the Palestinian territory.

share of Palestine but the Arab share as well. On May 14, the state of Israel was proclaimed. Since that time there has been continual strife between Israel and its surrounding Arab neighbors. The first outbreak of violence was the Suez War in 1956, when Israel staged a surprise attack on Egypt in the Sinai area. In 1967, the tensions broke into war again, and in what is called the Six-Day War, Israel made large territorial gains, taking land from Egypt and Jordan. Israel continued to occupy the territory it won in the war, citing the need for national security. In 1973, Arab forces attacked Israel in an attempt to regain their land, and sporadic fighting continued until mid-1974 when both sides agreed to a cease-fire.

In 1974, the UN General Assembly passed what has come to be known as **Resolution 242,** which called for the return of land and property taken by Israel during the wars and recognized the Palestine Liberation Organization (PLO), giving it permanent observer status in the UN. Israel rejected this, citing security reasons and arguing that it could not give land back to a group committed to the annihilation of Israel. In response, Israel began to settle the occupied land.

Some hope of accord existed in 1979 as Egypt and Israel agreed to a peace treaty calling for Israel's withdrawal from the Sinai Peninsula, but the more difficult Palestinian question was skirted. That question eventually led to continued fighting and war as Israel invaded Lebanon in 1982 in an attempt to eliminate the PLO. As a result of this fighting, much of Beirut, the capital of Lebanon, fell into ruins as Israel, the PLO, and Syria struggled for political power in the area. In Lebanon, the many internal groups are differentiated by intense religious, political, and economic rivalries, and they fight bitterly with each other while at the same time outside interests, such as those of Syria and Israel, attempt to enforce their own versions of order on the country. In the early 1990s, a Syrian-backed faction took control, and it looked as though the long ordeal in Lebanon was finally coming to an end. Conflict still existed, however, in south Lebanon, where Lebanese troops attempted to regain land occupied by fighting PLO guerrillas and Israelis. The Golan Heights, which was once part of Syria but was annexed by Israel in 1984 and settled by Israeli citizens, remained in dispute.

In August 1993, Israeli Prime Minister Yitzhak Rabin and the chairman of the PLO, Yasser Arafat, signed a historic peace accord to bring to a conclusion almost five decades of incessant turmoil and conflict. Israel agreed to turn over specific regions of the West Bank and Gaza Strip to the Palestinian Arabs, who would administer them as autonomous divisions. The negotiations leading toward final settlement continued but with enormous fights and complaints on both sides. Those fights and complaints continued through the 1990s and in 2003; in retaliation for suicide bombings, Israel sent in its army and occupied much of the West Bank and Gaza, destroying and laying siege to PLO headquarters and houses of suspected terrorists and their relatives. In 2003, the United States and other Western countries established a Roadmap to Peace, which required both Palestinians and Israelis to move simultaneously toward peace, with the Palestinian police force stopping the militant Palestinians from attacking Israelis and the Israeli forces withdrawing from Palestine and stopping settlements. Few believed that the Roadmap would work, but all believed that it was best to try.

In 2006, Israel conducted a unilateral withdrawal from part of the Palestinian state, annexed other parts of the Palestinian territory that Israel had occupied in previous wars, and began building a war separating Palestinians from the annexed territories.

Arafat's successor party Fatah signed a peace treaty with Israel, then lost an election to Hamas, which did not accept the existence of Israel and was far more militant. Hamas vowed never to accept Israel's right to exist, leading Israel to break off peace negotiations and to begin a policy of assassinating Hamas leaders. That led to further violence, and in 2006 Hizballah, a militant group in Lebanon, entered the fight. Israel attacked Lebanon as well as the Palestinian state, arguing that the Lebanese government had not contained Hizballah. Israeli bombing raids killed thousands of Lebanese civilians, and Hizballah indiscriminantly launched thousands of missiles at Israel. Moderates were caught in the middle, as both sides became more and more radicalized. In 2009, President Obama reached out to the Arab and Palestine communities and took a strong stand against expansions of Israeli settlements in occupied territory of Palestine. This had always been the U.S.'s stated policy, but earlier it had looked the other way and not imposed any penalties on Israel, as it repeatedly violated the U.S.'s stated policy against expanding settlements. Whether Obama will impose penalties, such as a reduction in aid or a witholding of military equipment, remains to be seen. Whatever happens, this will likely remain a highly troubled area.

Other Mideast areas also remain unstable. Islamic militants oppose the Saudi Arabian monarchy, and after the 2003 Iraq invasion, in which the Sunni leader Saddam Hussein was removed from Iraq, the Saudi monarchy worried that its Shiite majority would revolt against the monarchy. Two other countries in the area, Iran and Syria, were classified by President Bush as part of the Axis of Evil and, soon after the 2003 Iraq invasion, the United States started claiming that Iran was harboring terrorists and developing nuclear weapons. Most observers believed that Iran was not harboring major terrorists, but they also believed that Iran learned the North Korean lesson—that the United States would not attack a country that has nuclear weapons and would use them. So Iran could very well be trying to develop such weapons in an attempt to forestall a U.S. preemptive war. The possibility became more likely as Iran announced it was developing its nuclear energy program, which would give it a source of fuel for nuclear weapons. In response, Iran, the United States, and the UN entered into tense negotiations about what Iran would and would not do in its nuclear energy program. As of 2009, these negotiations were continuing.

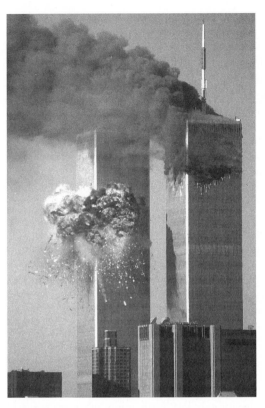

World Trade Center attacks, September 11, 2001.

Because of its multiple hot areas, the Mideast remains the most likely place a new worldwide war might emerge.

The War on Global Terrorism

As stated at the beginning of this chapter, the United States currently is engaged in a war on terrorism, and for U.S. citizens, this terrorism is very likely to disrupt aspects of their lives. The question is what to do about it. What drives people to be willing to commit terrorist acts, and what will stop them? Is it possible for a country to be so strong and forceful that it can prevent terrorist attacks, or does such force simply create more terrorists? Views differ enormously on these questions, and in the early 2000s the United States embarked on a policy based on the Bush Doctrine of preemption, which was designed to use U.S. economic and military power to rid the world of terrorism. That policy has not worked out; Iraq has become a festering quagmire, fighting continues in Afghanistan, and the number of people throughout the world who hate the United States and are committed to terrorism has increased, not declined. Supporters of preemption argued that, given time, the policy would work—we just had to stay the course. Opponents argued that we needed to follow a different course. In 2008, U.S. voters chose a different course by electing Barack Obama as president. Obama promised commitment toward a more cooperative foreign policy. The coming years will determine whether this different course will work.

Key Points

- If countries don't get what they want, and they have the power to do so, they often go to war to get what they want.
- International law is a good idea, but it lacks any way of enforcing its decisions.
- Three principal organs of the UN are the General Assembly, the Security Council, and the Secretariat.
- The United States didn't pay its dues for UNESCO for the same reason that Billy takes his ball away if he doesn't like the way the game is going.
- The new world order is to be determined collectively by the major powers, primarily the United States. The U.S. policy of preemption makes it the ultimate arbiter of right and wrong in the world.
- The Arab–Israeli conflict has many dimensions and affects the area like a cancer that has metastasized.

Some Important Terms

al Qaeda (418)
General Assembly (424)
international law (422)
mediation (421)
new world order (430)

North Atlantic Treaty
   Organization (NATO) (429)
policy of preemption (418)
Resolution 242 (435)
sanctions (426)

Secretariat (424)
Security Council (423)
United Nations (UN) (422)
veto (424)
Zionist (434)

Questions for Review and Discussion

1. How do you explain the prevalence of wars throughout human history?
2. Is the threat of war over with the end of the cold war? Explain your position.
3. Give what you think are some of the causes of war.
4. Explain the statement that war is "merely a continuation of politics by other means."
5. Explain how diplomacy is used to prevent war.
6. What are some of the reasons that international government cannot prevent all wars?
7. What are the three most important organs through which the UN acts?
8. What is the difference between the UN General Assembly and the UN Security Council?
9. How does the veto power of the Security Council hinder the search for peace? Are there any ways the veto power helps the search for peace?
10. Discuss some of the accomplishments of the UN.
11. What are some of the worst trouble spots in the world today? Can you think of ways to deal with any of these problems?
12. Give a brief history of the Arab–Israeli conflict.
13. What is the new world order? Do you think there is going to be more or less stability in the world under this order?
14. What is the most significant problem the world faces?
15. How would we know if the war on terrorism is justified?
16. If Mexico established a policy of preemption, how would the United States likely respond?
17. If the amount of money now spent on weapons systems could be used for something else, what do you think the money should be spent on?

Internet Questions

1. Go to www.un.org/Depts/dpko/dpko/ops.htm. What are the current UN peacekeeping operations?
2. What is the mission statement of the International Committee of the Red Cross? Consult its website, www.icrc.org.
3. According to Graça Machel, the UN expert on the impact of war on children (see www.unicef.org/graca), why are children particularly vulnerable to land mines?
4. According to Women Building Peace, www.international-alert.org/women, what are some of the activities women can perform in order to work toward constructing peace?
5. Using the International Peace Bureau site, www.ipb.org/web/index.php, what is the Hague Appeal for Peace program?

For Further Study

Basic Facts About the United Nations, New York: United Nations Publications. Updated regularly.

Boot, Max, *The Savage Wars of Peace: Small Wars and the Rise of American Power*, New York: Basic Books, 2002.

Carter, Jimmy, *Palestine: Peace not Apartheid*, New York: Simon and Schuster, 2006.

Diamond, Jared, *Guns, Germs, and Steel: The Fates of Human Societies*, New York: Norton, 1997.

Ferguson, Niall, *The War of the World: Twentieth-Century Conflict and the Descent of the West*, New York: Penguin, 2006.

Kennedy, Paul, *The Parliament of Man: The Past, Present, and Future of the United Nations*, New York: Random House, 2006.

Kuklick, Bruce, *Blind Oracles: Intellectuals and War from Kennan to Kissinger*, Princeton, NJ: Princeton University Press, 2006.

Rawls, John, *The Law of Peoples*, New York: Oxford University Press, 2000.

Shultz, Richard H., Jr., and Andrea J. Dew, *Insurgents, Terrorists, and Militias*, New York: Columbia University Press, 2006.

WWW   Center for War/Peace Studies   www.cwps.org

WWW   The International Court of Justice   www.icj-cij.org

WWW   Organization for Economic Co-Operation and Development   www.oecd.org

WWW   The United Nations www.un.org/english

WWW   United Nations Charter. en.wikipedia.org/wiki/United_Nations_charter.

WWW   United Nations Educational, Scientific and Cultural Organization www.unesco.org

WWW   Women's Federation of Peace International   www.wfwp.org/home.html

WWW   The World Health Organization   www.who.int/en

Index

Photo Credits